JAMES BOND ENCYCLOPEDIA

JAMES BOND
ENCYCLOPEDIA

JOHN CORK AND COLLIN STUTZ

CONTENTS

FOREWORD

When producing partners Albert R. Broccoli and Harry Saltzman began filming *Dr. No* in January 1962, they could not have imagined that the Bond series would be still going strong in the 21st century. Likewise, Ian Fleming, creator of the Bond character, would not have believed his secret agent would become a cinema legend delivering the most memorable line in film history—"Bond, James Bond."

John Cork and Collin Stutz have undertaken the monumental task of creating a Bond encyclopedia. Their research has been exhaustive. They have combed the MGM and Eon archives through documents, photographs, and film. They have interviewed actors and key production personnel and researched other archives and libraries. In short, they have been meticulous and thorough. The result is a definitive history of the Bond series over the past five decades.

Their effort is both a celebration and a tribute. It is a celebration of the Bond series and some of the best-loved and most exciting moments in cinema history. And it is a tribute to those who labored both in front and behind the camera to make Bond a legend. All are recognized, from the six exceptional actors who took up the challenge to play Bond and their magnificent leading ladies down to the day player and the background stunt artist. Directors, writers, designers, costumiers, cinematographers, camera crews, special effects, production, etc. are all acknowledged. Film is a collaborative process; every member of the team is essential right down to the most junior member of any department. This book is a tribute to their efforts, for which we are most grateful.

Michael G. Wilson
Barbara Broccoli

Broccoli and Saltzman in Jamaica, 1962

INTRODUCTION

Nobody does it better than Bond...James Bond. From the first reader who opened the first copy of *Casino Royale* in 1953 to the most recent viewer of the twenty-first century *Casino Royale*, the public's imagination has been ignited by 007. What you hold in your hands is a visual encyclopedia, a window into the remarkable world of James Bond.

The first attempt to cover this ground was an unofficial tome written by Steven Jay Rubin, published nearly two decades ago. As the initial and often updated attempt at a Bond encyclopedia, all who follow must tip our hats to his mighty effort. We should note that this book looks at 007 quite differently. We have chosen to focus mainly on the world inside the Bond adventures, eschewing behind-the-scenes details in all but a few select areas. We also chose to focus only on the Bond films created by EON Productions, and not the two films made by other production companies: the 1967 parody version of *Casino Royale* and 1983 *Thunderball* remake, *Never Say Never Again*. This was not because of restrictions placed on us by EON, but because the central characters in these films are represented for the most part in the EON series and would make the composition of entries on a character like Emilio Largo or Vesper Lynd far more convoluted than necessary.

Like the Bond films themselves, this book is a collaborative effort. While we wrote the vast majority of the text, we certainly did not do it all alone. Bruce Scivally not only proofread all the text but also wrote a significant number of filmmaker profiles and many entries for the Vehicles and Weapons & Equipment sections. Music historian Jon Burlingame contributed the profile on John Barry. Alastair Dougall at DK took all the text and added his special magic. Jenni McMurrie at EON Productions, working with Michael G. Wilson and Barbara Broccoli, provided valuable guidance that helped us stay on target.

Through all 007's filmic adventures, the Bond series has prospered by both satisfying and defying audience expectations. It seems rather elementary to define James Bond's universe by creating categories such as listed in the table of contents of this book, but it is not quite so simple. We quizzed ourselves endlessly about the placement of and space devoted to every entry. Is Miss Taro a Bond villain or woman? Is General Moon a Bond villain or supporting character? Is a jet pack a vehicle or a piece of equipment? The Aston Martin DB5 is filled with gadgets, but, for this book, one needs to look in the Vehicles chapter to find them. We also decided that unless a gadget was utilized by Bond or a principle character in the field, it would not receive an entry in the Weapons & Equipment section. The many gadgets demonstrated in Q's lab, but never used by Bond in the field, are paid tribute to under Q's character entry in Supporting Cast. Nonetheless, we have tried to have fun with this book and make it somewhat like James Bond's world. The enjoyment is not in the logic, but in the discovery, the visual sweep, and the intricate details. Just as with Ian Fleming's novels, one shouldn't be able to anticipate exactly what one will find on the next page, but one should know it will be exciting, exotic, deadly, and beautiful. Welcome to the world of 007.

John Cork
Collin Stutz

Ian Fleming at Goldeneye, his Jamaican home

IAN FLEMING

BORN May 28, 1908
DIED August 12, 1964
FULL NAME Ian Lancaster Fleming

No other writer influenced popular literature in the 20th century more than Ian Fleming. His erudite, sensual, sardonic prose, coupled with the epic scope of his stories, captured a readership in the tens of millions in the 1950s and 1960s. While not the creator of the spy thriller, he so changed the genre that everything that came after was influenced by his twelve novels and nine short stories featuring James Bond.

Ian Lancaster Fleming entered the world cocooned by wealth and privilege. His grandfather Robert Fleming made millions creating overseas investment trusts. His father, Valentine, became part of the landed gentry and was elected to Parliament two years after Fleming's birth. Valentine died in combat in May, 1917, fighting in World War I. He left a modest fortune for his four sons in trust, although they would not have access to the funds until after their mother, Eve's, death or remarriage.

Fleming studied at Durnford School and then Eton, where he won the Victor Ludorum athletic prize twice. He left before the end of his final term, ostensibly to prepare to enter the Royal Military College at Sandhurst. He attended the Villa Tennerhof school in Kitzbuhel, Austria, where his teachers, Ernan Forbes-Dennis and Phyllis Bottome, encouraged his talent for creative writing. Fleming dropped out of Sandhurst before graduating after a scandal involving a London showgirl. He continued his education in Europe, hoping for a career in the Foreign Office, but did not test well enough for placement. He then turned to journalism and excelled in

VIP VISIT *Sean Connery (Bond) and Shirley Eaton (Jill Masterson) chat with Fleming on the set of* Goldfinger *at Pinewood Studios.*

> "To give my idle hands something to do... I decided one day to damned well sit down and write a book."

(the first child died shortly after birth), Anne left Rothermere and met Ian in Jamaica. As they awaited Rothermere's divorce decree, Fleming spent his mornings writing a spy novel he entitled *Casino Royale*.

For the next 14 winters, Fleming continued to write more James Bond adventures. Success was slow in coming. Although *Casino Royale* made quite a splash in 1953, culminating with a live television production on CBS in the US in 1954, the subsequent three novels did not see an increase in sales. However, Fleming gained some publicity when Sir Anthony Eden stayed at Goldeneye to recover from the fallout of the Suez Crisis. The *Daily Express* began serializing the Bond novels as comic strips. In the US, an endorsement from President J. F. Kennedy sent sales rocketing.

ON LOCATION *(left) Ursula Andress talks with Bond's creator in Jamaica while filming* Dr. No.

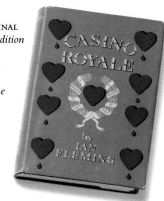

THE ORIGINAL *The first edition of* Casino Royale, *a book that changed the spy novel forever.*

By 1962, when *Dr. No* premiered in London, Bond had become a literary phenomenon.

Fleming always lived life on his own terms. He smoked up to 70 cigarettes a day and drank a half-bottle of spirits each evening. In 1964, with two heart attacks already behind him, Fleming suffered a coronary hemorrhage and died just weeks before the premiere of *Goldfinger*. He was 56 years old and the most-read author in the world.

GOLDEN YEARS *(from far left) Fleming's Jamaican home Goldeneye, where he wrote the Bond novels; Fleming, Pedro Armendariz, and Robert Shaw; Fleming with the crew of* From Russia With Love *in Istanbul; (below) Saltzman, Fleming, and Broccoli created a legacy of adventure and entertainment that inspires to this day.*

a brief career at Reuters. When his wealthy grandfather died, leaving nothing to Ian and his brothers, Fleming tried his hand at becoming a stockbroker. Traipsing to France and Austria on weekends and vacations, playing golf and seducing women, he wandered through his twenties. To many, he lived in the shadow of his brother Peter, an acclaimed writer, although the brothers always remained close.

In the months leading up to World War II, Fleming took on an assignment for *The Times* to report on a trade mission to Moscow. He turned over his observations to the Foreign Office and was soon employed as personal assistant to Admiral John Godfrey, Director of Naval Intelligence.

Fleming's work during World War II brought out the best in him. His imagination, forthrightness, and eye

for detail helped shape many important intelligence missions. While he did not see much active combat, he was at the forefront of the British espionage community.

For five winters after the war, Fleming traveled to his house Goldeneye on the north shore of Jamaica, living a life that was equal parts sybaritic and Spartan. In London, Fleming worked as foreign editor for Kemsley newspapers, managing reporters around the globe, much like a spymaster.

During this period, a long-term affair with Lady Anne Rothermere came to a head. He had known Anne while she was single and during her marriage to Lord O'Neill, who was killed during the war. She then married the press baron Lord Rothermere but continued her affair with Fleming. Eventually, pregnant with Ian's child for a second time

THE BOND STYLE

Bond's job consists of saving the world from chaos and catastrophe, so the order Bond places in his own life, from the way he ties his tie to the way he orders a drink, defines the world he fights so hard to save. Enter the world of Bond, James Bond, as seen through the details of his life, his many talents and his carefully acquired personal preferences. On the following pages you will dine, drink, and dress like a spy who knows that every pleasure may be his last. You will discover Bond's tastes, which, while easily copied, can only be fully savored by the embrace of adventure that serves as the main course of Bond's life.

CURRICULUM VITAE

THE JAMES BOND OF IAN FLEMING'S NOVELS is a veteran of World War II, whose path to becoming a "00" agent is shaped by his work with Naval Intelligence. The Bond of the early films appears to have a similar background, although he is too young to have served in any serious capacity in World War II. With *Casino Royale* (2006), the Bond filmmakers re-examined the character and his history for the post-Cold War era.

Fleming intended Bond to be a modern character, always in his thirties, always current, with a personal history as fluid as one might expect from a spy. Later Bond authors and historians have attempted to lock James Bond into a timeline, yet the best approach is clearly that taken by Fleming: Bond is, in the long run, timeless. He is old enough to be a seasoned professional, yet young enough to be in top physical condition.

In the films, Bond's age has changed as the series has progressed. Various passports have shown different dates that may or may not reflect Bond's actual birth date. For *Casino Royale*, Bond's birth date is set as April 13, 1968. This matches Bond's age to that of actor Daniel Craig, while the date of April 13 is the date of the publication of the novel *Casino Royale* in 1953. The filmmakers also set the location of Bond's birth in West Berlin.

Bond's pre-espionage life is never explored in the Bond movies. His parents are barely mentioned in the films (briefly in 1995's *GoldenEye*). The novels record that his father, Andrew, a Scot working for Vickers Defence Systems, and his Swiss mother, Monique Delacroix, died during a climbing accident in the French Alps when Bond was 11 years old. Bond was brought up by his Aunt Charmian and received a solid education, first at Eton College (from which he was soon expelled) and, from age 13, Fettes in Edinburgh, Scotland.

Bond traveled to Austria in his youth. There he found a mentor in ski instructor Hannes Oberhausser, whom Bond described as a "second father." In Fleming's short story *Octopussy*, Oberhausser is killed by a British officer at the end of World War II during the theft of a cache of Nazi gold. Oberhausser's body is dumped in the crevasse of a glacier, only to reappear years later, revealing the identity of the killer—Major Dexter Smythe. Bond is given the assignment of confronting Smythe with the murder. The incident is also referenced in the film *Octopussy* (1983).

For *Casino Royale* the filmmakers developed the following backstory: at the age of 17, Bond entered Britannia Royal Naval College. A

In the novel *On Her Majesty's Secret Service*, James Bond is confronted with a history of the Bond family of Bond Street fame, but disclaims any relationship. Despite being repelled by the snobbery associated with heraldry, Bond politely says he will adopt the crest's motto, *Orbis non sufficit*—"The world is not enough"— as his own. The phrase was used as the title of the 19th Bond film. In one scene, Bond proclaims it to be his family motto.

quick learner, he was deemed a born leader. Bond served on the Type-42 destroyer HMS *Exeter* and the Trafalgar-class hunter-killer submarine HMS *Turbulent*. Bond volunteered for the Special Boat Service and later served with the elite commando 030 Special Forces Unit, undertaking covert assignments in Iraq, Somalia, Iran, and Libya. He also participated in combat operations in Bosnia. Having risen to the rank of Commander, Bond was recruited by the RNR Defence Intelligence Group. His assignments included gathering information on the Pan Am 103 case (the Lockerbie bombing), the S-300 missile crisis in Cyprus, the Hong Kong handover, Iraq's weapons programs, and a rescue mission in Taliban-controlled Afghanistan. Bond also studied at various universities, including Oxford and Cambridge, earning a First in Oriental Languages at the latter.

Around this time, Bond was recruited by the branch of Her Majesty's Secret Service known as MI6, based in the Ministry of Intelligence building, Vauxhall Cross, London. There have been various attempts to tell the story of how Bond became a spy. Fleming himself never detailed this part of Bond's career. What Fleming did record is how Bond became a "00" agent. In the novel *Casino Royale*, Bond achieves "00" status by first assassinating a Japanese cipher expert in New York and then a Norwegian spying for the Germans. Bond has to perform the job silently and uses a knife to attack and kill the man in an apartment in Stockholm. "He just didn't die very quickly," Bond recalls.

The film *Casino Royale* introduces James Bond before he has achieved his licence to kill. However Bond is no less dangerous and, after accomplishing two professional assassinations in rapid succession, he is elevated to double-0 status.

The first kill is a messy death and occurs in a public restroom in Pakistan. The second is "considerably" easier—Bond assassinates Dryden, an MI6 Section Chief selling secrets, in his office in Prague. The dramatic pre-title sequence ends with Bond turning and firing his gun at his victim, revealing the origin of the signature, through-the-barrel graphic that starts each Bond film.

PERFECT HEALTH *Bond's medical report indicates good blood pressure, perfect vision, excellent reflexes, and a date of birth of 6 May, 1961. Bond's birth date has changed as both the novels and films have progressed.*

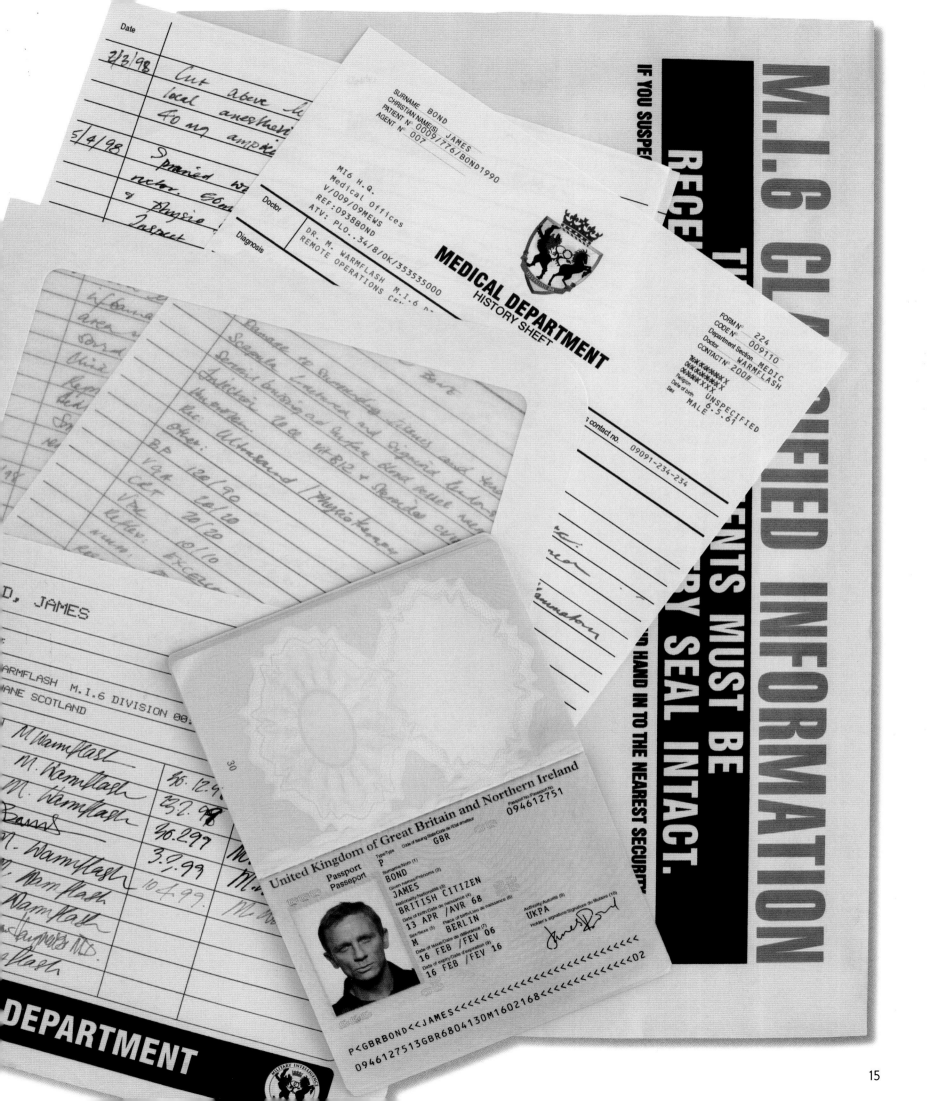

BOND'S SKILLS

JAMES BOND MAINTAINS HIS ATHLETIC ABILITIES for one simple reason: his life depends on being in top physical condition. Bond possesses a high tolerance for pain and incredible stamina, two attributes not only vital to his survival, but also qualities that give him great confidence in taking on new physical challenges. 007's keen conditioning makes him a deadly foe on land, sea or in the air.

On the ground, Bond possesses legendary fighting skills. He has privately worked on a training manual for unarmed combat entitled *Stay Alive!* that he hopes will be added to the list of internal MI6 publications. He is skilled at karate, judo, jujitsu, tae kwon do, boxing, wrestling, and knows five ways to kill a man with a single blow. Whether battling enemies aboard speeding vehicles or in the confines of a lift or stairway, 007 knows how to inflict the most damage on an opponent. Because of his physical conditioning, he can adapt to new challenges. Although never trained in Free Running techniques, sheer determination allows him to keep pace with a highly skilled practitioner/bomb-maker during one mission in Madagascar.

On the snow, Bond's skills prove prodigious. Bond learned to ski at an early age at the Hannes Schneider School in Arlberg, which is notable because Schneider is credited as the father of modern skiing. Hannes Oberhausser taught Bond the finer points of the sport during 007's school vacations in Austria during his teens, and his skills improved to championship level by his twenties. Bond can ski in extremely icy conditions, including in a bobsled run and on one ski. He has also mastered snowboarding. His skiing expertise helps him elude SPECTRE guards in Switzerland and KGB assassins in Austria, the Soviet Union, and Italy, as well as evade pursuing parahawks in the mountains of Azerbaijan. Bond has also spent time practicing the dangerous sports of bobsledding and the luge.

Bond's high-altitude skills include mountain climbing, another activity he learned in his youth while in Austria. Bond's mountaineering abilities have allowed him to scale sheer walls, cliff faces, and ice. His familiarity with climbing techniques, equipment, and safety procedures make it easy for him to learn commando skills utilizing ultra-fast rappelling, piton guns, and suction devices for 90°-plus ascents and descents.

Bond is just as proficient in water as he is on land. A superb

Bond's driving skills have allowed him to survive some very close calls. From Jamaica to Iceland, Bond has driven under the most treacherous conditions. 007 feels comfortable and confident behind the wheel of virtually every type of vehicle, from an Aston Martin sports car to a prototype lunar rover or a military hovercraft.

swimmer and high diver, Bond excelled in underwater commando training in the Royal Navy, becoming a champion scuba diver and an expert in underwater combat, as revealed during Operation Thunderball. On the water's surface, Bond excels at barefoot skiing and surfing. He employs both these skills during missions in the Caribbean and North Korea.

A confident pilot of all forms of watercraft, Bond drives both large and small boats at high speeds and can also operate military and personal submarines. His near instinctual feel for the operational limits of a craft serve him well during missions in all kinds of conditions and locations, including off the Dalmatian Coast, in Louisiana, Bangkok, the Mediterranean, Venice, Brazil, and the River Thames.

007's most remarkable set of skills reveal themselves in the air. In the Royal Navy, Bond undertook intensive parachute training, developing skills that save his life on numerous occasions. Bond relies on his aerial expertise when the assassin Jaws shoves him out of a chartered jet without a parachute. Bond maneuvers through the air to intercept an enemy skydiver and steal his chute, then battles Jaws in freefall. Bond's confidence in the air has allowed him to climb along the exterior of a helicopter being flown by remote control, to leap onto the exterior of a Beech 18 during take off and to be lowered by helicopter to snare the tail of a plane. He has performed a High Altitude, Low Opening (HALO) jump to locate the sunken HMS *Devonshire* off the Vietnamese coast by jumping from the back of a plane at 29,000 ft (8,839 m), freefalling for 5 miles (8 km) using his oxygen tank to breathe, and then opening his parachute 200 ft (60.9 m) below Vietnamese radar. Bond has also participated in aided skydiving operations with Programmable High Altitude Single Soldier Transport units, also known as Switchblades. An excellent hang glider/paraglider pilot, Bond can maneuver the craft through extreme conditions, such as the updrafts from waterfalls.

Bond maintains his skills as an expert pilot, able to fly virtually any aircraft, from a rocket belt and attack helicopters to prop planes and jet fighters.

Bond's unique combination of skills make him probably the most versatile and lethal secret agent to ever serve in Her Majesty's Secret Service, well equipped to face the deadliest of foes in the most challenging conditions. His determination to maintain his body in top physical condition is only matched by his drive to do the best work possible in the service of his country. Wherever 007's missions may take him, from icy slopes to the murky ocean depths, one can be certain that *nobody* does it better.

SURVIVAL INSTINCT *When in peril for his life, Bond knows his very existence depends on his ability to use his wits and never give up. Top: Bond pursues a terrorist bomber in* Casino Royale *in a lung-busting chase that also fully tests 007's agility and ability to think on his feet. Left to right: Bond uses martial arts training to fend off an assailant in* On Her Majesty's Secret Service; *Bond's mountain-climbing skills prove crucial to the mission's success in* For Your Eyes Only; *Bond perfoms a death-defying leap from a plane onto a tanker truck in* Licence To Kill; *Bond's years in the Royal Navy taught him numerous essential skills, enabling him to win through thanks to his courage and resourcefulness, not to good fortune or gadgets; Bond's skiing abilities save his life in* The World Is Not Enough.

WARDROBE

Costume designer Lindy Hemming, who has dressed 007 since 1995's *GoldenEye*, said it best: "When Bond enters a room, he has to have status. You have to believe he could enter a room anywhere in the world and be perfectly dressed for the occasion, but not stand out from his surroundings in a way that would make him a target of suspicion. He's kind of an elegant chameleon."

No moment better illustrates this point than Bond's transformation after he has planted explosives inside a heroin lab in Mexico in *Goldfinger* (1964). Bond strips off a waterproof suit to reveal an immaculate white dinner jacket and bow tie. He plucks a red carnation and places it in his lapel. The transformation from commando to connoisseur is complete.

James Bond's wardrobe redefined the look of a spy. Bond eschewed fedoras and trench coats, opting for finely tailored suits, stylish casual wear, and sleek commando gear. 007's clothes exude elegance through their practical durability. Their perfect styling echoes the inner confidence of Bond's character. Bond, of course, requires bespoke suits to hide the shape of his Walther PPK in its shoulder holster and to look good walking into a fine restaurant after a back alley fight.

The attention to the details of Bond's clothing in Ian Fleming's novels directly inspired Bond's cinematic wardrobe. Fleming's Bond always dressed for the occasion. In major cities and when traveling, Bond favored a dark-blue, single-breasted suit, often described as "navy serge" or "tropical worsted," with a black knitted tie, knotted with a simple four-in-hand knot (Bond was always suspicious of a man who used a Windsor knot to tie his tie).

In the early film adventures, Bond often wore gray suits and opted for lightweight tropical fabrics. By *Goldfinger*, 007's suits included waistcoats, a choice that gave way in the 1970s and 1980s to tailored sports jackets, reflecting a more casual era. In the late 1980s, Bond returned to wearing the kind of tailored suits that reflected both position and self-assurance.

Sean Connery is measured for one of James Bond's suits by Anthony Sinclair, a stylish Savile Row tailor of the 1960s, who provided many significant pieces of Bond's early wardrobe, including the tuxedo he wears in the opening scenes of *Dr. No*.

In 2006's *Casino Royale*, Vesper Lynd seems to mock Bond's style, correctly pegging him as an alumnus of Eton by the bespoke tailoring of his suit. She later presents him with the icon of 007's wardrobe, a tailored tuxedo. The moment Bond pulls his bow tie taut provides an important glimpse into the complementary nature of Bond to his wardrobe. While soldiers have their uniform, Bond's tuxedo serves as his battle gear as he engages his enemies in the most exclusive places in the world.

007's casual attire is just as important as his sartorial choices for formal situations. In Fleming's novels, Bond's regular visits to the tropics saw him wearing short-sleeved Sea Island cotton shirts—usually either white or dark blue—with dark slacks, leather sandals, or rope-soled shoes. These choices directly influenced Bond's look in the films. Bond's sky blue polo shirt and dungarees in *Dr. No* (1962) may have been a brighter color, but they come straight from the novel, and his dark blue tropical shirt, sandals, and slacks, as featured in *Thunderball* (1965), are taken nearly item for item from Fleming.

In the late 1960s and early 1970s, Bond dabbled in some of the styles of the time. Bond's golfing suit from 1969's *On Her Majesty's Secret Service* and safari suit from 1974's *The Man With The Golden Gun* stand out as prime examples. James Bond's identity, however, comes through in the way he wears his clothes, not in what he wears. When 007 dons a pink shirt in *Diamonds Are Forever* (1971) or a blue terrycloth one-piece bathing suit cover in *Goldfinger*, he does so with masculine confidence. He selects quiet sweaters that never bag, such as the one he wears while driving to Monaco in *GoldenEye*. From the silk shirts worn by Bond in Nassau and Venice in *Casino Royale* to the riding jacket he wears in *A View To A Kill* (1985), Bond's choices reflect his acute sense of what is appropriate to the occasion.

At the end of *Casino Royale*, after the deeply emotional loss of Vesper, Bond steels himself against the pain, literally armoring himself psychologically and physically as he tracks down Mr. White. Shooting him in the leg, Bond steps into view. His dark, bespoke three-piece suit would gain him the best table at any restaurant in the world. This is his armor. 007 is literally dressed to kill.

FOR EVERY OCCASION *Opposite page, top to bottom: an impeccably groomed Bond sports a white lace jabot as part of the Scottish Highland formal dress he adopts to impersonate Sir Hilary Bray in* On Her Majesty's Secret Service; *in* Live And Let Die, *Bond's look included a more casual, open-necked style befitting the steamy Caribbean climate; a leather-jacketed Bond readies his weapon in this publicity photo from* The Living Daylights; *Bond conveys elegance and danger with a gray Brioni suit and a silenced Walther P99 in this publicity shot from* The World Is Not Enough.
CLASSIC STYLE *Opposite page, right: Bond strides through* Casino Royale, *a man in his element in his ultimate uniform.*

LIFESTYLE

According to Ian Fleming, James Bond lives in a "comfortable flat" in a converted Regency house in a square off King's Road in Chelsea, London. On the ground floor, Bond has a "book-lined sitting room" and an "ornate Empire desk" by a broad window. Upstairs, 007 sleeps in a double bed with a dark blue counterpane in a smallish bedroom with white and gold Cole wallpaper accented with deep red curtains. He has a large white-tiled bathroom with an American-style shower. He also employs a devoted elderly Scottish housekeeper named May.

The Bond of the films has moved on from Fleming's portrait of bachelordom 1950s-style. Throughout the series, Bond retains an acute appreciation of classic excellence and elegance in every aspect of his life, while at the same time remaining perfectly in tune with his times. Bond's London home is seen in two films. In *Dr. No* (1962), we can see that Bond has a penchant for prints of vintage cars, owns a television, and has a spectacular entrance hall. In *Live And Let Die* (1973), Bond lives in a modern, ground-floor flat with a bedroom that opens into the living room and a state-of-the-art kitchen with a coffee grinder and espresso machine.

Bond enjoys good food served without pretense. He explains his attitude to food in the novel *Casino Royale*: "I take ridiculous pleasure in what I eat and drink. It comes partly from being a bachelor, but mostly from a habit of taking a lot of trouble over details..." In the novels, Bond relishes asparagus with sauce béarnaise, eggs Benedict with mousseline sauce, avocado with French dressing (a delicacy in post-war Europe), tagliatelle verdi with pesto sauce, langouste, stone crabs with melted butter, and a good pâté. Bond also savors well-prepared basics. Fleming had 007 comment once that the best food in the world is English food when cooked properly.

In the films, Bond's knowledge of food sets him apart from the average tourist or business traveler. He knows what to order and why. In *Thunderball* (1965) and *You Only Live Twice* (1967), Bond chooses conch chowder and oysters respectively because of their reputation as aphrodisiacs. In *On Her Majesty's Secret Service* (1969), Bond tastes the caviar at the Palacio Estoril Hotel in Portugal, and immediately knows it is Royal Beluga.

In foreign countries, Bond samples the local cuisine, such as Blue Mountain coffee in Jamaica, green figs and yogurt in Istanbul, preveza prawns, savara salad, and bourdetto in the village of Gastouri

In the films, Bond's tastes in champagne are aligned with Dom Perignon, Taittinger, and Bollinger. He prefers his champagne no warmer than 38° Fahrenheit. Bond believes the best vintage champagne is Dom Perignon '53. He mentions this preference to Dr. No, who serves Dom '55, and also to Jill Masterson in *Goldfinger* (1964).

outside of Corfu, and lobster with quail's eggs and sliced seaweed in Hong Kong. Bond cooks only once in the films, expertly preparing quiche for Stacey Sutton in *A View To A Kill* (1985). Bond's culinary knowledge extends to knowing where best to dine anywhere, from Miami Beach to Karachi.

The phrase, "shaken, not stirred" is synonymous with James Bond. Bond's opinion on how to prepare his vodka martini establishes him as a man who appreciates the subtle efforts that separate a mediocre drink from a remarkable cocktail. In both the novel and the film *Casino Royale* (2006), Bond orders a particularly fussy martini, which he names The Vesper: 3 measures Gordon's Gin; 1 measure vodka; a half measure Kina Lillet (now available as Lillet Blanc). Shake very well until ice-cold. Serve in a deep champagne goblet with a large thin slice of lemon peel. In Bond's other adventures, his martini is not quite so elaborate, and later in *Casino Royale* Bond asks one bartender if he looks like he gives a damn if the drink is shaken or stirred.

In the novels, Bond enjoys champagne, particularly the best. He orders the famed Taittinger Blanc de Blanc Brut '43, "probably the finest champagne in the world," Dom Perignon '46, the '53 Taittinger Blanc de Blanc, Bollinger, Krug, and Pommery. Bond also drinks pink champagne, such as Cliquot rosé, and Black Velvet, a mix of champagne and Guinness.

Fleming's Bond is happy to imbibe the local cocktail, liqueur, or brew. In the films, Bond largely confines himself to martinis or bourbon and branch water. However he does enjoy local specialties, such as a mint julep in Kentucky, raki in Turkey and saké in Japan. Bond is an infallible judge of brandy and sherry and a connoisseur of fine wines, his favorite being Château Mouton-Rothschild,

In the films, 007's winemanship has proved essential. In *From Russia With Love* (1963) Bond knows no self-respecting British agent would order red wine with fish, so he is not surprised when Captain Nash turns out to be SPECTRE assassin Donald Grant. In *Diamonds Are Forever* (1971), Bond's knowledge that Château Mouton-Rothschild is a claret allows him to spot the assassin Mr. Kidd posing as a wine steward.

James Bond is an expert gambler, noted as the best in MI6. He understands the strategy and odds in all casino games, knows how to spot cheats and, most importantly, how to handle himself when playing for very high stakes. Bond gambles in casinos in three novels and 11 films. He also plays roulette in the novels, and in the films shows his skills at baccarat, blackjack, craps and backgammon. Most importantly, Bond plays the complex game of Texas Hold'em poker in the film *Casino Royale* for stakes totaling well over £100 million.

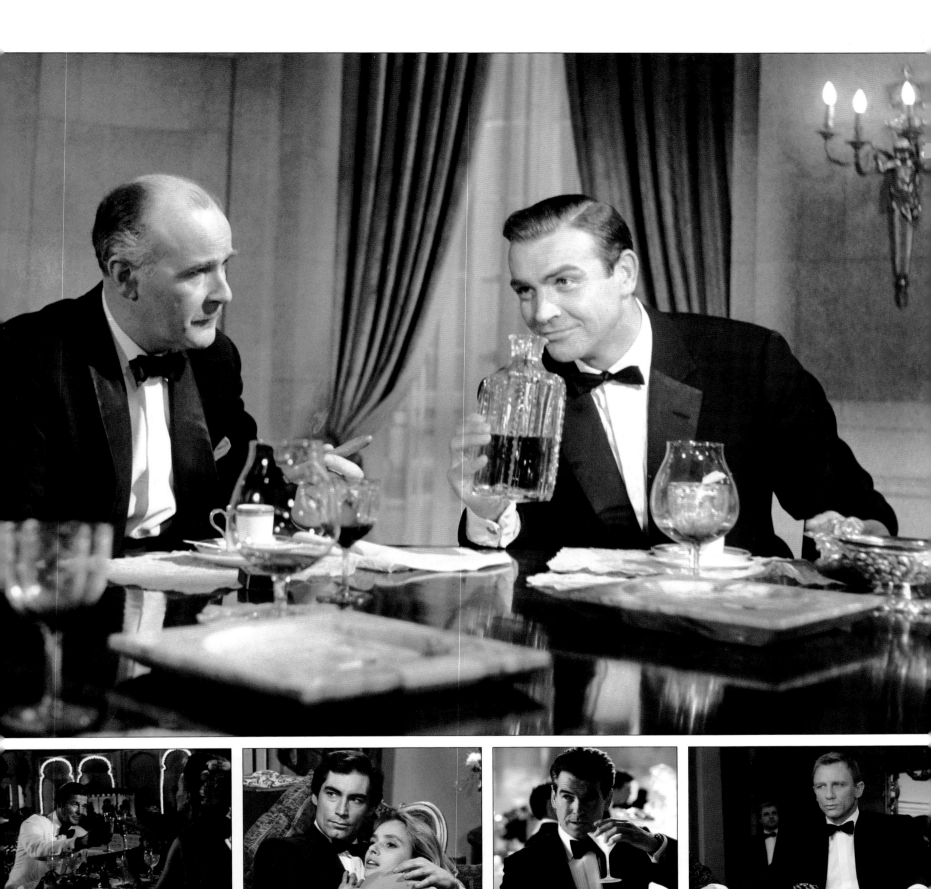

THE BOND LIFESTYLE *Ian Fleming wrote, "There are moments of great luxury in the life of a secret agent." Top: 007 offers his assessment of a "rather disappointing brandy" in* Goldfinger; *(left to right) Bond enjoys a fine meal in India with Magda in* Octopussy; *life or death situations add spice to Bond's relationships with the opposite sex and Kara Milovy brought out his protective side in* The Living Daylights; *Bond drinks a vodka martini with "plenty of ice" in Graves's Ice Palace in* Die Another Day; *Bond tests his gambling skills against Le Chiffre in* Casino Royale.

THE ROLE OF BOND

It takes a special kind of man to convince the world he is James Bond. One can slip on a dinner jacket, drive an Aston Martin and drink vodka martinis, but it takes more than surrounding oneself with 007's props to look the world in the eye and convincingly utter the words, "The name is Bond, James Bond." This requires an inner, elusive quality not easily put into words. Each actor must not only look the part, but also bring something to the role beyond the requisite good looks, sense of timing, and ability to portray grace under pressure.

Each of the six actors to play 007 has brought a unique personal touch to Ian Fleming's "blunt instrument." Each has interpreted 007 their own way yet remained true enough to the core of Bond's character to feel part of the cinematic continuum. Thanks to them, James Bond's name has ceased to be, as Fleming wrote, "flat and colorless." The very words "James Bond" define our fantasy of stylish masculinity thanks in large part to these men. Bond, through them, is our shorthand for urbane aplomb.

Meet the actors who made the man more than a number. Discover their journeys to the role that changed their lives and in some small way ours. Meet the men who became secret agent 007.

SEAN CONNERY

MISSIONS Dr. No (1962), From Russia With Love (1963), Goldfinger (1964), Thunderball (1965), You Only Live Twice (1967), Diamonds Are Forever (1971)

BORN 25 August, 1930, Edinburgh, Scotland

FULL NAME Thomas Sean Connery

Sean Connery defined the cinematic James Bond. His style, grace, sense of self, and sheer magnetism brought Ian Fleming's character to life. It was Connery's interpretation of 007 that helped establish the foundation of success upon which the entire James Bond series has been built.

Connery's upbringing in the working-class Fountainbridge neighborhood of Edinburgh was a far cry from the privileged British "old boy" network of Ian Fleming and James Bond. Connery's father, Joseph, was a lorry driver who prided himself on never missing a day's work.

After leaving school in his early teens, Connery worked on a milk delivery route which included Fettes, the exclusive Edinburgh boarding school where Ian Fleming placed a young James Bond after expulsion from Eton. While the fictional Bond learned the classics at Fettes, Connery worked to support his family.

Connery had many jobs before he joined the Royal Navy, hoping to see the world. He served as an able seaman assigned to battleships, training in gunnery school. Discharged with ulcers, he returned to Edinburgh, where he trained as a French polisher before deciding to enter the Mr. Universe contest in

"The person who plays Bond has to be dangerous."

London in 1953. Connery earned a bronze medal in his weight division, but it was clear that he had no future as a professional bodybuilder. Another competitor mentioned auditions for a touring company of *South Pacific*. They were looking for male dancers for the sailor's chorus. Connery, who had appeared as an extra in a play in Edinburgh, landed a role in the chorus and soon afterwards set off around the country as a professional actor.

Connery's new job as an actor almost lost out to a career as a professional footballer for Manchester United. On tour with *South Pacific* in Manchester, the production played against the football club's junior team. Matt Busby, the United manager, approached Connery and offered him a contract to play. Connery asked fellow actor Robert Henderson for advice. The older actor advised Connery to take the long view. Connery considered that a footballer's career would end by 30, but an actor could act forever. He dedicated himself to studying the classics at local libraries, around the UK during his time off from his duties with the chorus.

PLAYING THE GAME *(above left)* James Bond meets Sylvia Trench (Eunice Gayson) in Dr. No *at the Le Cercle gaming tables.*

BOND'S CREATOR *(above)* Sean Connery and Ian Fleming deep in conversation on Dr. No's *reactor set.*

CHECKING THE LIGHT *(left)* Honor Blackman (Pussy Galore) and Sean Connery on the Auric Stud set at Pinewood Studios.

BEACHCOMBER *(below left)* 007 introduces himself to Honey Ryder (Ursula Andress) on Crab Key beach in Dr. No.

Connery struggled to build his reputation as an actor, barely earning enough to live on as part of a suburban London repertory company. However, the small company gave him the chance to perform new dramatic roles each week. His developing skills and physical presence gained Connery roles in low-budget films, including 1957's *Action Of The Tiger*. The film's director, Terence Young, told Connery that the part would not do much for Connery's career, but that he would hire Connery for a better role one day.

Connery began working in BBC live drama productions and, when Jack Palance could not star in *Requiem For A Heavyweight*, Connery won the lead role. Rave reviews led to a contract with 20th Century-Fox, more television, and a role in the 1958 Lana Turner film, *Another Time, Another Place*, shot in England. The following year, Walt Disney and the director Robert Stevenson cast Connery in *Darby O'Gill And The Little People*, which brought him to Hollywood for the first time. The next two years provided a variety of television, theater, and small films but no break-out roles. Then, in the summer of 1961, now free of his Fox contract, Connery entered the Mayfair offices of American film producer Albert R. Broccoli. Connery walked with smooth, graceful strides, learned in part from classes with the Swedish dancer and drama teacher Yat Malmgren. His working-class background was by then leavened by relationships with beautiful upper-class women such as Julie Hamilton and Diane Cilento, his future wife. His air of confidence stemmed from succeeding against the odds. The producer, Albert R. Broccoli, his producing partner, Harry Saltzman, and United Artists executive Bud Ornstein watched Connery stride across the street after leaving. "He moved," Saltzman recalled, "like a big jungle cat." He would, they felt, be perfect for the role of James Bond.

By the time Connery retired from playing 007 in EON Productions's Bond films, his 007 adventures had grossed over

LOVE SCENE *Bond gets to know Tatiana Romanova (Daniela Bianchi) better in* From Russia With Love.

$600 million. He had also starred in movies directed by Alfred Hitchcock, Sidney Lumet, and Martin Ritt. In the 1970s, Connery established himself as an actor who could bring success to diverse films. He took on larger-than-life roles, such as the Raisuli in *The Wind And The Lion* (1975), Kipling's legendary Daniel Dravot in *The Man Who Would Be King* (1975), and Robin Hood in *Robin And Marian* (1976). In the 1980s, he won an Academy Award for Best Supporting Actor in *The Untouchables* (1987) and played the irascible father of Indiana Jones in *Indiana Jones And The Last Crusade* (1989), for which he was nominated again by the Academy in the same category.

By the 1990s, Connery could develop and produce films in which to star. He received a Lifetime Achievement award at the 1996 Golden Globes, a gala tribute at Lincoln Center, and praise from President Bill Clinton for his contribution to the arts. Connery received a knighthood on New Year's Day, 2000. In 2006, the American Film Institute awarded him a Lifetime Achievement award, and he is recognized as one of the most influential and successful actors of the past half century.

> "I care about Bond and what happens to him."

PUNCHED OUT *Bond and Red Grant (Robert Shaw) fight in* From Russia With Love.

GEORGE LAZENBY

OFFICIAL MISSIONS
On Her Majesty's Secret Service
(1969)
BORN 5 September, 1939
Queanbeyan, Australia
FULL NAME George Robert Lazenby

George Lazenby has always pushed himself to the limit. His confidence, pride, striking good looks, and charm made him a natural choice to become the successor to Sean Connery as James Bond.

Growing up in Australia, George Lazenby always dreamed big. He moved to Canberra in his teens and through sheer perseverance became the leader of a rock 'n' roll band as well as a booker for larger acts coming from Sydney. Recalling that early success, Lazenby relates it to his one performance as 007:

"I was basically doing it just to get out there. I didn't know I wanted to be an entertainer at the time. But, what was in the back of my mind, I guess, was to show off, to be somebody. And that's why, I think, when Bond came up, the odds were I'd get it because I wanted it more than anybody else."

Lazenby came to London to reunite with a girlfriend, but by the time he arrived, she had moved on. He lined up a car salesman job and

GEORGE AND HARRY *Producer Saltzman championed Lazenby's casting and remained friends with him for years.*

then advanced to selling Mercedes on Park Lane in London. His looks gained the notice of photographer Chard Jenkins. Soon, Lazenby was one of the highest-paid male models in Europe. He starred in a series of television commercials for Big Fry's chocolates, which made his face recognizable around the UK.

A chance blind date with casting director Maggie Abbott led her to suggest he try out for James Bond. Lazenby liked the idea of playing Bond, and he set about becoming

> "People think: Let's go and see a Bond film. It's always entertaining."

the perfect candidate. Lazenby purchased a suit that had been made for Connery in *You Only Live Twice* (1967) but was never used. At the Dorchester Hotel, Lazenby visited Kurt the Barber and asked for a haircut like Sean Connery's. It turned out producer Albert R. Broccoli was in the next chair, but Broccoli thought Lazenby was simply a businessman. Sporting a Rolex watch like 007's, Lazenby appeared at the door of the casting director's office saying, "I heard you were looking for James Bond."

After a meeting with producer Harry Saltzman, Lazenby confessed to director Peter Hunt later that he had no real acting experience. Hunt told him that if they stuck together, he could turn him into the new Bond. During a particularly energetic screentest, Lazenby bloodied the nose of stuntman Yuri Borienko. Bond producer Harry Saltzman walked over and told him, "We're going with you."

Producer Cubby Broccoli wrote in his autobiography *When The Snow Melts*: "Lazenby, in my judgment, made a good James Bond. He could easily have fallen into the trap of doing a smart but fatal imitation of Sean. Instead, he fought his corner as a fledgling actor, avoided tricks and gave a surprisingly effective performance."

The aftermath of *On Her Majesty's Secret Service* was difficult for Lazenby. He failed to capitalize on the effort he had put into playing Bond. Following what he now feels was some very bad career advice, Lazenby walked away from any chance he had to return as 007.

READY FOR ACTION
Lazenby's physical grace made him a natural successor to Sean Connery.

MONEYPENNY REPORTS *The actress Lois Maxwell remembers, "George was young and delicious and girls were falling in front of him like pieces of confetti."*

"At the time, I didn't know how big James Bond was. I didn't realize that no one's going to treat you the same again," Lazenby recalled. "All the doors open for you. I had that experience, and it was kind of fun. Later on, the opposite happened. They all closed. That was another part of life that I had to endure that wasn't so much fun."

He co-wrote, executive produced, and starred in the film *Universal Soldier* (1971), which died at the box office. By the mid-1970s, Lazenby was returning to Bond in a way. He appeared in a stylish commercial for Sony, playing a secret agent impressed by the technological wizardry of

ON SET *Lazenby discusses a scene with director Peter Hunt and actor Telly Savalas on location at Schilthorn, Switzerland.*

"It's hard to top a Bond film. There's nothing bigger."

Sony's off-the-shelf products. Lazenby subsequently played Bond-like characters in several films and television shows, but he also demonstrated real strength as an actor, a strength that has all-too-rarely been tapped. He played a US senator in Peter Bogdanovich's moving film *Saint Jack* (1979) and appeared as General Pettigrew in *Gettysburg* (1993). Lazenby has played other iconic roles, including Superboy's father Jor-El, as well as providing the voice of the Batman villain King in the *Batman Beyond* television series.

Outside of acting, Lazenby has been tremendously successful in real estate and sports, particularly off-road motocross racing.

MRS. JAMES BOND *"Diana Rigg was a star in her own right from The Avengers series. And I was this young upstart guy who probably didn't know a tenth of what she knew about the business."*

ACTION MAN *Lazenby enjoyed the role's physical challenges and complained when prevented from doing some of his own stunts.*

THE NEW 007 *Director Peter Hunt felt Lazenby had star quality. "He should've gone on and done the other Bonds. He would have made a very credible Bond and been very good indeed."*

ROGER MOORE

MISSIONS
Live And Let Die (1973), The Man With The Golden Gun (1974), The Spy Who Loved Me (1977), Moonraker (1979), For Your Eyes Only (1981), Octopussy (1983), A View To A Kill (1985)

BORN 14 October, 1927, London, England

FULL NAME Roger George Moore

Roger Moore's good looks, charm, and wit made him a natural for stardom. A worldwide star before being cast as Bond, Moore's easy sense of grace and savoir-faire brought the cinematic 007 unparalleled success in the 1970s and 80s. Moore's James Bond brought fantasy to the films at a time when movie audiences needed escapist entertainment of the highest caliber.

Born in Stockwell, South London, Moore excelled at art as a youth. After school, he took a job at an animation studio working on War Office short films in the middle years of World War II. Moore lost this job but quickly reentered the film world. His father was a detective sergeant with the London Police and an amateur actor himself. He had met director Brian Desmond Hurst while investigating a robbery. Moore's father took Roger to meet Hurst and asked him to help his son become an actor. Soon, Moore's strikingly handsome looks were noted when he worked as an extra on Caesar And Cleopatra (1945). With Hurst's

guidance, Moore found other small roles before joining the Royal Academy of Dramatic Arts, where one of his classmates was Lois Maxwell, the future Miss Moneypenny. Elocution lessons at RADA smoothed the rough edges of Moore's South London accent, enabling him to play sophisticated leading men convincingly.

In 1945, Moore was called up for military service. He has said he was recommended for officer training in part because of his good looks. After enduring postings in Germany, a car accident, and appendicitis, Moore transferred to the Combined Services Entertainment Unit, becoming friends with many other actors and future directors.

GLAMOR ON SET *Roger Moore poses with the actresses portraying Octopussy's beautiful but lethal girls.*

OTHERWISE ENGAGED *(above) 007 stalls M on the phone so that he can make love to Mary Goodnight (Britt Ekland) in* The Man With The Golden Gun.

TAKING A BREAK *(left) Albert R. Broccoli, Harry Saltzman, and new Bond Roger Moore relax before boat work begins for* Live And Let Die.

DEADLY DUEL *Bond pursues a mysterious assassin in* A View To A Kill.

HOW DOES THAT GRAB YOU? *(right) Jaws (Richard Kiel) has Bond in his grasp in* The Spy Who Loved Me.

as Simon Templar, the legendary adventurer created by Leslie Charteris, made him one of the most recognizable actors of the 1960s. As his fame grew, so did the interest in casting him as 007.

When Sean Connery announced he was leaving the role of Bond in 1966, producers Albert R. Broccoli and Harry Saltzman discussed casting Moore as Bond in *The Man With The Golden Gun*. The film was to have begun production soon after *You Only Live Twice* was completed, with Cambodia as a key locale. When political violence erupted in the country, the producers shelved the idea of making the film. Moore's commitment to *The Saint* prevented him from assuming the role when they decided to make *On Her Majesty's Secret Service* a year later. When the producers needed to replace George Lazenby, they again reached out to Moore, but his commitment to a new television series *The Persuaders* prevented him from taking the role. Finally, in 1972, the stars aligned, and Moore accepted the role of James Bond.

Roger Moore's first 007 film *Live And Let Die* significantly outgrossed

Connery's previous Bond, *Diamonds Are Forever*, firmly establishing Moore as a success as Bond. By the time Moore retired from the role of 007 in 1985, he had redefined the character of Bond and brought in over one billion dollars in worldwide box office. Moore earned a reputation for being an affable presence on the set, often engaging in practical jokes, or backgammon matches with producer Broccoli.

Moore continued to star in other films during his years as Bond, including numerous action–adventures, such as *Shout At The Devil* (1976) and *The Wild Geese* (1977). After 007, Moore continued to make film and television appearances, but at the request of his friend Audrey Hepburn, he began work as a Goodwill Ambassador for UNICEF (the United Nations International Children's Emergency Fund). Moore's work has taken him around the world, helping to raise money and awareness for global issues facing the planet's children. As James Bond, Roger Moore saved the world onscreen. As a UNICEF Goodwill Ambassador, his efforts have helped save real lives on a global scale.

After leaving military service, Roger Moore acted in various television and stage productions in London and New York. His New York work attracted the attention of MGM Studios, who signed him to a contract to begin work on April 1, 1954. His first significant role was in *The Last Time I Saw Paris* (1954) opposite Elizabeth Taylor. Moore quickly became friends with many top names in show business, including Frank Sinatra, a good friend of Bond producer Albert R. Broccoli. His contract lasted only three years, but it gave Moore a foothold in the film industry.

Moore appeared in many films in the 1950s, but he really made his mark on television. In 1957, he starred in *Ivanhoe*, which was followed by *The Alaskans*, *Maverick*, and then *The Saint*, which lasted from 1962 to 1969. Moore was one of the names considered for the role of James Bond in 1961 when Connery was cast. Moore's worldwide success

"I'm not that cold-blooded killer type. Which is why I play it mostly for laughs."

TIMOTHY DALTON

OFFICIAL MISSIONS

The Living Daylights (1987),
Licence To Kill (1989)

BORN 21 March, 1946,
Colwyn Bay, Wales

FULL NAME Timothy Peter Dalton

Timothy Dalton approached the role of Bond with the desire to bring the character of 007 as written by Ian Fleming to the screen. Dalton made the role his own by rereading all the Fleming novels and emphasizing the undercurrent of bitterness and ruthlessness that he felt defined the literary Bond while still embracing Bond's élan and extraordinary skills and determination.

Timothy Dalton was born in the coastal town of Colwyn Bay in North Wales where his father was stationed during World War II. The oldest of five children, Dalton came from a show business family. Both of his grandfathers were vaudevillians, while his grandmother was a theatrical agent who was once a variety performer with Charlie Chaplin. In the late 1940s, Dalton's father moved his American wife and growing family to Belper in Derbyshire, England, near Manchester where he could work in advertising. This is where the young Dalton soon found himself attracted to the cinema. Dalton remembers seeing *The Red Beret* in 1953, and imitating the soldiers with his friends. The Red Beret was the first UK production of the future Bond producer Albert R. "Cubby" Broccoli. At the age of 16, Dalton saw a production of *Macbeth* at the famous Old Vic theater and decided that he wanted to become an actor.

Dalton began his training at London's Royal Academy of Dramatic Art (RADA) in 1964 and spent his summers studying at the National Youth Theatre. He made his debut on stage in Shakespeare's *Coriolanus* at the Queen's Theatre. He left RADA after almost two years and joined the Birmingham Repertory Theatre. Actor John Rhys-Davies, a classmate of Dalton's at RADA and later his co-star in *The*

Living Daylights, has commented on Dalton's incredible sexual presence on stage during the late 1960s and how women would wait outside the stage door for him.

It wasn't long before movie producers came calling. He made his film debut in 1968's *The Lion In Winter*, starring Peter O'Toole and Katharine Hepburn, and went on to star in such films as *Wuthering Heights* (1970), *Cromwell* (1970), and *Mary, Queen Of Scots* (1971). Dalton commented in 1987 that after these films, he had felt "the need to go back to the stage." Devoting himself to the theater, Dalton made only one film between 1972 and 1978.

In 1987, after being cast as Bond, Timothy Dalton spoke about his long path to slipping on the shoulder-holster. "When I was about 25, Mr. Broccoli kindly asked me if I would be interested in taking over from Sean Connery who was about to relinquish Bond," he recalled. "It was not a firm offer, but an expression of interest. Frankly, I thought it would have been a stupid move for me. I was too young—Bond should be between 35 and 40 years old." Dalton continued acting, playing a wide variety of roles. "Then, several years ago, when Roger Moore was uncertain about continuing as 007, I was approached again. The situation was very vague, there wasn't a script yet, and I had already been asked to do *Flash Gordon*. But I was pleased to have been considered. When I was asked in early 1986, I was unavailable. I was doing my own stage productions of *Antony And Cleopatra* and *The Taming Of The Shrew* so the schedules conflicted and the idea went out the window again." Dalton's inability to sign in early 1986 led the filmmakers to pursue Pierce Brosnan, but when Brosnan proved unavailable

> "I tried to bring the movies back to something that was more like Ian Fleming."

> "I don't think anyone except the few people who have played James Bond can tell you how strange and special it is."

BETTER MAKE THAT TWO *(left) Bond prepares to spend some quality time with Linda (Kell Tyler) in* The Living Daylights.

GONE FISHING *007 uses a Coast Guard helicopter's winch to capture drug baron Franz Sanchez in mid-air in* Licence To Kill.

LATE ARRIVAL *(below center) In* Licence To Kill, *007 parachutes in to Felix and Della Leiter's wedding in Key West, Florida.*

PUT-UP JOB *In* The Living Daylights, *Bond "assassinates" General Pushkin at the North African Trade Convention.*

EYE ON THE TARGET *(left) In a deleted scene from* Licence To Kill, *Bond watches Franz Sanchez on TV in his Key West hotel room.*

AFGHAN NIGHTS *(right) In* The Living Daylights, *007 assures Kara Milovy (Maryam d'Abo) that she will see him again.*

owing to the renewal of his *Remington Steele* television contract, producers Cubby Broccoli and Michael G. Wilson returned to Dalton, who again had conflicts, as he was working on the film *Brenda Starr*, released in 1989. The producers agreed to delay the start of production of *The Living Daylights* if Dalton were willing to start immediately after *Starr* wrapped. Dalton accepted, becoming the fourth 007 in EON Productions' Bond series.

From the set of the TV mini-series *Scarlett* in April 1994, Dalton announced that he would not portray James Bond for a third time.

He continued to alternate between film, television, and stage work. Highlights included the comedy *The Beautician And The Beast* (1997), the western *American Outlaws* (2001), the animated/live-action film *Looney Tunes: Back In Action* (2003), the television epics *Cleopatra* and *Hercules*, and the comedy *Hot Fuzz* (2007). His most noted stage work of recent years is Philip Pullman's *His Dark Materials*, in which he portrayed Lord Asrael at London's National Theatre.

Dalton is married to Ukranian actress-model Oksana Grigorieva and lives in Los Angeles. His favorite pastimes are fishing, opera, and jazz.

PIERCE BROSNAN

MISSIONS
GoldenEye (1995), Tomorrow Never Dies (1997), The World Is Not Enough (1999), Die Another Day (2002)
BORN 16 May, 1953, Drogheda, County Louth, Ireland
FULL NAME Pierce Brendan Brosnan

Pierce Brosnan successfully brought James Bond into the 1990s and the 21st Century. His portrayal of 007 in 1995's *GoldenEye* ensured Bond's relevance after the end of the Cold War, and the success of *Die Another Day* in 2002 showed 007's enduring appeal after 9/11.

Pierce Brendan Brosnan was born in Ireland in 1953. Pierce's father left his mother May shortly after the birth. When May moved to London to study nursing, Pierce was raised by his maternal grandparents. They died when Pierce was six, so various relatives raised him until boarding house owner Eileen Reilly took him into her home.

On the day Ian Fleming died, August 12, 1964, eleven year old Pierce arrived in London to live with his mother. One month later, his mother took him to see his first movie since arriving in England,

UNKEMPT *(far left)*
Bond prepares to be traded for North Korean terrorist Zao in **Die Another Day.**

IMPECCABLY GROOMED
(left) Brosnan strikes a suitably cool, unruffled pose while shooting the tank chase in **GoldenEye.**

Goldfinger. Young Pierce was mesmerized by what he saw on the big screen. "I was an 11-year-old boy from the bogs of Ireland and there was this beautiful gold lady on a bed—naked. It made quite an impression on me," Brosnan recalled in 1995.

After attending Elliot School in London, Pierce worked as a commercial artist and a circus fire eater before studying at the London Drama Centre for three years. After graduating in 1976, he became assistant stage manager at the Theatre Royal, York, where he was handpicked by playwright Tennessee Williams to star in the British premiere of *The Red Devil Battery Sign.* Brosnan received rave reviews—his acting career had begun.

During this time, Brosnan fell in love with Australian actress Cassandra Harris, a divorced mother of two young children. They married on December 27, 1980, a few months after Cassandra had completed filming in Corfu as one of Bond's leading ladies in *For Your Eyes Only.* When

> ## "Bond is an enigma."
> **Pierce Brosnan**

Pierce visited Cassandra on the set, a number of people, including producer Albert R. "Cubby" Broccoli and actor Julian Glover, felt that Brosnan had the looks and bearing of a future 007.

While in Corfu, Brosnan received the script for a six-hour US TV mini-series *The Manions Of America.* When he returned to London and auditioned, he won a key role.

The show aired on ABC in September 1981, and Pierce and Cassie flew to Hollywood for Pierce to go on a round of auditions. During the trip, Pierce and Cassie dined at Cubby Broccoli's house in Beverly Hills. Driving back to their hotel, Pierce couldn't resist attempting the famous line, "The name is Bond, James Bond."

Brosnan soon signed a seven year contract with NBC, and, in the fall of 1982, *Remington Steele* premiered. After *Octopussy* was released in cinemas in June 1983, Roger Moore made noises about retiring as Bond. In numerous polls asking who people thought should be the next 007, Brosnan won by a landslide. However, Moore announced that he would make another Bond film, *A View To A Kill.* Meanwhile, Brosnan enjoyed continued success as Steele as well as the personal joy of the birth of his son Sean in September 1983.

When Moore finally resigned from the role, the world's press touted numerous actors, including Pierce, as the next 007. NBC announced the cancellation of *Steele* on May 15, 1986—although the network kept a 60-day option to renew the show.

On the day of cancellation, *The New York Post* announced that Brosnan would become the fourth actor in the EON Bond series to play 007. As a result of all the publicity, summer reruns of *Steele* posted record-breaking ratings for the series. On July 15, 1986—the 59th day of the option period—NBC head Brandon Tartikoff changed his mind and renewed *Remington Steele,* just as Brosnan was celebrating his selection as the next Bond with Cubby. Although Tartikoff offered to film *Steele* in conjunction with the Bond film, Broccoli refused. On August 6, 1986, Timothy Dalton was announced as the fourth 007.

A devastated Brosnan made three two-hour *Remington Steele* TV movies before NBC cancelled the series. Brosnan pursued film roles, but heartbreak followed when his wife, Cassie, was diagnosed with cancer. Brosnan's career took a backseat while he helped care for his wife, who sadly passed away on December 28, 1991. Brosnan became an advocate for women's health issues, working with numerous charities and lobbying the US

DRESSED TO KILL
A tuxedo-clad Brosnan poses in the traditional 007 uniform for **GoldenEye.**

Congress for research funding for ovarian cancer.

On April 11, 1994, Timothy Dalton announced his resignation as Bond. Although Brosnan found himself again in negotiations to play Bond, Brosnan was reluctant to get his hopes up, despite numerous polls that showed him as the top choice to be the new 007. Finally, on June 1, 1994, at 12:35 p.m., Brosnan received a phone call from his agent, Fred Spektor, saying "Hello, Mr. Bond, you've got the part." At a press event on June 8, 1994 in London, producers Michael G. Wilson and Barbara Broccoli announced Brosnan as the fifth James Bond.

Brosnan is now happily married to Keely Shaye-Smith, and they have two children. Pierce has his own production company, Irish Dreamtime, and, since retiring as 007, has starred in diverse movies, including *Laws of Attraction* (2004), *The Matador* (2005), and *Seraphim Falls* (2007). He has also become an advocate for environmental issues, lending his name, time, and stature to a wide array of initiatives.

DANIEL CRAIG

OFFICIAL MISSIONS
Casino Royale (2006)
BORN 2 March, 1968,
Chester, England
FULL NAME
Daniel Wroughton Craig

Daniel Craig redefined the character of James Bond in *Casino Royale*, stepping out of the shadows cast by his predecessors in the role and making 007 feel new, fresh, and dangerous. Craig brought a physical rawness, emotional focus, and darkly seductive air to Ian Fleming's creation; critics, fans, and moviegoers around the world embraced his performance, which helped to make *Casino Royale* the highest-grossing Bond film ever released.

Daniel Craig decided that he wanted to be an actor at the age of six when his mother took him to the Everyman Theatre in Liverpool, England. By the age of 16 he had made up his mind, leaving school and turning his back on a university career. Instead, his mother helped him apply to study at the National Youth Theatre in London. There he earned a reputation as a diverse and dedicated actor. He later took courses at the Guildhall School of Music and Drama at the Barbican, where he was considered one of the finest actors in his class. At the age of 22, before completing his studies, Craig landed a small but important role in the movie *The Power Of One*.

Craig appeared in numerous television productions, including his first brush with a major film series character in *The Young Indiana Jones Chronicles*, in which he played a Nazi

soldier. In 1996 he took a role in BBC television's political and social drama *Our Friends In The North*. His performance, which targeted him as a rising star in the UK, could have typecast him as a specialist in regional roles, but Craig turned down opportunities to play similar parts. Instead, he looked for a variety of challenging roles. In 1998, his performance as a petty crook who becomes the lover of the artist Francis Bacon in *Love Is The Devil*

> " Nobody knows more than I do how important this is, and it's my job to get it right."

BRAND NEW BOND *Daniel Craig wanted to develop and expand the role of Bond: "It's a question of taking it somewhere maybe where it's never gone before."*

ACTION HERO *Craig performed a lot of his own stunts in* Casino Royale.

won critical accolades. A series of solid but small roles in major films followed, including a turn as Lara Croft's boyfriend in *Tomb Raider* (2001). The size and quality of the roles offered to him steadily grew, and he worked with such respected film directors as Hugh Hudson, Sam Mendes, and Christine Jeffs. The lead role in *Layer Cake*, a hard-edged underworld thriller, finally brought Craig worldwide acclaim. Three fans of the film were Michael G. Wilson and Barbara Broccoli, producers of the James Bond films, and Debbie McWilliams, the casting director. "He's a phenomenal actor," Broccoli commented.

With the decision in early 2004, to recast the role of James Bond, the

kept in touch. When the filmmakers finally had a script they felt was ready to show, they sent it to Craig. "Once I sat down and read the story, I just thought that I wanted to tell this story," recalled Craig. "I'm a big Bond fan, and I love what he represents."

During 2005, MGM, the distributor of the Bond films, was sold to a consortium that included Sony Pictures, and Sony became the studio that would distribute *Casino Royale* around the globe. This meant the producers needed the approval of Sony's production executives on their choice for a new 007. "I screen-tested, because there was a new studio on board with Sony who wanted to see if I could do it or not," stated Craig.

CASINO ROYALE *(above) The stakes are high for Craig's James Bond.*

ASSASSIN *(far left) Daniel wanted to portray an element of cruelty in Bond's character.*

TENDER MOMENT *(left) Eva Green on Craig: "When you see him onscreen, he's always very intense and still."*

OFF-SCREEN *(below left)* Casino Royale *director Martin Campbell with Craig, whom Campbell has likened to Steve McQueen.*

THE HOTEL SPLENDIDE *(below) Craig's Bond is ready for trouble however luxurious the setting.*

"If you don't get bruised playing Bond, you're not doing it properly."

filmmakers' thoughts soon turned to Daniel Craig. Broccoli recalls, "When we decided we were going to make *Casino Royale*, it was obviously a big decision who we were going to use, and he [Craig] was always in the forefront of our minds." Craig was not so certain. Michael G. Wilson recalled, "He said to us, 'If I take this part, I will do it wholeheartedly. But I can't say I will till I've read the script.'" It was many months after that meeting before the script was completed, but the Bond producers

The screen test showed Craig's remarkable ability to transform himself into Bond and make the character his own. Sony chief production executive Amy Pascal watched the test and commented, "He has a kind of intensity, and a sexuality, and a roguishness." Sony gave the producers the green light to his casting, and on October 14, 2005, Daniel Craig arrived at the banks of the River Thames, stepped onto a rigid raider boat piloted by a Royal Navy escort, and raced across the

water to HMS *President* for his introduction to the world's media.

Just over 14 months later, Craig became the only 007 actor to have starred in a Bond film which took over $593 million in worldwide box office. Craig's portrayal of Bond has the sense that beneath the veneer of 007's implacable outer shell exists a dark, damaged, and extraordinary man. His remarkable transformation of the character has brought a new sense of emotional reality and danger to the Bond films.

BOND
VILLAINS

"G oodbye, Mr. Bond." The absolute certainty with which Goldfinger dismisses 007 is but the pride that goeth before the fall. All Bond villains must fail in their schemes, but still, let us pay our respects to the greatest minds to ever twist an evil plot. Bond villains are towering figures, billionaires, captains of industry, born leaders, visionaries. Bond villains such as Ernst Stavro Blofeld, Karl Stromberg, and Hugo Drax embark upon monumental undertakings that could only be realized by individuals capable of changing the world. That is their dream. To accomplish it, to wipe away our comfortable lives in one stroke, they employ hordes of slavishly devoted henchmen, drawn to their magnetic personalities. On the following pages, meet the men and women whose ambitions proved too big for this world.

ADAM

APPEARANCE
Live And Let Die (1973)
STATUS Dead; killed in a boating accident while pursuing 007
CHARACTERISTICS Stern, determined
PLAYED BY Tommy Lane

Dr. Kananga/Mr. Big henchman Adam confronts Bond at Lakeside Airport. Bond escapes in a speedboat headed for the Irish Bayou and Adam pursues him by car. Adam first eludes Sheriff Pepper, then steals the fastest boat on the river from Pepper's brother-in-law, Billy Bob. Adam chases Bond through the bayou until Bond throws fuel in Adam's eyes and his boat crashes into the rusting hulk of a ship.

ALVAREZ, DR.

APPEARANCE
Die Another Day (2002)
STATUS Dead; shot by Jinx
CHARACTERISTICS Proud, pompous
PLAYED BY Simón Andreu

Based in a clinic on Los Organos off the coast of Cuba, Dr. Alvarez is a leader in the field of gene therapy, genetically transforming individuals into other races. He also "increases the life expectancy of our beloved leaders and the richest westerners." Having successfully transformed Colonel Moon into Gustav Graves, Alvarez is in the process of turning North Korean Zao into a Caucasian when NSA agent Jinx assassinates him and destroys his clinic with a cell phone bomb.

LAST WORDS *Dr. Alvarez explains that his research depends on a supply of healthy donors, such as "orphans, runaways, people that won't be missed." He believes NSA agent Jinx is a new patient, but she is his assassin.*

APOLLO JET CREW

APPEARANCE
Moonraker (1979)
STATUS Pilot dead; fate of hostess unknown
CHARACTERISTICS Service—and death—with a smile
PLAYED BY Jean-Pierre Castaldi (pilot), Leila Shenna (hostess)

The villainous Apollo jet crew hijack Bond's chartered Dakar—London flight. They hope to stage a plane crash in which Bond's body will be found. After kissing Bond, the hostess produces a gun and trades her weapon for a parachute held by the pilot, who shoots out the controls. Bond shoves the pilot out of the plane, but is then himself pushed out by Jaws. Bond skydives after the pilot, steals his parachute, and evades Jaws. The pilot dies on impact, although the hostess probably survives.

HAVE A SAFE FLIGHT *The flight crew on Apollo demonstrates the proper use of a parachute in case of an in-flight emergency.*

APOSTIS

APPEARANCE
For Your Eyes Only (1981)
STATUS Dead; killed by Bond
CHARACTERISTICS Silent, restrained, merciless, relentless
PLAYED BY Jack Klaff

Apostis serves not only as a chauffeur for intelligence informant Kristatos, but also as a fierce killer in Kristatos's organization. Kristatos invites Bond to utilize Apostis as a chauffeur one evening and Apostis apparently informs Kristatos and killer Emile Locque of Bond's location, resulting in an attack that causes the death of Columbo's mistress Countess Lisl Von Schlaf.

Bond confronts Apostis when climbing to Kristatos's clifftop hideaway. Apostis kicks Bond over a cliff and begins to dislodge the pitons securing Bond's climbing ropes. Bond hurls a piton into Apostis, causing him to fall to his death.

ARKOV, DR.

APPEARANCE
The World Is Not Enough (1999)
STATUS Dead; identity used by others
CHARACTERISTICS Apprehensive, hesitant, worried, distressed
PLAYED BY Jeff Nuttall

A scientist in league with terrorist Renard and Elektra King, Arkov provides Renard with the Parahawks that attack Bond. However, when Bond destroys the Parahawks, Arkov blames the failure to kill Bond on Elektra's sidekick Davidov. Renard has Arkov killed for failing "his test of devotion." Bond later uses Arkov's identity to enter a nuclear site in Kazakhstan.

ASIAN CARTEL

APPEARANCE
Licence To Kill (1989)
STATUS Living; whereabouts unknown
CHARACTERISTICS Ruthless but cowardly; eager to profit from drugs trade, but unwilling to get hands dirty
PLAYED BY Unknown

Drug lord Franz Sanchez hopes to create an Asian drug cartel, with members from Japan, Taiwan, South Korea, and Malaysia. To create a drug empire from Chile to Alaska, Sanchez prepares to grant them exclusive cocaine franchises in Asian territories and guarantee prices for five years. At the Olympatec Meditation Institute, he asks each cartel member to pay $100 million in negotiable bearer bonds. When Bond destroys the institute, the members escape.

BAMBI & THUMPER

APPEARANCE
Diamonds Are Forever (1971)
STATUS Arrested by the CIA
CHARACTERISTICS Great gymnasts, powerful hand-to-hand combatants
PLAYED BY Lola Larson (Bambi), Trina Parks (Thumper)

Bambi and Thumper work for the unscrupulous casino manager Bert Saxby and less directly Ernst Stavro Blofeld. They guard millionaire recluse Willard Whyte, keeping him a prisoner in his desert home.

When James Bond arrives, Bambi and Thumper greet him with mocking insouciance and seductive warmth. It is all just a ploy to get Bond in a position where they can hurt him. Both trained gymnasts, they use their lithe but powerful bodies to knock Bond around. After throwing Bond into a pool, they dive in after him, only to discover that Bond's superior swimming skills put them both at a grave disadvantage. Rather than drown, they confess Whyte's true location before Felix Leiter and CIA agents arrest them.

BARSOV, SERGEI

APPEARANCE
The Spy Who Loved Me (1977)
STATUS Killed by Bond
CHARACTERISTICS Experienced KGB agent and assassin; superb skier
PLAYED BY Michael Billington

KGB agent Sergei Barsov attempts to chase and shoot James Bond on skis near Berngarten in the Austrian Alps, but Bond whirls around and eliminates him with a ski-pole rocket gun. Despite his death, Barsov still poses a danger to Bond. On his next mission, Bond finds himself working with Major Anya Amasova, Barsov's former lover.

GUNNING FOR BOND *KGB agent Sergei Barsov, the lover of Major Anya Amasova, takes on 007 in the Austrian Alps and loses.*

Bambi: Hi, there. I'm Bambi.
Thumper: And I'm Thumper. Is there something we can do for you?

BLOFELD, ERNST STAVRO

APPEARANCES
From Russia With Love (1963), Thunderball (1965), You Only Live Twice (1967), On Her Majesty's Secret Service (1969), Diamonds Are Forever (1971), For Your Eyes Only (1981)

STATUS Presumed dead

CHARACTERISTICS A brilliant criminal mind; ruthless, calculating, enigmatic, snobbish, messianic, erudite

PLAYED BY Anthony Dawson (body in From Russia With Love, Thunderball), Eric Pohlmann (voice in From Russia With Love, Thunderball), Donald Pleasence (You Only Live Twice), Telly Savalas (On Her Majesty's Secret Service), Charles Gray (Diamonds Are Forever), John Hollis (body in For Your Eyes Only), Robert Rietty (voice in For Your Eyes Only)

Ernst Stavro Blofeld, founder of the terrorist organization SPECTRE, remains one of the greatest geniuses in the history of crime. He would be one of the world's richest and most influential men if it were not for James Bond. Blofeld has hijacked hydrogen bombs, built two operational space weapons, and developed a powerful bacteriological weapon. He has mounted numerous smaller criminal operations and inspired slavish loyalty in hundreds of associates, many of whom have been willing to go to their deaths on his behalf. He eluded capture for years. MI6 even launched a major campaign to capture or kill Blofeld—Operation Bedlam—which ended

> **"Allow me to introduce myself. I am Ernst Stavro Blofeld."**

with uncertain results.

Blofeld has the remarkable ability to significantly alter his appearance, both in the James Bond novels and films. According to Fleming, Blofeld was born on 28 May, 1908 in what is now Gdynia, Poland to a Greek mother and Polish father. Athletic as a youth, he competed in amateur weight-lifting contests. Blofeld studied economics and political history at the University of Warsaw. Realizing that wealth and power flow to those who have early access to information, he took a job at the Ministry of Posts and Telegraphs. In the build-up to World War II, Blofeld, using top secret communications, formed a fictional spy network—TARTAR—and began selling secrets. He sold to the Germans, the Americans, and the Swedish, amassing a small fortune.

Blofeld destroyed his birth records and left Poland before Germany invaded. In Istanbul, Blofeld worked for Ankara Radio. Once it became clear that the Germans were losing

FIRST APPEARANCE *Blofeld briefs subordinates Rosa Klebb, Morzeny, and Kronsteen in* From Russia With Love.

the war, he set up another fake spy ring and sold government communications to the Allies. Blofeld finished the war rich and decorated by the Allies.

After years in South America, Blofeld returned to Europe ready to make his mark. He formed SPECTRE, which made him tremendously powerful.

By the early years of SPECTRE, he weighed roughly 280 lbs and sported a crew-cut. His eyes showed whites all the way around above a squat nose. A mere two years later, Blofeld looked very different. His now long, white hair was carefully groomed. He had lost over 100 lbs, and his formerly even voice sounded more animated. His eyes looked normal behind green contacts and his nose, reshaped by surgery, appeared aquiline but damaged by tertiary syphilis. Nine months later, Blofeld had again altered his

FACE TO FACE *Cradling his white Persian cat, Blofeld confronts Bond in SPECTRE's volcano rocket base.*

COUNT DOWN *Blofeld briefly showed a romantic side to Tracy in* On Her Majesty's Secret Service.

MAN OF MYSTERY *An attack on Bond in* For Your Eyes Only *may or may not have been masterminded by Blofeld.*

appearance, repairing the damage to his nose and growing a drooping black mustache. The literary Blofeld dies at the end of the novel *You Only Live Twice*, when Bond strangles him to death at his Castle of Death in Japan.

In the films, Blofeld first appears in *From Russia With Love*, demonstrating his philosophy of letting two competing forces think they are battling each other before opportunistically attacking the weakened victor. He has medium length black hair, but his face remains unseen. He wears a signet ring with an octopus design and strokes a white Persian cat that reflects his relaxed but predatory indifference to all that surrounds him.

The Blofeld of *Thunderball* is nearly bald, lean, and fit. He is briefly glimpsed, face obscured, at the SPECTRE board meeting in Paris, once again stroking his white cat.

In *You Only Live Twice*, Blofeld moves his operation to Japan where,

> "I shall look forward personally to exterminating you, **Mr. Bond.**"

with financing from Communist China, he builds a rocket base inside a hollowed-out volcano. When he reveals his face to Bond for the first time, he has a scar down the right cheek and around one eye. Wearing a traditional Mao jacket and slacks, he obsessively strokes his cat. His decrepit physique appears to be an outward expression of his mental perversions.

By *On Her Majesty's Secret Service*, Blofeld is unscarred, physically robust and sexually aggressive. He confidently fights, skis, and handles a bobsled. In *Diamonds Are Forever*, Blofeld not only endures numerous plastic surgeries, but also convinces many others to have their appearance and voice altered to double him. He seems to have modeled his looks on

Dikko Henderson, Bond's contact in Japan in *You Only Live Twice*—if, in fact, the character Bond battles at the end of the film *is* Blofeld. Certainly the assassination attempt on Bond at the end of *Diamonds Are Forever* after Blofeld's apparent demise would seem to imply that the master criminal may have survived through sheer stamina or cunning.

In *For Your Eyes Only*, a wheelchair-bound, bald man holding a white cat attempts to assassinate Bond. Despite his physical similarity to Blofeld from *On Her Majesty's Secret Service*, it is unclear if the man in the wheelchair is indeed the notorious mastermind. It is possible Blofeld has gone half-mad while plotting Bond's death, totally losing his sophisticated veneer. He makes brittle jokes for his own pleasure and laughs maniacally. Despite being dropped down a gasworks chimney, no positive identification has ever been made of Blofeld's corpse. His ultimate fate remains a mystery.

CHANGING FACES *A series of medical models reveals the extent of Blofeld's plastic surgery from* You Only Live Twice *to* Diamonds Are Forever.

SWORN ENEMIES *Bond eliminates one of Blofeld's doubles at the beginning of* Diamonds Are Forever. *Thinking he has avenged the murder of his wife, Bond soon finds he has a seemingly limitless number of Blofelds to kill.*

A LADY'S TOUCH *Boitier, dressed in drag for his own funeral, attacks 007 with a poker.*

BOITIER, COL. JACQUES

APPEARANCE
Thunderball (1965)
STATUS Beaten, whipped, and throttled
CHARACTERISTICS Looks good in
a dress
PLAYED BY Rose Alba, Bob Simmons

SPECTRE No. 6, Colonel Jacques Boitier (pronounced "Boovarr"), is a murderer of two British Secret Service agents. The wealthy Boitier attempts to alter his identity and thus elude authorities and James Bond. He stages his own death and poses as his widow at the funeral. Bond becomes aware of his deception, and waits for the Colonel in the drawing room of his chateau. There, the two engage in a brutal fight, destroying many priceless antiques in Boitier's collection. Bond eventually kills Boitier with a fire poker, choking the life out of him over the hearth.

> " My dear Colonel Boitier, I don't think you should have opened that car door **by yourself.** "
> **007 to Boitier**

NICE MOVES *Bonita dances the tarantella before an explosion at Mr. Ramirez's heroin lab interrupts her show.*

BONITA

APPEARANCE
Goldfinger (1964)
STATUS Living; whereabouts unknown
CHARACTERISTICS Deceitful dancer
PLAYED BY Nadja Regin

Bonita, a young woman from Turkey, dances the tarantella at the El Scorpio nightclub in coastal Mexico. She works with Mr. Ramirez, a major heroin smuggler with a local base of operations. After Bond destroys a heroin lab at the Ramirez Export Compania grounds, he visits Bonita, only to discover she has enticed him into a trap in her dressing room. As Bond and Bonita embrace, Bond sees a capungo—a Mexican thug—reflected in Bonita's eyes. Bond flings her into the path of the capungo's cosh, knocking her out. After killing the Mexican bandit, Bond leaves Bonita nursing her sore head.

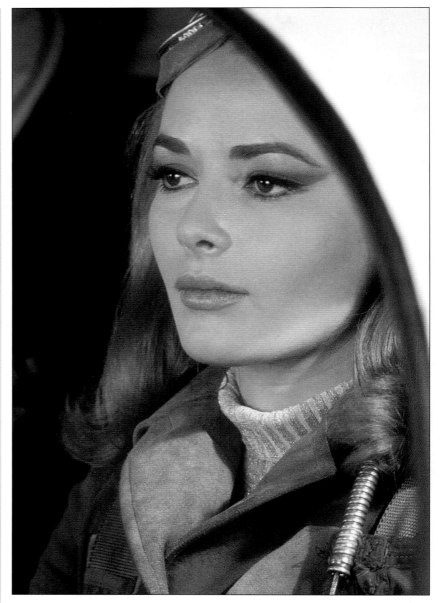

BRANDT, HELGA

APPEARANCE
You Only Live Twice (1967)
STATUS Dead; fed to piranhas
CHARACTERISTICS Cunning, but
not ruthless enough for SPECTRE
PLAYED BY Karin Dor

SPECTRE No. 11, Helga Brandt, is the confidential secretary to chemical tycoon and SPECTRE operative, Mr. Osato. An accomplished pilot, seductress, and murderess, she aids Ernst Stavro Blofeld in his plot to launch World War III on behalf of the Communist Chinese.

Brandt first meets Bond when he poses as Mr. Fisher, managing director of Empire Chemicals. She knows Bond engaged in the theft of documents in Osato's office the previous night, yet Brandt and Osato are uncertain of Bond's real identity, believing earlier newspaper reports of his death in Hong Kong. After the meeting, Osato orders Brandt to kill "Mr. Fisher," and she tries to accomplish this with a carload of assassins and no fewer than 25 assailants at the Kobe docks. When she captures Bond, Brandt insists on questioning him herself and pretends to be seduced. Bond claims to be an industrial spy and offers her $150,000 to help him escape. Brandt flies him to Tokyo the next day but, airborne, she triggers a device to pin Bond in his seat, tosses a lipstick magnesium flare into the cockpit and parachutes away, sending Bond to what she believes will be certain doom. Later, Brandt and Osato learn from Blofeld that Mr. Fisher is in fact James Bond and is very much alive. Blaming Brandt for the failure to eliminate Bond, Blofeld feeds her to a school of hungry piranhas.

BRAUN

APPEARANCE Licence To Kill (1989)
STATUS Fried
CHARACTERISTICS Silent; obeys orders without question
PLAYED BY Guy De Saint Cyr

NO HEART *Braun holds Lupe Lamora's boyfriend Alvarez helpless.*

Braun is a henchman of drug lord Franz Sanchez. With Sanchez, Perez, and Dario, he participates in the murder of Alvarez, lover of Sanchez's girlfriend Lupe. He also aids in the stabbing of Della Leiter and the maiming of Felix Leiter. When Sanchez's security chief, Heller, tries to steal Sanchez's stinger missiles, Braun drives a forklift blade through Heller's chest. Later, on a winding road, Braun's flame-engulfed truck careens off a cliff, just missing Pam Bouvier's plane.

BULL, THE

APPEARANCE
The World Is Not Enough (1999)
STATUS Dead; shot by Zukovsky
CHARACTERISTICS Smug, cocky, deceitful; not as tough as he looks
PLAYED BY Goldie

The Bull, alias Mr. Bullion, works for Valentin Zukovsky as his bodyguard. He is secretly in the employ of Elektra King and her terrorist lover, Renard.

When Elektra is convinced Bond has died in an explosion, The Bull calls to inform her that Bond is in fact alive. Elektra orders an attack on Bond and Dr. Christmas Jones at Zukovsky's caviar factory. When this fails, The Bull sabotages the Istanbul building where Bond, Jones, and Valentin meet. The explosion injures Valentin, but Bond and Christmas escape. The Bull captures Bond and Jones and takes them to Elektra's base at Maiden's Tower, Istanbul. Zukovsky soon arrives and promptly shoots The Bull.

NAME CHANGE *In an early script draft, The Bull was known as "The Boa."*

BUNT, IRMA

APPEARANCE On Her Majesty's Secret Service (1969)
STATUS Living; whereabouts unknown
CHARACTERISTICS Humorless and determined; blindly loyal to Blofeld
PLAYED BY Ilse Steppat

Irma Bunt is the personal secretary of Ernst Stavro Blofeld. She actively participates in his plot to threaten the world with the biological warfare agent, Virus Omega.

Bunt watches over the female allergy patients at Bolfeld's clinic, Piz Gloria. To help Blofeld secure an hereditary title, she escorts James Bond (posing as Sir Hilary Bray of the Royal College of Arms), to Blofeld's mountain clinic. After Blofeld learns from British agent Campbell that Bray is in fact James Bond, Bunt aids in his capture. She sneaks into Ruby Bartlett's bed where she knows Bond will come to visit. When Bond enters, she has a guard knock him over the head with a nightstick.

After Bond escapes Piz Gloria on skis and arrives in the village below, Bunt supervises the pursuit, but she narrowly escapes with her life when her car overturns and explodes. When Bond marries Tracy, it is Bunt, not Blofeld, who fires the machine gun burst that kills Bond's bride.

Irma Bunt appears in the novels *On Her Majesty's Secret Service* and *You Only Live Twice*. In the former, Bond quickly becomes annoyed with her and it is "quite an effort to restrain his right shoe from giving Irma Bunt a really tremendous kick in her tight, bulging behind."

In the latter, Bond knocks her unconscious in a Kyushu castle, strangles Blofeld to death, and then rigs a geyser to destroy the castle.

"Bunt. Interesting name... Nautical term meaning the baggy or swollen parts of a sail. Nothing personal, of course."
007 to Bunt

BUTCHER, PROFESSOR JOE

APPEARANCE
Licence To Kill (1989)

STATUS Living, still blessing people's hearts for cash

CHARACTERISTICS Lecherous conman

PLAYED BY Wayne Newton

American televangelist Professor Joe Butcher, whose catchphrase is "Bless your hearts," secretly works as a cocaine price fixer for drug baron Franz Sanchez. The author of a self-help book, *The Secrets Of Cone Power Revealed*, Butcher hosts his television program from the Olympatec Meditation Institute near Isthmus City. The Institute also houses Sanchez's cocaine labs. Butcher helps set the price of Sanchez's cocaine in an ingenious way.

When Butcher announces a fundraising goal for his meditation chapters, he is actually informing drug dealers around the world of the current month's cost per kilo. The drug dealers then call 555 LOVE with their orders disguised as pledges. CIA contract pilot Pam Bouvier pretends to be infatuated with Butcher to gain access to the cocaine labs and help Bond destroy Sanchez's operation.

TV SHOPPING *A pledge of $100 to Professor Butcher's Institute secures the pledger a copy of his book, valued at $49.95, for free.*

CAPUNGO

APPEARANCE
Goldfinger (1964)

STATUS Dead, gone in a flash

CHARACTERISTICS Brutal, evil

PLAYED BY Alf Joint

"A capungo is a bandit who will kill for as little as forty pesos," writes Ian Fleming in the novel *Goldfinger*. In the film, the capungo, a thug working for the heroin producer and smuggler Mr. Ramirez, attacks Bond in the dressing room of the tarantella dancer Bonita in an unnamed coastal Mexican town. Bond spies the capungo's reflection in Bonita's betraying eyes as he sneaks up behind with a club. Bond hurls Bonita into the path of the club, then, after a brutal fight, tosses the thug into Bonita's filled bathtub, knocking in a portable heater and electrocuting the capungo with a crackling flash.

SNEAK ATTACK
The capungo prepares to strike, but Bond is not to be caught off guard so easily.

CARLOS

APPEARANCE
Casino Royale (2006)

STATUS Dead, detonated

CHARACTERISTICS Silent, cold, skilled driver under pressure

PLAYED BY Claudio Santamaria

Alex Dimitrios hires terrorist Carlos to destroy the Skyfleet S570 prototype airplane at its unveiling. Using false ID and the pass code—ELLIPSIS—he enters the secure area of Miami International Airport, where he kills the driver of a runway fuel tanker. He plans to turn the truck into a giant bomb using a small detonator disguised as a keyfob, triggered by his mobile phone. James Bond, who has been following him, leaps onto the tanker and, after a brutal fight, Carlos jumps from the tanker. He sees Bond stop the truck short of the plane, but is confident the tanker will still blast the plane to bits. After pressing the trigger code on his mobile phone, Carlos discovers the detonator keyfob has been attached to his belt by Bond. He blows himself up, prompting a wry smile from 007.

CARVER, ELLIOT

APPEARANCE
Tomorrow Never Dies (1997)
STATUS Dead; according to press
reports, committed suicide
CHARACTERISTICS Power-hungry,
flamboyant, seething with rage
PLAYED BY Jonathan Pryce

Worldwide media mogul Elliot
Carver may be the most powerful
man on the planet. According to
James Bond, Carver can "topple
governments with a single broadcast."
This stylish villain plans to create
war between Britain and China and
install a sympathetic government in
China that will grant his Carver
Media Group (CMG) network
exclusive satellite transmission rights
for the next 100 years.

Carver was born in Hong Kong,
the illegitimate son of a German

woman, who died in childbirth, and
press tycoon Lord Roverman. A
Chinese family subsequently paid
£50 for the boy. Aged 16, he went to
work for a Hong Kong paper, whose
editor taught him the key to any
great story: "Why?"

When he turned
30, Carver took
revenge against his
father by building a
rival chain of
newspapers that
drove Roverman to
bankruptcy and
suicide.

Now in his fifties,
Carver, nicknamed
"The Emperor of the Air" by his
wife Paris, lives the life of a media
baron. He views himself as a
modern-day Caesar or Napoleon;
instead of legions and armies, he
commands television channels,
newspapers, magazines, and 8,000

MEDIA MOGUL *Carver proudly announces
the launch of his satellite news network.*

journalists in 132 countries. He uses
information as a weapon. For
example, he hopes to blackmail a US
President into signing a bill lowering
cable rates by
threatening to release a
compromising tape of
him with a cheerleader.
After the President
signs, Carver releases
the tape anyway.

Carver has
everything he could
want except for
exclusive broadcasting
rights in China.
Working from a stealth ship invisible
to radar, Carver uses a stolen GPS
encoder to send HMS *Devonshire* off
course into Vietnamese waters. The
Chinese, believing the ship is in their
waters, respond by sending two MiG
fighters to fly over the *Devonshire*.

> "Words are the
> new weapons,
> **satellites**
> the new artillery"
>
> **Elliot Carver**

Carver orders the sinking of the ship
with his Sea-Vac underwater drill and
the killing of any survivors. He also
orders the shooting down of a
Chinese MiG fighter.

Searching through the wreckage of
the *Devonshire*, Carver's men recover
a Tomahawk-class missile, which
Carver plans to fire at the building
hosting an emergency meeting of the
Chinese high command in Beijing.
A member of the high command,
General Chang, who is in league
with Carver, will deliberately delay
his arrival, allowing him to survive
the attack and ascend to power.

The suspiciously early reporting by
Carver's media empire of the
Devonshire's sinking, plus the fact that
his satellites were the source for the
GPS signals that sent the ship off
course, make Carver and his media
empire the focus of British and
Chinese investigations, led by James
Bond and Colonel Wai Lin.

Bond's past relationship with
Carver's wife Paris makes Bond a
particular target of Carver's wrath,
resulting in Carver ordering the
murders of Paris and Bond. When
Bond steals the incriminating GPS
encoder, Carver pulls no punches
trying to have Bond killed. Carver
fails and his men later find Bond and
Wai Lin searching the wreckage of
the *Devonshire*.

Carver confronts Bond in Vietnam,
but once again fails to kill him and
Wai Lin before they escape.
Regardless, Carver travels to his
stealth ship to instigate his war. Bond
and Wai Lin infiltrate the ship and
Bond eventually kills Carver using
the Sea-Vac drill to chew him to
pieces. The media report that Carver
has committed suicide on his luxury
yacht in the South China Seas.

CARVER, ROSIE

APPEARANCE
Live And Let Die (1973)
STATUS Killed by Kananga's scarecrows
CHARACTERISTICS naive secret agent, naive double agent, very superstitious
PLAYED BY Gloria Hendry

Rosie Carver works as a double agent for Dr. Kananga, prime minister of the Caribbean island of San Monique. Kananga, as "Mr. Big," schemes to corner the US drugs market with supplies of heroin produced on the island. Rosie feeds his organization valuable intelligence from her other job—field agent for the CIA. She does little to inspire confidence from James Bond. Her superstition and fear seem genuine, but her motivations remain unclear.

Rosie takes the liberty of checking into Bond's San Monique hotel as his wife and tries to sneak into his suite with her Smith & Wesson .38 drawn. Rosie later finds a voodoo sign in her bedroom—a small top hat with bloody feathers—and is so frightened that she begs Bond not to leave her alone for the night.

The next morning, Bond receives a Queen of Cups tarot card in an upside-down position (anonymously sent by Solitaire)—a sign that Rosie is not to be trusted. Bond and Rosie travel by boat to Kananga's plantation, and Bond tries to get her to take him to the spot in the hills where the authorities recovered the body of Baines, another British agent (whom Rosie, on her first CIA assignment, previously betrayed). Rosie appears afraid and confused, although her assignment from Kananga is clear: to lead Bond into a trap.

After making love to Rosie in a jungle clearing, Bond confronts her with the incriminating tarot card. She says she dare not tell him anything saying, "They'll kill me if I do." When Bond aims his gun at her, Rosie runs away in a panic. A gun concealed in the mouth of one of Kananga's scarecrows shoots her dead.

> "**Look after Mr Bond. See** that **some harm** comes to him."
>
> **Drax to Chang**

CHANG

APPEARANCE
Moonraker (1979)
STATUS Dead; fell through a clockface
CHARACTERISTICS Good at aikido and other martial arts, but not good enough
PLAYED BY Toshiro Suga

TIME TO KILL *Bond and Chang fight to the finish in Venice's historic Torre dell'Orologio. Chang's death prompts Hugo Drax to hire a new henchman, Jaws.*

Chang is billionaire Hugo Drax's loyal manservant and hitman. Drax orders him to prevent Bond from prying into his affairs. Chang's first attempt to kill Bond occurs when he deliberately over-revs a centrifuge Bond tests at Drax's technical facilities. Later, Chang releases Drax's pet Doberman dogs to hunt and kill Bond's ally and lover, Corinne Dufour, in the woods of Drax's country estate.

Finally, Chang, dressed in full Aikido gear, confronts Bond outside the showrooms of Venini Glass in Piazza San Marcos, Venice. He battles Bond inside the gallery, smashing shelves of priceless glassworks. The fight proceeds into the Torre dell'Orologio—the St. Mark's Clocktower—where Bond throws Chang through the famed stained-glass clockface. Chang crashes down onto a grand piano, fatally disrupting a classical music recital.

CHULA

APPEARANCE
The Man With The Golden Gun
(1974)
STATUS Living
CHARACTERISTICS Karate expert
PLAYED BY "Charlie" Chan Yiu Lam I

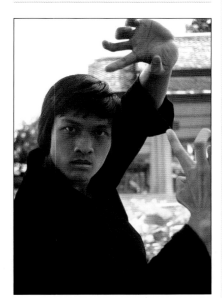

MARTIAL ARTIST *Bond is faced by Chula, the star of Hai Fat's school. Fortunately Bond has a few moves Chula does not anticipate.*

After being knocked unconscious by Scaramanga's assistant, Nick Nack, Bond awakens at a Bangkok martial arts academy run by tycoon Hai Fat. Bond soon realizes he is to be used as sport by assassins–in–training at the academy. After Bond seriously injures one student in an initial bout, the others chant for Chula, the school's most deadly student, who sits at the right hand of the master. Chula initially inflicts a great deal of pain on Bond but, using judo and kick-boxing techniques, Bond floors him. While Chula recovers, Bond breaks out of the fighting school. After Bond's ally Lt. Hip and his nieces, Cha and Nara, battle a swarm of pursuing students, Bond steals a longtail boat and races down Bangkok's klongs with Chula and other students in pursuit. Bond eventually lies in wait and, when Chula and crew stop, guns his engine and splits their boat in two. Chula is last seen flailing in the klong as Bond drives safely away.

CIGAR GIRL

APPEARANCE
The World Is Not Enough (1999)
STATUS Dead; blown to pieces
CHARACTERISTICS Accomplished assassin; totally committed to the cause
PLAYED BY Maria Grazia Cucinotta

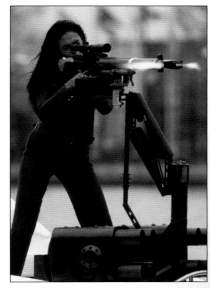

KILLER ON THE RIVER *The assassin known as Cigar Girl takes aim at 007 during a chase on the river Thames.*

The Cigar Girl is the nickname for an extremely accomplished assassin working for anarchist Renard. She is first seen bringing Bond a cigar in Lachaise's office in Bilbao, Spain. Just as Lachaise is about to reveal to Bond the identity of the person who sold Sir Robert King a stolen Soviet Atomic Energy Commission report, she expertly throws a knife, hitting Lachaise in the neck.

Cigar Girl: Would you like to check my figures?
007: Oh, I'm sure they're perfectly rounded.

After an explosion inside the MI6 building blasts a massive hole in a wall facing the River Thames, Bond spots the Cigar Girl on board a Sunseeker powerboat. She fires at Bond, but misses him.
Determined to catch her, Bond jumps into a prototype Q boat and speeds out of the rubble onto the Thames in pursuit. Bond and the Cigar Girl engage in a hair-raising high-speed chase, each attempting to outmaneuver the other. Spotting the launch of a hot-air balloon at the nearby Millennium Dome, Cigar Girl beaches her vessel and leaps out of the boat, shooting the balloon pilot.

As she ascends in the balloon, Bond jumps the Q boat into the air and seizes one of the balloon's tethers. Bond offers to protect her if she will reveal the identity of her employer. But the Cigar Girl, believing that Bond would never be able to protect her from Renard, fires a bullet into a propane gas tank, blowing herself up. Bond falls onto the Millennium Dome roof, dislocating his collar bone.

CONLEY, BOB

APPEARANCE
A View To A Kill (1985)
STATUS Mining disaster victim
CHARACTERISTICS Corrupt
PLAYED BY Manning Redwood

Bob Conley works as Max Zorin's mining engineer for Operation Main Strike. In addition, he handles Zorin's oil interests in the East Bay. Before linking with Zorin, Conley worked as chief engineer for a South African gold mine where a cave-in killed 20 miners. This led to his hasty departure from South Africa.

When Conley realizes that Zorin intends to betray assassin May Day and his fellow loyal miners, he objects. Zorin's chief henchman Scarpine knocks Conley unconscious, and he drowns in the flooding of the mine.

DAMBALA

APPEARANCE
Live And Let Die (1973)
STATUS Dead; shot by 007
CHARACTERISTICS Good with reptiles; has a flair for showmanship
PLAYED BY Michael Ebbin

Dambala is the high priest of a voodoo cult on the Caribbean island of San Monique. He dresses in a goat's head cowl and performs deadly rituals at the behest of Kananga, the island's despotic ruler.

Dambala does not participate in any of the more mundane criminal activities associated with Kananga's plot to flood the US with heroin. His role is to perform ceremonial sacrifices of anyone that Kananga wishes to have killed, such as the British secret agent Baines.

Dambala's voodoo ceremonies involve him leading crowds of excited believers in trance-like dancing and chanting. Dambala then carefully selects a poisonous snake from a coffin and waves the snake in the face of his victim until the

enraged creature strikes. Fortunately, Bond arrives in time to prevent Dambala visiting this grisly fate on the beautiful Solitaire.

RITUAL MURDER *Dambala performs his deadly voodoo ceremony, closing in on a helpless victim.*

DARIO

APPEARANCE
Licence To Kill (1989)
STATUS Pulverized
CHARACTERISTICS Cocky, menacing, pitiless; handy with a knife
PLAYED BY Benicio Del Toro

Dario works as a key enforcer for Franz Sanchez, a Central American drug lord. Sanchez treats Dario, the youngest member of his inner circle, like a younger brother.

Dario demonstrates his skill with a Bowie knife when he arrives in Cray Cay with Sanchez to retrieve the drug lord's girlfriend, Lupe Lamora. Dario removes the heart of her illicit lover, Alvarez, and provides Sanchez with a "little valentine." After DEA agent Felix Leiter, who has been hunting Sanchez for years, finally captures him, Dario exacts revenge by stabbing Della, Felix's bride. Dario

then helps Sanchez lower Leiter into a shark tank.

Dario acquires Leiter's secret files and eliminates all of Leiter's contacts in his investigation of Sanchez except one—Pam Bouvier. Dario travels to the Barrelhead Bar in Bimini to kill her and shoots her in the back as she speeds away in a boat with 007. Dario thinks she is dead, unaware that her Kevlar vest stopped the bullets.

When Bond participates in a tour of Sanchez's drug processing plant, Dario reconizes him. His cover exposed, Bond sets the lab ablaze, but Sanchez captures and interrogates him. When Bond refuses to speak, Dario throw him onto a conveyor belt leading to a pulverizer. Before Dario can kill Bond, Pam appears through the cocaine mist and Dario momentarily thinks she is a ghost. Pam shoots Dario, and Bond hurls him into the pulverizer.

DAVIDOV

APPEARANCE
The World Is Not Enough (1999)
STATUS Dead; killed by Bond
CHARACTERISTICS Quiet, nervous
PLAYED BY Ulrich Thomsen

Sasha Davidov runs security for King Industries. Although he acts out the charade that terrorist Renard is threatening Elektra King's life, Davidov, in fact, is in league with Elektra, Renard, and Dr. Arkov in a plot to steal a nuclear bomb from an abandoned facility in Kazakhstan. When Renard orders Arkov's death, Davidov takes Arkov's place to gain entry to the nuclear facility. Bond shoots Davidov and assumes Arkov's identity.

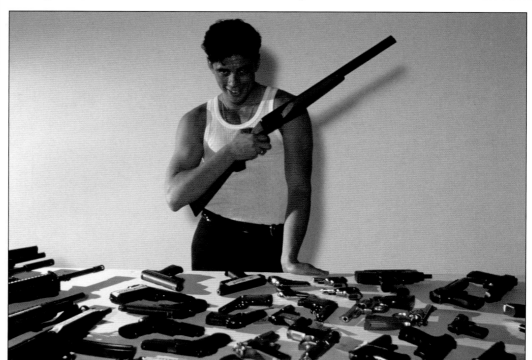

MENACING MAN
Totally loyal to Sanchez, Dario enjoys inflicting pain and terrorizing victims of his boss's displeasure.

DAY, MAY

APPEARANCE
A View To A Kill (1985)
STATUS Dead; blown up
CHARACTERISTICS Strong, dedicated, stylish, deadly
PLAYED BY Grace Jones

Of all the foes faced by 007, none can claim to be more exotic than the couture killer May Day. With strength allowing her to lift a grown man over her head and the poise to base jump from the top of the Eiffel Tower, May Day appears to be the perfect ally and lover for Max Zorin. Both have near-total disregard for human life and manic personalities.

May Day's main role in Zorin's plot appears to be killing his opponents. She murders French private detective Aubergine, MI6 agent Sir Godfrey Tibbett, and CIA agent Chuck Lee. She makes love to Bond on her terms, but remains perfectly willing to kill him. Yet, events at the Main Strike mine change her mind. After loyally murdering Zorin's potential enemies, she discovers that Zorin sees her as expendable. He floods the Main Strike mine with her in it, killing numerous other associates. Overcome with a newfound sense of decency, she helps Bond disrupt Zorin's plan to set off a double earthquake, flood Silicone Valley, and monopolize microchip production. Using her enormous upper body strength, May Day cranes up a detonator from a pit of explosives then personally guides the timed device outside the mine. Knowing she will die when the detonator explodes, May Day asks one favor from Bond: "Get Zorin for me!"

007: I can see you're a woman of very few words.
May Day: What's there to say?

DENT, PROF.

APPEARANCE
Dr. No (1962)
STATUS Dead; shot by 007
CHARACTERISTICS Suspicious, rash; dislikes doing his own dirty work
PLAYED BY Anthony Dawson

According to the script of *Dr. No*, Professor R. J. Dent is "40, distinguished-looking, and a metallurgist by profession." He is also the leader of Dr. No's organization in Jamaica. He oversees the murder of anyone too curious about Dr. No's activities on his island Crab Key, such as British agent Strangways and his secretary, Mary.

When James Bond arrives in Jamaica to investigate Strangways's disappearance, Dent sends an assassin, Mr. Jones, to intercept him. Jones, confronted by Bond, ends up dead, weakening Dent's suggestion that Strangways might simply have run off with his secretary.

Bond's discovery of a receipt from Dent's metallurgist lab forces Dent to lie about the radioactive rock samples Strangways brought to him from Crab Key. Knowing Bond may discover the truth, Dent plots several attempts on Bond's life. He arranges for a tarantula to be placed in Bond's bed and, when this fails, he instructs his associate, Miss Taro, to invite Bond to her house, ordering the Three Blind Mice assassins to attack Bond on the way.

Bond survives and arrives at Miss Taro's unscathed, much to her surprise. She phones Dent, who tells her to delay Bond. Suspecting a trick, Bond makes love to Miss Taro before having her arrested. He then waits for Dent to arrive. After Dent fires all his bullets into pillows Bond has placed under the bedclothes to resemble his body, Bond coolly shoots Dent twice.

DOCTOR'S ORDERS *Summoned by Dr. No, Professor Dent takes delivery of a deadly tarantula with which to eliminate 007.*

DIMITRIOS, ALEX

APPEARANCE
Casino Royale (2006)
STATUS Dead; killed by Bond
CHARACTERISTICS Quick-tempered, jealous, sleazy, vengeful
PLAYED BY Simon Abkarian

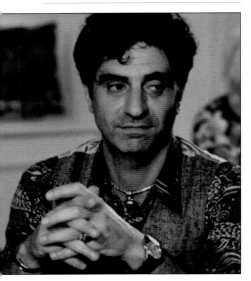

Dimitrios organizes professional saboteurs for terrorist banker Le Chiffre in his plot to manipulate the stock price of the aircraft manufacturer Skyfleet. According to the MI6 database, Dimitrios has been a government contractor in Iraq, Afghanistan, Chechnya, Rwanda, Nicaragua, and El Salvador for the past 30-odd years. Working as an arms dealer, Dimitrios has ties to death squads and right-wing paramilitary groups. MI6 Intelligence believes most of Dimitrios's associates have been killed, including the very much alive Le Chiffre.

When Bond finds a cell phone number in the belongings of bomb-maker Mollaka, he traces a mysterious text message to Dimitrios in the Bahamas. There, Bond humiliates Dimitrios at poker, wins possession of his vintage Aston Martin DB5, and seduces his wife, Solange. When Dimitrios has to travel to Miami to provide payment to another saboteur, Carlos, Bond follows him. Dimitrios tries to kill Bond at the Body Worlds Exhibition, but Bond turns the tables on him, stabbing Dimitrios with his own stiletto.

DRAX, HUGO

APPEARANCE Moonraker (1979)
STATUS Dead; orbiting
CHARACTERISTICS Dignified, messianic, brilliant, softly spoken, cultured
PLAYED BY Michael Lonsdale

Aerospace mogul Hugo Drax secretly launches a deadly attack on humanity in order to eradicate the human race from the earth. He plans to repopulate it with hand-picked, genetically ideal humans and create an "ultimate dynasty."

Drax is, as James Bond notes, "obsessed with the conquest of space." He has built an aerospace empire in Southern California, including a state-of-the-art manufacturing facility for the *Moonraker*, a space shuttle created ostensibly for NASA. Drax has also launched a personally funded training program for a new astronaut corps, reputedly to man the *Moonraker* fleet. In fact, he has built the shuttles and trained the astronauts to help him carry out his masterplan.

Little of Drax's background is known, but the scale of his operation provides evidence that he has built his empire over many years. Drax's austere, emotionless manner masks an inner belief in himself as a godlike figure. His aristocratic lifestyle rivals that of King Louis XIV of France—Drax even lives in a French chateau brought stone by stone to California.

Drax's other base, the launch site for his shuttles, lies deep in the South American jungle inside a ruined Mayan temple. Here Drax dresses in the style of Chinese dictator Mao Zedong.

" James Bond. You appear with the tedious inevitability of an **unloved season.** "
Drax to 007

RENAISSANCE MAN *Drax prides himself on being a man of culture and taste. When Bond first meets him, he is playing the piano for two guests, Countess Labinsky and Lady Victoria Devon.*

A MODEL CREW *Hugo Drax's astronaut corps, hand-picked for their physical attractiveness, arrive on Drax's space station as part of his scheme to create an "ultimate dynasty."*

While supposedly building the *Moonraker* shuttle fleet for the US government, Drax secretly manufactures and launches an orbiting space station. He also creates radar cloaking devices that hide both the launches and the station from detection. Drax's scientists have distilled a nerve gas, derived from the rare orchid *Orchidacea Negra,* that only kills humans. Drax plans to convey his astronauts into space and rain down globes of this nerve gas onto the Earth, killing all humanity.

When one of Drax's shuttles develops a problem, he arrogantly steals another delivered to the US government. Since that shuttle was in the possession of the Royal Air Force at the time, MI6 sends Bond to investigate. This leads to many overt attempts by Drax to have Bond killed, arousing further suspicion on Bond's part. 007 discovers Drax's South American base and, after a series of escapades, finally confronts Drax on his space station. Bond eliminates Drax with his wrist-dart gun and destroys the globes of gas before they can strike the Earth.

In the novel *Moonraker*, Drax is a Nazi mistaken for a burned British soldier. After the war, Drax builds his empire to launch a rocket with an atomic warhead at London.

DRYDEN

APPEARANCE
Casino Royale (2006)
STATUS Dead; shot by Bond
CHARACTERISTICS Devious, fatalistic
PLAYED BY Malcolm Sinclair

Prague station chief Dryden becomes James Bond's second kill in his progress to become a double-0 agent. Dryden has turned traitor, selling MI6 secrets through a network that includes Fisher, a contact in Pakistan. After Bond kills Fisher, he visits Dryden and assassinates him in his office.

FAT, HAI

APPEARANCE
The Man With The Golden Gun (1974)
STATUS Interred in his own mausoleum
CHARACTERISTICS Ruthless, arrogant, fatally over-confident
PLAYED BY Richard Loo

Bangkok businessman Hai Fat hopes to monopolize the solar energy market by obtaining a highly efficient solar cell, the Solex. To this end, he partners with hit man Scaramanga, finances a solar power plant on a remote Chinese island, and lures expert Gibson away from the British. When Bond investigates, Fat expresses regret at involving Scaramanga in his plan. In response, Scaramanga shoots Fat dead.

FEYADOR, COL.

APPEARANCE
The Living Daylights (1987)
STATUS Dead; blown up
CHARACTERISTICS Corrupt comrade
PLAYED BY John Bowe

Colonel Feyador is commander of a Soviet airfield in Afghanistan. An old comrade-in-arms of Soviet General Georgi Koskov, Feyador is the only one on his base aware of Koskov's duplicitous defection to the West. He is involved with Koskov and Whitaker's opium-smuggling scheme. When Kamran Shah and his mujahedeen rebels attack the base, Shah throws a grenade under former captor Feyador's petrol truck, blowing him up.

FILLET OF SOUL WAITER

APPEARANCE
Live And Let Die (1973)
STATUS Living
CHARACTERISTICS Outwardly deferential, but capable of nasty turns
PLAYED BY Dan Jackson

The Fillet of Soul waiter works for Kananga/Mr. Big. When Bond orders a bourbon and water "neat" (no ice), the waiter tells him this will cost him extra. The same waiter delivers Bond into Mr. Big's clutches at two different clubs: once by seating Bond in a pivoting booth and second at a sinking table.

FISHER

APPEARANCE
Casino Royale (2006)
STATUS Dead; killed by Bond
CHARACTERISTICS Hard to kill
PLAYED BY Daud Shah

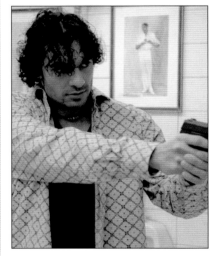

Fisher is in league with MI6 station chief Dryden selling British government secrets. As such, he becomes James Bond's first assassination assignment, one of two government-sanctioned killings necessary to achieve "00" status.

In a bathroom at a cricket stadium in Pakistan, Bond believes he has drowned Fisher and turns away. Fisher, still alive, grabs his gun and takes aim. Bond's lightning reactions serve him well as he turns and shoots Fisher dead.

FLEX, JENNY

APPEARANCE
A View To A Kill (1985)
STATUS Dead; submerged
CHARACTERISTICS Charming, cruel
PLAYED BY Alison Doody

Jenny Flex works as one of Max Zorin's deadly female accomplices. An avid horsewoman, Flex meets James Bond at Zorin's French chateau. She assists in the kidnapping and murder attempt on Bond in France as well as starting the fire in San Francisco City Hall.

In Zorin's Main Strike Mine, Flex delivers a bomb disguised as a coffee thermos to Scarpine and helps position the detonator Zorin plans to use to create a double earthquake. She chases after Bond

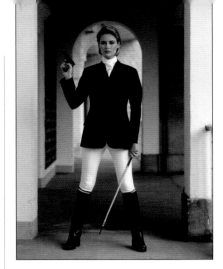

and geologist Stacey Sutton when Zorin finds them hiding in the mine. Along with many others, Zorin betrays Flex, flooding the mine with her in it.

FRANKS, PETER

APPEARANCE
Diamonds Are Forever (1971)
STATUS Dead; killed by Bond
CHARACTERISTICS Experienced smuggler; skilled at close quarters combat
PLAYED BY Joe Robinson

Smuggler Peter Franks unwittingly provides cover for Bond to infiltrate Blofeld's diamond smuggling operation. Before Franks can move a hoard of diamonds from Amsterdam to Los Angeles for $50,000, British officials arrest him. Bond poses as Franks, complete with fake fingerprints, to meet his contact Tiffany Case. When Franks escapes custody, Bond must prevent him from contacting Case. Bond and Franks fight in the elevator in Case's apartment building and, after a brutal struggle, Bond kills Franks. Bond convinces Case that the dead man is 007 and smuggles the diamonds into the US in Franks's coffin.

FROST, MIRANDA

APPEARANCE
Die Another Day (2002)
STATUS Dead; killed by Jinx
CHARACTERISTICS Aloof, articulate
PLAYED BY Rosamund Pike

Cold-hearted Miranda Frost is an MI6 agent, Olympic fencer, and the secret lover of Gustav Graves/Colonel Moon.

Miranda meets Colonel Moon when they both compete for the Harvard Fencing Team. They fall in love, and, after completing his education, Moon returns to North Korea corrupt and power-hungry. Miranda wins the 2000 Olympic Gold Medal in Fencing by default when Moon arranges for the true victor to overdose on steroids. Frost is soon recruited by MI6 and the three years she spends working in cryptology place her in the ideal position to keep her lover abreast of ministry secrets.

Miranda betrays Bond in North Korea by informing Moon's associate Zao of his true identity. Bond's infiltration of Moon's organization forces Moon to change his identity to Gustav Graves via DNA replacement therapy. Although his face is different, Miranda still loves him, and pretends to spy on him for MI6 while working as his publicist. She battles NSA agent Jinx aboard Graves's Antonov plane using various knives and swords until Jinx fatally stabs her in the heart.

> " I know all about you 007. **Sex for dinner, death for breakfast.** Well it's not going to work with me. "
> Miranda Frost

GABOR

APPEARANCE
The World Is Not Enough (1999)
STATUS Dead; guarded
CHARACTERISTICS Silent, protective
PLAYED BY John Seru

Gabor is the loyal bodyguard of Elektra King and has been at her side since her kidnapping by the terrorist Renard. Gabor follows Elektra wherever she travels and also works to protect her more nefarious interests.

Bond shoots Gabor dead at the Maiden's Tower, Istanbul, immediately after Baku-based casino and caviar factory owner Valentin Zukovsky frees Bond from Elektra's torture chair.

GETTLER

APPEARANCE
Casino Royale (2006)
STATUS Dead; killed by Bond
CHARACTERISTICS Methodical killer
PLAYED BY Richard Sammel

Gettler, distinguished by his Panama hat and glasses with one dark lens, works for terrorist Mr. White, who sends him to Venice to acquire the money Vesper Lynd has embezzled from Bond's holding account. Bond discovers Vesper's treachery and pursues her through the streets, but Gettler spots him and takes Vesper hostage in a building under restoration on one of Venice's canals. Bond kills Gettler by firing a nail gun into the dark lens of his glasses.

In the novel, SMERSH agent Gettler hunts down Vesper when she refuses to cooperate with SMERSH.

GOLDFINGER

APPEARANCE
Goldfinger (1964)
STATUS Dead; depressurized
CHARACTERISTICS The personification of greed, a compulsive cheater, brilliant criminal strategist
PLAYED BY Gert Frobe

One of the most audacious criminal masterminds in history, Auric Goldfinger assaults and successfully penetrates the United States Bullion Depository at Fort Knox, nearly succeeding in his Operation Grand Slam to irradiate $15 billion of gold—the entire Federal Gold Reserve.

One of the world's richest men, obsessed with gold and its acquisition, Goldfinger, a British citizen, owns gold deposits in Zurich, Amsterdam, Hong Kong, and Caracas worth roughly £20 million. According to the Fleming novel, Goldfinger's father and grandfather worked for Gustav and Carl Fabergé, jewelers to the Imperial Court of Russia. Born in 1916, Auric immigrated to England from Riga, Lithuania, at the age of 21. By purchasing gold coins and jewelry through a chain of pawn shops, Goldfinger amassed a fortune.

In the film, Goldfinger plots to place an atomic device, obtained from the Communist Chinese government, inside Fort Knox. By

GOBINDA

APPEARANCE
Octopussy (1983)
STATUS Dead; fell from airplane
CHARACTERISTICS Commanding, silent, murderous, exceptionally loyal; practiced with various antique weapons
PLAYED BY Kabir Bedi

Gobinda works in the service of amoral exiled Afghan prince Kamal Khan. He grimly eliminates anyone who interferes with Khan's plans.

Described in the script as a "tall, imposing Sikh in Indian suit and turban," Gobinda demonstrates his strength when, after Bond defeats Kamal Khan at backgammon using Khan's own loaded dice, he crushes the dice into sand in front of Bond.

Gobinda attempts to kill Bond numerous times—firing a blunderbuss at him from a tuk-tuk taxi, shooting at him during a supposed tiger hunt, and attempting to cut him in half with a sword while on top of smuggler Octopussy's circus train. Despite his repeated failures to end Bond's life, Gobinda

GUNNING FOR 007 *Gobinda attempts to bring down Bond with his blunderbuss during a spectacular chase through a crowded market.*

remains undeterred and implacable.

Gobinda and Khan hire a band of local thugs, led by the sinister Mufti, to assassinate Bond. The thugs make their attempt on Bond's life while Bond visits Octopussy's magnificent floating palace. Under Gobinda's command, the thugs kill Bond's contact Vijay with a deadly yo-yo buzz saw and then use snorkels disguised as lilypads to cross the lake surrounding the palace. They then sneak into the palace, unsuccessfully attempting to kill Bond with the same buzz saw while he and Octopussy make love.

Alhough Khan betrays Octopussy and Magda, he remains loyal to Gobinda until he orders him to climb out of his Beech 18 plane in mid-air and battle Bond, at which point Gobinda realizes that Khan will even sacrifice him. As Gobinda and Bond struggle, Bond bends back an antenna on top of the plane's fuselage and whips it into Gobinda's face, causing him to lose his grip and fall to his death.

AN ODD COUPLE *Goldfinger and his Korean manservant and caddy Oddjob calmly prepare for a round of golf.*

this coup, Goldfinger plans to increase the market value of his own sizeable gold hoard tenfold; the Communist Chinese hope to induce economic chaos in the West.

Bond gains a valuable insight into Goldfinger's ultra-competitive, devious, and ruthless nature when he catches him cheating at gin rummy in Miami Beach. Goldfinger's anger that his paid companion Jill Masterson betrayed him to Bond results in her horrific death from skin suffocation; he has her painted gold. Rumors that Goldfinger has been smuggling gold ignite the interest of the British Secret Service and MI6 sets Bond on Goldfinger's

tail. Bond infuriates Goldfinger by out-tricking him in a golf match and then follows him to his factory in Switzerland. There Bond discovers that Goldfinger has been smuggling gold from England in the body panels of his Rolls-Royce.

Goldfinger then kidnaps Bond, who, having chanced to overhear mention of "Operation Grand Slam," convinces Goldfinger to keep him alive, instead of cutting him in half with an industrial laser.

Using most of the organized crime families in the US to smuggle in the components he needs to carry out his plan, Goldfinger gathers the crime bosses together at his stud farm in Kentucky, boastfully informs

GRAND SLAM *Auric Goldfinger explains his masterplan to a convention of American hoods. He twists the details to make them think he plans to steal the gold in Fort Knox.*

them of some of the details of Operation Grand Slam, and then proceeds to gas them all.

One ally he cannot afford to betray, Pussy Galore, proves to be his downfall. Goldfinger enlists Galore's pilots from her Flying Circus to spray Delta-9 nerve gas over the Fort Knox area. Bond convinces Galore to reconsider. She works with the authorities to replace the deadly gas in the canisters. When Goldfinger makes his assault, he finds himself

involved in a battle. Nevertheless, he manages to get his atomic device locked inside the depository, with Bond handcuffed to it, before escaping. The authorities defuse the bomb, but Goldfinger has one last trick. He hijacks a presidential jet flying Bond to the White House. During a fight on board, Goldfinger fires his pistol. The shot shatters a window. As the cabin depressurizes, Goldfinger is sucked through the opening to his doom.

FACING DEATH *Strapped to a golden table, helpless beneath Goldfinger's industrial laser, Bond racks his brains for an escape route.*

007:
Do you expect me to talk?
Goldfinger:
No, Mr. Bond.
I expect you to die!

GONZALES, HECTOR

APPEARANCE
For Your Eyes Only (1981)
STATUS Assassinated
CHARACTERISTICS Arrogant and
deadly assassin-for-hire
PLAYED BY Stefan Kalipha

Cuban hit man Hector Gonzales poses as a pilot for the Athens-based Kerkyra Charter Service in order to murder British agent Sir Timothy Havelock and his wife, Iona. Gonzales flies Timothy and Iona's daughter Melina to her parents' research ship, *Triana* in Corfu Harbour. He then turns his seaplane around and guns down her parents.

The Greek police identify Gonzales using Melina's description. Through a detective agency, Melina tracks Gonzales to a villa outside Madrid, Spain. After Gonzales receives a payment from henchman Locque for the Havelock murders, Melina, hiding in nearby bushes, shoots him with her crossbow.

Major Hector Gonzales appears in Ian Fleming's short story *For Your Eyes Only*, set in Jamaica. Gonzales works for a man named Von Hammerstein, and he murders the Havelocks when they refuse to sell their land.

GRANT, DONALD "RED"

APPEARANCE
From Russia With Love (1963)
STATUS Dead; eliminated by 007
CHARACTERISTICS A cunning killer
who enjoys playing a waiting game; very fit, bitter, psychotic, greedy for money
PLAYED BY Robert Shaw

Donald Grant is SPECTRE's ultimate killing machine. His physical strength and methodical determination set him apart from other assassins.

Named Donovan Grant in Ian Fleming's novel, he hails from Northern Ireland where he won a boxing title in 1945. Defecting in Berlin, Grant works as the chief executioner for SMERSH and has adopted the Russian name Krassno Granitski. His murderous moods are linked to lunar cycles.

In the film, Grant is a convicted murderer who escaped from Dartmoor Prison in 1960. SPECTRE recruited him in Tangier in 1962. A homicidal paranoiac, Grant responded well to SPECTRE training, changing his crude killing techniques. He has one affectation: he pulls on gloves before committing a murder. He also often garrotes his victims with a wire concealed inside his watch.

SPECTRE member Rosa Klebb selects Grant to carry out Kronsteen's plot to humiliate the British Secret Service, exact vengeance on James Bond for the death of Dr. No, and sell a Lektor decoder back to the Soviets.

Grant initially serves as Bond's guardian angel, protecting him from assassination until Bond can steal the decoder. Grant then isolates Bond by murdering both Head of Station T Kerim Bey and Soviet security agent Benz aboard the Orient Express. He assassinates the British agent sent by M to meet Bond in Zagreb and takes the alias of Captain Nash. Bond

becomes suspicious when Grant orders red wine with fish at dinner. Grant drugs Soviet cipher clerk Tatiana Romanova before confronting Bond on board the train. Faced with certain death, Bond exploits Grant's greed by telling him that his attaché case and another one in the compartment both have gold sovereigns in them. When Grant opens the second case, he sets off a tear-gas canister. After a brutal fight, Bond strangles Grant with the garrote-wire watch.

THE IMPOSTER *To get the drop on Bond aboard the Orient Express, Grant pretends to be a British agent named Captain Nash.*

> "He seems fit enough. **Have him report to me in Istanbul in 24 hours.**"
>
> Rosa Klebb

GRAVES, GUSTAV / MOON, COLONEL

APPEARANCE
Die Another Day (2002)

STATUS Dead; electrocuted

CHARACTERISTICS Suffers from anger-management issues; obsessed with victory; cannot sleep so he attempts to live his dreams.

PLAYED BY Toby Stephens/ Will Yun Lee

ON THE TAKE *Moon abuses his position in the North Korean army to gain considerable wealth for himself.*

Colonel Tan-Sun Moon, alias Gustav Graves, is a psychotic North Korean officer who hopes to forcefully unite South Korea with the North and form a new superpower. Moon is the son of peaceful North Korean General Moon, who wishes to form a bridge between his country and the West by sending his son to Harvard to receive a Western education. There the younger Moon falls for beautiful British fencer Miranda Frost, and becomes consumed with dreams of power. After further study at Oxford University, Moon returns to North Korea where his father awards him

the rank of Colonel.

Moon subsequently arranges for the winner of the fencing gold medal at the Sydney Olympics to overdose on steroids so that the runner-up, Miranda Frost, can claim the gold by default. In return for this service, Miranda gives Graves full access to the Ministry's secrets when she begins working for MI6.

When 007 arrives in North Korea to stop Moon's trade in African conflict diamonds, Miranda tips off Moon's henchman Zao to Bond's real identity via PDA mobile phone. Bond and Moon battle on board a hovercraft amid the minefields of the Korean Demilitarized Zone (DMZ), resulting in Moon plunging over a high waterfall.

Moon is thought dead, but he is actually only injured. He secretly travels to Dr. Alvarez's Cuban clinic to undergo painful DNA replacement therapy. Several months later, he emerges with a new face and identity. He reappears as Argentinean orphan Gustav Graves, an engineer who has discovered a fortune in diamonds in Iceland (they are really African conflict diamonds). Graves amasses great wealth and presents himself as an environmentalist, a humanitarian and a relentless sportsman training for the British Olympic fencing team. Only the latter is true, but soon his adoptive nation of Britain offers him a knighthood.

With his great wealth, he announces a grand humanitarian project at a party at his Ice Palace in Iceland: the Icarus space mirror. Graves claims the Icarus will act as a second sun, growing crops and preventing hunger. In fact, Icarus is a deadly weapon

capable of destruction on a massive scale. Bond eventually battles Graves to the death aboard his Antonov plane, electrocutes Graves with his own battlesuit, and sends him into the jet engines.

Graves/Moon is based on the character of Hugo Drax in the novel *Moonraker*—a Nazi who changes his face and lives as a knighted Englishman with plans to use his Moonraker rocket to destroy London. The name Colonel Moon is a nod to the first non-Fleming James Bond novel *Colonel Sun* by Kingsley Amis (under the pseudonym Robert Markham), in which the villain's name is Colonel Sun Liang-tan.

> "You see, Mr. Bond, you can't kill my dreams. But my dreams can kill you."
>
> Gustav Graves

ELECTRIC WARRIOR *Graves's battlesuit, possessing a taser defense system and allowing Graves to control his Icarus superweapon, greatly enhances his strength.*

CROSSING SWORDS *Bond gets under the skin of Gustav Graves by defeating him in a spectacular duel at Blades, Graves's fencing club.*

GRISHENKO, BORIS

APPEARANCE
GoldenEye (1995)
STATUS Dead; frozen stiff
CHARACTERISTICS Talented computer programmer, highly inflated opinion of himself, not invincible
PLAYED BY Alan Cumming

PASSWORD PROTECTED *Boris teases Natalya with another prank on her computer, making her guess the password—"Knockers."*

Boris Grishenko provides former MI6 agent Alec Trevelyan with the hacker skills to carry out a plot to zap London with an electromagnetic pulse weapon named GoldenEye and illegally transfer billions of pounds from the Bank of England.

Grishenko works at the Severnaya Space Weapons Control Centre in Siberia as the senior computer programmer. In his spare time, he hacks into secure computers around the world. He loves riddles, which he uses to create passwords. Boris, who has the maturity of a pre-adolescent, sees the world as

BLIND AMBITION *Boris Grishenko believes he is the best hacker in the world, and with Trevelyan's grand scheme, he plans to prove it.*

though it is a computer game, with little or no moral consequences to his action. His victory yell is, "I am invincible!"

Boris gives the signal for General Ourumov and Xenia Onatopp to start the massacre at Severnaya and later lures programmer Natalya Simonova into a trap in St. Petersburg. In Cuba, Boris not only programs the surviving GoldenEye satellite to detonate over London, but he also hacks into the Bank of England mainframe. When Bond and Natalya infiltrate the Cuban control complex, Boris seems happy to see Simonova alive, and is unprepared for her anger at his actions.

More worrisome for Boris, Simonova alters the GoldenEye's course, programming the satellite to burn up over the Atlantic. Boris tries to break her pass codes as Bond and Simonova work to destroy the satellite control station. He survives the crash of the transmitter and antenna through the complex's roof, but, as he celebrates, a cascade of liquid nitrogen freezes him solid.

LAST ACT *Trevelyan and Grishenko move into the final stages of their plan to blast London with GoldenEye.*

"I am invincible!"

Boris Grishenko

GRUNTHER

APPEARANCE
On Her Majesty's Secret Service (1969)
STATUS Dead; reached a prickly end
CHARACTERISTICS Quiet, merciless
PLAYED BY Yuri Borienko

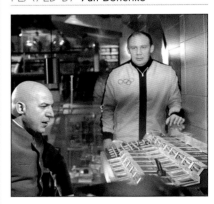

SIDEKICK *Grunther helps Blofeld in the brainwashing of his 12 allergy patients.*

Described in the script as a "professional winter-sports man," Grunther is security chief at Ernst Stavro Blofeld's allergy clinic Piz Gloria. He prevents Bond's contact Campbell from boarding the cable car leading to Blofeld's mountaintop retreat and later leads Blofeld's men down the alpine slopes in a frantic race to kill 007, who is armed with information regarding Blofeld's bacteriological warfare plot. Grunther eventually dies struggling with Bond's fiancée Tracy at Piz Gloria. She defeats him by spinning him into a spiked wall decoration.

GUPTA, HENRY

APPEARANCE
Tomorrow Never Dies (1997)
STATUS Dead; shot by Elliot Carver
CHARACTERISTICS A dedicated
anarchist, mild-mannered, cunning
PLAYED BY Ricky Jay

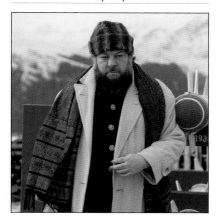

Employed by media mogul Elliot
Carver, Henry Gupta plays a key role
in Carver's plot to foment war
between Britain and China. Formerly
a student radical at Berkeley in the
1960s, Gupta developed the concept
of techno-terrorism. He purchases a
GPS encoder and barely escapes with
his life when Bond raids a terrorist
arms bazaar in the Khyber Pass. With
the aid of Carver's satellites, Gupta
uses the GPS encoder to send HMS
Devonshire off course into Vietnamese
waters, igniting an international
incident. He also acts as a security
advisor to Carver, declaring Bond to
be a government agent and showing
Carver a security camera recording of
his wife, Paris, admitting that she once
had an affair with 007. Carver kills
Gupta when he outlives his usefulness.

HANS

APPEARANCE
You Only Live Twice (1967)
STATUS Dead; eaten by piranhas
CHARACTERISTICS Strong, impassive
PLAYED BY Ronald Rich

Hans serves as Ernst Stavro Blofeld's
bodyguard during Blofeld's time in
Japan. Tall, quiet, and tremendously
strong, Hans performs a
demonstration feeding of Blofeld's
piranhas for the representatives of
the Communist Chinese government
to encourage them to pay Blofeld in
advance for his services.
   During the Japanese SIS ninja
attack on the rocket base, Blofeld
entrusts Hans with the key to the
Bird 1 exploder button so that Hans

can destroy the spacecraft once it has
engulfed the US Jupiter orbiter.
James Bond confronts Hans, steals
the exploder key, and flips him into
Blofeld's piranha pool where the fish
promptly eat him.

HELLER

APPEARANCE
Licence To Kill (1989)
STATUS Forked; came to a dead end
CHARACTERISTICS Protective,
aggressive
PLAYED BY Don Stroud

Heller, an ex-Green Beret colonel, is
drug lord Franz Sanchez's security
chief. He inadvertently saves Bond's
life when he attacks a safe house run
by narcotics agents Kwang and Loti.
   Pam Bouvier gives Heller a letter
from the US Attorney General
granting him immunity if he safely
returns four Stinger missiles bought
by Sanchez from the Contras. Bond
later uses this information to further
the distrust between Sanchez and his
men. Pam and Bond discover Heller
impaled on a forklift blade, courtesy
of Sanchez's henchman Braun.

WRESTLING MATCH *Bond tangles with Hans
in Blofeld's apartment, trying to grab the key
that will blow up Blofeld's* Bird 1 *rocket.*

HOWE, W. G.

APPEARANCE
A View To A Kill (1985)
STATUS Dead; shot by Zorin
CHARACTERISTICS A weak-willed
yes-man, misguidedly loyal to Zorin
PLAYED BY Daniel Benzali

Based at San Francisco City Hall,
office of the State Department of
Conservation, Division of Oil and
Mines, W. G. Howe unwittingly aids
industrialist Max Zorin in his plot to
destroy California's Silicon Valley. He
barely tolerates State Geologist
Stacey Sutton, and when she
continues to question Zorin's
activities, Howe fires her at Zorin's
request. Zorin does not reward
Howe for his help; he kills him with
Bond's Walther PPK in order to
frame Bond for Howe's murder.

IMPOSTER 00 AGENT

APPEARANCE
The Living Daylights (1987)
STATUS Dead; cover blown
CHARACTERISTICS Determined
PLAYED BY Carl Rigg

The Imposter 00 Agent works for
General Koskov to ignite a secret
war between Britain and the Soviet
Union. He infiltrates a training
mission for three 00 agents who
parachute onto Gibraltar for a
routine training exercise with the
SAS. The Imposter kills an SAS
guard and 004. This is the beginning
of the *Smiert Spionam*—"Death to
Spies"—plot hatched by Koskov and
US arms dealer Brad Whitaker to
convince the British that KGB head
General Pushkin should be killed.
Bond battles the Imposter in a stolen,
explosive-filled British Army Land
Rover, which eventually plummets
over a cliff toward the water. Bond
deploys his back-up parachute,
escaping the vehicle as its cargo
explodes over the Mediterranean.

ANONYMOUS *The Imposter 00 Agent
eliminates an SAS guard on Gibraltar.*

JAILER

APPEARANCE
The Living Daylights (1987)
STATUS Unknown
CHARACTERISTICS Sadistic and
brutal; laughs at his own jokes
PLAYED BY Ken Sharrock

The jailer working for Colonel
Feyador at a Soviet air base in
Afghanistan is charged with holding
Bond and cellist Kara Milovy before
sending them to Moscow. After
threatening mujaheddin leader
Kamran Shah with execution and
Kara with a strip search, the jailer beats
Bond before taking his key fob from
him. However, when Bond whistles
Rule, Britannia! his key fob emits a
cloud of stun gas, dazing the Soviet
jailer long enough for 007 to get the
better of him and escape with Kara.

WHISTLE WHILE YOU WORK *The Soviet army
jailer plays with Bond's key fob.*

JANNI

APPEARANCE
Thunderball (1965)
STATUS Dead; killed in explosion
CHARACTERISTICS Likes his dirty work
PLAYED BY Michael Brennan

Janni works for SPECTRE No. 2,
Emilio Largo, and is often paired
with Vargas. Janni helps Vargas kidnap
James Bond's Nassau contact Paula
Caplan and also searches for Bond in
the Junkanoo parade. Janni dies when
the hydrofoil portion of Largo's
yacht, *Disco Volante*, crashes into a
coral reef and explodes.

TIED UP *Janni works
enthusiastically with Vargas
to kidnap Paula Caplan.*

JAWS

APPEARANCE
The Spy Who Loved Me (1977);
Moonraker (1979)
STATUS Alive and living large
CHARACTERISTICS Orally fixated,
deadly bite; seemingly indestructible
PLAYED BY Richard Kiel

This seven-foot-two-inch monster of
a man with steel teeth is one of the
most awe-inspiring figures in the
history of villainy.

Nothing of the background of
Jaws exists in the Bond films, but
screenwriter Christopher Wood
reveals quite a bit of the history of
Jaws in his novelization of *The Spy
Who Loved Me*. Born Zbigniew
Krycsiwiki in Poland, his father was a
circus strongman and his mother a
prison warden. A police arrest in
1972 led to a beating that destroyed
his teeth and jaw. Eventually, the
megalomaniac Karl Stromberg found
him and coerced a former
concentration camp doctor into
saving Krycsiwiki. Fourteen
operations later, Krycsiwiki's jaw
worked again, but now with razor-
sharp steel teeth.

Working as an enforcer for
Stromberg, Jaws initially attempts to
obtain a microfilm of the plans of
Stromberg's submarine tracking
system from Max Kalba in Cairo.
James Bond and Major Anya
Amasova steal it back that evening.
Jaws later attacks them on a train, but
Bond kicks him out a window.

Jaws is nothing if not persistent. In
Sardinia, Bond sprays his windshield

" He just dropped
in for a
quick bite. "
Bond to Anya Amasova

HIGH AMBITION *(top) Jaws prepares to try to kill James Bond again in* Moonraker.

HOT SHOTS *(top right) Jaws and a henchman fire gunshots at Bond and Anya Amasova in* The Spy Who Loved Me.

HEAVY WEIGHT *(above) Jaws moments before he accidentally drops a stone block on his own foot in* The Spy Who Loved Me.

PERFECT MATCH *(right) Jaws with the petite Dolly, his true love, in orbit in* Moonraker.

with cement, sending his car full of killers off a cliff. Later, in Stromberg's *Atlantis* base, Bond uses an electromagnet to lift Jaws by his teeth and drop him in a shark tank. Somehow Jaws survives all of these indignities.

Later, working for an unnamed employer, Jaws shoves 007 out of a charter jet, then skydives after him, only to tear loose his own ripcord and plunge into a circus tent. The industrialist Hugo Drax soon hires Jaws to work for him. Jaws attempts to kill Bond at Rio's Carnival and then tries to end 007's life on the cable cars at Sugarloaf Mountain. For his troubles, Jaws crashes at high speed into the control station. In the rubble, he meets Dolly, and the pair immediately falls in love.

Jaws travels with Drax to his secret rocket base, where he helps Drax

with security issues, such as chasing Bond over a waterfall in a boat and later policing 007 while Drax gives Bond a tour of his control room.

Jaws soon travels to Drax's space station with Dolly. After capturing Bond and Dr. Holly Goodhead, he eventually realizes that, when Drax has accomplished his plan to repopulate the earth with beautiful people, both he and Dolly will be eliminated. He fights Drax's men alongside Bond and then frees a *Moonraker* shuttle so that Bond and Holly can escape Drax's exploding space station. When it looks like Jaws will die in space, he shares a bottle of champagne with his lover, speaking his only words, "Well, here's to us." Space Marines later rescue him and Dolly from the wreckage of the station.

JONES, MR.

APPEARANCE
Dr. No (1962)
STATUS Dead; suicide by poison
CHARACTERISTICS Shifty, fearful
PLAYED BY Reginald Carter

One of Dr. No's agents, Mr. Jones, poses as a chauffeur in an attempt to kidnap James Bond. Jones meets 007 at Jamaica's Palisadoes Airport claiming Government House has sent him. Bond confirms that government official Pleydell-Smith did not send a car but nevertheless agrees to ride with Jones. After losing a car that tails them, Bond demands to know who really sent Jones. A fight ensues, which Jones loses. Rather than betray his terrifying employer, Jones opts to kill himself. Biting into a cigarette that contains a cyanide capsule, he tells Bond to "go to hell" and dies instantly.

KANANGA, DR.

APPEARANCE
Live And Let Die (1973)
STATUS **Dead; exploded**
CHARACTERISTICS **Immensely
ambitious, contemptuous, superstitious**
PLAYED BY **Yaphet Kotto**

MAN OF THE PEOPLE *To the world at large, Dr. Kananga presents himself as a humanitarian politician, campaigning for San Monique at the United Nations.*

Dr. Kananga serves as Prime Minister of the Caribbean nation of San Monique while maintaining another identity as Mr. Big, underworld boss and head of the chain of Fillet of Soul clubs. Having created a pipeline for heroin into the US, Kananga plans to flood the country with the drug and monopolize the market. Kananga supports his bold ambition with a surprisingly large underworld network of willing followers.

Kananga encourages a belief in voodoo among the local population. He also maintains an interest in Obeah, the Caribbean folk religion that includes spells, fortune-telling, and black magic. Kananga travels with a man

claiming to be the human embodiment of Baron Samedi, one of the most feared figures in voodoo culture and chief of the legion of the dead.

Over the years, Kananga employs at least two women whom he believes have the power to tell the future with tarot cards: Solitaire and, previously, her mother. He has done everything possible to cut these women off from outsiders, declaring that their power exists only to serve him.

All of this dabbling in the occult and folk religions appears to play a key role in creating a vast network of followers of Kananga both in San Monique and the US. When the British Secret Service and CIA investigators begin to suspect that Dr. Kananga and Mr. Big may both

be linked to drug smuggling, Kananga pulls off a triple killing of British agents—Dawes at the UN, Hamilton in New Orleans, and Baines in San Monique.

The killings naturally draw more attention to Kananga's activities, most notably bringing James Bond to New York to investigate. Kananga immediately orders Bond's death. Bond survives numerous attacks during the visit, which includes a brief meeting with Kananga disguised as Mr. Big. Kananga returns to San Monique and Bond immediately follows. On the island, Kananga attempts to have his CIA mole Rosie Carver lead Bond to a location where he will be killed. Not only does Bond foil this plot, he also escapes San Monique with Solitaire.

> **"The question still stands, Mr. Bond... Did you touch her?"**
>
> **Kananga to 007**

Kidnapping them both in New Orleans, Kananga discovers Solitaire has slept with Bond, negating her supposed power to see the future, which was linked to her virginity.

Bond again escapes from Kananga's men, destroying Kananga's heroin processing lab along the way. Kananga returns to San Monique and stages a massive voodoo ceremony at which his High Priest Dambala will execute Solitaire. He correctly believes this will draw Bond, allowing him one more chance to kill Bond. Not only does Bond save Solitaire, but he also blows up Kananga's poppy fields, kills Dambala and, seemingly, Baron Samedi. Kananga's trap nonetheless snares Bond and Solitaire. He has the pair tied to a winch platform so they can be lowered into a shark tank and eaten by the sharks. Bond escapes and fights Kananga. They fall into the shark pool, but Bond shoves a compressed-air shark pellet into Kananga's mouth. Kananga's body fills with carbon dioxide gas, causing

"Drown, Mr Bond? I doubt you'll get the chance to drown!"

Kananga to 007

SHARK BAIT *Kananga looks forward to the imminent deaths of Bond and Solitaire.*

him to literally explode.

Mr. Big, but not the alter-ego Dr. Kananga, exists in the Ian Fleming novel. A Haitian of French and African ancestry and named Buonaparte Ignace Gallia, Mr. Big is an agent for SMERSH, financing Communist interests in the US through the sale of gold coins from treasure discovered in Jamaica. Mr. Big sees himself as "a wolf, and I live by a wolf's laws. Naturally, sheep describe such a person as a 'criminal'." Mr. Big suffers from heart disease, which has turned his skin grey.

KANANGA'S CAB DRIVER

APPEARANCE
Live And Let Die (1973)
STATUS Unknown
CHARACTERISTICS Good natured and humorous with a winning smile
PLAYED BY Arnold Williams

If only all cab drivers had the cheerful personality of Kananga's unnamed cab driver, who is assigned to pick up 007 in New York and New Orleans. He delivers Bond to the Fillet of Soul in Harlem and subsequently kidnaps Bond and Solitaire in New Orleans.

KAUFMAN, DR.

APPEARANCE
Tomorrow Never Dies (1997)
STATUS Dead; killed by Bond
CHARACTERISTICS Professor of forensics; expert marksman; sadistic, arrogant
PLAYED BY Vincent Schiavelli

Dr. Kaufman is a softly spoken hitman employed by media mogul Elliot Carver to assassinate those who betray him, such as his wife, Paris. At the time of his death, Kaufman was schooling Carver's henchman Stamper in Chakra torture. Kaufman has kept a victim alive for 52 hours, a record Stamper, who views Kaufman as a father figure, hopes to break.

KHAN, KAMAL

APPEARANCE
Octopussy (1983)
STATUS Dead; killed in plane crash
CHARACTERISTICS Charismatic, thoroughly corrupt, enjoys cheating
PLAYED BY Louis Jourdan

Exiled Afghan prince Kamal Khan is an international art dealer and marginal politician who works with Soviet General Orlov to stage a nuclear "accident" on a US Air Force base in West Germany.

Based in Udaipur, India, Khan is a sportsman, hunter, and backgammon player. He and his partner Octopussy steal Soviet art treasures from the

BIDDING WAR *Kamal Khan and Magda watch as Bond raises his bid on a Fabergé egg. Khan must win the auction or risk exposing his smuggling operation.*

"Mr. Bond is indeed a very rare breed. Soon to be made extinct."

Kamal Khan

Kremlin Art Repository and replace them with near perfect forgeries designed in the basement workshop of his Monsoon Palace. After smuggling the real treasures into the West via Octopussy's train, Khan and Orlov betray her by removing the treasures, replacing them with a nuclear bomb, and leaving her to die. Khan's reward will be the treasure all for himself.

After Bond foils Khan's and Orlov's plot, Khan kidnaps Octopussy and escapes in his plane with international monies that he can reprint. Bond rescues Octopussy from Kamal's plane seconds before it crashes.

KIL, MR.

APPEARANCE
Die Another Day (2002)
STATUS Dead; lasered by Jinx
CHARACTERISTICS Has a name to die for, incredibly strong, silently intimidating
PLAYED BY Lawrence Makoare

Mr. Kil works for Gustav Graves as head of security at Graves's Ice Palace in Iceland. Mr. Kil's job encompasses everything from carrying Bond's luggage to attempting to decapitate Bond's ally, NSA agent Jinx, with a diamond-cutting laser. When Bond arrives to rescue Jinx, he and Kil fight in a laser fire maze, with Kil trying to stab Bond with his Maori bone hair comb. A tied-down Jinx reaches the remote control switch and fires a laser through Kil's head. She later lasers off Kil's hand and uses his palm print to gain access to other areas of Graves's diamond mine.

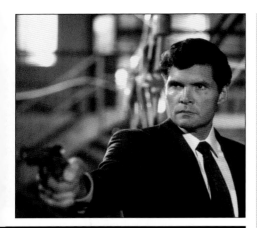

KILLIFER

APPEARANCE
Licence To Kill (1989)
STATUS Dead; shark bait
CHARACTERISTICS Opportunistic and devious; not as clever as he thinks
PLAYED BY Everett McGill

Ed Killifer is a cigar-chomping DEA agent and a friend of Felix Leiter, who turns traitor when he accepts a $2 million bribe to free drug baron Franz Sanchez from US custody. Killifer crashes the van carrying Sanchez off Key West's Seven Mile Bridge into the sea, and they escape in a Shark Hunter two-man submersible, courtesy of Sanchez's associate, Milton Krest.

After Killifer frees Sanchez, he enters the murky world of drug lord justice. He collects his payment, but then must endure watching Leiter lowered into a shark tank.

Waiting to be picked up at Krest's Ocean Exotic warehouse, Killifer hears gunshots and finds Bond has killed all the guards. Knocked off balance by Leiter's fisherman friend Sharky, Killifer offers Bond a million dollars to save him from falling into the shark tank. Bond refuses, slinging Killifer's heavy suitcase full of bribe money at him, and sending the treacherous DEA agent to his death.

KING, ELEKTRA

APPEARANCE
The World Is Not Enough (1999)
STATUS Dead; shot by Bond
CHARACTERISTICS Bitter, vengeful, ambitious; virtually irresistible to men.
PLAYED BY Sophie Marceau

Elektra Vavra King secretly teams with her terrorist kidnapper Renard in a scheme to kill her father, Sir Robert King, monopolize oil distribution from the Caspian Sea, and destroy Istanbul.

Elektra's great-grandfather discovered oil in the Caspian at the turn of the 20th Century. The Bolsheviks slaughtered him and many of his people, the Vavras, in order to gain control of the reserves. British industrialist Robert King married into the Vavra family, and, after the Soviet Union collapse, the renamed family business King Industries established a strong presence in the Caspian.

Before the film begins, international terrorist Renard kidnaps Elektra, holds her in Cyprus, and demands $5 million for her release. During captivity, Elektra realizes her father refuses to pay her ransom. Fueled by a sense of betrayal, Elektra turns Renard toward a much darker and more far-reaching plot. First, she makes it appear that Renard cut off part of her ear and that she killed two captors to escape. In the aftermath of the kidnapping, MI6 agent 009 shoots Renard. The bullet lodges in his brain, slowly destroying his tactile senses and condemning him to certain death. With his fate sealed, Elektra knows that the obsessed Renard will undertake any risk for her.

> "There's no point in living if you **can't feel alive.**"
>
> **Elektra to 007**

Elektra and Renard then arrange a complex financial transfer that results in Sir Robert blowing himself up with a bomb concealed inside a case of money at MI6 headquarters. With the death of her father, Elektra sets her sights on two goals: killing M for persuading Sir Robert not to pay the ransom and gaining complete control of Caspian Sea oil distribution.

Elektra anticipates that her father's death will result in M sending someone to protect her. She soon finds herself in the company of James Bond. Taking advantage of Bond's protective impulses, she uses him to convince M that Renard continues to pose a threat. Elektra sleeps with Bond, drawing him in emotionally. She is attracted to him but even more enchanted by her own power over men. Next, she convinces M that a nuclear warhead stolen by Renard has been used to blow up her pipeline. Elektra then obtains a Russian nuclear submarine and crew for her plot to destroy Istanbul—the only other channel for Caspian Sea oil to reach the West, apart from her pipeline.

As a final act of devotion, Renard plans to place part of the stolen warhead's plutonium in the submarine's reactor, turning the sub into a nuclear bomb.

Elektra takes Bond prisoner at the Maiden's Tower on the Bosphorus. When Russian casino and caviar factory owner Valentin Zukovsky, confronts her, she shoots him. However he fires one final shot, which frees 007.

ACCESSING THE FILES (right) Bond searches the MI6 archives to search for clues related to Elektra's kidnap ordeal.

ACT OF BETRAYAL (far right) M lashes out at Elektra, furious at the duplicity of a young woman she looked on as a daughter. Elektra responds by imprisoning M in Istanbul's Maiden's Tower.

TURN OF THE SCREW *Elektra taunts Bond, held captive in an antique torture chair.*

> "You should have killed me when you had the chance. But you couldn't —not me— not a woman you've loved."
>
> **Elektra to 007**

FINAL FAREWELL *Elektra and Renard share a last embrace before he goes to his death. "The future is yours—have fun with it," he tells her.*

Elektra, unarmed, faces Bond at the top of the tower. Bond trains a gun on her, making it clear he will spare her life if she calls off Renard's attack. She feels certain Bond will not kill her—a former lover—in cold blood. The moment she gives the final command to Renard via radio, Bond shoots her in the heart.

KISCH

APPEARANCE
Goldfinger (1964)
STATUS Dead; killed by Oddjob
CHARACTERISTICS Quiet, efficient
PLAYED BY Michael Mellinger

Goldfinger uses Kisch, his loyal lieutenant, for many key tasks. Kisch shoots Bond with a tranquilizer gun, gasses a group of American gangsters, and handcuffs Bond to an atomic device inside the vault at Fort Knox. When Goldfinger seals Kisch inside the depository, Kisch makes a dash to remove the bomb's fuse, but Oddjob hurls him off a gangway to his death. Bond retrieves the handcuff key from Kisch's body and frees himself to battle Oddjob.

TIME BOMB *Kisch prepares to lock James Bond to an atomic device inside Fort Knox.*

KLEBB, ROSA

APPEARANCE
From Russia With Love (1963)
STATUS Dead; shot by Tatiana Romanova
CHARACTERISTICS Viciously cruel, phlegmatic, repulsive
PLAYED BY Lotte Lenya

Colonel Rosa Klebb, a.k.a. SPECTRE Number 3, is the former head of operations for SMERSH. She relishes the mechanisms of authoritarian structure with a sadomasochistic delight. In the presence of Blofeld, she obsequiously hangs on his every word. Outside Blofeld's presence, Klebb becomes a dominatrix, issuing orders with glee and luxuriating in her power.

Klebb, as described by Ian Fleming, is a squat, toadlike woman with her orange hair tightly scraped back. She is bisexual and makes a crude pass at Tatiana Romanova in both the novel and film.

Klebb defected from the Soviet Intelligence apparatus to run operations for SPECTRE. She implements Kronsteen's plan by selecting assassin Donald Grant and recruiting Soviet cipher

clerk Tatiana Romanova to entice Bond to steal a Lektor decoder. She also guides Grant to commit acts of sabotage and murder to heat up the Cold War in Istanbul. When Bond survives Grant's attempt to kill him on the Orient Express, Klebb, under personal orders from Blofeld, goes after Bond herself in Venice. Disguised as a hotel maid, she tries to steal the Lektor and assassinate Bond. Tatiana knocks the gun away, leading to Klebb's attack with the poison-tipped blade in her shoe. Tatiana shoots Klebb before she can fatally kick Bond.

In the novel, Klebb is one of the most powerful and feared women in the Soviet Union. She rose to power working for Moscow during the Spanish Civil War. In 1953, she became the head of operations for Otdyel II, SMERSH, where she reportedly let no torture take place without her presence and had a special blood-spattered smock for such occasions. She is said to have killed—or ordered the killing of—more people than anyone in the world. She attempts to stab Bond with poisoned knitting needles at the Ritz in Paris but fails. As French authorities arrest her, she nearly kills 007 with a kick from the poison-tipped blade in her shoe.

M later reports that Klebb died in custody.

> "You are not here to ask questions!"
>
> **Rosa Klebb**
> to Tatiana Romanova

KOSKOV, GENERAL

APPEARANCE
The Living Daylights (1987)
STATUS Arrested; probably executed by the KGB
CHARACTERISTICS Veneer of charm conceals a cunning criminal brain
PLAYED BY Jeroen Krabbe

Soviet mastermind General Georgi Koskov plots an elaborate scheme with American arms dealer Brad Whitaker to take over the KGB for personal gain.

When Koskov informs the British Secret Service that he wishes to defect to the West, he specifically asks for James Bond to protect him from a KGB sniper assigned to watch him. In actuality, Koskov's defection is part of an elaborate plot to convince MI6 to assassinate General Leonid Pushkin, the new head of the KGB. He sets up his cellist girlfriend Kara Milovy as the supposed sniper so that Bond will assassinate her. He wants her out of the way, since she knows too much about his operations. Sensing Kara doesn't know what she's doing, Bond shoots the rifle out of her hands and successfully brings Koskov to England.

At MI6's Blayden safe house, Koskov claims to M, the Minister of Defense, and Bond that General Pushkin is "sick like Stalin" and has restarted the assassination program Smiert Spionam ("Death to Spies"), deactivated for 20 years, to eliminate British and American agents. Minutes later, the KGB supposedly recaptures Koskov. Actually, Koskov's accomplice Necros captures him and delivers him safely to Brad Whitaker's palatial home in Tangier.

Once Bond eliminates Pushkin,

LIVING IT UP *Georgi Koskov relaxes poolside at arms dealer Brad Whitaker's luxurious mansion in Tangier.*

Koskov and Whitaker plan to use the down payment on a large Soviet order of American high-tech weapons to buy a vast supply of opium from Afghan drug dealers the Snow Leopard Brotherhood. They will make a fortune when they sell the opium to various parts of the world and still be able to supply the Soviets with their initial arms order. Claiming his defection was just a clever ruse, Koskov will then heroically return to the Soviet Union with Bond, Pushkin's killer, in line to become the next head of the KGB.

Bond, however, does not believe that Pushkin is a psychopath, and the two men join forces to turn the tables on Koskov and Whitaker by

> **"I'm sorry, James. For you I have great affection,** but we have an old saying: duty has no sweethearts.**"**
>
> **Koskov to 007**

faking Pushkin's assassination. When Koskov convinces Kara to drug Bond, claiming he is a KGB agent pursuing him, Bond proves Koskov is a liar by revealing that he was assigned to kill her by British Intelligence but spared her life.

Koskov captures Bond and takes him and Kara to Colonel Feyador's airbase in Afghanistan. Bond and Kara escape custody, and Bond destroys Koskov's and Whitaker's opium shipment. Bond then returns to Tangier to eliminate Whitaker. Pushkin recaptures Koskov and ships him in a "diplomatic bag" back to Moscow, where he faces execution.

KRA

APPEARANCE
The Man With The Golden Gun (1974)
STATUS Dead; killed by Goodnight
CHARACTERISTICS Skilled with machines
PLAYED BY Sonny Caldinez

Kra works in maintenance and security for Scaramanga, operating his solar energy system. He finds life lonely on Scaramanga's island, and the sight of Mary Goodnight in a bikini proves too much for him. She hits him over the head with a spanner, sending his body into the temperature-controlled vats. The heat from Kra's body sets off a series of explosions that destroy the island.

KRATT

APPEARANCE
Casino Royale (2006)
STATUS Dead; shot by Mr. White
CHARACTERISTICS Intimidating and watchful; good with a knife
PLAYED BY Clemens Schick

Le Chiffre's shaven-headed bodyguard Kratt accompanies his boss to Uganda to make a deal with terrorist leader Steven Obanno. Back in the Bahamas, Kratt informs Le Chiffre that MI6 has eliminated the bomber Mollaka. Later, using a knife, Kratt cuts a tracking device from Bond's arm and the seat from a cane-bottomed chair. He strips 007 and places him in the chair so Le Chiffre can torture him. Kratt dies when Mr. White arrives, killing Le Chiffre and his men.

KREST, MILTON

APPEARANCE
Licence To Kill (1989)
STATUS Dead; killed by Sanchez
CHARACTERISTICS Frequently drunk, belligerent, extremely unlucky
PLAYED BY Anthony Zerbe

American Milton Krest owns the Ocean Exotica Warehouse in Key West and the *Wavekrest*, a marine research vessel. Both serve as covers for drug lord Franz Sanchez's US and Caribbean drug operations.

Once an imposing man, Krest is now Sanchez's alcoholic puppet, who peeks through windows at his boss's girlfriend Lupe Lamora. After aiding in Sanchez's escape from US custody, Krest becomes a pawn in Bond's vengeance plot to turn the drug lord against his many underlings. Bond steals $5 million in drug money from Sanchez and plants the money on the *Wavekrest* in Isthmus City. Krest pleads his innocence to his boss

CRUEL DEATH *Sanchez metes out the ultimate punishment to his associate Krest.*

claiming that he has no idea how the money ended up there, but Sanchez believes Krest stole the money to pay a freelance hit team to kill him. Sanchez throws Krest into the ship's decompression chamber, causing his head to explode.

Krest appears in Fleming's short story *The Hildebrand Rarity*. Bond helps Krest and fisherman Fidele Barbey capture a rare fish, the Hildebrand Rarity, in the Seychelles for the Smithsonian Institute. Bond dislikes Krest, whom he discovers whips his wife with a stingray tail known as "The Corrector." Bond later finds Krest dead with the rare fish stuffed in his mouth.

KRIEGLER, ERICH

APPEARANCE
For Your Eyes Only (1981)
STATUS Dead; shoved out the window by 007
CHARACTERISTICS Extremely fit, quietly menacing; expert skier and shot
PLAYED BY John Wyman

KGB agent Erich Kriegler is an assassin as well as the East German biathlon champion, who, according to Bibi Dahl, "doesn't smoke, only eats health foods, and won't even talk to girls." The KGB assigns Kriegler to help their agent Aris Kristatos salvage the Automatic Targeting Attack Communicator (ATAC) from the wreck of the *St. Georges*.

Bond encounters Kriegler while the latter competes on a biathlon course at Cortina D'Ampezzo in the Italian Alps. Kriegler first pursues Bond on skis and then chases him on the snow and down a bobsled run while riding a Yamaha XJ500 motorcycle equipped with machine guns. Bond escapes, but Kriegler crashes the motorcycle.

When Kristatos retrieves the ATAC from Bond, Kriegler guards it until the KGB arrives at St. Cyril's Monastery to pay for its delivery. Bond then raids the monastery and uses a heavy spiked candelabra to push Kriegler headlong through a window, causing the KGB assassin to fall to his death.

KRILENCU

APPEARANCE
From Russia With Love (1963)
STATUS Assassinated by Kerim Bey
CHARACTERISTICS Enjoys killing
PLAYED BY Fred Haggerty

Bulgarian Krilencu works as a killer for the Soviets in the Balkans. He twice attempts to assassinate Kerim Bey. He plants a limpet mine outside Bey's office and, during a gun battle at a gypsy camp, he shoots Bey in the arm. The next night, Kerim Bey sets a trap. He brings Bond to Krilencu's home, a building with a poster for the Bob Hope comedy *Call Me Bwana* (1963) painted on the side. Bey's sons, dressed like police, ring the doorbell. Bey and Bond watch as a secret trapdoor, concealed in Anita Ekberg's mouth, opens. As Krilencu escapes, Bey shoots him.

In the novel, Marilyn Monroe's mouth on the poster of *Niagara* (1953) hides the trapdoor.

> "This man
> # kills for
> ## pleasure."
> **Kerim Bey
> on Krilencu**

KRISTATOS, ARIS

APPEARANCE
For Your Eyes Only (1981)
STATUS Dead; knifed by Columbo
CHARACTERISTICS Cultured manner hides a cruel and ruthless nature
PLAYED BY Julian Glover

Aristotle Kristatos leaves a trail of murder and mayhem in his quest to obtain the British Automatic Targeting Attack Communicator (ATAC) transmitter and sell it to the Soviets.

Originally from Kefalonia, Greece, Kristatos appears to be an Anglophilic shipping magnate with additional businesses in insurance and oil exploration. The British awarded him the King's Medal for his resistance fighting against the Nazis on Crete during World War II, but in actuality Kristatos worked as a double agent during the war and the Greek Civil War. His arch-rival, smuggler Milos Colombo, knows his secret history

NO WAY OUT
His plans in tatters, Kristatos tries to escape, but Melina has him in her crossbow sights.

KRONSTEEN

APPEARANCE
From Russia With Love (1963)
STATUS Assassinated by Morzeny
CHARACTERISTICS Tactical genius; methodical, arrogant, vain
PLAYED BY Vladek Sheybal

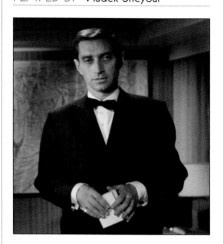

and his current work of smuggling heroin from Albania into England through newsprint rolls. The proud sponsor of Olympic hopeful ice skater Bibi Dahl, Kristatos lives for the day she will win the gold medal. According to British agent Luigi Ferrara, Kristatos spends a few months every year at his chalet in Cortina d'Ampezzo and "knows everything going on."

To obtain the ATAC, Kristatos apparently arranges for a World War II-era contact mine to be placed in the fishing nets of the *St. Georges*, a British vessel that secretly serves as an electronic surveillance ship. The mine explodes but the *St. Georges* sinks in water too deep for Kristatos to mount a recovery operation. The British send marine archaeologist Sir Timothy Havelock to secretly locate the ATAC. Kristatos orders his murder, failing to account for the vengeful dedication of Havelock's daughter, Melina.

When Kristatos meets Bond in Cortina, he stages the murder of British agent Ferrara and orders assassination attempts on Bond and Melina Havelock. Kristatos temporarily misleads Bond into believing that Columbo, Kristatos's hated rival, ordered the Havelock assassination, but finds the tables have turned when Bond and Columbo raid his Albanian warehouse. Realizing Bond and Melina will lead him to the location of the ATAC, he has them shadowed. Once Bond and Melina recover the ATAC, he seizes it and attemptss to murder them by dragging them over a coral reef in shark-infested waters.

Kristatos retires to St. Cyril's Monastery in Greece, where he awaits payment from the KGB. After he completes the transaction, he plans to leave Greece for Cuba. He never gets the chance. Bond, Melina, and Columbo raid the monastery as General Gogol arrives with the payment for the ATAC. Before Kristatos can complete the transaction, Columbo hurls a knife in his back, killing him. Kristatos dies surrounded by those he betrayed.

> "**I have anticipated every possible variation of counter move.**"
> Kronsteen

Czechoslovakian chess champion Kronsteen secretly serves as SPECTRE's Number 5, the director of planning. He devises a plan to have the British Secret Service steal a Lektor decoder with the aid of Soviet cipher clerk Tatiana Romanova, who believes she is on a top-secret mission for SMERSH, the murder apparat of the Soviet Union.

SPECTRE plans to recover the decoder and sell it back to the Soviets. But first, Kronsteen's plan calls for the humiliating death of James Bond to avenge his killing of SPECTRE operative Dr. No.

Kronsteen's scheme would ultimately encompass the faked suicide of Bond and a letter, supposedly from Tatiana, threatening to turn over to the press a film of her making love to Bond if he does not marry her. When Kronsteen's cunning plot fails, SPECTRE Number 1 Ernst Stavro Blofeld orders his death. In the novel, Kronsteen is known as the "Wizard of Ice" for his emotionless chess style, which has helped him win the title of Champion of Moscow twice.

> "**Leave the legs free.**
> **They'll make appetizing bait.**"
> Kristatos

THE SECRET AGENT
Kristatos maintains an outward appearance of a respectable business tycoon, a war hero, and pro-British. Bond is only taken in for a while.

KUTZE, LADISLAV

APPEARANCE
Thunderball (1965)

STATUS Presumed dead; lost at sea

CHARACTERISTICS Meticulous

PLAYED BY George Pravda

Polish nuclear physicist Ladislav Kutze is Emilio Largo's chief technical engineer, preparing hijacked nuclear weapons to extort money from the West. Kutze becomes increasingly ambivalent about his role and disturbed when he finds Largo torturing Domino Derval. When Largo later tries to escape the Royal Navy in the *Disco Volante*, Kutze frees Domino and tells her that he has thrown the arming device for the one remaining bomb into the sea. Kutze leaps from the *Disco Volante* hydrofoil before it explodes, never to be seen again.

LACHAISE

APPEARANCE
The World Is Not Enough (1999)

STATUS Dead; knifed in the neck

CHARACTERISTICS Well-groomed, tight-lipped, professional, procedural

PLAYED BY Patrick Malahide

An executive at La Banque Suisse de L'Industrie in Bilbao, Spain, Lachaise operates as a middleman, baiting a trap set by Elektra King and terrorist Renard to kill Sir Robert King, Elektra's father. Lachaise contacts MI6, offering to return money paid by Sir Robert for a secret Russian Atomic Energy Commission Report that turned out to be worthless. Just as Lachaise is about to reveal the name of the person behind the scam to Bond, another Renard agent—The Cigar Girl—kills him.

LARGO, EMILIO

APPEARANCE
Thunderball (1965)

STATUS Dead; harpooned

CHARACTERISTICS Authoritative, arrogant, amoral, cruel; enjoys impressing others with his beautiful possessions

PLAYED BY Adolfo Celi

SPECTRE Number 2 Emilio Largo leads a plot to hijack a bomber carrying two hydrogen bombs and extort $280 million from the NATO nations. According to Ian Fleming in his novel *Thunderball*, Largo hails from Rome. His ruthlessness, social position, nerves of steel, and most of all, his "exquisite fineness" make him a perfect match for SPECTRE.

Largo has seduced Dominique (Domino) Derval in Capri. She is the sister of François Derval, a NATO pilot whom SPECTRE eventually murders. Domino proves to be Bond's avenue to Largo.

After arranging for the hijacked

BAD LOSER
Bond defeats Largo at the baccarat tables while Domino looks on.

NATO bomber to crash-land at sea, Largo kills SPECTRE-hired pilot Angelo Palazzi. Largo's men then camouflage the bomber at rest on the seabed and transport the nuclear weapons to a sealed underwater cave.

In Nassau, Largo discovers Bond has been dispatched to observe him. Both know they are watching each other. Both also know that Largo has nothing to fear directly from 007 as long as Bond does not know where the nuclear warheads are hidden.

As the deadline approaches, Largo retrieves the bombs but discovers 007 has infiltrated his underwater crew. Largo traps Bond behind the hydraulic doors of the underwater pen. He then takes the *Disco Volante* to Biscayne Bay but discovers that Domino has betrayed him by trying to signal to the CIA that the bombs are on board. Furious, he tortures her. Largo and his crew slip out through the underwater hatch to plant one bomb to be used should the NATO nations fail to pay up. However, as he guides his men underwater, Aquaparas from the US Navy attack them. Bond soon joins them, and they capture one hydrogen bomb.

"You wish to put the **evil eye** on me. We have a way to deal with that where I come from."

Largo to Bond

Largo escapes to the *Disco Volante*, which he converts into a high-speed hydrofoil. Bond manages to climb aboard the speeding craft and battle Largo and much of the remaining crew.

When the *Disco* glances off a coral reef at tremendous speed, Largo gains a crucial advantage in the fight. He levels his gun at Bond, but before he can shoot, Domino fires a speargun into his back. Largo, dying, lurches to the yacht's controls and collapses over the wheel, guaranteeing him and his ship a ghastly fate.

FINAL RECKONING *Largo and Bond grapple aboard the* Disco Volante.

LE CHIFFRE

APPEARANCE
Casino Royale (2006)
STATUS Dead; shot by Mr. White
CHARACTERISTICS Conniving,
ruthless, enigmatic
PLAYED BY Mads Mikkelsen

Le Chiffre provides private banking services for the world's terrorists. He invests their money, then gives them access to it wherever they need it. To make his personal fortune, he employs terrorists to manipulate stock values.

Le Chiffre's background remains murky. MI6 knows him only as Le

BUSINESS TALKS *Le Chiffre and the mysterious Mr. White meet with Steven Obanno, leader of the Lord's Resistance Army, to discuss Obanno's substantial investment.*

Chiffre, or "the cipher." Born, it is believed, in Albania, Le Chiffre earned a reputation as a chess prodigy and mathematical genius. As a poker player, his ability to quickly determine the odds made him a formidable opponent. Le Chiffre associated with Saddam Hussein but the Iraqi leader reportedly turned against him after the 1991 Gulf War and ordered him beheaded. Although MI6 long believed Le Chiffre to be dead, he remained alive and prospered as terrorist networks grew during the 1990s.

Le Chiffre's distinguishing features include a scar surrounding his left eye and "a derangement of the tear duct" that causes him to weep blood. He often uses an inhaler.

After receiving a large investment from Steven Obanno, leader of the Lord's Resistance Army in Uganda, Le Chiffre writes put options on Skyfleet (a "put option" is an agreement to buy a stock at a certain price), an aerospace consortium about to unveil the world's largest airliner. He plans to destroy the plane

but Bond foils the plot, causing Le Chiffre to lose over $100 million. To win back the money, Le Chiffre sets up a high-stakes poker tournament in Montenegro.

Bond, staked first by the British government and later by the CIA, defeats Le Chiffre. Facing financial ruin, Le Chiffre captures and tortures Bond, but 007 refuses to give him the password to access the account holding the winnings. Before Le Chiffre can kill Bond, Mr. White, a shadowy figure from the terrorist underworld, murders Le Chiffre, leaving Bond alive.

In the Ian Fleming novel, Le Chiffre works as a Soviet operative in France.

"The only question remains. Will you yield... in time?"

Le Chiffre to Bond

LING, MR.

APPEARANCE
Goldfinger (1964)
STATUS Dead; killed by Goldfinger
CHARACTERISTICS A methodical man
PLAYED BY Burt Kwouk

COUNTDOWN *Outside the Fort Knox vault, Mr. Ling sets the timer on the atomic device.*

Nuclear fission specialist Mr. Ling accompanies the atomic device provided to Auric Goldfinger by the Communist Chinese. Bond overhears Goldfinger speak the phrase "Operation Grand Slam" to Ling in Switzerland. When Goldfinger captures Bond, Ling advises keeping him alive. When the atomic device arrives at Fort Knox, Ling primes it to explode in four minutes. Goldfinger shoots Ling dead when US Army troops attack.

LIPARUS CAPTAIN

APPEARANCE
The Spy Who Loved Me (1977)
STATUS Dead; killed in an explosion
CHARACTERISTICS Loyal to his chief, good at complex tasks
PLAYED BY Sydney Tafler

The captain of the *Liparus* manages one of the most complex ships ever built—a craft large enough to hold an operations center to launch a nuclear war, three Polaris-class submarines, and hundreds of prisoners and crew. The captain nervously reports to shipping magnate Karl Stromberg that fighting has broken out among his crew and the captured sailors. When Bond attacks the operations center, an explosion fatally injures the captain. He tells Bond that only four minutes remain before nuclear missiles launch to destroy New York and Moscow.

LIPPE, COUNT

APPEARANCE
Thunderball (1965)
STATUS Dead; killed by Fiona Volpe
CHARACTERISTICS Cruel, rash
PLAYED BY Guy Doleman

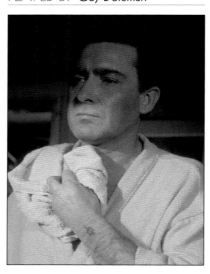

Count Lippe recruits and coaches Angelo Palazzi to impersonate NATO pilot Major François Derval as part of a plot to hijack two atomic weapons. A SPECTRE agent, Lippe stays with Palazzi at the Shrublands health clinic, where James Bond notices the symbol of the Red Dragon of Macau Tong tattooed on his wrist. Lippe, aware of Bond's suspicion about the tattoo, tries to kill him on a motorized traction machine. Bond survives and traps Lippe in a steam cabinet with the heat turned up high.

After helping switch Palazzi for Derval, Lippe tries once more to kill Bond. Yet, Lippe is unaware that Blofeld has ordered his death. As he chases and fires at Bond's Aston Martin DB5, SPECTRE killer Fiona Volpe shoots rockets into his car, incinerating him.

LOCQUE, EMILE LEOPOLD

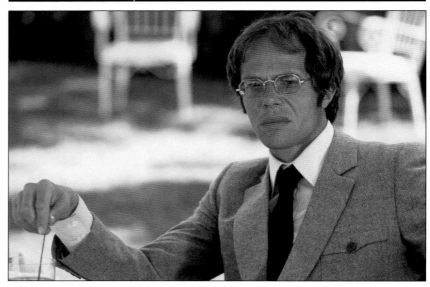

APPEARANCE
For Your Eyes Only (1981)
STATUS Dead; killed by Bond
CHARACTERISTICS Silent, psychotic, murderous, unemotional
PLAYED BY Michael Gothard

Emile Leopold Locque commits murders for corrupt smuggler Kristatos. A former enforcer for the Brussels underworld, Locque escaped a murder sentence at Namur prison after strangling his psychiatrist.

Locque pays Hector Gonzales in Spain for assassinating Sir Timothy Havelock and his wife. When daughter Melina Havelock kills Gonzales, Locque takes back the cash. Locque aids Kristatos in convincing James Bond that rival Milos Columbo murdered the Havelocks. Locque kills MI6 contact Luigi Ferrara, leaving a columbo (dove) pin on his body. He later runs over Columbo's mistress Countess Lisl Von Schlaf. Locque faces Bond in Albania, where 007 shoots him and then kicks him and his car off a cliff.

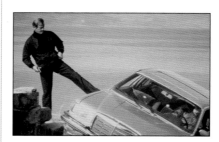

EYES OF A KILLER *Locque's unusual octagonal glasses help Bond identify him using Q's Visual Identagraph machine.*

LOG CABIN GIRL

APPEARANCE
The Spy Who Loved Me (1977)
STATUS Living; whereabouts unknown
CHARACTERISTICS Stunning, passionate, duplicitous
PLAYED BY Sue Vanner

"He had **no head** for heights."

007

James Bond makes love to a beautiful woman in a cabin near Berngarten, Austria, unaware that she works for the KGB. Her passion seems genuine enough. However, when Bond receives word that M needs him and quickly leaves, she notifies agent Sergei Barsov and his team of assassins via radio, igniting a dangerous and deadly chase on skis culminating in Bond leaping off the side of a mountain.

MARKOVITZ & BECHMANN

APPEARANCE
The Spy Who Loved Me (1977)
STATUS Dead; blown up
CHARACTERISTICS Nervous, greedy
PLAYED BY Milo Sperber
(Markovitz), Cyril Shaps (Bechmann)

The two brilliant scientists Professor Markovitz and Dr. Bechmann develop a submarine tracking system for shipping magnate Karl Stromberg. After the successful capture of HMS *Ranger* and the *Potemkin*, Stromberg instructs his assistant to pay $10 million each into the scientists' Swiss bank accounts. But as they fly from his ocean laboratory, *Atlantis*, Stromberg blows up the helicopter in which they are riding.

METZ, PROF. DR.

APPEARANCE
Diamonds Are Forever (1971)
STATUS Missing; presumed dead
CHARACTERISTICS Brilliant scientist;
idealistic, pompous, gullible
PLAYED BY Joseph Furst

Known as the world's leading expert on laser refraction, Metz builds Ernst Stavro Blofeld the ultimate weapon, a diamond-encrusted satellite laser. Metz believes he and Blofeld have the same goal: total disarmament of the nuclear powers, resulting in world peace. Once Metz's satellite begins blasting military targets, Metz foresees war and begs Blofeld to surrender.

With horror, he realizes Blofeld wants world domination. Metz dies in the assault on Blofeld's oil rig command center.

MISCHKA & GRISCHKA

APPEARANCE
Octopussy (1983)
STATUS Dead; both killed by Bond
CHARACTERISTICS Fiercely loyal to
each other; implacable killers
PLAYED BY David and Tony Meyer

Twin knife throwers Mischka and Grischka feature prominently in Octopussy's circus. Kamal Khan and General Orlov also secretly employ the pair as assassins.

When Agent 009, disguised as a circus clown, steals a fake Fabergé egg from Octopussy's circus in East Berlin, Mischka and Grischka give chase. They eventually throw a knife into his back, fatally wounding him. 009's murder and the recovery of the fake Fabergé egg from his body bring James Bond to investigate.

Later, on board Octopussy's train, Mischka uses a welding torch to attack Bond as he enters a car housing Khan's and Orlov's atomic bomb. Momentarily blinded, Bond pulls a lever just in time, bringing the circus's heavy cannon down on Mischka, instantly killing him. Bond then disguises himself in Mischka's clothes. When Grischka sees Khan's henchman Gobinda battling Bond, who is dressed in his brother's clothes, he realizes his brother has been murdered. Bond and Grischka fight and fall off the train. Grischka pursues 007, pinning him to a cabin door with his knives. Bond turns the tables on the vengeful twin by throwing one of Grischka's own knives into his stomach, avenging the murder of 009.

The origins of Mischka and Grischka stem from an early script draft of *The Spy Who Loved Me* (1977).

SMOOTH MOVES *Mollaka races through a construction site in Madagascar to elude Bond.*

MOLLAKA

APPEARANCE
Casino Royale (2006)
STATUS Dead, shot by Bond
CHARACTERISTICS Fast on his feet;
amazing free runner; burn scars on body
PLAYED BY Sébastien Foucan

Mollaka earns his living as a bomb-maker and saboteur. Alex Dimitrios, a middleman working with terrorist banker Le Chiffre, contacts him to destroy the prototype of the world's largest airliner, built by Skyfleet.

In Madagascar, Mollaka realizes that MI6 operative Carter has him under surveillance and knowing that the bomb in his backpack will incriminate him, he runs. He eludes Carter, leaping through an empty swimming pool where a cobra-mongoose fight takes place. Carter fall foul of the cobra, but Mollaka soon discovers that another

MI6 agent is pursuing him—James Bond. Racing for the sanctuary of the Nambutu Embassy, Mollaka charges into a construction site. An expert free runner, Mollaka races up the girders forming the skeleton of a building, assuming that Bond will be forced to remain on the ground. Bond, however, refuses to quit, doggedly pursuing his quarry even when Mollaka scales a construction crane, springs across to another crane, and then leaps down onto a rooftop.

Bond follows Mollaka into the Nambutu Embassy, determined not to let him escape. When embassy guards finally corner Bond, he shoots Mollaka dead and escapes in a cloud of flame and smoke with Mollaka's backpack. This explosive incident, faithfully captured on the embassy's security cameras, becomes front-page news in England. Mollaka's death forces Dimitrios to hire Carlos, a new bomber.

MOON, GENERAL

APPEARANCE
Die Another Day (2002)
STATUS Dead; victim of patricide
CHARACTERISTICS Dignified; over-indulgent parent
PLAYED BY Kenneth Tsang

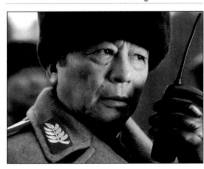

"The son I knew
died long ago."
General Moon to Gustav Graves

North Korean General Moon yearns for peace between North Korea and the West, but his son has other plans. Moon hoped his son's Western education would broaden his mind, but it only corrupted him. Colonel Moon's apparent death during a hovercraft chase with 007, crushes his father. General Moon takes Bond prisoner and discovers that Bond's incursion into North Korea has given a stronghold to a group of warmongering generals in the North Korean government. He also believes Bond knows his son's Western ally. He learns nothing from 007 and eventually frees him for Zao in a prisoner exchange. The General later learns that his son has used gene therapy to transform himself into Gustav Graves and plans to launch a war with South Korea. When General Moon rejects the plan and his son, Graves murders him.

MORTNER, DR.

APPEARANCE
A View To A Kill (1985)
STATUS Dead; killed in airship explosion
CHARACTERISTICS Protective, paternal
PLAYED BY Willoughby Gray

Dr. Carl Mortner's real name is Hans Glaub, a Nazi scientist who experimented with steroids on pregnant Jewish women in concentration camps to enhance intelligence. A number of women aborted, although several children were produced with phenomenal IQs. The only side-effect was that the children, who included Max Zorin, matured into psychotics. The Soviets then grabbed Glaub and had him develop steroids for their athletes. Glaub eventually appears in the West with Zorin as Dr. Carl Mortner, a horse breeding consultant who injects steroids into Zorin's horses. Mortner is later distraught at his "creation's" death and dies when Zorin's airship explodes.

MORZENY

APPEARANCE
From Russia With Love (1963)
STATUS Unknown
CHARACTERISTICS Lethal, bureaucratic
PLAYED BY Walter Gotell

Morzeny trains personnel on SPECTRE Island, where he introduces SMERSH defector Rosa Klebb to assassin Donald Grant. Under orders from Blofeld, Morzeny kills SPECTRE No. 5, Kronsteen, when his plan to acquire the Lektor decoder fails. Klebb orders Morzeny to complete the mission. He suffers burns when Bond ignites a fuel slick around his boat off the Dalmatian coast. It is rumored he returned to the Soviet Union and had a career with the KGB.

KILLER TACTICS *Morzeny, Rhoda, and Klebb plot the demise of 007.*

NAOMI

APPEARANCE
The Spy Who Loved Me (1977)
STATUS Dead; blasted out of the sky
CHARACTERISTICS Great helicopter pilot, even better at flirting
PLAYED BY Caroline Munro

Naomi works for Karl Stromberg as his beautiful but murderous helicopter pilot/assistant. Naomi's dazzling smile and sparkling eyes conceal a deadly fascination with killing. She collects James Bond and Anya Amasova at the Hotel Cala di Volpe and brings them to *Atlantis*, Stromberg's ocean laboratory. Her flirtations with Bond raise Anya's ire. When Bond and Anya later drive in 007's Lotus Esprit, Stromberg's assassins, including Naomi, set upon them. Naomi blasts the Lotus with the machine guns mounted on her Bell Jet Ranger helicopter. She appears to drive Bond and Anya into the sea, unaware that Bond's Lotus can transform into a well-armed submarine. She ends up a sitting duck, blown away by a sea-air missile.

NECROS

APPEARANCE
The Living Daylights (1987)
STATUS Dead; given the boot by 007
CHARACTERISTICS Extremely strong, fit, and cunning; often employs disguise
PLAYED BY Andreas Wisniewski

Soviet assassin Necros works for KGB General Koskov and arms dealer Brad Whitaker. A true chameleon, he convincingly adopts various accents, and impersonates a runner, a milkman, a doctor, a balloon vendor, and a lighting technician to accomplish his various objectives. He uses his Walkman headphone wires as a garrote to assassinate his victims.

Necros plays a central role in Koskov's kidnapping from the Blayden safe house. He also kills Saunders, head of Section V, and kidnaps Bond in Tangier, helping to transport him to Afghanistan.

Necros assists in Koskov's opium smuggling scheme and fights with Bond on a cargo net hanging out of the back of a Soviet transport plane. The assassin grabs Bond's boot to prevent himself from falling, but Bond cuts his boot's laces, causing Necros to plummet to his death.

NICK NACK

APPEARANCE
The Man With The Golden Gun (1974)
STATUS Living; serving a life sentence in a very small cell
CHARACTERISTICS Impish, conniving
PLAYED BY Hervé Villechaize

Nick Nack works for master assassin Francisco Scaramanga as a most evil gentleman's gentleman, serving the functions of butler, chef, accomplice, and occasional assailant.

Nick Nack resides on Scaramanga's island in the South China Seas. He arranges for hitmen to try to kill Scaramanga in his private fun house maze. These exercises help to keep his boss in peak condition for killing. On one occasion, Nick Nack remarks that, should Scaramanga die, the island will become his.

Nick Nack helps Scaramanga in his mission to auction off the world's first solar energy system. He also steals the vital Solex Agitator from the lifeless body of the scientist Gibson after Scaramanga kills him.

When Bond faces off with Scaramanga on the island, Nick Nack officiates the duel. After Bond kills Scaramanga and escapes with Mary Goodnight in Scaramanga's junk ship, Nick Nack attacks. Bond shuts Nick Nack in a suitcase and places him in a wicker basket hung from the boat's mainmast.

" I may be small, but I never forget. "

Nick Nack to 007

NO, DR.

APPEARANCE
Dr. No (1962)
STATUS Dead; boiled alive
CHARACTERISTICS A scientific genius, egotistical, impassive, commanding; rules subordinates by fear
PLAYED BY Joseph Wiseman

Dr. No masterminds a plot to sabotage or "topple" American rocket launches from Cape Canaveral. Using a secret base on the Caribbean island of Crab Key off the coast of Jamaica, Dr. No employs a nuclear reactor to beam radio signals that interfere with the rockets' gyroscopic controls.

By Dr. No's own account, he is "the unwanted son of a German missionary and a Chinese girl of good family." He became "treasurer of the most powerful criminal society in China," before stealing $10 million of their money and escaping to the US. Rejected by the scientific communities of both East and West, Dr. No joined the terrorist organization SPECTRE and became one of their top operatives. He now plans to exact revenge against East and West, with SPECTRE deciding which side will win the Cold War and be first to reach the moon.

Dr. No's great strength is his ability to instill fear into the men and women he employs. Metallurgist Professor Dent heads his criminal organization in Jamaica. Dr. No, through Dent, apparently controls the actions of the so-called Three Blind Mice killers, Mr. Jones, a

MASTER VILLAIN *Dr. No congratulates 007 for damaging his organization and his pride before calling him "a stupid policeman."*

> ## "I never fail, Mr. Bond."
>
> ### Dr. No to 007

woman posing as a *Daily Gleaner* photographer, Miss Taro, and likely others. Together, they keep a watchful eye on anyone in the Jamaica area who shows interest in Dr. No or Crab Key. It is this team who is responsible for the deaths of Commander John Strangways and his secretary Mary Prescott. Dr. No's guards on the island also killed Honey Ryder's father and several of Quarrel's friends.

On Crab Key, Dr. No employs a small army of guards. He also uses a flame-throwing swamp vehicle painted to resemble a dragon to frighten away or kill any curious visitors.

Equipped with mechanical hands as a result of radiation experiments gone wrong, Dr. No considers himself one of the great radiation power experts in the world. The owner of Goya's portrait of Wellington, stolen in August, 1961 from London's National Gallery, Dr. No exhibits impeccable taste, expertly mixing antiques and modern design. (The real painting was recovered in May, 1964.)

Dr. No's men capture Bond and Honey, and at first they treat them well, since Dr. No hopes 007 will join his organization. Bond refuses, and Dr. No incarcerates him and Honey. Dr. No prepares to topple a NASA moon launch, unaware that 007 has escaped and entered the nuclear reactor room disguised as a technician. When Dr. No realizes Bond is overheating the reactor, he

charges. The pair battle on the fuel elements carriage as it is lowered into the reactor core. Bond knocks Dr. No into the reactor pool. Dr. No's metal hands uselessly claw at the carriage as the genius scientist boils to death in the churning water.

In the novel, Fleming describes Dr. No as "a giant venomous worm wrapped in grey tin-foil." When Dr. No steals $1 million in gold from the Tongs, they catch him, cut off his hands, and shoot him through the heart. However, Dr. No is one of those rare individuals whose heart is on the right hand side of his body. He miraculously survives and invests the stolen gold in rare stamps, so that his money can be easily moved. He changes his appearance and takes the name Julius No: "Julius," after his father; "No," for his rejection of him and all authority. Backed by the Soviets, he buys the island of Crab Key and plans to destroy American rockets. The great doctor meets his demise when Bond buries him under a giant mound of guano.

TOPPLING TIME *Attired in protective clothing, Dr. No prepares to send a moon launch from Cape Canaveral off course.*

DOCTOR'S ORDERS *(below left) Dr. No brings Bond and Honey into his inner sanctum; (below) Dr. No demonstrates the power of his mechanical hands, crushing a metal Buddha figurine.*

> "The successful criminal brain is **always superior.** It has to be!"

Dr. No to 007

NORTH KOREAN GENERALS

APPEARANCE
Die Another Day (2002)
STATUS Dead; sucked out of decompressing aircraft cabin
CHARACTERISTICS Power-mad, greedy
PLAYED BY Daryl Kwan (General Han), Vincent Wong (General Li), Stuart Ong (General Dong)

The generals plan to make North Korea a dominant Asian power.

Han, Li, and Dong are three top North Korean generals who stage a coup to remove General Moon from power so that his psychotic son can use the Icarus satellite to destroy the Korean DMZ. Once this occurs, they plan to attack South Korea and then Japan. When James Bond's Walther P99 accidentally fires inside the flying command center, the plane depressurizes, sucking the generals into the upper atmosphere.

OBANNO

APPEARANCE
Casino Royale (2006)
STATUS Dead; throttled by Bond
CHARACTERISTICS Callous; rules
by inflicting violence and creating terror
PLAYED BY Isaach de Bankole

Steven Obanno leads the Lord's Resistance Army, an actual rebel force based in Uganda accused of acts of terrorism and war crimes. The real leader of the LRA, Joseph Kony, partly inspired the character of Obanno in *Casino Royale*.

Obanno entrusts an investment of millions of dollars to Le Chiffre, a banker to terrorists introduced to him by Mr. White. When that investment is lost by Le Chiffre, Obanno threatens him and his girlfriend Valenka during a break in Le Chiffre's poker tournament at Casino Royale. Obanno's lieutenant realizes that Bond has been listening in on Obanno's heated confrontation with Le Chiffre. Obanno and his lieutenant attack Bond, who, after a vicious struggle in a stairwell at the Hotel Splendide, kills them both.

FEAR FACTOR *Obanno and his henchman terrorize Le Chiffre's girlfriend Valenka.*

ODDJOB

APPEARANCE Goldfinger (1964)
STATUS Dead; electrocuted
CHARACTERISTICS Martial arts
expert, staunchly loyal, deadly aim
PLAYED BY Harold Sakata
(Tosh Togo)

Oddjob is the dean of all henchmen, a perfect combination of strength, skill, and loyalty. Ostensibly the manservant, chauffeur, and caddy of Auric Goldfinger, Oddjob is an impassive killer who knows seven ways to kill a man with one blow. For long range attacks, Oddjob throws his metal-rimmed hat, which can sever the head of a statue or break a person's neck.

Oddjob knocks Bond out at the Fontainebleau Hotel in Miami Beach. In England, Oddjob abets Goldfinger in his attempt to cheat during a golf match with Bond. Following Goldfinger's defeat, Oddjob crushes a golf ball with one hand as a show of strength.

When Bond and Tilly Masterson trip an alarm at Goldfinger's factory, Oddjob supervises their pursuit by Korean guards and kills Tilly with a throw of his hat. In Kentucky, Oddjob shoots Mr. Solo, the one gangster who opts out of Goldfinger's scheme, and has his body crushed inside a Lincoln Continental. After priming an atomic device to irradiate the US gold supply, Goldfinger locks Oddjob inside the vaults along with Bond and Kisch, a trusted lieutenant. Rather than join forces to try to escape, Oddjob kills Kisch and turns on Bond, who kills Oddjob by sending a surge of electricity through the brim of his hat.

SHOCK TACTICS *Oddjob dies in a shower of sparks, electrocuted by Bond during their epic battle inside Fort Knox.*

ONATOPP, XENIA

APPEARANCE
GoldenEye (1995)
STATUS Crushed to death
CHARACTERISTICS Seductive, sadistic, outlandish, psychotic
PLAYED BY Famke Janssen

Ex-Soviet fighter pilot Xenia Onatopp is a key figure in the Janus crime syndicate run by Alec Trevelyan, and one of the most beautiful and unusual femme fatales ever to seduce a man to his doom. Xenia gains great sexual pleasure from killing. She dresses in leather or in elaborate gowns, basking in her perverse sexuality.

Xenia first meets Bond in the South of France. Driving her red Ferrari, she races Bond's Aston Martin down the twisting corniche toward Monte Carlo. After a further brush with Bond in the casino, she kills Canadian Navy Admiral Chuck Farrel by crushing him between her thighs—her favored method of

> "This time, Mr. Bond, the pleasure will be all mine."
>
> Onatopp to 007

murder. She shoots two French pilots and steals the latest NATO helicopter, the Tiger, which is immune to all electronic interference. With General Ourumov, she participates in the mass murder of staff at the Severnaya satellite station in Siberia and the destruction of the area with the GoldenEye weapons system.

Xenia kidnaps Natalya Simonova in St. Petersburg and attempts to kidnap Bond. Following a sexually charged battle in his hotel's spa, Bond forces Xenia to take him to Trevelyan, then knocks her unconscious. Bond rescues Natalya but Xenia helps Ourumov recapture her, bringing her on board an armored train and luring Bond to save her. Xenia later escapes with Trevelyan to Cuba.

When 007 and Natalya arrive in Cuba, Xenia attacks them, abseiling from a helicopter. Bond shoots the pilot, sending the helicopter out of control and flinging Xenia into the fork of a tree. With the weight of the helicopter cinching her between the branches, Xenia discovers the reality of death by crushing.

GIRL POWER In the Cuban jungle, Xenia Onatopp puts the squeeze on Bond.

DREAMS OF GLORY Dismayed at improving political relations between East and West, Orlov plots to bring about World War III.

ORLOV, GENERAL

APPEARANCE
Octopussy (1983)
STATUS Killed as a traitor
CHARACTERISTICS Fanatical, warmongering, conniving, power-hungry
PLAYED BY Steven Berkoff

General Orlov is a war-obsessed Soviet general who is in league with exiled Afghan prince Kamal Khan in a scheme to detonate an atomic bomb on the American Air Force Base in Feldstadt, West Germany.

Failing in his never-ending attempt to convince the Soviet leadership council that the USSR can successfully invade Western Europe, Orlov secretly sets up his plot. He funnels precious jewels from The Kremlin Art Repository, replacing them with duplicates created by expert forger Lenkin. Working with smugglers Kamal Khan and Octopussy, Orlov offers the originals for auction in the West and uses some of the money to pay Khan. Orlov and Khan double-cross Octopussy by smuggling a nuclear weapon rather than jewels on her circus train when it travels from East Germany to West Germany, where it is to be detonated. If the world believes an American nuclear weapon blasted a base and town in West Germany, Orlov knows the US will be required to remove its nuclear deterrent from Europe. Soviet tanks and armies would be better positioned to invade the West.

Once Bond learns of Orlov's scheme, he races to stop the train with the bomb. Orlov pursues Bond, unaware that General Gogol has uncovered his jewel-smuggling racket. When the train crosses the border, Orlov runs after it, and East German guards gun him down. As Gogol stands over him, Orlov hints at his much larger plot as he dies.

GUNNED DOWN Orlov races to catch and kill Bond, but East German guards shoot him first.

> "Tomorrow I shall be a hero of the Soviet Union."
>
> Orlov to Gogol

OSATO

APPEARANCE
You Only Live Twice (1967)
STATUS Dead; paid the price of failure
CHARACTERISTICS Ruthless, fearful
PLAYED BY Teru Shimada

Owner of Osato Chemicals & Engineering Co. Ltd., Mr. Osato provides Ernst Stavro Blofeld with liquid oxygen and various other components for his plot to launch World War III on behalf of the Communist Chinese.

As one of the leading manufacturers of chemicals in Asia, Osato manages his own empire. The depth and length of his relationship with SPECTRE remains unclear, but, by the events depicted in *You Only Live Twice*, much of Osato's organization exists totally to serve SPECTRE's needs. His confidential secretary, Helga Brandt, also serves as SPECTRE No. 11, and Osato's assistant doubles as SPECTRE No. 4. Osato's freighter, *Ning-Po*, ships liquid oxygen and various other supplies to Blofeld. Despite his position of power, Osato views Blofeld with great respect and also with great fear.

Osato apparently helps arrange for the murder of Dikko Henderson, Bond's Tokyo contact. When Bond doubles as the assassin and pretends to be wounded, the getaway car driver delivers him to Mr. Osato's office. There, Bond kills the driver and steals important clues from Osato's safe.

Blofeld orders Osato to kill 007, but Bond survives numerous attempts on his life. When Blofeld captures Bond in his volcano rocket base and finds that Japanese SIS ninjas have followed, he shows 007 "the price of failure" and shoots Osato at point blank range.

OURUMOV, GENERAL

APPEARANCE
GoldenEye (1995)
STATUS Dead; shot by Bond
CHARACTERISTICS Unctuous, corrupt, self-serving, ruthless
PLAYED BY Gottfried John

General Ourumov conspires with Alec Trevelyan to use the GoldenEye weapon system to make himself tremendously wealthy. The head of the Arkangel Chemical Weapons Facility during the Soviet years, he helps to fake the death of 006 and then build and position the Janus crime syndicate.

After the fall of the Soviet empire, he is promoted from colonel to general and becomes Head of the Space Division of the Russian Army.

The British believe Ourumov wants to be the next iron man of Russia. Along with Xenia Onatopp, he stages an unscheduled test of the Severnaya Space Weapons Control Centre to obtain command of the GoldenEye space weapons. He has Xenia kill everyone inside with the exception of accomplice Boris Grishenko. Ourumov informs the Minister of Defence, Dimitri Mishkin, and the Russian Defence Council that Siberian Separatists committed the crime.

After learning that programmer Natalya Simonova escaped Severnaya, Ourumov discovers Mishkin has arrested both James Bond and Natalya and plans to interrogate them. When Ourumov interrupts, Mishkin reveals that he now suspects Ourumov in the massacre at Severnaya. In response, Ourumov kills Mishkin. Natalya temporarily escapes with Bond, but Ourumov recaptures her and takes refuge in Trevelyan's train. He holds a gun to Natalya's head when 007 enters, but Bond shoots Ourumov anyway.

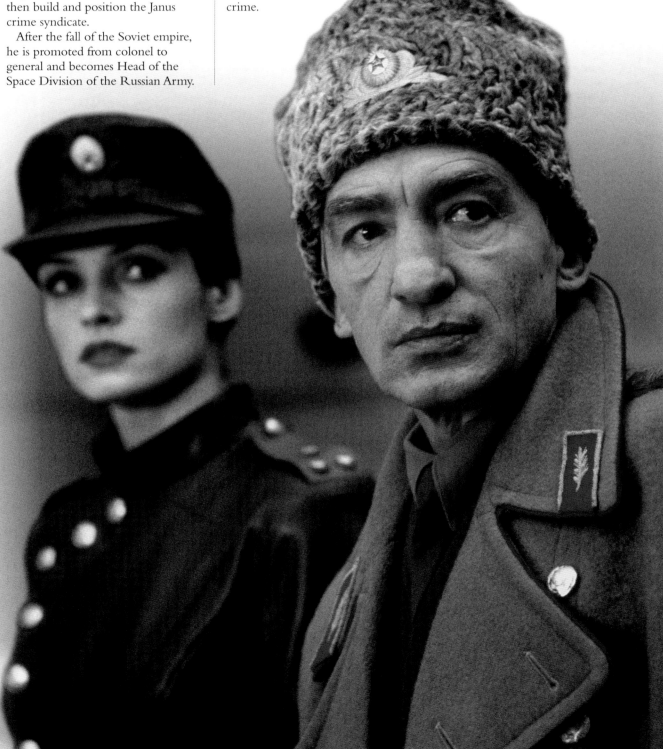

PALAZZI

APPEARANCE
Thunderball (1965)
STATUS Dead; drowned by Largo
CHARACTERISTICS Experienced
pilot; efficient, but a little too greedy
PLAYED BY Paul Stassino

SPECTRE hires Angelo Palazzi to impersonate pilot Major Derval on a NATO training mission. His brief is to gas the crew and to fly the Vulcan bomber to waters off the Bahamas. The job requires two years of plastic surgery. Palazzi agrees to a fee of $100,000, but after killing the real Derval, he demands $250,000 instead. He accomplishes his mission and delivers the plane and its two nuclear warheads to Emilio Largo. While the plane rests underwater with Palazzi strapped into the cockpit, Largo renegotiates Palazzi's fee. He cuts his airhose, settling SPECTRE's account permanently.

PAN HO

APPEARANCE
A View To A Kill (1985)
STATUS Dead; drowned in a mine
CHARACTERISTICS Calculating;
ruthless in the execution of her duties
PLAYED BY Papillon Soo Soo

Pan Ho, along with Jenny Flex, is one of Max Zorin's many assistants. She greets Bond at Zorin's French chateau, carefully checking 007's invitation to a sale of racehorses. She later pours gasoline all over the floors of San Francisco City Hall which Zorin then sets ablaze in order to kill Bond and geologist Stacey Sutton.

When Zorin floods his Main Strike Mine, Pan Ho and Jenny both drown in the torrent, leaving May Day grief-stricken at their deaths.

PEREZ

APPEARANCE Licence To Kill (1989)
STATUS Dead; flame-broiled
CHARACTERISTICS Loyal, sadistic
PLAYED BY Alejandro Bracho

Perez and fellow henchmen Dario and Braun are employed by drug lord Franz Sanchez to kill his enemies. Perez helps to maim CIA agent Felix Leiter and to kill his wife, Della. Perez later fires a Stinger missile at a tanker truck driven by 007 and gets covered with insecticide powder by CIA informer Pam Bouvier. He is in Braun's truck when it is engulfed in flames and veers off a cliff, plunging to certain doom.

PHOTOGRAPHER, THE

APPEARANCE
Dr. No (1962)
STATUS A mystery
CHARACTERISTICS Defensive, scared
PLAYED BY Marguerite LeWars

This unnamed photographer, identified as Annabel Chung in the novel, works for Dr. No. She fails to take Bond's picture at Palisadoes International Airport, Jamaica, when he conceals his face with his hat, so she tries again at Puss-Feller's

nightclub. Local islander and 007 ally, Quarrel, grabs her and her camera, but she refuses to reveal the identity of her employer, cutting Quarrel's face with the broken lightbulb from her camera.

> ❝You'll be sorry. You'll all be sorry. You rats.❞
>
> The Photographer to 007, Quarrel, and Leiter

EXPOSED *Bond and Quarrel corner the photographer in Puss-Feller's club and try to discover the identity of her employer. Bond exposes the film she has taken, which contains shots of him.*

QUIST

APPEARANCE
Thunderball (1965)
STATUS Dead; eaten by sharks
CHARACTERISTICS Out of his
depth; lacks the killer instinct
PLAYED BY Bill Cummings

IN THE DEEP END *Largo's men prepare to throw Quist (center) into the shark pool.*

Quist works for Emilio Largo in Nassau, shadowing his mistress Domino and performing other bits of dirty work. Largo sends Quist to investigate Bond at the Coral Harbour Hotel, but while he snoops in Bond's hotel room, 007 returns and Quist hides in the shower. Bond cranks the hot water then knocks Quist about. Bond sends him back to Largo, calling him "the little fish I throw back into the sea." Largo does 007 one better, tossing Quist into his shark pool.

RAMIREZ

APPEARANCE
Goldfinger (1964)
STATUS Living; operation damaged
CHARACTERISTICS Powerful heroin
manufacturer

One of the few unseen villains in the Bond films, Mr. Ramirez operates a heroin manufacturing lab in Mexico. The profits from the drug sales go to finance Communist revolutionaries in Central America and the Caribbean. Ramirez has a state-of-the-art lab in a fake oil storage tank, which Bond sabotages. Ramirez later sends one of his goons—a capungo—to try and kill Bond in dancer Bonita's dressing room. The damage Bond inflicts on Ramirez's operation effectively shuts down his political activities.

OVERPOWERED *Armed guards cannot stop Bond infiltrating Ramirez's heroin lab.*

RENARD

APPEARANCE
The World Is Not Enough (1999)
STATUS **Dead; killed by Bond**
CHARACTERISTICS **Detached, psychotic, apolitical, devoted, unrelenting**
PLAYED BY **Robert Carlyle**

Viktor Zokas—alias Renard—wishes to spread anarchy, but he changes his goal when he falls in love with his kidnap victim Elektra King. While he previously spent his life creating chaos around the globe, now facing death, he devotes his remaining days to helping Elektra carry out a megalomaniacal plot of revenge that will leave her as one of the most powerful women in the world.

Renard once worked for the KGB, but his ruthless methods led them to declare him a liability after the Afghan conflict. He then became a freelance terrorist, working for anyone who would hire him. He operated in Pukch'ong, North Korea and in Moscow in 1996. He has, according to MI6 records, also been spotted in "all the romantic vacation spots," such as Bosnia, Iraq, Iran, Beirut, and Cambodia.

Renard kidnaps oil heiress Elektra King, but when Elektra's father, Sir Robert, refuses to pay, Elektra seduces Renard, turning him into a tool for her goals. She stages an escape with Renard's help. A week later, MI6 agent 009 shoots Renard in the head. However, the bullet does not kill him, but starts a slow path through his brain, gradually killing off his senses. Renard, now unable to feel agony or sensual pleasure, can push his body harder and for longer than a

SLOW DEATH *Viewing a hologram, Bond learns that a bullet fired by an MI6 agent is moving through Renard's brain, destroying his senses.*

BOMB RAID *Renard steals a nuclear weapon from a former Soviet test site in Kazakhstan.*

FIGHT TO THE DEATH *Bond enrages Renard by telling him that his beloved Elektra is dead, but Renard refuses to be distracted from his deadly purpose: to blow up a nuclear submarine.*

normal person. He will grow stronger until the day the bullet cuts off his entire nervous system, killing him.

Renard and Elektra first stage the killing of Elektra's father, by blowing him up with the exact amount of explosive-laced money he refused to

> Renard: **You can't kill me. I'm already dead.**
> 007: **Not dead enough for me.**

pay for Elektra's release. They anticipate this will lure M, Sir Robert's personal friend, into their trap, allowing them to kidnap her. Renard attempts to kill Bond when 007 stumbles on a plot to steal a nuclear weapon in Kazakhstan.

Renard next attempts to stage a small nuclear explosion in a pipeline controlled by Elektra King, an act designed to distract the world from her more deadly plot to destroy Istanbul. Using a stolen Russian nuclear submarine, Renard plans to place a rod made from the stolen weapon's plutonium core into the sub's reactor. This will cause the submarine to explode in the Bosphorus, creating a highly toxic dirty bomb, killing eight million people, and ensuring that Elektra's pipeline is the only source of oil from the Caspian to the West. Renard brings Dr. Christmas Jones, a nuclear physicist working with Bond, onboard to die with him. 007 gains access to the sub as it submerges, battles Renard, and eventually impales him on his own plutonium rod, bringing his fatalistic suicidal dream to an end.

RHODA

APPEARANCE
From Russia With Love (1963)
STATUS **Unknown**
CHARACTERISTICS **Silent, obedient**
PLAYED BY **Peter Brayham**

SPECTRE operative Rhoda serves as Morzeny's attaché, helping to coordinate agent training. Rhoda has an important role in SPECTRE's plot to kill 007 and sell a stolen Lektor decoder back to the Soviets. He creates a road block on the Orient Express train line, providing an escape route for Donald Grant. Bond, with Tatiana Romanova, takes Rhoda hostage and steals his truck, using Grant's escape plan. Bond sets of in SPECTRE's Fairy Huntress speedboat and shoves Rhoda overboard in the Gulf of Trieste.

SALES GIRL

APPEARANCE
Live And Let Die (1973)
STATUS **Living, whereabouts unknown**
CHARACTERISTICS **Observant**
PLAYED BY **Kubi Chaza**

The unnamed Sales Girl is another of Dr. Kananga/Mr. Big's US operatives. After the death of CIA driver Charlie in New York, James Bond tracks the assassin Whisper's white Corvorado to the Oh Cult Voodoo Shop at 33 E. 56th Street. Bond distracts the Sales Girl in order to slip into the store's garage, which is shared with Dr. Kananga's San Monique Embassy offices. Bond then follows a Cadillac with Texas plates out of the garage, but the Sales Girl reports his movements. She later briefly appears in New Orleans as a flight attendant on Mr. Big's personal jet.

SAMEDI, BARON

APPEARANCE
Live And Let Die (1973)
STATUS **Unknown**
CHARACTERISTICS **Intimidating, with a deliberately threatening laugh**
PLAYED BY **Geoffrey Holder**

The legendary figure of Baron Samedi is a mischief-maker who both tempts and punishes humans. The host at a show for tourists in San Monique describes Baron Samedi as the "voodoo god of cemeteries and Chief of the Legion of the Dead, the man who cannot die." Dr. Kananga employs a man who claims to be the Baron to instill fear in his minions and to protect his thousands of acres of poppy fields.

Bond and Solitaire briefly meet Baron Samedi in a graveyard. He later appears in New Orleans at Mr. Big's office taunting Kananga and Solitaire with a flaming High Priestess tarot card and a Death card.

On San Monique, Baron Samedi, painted with a skeleton design, rises from a grave. Bond shoots him, revealing that this Baron Samedi is just a mannequin. Another Baron Samedi, this time human, then rises from the grave. Bond tosses him into a coffin filled with poisonous snakes, apparently killing him. But nothing is certain where the God of Cemeteries is concerned, and Baron Samedi sits mocking human conceit on the front of the Crescent train at the film's end.

SANCHEZ, FRANZ

APPEARANCE
Licence To Kill (1989)
STATUS Dead; burned to death
CHARACTERISTICS Authoritative;
tendency towards violence and paranoia
PLAYED BY Robert Davi

Drug baron Franz Sanchez plans to create a cocaine cartel that stretches from Central America to the Far East. To Sanchez, loyalty is more important than money, and a vengeance-seeking James Bond seizes upon this belief to bring down the drug lord and his empire.

Under his personal law of *plomo o plata* (lead or silver), Sanchez has killed, intimidated, or bribed government officials in countries stretching from the US to Chile, and he faces 139 felony counts and 936 years in prison if caught by the US government. Constant pressure from the Drug Enforcement Agency (DEA) leads Sanchez to purchase four Stinger missiles from the Contras. He threatens to shoot down a US airliner if the DEA doesn't back off. Using the small nation of Isthmus as his operational base, Sanchez maintains full control over "President for life" Hector Lopez. Sanchez operates the world's largest, albeit illegal, private investment fund, which is linked to his illegal drug network. He sells cocaine worldwide through the coded sermons of televangelist Professor Joe Butcher,

and his casino operation enables him to launder large quantities of cash.

Sanchez makes a rare foray into US territory when he discovers his mistress Lupe Lamora has joined her illicit lover Alvarez. DEA agents, including Felix Leiter and MI6 "observer" James Bond, capture Sanchez in an aerial chase as he attempts to fly into international airspace.

Sanchez bribes DEA agent Ed Killifer with $2 million to spring him from US custody. He then exacts revenge on Leiter by having Felix's bride Della murdered and Felix himself lowered into a shark tank. He leaves Leiter maimed but alive as a warning of what happens to those who cross him. He then returns to Isthmus City

and restarts his drug manufacturing and smuggling operation.

Sanchez soon learns that a major cocaine shipment to the US has gone awry, with the cocaine ruined and the payment stolen by a mysterious stranger. He does not realize the stranger is Bond, now on a personal mission of vengeance. Armed with the drug lord's money, 007 arrives in Isthmus City and offers his services to Sanchez. He comes to trust Bond after wrongly concluding 007 foiled an assassination attempt against him. Realizing that Sanchez values loyalty above anything else, Bond cunningly sows the seeds of distrust between the drug lord and his henchmen.

Bond discovers Sanchez's master plan: a scheme with an Asian drug cartel to smuggle vast quantities of cocaine by dissolving the drug in ordinary gasoline, shipping it

LIZARD KING *Sanchez sees himself as calculating and cold-blooded—as reflected by his choice of an iguana as a pet. The creature wears a diamond-encrusted collar, advertising Sanchez's wealth.*

by ocean-going tanker, and then reconverting it to cocaine. In a spectacular battle, Bond, assisted by Pam Bouvier, destroys each tanker truck one-by-one. He then takes a cigarette lighter given to him by Felix and Della and uses it to torch a gasoline-soaked Sanchez.

THE FINAL CUT *Sanchez prepares to strike Bond with a machete seconds before the drug baron meets his own death.*

Felix Leiter: Killing me won't stop anything, Sanchez!
Sanchez: There are worse things than dying, *hombre*.

SANDOR

APPEARANCE
The Spy Who Loved Me (1977)
STATUS **Dead; killed by Bond**
CHARACTERISTICS **Hugely strong, intimidating; kills without question**
PLAYED BY **Milton Reid**

Sandor works for shipping magnate Karl Stromberg, who instructs him to travel with Jaws and eliminate anyone who comes into contact with the stolen microfilm of Stromberg's remarkable submarine tracking system. Sandor attempts to assassinate Bond at the house of middleman Aziz Fekkesh in Cairo but shoots Felicca instead. A fierce struggle with Bond leaves Sandor hanging precariously over the edge of a rooftop, clinging to Bond's tie. After Sandor tells Bond that Fekkesh can be found at the pyramids, Bond flips his tie away, sending Sandor to his death. "What a helpful chap," comments Bond.

TIGHT SQUEEZE *Despite his great strength, Sandor meets his match when he comes up against Bond in Cairo.*

SAXBY, BERT

APPEARANCE
Diamonds Are Forever (1971)
STATUS **Dead; shot by the CIA**
CHARACTERISTICS **Gruff, businesslike, laconic, treacherous**
PLAYED BY **Bruce Cabot**

Casino manager Albert R. Saxby is the reclusive billionaire Willard Whyte's right-hand man—until he decides to join Ernst Stavro Blofeld in a plot to kidnap Whyte, take over his empire, and use it to create the ultimate weapon. Saxby manages the Las Vegas end of Blofeld's diamond smuggling operation. When Whyte discovers that Saxby has betrayed him, he demands that Saxby be told he's fired, unaware that a CIA sharpshooter has just killed the traitorous employee.

SCARAMANGA, FRANCISCO

APPEARANCE
The Man With The Golden Gun
(1974)
STATUS Dead; shot by Bond
CHARACTERISTICS Superb marksman,
sophisticated manner hides a ruthless
craving for power
PLAYED BY Christopher Lee

Francisco Scaramanga, known as The
Man With The Golden Gun, plans to
auction the world's most efficient
solar energy system to the highest
bidder. Already the world's highest
paid assassin, Scaramanga schemes to
transform himself into an immensely
powerful underworld figure.

007: Six bullets
to your one?
Scaramanga:
I only need
one.

SIGN OF POWER *Andrea Anders dries off
Scaramanga after a swim. Some believe his
third nipple is a sign of invulnerability.*

Born to a Cuban ringmaster father
and an English snake-charmer
mother, Scaramanga grew up in the
circus where he gained a reputation
as a trick shot artist and where his
only real friend was an African bull
elephant. Scaramanga murdered the
elephant's cruel handler and then,
realizing he loved killing more than
animals, he decided to devote his life
to the "art" of murder.

The KGB recruited and trained
him, turning him into an
overworked and underpaid
assassin. In the late 1950s,
Scaramanga left the Soviets,
offering his services to anyone
who could afford his price—one
million dollars a kill. No known
photographs of him exist,
although the CIA has his
fingerprints on file. He has one
distinguishing feature—a
superfluous papilla—a third nipple.

Scaramanga kills his victims with
golden bullets and uses a number of
golden guns, including one made
from seemingly innocuous objects—

SHOOTING MATCH *Scaramanga searches for James Bond in his fun house, failing to notice that 007's mannequin has regrown the fingers he previously shot off.*

a lighter, a pen, a cigarette case, and a cuff link.

Living on a remote island in Chinese waters with his valet Nick Nack and mistress Andrea Anders and traveling by Chinese junk, Scaramanga performs the occasional favor for his Communist landlords. To hone his assassin skills, Scaramanga instructs Nick Nack to bring in hitmen to engage him in shootouts in a specially designed fun house maze. The maze contains a lifelike mannequin of Bond, the only man Scaramanga sees as a peer.

Scaramanga becomes corrupt industrialist Hai Fat's junior partner in a scheme to monopolize a new solar energy process designed by British scientist Gibson. Hai Fat and Gibson house the test plant in the rock spires on Scaramanga's island.

Unknown to Scaramanga, Andrea wants him dead, and she sends the British Secret Service a golden bullet inscribed "007," hoping Bond will be dispatched to kill him.

Cracks appear in Scaramanga and Hai Fat's scheme when Gibson opts to re-defect to the British using the Solex Agitator, the key to converting solar energy into electricity, as a bargaining chip for immunity. Scaramanga assassinates the scientist and recovers the Solex, but Gibson's overtures launch Bond on Scaramanga's trail.

Scaramanga kills Hai Fat to consolidate his position as lone controller of the solar technology. He murders Andrea for betraying him, kidnaps Bond's assistant, Mary Goodnight, and sets up a showdown with James Bond.

Bond tracks Scaramanga to his island, where a duel of the titans—Scaramanga versus 007—occurs. Scaramanga leads Bond on a chase through Nick Nack's fun house, but Bond outwits him by posing as his own mannequin and shooting him.

In Fleming's novel, KGB assassin "Pistols" Scaramanga, who always uses a gold-plated Colt .45, operates in the Caribbean. M orders Bond to assassinate Scaramanga, who has eliminated numerous agents. It is Bond's first assignment since the Soviets captured and brainwashed him. Bond eventually kills Scaramanga in a Jamaican swamp.

SCARPINE

APPEARANCE
A View To A Kill (1985)
STATUS Dead; killed in an airship explosion
CHARACTERISTICS Suave and well-dressed; a calm and ruthless mass killer
PLAYED BY Patrick Bauchau

Scarpine, a French killer with a deep scar on his cheek, works as Max Zorin's trusted and valued head of security at his French chateau and at his oil pumping station in San Francisco. After Zorin betrays May Day in the Main Strike Mine, Scarpine becomes Zorin's number two man, machine-gunning Zorin's mineworkers and later piloting his airship. He prepares to kill Bond on the Golden Gate Bridge, but Stacey Sutton knocks him unconscious with a fire extinguisher. He meets his demise when Zorin's airship blows up over San Francisco Bay.

UNDER SUSPICION *At a party at Max Zorin's chateau, Scarpine keeps an eye on James St. John Smythe, alias James Bond.*

SCORPION GUARD

APPEARANCE
Die Another Day (2002)
STATUS Alive; whereabouts unknown
CHARACTERISTICS Vicious, sadistic
PLAYED BY Tymarah

This seemingly emotionless army officer in charge of a North Korean prison tortures Bond for 14 long months with the stings of *Parabuthus* and death stalker scorpions. She then provides Bond with an antiserum in an attempt to extract information from him. A defiant Bond, however, refuses to give away any MI6 secrets. His ironic nickname for her is "The Concierge."

SISTER LILY & SISTER ROSE

APPEARANCE
Dr. No (1962)
STATUS Unknown
CHARACTERISTICS Duplicitous, over-friendly, and coy
PLAYED BY Yvonne Shima (Sister Lily), Michel Mok (Sister Rose)

The script for Dr. No describes these two Chinese hostesses based in Dr. No's bauxite mine base as "bright, helpful, inquisitive." Sister Lily beams from ear to ear as she shows Bond and Honey their rooms in Dr.No's luxurious underground bunker. She seems to genuinely want her guests to feel as comfortable as possible,

despite her knowledge that Bond and Honey are Dr. No's prisoners. Sister Lily's smile only becomes a trifle forced when Bond requests two tickets to London.

CORDIAL WELCOME *Inside Dr. No's lair, Sister Lily greets Bond and Honey after their decontamination shower.*

SLUMBER, MORTON

APPEARANCE
Diamonds Are Forever (1971)
STATUS Living; whereabouts unknown
CHARACTERISTICS Solicitous, unctuously charming, unscrupulous
PLAYED BY David Bauer

Morton Slumber, President of Slumber, Inc. Mortuary, plays a key role in Ernst Stavro Blofeld's diamond-smuggling operation. When Bond, using the identity of Peter Franks, arrives with a shipment of fake diamonds concealed in a coffin, Morton Slumber greets him effusively. The coffin is incinerated and Bond is presented with an urn containing the diamonds. The assassins Wint and Kidd then attack Bond as he collects his $50,000 fee, dump him in a coffin and send him to be cremated alive. Slumber and his accomplice, Shady Tree, discover that the diamonds are fake and manage to rescue Bond just in time. Bond remarks that he must have been given fake money, too, as no one would burn up 50,000 real dollars. "You get me the real money and I'll bring you the real diamonds," is Bond's parting shot.

SMERSH

APPEARANCES From Russia With Love (1963), The Living Daylights (1987)

SMERSH, a real Soviet intelligence directorate, has a murky history. Even the date of its formation remains in dispute. SMERSH was a contraction of two words: *smiert spionam* (or *spionom)*, meaning "death to spies." SMERSH's autonomy and ruthlessness gave it broad power and instilled fear in defectors.

SMERSH appears as the villainous organization in four of Ian Fleming's novels, although it was most likely disbanded by 1953. In the Bond films, Rosa Klebb is former head of operations for SMERSH in *From Russia With Love*. Although the word "SMERSH" is never used in the film, the concept of a Soviet murder organization is revived under the root phrase *smiert spionam* in *The Living Daylights*.

SOLO, MR.

APPEARANCE
Goldfinger (1964)
STATUS Dead; killed by Oddjob
CHARACTERISTICS Brash but sensible
PLAYED BY Martin Benson

Mr. Solo is the lone gangster who refuses Goldfinger's invitation to loot the Bullion Depository at Fort Knox. Goldfinger's owes Solo $1 million in gold for smuggling his industrial laser into the US. Goldfinger has Oddjob ostensibly drive Solo to the airport with the gold. Instead, Oddjob shoots Solo and has the car crushed. It is an expensive death since Goldfinger must then separate his gold from the car.

SPECTRE

APPEARANCES
Dr. No (1962), From Russia With Love (1963), Thunderball (1965), You Only Live Twice (1967), On Her Majesty's Secret Service (1969), Diamonds Are Forever (1971)

There stands but one criminal organization which can make governments tremble at the very mention of its name: SPECTRE.

The brainchild of Ernst Stavro Blofeld, SPECTRE stands for Special Executive for Counter-intelligence, Terrorism, Revenge and Extortion. This acronym should never be spelled with periods after each letter.

SPECTRE gleefully exploits global fears and international rivalries to make a profit. Aside from Blofeld, major operatives include Dr. No, Rosa Klebb, Donald Grant, Kronsteen, Jacques Boitier, Count Lippe, Emilio Largo, Fiona Volpe, Mr. Osato, Helga Brandt, and Irma Bunt, as well as hundreds of other associates. SPECTRE's symbol is an octopus, its tentacles able to work independently and together. Some agents have been known to wear an octopus signet ring. Fortunately for world peace, Bond has destroyed so many SPECTRE plots that the organization has all but ceased to exist.

In the novels, Ian Fleming introduces SPECTRE in *Thunderball* (1961), but his fascination with the name predates this. In *Diamonds Are Forever* (1956), he names a ghost town Spectreville, and in *From Russia With Love* (1957), Bond seeks an encoding machine called the Spektor.

CALLED TO ACCOUNT *The International Brotherhood for the Assistance of Stateless Persons is a front for SPECTRE's Paris base. It is here that top operatives, including SPECTRE No. 2 Emilio Largo (far left), gather to report to their chief, Blofeld.*

STAMPER

APPEARANCE
Tomorrow Never Dies (1997)
STATUS Dead; blown up
CHARACTERISTICS Sadistic killing machine; nearly impervious to pain
PLAYED BY Götz Otto

Stamper works as Elliot Carver's murderous assistant, abetting the media mogul in his plot to stage and profit from a military crisis between the UK and China. At well over 6 ft tall, with one blue and one brown eye, Stamper is a truly imposing presence. More than just muscle, he is a genuine psychopath, a protégé of the assassin Dr. Kaufman, who teaches him the fine arts of chakra torture.

Stamper oversees Carver's operation in the South China Sea by sending the Sea Vac drill from Carver's stealth ship into the hull of HMS *Devonshire*. When seventeen British sailors survive the sinking, Stamper personally machine-guns them in the water.

Stamper subsequently oversees numerous attempts to kill Bond and the Chinese agent Wai Lin. He captures them in Vietnamese waters and delivers them to Carver's Saigon headquarters. There, Elliot Carver instructs Stamper to kill Bond slowly using chakra torture tools. Stamper hopes to break Kaufman's 52-hour record of inflicting agony before the victim dies. Bond and Wai Lin manage to escape, with Bond burying a chakra blade deep in Stamper's thigh.

Stamper returns to Carver's stealth ship where he helps prepare the launch of a Tomahawk-class missile at Beijing. When Bond and Wai Lin board the ship, Stamper leads the hunt for them. After Carver's death, Stamper tries to stop Bond from sabotaging the missile. When the missile's engine explodes, the blast kills Stamper.

STROMBERG, KARL

APPEARANCE
The Spy Who Loved Me (1977)
STATUS **Dead; shot by Bond**
CHARACTERISTICS **Webbed hands; misanthropic, impatient; obsessed with life beneath the sea**
PLAYED BY **Curt Jurgens**

One of the richest men in the world, Karl Stromberg owns the Stromberg Shipping Line. He hopes to destroy humanity and rebuild civilization beneath the sea. If not for the alliance of James Bond and KGB agent Major Anya Amasova, Stromberg would very likely have achieved his dream.

Named Sigmun Stromberg in the film's novelization, he hails from Apvorst, Sweden, where his interest in marine life and immeasurably high IQ brought him respect and power. After first making a small fortune as a corrupt undertaker, Stromberg went into insurance following World War II, and took over a large shipping line.

Stromberg hires scientists Professor Markovitz and Dr. Bechmann to develop a submarine tracking system that he uses to capture the SLBM-equipped submarines, Britain's HMS *Ranger* and the Soviet *Potemkin*. With these, he plots nuclear strikes against New York and Moscow, counting on global nuclear warfare to follow and destroying a world he sees as irredeemably decadent.

Stromberg's plan begins to unravel close to home. He discovers his assistant has placed a microfilm of the tracking system up for sale. After killing the culprit, Stromberg

TAKING CONTROL *Stromberg confronts James Bond and Major Anya Amasova aboard his* Liparus *supertanker headquarters.*

D–DAY *Stromberg tells the* Liparus's *Captain to proceed with their plan for Armageddon.*

SEAFOOD SUPPER *Stromberg dines in his luxurious dining room aboard* Atlantis.

ATLANTIS RISING *Stromberg's marine research lab surfaces from the sea off the coast of Sardinia.*

007: Don't you miss the outside world?
Stromberg: For me, this is all the world. There is beauty... there is ugliness... and there is death.

launches a campaign to kill anyone who has come into contact with the microfilm. The microfilm draws the attention of Amasova and Bond, who arrange to visit Stromberg's marine research laboratory *Atlantis* off the coast of Sardinia undercover as a marine biologist and his wife. Stromberg, seeing through the charade, orders his personal henchman, the metal-toothed Jaws, to kill Bond and Amasova. The pair

survive a barrage of attacks.

The use of a Stromberg Shipping Line helicopter in one instance brings more attention to Stromberg's plot, as does a model of the *Liparus* with an all-too accurate depiction of its custom hull design. As a result, Bond and Amasova join the submarine USS *Wayne*, which is sent to attack the *Liparus*. Stromberg captures the *Wayne*, takes custody of Amasova, and orders the positioning of the *Ranger*

and *Potemkin* so that they may launch their SLBMs.

Stromberg retires to *Atlantis* to await Armageddon, an optimistic outlook considering the USSR, US, and British are by now fully cooperating. Bond leads an attack of British, American, and Soviet sailors that foils Stromberg's plot. 007 travels on the *Wayne* to *Atlantis*, confronting Stromberg and killing him with four shots from his Walther PPK.

SWISS GATEKEEPER

APPEARANCE
Goldfinger (1964)
STATUS Unknown
CHARACTERISTICS Friendly, unless
told to kill; handy with a machine gun
PLAYED BY Varley Thomas

Working at Auric Enterprises, this
grandmotherly gatekeeper politely
lets the captured James Bond into
the compound while under armed
guard and escort. Later, after Bond
ejects his unwelcome passenger out
of his Aston Martin DB5, he charges
for the gate. The gatekeeper fearlessly
stands in 007's way, spraying Bond's
windscreen with machine gun fire.

TEE HEE

APPEARANCE
Live And Let Die (1973)
STATUS Dead; disarmed by Bond
CHARACTERISTICS A smiling
assassin; the least little thing amuses him
PLAYED BY Julius W. Harris

One could call Tee Hee the
right-hand man for Dr. Kananga/Mr.
Big—except he has neither a right
hand nor a right arm. He lost the
limb to Albert, an old crocodile. In its
place, he boasts a deadly set of
pincers that can grab, cut, or claw at
a victim. The strength of these can be
seen when Tee Hee twists the barrel
of Bond's Walther PPK when they
meet in New York. His nickname
results from his omnipresent snicker.

In New Orleans, under orders
from Dr. Kananga/Mr. Big, Tee Hee
threatens to snip off Bond's little
finger. He knocks Bond unconscious
and escorts him to a drug lab outside
the city. He then leaves 007 stranded
on an island surrounded by hungry
crocodiles.

After 007 escapes and destroys
Kananga's operation, Tee Hee
sneaks aboard a train, battles
Bond, and slams him around
with his mechanical arm. 007
uses nail clippers to force Tee
Hee's claw to lock onto the
window handle, then throws
him out, ripping his prosthesis
off in the process.

Bond kills a character
named Tee-Hee Johnson in the
Fleming novel.

DISARMING THE VILLAIN *Tee Hee attempts
to avenge the death of his boss, Kananga, on*
The Crescent *passenger train.*

> "Tee Hee, on the first
> wrong answer from Miss
> Solitaire, you will snip
> **the little finger
> of Mr. Bond's
> right hand.**"
>
> Kananga to Tee Hee

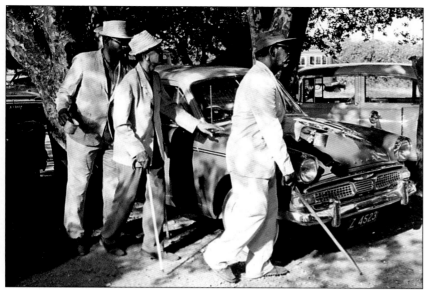

THE PERFECT COVER *Three killers disguised as blind beggars approach The Queen's Club to assassinate Strangways.*

THREE BLIND MICE, THE

APPEARANCE
Dr. No (1962)
STATUS Dead; killed in car crash
CHARACTERISTICS Sharp-eyed killers
PLAYED BY Eric Coverley (1st Beggar), Charles Edghill (2nd Beggar), Henry Lopez (3rd Beggar), Adrian Robinson (Hearse Driver)

These three blind beggars actually possess 20/20 vision and work for Dr. No. They shoot British Secret Service representative Strangways with silenced revolvers and later murder Mary Prescott, the secretary working with Strangways. The killings bring Bond to Jamaica to investigate. The Three Blind Mice attempt to eliminate Bond as he exits a taxi at his hotel. When this fails, they pursue Bond's Sunbeam Alpine through the mountains in their hearse. An adroit maneuver by Bond leads them to crash in flames.

TORO, COLONEL

APPEARANCE
Octopussy (1983)
STATUS Dead; blown up by Bond
CHARACTERISTICS Sure, authoritative
PLAYED BY Ken Norris

In an unnamed Latin American country, Bond impersonates army officer Colonel Toro in order to destroy a spy plane prototype housed

SEEING DOUBLE *Colonel Toro comes face to face with his lookalike, James Bond.*

in a hangar. Unfortunately, the real Colonel Toro arrives, and his men quickly capture 007. With his beautiful assistant Bianca's help, Bond plans his escape in the Acrostar Bede jet, but Toro's men fire a rapier surface-to-air missile at the jet. Bond flies through the hangar just before the doors close. The missile hits the doors, causing a massive explosion.

TREE, SHADY

APPEARANCE
Diamonds Are Forever (1971)
STATUS Dead; killed by Wint and Kidd
CHARACTERISTICS Crotchety, cynical; enjoys crossword puzzles
PLAYED BY Leonard Barr

Shady Tree is not only a comedian at The Whyte House's Lincoln Lounge but also a final link in Ernst Stavro Blofeld's complex diamond-smuggling pipeline.

Tree confronts James Bond, whom he believes to be smuggler Peter Franks, at Slumber Mortuary, cursing him for delivering a consignment of fake diamonds. Bond calmly tells Tree to get him the real money, instead of forged notes, and he will deliver the real diamonds.

FAREWELL PERFORMANCE *Shady Tree and his Acorns perform at The Whyte House.*

At The Whyte House, the killers Mr. Wint and Mr. Kidd, posing as fans wishing to sell comedy material, visit Tree, who claims he hasn't changed his act for 40 years. Wint and Kidd shoot him before casino manager Bert Saxby informs them that Tree has yet to acquire the real diamonds. The killers reply, "That's most annoying."

> "On behalf of the Whyte House, I'd just like to say you've been a lousy audience..."
>
> **Shady Tree**

TREE ASSASSIN

APPEARANCE
Moonraker (1979)
STATUS Dead; shot by Bond
CHARACTERISTICS Good at climbing into and falling out of trees
PLAYED BY Guy Delorme

Little is known about this henchman who works for billionaire aerospace mogul Hugo Drax. Under orders from Drax, the marksman climbs into a tree. When Bond appears, Drax sets him up to be killed, handing him a gun and asking him to shoot at a pheasant during a hunt on Drax's country estate.

Drax counts on the lack of interest of US police in hunting-related shooting deaths to cover up what he hopes will be Bond's death. The tree assassin fails to take his shot quickly, and Bond picks him off while pretending to shoot at a pheasant.

TREVELYAN, ALEC

APPEARANCE GoldenEye (1995)
STATUS Dead
CHARACTERISTICS Vengeful, highly skilled at the art of espionage
PLAYED BY Sean Bean

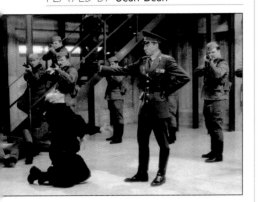

MISSION ACCOMPLISHED *006 convincingly fakes his own death with the help of Colonel Ourumov and his soldiers.*

Alec Trevelyan launches a plot to destroy London as an act of vengeance for the betrayal of his parents by the British Army at the end of World War II. Trevelyan's parents were Cossacks who opposed Stalin and fought with the Nazis. When the British captured many Cossacks near Lienz, Austria, they were turned over to the Soviets who swiftly executed them. Trevelyan's parents survived, but his father could not live with the shame and killed himself and his mother.

Trevelyan quickly rose through the ranks of MI6 to become 006. While MI6 knew about his parents' fate, the service believed that Trevelyan was too young to be affected by what

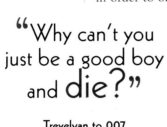

> "Why can't you just be a good boy and die?"
>
> Trevelyan to 007

had happened.

Trevelyan convinces MI6 to send Bond with him on a mission to the Soviet Union to destroy the Arkangel Chemical Weapons Facility, managed by Colonel Ourumov. In fact, the raid gives Trevelyan an opportunity to fake his own death. While the original plan anticipated the capture of Bond, 007 survives and causes explosions that scar Trevelyan.

After the fall of the Soviet Union, Trevelyan and Ourumov sell arms to illegal clients, such as Iraq. Trevelyan calls himself Janus after the two-faced Roman god and makes his residence on an armored train once used to transport nuclear missiles.

All this is a prelude to Trevelyan's master plan: to transfer billions of pounds from the Bank of England and set off the electromagnetic pulse space weapon GoldenEye over London to erase any record of the transaction. With the aid of hacker Boris Grishenko, assassin Xenia Onatopp, and Ourumov (now a General), he organizes a massacre of staff at the Russian Space Weapons Centre, Severnaya, in order to obtain his hands on the GoldenEye satellite system. A minor hitch occurs when one of the staff, Natalya Simonova, survives. This draws 007 to Russia. Trevelyan meets Bond once again after Xenia Onatopp fails to kill him. Through a series of cat-and-mouse maneuvers, Trevelyan ends up in Severnaya's sister control station in Cuba, where he and Bond fight to the death on a giant satellite dish transmitter. Competitive to the last, Trevelyan taunts 007: "I was always better." Bond responds by dropping his former friend and colleague from the antenna, which falls and crushes Trevelyan to death.

UNWANTED ATTENTIONS *Trevelyan toys with Natalya Simonova on his converted armored train.*

GUNNING FOR 007 *Trevelyan threatens Bond if Natalya does not reveal a passcode. "Shoot him. He means nothing to me," she replies.*

TRUMAN-LODGE

APPEARANCE
Licence to Kill (1989)
STATUS Dead; casualty of cutbacks
CHARACTERISTICS Whiny fiscal whiz
PLAYED BY Anthony Starke

Harvard Business School graduate William Truman-Lodge oversees the financial side of drug lord Franz Sanchez's cocaine empire. Wanted for insider trading on Wall Street, Truman-Lodge creates the business plan for Sanchez to supply an Asian drug cartel with cocaine. He also sets the prices for the US distribution of cocaine.

Eventually, Truman-Lodge's frequent nagging about money matters prompts Sanchez to "fire" him—using a submachine gun.

VALENKA

APPEARANCE
Casino Royale (2006)
STATUS Dead; shot by Mr. White
CHARACTERISTICS Devoted but lethal
PLAYED BY Ivana Milicevic

Le Chiffre's girlfriend Valenka revels in the luxurious life his illicit banking activities provide. She accompanies him to his high-stakes poker tournament in Montenegro. During the tournament, the Ugandan terrorist Obanno, who had entrusted Le Chiffre with a vast amount of money, attacks Valenka. Obanno and his lieutenant force Valenka to call Le Chiffre to his room. Obanno informs Le Chiffre that if he does not pay back the money he has lost, he will cut off Valenka's arm. Obanno notes that Le Chiffre raises no protest and sarcastically suggests that Valenka should find a new boyfriend.

Valenka ignores this advice and helps Le Chiffre in his bid to win the all-important poker game by poisoning Bond's "Vesper" martini.

TO YOUR HEALTH *Valenka looks on as a poisoned "Vesper" martini is delivered to 007.*

The poison sends 007 into cardiac arrest, and he only survives thanks to the quick thinking of his colleague, Treasury financial officer Vesper Lynd.

After Bond defeats Le Chiffre at poker, Valenka and her lover take Bond aboard a barge, where Le Chiffre tortures 007. Mr. White arrives and kills Le Chiffre and his entourage, including Valenka, but allows Bond to live.

VAN BIERK

APPEARANCE
Die Another Day (2002)
STATUS Serving time, per his sentence from the World Court
CHARACTERISTICS Debonair, smart
PLAYED BY Mark Dymond

Van Bierk, a South African trader of Sierra Leone conflict diamonds, bears a passing resemblance to James Bond. He sells the illegal diamonds to North Korean Colonel Moon in exchange for weapons. Bond uses a beacon device to divert Van Bierk's helicopter to his location and then impersonates Van Bierk to penetrate Moon's compound and plant an explosive device.

VARGAS

APPEARANCE
Thunderball (1965)
STATUS Dead; shot by Bond with a spear gun
CHARACTERISTICS Does not drink, smoke, or make love; his passion is killing.
PLAYED BY Philip Locke

Vargas works for Emilio Largo. His gaunt looks mirror his sinister nature. One of a group of SPECTRE thugs who toss Largo's hapless henchman Quist into a shark pool, Vargas later tries to kill Bond when 007 searches below the *Disco Volante*. He participates in the kidnapping of Bond's ally Paula Caplan and is interrogating her when she poisons herself. Vargas sees Bond talking to Domino on a beach and moves in for the kill. Bond shoots him with a speargun, saying, "I think he got the point."

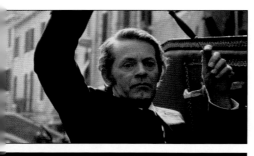

VENICE ASSASSINS

APPEARANCE
Moonraker (1979)
STATUS One dead; one escaped
CHARACTERISTICS Ingenious at springing surprise attacks, but ineffective
PLAYED BY Unknown

Industrialist Hugo Drax sends two assassins to kill Bond while he travels through Venice in a gondola. One tries to murder 007 from a funeral boat, emerging like Dracula from a coffin and hurling knives at Bond's gondolier and 007. Bond retrieves the knife meant for him and kills the attacker. The other assassin fires a machine gun at Bond as he flees in his specially equipped gondola.

VLAD

APPEARANCE
Die Another Day (2002)
STATUS Dead; flying high
CHARACTERISTICS Keen, nervous
PLAYED BY Michael Gorevoy

Russian scientist Vladimir Popov, called Vlad by his associates, is the brains behind the Icarus space program. He also designs an ice dragster and an armored battlesuit that can control the Icarus satellite. Gustav Graves is surprisingly rude to Vlad, taking his amazing technical accomplishments for granted. Vlad dies when a shot from Bond's Walther P99 decompresses Graves's Antonov transport plane, sucking Vlad into the stratosphere.

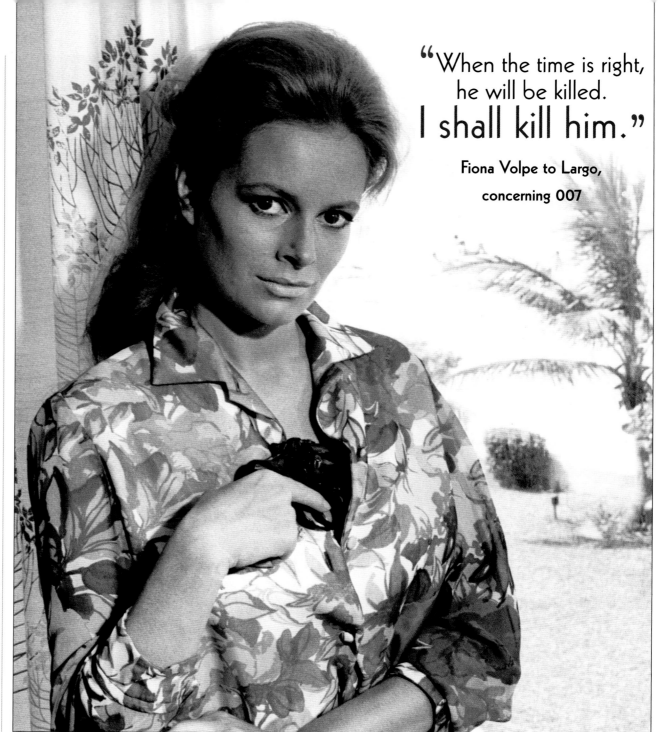

> "When the time is right, he will be killed. **I shall kill him.**"
>
> Fiona Volpe to Largo, concerning 007

VOLPE, FIONA

APPEARANCE Thunderball (1965)
STATUS Dead; shot by her own men
CHARACTERISTICS Cunning strategist; weapons expert; often makes love to her victims before killing them
PLAYED BY Luciana Paluzzi

As the Head of SPECTRE's Execution Branch, Fiona Volpe serves as the ultimate femme fatale. She not only kills anyone deemed a security risk, she enjoys seducing her targets, teasing their egos and libidos, and sending them to their doom.

Volpe plays an important role in SPECTRE's plan to ransom two atomic weapons. She sets up NATO pilot François Derval to be killed by SPECTRE mercenary Angelo Palazzi, then kills her colleague Count Lippe for bringing the conniving Palazzi onboard.

Volpe bides her time rather than lashes out in anger. She scolds key SPECTRE figure Emilio Largo for trying to kill James Bond. As she points out, Bond's death would have led the British to discover SPECTRE's plan.

Volpe meets Bond when he flags down her car in the Bahamas. As she drives him to the Coral Harbour hotel, he notices her SPECTRE signet ring. She later orders the kidnapping of Bond's contact, Paula

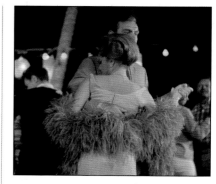

DANCE OF DEATH *Fiona Volpe dies in Bond's arms at the Kiss Kiss Club.*

Caplan, seduces Bond, then arranges for him to be abducted. When Bond escapes, Volpe tracks him to a club where she plots for him to be shot as they dance. Bond sees the trap and spins her into the bullet's path.

WHISPER

APPEARANCE
Live And Let Die (1973)
STATUS Unknown
CHARACTERISTICS Methodical and
slow-moving; soft-spoken to the extreme
PLAYED BY Earl Jolly Brown

Whisper works as one of Dr. Kananga's henchmen. He gets his nickname from his quiet, hoarse voice. Whisper tries to kill 007 upon his arrival in New York by firing a poison dart from the side mirror of his white Corvorado "pimpmobile" into the temple of Bond's driver. He hopes the car will crash, but Bond manages to bring it to a stop.

On the island of San Monique, Whisper delivers champagne to Bond's hotel bungalow shortly before 007 battles a desert kingsnake. Whisper later becomes the butt of one of Kananga's jokes when Kananga fires a CO_2 shark pellet into a sofa on which Whisper sits, making it explode. Bond later kicks Whisper into a drug shipment container and then locks him inside.

In the novel, he is known as The Whisper and runs Mr. Big's switchboard in Harlem, New York, which tracks the enemy's movements. His quiet voice is a result of a childhood illness that left him with only half a lung.

WHITAKER, BRAD

APPEARANCE
The Living Daylights (1987)
STATUS Dead; killed by Bond
CHARACTERISTICS Egotistical, war-hungry, brash, over-confident
PLAYED BY Joe Don Baker

Based in Tangier, American arms dealer Brad Whitaker has a museum containing statues of military leaders such as Hitler, Napoleon, and Caesar, —all in his own likeness—and dioramas of great battles. Expelled from West Point for cheating, Whitaker was a mercenary in the Belgian Congo and then worked with criminal organizations that financed his first arms deals. He now partners General Koskov in a scheme to eliminate KGB head Pushkin, and misuse Soviet government funds to trade diamonds for opium.

"He met his Waterloo."
007

When Bond confronts him in his home, Whitaker nearly kills 007 with a high-tech assault rifle. Bond kills Whitaker by attaching his explosive key fob to a statue of Wellington. When Bond emits a wolf whistle, the statue explodes and crushes Whitaker into his diorama of the battle of Waterloo.

WHITE, MR.

APPEARANCE
Casino Royale (2006)
STATUS Shot by Bond; eventual fate unknown at present
CHARACTERISTICS Genius of betrayal
PLAYED BY Jesper Christensen

A mysterious representative for an unidentified network that helps finance chaos and instability calls himself Mr. White.

He introduces Steven Obanno of The Lord's Resistance Army to Le Chiffre, private banker to world terrorists. Le Chiffre loses Obanno's money by sponsoring his own, financially-motivated terrorist plot that goes wrong. Mr. White's involvement and knowledge of Le Chiffre's attempt to regain his money through a poker tournament are unclear. However, White's organization and Le Chiffre, using Financial Action Task Force liaison officer Vesper Lynd, weave an elaborate web to ensure the money ends up in their possession.

When Bond wins the poker game, Le Chiffre kidnaps and tortures 007, who refuses to reveal the password that will allow access to get the tournament prize money. Mr. White arrives moments before Le Chiffre plans to kill 007. White kills Le Chiffre, but spares Bond's life, seemingly as part of a deal with Lynd to gain access to the winnings.

In Venice, when the transfer of funds between Lynd and organization operative Gettler goes wrong, Mr. White collects Lynd's briefcase full of cash. White appears to be Lynd's key contact in the organization. Apparently through White, she thinks her French-Algerian lover has been kidnapped, and should she fail to cooperate, she believes her lover will be killed. After Lynd drowns in the sinking house in Venice, she leaves White's cell phone number for Bond on her cell phone.

007 tracks White down to a European lakeside villa. Bond calls White's mobile and then shoots him in the leg. Finally, 007 introduces himself to White in preparation for his attack on the organization.

WINT, MR. & KIDD, MR.

APPEARANCE
Diamonds Are Forever (1971)
STATUS Dead; lost at sea
CHARACTERISTICS Methodical killers with a macabre sense of humor; able to finish each other's sentences
PLAYED BY Bruce Glover (Wint), Putter Smith (Kidd)

Wint and Kidd work as killers for Ernst Stavro Blofeld, murdering the members of Blofeld's diamond smuggling ring as the final consignment of stones works its way through the pipeline. Starting with Dr. Tynan in South Africa, Wint and Kidd follow the chain of smugglers to Amsterdam, Los Angeles, and Las Vegas, leaving a trail of corpses in their wake.

> **"Everyone who touches those diamonds seems to die."**
>
> Mr. Wint

Although Wint and Kidd knock Bond unconscious at Slumber, Inc. and later place his body in a buried pipeline, Bond never sees the pair until the very end of the mission.

A homosexual couple, Wint and Kidd indulge in macabre banter as they work. For example, when Kidd takes pictures of police pulling Mrs. Whistler's body from the Amster River, he notes that she wanted photos of the canals for the children at her school.

Wint's liking for pungent cologne stays with 007, after he smells it on his clothes when he awakes in a desert pipeline. When Wint and Kidd, posing as stewards, try to kill Bond and Tiffany Case aboard Willard Whyte's cruise ship, Bond recognizes the scent. He mentions that it would have been more appropriate to serve a claret rather than Mouton Rothschild '55 with their meal. Wint apologizes, but Bond points out that Mouton Rothschild *is* a claret. Realizing their cover is blown, Wint and Kidd attack. Bond sets Kidd ablaze with brandy; he then tosses Wint over the side with the bomb (disguised as a dessert called a "Bombe Surprise") meant to kill him and Tiffany. Wint explodes before hitting the water.

Wint and Kidd appear in the novel as enforcers for The Spangled Mob. Bond kills them aboard a ship—the *Queen Elizabeth*.

ZAO

APPEARANCE
Die Another Day (2002)
STATUS Dead; smashed by a lighting fixture while battling Bond
CHARACTERISTICS Experienced and sadistic assassin and terrorist
PLAYED BY Rick Yune

Zao is a North Korean terrorist in league with Colonel Moon, selling conflict diamonds and illicit weapons. At Moon's North Korean compound, Zao takes a PDA cell phone photo of Bond, who is posing as conflict-diamond trader Van Bierk, and transmits it to MI6 double agent Miranda Frost. She quickly identifies "Van Bierk" as Bond. Unmasked, Bond sets off an explosion th,at embeds diamonds in Zao's face. Bond then seemingly kills Moon before being taken prisoner.

Zao later attempts to blow up a summit meeting between South Korea and China, killing three Chinese agents before being captured. To secure Zao's release, Colonel Moon, altered by gene therapy and now known as Gustav Graves, asks Miranda Frost, his lover, to reveal to the North Koreans the identity of the top US agent in the North Korean High Command. The spy is executed, leading the US and British Secret Services to assume that Bond has cracked under torture and revealed this information. They hastily arrange

> 007: Your time will come
> Zao: Not as soon as yours.

UNMARKED *Zao before Bond gives him the world's most expensive face (top).*

for Zao to be released in a prisoner exchange with Bond.

Zao travels to a Cuban medical clinic for DNA replacement therapy, which will morph him into a German Caucasian. Bond disrupts Zao's transformation, but Zao escapes in a helicopter, his face still pockmarked with diamonds, his body chalk white from the unfinished transformation. Zao arrives in Iceland and, driving a Jaguar XKR loaded with weaponry, attacks Bond in his Aston Martin Vanquish. Inside Gustav Graves's melting and crumbling Ice Palace, Bond tricks Zao into crashing his car. 007 then fires a single shot that severs a cable holding a giant ice chandelier. It comes crashing down upon Zao and kills him.

ZORIN, MAX

APPEARANCE
A View To A Kill (1985)
STATUS Dead; at the bottom of San Francisco Bay
CHARACTERISTICS Brilliant but unstable; relishes killing
PLAYED BY Christopher Walken

Max Zorin's boundless ambition leads him to create a plot to corner the world's microchip market. The result of Nazi steroid experiments on pregnant women in concentration camps, Zorin was born in Dresden and quickly deemed a genius (He speaks five languages without accent). But, like all the "steroid kids," he is a psychotic. According to the script, Zorin is "tall, slender, impeccably dressed, in his late thirties. Unusually handsome, he has one grey eye and one blue eye."

In the 1960s, Zorin fled East Germany for France with his "creator," Hans Glaub, the scientist who ran the steroid experiments and changed his name to Dr. Carl Mortner. Zorin built a fortune in oil and gas trading and then expanded into electronics. Gaining a reputation as a staunch anti-Communist and a penniless refugee who made good, Zorin acquired influential friends in European governments.

Zorin's success proves a perfect cover for his second life as a KGB agent who, working for General Gogol, funnels important technology into the Soviet Union. Zorin also works behind the KGB's back, providing technology to a group of microchip manufacturers whom he hopes will join him in a microchip production and distribution cartel. M becomes suspicious of Zorin when a microchip recovered by 007 in Siberia matches a chip impervious to electromagnetic pulse damage developed by a Zorin Industries company. Zorin plans to trigger a massive double earthquake that will flood the entire San Francisco Bay area, including Silicon Valley, home of 80 percent of world microchip production. Calling his plan Operation Main Strike, he foresees that his cartel's chips will then rule the market.

Zorin faces two obstacles. The first is his questionable obsession with

THE BOSS FROM HELL *Max Zorin ruthlessly guns down his loyal workers in his Main Strike mine prior to flooding it.*

THE IMPERFECT COUPLE
Super-intelligent but psychotic Max Zorin and super-strong but amoral May Day make a lethal partnership.

horse racing. Zorin and Mortner use remote-triggered microchips to inject steroids in racehorses during competition. This draws attention to his activities and compels him to order his accomplice May Day to murder two investigators in France—Achille Aubergine and Sir Godfrey Tibbett—and to personally attempt to murder 007. Additionally, Zorin engages in an ugly battle for control of Sutton Oil. He takes over the company in a rigged proxy fight, but this sparks a legal challenge from oil heiress Stacey Sutton. Zorin offers her $5 million for her shares in the company, but Stacey tears up the check and vows to regain what is rightfully hers.

As Operation Main Strike nears, Zorin severs all ties with the KGB and commits grander crimes. He orders May Day to murder CIA agent Chuck Lee. He assassinates state geologist W. G. Howe and sets San Francisco City Hall afire. He even machine guns his own employees at his mine and betrays May Day. This final act proves the undoing of Operation Main Strike. May Day sacrifices her life to remove the detonator from the tons of explosives set to trigger the fateful earthquake.

When Zorin attempts to escape in his airship, Bond grabs onto the mooring line and ties it to the vertical struts of the Golden Gate Bridge, where Zorin and Bond battle. Bond gains the advantage, and Zorin falls to his death.

BOND
WOMEN

More than any other characters in the Bond canon, it is often the women who issue Bond a challenge. They test his confidence. They demand he rise to their standards. When Anya Amasova discovers that Bond killed her lover, he must prove his integrity to her or be killed. The women of the Bond films usually know what they want—and how to get it. They understand the world and are not afraid of it. Whether secret agents or mistresses, smugglers or cellists, they are the smartest, most beautiful, most life-embracing women around. Some, such as NSA agent Jinx and Wai Lin of the Chinese People's External Security Forces, are very much Bond's equal. If Bond represents masculinity, these women are the epitome of modern femininity: strong, sensual, brilliant, and self-possessed.

AKI

APPEARANCE
You Only Live Twice (1967)
STATUS Poisoned in Bond's arms
CHARACTERISTICS Excellent spying
skills; remains calm under pressure;
superior driver and athlete
PLAYED BY Akiko Wakabayashi

The first Bond woman to be
considered a comrade in arms to 007,
Aki works for the Japanese Secret
Service (SIS) as Agent 294. Aki makes
contact with 007 at a sumo wrestling
match in Tokyo. When Bond gives
her the recognition signal, "I love
you," she takes him to see British
secret service operative Dikko
Henderson at his home. An assassin
kills Henderson before he can give
007 important information, and Aki
trails Bond and the killer's accomplice
in her Toyota 2000GT to the
headquarters of Osato Chemicals &
Engineering. She rescues Bond from
Ostato's guards and delivers him to the
office of Tiger Tanaka, head of the SIS.

The following day, Aki once again
saves Bond from gunmen, and the
two travel to the Kobe docks,
escaping a multitude of attackers.
Tanaka informs Bond he will have to
take a wife as part of his cover as a
Japanese fisherman. He forbids a
disappointed Aki from playing the
role, but she supervises Bond's
cosmetic transformation into a
Japanese fisherman. Bond and Aki
then share a bed for the night. As they
sleep, a SPECTRE assassin climbs
above the bed and drips a deadly
poison down a string directed at
Bond's mouth. Aki, however, shifts in
her sleep, and the poison drips onto
her lips, killing her instantly.

AMASOVA, MAJOR ANYA

APPEARANCE
The Spy Who Loved Me (1977)
STATUS Living; whereabouts unknown
CHARACTERISTICS The KGB's top
agent; graduate of a Siberian survival
course; positive mental attitude; patriotic
and vengeful
PLAYED BY Barbara Bach

Major Anya Amasova, Agent Triple X
of the KGB, works with James Bond
in an uneasy alliance to locate two
hijacked nuclear submarines.

Anya arrives in Moscow after a
period of leave with her KGB agent
lover, Sergei Barsov. KGB chief
General Gogol informs her that the
nuclear submarine *Potemkin* has
disappeared and instructs Anya to

> **"Then when this mission is over, I will kill you."**
>
> **Anya to 007**

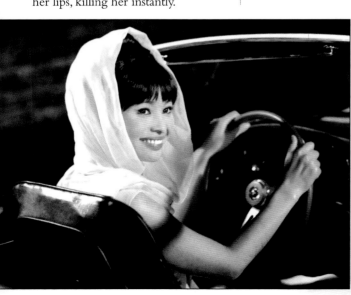

pursue a connection in Cairo. He then tells her of Barsov's tragic death in a British Secret Service operation. Anya replies, "I would very much like to meet the person responsible."

In Egypt, Anya pursues the submarine tracking system microfilm offered for sale by Max Kalba. She encounters Bond at the Pyramids of Giza while meeting contact Aziz Fekkesh. She meets 007 again at the Mujaba Club, where the pair shares knowledge of each other's dossiers and attempt to bid for the microfilm. When a huge hulking figure—Karl Stromberg's henchman Jaws—kills Kalba, Anya and Bond follow and

MAJOR PLAYER *Anya Amasova learns of the tragic death of her lover, Sergei Barsov, from her chief, General Gogol.*

THE LAST CALL *Anya decides Bond's fate at the end of their mission.*

successfully battle the giant for the microfilm. Anya then wins the microfilm for the KGB by blowing narcotic dust from a trick cigarette into Bond's face.

When Anya contacts General Gogol, she discovers the Soviets and British have agreed to pool their resources. After another attack by Jaws, Anya and Bond give in to their romantic attraction, but when Anya discovers that 007 killed her lover, she vows to kill him when the mission is over. Realizing that shipping magnate Stromberg is behind the nuclear submarine hijack, Bond and Anya hunt Stromberg's *Liparus* supertanker on the USS *Wayne* submarine, but Stromberg captures the craft.

Stromberg takes Anya to *Atlantis,* his marine research laboratory. Having destroyed the *Liparus,* Bond rescues Anya as the *Wayne* torpedoes *Atlantis,* and they flee in Stromberg's escape pod. Anya must decide whether or not to fulfill her vow to kill Bond. She decides to put the Cold War behind her, and, as a result, Gogol, M, Q, and the Minister of Defence catch the two spies making love, oblivious to their rescue by the Royal Navy.

ANDERS, ANDREA

APPEARANCE
The Man With The Golden Gun (1974)
STATUS Dead; shot by Scaramanga
CHARACTERISTICS Desperate to free herself from a man she fears
PLAYED BY Maud Adams

Trapped in a relationship with master assassin Francisco Scaramanga, Andrea Anders sends a golden bullet engraved with the number "007" to the British Secret Service. She hopes it will spur James Bond to come after Scaramanga, kill him, and free her from a life she loathes. Her plan succeeds but too late for her to reap the rewards.

When Bond appears at her hotel room in Hong Kong, Andrea pretends not to know Bond's identity. She suffers 007's rough treatment, eventually confessing that Scaramanga has an appointment at the Bottom's Up Club in Hong Kong. Andrea finds Bond again in Bangkok, slipping into his room to warn him that Scaramanga wants to kill him. She admits that she sent the bullet and offers to sleep with him if he will kill Scaramanga. Bond asks her to acquire for him the Solex Agitator, the key component of the world's most efficient solar energy system. She steals it for Bond, but Scaramanga discovers her betrayal and shoots her through the heart at their rendezvous, a Thai kick-boxing match.

A SUITABLE SUBJECT *Ruby appears in the novel* On Her Majesty's Secret Service *with the surname Windsor. She is portrayed as not terribly bright ("I failed my GCE twice"), which was part of her selection criteria by Ernst Stavro Blofeld.*

BLOFELD'S ANGELS OF DEATH

APPEARANCE On Her Majesty's Secret Service (1969)
STATUS Living; whereabouts unknown
CHARACTERISTICS International, impressionable, naïve
PLAYED BY Angela Scoular (Ruby), Catherina von Schell (Nancy), Julie Ege (Scandinavian Girl), Mona Chong (Chinese Girl), Sylvana Henriques (Jamaican Girl), Dani Sheridan (American Girl), Joanna Lumley (English Girl), Zara (Indian Girl), Anoushka Hempel (Australian Girl), Ingrit Back (German Girl), Helena Ronee (Israeli Girl), Jenny Hanley (Italian Girl)

BREAKING AND ENTERING *Bond discovers Nancy in his bedroom at Piz Gloria. She circumvented the security doors with a nail file.*

BARTLETT, RUBY

APPEARANCE On Her Majesty's Secret Service (1969)
STATUS Living; whereabouts unknown
CHARACTERISTICS Good-natured
PLAYED BY Angela Scoular

Ruby Bartlett unwittingly helps 007 gain insight into Blofeld's operation at his Swiss mountain allergy clinic. In her room, Bond witnesses Blofeld's brainwashing techniques. Raised on a poultry farm in Morecambe Bay, Lancashire, England, Ruby became allergic to chickens. Blofeld has cured her allergy; however, brainwashing has now primed her to return to England and spread the bacteriological warfare agent Virus Omega among poultry populations.

BERGSTROM, PROF. INGA

APPEARANCE Tomorrow Never Dies (1997)
STATUS Living; whereabouts unknown
CHARACTERISTICS Cunning linguist
PLAYED BY Cecilie Thomsen

Professor Inga Bergstrom is a Danish Professor at Oxford University with whom Bond brushes up on "a little Danish" and "learns a new tongue." Moneypenny disrupts their afternoon tryst with a phone call. She summons Bond to the Ministry of Defense to deal with a crisis in the South China Sea, where 17 British sailors have been murdered.

BIANCA

APPEARANCE Octopussy (1983)
STATUS Living, whereabouts unknown
CHARACTERISTICS Resourceful; improvises on the spot
PLAYED BY Tina Hudson

Bond's colleague Bianca aids him when he arrives in a Latin American country to destroy a spy plane. She places a fake mustache on his upper lip and attaches a fake ID to his jacket to aid in his convincing disguise as Colonel Luis Toro.

Minutes later, Bianca notices Toro's paratrooper guards driving away with a captured Bond. She speeds up to the vehicle in a Range Rover Convertible and uses her feminine wiles to distract the guards, allowing Bond to pull the rip cords on the guards' parachute harnesses. Before Bond escapes in the Acrostar Bede jet, which he and Bianca have stowed in the back of a horsebox, 007 kisses Bianca goodbye, telling her he will see her in Miami.

DRESSED TO THRILL *Beautiful Bianca proves to be a resourceful and skilled accomplice on Bond's mission to destroy a spy plane.*

Ernst Stavro Blofeld gathers twelve beautiful women from around the globe who will unwittingly act as his Angels of Death, spreading his Virus Omega to crops and livestock if his demands are not met.

"The first impression of them is of contestants in an international beauty contest." This is how these women are described in the script. They all suffer from different allergies, including sensitivities to chicken, potatoes, bananas, and rice. They convene in a Swiss clinic known as The Bleuchamp Institute for Allergy Research at Piz Gloria hoping to find a cure for their allergies. Blofeld, posing as the Count Balthazar de Bleuchamp, uses

the clinic as cover to develop and distribute his bacteriological warfare agent. The twelve brainwashed women, along with several unidentified others, will return to their respective countries and, on his command, spray the deadly Virus Omega agent using innocent-looking atomizers, destroying crops and decimating livestock.

Bond arrives at Piz Gloria disguised as the genealogist Sir Hilary Bray, whom Blofeld has hired to prove his claim to the title of Comte de Bleuchamp. Bond seduces two women, Ruby and Nancy, and flirts with the Chinese woman in an attempt to discover Blofeld's plans. Although captured after sneaking into Ruby's room late at night, Bond uncovers the bacteriological warfare plot and escapes Piz Gloria on skis.

Bond returns later with his future father-in-law Marc Ange Draco and Draco's men, firstly to rescue his fiancée Tracy, who has been kidnapped by Blofeld, and secondly to destroy Blofeld's base, Piz Gloria. This communications center controls the women in their respective countries, and its destruction removes the world threat posed by the twelve "Angels of Death."

There are only ten beautiful women in Fleming's novel. Instead of arriving from all over the world, they come solely from the United Kingdom. All in their twenties, they are described as "working girls probably. Sort of air-hostess type."

"I'll tell you what to do,
I will tell you when, and
I will tell you how."

Ernst Stavro Blofeld

103

BOUVIER, PAM

APPEARANCE
Licence To Kill (1989)
STATUS Living; whereabouts unknown
CHARACTERISTICS Professional,
superb pilot; has a possessive streak
PLAYED BY Carey Lowell

in order to break into The Olympatec Meditation Institute, a cover for Sanchez's cocaine labs. She rescues Bond and then flies him above one of the tanker trucks to stop Sanchez. At a party celebrating the end of Sanchez's reign, Pam expresses disappointment when she sees Bond kissing Lupe. In the end, Bond chooses to be with Pam.

Pam Bouvier works as a CIA contract pilot and agent trying to contain drug lord Franz Sanchez's operation in Isthmus City.

Bond meets her at DEA agent Felix Leiter's wedding reception and then later at the Barrelhead Bar in Bimini where her drink of choice is "Bud with lime." While at the bar, she finds herself under attack from Sanchez's henchman Dario and his gang. She successfully defends herself with a 12 gauge shotgun. She escapes with Bond and informs him that she was an army pilot who has flown to the toughest hellholes in South America. Bond pays her $75,000 for a private flight to Isthmus City, where he continues to pay her to pose as his secretary, Ms. Kennedy. She even cuts her hair very short to look the part but keeps a Beretta in her garter belt for her own security.

Pam delivers a letter from the US Attorney General to Heller, Sanchez's Chief of Security, granting him immunity if he can retrieve the four Stinger missiles Sanchez purchased from the Contras. Pam harbors concern for Bond's safety during the mission but displays anger and jealousy when she learns Bond has had an affair with Lupe Lamora, Sanchez's girlfriend. She still comes to Bond's aid by posing as a Bible Belt churchgoer from Wichita Falls

STRAIGHT SHOOTER
Pam encounters Bond for the second time in a sleazy Bimini bar, where she proves herself adept with a shotgun.

"If it wasn't for me, your ass would've been nailed to the wall."
Pam Bouvier

CAROLINE

APPEARANCE GoldenEye (1995)
STATUS Retired from MI6, now a guidance counselor at Eton
CHARACTERISTICS Easily flustered
PLAYED BY Serena Gordon

A woman of impeccable background, Caroline works for MI6 evaluating the psychological health of agents. M sends her to report on 007, and she rides with him on a twisting corniche into Monaco in Bond's Aston Martin DB5. When 007 engages in a high-speed flirtatious chase with Ferrari-driving Xenia Onatopp, a terrified Caroline demands he stop. Bond pulls the car to the edge of a cliff overlooking Monaco and produces a bottle of Bollinger as Caroline melts into his arms.

CARUSO, MISS

APPEARANCE
Live And Let Die (1973)
STATUS Alive; whereabouts unknown
CHARACTERISTICS Covert worker
PLAYED BY Madeline Smith

Little is known about the secretive Miss Caruso. After helping James Bond on a mission in Rome, she leaves the country to spend time with him without informing her superiors. This causes the Italians to query M as to her whereabouts. When M arrives at Bond's home at 5:48 a.m. to give 007 an assignment, he asks Bond about her. 007 does not answer, since Caruso is hiding in his closet. Miss Moneypenny witnesses this and helps Bond keep Caruso concealed from M, allowing the pair to spend additional time together before 007 flies to New York.

Miss Caruso: Such a delicate touch.
007: Sheer magnetism, darling!

CARVER, PARIS

APPEARANCE
Tomorrow Never Dies (1997)
STATUS Assassinated
CHARACTERISTICS Sophisticated, cosmopolitan, unhappy; still carrying a torch for 007
PLAYED BY Teri Hatcher

Paris Carver is the stunning American wife of British media baron Elliot Carver and a former flame of James Bond.

Paris and 007 meet again at a party in Hamburg, Germany, celebrating the launch of Elliot Carver's new global satellite network. Paris slaps Bond hard when she sees him again, still angry that his last words to her were, "I'll be right back." When Bond knew her, she used to drink straight shots of tequila. Now she prefers to take a sip of her husband's champagne. She knows Bond very well, asking him if he still sleeps with a gun under his pillow. A jealous Elliot asks his wife how she knows Bond. She lies, saying that James dated her roommate in Zurich.

Paris later goes to Bond's hotel room and tells him that she used to look for his obituary in the papers every day. Bond confesses to her that the reason he backed out of their relationship was because she had become "too close for comfort." The two spend a passionate evening together, and with the help of Paris, Bond locates Elliot Carver's secret lab. When Carver learns of his wife's betrayal, he sends Dr. Kaufman, a professional hitman, to assassinate her. Bond returns to his hotel room to find Paris still in his bed—dead.

007: Was it something I said?
Paris: How about the words I'll be right back?

CASE, TIFFANY

APPEARANCE
Diamonds Are Forever (1971)
STATUS Living; whereabouts unknown
CHARACTERISTICS Confident, mercenary, clever, seductive
PLAYED BY Jill St. John

Smuggler Tiffany Case plays a vital role in the downfall of Ernst Stavro Blofeld. Part of a smuggling pipeline of South African diamonds, Tiffany finds herself in the middle of a battle between Bond, the CIA, and Blofeld's organization—with world domination in the balance.

Tiffany reveals little of her background except that she was born on the first floor of Tiffany & Co. while her mother shopped for a wedding ring. She has grown up with a mercenary attitude toward wealth and uses her feminine wiles to get what she wants and to protect herself and her interests.

When she meets James Bond, he poses as smuggler Peter Franks. When Bond kills the real Franks, he convinces her the dead man is actually 007. She urges Bond to leave with her and the diamonds immediately. She parts ways with Bond in Los Angeles, only to be called back into service by her contacts in Las Vegas because Bond has delivered fake diamonds. After collecting the real diamonds and eluding over 30 US government agents, Tiffany discovers from Bond that someone is killing all the smugglers in the pipeline. The body of Plenty O'Toole, drowned in her pool, confirms that Tiffany herself is the next target.

Tiffany agrees to help Bond, leading him to the diamonds. She soon finds herself in a guarded suite in Las Vegas, uncertain if she will be rewarded or prosecuted. After Bond discovers Blofeld is behind the smuggling operation, Tiffany convinces the CIA of her willingness to cooperate.

When she sees a woman with a white Persian cat leaving the Whyte House, she follows, thinking it could be Blofeld in drag. It is, but Blofeld kidnaps Tiffany. She pretends to cooperate, traveling with Blofeld to the oil rig from where he launches his satellite attacks against military targets belonging to the world's

007: Weren't you a blonde when I came in?

Tiffany Case: Could be.

007: I tend to notice little things like that— whether a girl's a blonde or a brunette.

MORE THAN MEETS THE EYE *Tiffany Case schemes to obtain a cache of diamonds. Bond has other plans.*

DIVIDED LOYALTIES *Case appears to side with Blofeld when 007 ejects a satellite guidance tape from the command center on an oil rig.*

superpowers. Case maintains the illusion of allegiance to Blofeld when Bond arrives, but surreptitiously tries to help 007.

At the end of the adventure, Tiffany and Bond go on a sea cruise together. After Bond has disposed of the assassins Wint and Kidd, Tiffany asks Bond: "James, how the hell do we get those diamonds down again?"

In Fleming's novel, Tiffany has led a troubled life. Her mother worked as a madam, and Tiffany became an alcoholic. After she saved a child from drowning, she turned her life around and became a smuggler for the Spangled Mob. At the story's conclusion, Tiffany moves in with Bond—the only woman to do so in the novels or films—but the affair soon ends.

CHEW MEE

APPEARANCE The Man With The Golden Gun (1974)
STATUS Living; whereabouts unknown
CHARACTERISTICS Enjoys swimming
PLAYED BY Françoise Therry

When Bond sneaks into industrialist Hai Fat's estate impersonating his employee Francisco Scaramanga, he meets beautiful Chew Mee swimming in Fat's pool. She invites Bond to join her. When Bond informs her he has no bathing suit, Chew Mee admits that neither has she. Bond starts to unbutton his shirt, but Hai Fat interrupts.

AUDIENCE CONCERN
Bibi and Bond observe East German biathlon champion Erich Kriegler's expert shooting.

DAHL, BIBI

APPEARANCE
For Your Eyes Only (1981)
STATUS Living; retired from ice-skating
CHARACTERISTICS Cute, libidinous
PLAYED BY Lynn-Holly Johnson

Bibi Dahl is an Olympic-caliber ice skater whose fresh-faced innocence belies her irrepressible sexual drive.

Bond meets the teenager at an ice rink in Cortina through her sponsor, Aris Kristatos, and her coach, Jacoba Brink. Bibi immediately falls for Bond and later tries to seduce him in his room at the Hotel Miramonte. Mindful of her youth, Bond politely, but firmly, shows her the door.

She is also a fan of East German biathlon champion Erich Kriegler (secretly a hitman working for Kristatos), who rudely ignores her.

Later, when Kristatos retreats with his entourage to an abandoned monastery in Greece, Bibi, sick of his bullying, tries to flee with Jacoba Brink. After Milos Columbo kills Kristatos, Columbo apparently becomes Bibi's new sponsor.

> ❝She's completely absorbed in her skating, but innocent in the ways of the world.❞
>
> Aris Kristatos to 007

PAINFUL REVELATIONS *Bond explains to Domino that Largo killed her brother.*

DERVAL, DOMINO

APPEARANCE
Thunderball (1965)
STATUS Alive; whereabouts unknown
CHARACTERISTICS Good swimmer, excellent dancer, lonely; seeking escape from a suffocating relationship
PLAYED BY Claudine Auger

Dominique Derval, the kept woman of Emilio Largo, becomes the sole link for James Bond to stop a nuclear extortion plot.

Domino, as her friends call her, grew up in France with her brother François, a Major with the *Armée de l'air* serving with NATO. Through him, Domino met Largo in Capri, and they began an affair. Despite a life of luxury, she finds the relationship empty. The only person to whom she feels connected is her brother.

Domino has been in Nassau for about three weeks when she meets 007 while snorkeling. Although attracted to him, she cannot act on her impulses, due to the watchful eye of Largo. When she spends time with Bond at the Café Martinique, she openly talks about her disenchantment.

Domino and Bond flirt during a few brief meetings and eventually,

while scuba diving, they make love underwater. On the beach afterward, Bond reveals that Largo killed her brother and stole two atomic weapons. She agrees to help Bond by taking a Geiger counter camera with her to the *Disco Volante,* Largo's yacht, to learn whether the missing bombs are aboard.

Largo catches Domino with the gadget and tortures her to find out what she knows, leaving her in a mild state of shock. Largo's chief scientist, Ladislav Kutze, nervously enters her cabin and unties her. Domino goes up to the bridge with a spear gun and shoots Largo in the back just as he prepares to kill Bond. Bond grabs her, and they leap into the sea before the speeding *Disco Volante* crashes and explodes.

In the novel *Thunderball,* Domino's surname is Vitali.

> ❝Promise me one thing. You will **kill Largo** for me whatever happens.❞
>
> **Domino to 007**

DINK

APPEARANCE
Goldfinger (1964)
STATUS Alive; whereabouts unknown
CHARACTERISTICS Cheerful, obliging
PLAYED BY Margaret Nolan

Dink massages the kinks out of Bond's body while he is on brief leave in Miami after dismantling Mr. Ramirez's drug operations in Mexico. Bond summarily dismisses Dink, described in the script as "a sumptuous bunny girl," when Felix Leiter arrives for a chat.

DI VICENZO, TRACY

APPEARANCE On Her Majesty's Secret Service (1969)
STATUS The late, beloved wife of James Bond
CHARACTERISTICS Headstrong, susceptible to depression, athletic, honest
PLAYED BY Diana Rigg

ON THE BEACH *Bond rescues Tracy from drowning herself.*

Teresa Di Vicenzo is the only woman ever to marry James Bond. Preferring to be called Tracy because Teresa was a saint, she remains one of only two women with whom Agent 007 has truly fallen in love.

> ❝Why do you persist in trying to **rescue me** Mr. Bond?❞
>
> **Tracy Di Vicenzo**

Tracy was born in 1943 to an English mother and a Corsican bandit, Marc Ange Draco, who went on to lead the biggest crime syndicate in Europe, the Union Corse. Tracy's mother died when she was 12, and she became involved in numerous scandals until Draco cut off her allowance. She then secretly married an Italian count who died when he crashed his Maserati while driving with one of his mistresses.

At her very lowest point, Tracy attempts suicide, walking into the sea in Portugal. Bond saves her, but she soon flees. In the casino at Estoril, she recklessly gambles with money she does not have, and Bond volunteers to cover her losses. They meet in 007's suite, but Tracy remains in a very self-destructive mind frame. After a night of lovemaking, Tracy's suicidal mood passes. She meets

Bond again at her father's birthday celebration. There, she discovers that her father has offered 007 information if he will spend time with her. Angry, Tracy nearly leaves, but Bond confirms his feelings for her are genuine. They remain together until Bond disappears on assignment to Switzerland to find Blofeld.

Tracy pries his location out of her father and rescues James from Irma Bunt and a host of SPECTRE killers. During a blizzard, Bond and Tracy take refuge in a barn, where Bond proposes marriage. They discuss potential residences once married: Acacia Avenue, Tunbridge Wells; Belgrave Square, London; Via Veneto, Rome; Paris; and Monaco. The next morning, Blofeld captures Tracy and holds her prisoner

WEDDING DAY *Tracy and Bond marry in a spectacular ceremony held in Draco's picturesque Portuguese estate.*

at his clinic, Piz Gloria, until her father and 007 arrive, rescue her, and destroy Blofeld's labs.

Bond returns to Portugal and buys Tracy an engagement ring. At their wedding, Draco offers Bond a dowry of £1 million, but 007 refuses. Leaving on their honeymoon, Tracy expresses her desire to have three boys and three girls. Bond tells Tracy, "We have all the time in the world." A Mercedes approaches with Blofeld at the wheel. From a rear window, Irma Bunt fires nine shots from an MP40 submachine gun. One bullet hits Tracy in the head, killing her instantly.

Tracy's death remains one of Bond's few unhealed wounds. In *For Your Eyes Only*, he visits Tracy's grave in England. On other occasions, Bond reacts with uncharacteristic sensitivity whenever anyone refers to his marriage.

In the Fleming novel, Tracy married Count Guilo di Vicenzo, who stole a large portion of her money. She also gave birth to a child who died of spinal meningitis. These factors explain Tracy's suicidal tendencies. Her death sends Bond into a self-destructive spiral.

TIME RUNS OUT *Tracy dies from a bullet fired by Irma Bunt. Sadly, Bond could not save her from his enemies.*

109

DUFOUR, CORINNE

APPEARANCE
Moonraker (1979)
STATUS Dead; killed by Drax's dogs
CHARACTERISTICS Top-notch pilot;
idealistic, romantic, good-hearted
PLAYED BY Corinne Clery

A helicopter pilot of French descent working for the Drax Corporation, Corinne Dufour reveres billionaire Hugo Drax, seeing him as an inspirational success story. She flies Bond from Los Angeles International Airport to the Drax Estate in the Mojave Desert. During the flight, she gives Bond an overview of the Drax Aerospace facilities where the Moonraker shuttle is constructed and Drax's château, brought to California stone-by-stone from France. She introduces 007 to Drax and then takes Bond to meet Dr. Holly Goodhead. Bond slips into Corinne's room as she's getting ready for bed and asks her to help him acquire

information. She tells Bond that some secret projects at the facilities have been moved to other locations. After sleeping with 007, she finds him searching Drax's office. She inadvertently reveals the location of Drax's safe. Bond cracks the safe and photographs the documents inside while she watches. The next day, Drax fires her during a pheasant shoot on his estate. He then sends his Dobermans to kill her.

FEARING, PATRICIA

APPEARANCE
Thunderball (1965)
STATUS Living; whereabouts unknown
CHARACTERISTICS Good masseuse; loves a touch of mink
PLAYED BY Molly Peters

Patricia Fearing is an osteopath at Shrublands health clinic. When she finds Bond passed out on a motorized traction table set at full throttle, she fears she will lose her job. Bond remains silent, at a price, and they adjourn to a nearby steam bath. Later that evening, she is enjoying a massage by Bond, when he suddenly leaves her to investigate the arrival of a body at the clinic.

FELICCA

APPEARANCE
The Spy Who Loved Me (1977)
STATUS Dead; shot by Sandor
CHARACTERISTICS Easily led
PLAYED BY Olga Bisera

Felicca meets Bond at the apartment of black market trader Aziz Fekkesh. She has been instructed to keep Bond occupied while Fekkesh arranges to sell a microfilm of shipping boss Stromberg's submarine tracking system to Major Anya Amasova. When she sees Sandor, Stromberg's henchman, preparing to shoot 007, she screams. Bond spins her around so that she takes the bullet meant for him and he chases after Sandor. The nature of her relationship to Fekkesh, Sandor, and Stromberg remains unknown.

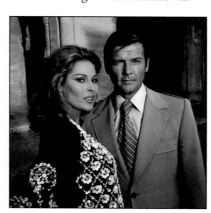

GALORE, PUSSY

APPEARANCE
Goldfinger (1964)
STATUS Living on a private island
CHARACTERISTICS Ambitious, strong, uncompromising, self-assured; a superb pilot and expert at judo
PLAYED BY Honor Blackman

A born leader who holds men in contempt, Pussy Galore leads an all-female aerial acrobatic troupe—Pussy Galore's Flying Circus—that serves as cover for various illegal activities. Employed as Goldfinger's personal pilot, Galore plays a key role in his plot, Operation Grand Slam, to irradiate the gold supply at Fort Knox. The plan calls for her pilots to spray the entire Fort Knox area with Delta-9 nerve gas, allowing Goldfinger to plant his dirty bomb inside the depository. She also helps bring in the nuclear device to Fort Knox. Galore plans to use the cash that she gains for her part in Operation Grand Slam to buy an island in the Bahamas.

Galore flies 007 from Switzerland to Goldfinger's Kentucky estate. Although Bond remains a prisoner, Pussy briefly treats him as a free man for the benefit of watching CIA agent Felix Leiter. Bond tells her that Goldfinger plans to use her pilots not to spray knock-out gas over Fort Knox, as she had thought, but to

"You can turn off the charm. **I'm immune.**"

Pussy Galore to 007

spray a lethal nerve gas. Felix Leiter later reports that Pussy Galore helped switch the nerve gas for a harmless substance, thereby saving thousands of lives and ruining the plot. Despite this good deed, Galore participates with Goldfinger in the hijacking of the President's plane with 007 aboard, before happily ending her adventure in Bond's arms.

In Ian Fleming's novel Goldfinger, Pussy Galore is American, not British, and she is the leader of a gang of lesbian cat burglars named The Cement Mixers. Hugely resentful of men, she nevertheless seduces Bond at the novel's end.

PUSSY GALORE AND HER FLYING CIRCUS Dressed in black, Pussy Galore and her loyal pilots begin on the side of greed and self-interest, but eventually see the error of their ways.

GOODHEAD, DR. HOLLY

APPEARANCE
Moonraker (1979)
STATUS Living
CHARACTERISTICS Secretive, clever, calm under pressure; a top-flight astronaut
PLAYED BY Lois Chiles

Fully-trained astronaut, CIA agent, and Vassar College graduate, Dr. Holly Goodhead works for the Drax Corporation, supposedly on loan from NASA. In reality, her job entails investigating billionaire Hugo Drax's suspicious activities for the CIA. Holly's skills as an astronaut allow her to travel into orbit with Bond and undermine Drax's plot to annihilate the Earth's entire population and repopulate the planet with his own squad of physically perfect humans.

Holly meets Bond after the disappearance of one of the Moonraker shuttles. She declines to share any of her concerns about Drax in California or when Bond confronts her about her CIA connection in Venice. Despite sleeping with Bond, she does not trust him until he saves her life on the Sugarloaf Mountain funicular railroad in Brazil.

BANG ON TIME *Dr. Holly Goodhead observes 007 destroying the air vent hatch in Drax's shuttle launch complex using his watch detonator.*

Drax's thugs kidnap Holly and bring her to his space shuttle launch complex. She remains a prisoner until Jaws throws Bond into her holding quarters. The pair escapes and takes over a shuttle. They travel to Drax's secret space station where they discover the extent of Drax's plan. Holly and Bond then work together to destroy his operation. She pilots Drax's personal shuttle while he uses the craft's laser weapon to destroy Drax's satellite globes filled with deadly nerve gas. Holly ends up in Bond's arms, orbiting the Earth.

ZERO GRAVITY LOVE *At the end of the mission, Bond and Holly float in each other's arms.*

GOODNIGHT, MARY

APPEARANCE
The Man With The Golden Gun (1974)
STATUS Living; whereabouts unknown
CHARACTERISTICS Enthusiastic, brave; desperate to be taken seriously; often finds herself in over her head
PLAYED BY Britt Ekland

Staff intelligence officer Mary Goodnight has been in Hong Kong two years before 007 arrives to kill Scaramanga. She helps Bond locate Andrea Anders, Scaramanga's girlfriend, but fails to notify Lt. Hip of Bond's presence, an oversight that gives Scaramanga and his servant Nick Nack a chance to steal the invaluable Solex Agitator from its designer, Gibson. After this, Goodnight suffers a series of indignities. When Bond propositions her, she slips into his room, only to have Bond shove her into a closet when Andrea arrives. She has to keep hidden while the pair makes love.

Goodnight soldiers on but soon finds herself kidnapped by Scaramanga. On the villain's island,

"**My hard-to-get act didn't last very long, did it?**"

Goodnight to 007

she awaits Bond's arrival.

During 007 and Scaramanga's duel, the technician Kra makes a crude pass at her. Goodnight hits him over the head with a spanner, sending him into the temperature-sensitive vats of Scaramanga's solar energy plant. After Bond kills Scaramanga, Mary helps him retrieve the Solex, accidentally triggering a lethal solar ray. When the island explodes due to Kra's body in the cooling vats, she escapes with Bond in Scaramanga's junk. After a final battle with Nick Nack, she ends up where she has hoped to be all along, in 007's arms.

Goodnight appears in three Fleming novels: *On Her Majesty's Secret Service*, in which she replaces Bond's secretary, Loelia Ponsonby, *You Only Live Twice*, and *The Man With The Golden Gun*.

HITWOMAN *Goodnight teaches Kra not to turn his back in Scaramanga's solar plant.*

HAVELOCK, MELINA

APPEARANCE
For Your Eyes Only (1981)
STATUS Living; whereabouts unknown
CHARACTERISTICS Experienced marine archaeologist; expert crossbow shot and scuba diver; passionate, courageous, protective, independent
PLAYED BY Carole Bouquet

The daughter of Timothy and Iona Havelock, Melina is a half-Greek, half-English marine archaeologist, who, according to the script, "reflects her ancestry: warmth overlaid with reserve." Melina grew up a water gypsy on her father's yacht, the *Triana*, traveling wherever his archaeological work took the family, including the Greek Islands, North Africa, and Turkey. In the script, Melina reveals that she later went to boarding school in England and attended Scripps Institution of Oceanography in La Jolla, California, where she earned a PhD.

As Melina returns to the *Triana* via seaplane, she has no idea her smiling pilot is Cuban hitman Hector Gonzales. Soon after she has gone aboard, Gonzales flies over Corfu harbor and machine-guns her mother and father.

Melina sets out to hunt her parents' killer. Through a detective agency, she tracks Gonzales to his Spanish villa and shoots him dead with her crossbow, inadvertently helping to free Bond from capture by Gonzales's men. She and Bond escape in her Citroen 2CV. That night, she confesses to Bond she will not rest until she discovers who paid Gonzales to kill her parents.

> "I'm half Greek, and Greek women, like Electra, always **avenge their loved ones.**"
>
> Melina to 007

Bond informs Melina that her father was on a mission for British Intelligence to recover the ATAC transmitter, recently lost in the wreck of the *St. Georges* surveillance ship. Melina deciphers her father's notes written in a special shorthand and uses her family's submarine, the *Neptune,* to help 007 salvage the ATAC. Smuggler Aris Kristatos captures the pair, takes the ATAC, and then drags Bond and Melina behind his ship over a coral reef. Bond and Melina survive and learn Kristatos has taken the ATAC to the abandoned St. Cyril's Monastery.

When Melina finally comes face to face with Kristatos, she tells Bond to step aside so that she can exact her revenge on her parents's killer. Before she can fire her crossbow, Kristatos's enemy Milos Columbo throws a knife into his back.

In Fleming's short story *For Your Eyes Only*, Melina's name is Judy. She tracks her parents's killers, Gonzales and Von Hammerstein, to the Vermont woods where she fires a crossbow bolt into Von Hammerstein's back. Bond observes that she has the "vibrations of a wild animal" and nicknames her "Robina Hood."

FLYING VISIT *(far left) Melina with her marine archaeologist father Sir Timothy Havelock, shortly before a joyful family reunion turns to tragedy.*

READY TO FIRE *(center left) Melina fires her crossbow bolt into the chest of one of Gonzales's goons in the woods near the hitman's Spanish villa.*

FOR YOUR EYES ONLY *(top) At the end of the mission, Melina prepares for a moonlight swim with 007.*

IVANOVA, POLA

APPEARANCE
A View To A Kill (1985)
STATUS Living; whereabouts unknown
CHARACTERISTICS Clever, devious
PLAYED BY Fiona Fullerton

HOT TUB *Bond and Pola Ivanova do their best to relieve lingering East–West tensions.*

Pola Ivanova works as a KGB agent and was once ordered to seduce James Bond in London while she toured with the Bolshoi.

With the aid of a waterproof Walkman and a microphone on the end of a telescoping rod, Pola and fellow agent Klotkoff record Max Zorin's activities at his oil pumping station in San Francisco. Pola then meets 007 again, and they retire to the Nippon Relaxation Spa in Chinatown. Bond steals the tape of the bugged conversation, much to the consternation of Pola and KGB chief General Gogol.

JINX

APPEARANCE
Die Another Day (2002)
STATUS Still working for the good guys
CHARACTERISTICS Self-assured, independent, sexual, feisty
PLAYED BY Halle Berry

Nicknamed Jinx because she was born on Friday the 13th and because her relationships never last, the enigmatic NSA agent Giacinta Johnson teams up with James Bond to prevent Gustav Graves from using his Icarus satellite superweapon to turn North Korea into a new superpower.

In Los Organos, Cuba, Jinx discovers that escaped North Korean terrorist Zao is a secret patient at a clinic run by Dr. Alvarez, who specializes in DNA replacement therapy. Jinx also catches Bond's eye, emerging from the sea in her bikini and knife belt. Bond and Jinx recognize each other's predatory nature and seduce each other.

The next morning, Jinx assassinates Dr. Alvarez. She makes a back-up disk of the files on Alvarez's computer and programs a cell phone bomb to destroy the clinic. After failing to assassinate Zao, she performs an amazing 200-ft (61-m) backdive and escapes in a Sunseeker 48-50 powerboat.

Jinx travels to Iceland to investigate Gustav Graves under the alias of Miss

KILLING AGENDA *Jinx infiltrates the clinic of geneticist Dr. Alvarez. After hearing him confess his evil practices, she shoots him dead.*

Jinx:
I'm so good.
007:
Especially when you're bad.

Swift of *Space and Technology Magazine* and arrives at his Ice Palace in a 2003 Ford Thunderbird. She attends the unveiling of the Icarus satellite by Graves. Bond later rescues her from being burnt to death by a diamond-cutting laser. 007 also saves her from drowning inside Graves's melting Ice Palace.

Jinx and 007 officially join forces to disable the Icarus satellite weapon. Entering North Korea on jet gliders known as switchblades, they parachute near an airfield. They sneak aboard an Antonov transport plane, from which Graves and a group of North Korean Generals plan to supervise Icarus's destruction of South Korea's defenses. After the plane depressurizes, Jinx takes over the cockpit and flies the plane into the beam of the Icarus satellite, destroying the satellite's control mechanism. Jinx and double agent Miranda Frost battle to the death, with Jinx finally defeating the gold medal-winning fencer by slamming a broken-off sword into her heart.

After escaping the disintegrating plane, Jinx and Bond helicopter to a South Korean Buddhist temple, where they make love on a bed covered with Graves's diamonds.

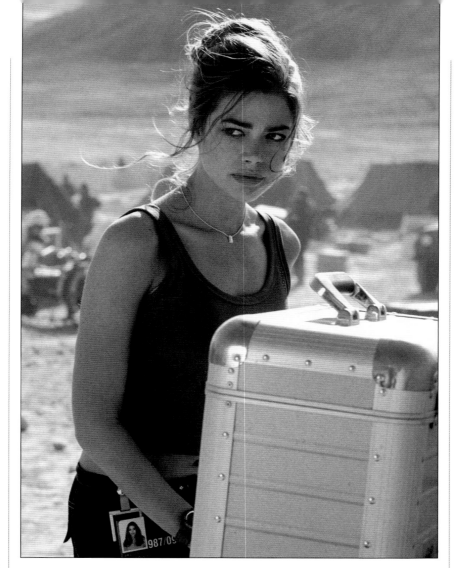

JONES, DR. CHRISTMAS

APPEARANCE
The World Is Not Enough (1999)
STATUS Living; whereabouts unknown
CHARACTERISTICS Gifted scientist, confident of her skills in a male-dominated profession; brave under pressure
PLAYED BY Denise Richards

> " Jones, Christmas Jones. And don't make any jokes. I've heard them all."

American nuclear physicist Dr. Christmas Jones works for the International Decommission Agency (IDA). She has a peace tattoo below her naval and speaks fluent Russian. Wearing a tank-top, shorts, and heavy duty boots, she uses a tactical fission HP Jornada 430SE palm-sized computer to acquire readouts on the makes of various nuclear devices.

Christmas meets Bond in Kazakhstan, where he poses as Russian atomic scientist Dr. Arkov. Christmas recognizes that Bond's credentials are forged and, in the confusion, anarchist terrorist Renard escapes with a nuclear weapon.

Christmas joins forces with Bond to find the weapon. They travel on an observation rig in a harrowing chase through an unused pipeline where it appears that a bomb has been placed in a "pig." At the last moment, Bond and Christmas realize that the pipeline explosion is just a diversion. Christmas helps 007 confront Baku-based casino and caviar factory owner Valentin Zukovsky to uncover Renard's and his accomplice, oil tycoon Elektra

FIRST MEETING *Christmas and Bond must work together to survive when Renard steals a nuclear device.*

IN THE DEEP END *Christmas Jones risks drowning to help 007 foil Renard's plot.*

King's, true plot. The pair plans to cause the meltdown of a Russian submarine's reactor by loading it with weapons-grade plutonium. This will destroy Istanbul, killing eight million people and giving Elektra's pipeline total control over oil supplies to the West.

Christmas eventually helps Bond prevent Renard loading a plutonium rod into the submarine's reactor. After Renard's death, she and Bond escape just as the hydrogen gas ignites, blowing the submarine apart.

At the end of the adventure, Dr. Jones and 007 find themselves in each other's arms, ready to welcome in the new millennium.

JONES, KIMBERLEY

APPEARANCE
A View To A Kill (1985)
STATUS Living; whereabouts unknown
CHARACTERISTICS Skillful submarine pilot; appreciates the finer things in life
PLAYED BY Mary Stavin

British agent and iceberg submarine pilot Kimberley Jones transports James Bond to and from the KGB's Siberian research center when he receives instruction to investigate the death of Agent 003. After completing his mission, Kimberley places the sub on automatic pilot, and the two plan to enjoy vodka, caviar, and each other during the five-day trip to Alaska.

LAMORA, LUPE

APPEARANCE
Licence To Kill (1989)
STATUS Living; whereabouts unknown
CHARACTERISTICS Discontented, mercenary, rueful
PLAYED BY Talisa Soto

> "You know, I love James so much."

Lupe to Pam Bouvier

LIN, WAI

APPEARANCE
Tomorrow Never Dies (1997)
STATUS On active duty
CHARACTERISTICS Martial arts expert; independent, intelligent
PLAYED BY Michelle Yeoh

Colonel Wai Lin, a top agent for the Chinese People's External Security Force, teams with Bond to stop a manufactured war from breaking out between Britain and China. Wai Lin remains among the most athletic of all the Bond women, displaying fighting skills beyond compare.

Described in the script as "a petite, stunningly beautiful Chinese woman," Wai Lin's investigation of media mogul Elliot Carver begins when her organization discovers stealth material is missing from one of the bases of General Chang, a key figure in the Chinese military. Wai Lin follows a lead to Carver's

headquarters in Hamburg, Germany. Believing that Chang and Carver might be building a stealth plane, she infiltrates the launch party of Carver's new satellite news network CMGN and poses as a representative of the New China News Agency. Carver suggests that she work in his Beijing bureau, but she reminds him that he doesn't have a bureau in Beijing; the Chinese have refused him broadcast rights.

> "I hate to disappoint you, but I don't even have a little red book."

Wai Lin to 007

Wai Lin tries to break into Carver's secret laboratory but discovers 007 has beaten her to it. As guards pursue Bond, Lin escapes with ease.

Wai Lin next encounters 007 diving in the sunken HMS *Devonshire* off the coast of Vietnam. They discover Carver has stolen a cruise missile from the ship. Captured by Carver's enforcer Stamper, Lin and Bond are flown to Carver's Saigon headquarters. There, she discovers the extent of Carver's plan to manipulate China and Britain into war and also confirms the participation of General Chang in the plot.

Handcuffed together, Wai Lin and Bond pull off a series of hairsbreadth escapes before she leaves Bond shackled to a pipe, telling him she "works alone." After Chang's men attack her, and Bond comes to her aid, 007 convinces her that preventing a war is also his goal. Wai Lin then learns that Carver and Chang have built a stealth ship, not a stealth plane.

Bond and Wai Lin locate, slip aboard, and plant limpet mines on Carver's stealth ship. When Stamper captures Wai Lin, Bond proves his loyalty by trying to bargain for her freedom. Bond sets off a grenade, blasting a hole in the ship's hull and allowing Lin to escape. During the ensuing battle, Carver attempts to launch his stolen British cruise missile at Beijing.

BREAK-IN *Bond catches Wai Lin infiltrating Carver's headquarters. The two agents soon become partners.*

EASY RIDERS *Bond and Wai Lin escape Carver's men in Saigon on a BMW Cruiser R1200 motorbike.*

BICYCLE SHOP SHOWDOWN *Wai Lin uses her martial arts skills to defeat General Chang's men.*

The beautiful mistress of drug baron Franz Sanchez, Lupe Lamora realizes that James Bond is the one man who can help her break free from her destructive and very dangerous relationship. Accordingly, she helps Bond in his quest to bring down Sanchez's empire.

Lupe comes from an impoverished background, which it took her 15 years to escape. Franz Sanchez first saw her in a Miss Galaxy beauty contest and, struck by her beauty, rigged the competition so that she won. He then gave her a job in his Isthmus City casino, and she eventually became his mistress.

When Lupe embarks on an affair with Alvarez, Sanchez enters US territory and whips her with a stingray tail for her betrayal. During Bond's and DEA agent Felix Leiter's attempt to capture Sanchez, 007

meets Lupe and offers assistance to the beaten young woman, which she refuses.

Lupe encounters Bond again on board Milton Krest's drug smuggling ship, the *Wavekrest*, and later in Isthmus City, where she helps 007 to deceive Sanchez and infiltrate his organization. She also sleeps with Bond and states that she has deep feelings for him.

When Lupe reveals how she feels about 007 to CIA contract pilot and agent Pam Bouvier, she ignites Pam's jealous streak. After Bond kills Sanchez, Lupe again makes a play for 007's affections. Bond understands Lupe's complex love/hate relationship with men and turns down her invitation. Lupe quickly shifts her amorous attentions to the wealthy President of Isthmus City, Hector Lopez.

Stamper recaptures Wai Lin and tries to stop Bond disabling the missile by threatening to kill her. Wai Lin tosses Bond detonators to cause the missile to self-destruct. Stamper then tries to drown her by lowering her into the water wrapped in a heavy chain, but Bond revives her with an underwater kiss of life. She ends her adventure in Bond's arms, amid the wreckage of Carver's ship.

LINDA

APPEARANCE
The Living Daylights (1987)
STATUS Living; whereabouts unknown
CHARACTERISTICS Wealthy, bored
PLAYED BY Kell Tyler

Linda, a single woman, finds life on the Mediterranean boring, full of "playboys and tennis pros." She hopes to find a real man. Within seconds of expressing this desire to her friend Margot, Bond parachutes onto her *Moonmaiden II* yacht. As 007 calls Exercise Control to tell them he will report on an attack on agents in one hour, Linda pours him a glass of champagne. Eyeing her and the drink, Bond delays his report time to two hours.

ADRIFT AT SEA *Linda hopes to meet a "real man." Moments later, 007 arrives via a smoldering parachute.*

LING

APPEARANCE
You Only Live Twice (1967)
STATUS Working undercover
CHARACTERISTICS Fun, but devious
PLAYED BY Tsai Chin

M's office arranges for Ling, a double agent, to aid in the fake murder of James Bond. Posing as Bond's lover in Hong Kong, Ling stages a betrayal, trapping Bond in a Murphy wall bed as two gunmen spray it with machine gun fire.

It is rumored Ling later married into a fortune, changed her name, and became a professional gambler of some repute.

LYND, VESPER

APPEARANCE
Casino Royale (2006)
STATUS Dead in Venice
CHARACTERISTICS Enigmatic,
conflicted, complicated
PLAYED BY Eva Green

Vesper Lynd both opens and shuts James Bond's heart. The internal torment she suffers and the pain she causes leave permanent scars on 007.

Lynd works for the Financial Action Task Force of Her Majesty's Treasury as an International Liaison Officer with experience with illicit banking practices. She supervises the British government's funds that finance Bond in a high-stakes poker tournament organized by Le Chiffre.

Bond speculates that she grew up an orphan. In a production draft of the script, Vesper reveals that her father killed her mother and then shot himself. When Bond meets Lynd, she wears an Algerian love knot necklace, a gift from her French-Algerian lover. At some point Vesper, comes to believe the terrorist network associated with Mr. White has kidnapped her lover. Should she fail to cooperate, she believes he will be killed.

Bond's arrogance initially angers Vesper, but she observes him closely enough to have a tuxedo hand tailored by eye. When Lynd witnesses Bond killing Ugandan warlord Obanno and his lieutenant, Bond's gentle sympathy for her shattered emotions draws her closer to him.

> **"Am I going to have a problem with you, Bond?"**
>
> **Vesper Lynd**

Even so, she denies him more Treasury funds to stay in the tournament when he over-plays his hand. After CIA agent Felix Leiter gives Bond funds to continue, Le Chiffre's girlfriend, Valenka, poisons him. Bond lapses into cardiac arrest, but Vesper saves him, reattaching a wire to his portable defibrillator and restarting his heart.

After Bond wins the poker game, Le Chiffre kidnaps Vesper, luring Bond into a trap in order to extort the tournament winnings. Vesper knows Bond will be brutally tortured, but she makes a deal with Mr. White to spare Bond's life in return for delivering the funds. Before she can transfer the funds to White's accomplice Gettler, Bond confesses his love for her and resigns from MI6.

In Venice, Bond uncovers Lynd's deception. Although he kills her enemies, Vesper cannot live with her actions. She locks herself in a submerged elevator and drowns. Bond closes himself off emotionally after her death, repressing his love for Vesper and transforming it into cold dedication to his work. Bond finds her betrayal bitter, telling M, "The bitch is dead."

Vesper does leave Bond an essential clue to help him trace the terrorist network—on her cell phone, she stores Mr. White's number.

In Ian Fleming's novel, Vesper

REST AND RECUPERATION *Vesper finds herself emotionally drawn to Bond during his recovery from the brutal torture inflicted by Le Chiffre.*

works for Section S, a part of the Secret Service devoted to the Soviet Union. Her lover, a Polish Free Fighter, has been in Soviet custody since the end of World War II, and she knows that if she fails to deliver key intelligence to her Soviet handlers, he will be murdered. After Bond's torture by Le Chiffre, she tries to forget her lover, but her burden of guilt for his inevitable death and Bond's suffering proves too great and she kills herself with an overdose of sleeping pills. Her death makes Bond vow to "go after the threat behind the spies, the threat that made them spy."

It is through his tragic affair with Vesper Lynd that James Bond finds the inner sense of purpose that drives him to rise to any challenge, to defeat any foe, to be the greatest secret agent the world has ever known.

MAGDA

APPEARANCE Octopussy (1983)

STATUS Living; whereabouts unknown

CHARACTERISTICS Extremely athletic, agile, enigmatic; performs sleight-of-hand magic tricks

PLAYED BY Kristina Wayborn

Magda is the associate of exiled Afghan prince Kamal Khan and also a member of Octopussy's circus troupe, where she performs magic tricks and juggles. She resides at Khan's Monsoon Palace and aids him, helping to deceive Octopussy and James Bond until she discovers that he planned for her to die in a nuclear explosion.

Magda helps Khan in his effort to re-purchase a Fabergé egg being sold at auction. When he learns the jeweled egg is a forgery, he instructs Magda to seduce Bond and take the original from him. During their lovemaking, Bond notices an octopus tattoo on Magda's rear, which she refers to as "my little Octopussy." After snatching the egg, she demonstrates her athletic ability by backflipping from Bond's hotel balcony and twirling to the ground using her sari.

Magda believes Khan only smuggles jewels from the Soviet Union. He does not reveal to her his plot to explode a nuclear weapon on a US Air Force Base in West Germany. She joins forces with Octopussy and 007 when she learns that Kamal left them to be

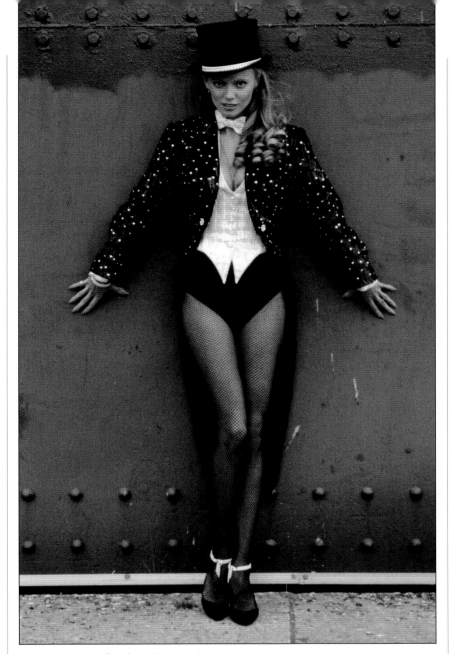

IN COSTUME *As well as being Octopussy's second in command, Magda also performs in Octopussy's Circus.*

killed in the explosion.

During a final assault on the Monsoon Palace by Octopussy's troupe, Magda leads the fight with stun grenades and weighted skirts. Using her acrobatic ability, she disables many better-armed guards. She is saved by Q when Kamal's men attack the troupe.

Magda: He suggests a trade. The egg for your life.
007: I'd heard the price of eggs was going up, but isn't that a little high?

MANUELA

APPEARANCE Moonraker (1979)

STATUS Living; whereabouts unknown

CHARACTERISTICS Good with martinis and Rio geography

PLAYED BY Emily Bolton

Manuela works for Station VH in Rio de Janeiro, Brazil. She follows Bond from the airport to his hotel suite, where she shakes him a martini. After spending five romantic hours with Bond, she takes him into Rio during Carnival. The pair slips through the crowds to an import/export subsidiary of the Drax Corporation, Carlos and Wilmsberg, Inc., on Carioca Avenue. Bond, who is investigating millionaire Hugo Drax following the disappearance of a shuttle, finds a clue: a sticker for Drax Air Freight. Meanwhile Jaws, dressed in a carnival costume, attacks

Manuela. Bond arrives just in time to save her, and crowds carry Jaws away. Manuela tells 007 that Drax Air Freight operates out of San Pietro Airport and Bond takes her home.

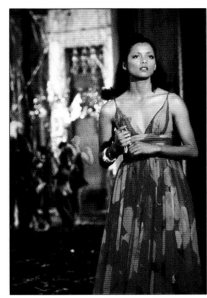

WATCHING AND WAITING *At the Rio Carnival, Manuela anxiously awaits Bond's return from his investigation of a warehouse.*

MARIE

APPEARANCE Diamonds Are Forever (1971)

STATUS Unknown

CHARACTERISTICS Seductive, surprisingly informative

PLAYED BY Denise Perrier

Marie resides at Ernst Stavro Blofeld's coastal compound. The nature of her relationship to Blofeld remains unexplained. She seems extremely happy to see the dashing Bond when he arrives at the compound from Cairo, Egypt. Her interest is short-lived. Bond immediately rips off Marie's bikini top, choking her with it until she finally reveals to him the whereabouts of Blofeld.

STRONG-ARM TACTICS *Bond wastes no time learning where Blofeld is hiding himself.*

119

MASTERSON, JILL

APPEARANCE
Goldfinger (1964)
STATUS Dead; by skin asphyxiation
CHARACTERISTICS Bored,
adventurous, fun-loving
PLAYED BY Shirley Eaton

When James Bond enters
Goldfinger's suite at Miami's
Fontainebleau Hotel, he discovers
Goldfinger's paid companion Jill
Masterson on the balcony with
binoculars. She is telling Goldfinger,
via radio, which cards are held by Mr.
Simmons in a game of gin rummy,
enabling Goldfinger to cheat.
When questioned by Bond, Jill
states that her relationship with
Goldfinger is purely professional.

Bond takes over the radio link
and commands Goldfinger to start
losing his ill-gotten gains.
Impressed, Jill accepts Bond's
invitation to dinner at his hotel
suite, seeing Bond as an escape
from a job she hates. Her
feelings of liberation
prove tragically short-lived.
Goldfinger's manservant
Oddjob knocks out Bond.
When he comes to, he finds
Jill dead, painted from head to
toe in gold leaf. Bond later

GOLDEN GIRL *In the
novel, Bond never sees Jill
painted gold. He hears
about Goldfinger's
murderous actions from
Jill's sister, Tilly.*

learns that she has died from skin
asphyxiation.

In the novel, Jill's last name is
Masterton. She does not die with
Bond, but Goldfinger kills her days
later. Fleming's rationale for Jill's
death has caused controversy. Some
claim there is no chance of Jill dying
by being painted gold. Others believe
that failing to leave a patch of skin
open on Jill's back could be fatal.

MASTERSON, TILLY

APPEARANCE
Goldfinger (1964)
STATUS Dead; broken neck
CHARACTERISTICS Vengeful, angry
PLAYED BY Tania Mallet

Tilly Masterson wants to kill Auric
Goldfinger for murdering her sister,
Jill. Bond meets Tilly on a Swiss
mountain road, when she takes a shot

"I'm beginning to like you, Mr. Bond."

Jill Masterson

at Goldfinger and nearly hits 007.
After a car chase, Bond shreds her
Mustang's tires with the wheel hubs
of his DB5. He spots her ArmaLite
AR-7 case, which she claims holds
her ice skates. Bond also realizes
that she has lied about her
name, which she claims to be
Tilly Soames.

That night, Bond finds
Tilly trying to stalk
Goldfinger at his factory.
When her rifle trips an
alarm wire, she admits
she is Jill's sister and
escapes with Bond.
Oddjob soon breaks
her neck with his
deadly, metal-rimmed,
dressage top hat.

In the novel, Tilly is a
lesbian with the last name
Masterton and survives until
near the end.

MILOVY, KARA

APPEARANCE
The Living Daylights (1987)
STATUS Alive; one of the world's virtuoso cellists
CHARACTERISTICS Talented, innocent, artistic, loyal, trusting
PLAYED BY Maryam d'Abo

Cellist Kara Milovy is the Czech lover of rogue KGB General Georgi Koskov. He sets her up as a sniper, instructing her to fire blank bullets at him to make his defection to the British appear genuine. Bond, sensing she doesn't know what she's doing, shoots the rifle from her hands.

When Koskov is snatched back,

TOBOGGAN RUN *Kara and Bond escape across the Czech border aboard her cello case.*

apparently by the KGB, Bond decides to investigate the mysterious sniper who, Moneypenny informs him, is a cellist on a scholarship to the Bratislava Conservatoire. Bond tracks Kara down and pretends to be Koskov's friend to win her trust and bring her out of Czechoslovakia to Austria.

Their romantic interlude in Vienna is cut short when Bond discovers that Kara's cello, a Stradivarius named The Lady Rose,

was purchased for her by arms dealer Brad Whitaker. Suspecting a link between Koskov and Whitaker, Bond takes Kara with him to Tangier, where Whitaker is based. Without Bond's knowledge, Kara telephones Whitaker's villa and discovers that "Georgi" is there. Now working with Koskov, she drugs Bond's martini. Just before he passes out, Bond tells her the truth: that he is not Koskov's friend but a British agent, and that Koskov has betrayed the Russians, the British, and Kara herself, setting her up to be killed.

Koskov kidnaps Bond and Kara accompanies them to Afghanistan. Bond has convinced Kara of Koskov's treachery and she becomes a valuable ally, helping Bond escape from a Soviet airbase and joining a group of mujaheddin fighters to rescue Bond when he becomes trapped in Koskov's drug convoy.

At the end of the adventure, Kara gives a concert at the Schonbrunn Palace Theater in Vienna. After the concert, General Gogol of the Foreign Service grants her a visa so that she can travel from East to West whenever she desires.

CLASSICAL SUBTERFUGE
Kara Milovy plays Mozart's 40th Symphony in G minor shortly before posing as a KGB assassin aiding in the fake defection of her lover General Georgi Koskov.

> "Whoever she was, I must have scared **the living daylights** out of her."
>
> 007

O'TOOLE, PLENTY

APPEARANCE
Diamonds Are Forever (1971)
STATUS **Dead, killed by assassins Wint and Kidd**
CHARACTERISTICS **Beautiful, unlucky**
PLAYED BY **Lana Wood**

Plenty O'Toole works the casino floor finding wealthy men who will ply her with money and favors. She has consistently bad luck. When she meets Bond, he tips her $5000 of his winnings at craps. She asks if he wants to get a drink. Left alone in Bond's suite at the Tropicana, she is attacked by Morton Slumber's thugs, who throw her, from several floors up, into the hotel pool. She survives, but ends up dead in Tiffany Case's pool, her feet tied to a flagstone.

In the original script, Plenty returns from the hotel pool to Bond's suite and finds him with Tiffany. She locates Tiffany's address and goes to her house. Wint and Kidd mistake her for Tiffany and kill her.

Plenty: Hi, I'm Plenty.
007: But of course you are.
Plenty: Plenty O'Toole.
007: Named after your father, perhaps?

OCTOPUSSY

APPEARANCE
Octopussy (1983)
STATUS Living, whereabouts unknown
CHARACTERISTICS Leader, morally ambivalent, spiritual, athletic
PLAYED BY Maud Adams

Octopussy leads a modern incarnation of a secret order of female bandits and smugglers. Fabulously wealthy, she lives at The Floating Palace on Lake Pichola in Udaipur, India. This splendid palace is populated solely by women and is only accessible via her private barge. Partnered with exiled Afghan prince Kamal Khan in a $300 million jewelry smuggling operation, Octopussy runs a European circus that provides the perfect cover for this operation.

Octopussy's father, Major Dexter Smythe, committed a murder and stole a cache of North Korean gold many years ago. James Bond traveled to Sri Lanka to bring Smythe to justice, but after meeting Bond, Smythe chose to commit suicide before his final arrest. When Octopussy meets Bond, she thanks him for giving her father an honorable alternative to public disgrace. Her father, a leading authority on octopi, gave his daughter the pet name of Octopussy.

Octopussy first discovered she had a knack for smuggling when she finished selling off her father's gold. Contacts in Hong Kong offered her a commission to smuggle diamonds. She needed an organization so she revived the ancient octopus cult and chose as her symbol the poisonous blue-ringed octopus. She assembled her all-female team, led by tall blonde Gwendoline and short brunette Midge, from young women discovered all over Southeast Asia who were looking for a guru and spiritual discipline. Octopussy gives them a purpose, a sisterhood, and a way of life.

Octopussy meets Bond when he sneaks into her compound to find information about the death of 009. She tries to induce Bond to work for her, unaware that her partner Khan wants 007 dead. After an emotional confrontation, Octopussy sleeps with

ARMED TO THE HILT *Octopussy's circus performers also train in commando tactics.*

PAINTED SMILE *The circus is the perfect front for smuggling.*

TWO OF A KIND *Bond and Octopussy strike up an almost instant rapport, united by a love of intrigue, danger, and passion.*

REVENGE *Octopussy attacks Kamal for his treachery.*

Bond before thugs attack the pair in an attempt to kill 007. When Bond falls into the lake with one attacker and a crocodile joins the fray, Octopussy believes Bond has been killed.

Octopussy travels to Europe for a scheduled tour of her circus that will take her across the border from East to West Germany. She supervises the transfer of Soviet jewels from General Orlov onto her train for smuggling into the West. At a performance of her circus at a US

Air Force Base in Feldstadt, the appearance of Bond, alive, stuns her. 007 reveals that Kamal has removed the smuggled jewels from her circus train and replaced them with an atomic bomb. Octopussy then provides vital help in disarming the bomb.

Later, with her troupe, Octopussy seeks revenge on Kamal Khan in India. She and her highly trained force of female guards attack Khan's Monsoon Palace, but Khan and his henchman Gobinda capture her and

flee. Bond rescues her from Khan's Beech 18 plane. At the film's close, she finds herself in 007's arms as he recuperates on her barge.

In Fleming's short story, Major Dexter Smythe gives the pet name Octopussy to an octopus in Jamaica. The story recounts Bond confronting Smythe with his past crime, Bond's personal connection to the event, and Smythe's subsequent death and consumption by the octopus that so intrigued him.

"Good evening. I wondered when you might arrive."

Octopussy to 007

PEACEFUL FOUNTAINS OF DESIRE

APPEARANCE
Die Another Day (2002)
STATUS Living; whereabouts unknown
CHARACTERISTICS Efficient, professional, competent
PLAYED BY Rachel Grant

The Hong Kong masseuse Peaceful Fountains of Desire is actually working for fellow Chinese Intelligence agent Mr. Chang, who doubles as the concierge at the Rubyeon Hotel in Hong Kong. James Bond checks into the hotel, and Peaceful arrives at his room. When he finds a Beretta stashed in Peaceful's garter, a suspicious Bond throws an ashtray at a closet mirror, breaking the glass and revealing Mr. Chang and his team prepared to film Peaceful's "interrogation" of Bond.

ROMANOVA, TATIANA

APPEARANCE
From Russia With Love (1963)
STATUS Living; whereabouts unknown
CHARACTERISTICS
Loyal, innocent, graceful, passionate
PLAYED BY Daniela Bianchi

Corporal of State Security Tatiana Romanova plays a key role in a SPECTRE plot to kill 007. Tatiana—Tania to her friends—works in the cryptographic section of the Soviet consulate in Istanbul, Turkey. She formerly lived in Moscow, where she worked in the English decoding group in the KGB Central Index. She studied ballet in Leningrad (now St. Petersburg) but was dismissed when she grew an inch over the regulation height.

Tatiana meets with Rosa Klebb, believing Klebb works for SMERSH. Under threat of death, she agrees to Klebb's assignment "to give false information to the enemy." She contacts Istanbul head of Station T, Turkey, Kerim Bey, claiming she wishes to defect with a Lektor decoder, but only on the condition that James Bond escorts her and the decoder to England. She meets 007 in his hotel room, slipping into his bed wearing only a black choker and black stockings. Unknown to Tatiana and Bond, Klebb and a SPECTRE cameraman film their lovemaking.

Tatiana helps Bond obtain the Lektor and escapes with him aboard the Orient Express bound for Paris.

Tatiana is deeply conflicted about her emotions for Bond versus her fear of Klebb and loyalty to her country. When Bond confronts her about the murder of Kerim Bey on the train, she truthfully professes ignorance but refuses to reveal Klebb's plot. SPECTRE assassin Donald Grant subsequently drugs her while he dines with her and Bond. During a fatal confrontation Grant reveals to 007 that Tatiana is a completely innocent pawn in SPECTRE's conspiracy.

After Grant's death, Bond escapes with Tatiana to Venice. Confronted by Rosa Klebb, Tatiana must decide where her true loyalties lie. As Klebb prepares to shoot Bond, Tatiana knocks the gun from her hand. She then shoots Klebb, choosing Bond's world rather than Soviet-style obedience. Her adventure ends on Venice's Grand Canal in 007's arms.

In the novel, Tatiana does not participate in Bond's final confrontation with Klebb, and her loyalties lie much more with Bond throughout the story.

THE INTERVIEW *Tatiana reports to Colonel Klebb, still thinking Klebb works for SMERSH.*
SECRET MEETING *Bond interrogates Tatiana on the Bosphorus about the Lektor decoder, using a tape recorder hidden inside a camera.*
ESCAPE *Tatiana and 007 flee Istanbul on the world's most romantic train, the Orient Express.*
THE CHOICE *Tatiana must decide between Mother Russia or Bond. She never learns that Klebb works for SPECTRE.*
THE SEDUCTRESS (left) *This classic scene where Bond meets Tatiana has been used by the Bond film producers to test actors for the role of 007.*

Tatiana: I think my mouth is too big.
007: No, it's just the right size. For me, that is.

RYDER, HONEY

APPEARANCE
Dr. No (1962)
STATUS Living; whereabouts unknown
CHARACTERISTICS Self-reliant, vulnerable, vengeful, passionate
PLAYED BY Ursula Andress

Honey Ryder stands as the archetypal Bond woman: strong, resilient, and beautiful. Searching Caribbean beaches for seashells, she becomes swept up in 007's mission to stop Dr. No "toppling" US rockets.

Before encountering James Bond, Honey traveled the world with her marine zoologist father. They arrived in the Caribbean to study seashells. When he visited Crab Key, he disappeared, and she never saw him again. Local authorities claimed that he must have drowned, but Honey believes Dr. No is responsible.

Honey meets Bond on Crab Key. Her iconic walk from the sea, clad in a white bikini, diver's belt, and knife, perfectly captures her radiant beauty and confidence.

Bond attracts Honey's attention by joining in as she sings a local calypso *Underneath The Mango Tree*. Later, Honey tells Bond that, after her father's death, she was raped by her landlord. Honey then relates how she took her revenge:

THE BIKINI *Ursula Andress and designer Tessa Welbourn could not find the right swimsuit for Honey, so they designed their own athletic-cut bikini.*

by placing a deadly black widow spider beneath her landlord's mosquito net.

Honey's arrival on the island via sailboat triggers Dr. No's radar system; his guards capture Honey and Bond and kill Bond's Cayman Islander ally, Quarrel.

> **Honey Ryder:** What are you doing here? Looking for shells?
> **007:** No, I'm just looking.

By visiting Crab Key, Bond and Honey have been exposed to radioactive waste from No's nuclear generator. They are cleansed before being taken to well-appointed rooms. Bond and Honey then pass out after drinking drugged coffee.

At dinner, Bond tells Dr. No that Honey has nothing to do with his mission, but No senses Bond's protective feelings for Honey and uses her to provoke 007. Dr. No's men manacle her in a chamber that slowly fills with water, but Bond rescues her. They escape in a boat seconds before Dr. No's nuclear reactor explodes, obliterating Crab Key. Honey ends up adrift in Bond's arms.

In the novel *Dr. No*, Fleming gives Honey the name Honeychile Rider and she has a broken nose. When Bond first sees her, she appears naked on the beach except for a belt and knife, resembling "Botticelli's Venus." Bond remembers Honeychile when he returns to Jamaica in the novel, *The Man With The Golden Gun*, noting that he had heard she had married a Philadelphia doctor and had two children. Her character appeared in later Bond novels.

SIMONOVA, NATALYA

APPEARANCE
GoldenEye (1995)
STATUS Living; whereabouts unknown
CHARACTERISTICS Excellent computer programmer, loyal, resourceful
PLAYED BY Izabella Scorupco

Natalya Simonova was just a second-level computer programmer for the Russian military in Siberia until fate conspired to make her a central figure in a globehopping adventure with James Bond.

At the Severnaya Space Weapons Research Centre, which the rest of the world believes is an abandoned radar station, Natalya programs the guidance systems of satellites. Her co-worker, Boris Grishenko, proves childishly irritating, but Natalya cares for him, as the screenplay notes, like a "pesky younger brother."

By a combination of quick thinking and good luck, Natalya survives a massacre at Severnaya carried out by the Janus organization's General Ourumov and Xenia Onatopp and a detonation of the Petya GoldenEye superweapon. Natalya travels to St. Petersburg, resolved to find out who was behind the killings. However, as the only witness and known survivor of the massacre, Natalya is suspected by Russian Intelligence and also targeted by Janus. Fortunately MI6 has dispatched Bond to find her and he saves her life several times.

Natalya discovers that Boris not only survived the Severnaya bloodbath, he actually aided the

DESOLATION (above) Natalya's co-workers lie dead in the Severnaya station moments before Petya's detonation.

JUBILATION (right) Natalya and James take a moment after wrecking Alec Trevelyan's plot.

Natalya: How can you be so cold?
007: It's what keeps me alive.
Natalya: No. It's what keeps you alone.

killers. Using her considerable computer skills, she traces Boris to Cuba. Discovering that Boris has joined a plot to detonate Mischa, the second GoldenEye satellite, she travels to Cuba with Bond, looking for a satellite dish and control center for the GoldenEye weapons system.

Natalya infiltrates Janus's secret command center with Bond and seizes the opportunity to reprogram the guidance of Mischa. Boris discovers her hacking and tries in vain to break the code of her password. He cannot, and Mischa burns up in the atmosphere, foiling Janus's plot to plunge Britain into economic chaos. Natalya hijacks a helicopter to rescue Bond after he kills Janus's mastermind, traitorous former MI6 agent Alec Trevelyan.

SOLANGE see page 128

SOLITAIRE

APPEARANCE
Live And Let Die (1973)
STATUS Living; whereabouts unknown
CHARACTERISTICS Clairvoyant; gifted reader of tarot pack; innocent of the ways of the world, sensitive, impressionable, courageous
PLAYED BY Jane Seymour

The corrupt president of the Caribbean island of San Monique, Dr. Kananga, alias Harlem gangster Mr. Big, believes Solitaire has the

IN THE CARDS *Solitaire ponders the dangerous consequences of losing her clairvoyant powers.*

power of the Obeah. She describes herself as the High Priestess, the wife to the Prince no longer of this world. She believes she is the spiritual bridge to the Secret Church where the present and the future can be seen through tarot cards. She lives in a guarded grand white house on a cliff above the Caribbean that no one dares enter except for Dr. Kananga. Her change of loyalties from Kananga to Bond is crucial to the collapse of Kananga's drug empire.

Solitaire's supposed powers exist only while she retains her virginity. Once compelled to earthly love, Solitaire believes the Gods will take away her gift. Her mother, Kananga claims, also had the power. Solitaire implies that Kananga killed her mother when he discovered she had taken a lover.

When Solitaire first meets Bond in Mr. Big's office, Bond selects the Lovers card from her tarot deck. The implications of this card and her attraction to 007 cause Solitaire to begin to doubt her relationship with Kananga. She sends Bond a tarot card warning him of CIA agent Rosie Carver's impending betrayal.

Bond later pays her a night time visit, using a tarot pack full of Lovers cards to help convince her to sleep with him. Bond and Solitaire escape from San Monique, but Kananga, furious at this perceived betrayal, kidnaps her and takes her back to his base to be sacrificed in a voodoo ritual. Bond heroically rescues her.

In the Ian Fleming novel, Solitaire's real name is Simone Latrelle. Mr. Big found her in a cabaret in Haiti doing a telepathic act. She escapes with Bond on a train to Florida. Mr. Big kidnaps her, taking her to Jamaica where he plans to kill her and Bond by dragging them over a coral reef.

> "When he finds out I've lost my powers, **he'll kill me.**"
>
> Solitaire to 007

SOLANGE

APPEARANCE
Casino Royale (2006)
STATUS Dead; killed by
Le Chiffre's men
CHARACTERISTICS Sad, lonely
PLAYED BY Caterina Murino

LONELY GIRL *Bond first sees Solange riding her horse along the beach in Nassau.*

STOLEN KISSES *Out of love with her boorish husband, Solange finds herself drawn to 007.*

Solange, wife of terrorist middleman Alex Dimitrios, inadvertently provides James Bond with information that allows him to stop a bomber destroying a Skyfleet prototype aircraft at Miami airport.

Solange lives a life of luxury with her husband. Nevertheless, she feels that she has wasted her chance of true happiness by getting involved with the wrong men. Aware that her husband is a bad man, she knows little about how he makes his money. She has long since become weary of his bad temper and coldness. When Bond emerges from the surf in Nassau, Solange watches, instantly attracted.

That evening, Solange arrives at a poker game where her husband plays against Bond. Losing, Dimitrios reacts coldly to his wife's affection. Bond soundly defeats her husband, even winning his car, a superb Aston Martin DB5. When Solange mistakenly gets into the Aston Martin, Bond invites her for a drink. Sensing a spark of humanity long absent from her life, she accepts, despite realizing that Bond may be using her to get closer to her

husband. Bond and Solange's passion is interrupted by a telephone call from Dimitrios, who tells Solange he is flying to Miami that night. Bond makes a quick exit to pursue him.

When the bomb plot goes awry, Le Chiffre tortures and kills Solange, leaving her body in a hammock.

In Fleming's story *007 in New York*, Bond hopes to meet a girlfriend

007: Can I ask you a personal question?
Solange: Now would seem an appropriate time.

named Solange who works in the old Abecrombie & Fitch. She was the inspiration for the name in *Casino Royale*, not the fanciful mention in the short story *From A View To A Kill*.

SUTTON, STACEY

APPEARANCE
A View To A Kill (1985)
STATUS Living; whereabouts unknown
CHARACTERISTICS Determined, skittish, emotional
PLAYED BY Tanya Roberts

Oil heiress Stacey Sutton becomes a vital ally to James Bond during his investigation of industrialist Max Zorin. Her knowledge of geology and mining uncover the nature of Zorin's Project Main Strike, a plot to cause a massive earthquake that will destroy Silicon Valley.

When Stacey's grandfather died, he left Sutton Oil to her father, who expected only child Stacey to take over the family business. In college, she studied geology. Zorin soon seized control of Sutton Oil in a rigged proxy fight. The resulting legal battles put a tremendous financial strain on Stacey, and she takes a position as a geologist with the State of California to help pay her legal fees. She has managed to hold onto her family home outside San Francisco, although she has had to sell most of her furnishings. Her only real remaining possessions include a

Himalayan Persian cat named Pussy, three canaries, and a Ming vase with her grandfather's ashes inside.

Her government job gives her access to information that might expose Zorin's plans for Main Strike. Knowing this, Zorin offers to settle Stacey's lawsuit for $5 million in exchange for her shares in his company. She refuses this large payoff after Zorin's goons attack her in her own home.

Stacey braves a deadly fire at San Francisco City Hall, drives an out-of-control fire truck, climbs mine shafts, and hangs from the Golden Gate Bridge all in her effort to help Bond stop Zorin. After Zorin's death, she and 007 retire to her steamy shower.

> "I'd sell **everything** and live in a **tent** before I give up."
>
> **Stacey to 007**

SUZUKI, KISSY

APPEARANCE
You Only Live Twice (1967)
STATUS Living
CHARACTERISTICS Intrepid, good with firearms, excellent swimmer
PLAYED BY Mie Hama

Kissy Suzuki serves as a local agent for Japanese Intelligence chief Tiger Tanaka on the island of Matsu where she works as an Ama diver. She possesses an adventurous spirit and appears willing to take on any challenge.

Kissy pretends to marry James Bond to give him cover for his investigation of captured US and Soviet spacecraft. Kissy offers a valuable clue to Bond and Tanaka

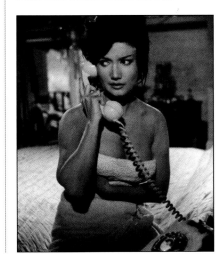

DEADLY SHOT *Suzuki fires a shot that saves Tanaka's life during the battle inside SPECTRE's volcano complex.*

when she explains that an Ama girl died in Ryuzaki, a cave on the mainland that served as an ancient vent for a nearby volcano. Kissy takes Bond to the cave the following morning, and they find it filled with lethal phosgene gas. Upon further examination, Bond and Kissy discover an apparent lake within the volcano's crater is only a canopy for the rocket base below. Kissy agrees to return to her village and bring back Tanaka and his SIS ninjas, an arduous journey. Kissy avoids an attack by a SPECTRE helicopter as she swims from the mainland to the island. Returning with Tanaka, she ably participates in the assault on the rocket base, saving Tanaka's life at least once. When Blofeld sets off explosions that destroy the base, Kissy and Bond escape out of Ryuzaki cave. They find a raft and relax in each other's arms until

rescued by M's submarine.

Kissy Suzuki appears in the original Ian Fleming novel. At 17, she was cast as an Ama diving girl in a movie. Not liking Hollywood, she returned to her family on the island of Kuro, and dives for awabi shells. Bond meets her when Tiger Tanaka asks him to kill Dr. Shatterhand (in reality, Blofeld). A local official arranges for Bond to live with the Suzuki family under the name of Taro Todoroki, a purported anthropologist. Kissy helps 007 get to Shatterhand's castle, rescues him when he falls, injured, into the sea, and takes him as her lover while he suffers from amnesia. Kissy becomes pregnant but never tells Bond. When Bond discovers the word "Valdivostok" on a scrap of newsprint, Kissy helps him travel to the city and away from her forever.

TARO, MISS

APPEARANCE
Dr. No (1962)
STATUS Living; whereabouts unknown
CHARACTERISTICS Charming but devious
PLAYED BY Zena Marshall

Miss Taro is Dr. No's Eurasian henchwoman and spy at Government House in Jamaica, where she works as Pleydell-Smith's secretary. As part of a trap, she invites Bond to her house, and the Three Blind Mice assassins nearly kill him en route. Surprised when Bond turns up alive, she makes love to him, hoping to delay him so that Professor Dent, another Dr. No minion, can arrive to kill him. Bond has Taro arrested instead and then kills Dent.

"The demure, efficient-looking little secretary in the horn-rimmed glasses," is how Fleming describes Miss Taro in the novel *Dr. No*.

TRENCH, SYLVIA

APPEARANCE Dr. No (1962),
From Russia With Love (1963)
STATUS Living; whereabouts unknown
CHARACTERISTICS She knows
what she wants but not how to get it
PLAYED BY Eunice Gayson

Sylvia Trench is the first James Bond woman. She plays a vital role in the cinematic history of 007 by introducing James Bond to audiences in *Dr. No*. It is from her discerning perspective that the world first sees 007 and hears him say, "Bond, James Bond." Described in the script for *Dr. No* as "willowy, exquisitely gowned, with a classic, deceptively cold beauty," Sylvia Trench battles Bond over a game of Chemin de fer at the Le Cercle casino at Les Ambassadeurs in London. She loses to Bond but finds him terribly intriguing. She follows him from the table when a Secret Service representative calls Bond away. Bond offers to take her golfing and to dinner the next day. Taking his card, she tells him she will let him know in the morning. She then travels to his home and lets herself inside, planning to spend the rest of the night with him. Slipping into one of Bond's pajama jackets, she practices her putting. She greets 007 when he arrives, and the pair spends a passionate time together before he flies to Jamaica.

Sylvia also appears in *From Russia With Love*. As she shares a picnic with Bond, he receives a phone call from Miss Moneypenny to meet with M, forcing Bond to cut their picnic short.

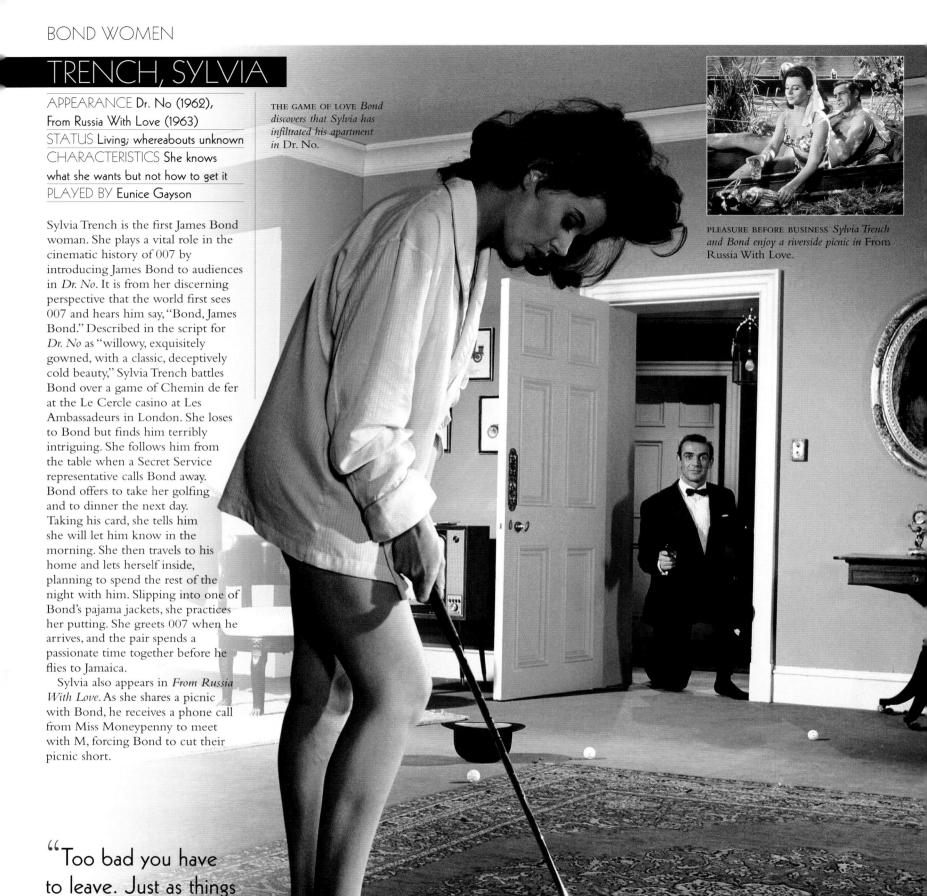

THE GAME OF LOVE *Bond discovers that Sylvia has infiltrated his apartment in* Dr. No.

PLEASURE BEFORE BUSINESS *Sylvia Trench and Bond enjoy a riverside picnic in* From Russia With Love.

"Too bad you have to leave. Just as things were getting interesting again."

Sylvia Trench to 007

VIDA & ZORA

APPEARANCE
From Russia With Love (1963)

STATUS Both living, thanks to Bond

CHARACTERISTICS Jealous, passionate; savage fighters when roused

PLAYED BY Aliza Gur (Vida), Martine Beswick, credited as Martin Beswick (Zora)

Zora and Vida love the same man—the son of the gypsy chief Vavra. Their rivalry must be settled the gypsy way. They agree to fight barehanded to the death. Vavra allows Head of Station T Kerim Bey and James Bond to witness the bitter death match. Bulgarian assassin Krilencu attacks the gypsy camp, interrupting the battle. After the gun battle, Bond asks that the fight be stopped. Vavra agrees but adds that Bond must decide who will marry his son. The winner is never revealed.

VON SCHLAF, COUNTESS LISL

APPEARANCE
For Your Eyes Only (1981)

STATUS Dead; run over by Locque's dune buggy

CHARACTERISTICS Expensive, regal

PLAYED BY Cassandra Harris

Countess Lisl Von Schlaf claims to be a member of the Austrian nobility but is in fact from Liverpool, England. She is engaged in both a business and personal relationship with Greek smuggler Milos Columbo. Bond notices her with Columbo while he dines with shipping magnate Aris Kristatos at Columbo's casino. Kristatos describes Lisl as an "expensive mistress… if she bets, it's with other people's money."

Thanks to a concealed bug, Columbo overhears Kristatos and Bond's conversation and realizes that Bond is a potentially dangerous spy. He stages a furious argument with Lisl; she leaves abruptly, and Bond, seeing an opportunity to find out more about Columbo, offers to drive her home. Kristatos wants Bond to investigate and hopefully kill Columbo, so he offers to lend Bond his own car and chauffeur.

Riding in the back of Kristatos's Rolls-Royce, Bond claims to be a writer researching a novel about Greek smugglers. "Do you know any?" he asks innocently.

When they arrive at Lisl's house, she invites Bond in for champagne and oysters. During a romantic evening together, Lisl freely admits to Bond that Columbo asked her to find out more about him.

The following morning, Bond and Lisl are strolling contentedly along the beach near her house. Under orders from Kristatos, Emile Locque and Claus, driving dune buggies, ambush them. Columbo's men then arrive and kill Claus, but Bond cannot prevent Locque from running Lisl down, killing her.

Countess Lisl:
My nightie's slipping.
007: So is your accent, Countess.

WARMFLASH, DR. MOLLY

APPEARANCE
The World Is Not Enough (1999)

STATUS Living; whereabouts unknown

CHARACTERISTICS Expert practitioner; excellent bedside manner for 007

PLAYED BY Serena Scott Thomas

Molly Warmflash is a striking MI6 doctor with a strong attraction to Bond. He visits her when he has been placed on the inactive roster for a dislocated collar bone. Dr. Warmflash warns Bond to stay out of action but, after the two of them spend an amorous afternoon together at Castle Thane in Scotland, Dr. Warmflash agrees to give 007 "a clean bill of health." At an MI6 briefing, Bond, M, and others listen as Dr. Warmflash uses a hologram to explain the unusual effects of a bullet fired by 009 into Renard's head.

SUPPORTING CAST

Who are those we relegate to the Supporting Cast? They are station chiefs, spymasters, astronauts, organized crime kingpins, ingenious scientists, and experts of all kinds. They may be close colleagues of 007 or even would-be enemies. More often than not, they are individuals who choose to stand by Bond at just the right instant. For a moment, their lives are swept up in adventure. If they are lucky, they encounter the eye of the storm as it passes; if not, they sacrifice their lives for a noble cause. For a moment, they are part of the world of 007.

"00" SECTION

APPEARANCES
Thunderball (1965), Octopussy (1983), The Living Daylights (1987), GoldenEye (1995), The World Is Not Enough (1999)
STATUS Some living, many deceased; 00 agents tend to have short life spans
CHARACTERISTICS Utterly dedicated
PLAYED BY Andy Bradford (009, Octopussy), Glyn Baker (002, The Living Daylights), Frederick Warder (004, The Living Daylights), Sean Bean (006, GoldenEye)

The "00" section designates the most elite and trusted agents in British Intelligence. While James Bond holds the number 007, many of his contemporaries make appearances in his adventures.

In Goldfinger and The Living Daylights, M threatens to replace 007 with 008 unless Bond can remain detached in his missions. In Thunderball, every 00 agent in Europe attends a briefing on Operation Thunderball. In The Man With The Golden Gun, Bond and Moneypenny discuss Bill Fairbanks, the late 002, assassinated by Francisco Scaramanga in the arms of dancer Saida. A new 002 accompanies 004 and 007 on a training exercise o the Rock of Gibraltar in The Living Daylights, but an assassin eliminates 004. 009 dies in Octopussy, dressed as a clown carrying a forged Fabergé Egg. In A View To A Kill, Bond discovers 003's frozen body in Siberia, with a vital microchip in a locket. In The World Is Not Enough, a new 009 shoots terrorist Renard in the head. In GoldenEye, Alec Trevelyan, 006, is a traitor who uses his position to plot the ultimate betrayal of Great Britain. In Ian Fleming's novels, 007 shares an office with 008 and 0011.

The agents who populate this section's ranks are the UK's secret aristocracy, the Western World's silent saviors, the civil servants entrusted with matters of life and death, who carry the burden of a licence to kill.

BROTHERS IN ARMS 006 and 007 infiltrate the Arkangel Chemical Weapons Facility in the USSR, but only one of them is loyal to Queen and country.

PAINTBALLED 002 suffers the humiliation of the SAS catching him during a training mission on Gibraltar.

OPERATION THUNDERBALL Bond arrives fashionably late for a meeting to discuss the theft of two atomic bombs.

AKAKIEVICH, COLONEL

APPEARANCE
The World Is Not Enough (1999)
STATUS Dead; shot by Renard
CHARACTERISTICS Not overly bright
PLAYED BY Claude-Oliver Rudolph

Colonel Akakievich serves as a commanding officer in the army of the Commonwealth of Independent States (CIS). Working with the International Decommissioning Agency (IDA), he has overseen the decommissioning of four nuclear test facilities in the past year. When James Bond, posing as Dr. Arkov of the Russian Atomic Energy Department, arrives in Kazakhstan, Akakievich informs him that he greatly admires his research. He also informs Bond that IDA physicist Dr. Christmas Jones is "not interested in men. Take my word for it."

Bond descends into the underground nuclear test chamber and confronts Renard, who is posing as one of Arkov's men. Akakievich and Jones arrive soon after with a photo of the real Dr. Arkov, who is 63 years old. They declare Bond an imposter and forbid Renard and his men to leave with the nuclear bomb. Renard proceeds to shoot Akakievich and his men and steal the bomb.

DEATH OF A CLOWN A dying 009 gatecrashes an embassy gathering to leave a vital clue.

ANNA

APPEARANCE
GoldenEye (1995)
STATUS Dead; killed by Xenia Onatopp
CHARACTERISTICS Hardworking
PLAYED BY Michelle Arthur

Anna works at the Severnaya Space Weapons Control Centre with her friend Natalya Simonova. She finds programmer Boris Grishenko's computer pranks irritating. When Boris changes Natalya's screen into a buxom cartoon figure, Anna says, "He wouldn't know a woman if one came up and sat on his head." Minutes later, Janus member Xenia Onatopp blasts Anna away with other Severnaya staff. Natalya finds her body in the wreckage.

ASTRONAUTS

APPEARANCE
You Only Live Twice (1967)
STATUS Welcomed home as heroes
CHARACTERISTICS Well-trained, brave
PLAYED BY Paul Carson, Norman Jones, Laurence Herder, Richard Graydon, Bill Mitchell, George Roubicek

When *Bird 1* engulfs *Jupiter 16*, its doors clip the lifeline of Chris, an astronaut performing an EVA (extravehicular activity). The other astronaut becomes a prisoner of SPECTRE. Later, Blofeld's plot snares two Soviet cosmonauts. When Bond invades Blofeld's rocket base, he frees the three astronauts and saves two more.

AUBERGINE, ACHILLE

APPEARANCE
A View To A Kill (1985)
STATUS Dead; poisoned
CHARACTERISTICS Jocular, pompous bon viveur out of his depth
PLAYED BY Jean Rougerie

With his carefully groomed mustache, Achille Aubergine is a classic European gentleman detective in the tradition of Agatha Christie's Hercule Poirot. A friend of Sir Godfrey Tibbett with connections within the Sureté, Aubergine lunches with Bond at Le Jules Verne restaurant in the Eiffel Tower. Aubergine does not know the secret of Max Zorin's success but feels it is to be found at Zorin's stud farm estate outside Paris. May Day kills Aubergine when she whips a hook, dipped in poison and attached to a butterfly marionette, into his cheek.

STUNG BY A BUTTERFLY French detective Aubergine suffers a fatal wound while dining at Le Jules Verne restaurant.

BAINES

APPEARANCE
Live And Let Die (1973)
STATUS Dead; poisoned
CHARACTERISTICS Scared witless
PLAYED BY Dennis Edwards

British secret service agent Baines is captured soon after arriving on the Caribbean island of San Monique. He hopes to investigate the activities of Dr. Kananga, the island's prime minister. Betrayed by double agent Rosie Carver, Baines becomes top billing at a voodoo ceremony featuring a human sacrifice. High Priest Dambala approaches Baines carrying a poisonous snake. The reptile administers the fatal bite. Local authorities find the body and report the death, much to the displeasure of Dr. Kananga.

BELL, MRS.

APPEARANCE
Live And Let Die (1973)
STATUS Alive; no thanks to Bond
CHARACTERISTICS Nonplussed
PLAYED BY Ruth Kempf

A student with the Bleeker Flying School, Mrs. Bell endures a horrifying ground check with 007 at Lakeside Airport, New Orleans. Riding in a Cessna 140 and thinking Bond may be a substitute instructor, Mrs. Bell finds herself in a student pilot's nightmare. Bond proceeds to elude pursuers working for drug lord Dr. Kananga/Mr. Big. In the process, he destroys a small fleet of planes, shears the wings of the Cessna, and leaves Mrs. Bell dumbfounded.

BENSON, CAPT.

APPEARANCE
The Spy Who Loved Me (1977)
STATUS Living; whereabouts unknown
CHARACTERISTICS Confident, intelligent, conscientious staff officer
PLAYED BY George Baker

Captain Benson is commander at Faslane Naval Base when HMS *Ranger*, one of the Royal Navy's four Polaris submarines, goes missing. When James Bond and Q arrive for a meeting at Faslane, a map of the *Ranger*'s course in Bond's possession shocks Benson. He realizes that the Soviets have technology that could enable them to track British submarines and sink them.

BENZ

APPEARANCE
From Russia With Love (1963)
STATUS Killed by Donald Grant
CHARACTERISTICS Watchful
PLAYED BY Peter Bayliss

Benz works for the Soviet Consulate in Istanbul under Koslovski, chief of security, often watching the airport and train stations. Benz spots Tatiana and Bond boarding the Orient Express and follows them, hoping to have Bond and Tatiana stopped at the border and recover the stolen Lektor decoder. Instead, Bond's ally Kerim Bey confronts Benz and jokingly refers to him as "Commissar." Tied up and gagged, Benz is forced to sit and listen to Kerim Bey recounting his colorful life story. Unfortunately SPECTRE assassin Donald Grant is also on board the train and kills both Kerim Bey and Benz.

BEY, KERIM

APPEARANCE
From Russia With Love (1963)
STATUS Dead; killed by Donald Grant
CHARACTERISTICS Robust,
confident, dependable, sagacious
PLAYED BY Pedro Armendariz

Head of Station T in Istanbul, Turkey, Kerim Bey provides essential aid to Bond on his mission to recover a Lektor decoder. Bey becomes a loyal friend and trusted companion of 007.

Bey worked as a strongman in a circus act in his youth. In Fleming's novel, he is named Darko Kerim, and the circus act enables him to spy on Soviets when traveling across the border. Kerim Bey employs his sons as agents in key positions. As in the novel, Bey appears to "consume a large quantity of women" and to be "greedy for life." His instincts, understanding, and attitude to his work greatly impress Bond.

Bey believes that the Soviets are luring Bond into a trap. Shortly after Bond arrives in Istanbul, a limpet mine explodes near Bey's desk. Bey takes Bond to a gypsy camp in order to escape any further attempts on his life. However, the Soviet-controlled agent Krilencu raids the encampment with a team of

> "All of my key employees are my sons.
> Blood is the best security
> in this business."
> Kerim Bey to 007

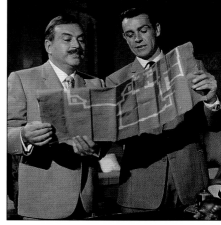

PLAN OF ATTACK *Kerim Bey and Bond look over a copy of the original architect's blueprints of the Soviet Consulate in Istanbul.*

Bulgarians. Bey, with Bond's help, later assassinates Krilencu. Kerim Bey helps Bond carry out an attack on the Soviet consulate. While on the Orient Express, Rosa Klebb's henchman Donald "Red" Grant kills him.

BORCHOI

APPEARANCE
Octopussy (1983)
STATUS Living; whereabouts unknown
CHARACTERISTICS
No-nonsense, influential art expert
PLAYED BY Gabor Vernon

CHEAP IMITATION *Art expert Borchoi recognizes that the real Romanoff Star has been stolen and replaced by a fake.*

Comrade Borchoi serves as a curator for Leningrad's Hermitage Museum, in the Soviet Union. When General Gogol, head of the KGB, becomes suspicious of General Orlov's activities within the Kremlin Art Repository, he brings Borchoi to its vaults to confront Lenkin, the curator of the Kremlin collection. Borchoi picks up the Romanoff Star and examines it with a jeweler's magnifier. When he recognizes that it is actually a fake, Borchoi drops it on the floor and crushes it to pieces with his shoe.

BRAY, SIR HILARY

APPEARANCE **On Her Majesty's Secret Service (1969)**

STATUS **Living; whereabouts unknown**

CHARACTERISTICS
By-the-book, stuffy

PLAYED BY **George Baker**

Genealogist Sir Hilary Bray works at Britain's Royal College of Arms. Ernst Stavro Blofeld asks Sir Hilary to establish his title, Count Balthazar de Bleauchamp. This gives Bond the chance to visit Blofeld disguised as Bray. Sir Hilary agrees to Bond's deception as the matter is of national importance. The real Sir Hilary then loses himself among the churches of Brittany, where he plans to do several brass rubbings. He informs 007 that the real de Bleauchamps are without earlobes and that the family tombs are located in the Augsburg Cathedral in southern Germany, although Blofeld later claims the tombs are located in the St. Anna Kirche.

BRINK, JACOBA

APPEARANCE
For Your Eyes Only (1981)

STATUS **Living; whereabouts unknown**

CHARACTERISTICS **Demanding, overprotective, motherly**

PLAYED BY **Jill Bennett**

Jacoba Brink, "once a world class skater herself," is the strict, overprotective ice-skating coach of Olympic hopeful Bibi Dahl. She clearly does not approve of her pupil's infatuation with men, especially Bond. When Bibi lashes out at Kristatos for being unable to practice at St. Cyril's Monastery, he accuses Brink of poisoning her against him. The two women decide to leave him and find a new sponsor. As Brink tries to engineer their departure, she finds Bond and his team plotting their attack and leads them to Kristatos.

BUKHARIN, GENERAL

APPEARANCE
Tomorrow Never Dies (1997)

STATUS **Living; whereabouts unknown**

CHARACTERISTICS **Diplomatic, hesitant, soft-spoken**

PLAYED BY **Terence Rigby**

Russian General Bukharin works with British Admiral Roebuck in the Ministry of Defence Situation Room to identify fanatics at a terrorist bazaar on the Khyber Pass. Unfortunately, they discover that the terrorists already have Soviet SB-5

TOP BRASS *General Bukharin works closely with the irascible Admiral Roebuck.*

nuclear torpedoes, prompting Roebuck to bark at Bukharin, "Can't you people keep anything locked up?"

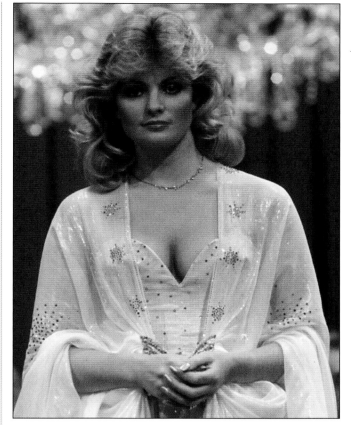

THE BUTTERFLY EFFECT *The Butterfly Girl prepares for her butterfly marionette act.*

BUTTERFLY GIRL

APPEARANCE
A View To A Kill (1985)

STATUS **Living; whereabouts unknown**

CHARACTERISTICS **Beautiful, talented whistler**

PLAYED BY **Carole Ashby**

As Bond lunches with the detective Aubergine at Le Jules Verne restaurant in the Eiffel Tower, the cabaret act *"Dominique et ses Papillons"* begins. The Butterfly Girl whistles a tune while a hooded figure uses a fishing pole to animate butterfly marionettes from the girl's hands. Assassin May Day knocks out the hooded figure and uses the fishing pole to embed a poisoned hook attached to a butterfly into Aubergine's cheek.

CAMPBELL

APPEARANCE **On Her Majesty's Secret Service (1969)**

STATUS **Frozen to death**

CHARACTERISTICS **Keen, foolhardy**

PLAYED BY **Bernard Horsfall**

British Secret Service agent Campbell works in Switzerland and tries to aid 007 on Operation Bedlam without much success.

Campbell first helps Bond by supervising a construction crane and basket to deliver a safecracking device and copy machine to Bond at Gebrüder Gumbold's Bern offices.

He later tries to take the cable car to The Bleuchamp Institute for Allergy Research atop Piz Gloria to assist Bond, but Blofeld's henchman Grunther tells him it is private property. A determined Campbell ignores him and climbs to Piz Gloria.

However, Blofeld's men capture him. Blofeld tortures Campbell, forcing the agent to reveal enough information to unmask his and Bond's true identities. This leads to Bond's capture. Campbell meets his end when Blofeld hangs him upside down by a rope from an ice wall, making his death look like a climbing accident.

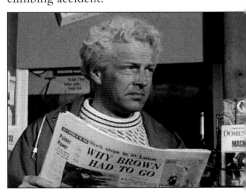

CAPLAN, PAULA

APPEARANCE Thunderball (1965)
STATUS Dead; suicide
CHARACTERISTICS Wry, knowing
PLAYED BY Martine Beswick

British Secret Service agent Paula Caplan aids Bond on his mission to recover two missing nuclear weapons by helping him make contact with Domino Derval, mistress of the mysterious Emilio Largo. Paula is later kidnapped by Largo's henchmen and she takes cyanide rather than give in to torture. Paula's full name does not appear in drafts of the shooting scripts. In the release script, her last name is spelled Kaplan.

CARTER

APPEARANCE Casino Royale (2006)
STATUS Dead; bitten by a cobra
CHARACTERISTICS Cannot play it cool
PLAYED BY Joseph Millson

Carter, Bond's Madagascar colleague, keeps bomb-builder Mollaka under surveillance in a crowd while he watches a cobra/mongoose fight.

Carter tries to talk with Bond, but his constant touching of his earpiece tips off Mollaka, sending him running. Carter gives chase, trips, accidentally fires his gun in the air, and falls headlong into the bottom of the pit where the cobra and mongoose fight.

CARTER, COMMANDER

APPEARANCE
The Spy Who Loved Me (1977)
STATUS Living; whereabouts unknown
CHARACTERISTICS Tough worker
PLAYED BY Shane Rimmer

Commander Carter leads the USS Wayne's attack on the Liparus supertanker owned by shipping magnate Karl Stromberg. When the Liparus captures his submarine, Carter and his crew, including Bond, surrender. Freed by 007, the Wayne's crew tries to stop Stromberg's plot to start a nuclear war. Carter helps 007 to blast open the operations room. When explosions wrack the ship, Carter uses the Wayne's torpedoes to destroy the Liparus's bows and reach safety. Carter then receives orders from the UN Security Council to destroy Stromberg's base Atlantis.

CARVER'S PR

APPEARANCE
Tomorrow Never Dies (1997)
STATUS Living; whereabouts unknown
CHARACTERISTICS Good at her job, but not good enough for Carver
PLAYED BY Daphne Deckers

Media mogul Elliot Carver's PR introduces Bond to Carver as a new banker at a party to launch his satellite network. When 007 later shuts down the power to the building, cutting Carver off in the middle of his speech, Carver angrily blames his PR for the incident and fires her.

CASINO ROYALE PLAYERS

APPEARANCE
Casino Royale (2006)
STATUS Living; whereabouts unknown
CHARACTERISTICS Mysterious, very big spenders
PLAYED BY Tsai Chin (Madame Wu), Lazar Ristovski (Kaminovski), Urbano Barberini (Tomelli), Veruschka (Gräfin von Wallenstein), Tom So (Fukutu), Ade (Infante), Charlie Levi Leroy (Gallardo), Andreas Daniel (Dealer), Carlos Leal (Tournament Director)

In addition to Bond, Le Chiffre, and CIA agent Felix Leiter, these seven characters make up the participants needed for a high stakes poker game set up by Le Chiffre at the Casino Royale in Montenegro. The players buy in to the game for $10 million. If they lose that amount, they may stake an additional $5 million each. This makes the total possible stake in the winner-takes-all tournament a staggering $150 million. Very little is known about these international casino players. Madame Wu is a Chinese woman who has played poker with Le Chiffre in the past. Kaminovski is an extremely wealthy Russian. Tomelli runs a media empire in Italy. Gräfin von Wallenstein is a German countess. The gentleman with the long, silver hair in a ponytail, Fukutu, is a computer software mogul in Japan. Infante is a larger-than-life exiled African dictator. Gallardo is an Argentinean billionaire.

Tomelli, Infante, and Felix Leiter are all impressed by the complexity of Bond's dry martini and, to Le Chiffre's irritation, order an identical one for themselves.

Bond eventually beats Le Chiffre and wins the jackpot. Generous to a fault, Bond leaves the highly efficient dealer a large $500,000 tip.

CHANG, MR.

APPEARANCE
Die Another Day (2002)
STATUS Living; whereabouts unknown
CHARACTERISTICS Sophisticated,
intelligent, well-groomed
PLAYED BY Ho Yi

The manager of Hong Kong's Rubyeon Royale Hotel, Mr. Chang also works for Chinese Intelligence. He knows Bond well and opens the Presidential Suite for 007 when he arrives unshaven and dirty. Bond asks Chang to get him into North Korea so he can kill the terrorist Zao, who has just murdered three Chinese agents. Chang tells Bond that Zao is in Havana, Cuba. He gives Bond a plane ticket and passport and asks him to say "goodbye" to Zao from the Chinese.

"Hong Kong's our turf now..."

Mr. Chang to 007

CHARLIE

APPEARANCE
Live And Let Die (1973)
STATUS Dead; killed by a poison dart
CHARACTERISTICS Loyal chauffeur
PLAYED BY Joie Chitwood

Charlie works for the CIA. Via a baggage tag that matches Charlie's license plate, Charlie collects Bond at JFK Airport. On FDR Drive, a white Corvorado fires a tiny metal dart into Charlie's temple. The dart kills Charlie, but not before triggering his right foot to stomp the accelerator, trapping Bond in Charlie's out-of-control car.

CHE CHE

APPEARANCE On Her Majesty's
Secret Service (1969)
STATUS Living; whereabouts unknown
CHARACTERISTICS Friend and foe
PLAYED BY Irvin Allen

Crimelord Marc Ange Draco's henchman Che Che engages Bond in a brutal fight in the room of Draco's daughter, Tracy di Vicenzo, at the Hotel Estoril in Portugal. Bond knocks out Che Che during the encounter. Undaunted, he returns to spy on 007 and, next morning, presses a knife into Bond's ribs and escorts him to his boss. Che Che later joins the assault on Piz Gloria, killing several of Blofeld's men with a flame-thrower. He also attends Bond and Tracy's wedding.

CLIVE, MAJOR

APPEARANCE
Octopussy (1983)
STATUS Living; whereabouts unknown
CHARACTERISTICS Trusting and gullible; an over-eager gambler
PLAYED BY Stuart Saunders

A retired British army officer, Major Clive loses 220,000 rupees to exiled Afghan prince Kamal Khan playing backgammon at the Shiv Niwas Palace Hotel casino in India. His loss comes as no surprise as Khan plays with loaded dice that reveal a winning double six when needed. Clive refuses Kamal's offer to increase the stakes to 100,000 rupees, and Bond takes his place at the table.

CHA & NARA

APPEARANCE
The Man With The Golden Gun (1974)
STATUS Living; whereabouts unknown
CHARACTERISTICS Inconspicuous, dangerous; superb martial artists
PLAYED BY Joie Pacharintraporn (Cha), Cheung Chuen Nam aka Yuen Qiu (Nara)

At first, the two nieces of Hong Kong detective Lieutenant Hip come across as giggling schoolgirls. In reality, these daughters of a karate school owner are tremendously skilled fighters who eagerly demonstrate their talents. When Hip arrives with them hoping to rescue 007, they flatten a squad of millionaire Hai Fat's martial arts students with their karate moves.

COLTHORPE

APPEARANCE
The Man With The Golden Gun (1974)
STATUS Living; whereabouts unknown
CHARACTERISTICS Has an excellent
eye for detail
PLAYED BY James Cossins

Armaments expert Colthorpe works with Q as a ballistics specialist. He examines the golden dum-dum bullet that killed 002, which Bond has retrieved from Beirut belly-dancer Saida. Colthorpe helps deduce who made it. Examining the bullet's nickel content, Colthorpe and Q determine that it was cast by the Portuguese specialist gun-maker Lazar, who lives in Macau. Bond sets off to discover who Lazar made the bullet for.

COLUMBO, MILOS

APPEARANCE
For Your Eyes Only (1981)
STATUS Living; whereabouts unknown
CHARACTERISTICS Possesses a zest
for life, well-groomed, ruggedly
handsome, pistachio nut lover
PLAYED BY Topol

Greek Milos Columbo smuggles gold, diamonds, cigarettes, and pistachio nuts using a fleet of intercoastal freighters in the Aegean Sea. He owns shares in the Achillion Casino in Gastouri, outside of Corfu, and is known as "The Dove" among members of the Greek underworld.

Smuggler Aris Kristatos fought with Columbo in World War II against the Nazis and Communists, but was, in fact, a double agent. When Columbo learned the truth, it resulted in a blood feud between the two. Hoping Bond will kill Columbo for him, Kristatos leads Bond to believe that it is Columbo who is involved in white slavery, heroin

UNITED FRONT *Columbo and his men, Santos, Nikos, and Karageorge watch with Melina as 007 climbs the Meteora mountain.*

"You have what the Greeks call *thrassos*—guts."

Columbo to 007

smuggling, contract murder, and the salvaging of the British spy ship, the *St. Georges*, to retrieve the vital ATAC transmitter.

Columbo asks his mistress, Countess Lisl Von Schlaf, to discover more about Bond, but after she spends the night with 007, hitmen working for Kristatos kill her on the beach. Columbo captures Bond and earns his trust by returning his Walther PPK. Columbo takes Bond to a warehouse in Albania where Kristatos refines heroin before shipping it to England, and they engage in a gun battle with Kristatos's men.

Armed with a clue that Kristatos has taken the ATAC to St. Cyril's Monastery, Bond contacts Columbo

ATAC ATTACK *Columbo and Kristatos battle to the death over the ATAC transmitter.*

as he is in great need of help. There are 439 St. Cyril's that exist in Greece, but Columbo knows which one Kristatos is using as a base. With his men and Melina Havelock, daughter of marine archaeologist Sir Timothy Havelock, Columbo helps 007 infiltrate the monastery. The feud between Columbo and Kristatos ends when Columbo throws a knife into Kristatos's back.

Wounded from his battle with Kristatos, Columbo appears to become the new sponsor of Kristatos's protegée Bibi Dahl, an Olympic ice-skating hopeful.

In Fleming's short story *Risico*, the character's name is Enrico Colombo and the name of his ship is the *Colombina*.

DAWES

APPEARANCE
Live And Let Die (1973)
STATUS Dead
CHARACTERISTICS Good listener
PLAYED BY James Drake

Dawes becomes one of three British agents killed within 24 hours under the orders of dictator Dr. Kananga, prompting M to send Bond to investigate. Dawes, representing the United Kingdom, watches Dr. Kananga at the UN. While listening to a procedural speech from the Hungarian delegate, an unknown assailant removes the translation audio feed, replacing it with a plunger device that sends a devastatingly painful signal to Dawes through his earpiece. Within seconds, Dawes falls over dead.

DAY, COMMANDER

APPEARANCE
Tomorrow Never Dies (1997)
STATUS Dead; drowned
CHARACTERISTICS Efficient, cautious
PLAYED BY Christopher Bowen

Commander Richard Day is Captain of the HMS *Devonshire* in the South China Sea. When two Chinese MiGs fly past, the pilots state that the *Devonshire* is in Chinese territorial waters. Day insists that his ship is in international waters and that his crew will defend themselves if attacked. Day believes the Chinese pilots have launched an aerial torpedo to sink the *Devonshire* and orders his crew to abandon ship.

DOLLY

APPEARANCE
Moonraker (1979)
STATUS Living; whereabouts unknown
CHARACTERISTICS Love-struck
PLAYED BY Blanche Ravalec

Dolly helps rescue Jaws at Sugarloaf Mountain in Rio de Janeiro, Brazil, when his cable car crashes into the tramway station. She falls in love with Jaws, accompanies him into space, and softens his cold-as-steel heart. When billionaire Hugo Drax explains his plan to repopulate Earth with physically perfect specimens, Dolly questions how she and Jaws would fit into this plan. She and Jaws help 007 escape from Drax's space station, and the pair enjoys champagne before space shuttle captain Colonel Scott rescues them.

DRACO, MARC ANGE

APPEARANCE On Her Majesty's Secret Service (1969)
STATUS Living; whereabouts unknown
CHARACTERISTICS Exudes strength, charm, animal magnetism, and authority, but also menace
PLAYED BY Gabriele Ferzetti

Corsican Marc Ange Draco is the head of the Union Corse, the biggest crime syndicate in Europe. He also briefly holds the title of Bond's father-in-law. His legitimate business fronts include construction, electrical supplies, and numerous agricultural holdings. Born in Corsica, his patriotic drink of choice is Corsican brandy.

Draco was a bandit hiding in the mountains when he met a romantic English girl. The two fell in love, married, and had a child, Teresa (Tracy), in 1943. Twelve years later, Draco's wife died. By then, Draco had been elected capu or "chief" of the Union Corse.

Never giving his daughter a proper home or supervision, Draco watched Tracy immerse herself in one scandal after another to spite him. Although he cut off her allowance, he instructed his men to follow her wherever she traveled and keep her safe.

> ## "On the day you marry her, I will give you a personal dowry of one million pounds. In gold."
>
> ### Draco to 007

Bond rescues Tracy from a suicide attempt and then brutally defeats Draco's men. Draco believes he has at last found the perfect man for his daughter and offers 007 £1 million on the day he marries her. Bond refuses but agrees to continue seeing Tracy in exchange for information regarding his archenemy Blofeld. Tracy sees through her father's motives and tells him to give Bond the information he wants or he will never see her again. Left with no alternative, Draco reveals to 007 that Blofeld's contact is Swiss lawyer Gebrüder Gumbold. However, Draco's wishes are fulfilled, as Bond and Tracy slowly fall in love.

Later, when Blofeld kidnaps Tracy, and holds her hostage at his alpine base Piz Gloria, Bond enlists Draco's help to mount a helicopter attack on Blofeld's lair and rescue her.

At Bond and Tracy's wedding, Draco presents Bond with a £1 million dowry for marrying his daughter, but 007 politely refuses the money. Bond and Tracy's happiness does not last as Draco's beloved daughter is gunned down by Blofeld's henchwoman, Irma Bunt.

TOUGH LOVE *(above) Draco tries to convince Tracy that 007 doesn't need her help.*

FOND FAREWELL *(right) Tracy tells her father she will obey her husband just as she has obeyed him.*

PROUD FATHER *(below) Draco never suspected the tragic price his daughter would pay for marrying 007.*

DUFF, SUPT.

APPEARANCE
Dr. No (1962)
STATUS Living; whereabouts unknown
CHARACTERISTICS Reliable,
knowledgeable; a great help to 007
PLAYED BY William Foster-Davis

Superintendent Duff, the Jamaican Police Commissioner, aids James Bond and Government House in the investigation into the disappearance of British Secret Service representative John Strangways and his secretary, Mary. Duff reports that the car a chauffeur named Mr. Jones used to pick up Bond at Palisadoes Airport was stolen and reveals that Mr. Jones does not hail from Kingston. Bond hands Duff a photograph of Strangways and Quarrel, a fisherman whom Bond noticed tailing him from the airport, and asks Duff to investigate him. 007 also requests a car from Duff when he has the traitorous Miss Taro arrested.

FALCO

APPEARANCE
Die Another Day (2002)
STATUS Living; whereabouts unknown
CHARACTERISTICS Wry, cynical;
initially sceptical of MI6's efficiency
PLAYED BY Michael Madsen

Damian Falco is the hard-bitten chief of the National Security Agency (NSA) and the boss of NSA agent Jinx. He does not trust Bond and has mixed feelings about joining forces with the British to stop billionaire Gustav Graves from destroying the Korean Demilitarized Zone so that North Korea can

> "Put your house in order, or we're gonna do it for you."

Falco to M

invade the South. He believes the Americans can handle the situation on their own.

When Falco becomes aware of information leaking from North Korea, he believes 007, who the North Koreans hold captive, to be the source. Falco subsequently engineers and supervises a prisoner exchange.

Falco then encourages M to imprison Bond on a British warship in Hong Kong Harbor. Later, at NSA headquarters, an angry Falco implies to M over a video link that she intentionally let 007 escape since Bond recently destroyed the Alvarez clinic in Los Organos. He fails to mention that his agent Jinx played a part in the clinic's destruction.

When Falco reluctantly agrees to send Jinx into North Korea with Bond to stop Graves, it is because he has no intention of leaving this situation solely in the hands of the British.

When Bond kills Graves and stops the destruction of the DMZ, Falco cannot admit that he was wrong about 007, allowing M to simply smile at what her best agent just accomplished.

FIREWORKS In the US Command Bunker in the DMZ, Falco tells 007, M, and Jinx that Defcon Two has been declared.

FALLON

APPEARANCE
Licence To Kill (1989)
STATUS Killed by tank blast
CHARACTERISTICS No-nonsense, businesslike, disciplined
PLAYED BY Christopher Neame

Fallon is MI6's man in Isthmus City, who M orders to bring Bond back to London at any cost. Fallon arrives at the safe house belonging to Hong Kong narcotics agents Kwang and Loti, who have just prevented Bond from assassinating Sanchez. Fallon prepares to drug Bond and ship him home, when Heller, Sanchez's head of security, fires a tank shell at the house, killing Fallon instantly.

FANNING, JIM

APPEARANCE Octopussy (1983)
STATUS Living; whereabouts unknown
CHARACTERISTICS Fussy art expert
PLAYED BY Douglas Wilmer

British Secret Service art expert Jim Fanning accompanies Bond to Sotheby's auction house in London to help spot the seller of a rare Fabergé Egg. Fanning predicts that the egg will fetch between £250,000 and £300,000. When exiled Afghan prince Kamal Khan and 007 become embroiled in a bidding war, which reaches £500,000, Fanning nearly faints.

FARREL, ADMIRAL

APPEARANCE
GoldenEye (1995)
STATUS Dead; crushed
CHARACTERISTICS Easily seduced
PLAYED BY Billy J. Mitchell

IDENTIFICATION CARD
SURNAME-NOM **FARREL**
GIVEN NAMES-PRENOMS **CHUCK**
STATUS-STATUT **ADMIRAL 2488**
DEPARTMENT OF NATIONAL DEFENCE

Canadian Navy Admiral Chuck Farrel has no clue that his betrayal of his country serves a Janus plot to steal a new Tiger helicopter. When he takes on Xenia Onatopp, a member of Janus, as a lover, he does virtually everything he can to please her, including buying her an expensive black-market Ferrari. During a night of lovemaking, Xenia suddenly crushes Farrel's rib cage with her thighs. His ID allows Alec Trevelyan to slip aboard the French warship and gain access to the Tiger.

FEKKESH, AZIZ

APPEARANCE
The Spy Who Loved Me (1977)
STATUS Dead; killed by Jaws
CHARACTERISTICS Furtive, nervous; realizes too late that he is in mortal peril
PLAYED BY Nadim Sawalha

Egyptian middleman Aziz Fekkesh tries to negotiate the sale of plans for Karl Stromberg's submarine tracking system. Fekkesh fails to meet Bond for an appointment in Cairo. At the Pyramids of Giza *Son et Lumière* show, Fekkesh sees Jaws and tries to run for safety. Bond follows the chase into an ancient tomb. Inside, Jaws kills Fekkesh with a fatal bite before Bond can reach them. After Jaws escapes, 007 finds Fekkesh's appointment book, which leads him to businessman Max Kalba.

FERRARA, LUIGI

APPEARANCE
For Your Eyes Only (1981)
STATUS Dead; neck sliced
CHARACTERISTICS Charming, enthusiastic, suspicious
PLAYED BY John Moreno

Luigi Ferrara works as MI6's young agent in the northern town of Cortina in Italy. On the steamed mirror in his hotel bathroom, Bond receives a message to meet this Italian contact at the peak of the Tofana ski lift at 10 a.m.

Ferrara introduces Bond to shipping magnate Aris Kristatos and later informs 007 that his office in Milan might be able to help with information on Milos Columbo, the arch rival of Kristatos. Locque, a hitman working for Kristatos, murders Ferrara by slicing his throat. Bond avenges his death by kicking Locque's crashed Mercedes, with Locque inside, off a cliff.

Ferrara: The snow this year is better at Innsbruck.
007: But not at St. Moritz.

APPOINTMENT IN CORTINA *Luigi Ferrara meets with James Bond to discuss Operation Undertow.*

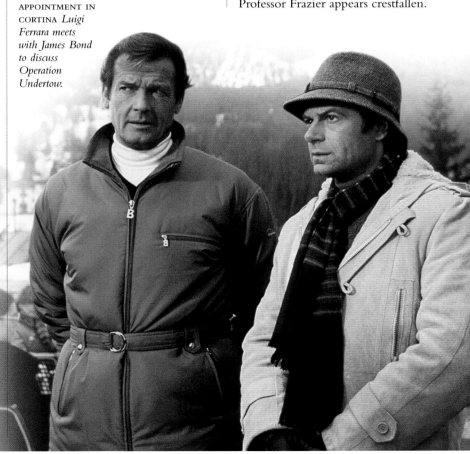

FRAZIER, PROFESSOR

APPEARANCE The Man With The Golden Gun (1974)
STATUS Living
CHARACTERISTICS Thrilled at the prospect of discovery
PLAYED BY Gerald James

SECRET MEETING *Prof. Frazier (fourth on the right) meets Bond and Lt. Hip aboard the partially sunken* Queen Elizabeth.

A solar energy expert retained by British Intelligence to work on bringing the defected scientist Gibson back to the British side, Professor Frazier becomes excited when he discovers Gibson brought the Solex Agitator, a device that turns the sun's power into electricity, to a meeting with Lt. Hip. When Bond and Lt. Hip tell him that the Solex was not found on Gibson after he was assassinated by Scaramanga, Professor Frazier appears crestfallen.

GIBSON

APPEARANCE
The Man With The Golden Gun (1974)
STATUS Dead; shot by Scaramanga
CHARACTERISTICS Mercenary, brilliant
PLAYED BY Gordon Everett

ONE FOR THE ROAD *Gibson orders a last drink at the Bottoms Up bar.*

British solar energy expert Gibson goes underground to work for Hai Fat, a Thai multi-millionaire. Gibson offers to re-defect to the British, but Scaramanga shoots him before he can turn over the Solex Agitator, a device that turns the sun's power into electricity.

GOGOL, GENERAL

APPEARANCES
The Spy Who Loved Me (1977), Moonraker (1979), For Your Eyes Only (1981), Octopussy (1983), A View To A Kill (1985), The Living Daylights (1987)
STATUS Living; retired
CHARACTERISTICS Détente-conscious; experienced in the ways of the world; something of a bon viveur
PLAYED BY Walter Gotell

General Anatol Gogol, the head of the KGB, crosses paths with Bond and British Intelligence on six assignments. Little is known about his personal life, but he enjoys a close relationship with his secretary, Miss Rublevich.

In *The Spy Who Loved Me*, Gogol and M team their top agents, 007 and Agent XXX, in an effort to discover the third party behind the disappearance of both nations' nuclear missile-equipped submarines. *Moonraker* finds Gogol in Moscow, assuring Colonel Scott of NASA that he will give the US 12 hours to determine the origins of billionaire Hugo Drax's space station before the Soviets attack. In *For Your Eyes Only,*

"How can I sleep? **Nothing but problems.**"

General Gogol

Gogol vies with the British as he prepares to purchase the ATAC transmitter from the evil Aris Kristatos. 007 destroys the ATAC and informs Gogol "That's détente, Comrade, you don't have it, I don't have it." Gogol takes Bond's advice to heart, because in *Octopussy*, the KGB chief opposes Russian General Orlov and his desire to launch war against the West. *A View To A Kill* sees Gogol trying to keep rogue KGB agent Max Zorin under control. He even awards Bond the Order of Lenin when 007 stops Zorin from destroying Silicon Valley. In his final appearance, in *The Living Daylights*, Gogol receives a promotion to the Foreign Service.

A MESSAGE FROM THE KGB General Gogol informs General Orlov that he is a disgrace to the Soviet Union.

GRANT'S MASSEUSE

APPEARANCE
From Russia With Love (1963)
STATUS Unknown
CHARACTERISTICS Tactile
PLAYED BY Jan Williams

The silent blonde who massages SPECTRE hitman Donald Grant is described in more detail in Ian Fleming's novel. She has been Grant's masseuse for two years but his perfect physique and malevolent essence repulse her. She is sometimes mysteriously told her services are not needed for a week or two. She has seen small wounds on Grant, but she knows nothing of his work and does not ever plan to ask.

GRAY, FREDERICK

APPEARANCE The Spy Who Loved Me (1977), Moonraker (1979), For Your Eyes Only (1981), Octopussy (1983), A View To A Kill (1985), The Living Daylights (1987)
STATUS Living; whereabouts unknown
CHARACTERISTICS Nonplussed and irritated by changes in his routine
PLAYED BY Geoffrey Keen

Sir Frederick Gray, the Minister of Defence, instructs Bond on the vital military and political factors for six of his missions. He plays a key role in 007's world, serving as the principle link between the Prime Minister and British Intelligence.

In *The Spy Who Loved Me*, Gray meets Bond at Faslane Naval Base in Scotland. *Moonraker* finds Gray furious with 007 for accusing billionaire Hugo Drax of illegal activities. When M is on leave in *For Your Eyes Only*, Gray briefs Bond on Operation Undertow. For *Octopussy*, Gray returns the stolen Romanoff Star to KGB chief General Gogol. *A View To A Kill* finds Gray concerned about the political implications of investigating the activities of industrialist Max Zorin.

Gray's final appearance in *The Living Daylights* sees the minister upset that the KGB has snatched back General Koskov only hours after he defected to the West.

GREENWALT, DR.

APPEARANCE
Tomorrow Never Dies (1997)
STATUS Living; whereabouts unknown
CHARACTERISTICS Nervous, cautious, well-educated
PLAYED BY Colin Stinton

OFF-TARGET *Dr. Greenwalt examines the tampered GPS encoder used by Elliot Carver and Henry Gupta to send HMS Devonshire off course.*

Dr. Dave Greenwalt is the US Air Force GPS (Global Positioning Satellite) expert. Bond arrives at the US Air Force base in Okinawa, Japan, to meet with Greenwalt and CIA contact Jack Wade. 007 brings the GPS encoder he stole from Henry Gupta's laboratory in Hamburg. Attaching the encoder to his GPS calibration unit, Greenwalt is able to determine the actual location where HMS *Devonshire* sank.

GUMBOLD, GEBRÜDER

APPEARANCE
On Her Majesty's Secret Service (1969)
STATUS Living; whereabouts unknown
CHARACTERISTICS Stern, precise
PLAYED BY James Bree

Gebrüder Gumbold, a lawyer based in Bern, Switzerland, represents the interests of SPECTRE chief Blofeld. Blofeld wants the College of Arms in London to verify his lineage as Count Balthazar de Bleauchamp and uses Gumbold to make the necessary contacts with Sir Hilary Bray of the College of Arms.

Criminal mastermind Marc Ange Draco informs 007 of Gumbold's connection to Blofeld. Bond breaks into the lawyer's office during Gumbold's lunch hour to crack his safe and photocopy the College of Arms letters. He exits the office just as Gumbold returns.

HAMILTON

APPEARANCE
Live And Let Die (1973)
STATUS Dead; assassinated while watching his own funeral
CHARACTERISTICS Unwisely curious
PLAYED BY Robert Dix

Hamilton is the second of three British agents killed by dictator Dr. Kananga's minions. On loan to American Intelligence, Hamilton watches the Fillet of Soul restaurant on Docker Street in New Orleans,. He sees a jazz funeral pass and asks another observer, "Whose funeral is it?" He gets a surprising answer: "Yours." The man jabs a switchblade between Hamilton's ribs, and his dead body falls to the street. The pallbearers place a bottomless coffin over his body. When they lift the coffin, Hamilton remains inside and the mourners break into a celebratory jazz dance.

HARGREAVES, ADMIRAL

APPEARANCE
The Spy Who Loved Me (1977)
STATUS Living; whereabouts unknown
CHARACTERISTICS Decisive leader
PLAYED BY Robert Brown

Admiral Hargreaves serves as Flag Officer of Submarines for the Royal Navy. He retains the ultimate responsibility for the four Polaris R-class submarines headquartered at Faslane Naval Base in Scotland. He is one of three individuals allowed to know the pre-arranged courses of the submarine fleet.

When Hargreaves meets Bond, he mentions HMS *Ark Royal* to 007, referencing Bond's service on the legendary World War II aircraft carrier sunk by a U-boat off Gibraltar. Hargreaves listens to the

Minister of Defence reveal how an enemy located HMS *Ranger* using a new submarine tracking system. Hargreaves acknowledges that such a system could undermine Western defense strategies.

After the submarine crisis, Hargreaves continued his career in public service, ultimately serving in other highly sensitive positions.

HAVELOCK, TIMOTHY & IONA

APPEARANCE
For Your Eyes Only (1981)
STATUS Dead; both murdered in cold blood
CHARACTERISTICS Attentive, patriotic
PLAYED BY Jack Hedley and Toby Robins

Marine archaeologists Timothy and Iona Havelock have traveled all over the world on their ship, the *Triana*, searching for relics in their Neptune 2-man sub. Proud parents of Melina, they currently work for British Intelligence on a mission to find the *St. Georges*, a missing British spy ship. Sir Timothy records his findings in a daily log written in a special kind of shorthand, which only Melina can decipher. Before Timothy can deliver his report to British Intelligence, Cuban hitman Hector Gonzales guns down him and Iona.

In Ian Fleming's short story *For Your Eyes Only*, Major Gonzales, who works for a man named Von Hammerstein, guns down Colonel Timothy Havelock and his wife. Gonzales kills them after they refuse to sell their 20,000 acres of Jamaican plantation land, which has been in the family for three centuries. M, who is best friends with the Havelocks and was best man at their wedding ceremony in Malta in 1925, asks James Bond to avenge their deaths.

WELCOME HOME, MELINA, MY DARLING
Timothy and Iona Havelock enjoy a happy reunion with their daughter Melina before tragedy strikes.

HAWKER

APPEARANCE
Goldfinger (1964)
STATUS Living; whereabouts unknown
CHARACTERISTICS Loyal caddy
PLAYED BY Gerry Duggan

Hawker caddies for Bond during his golf match with Goldfinger, watching admiringly as 007 outfoxes his cheating opponent. When Goldfinger loses his ball, Hawker suspects Oddjob is lying about finding it, and he is; Bond is standing on the real ball. Later, Hawker watches as 007 replaces Goldfinger's Slazenger 1 ball with a Slazenger 7. Goldfinger plays the wrong ball on the last hole and loses the match.

HAWKINS

APPEARANCE
Licence To Kill (1989)
STATUS Living; whereabouts unknown
CHARACTERISTICS By-the-book, athletic, hard-edged
PLAYED BY Grand L. Bush

IN OVER YOUR HEAD *Hawkins advises Bond to lay off the Sanchez case.*

DEA agent Hawkins, along with Agent Mullens, stops fellow agent Felix Leiter on Key West's Seven Mile Bridge and informs him that drug lord Franz Sanchez is in the Bahamas.

When Bond pursues his vengeance mission against Sanchez for the maiming of Leiter, Hawkins reminds 007 that he is out of his jurisdiction and in way over his head. Hawkins later leads Bond to the Hemingway House where M revokes Bond's licence to kill.

HENDERSON, DIKKO

APPEARANCE
You Only Live Twice (1967)
STATUS Dead; stabbed in the back
CHARACTERISTICS Guarded; never fully adopted Japanese culture
PLAYED BY Charles Gray

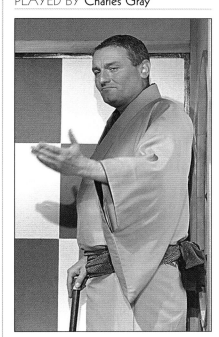

Dikko Henderson moved to Japan just before World War II, and lost his right leg in Singapore in 1942. He loves the Orient and works for MI6 as a station chief, although he expresses doubts about ever fully embracing the culture. Henderson maintains a close

> ## "Oh that's stirred not shaken.
> ### That was right, wasn't it?"
> **Henderson to Bond**

relationship with the Japanese SIS and has Japanese agent Aki meet 007 for him. Although Henderson gives Bond a martini "stirred, not shaken," 007 is too polite to correct him. Henderson believes a mysterious rocket capturing US spacecraft is being launched from Japan, and that a Japanese industrial concern is involved. Bond never finds out more because Henderson receives a knife in his back. It is rumored that a few years after Henderson's death, Blofeld used him as a model for his surgically-created looks.

HERGERSHEIMER, KLAUS

APPEARANCE
Diamonds Are Forever (1971)
STATUS Unknown
CHARACTERISTICS Friendly, conscientious, innocent
PLAYED BY Ed Bishop

Former NASA employee Klaus Hergersheimer works for WW Techtronics, a division of Whyte Enterprises, Inc. As a member of G Section for three years, he has the thankless duty of checking radiation shields for replacement. While making rounds in Section 5, Klaus finds Bond without a shield. Hergersheimer gives one to Bond but later discovers that 007 impersonated him while infiltrating Professor Dr. Metz's lab.

HIP, LT.

APPEARANCE The Man With The Golden Gun (1974)
STATUS Living
CHARACTERISTICS Good martial artist
PLAYED BY Soon-Taik Oh

British Secret Service contact in Hong Kong and a Lieutenant in the Hong Kong police force, Hip works to secure the re-defection of solar energy expert Gibson. Hip travels with Bond to Bangkok to investigate Hai Fat's connection to Gibson and Scaramanga. He shuttles Bond to Hai Fat's house and helps rescue Bond at Hai Fat's martial arts school. Hip collects the Solex from Bond and delivers it to Mary Goodnight. Shortly after he realizes she has been kidnapped, he disappears.

HOME SECRETARY

APPEARANCE Thunderball (1965)
STATUS Unknown
CHARACTERISTICS Extremely traditional, generally irritated
PLAYED BY Roland Culver

The Home Secretary represents the Prime Minister during Operation Thunderball. He has to decide if Britain should pay a ransom of £100,000,000 to recover two atomic bombs hijacked by SPECTRE. His fatalistic attitude places little faith in the work of 007. He orders his assistant Kenniston to secure $280,000,000 worth of flawless blue-white diamonds, which will be dropped in the Mergui Archipelago off the coast of Burma.

HOODS CONVENTION

APPEARANCE Goldfinger (1964)
STATUS Dead; gassed
CHARACTERISTICS Greedy, suspicious
PLAYED BY Bill Nagy (Mr. Midnight), Hal Galili (Mr. Strap), Roland Brand, Bill Brandon, Norman Chaucer, Bill Edwards, Laurence Herder, William Hurndell, John Maxim, John McCarthy, Lenny Rabin (other gangsters)

Goldfinger enlists top US crime figures to smuggle materials for Operation Grand Slam. The hoods are each to be paid $1 million in gold. Goldfinger offers them $10 million each in gold from Fort Knox if they help him rob it. All but Mr. Solo agree. Goldfinger decides to cover his tracks and orders Kisch to eliminate the group with nerve gas.

A BED FOR THE NIGHT *007 considers an offer of hospitality from Sheik Hosein.*

IRINA

APPEARANCE
GoldenEye (1995)
STATUS Living; whereabouts unknown
CHARACTERISTICS Gorgeous;
limited singing skills
PLAYED BY Minnie Driver

Irina, the mistress of Russian Mafia head Valentin Zukovsky, works as a country music singer in his club in St. Petersburg, Russia, performing with three backup singers. She is beautiful, but profoundly untalented—Bond compares her singing to strangling a cat. Irina finds it insulting when Zukovsky asks her to cut short her rehearsal of Tammy Wynette's "Stand By Your Man," and she storms off the stage.

HOSEIN, SHEIK

APPEARANCE
The Spy Who Loved Me (1977)
STATUS Living; whereabouts unknown
CHARACTERISTICS A gracious host who appreciates the treasures of Egypt
PLAYED BY Edward de Souza

A friend from Bond's student days at Cambridge University, Sheik Hosein lives the life of a hedonistic bedouin in the Egyptian desert, but he also has ties to the British Secret Service. Hosein helps 007 locate the men behind the sale of megalomaniac Karl Stromberg's submarine tracking system technology. He advises Bond to get in touch with the Egyptian Aziz Fekkesh and then businessman Max Kalba. After a member of Hosein's harem of beautiful wives suggestively presents 007 with a rose, Bond agrees to stay for the night at Sheik Hosein's camp.

"Well, what can I offer you? Sheep's eyes? Dates? Vodka Martini?"

Sheik Hosein to 007

HOTEL RECEPTIONIST

APPEARANCE
From Russia With Love (1963)
STATUS Living; whereabouts unknown
CHARACTERISTICS Nervous
PLAYED BY Arlette Dobson

SPECTRE bribes the Istanbul hotel staff to guide James Bond to a bugged room. When Bond objects to the arrangements, the hotel receptionist then offers 007 the Bridal Suite. Behind the suite's two-way mirrored wall, SPECTRE member Rosa Klebb films Bond's first meeting with Tatiana Romanova, a supposed defector from Soviet Intelligence.

"Who's strangling the cat?"

007 on Irina's singing

KALBA, MAX

APPEARANCE
The Spy Who Loved Me (1977)
STATUS **Dead; killed by Jaws**
CHARACTERISTICS **Cool, calm, collected; experienced black-marketeer**
PLAYED BY **Vernon Dobtcheff**

Owner of the Mujaba Club in Cairo, Egypt, Max Kalba receives the microfilm of megalomaniac Karl Stromberg's submarine tracking system from Stromberg's secretary via his underground network. Through middleman Aziz Fekkesh, Kalba offers to sell the microfilm to the Soviets or the British, whoever offers the highest bid. After Stromberg's enforcer, Jaws, kills Fekkesh, Kalba meets with KGB agent Anya Amasova and 007. Before a deal can be made, Jaws lures Kalba to a secluded phone booth, takes the microfilm and fatally bites him.

In an early script draft, Kalba and Bond engage in a duel over a game of backgammon. 007 wins, but Jaws kills Kalba before he can pay Bond.

KELLY, ADMIRAL

APPEARANCE
Tomorrow Never Dies (1997)
STATUS **Living; whereabouts unknown**
CHARACTERISTICS **Member of the Royal Navy, professional, focused**
PLAYED BY **Michael Byrne**

As HMS *Bedford* captain Admiral Kelly prepares his fleet of ships for war against the Chinese. The British and the Chinese governments determine that media mogul Elliot Carver has been pitting them off against each other. After Carver's

stealth ship becomes visible to radar. Kelly orders his crew to turn its attention from the Chinese and focus on destroying Carver's floating technological wonder.

KERIM BEY'S GIRLFRIEND

APPEARANCE
From Russia With Love (1963)
STATUS **Unknown**
CHARACTERISTICS **Bored, seductive**
PLAYED BY **Nadja Regin**

Kerim Bey's girlfriend enjoys the intrigue of liaising in the Istanbul office of the British Secret Service. She inadvertently saves Bey's life by inducing him to join her on the settee before a limpet mine explodes near his desk. After the shock of nearly being killed, she moved to Central America and studied dance.

KING, SIR ROBERT

APPEARANCE
The World Is Not Enough (1999)
STATUS **Dead; blown up in MI6 headquarters**
CHARACTERISTICS **Man of integrity**
PLAYED BY **David Calder**

Sir Robert King is the father of Elektra King. After reading law at Oxford University with M, Sir Robert married into the Vavra family, renaming their oil empire King Industries. When terrorist Renard kidnaps Elektra, Robert consults M, now head of MI6, who advises him not to pay the ransom.

Sir Robert ultimately becomes the victim of patricide. Elektra plots to kill him to take revenge for refusing to pay her ransom and also to seize what she believes to be her family's stolen heritage of Central Asian oil reserves. Elektra works with Renard to have her father obliterate himself with stacks of specially treated £50 notes. Sir Robert dies inside MI6 headquarters.

> ❝Be careful, M. I might try to **steal him from you.**❞
>
> **King on 007**

GOOD FRIENDS *(right) Sir Robert King and M share a drink as Bond enters her office.*

OIL KING *(below) Sir Robert's wealth and MI6 connections make him a target for terrorist Renard.*

KLOTKOFF

APPEARANCE
A View To A Kill (1985)
STATUS Dead; chopped into fish bait
CHARACTERISTICS Loyal, dutiful
PLAYED BY Bogdan Kominowski

KGB agent Klotkoff joins General
Gogol when he reprimands tycoon
Max Zorin for "assassinating" 007.
Klotkoff calls Zorin "a physiological
freak," prompting Zorin's lover
May Day to lift Klotkoff into the air
and hurl him to the ground.

At Zorin's oil pumping station,
Klotkoff and agent Pola Ivanova
record Zorin discussing plans to
destroy Silicon Valley. They then try
to detonate a mine at the station.
Pola escapes, but Zorin orders Klotkoff
be thrown into the intake pipe rotors.

KWANG

APPEARANCE
Licence To Kill (1989)
STATUS Dead; killed by cyanide
CHARACTERISTICS Decisive, driven
PLAYED BY Cary-Hiroyuki Tagawa

Disguised as an Asian drug lord,
Kwang, like his partner, Loti, is a
Hong Kong narcotics agent who has
spent years trying to infiltrate drug
lord Franz Sanchez's operations.
When Bond tries to kill Sanchez,
Kwang's ninja team attacks. They
take Bond to their safe house for
questioning, but then Heller,
Sanchez's security chief, attacks the
house. Kwang commits suicide by
biting into a cyanide tablet rather
than face Sanchez's wrath.

LAZAR

APPEARANCE
The Man With The Golden Gun
(1974)
STATUS Living
CHARACTERISTICS Skilled craftsman
PLAYED BY Marne Maitland

A Portuguese weapons maker based
in Macau, Lazar makes customized
bullets for assassin Francisco
Scaramanga and it is likely that he
made Scaramanga's unique
component golden gun for him.
Lazar prides himself on custom,
hand-crafted work. When Bond
meets Lazar, 007 turns a gun on the
weapons maker. Lazar agrees to let
Bond trace the delivery of the
golden bullets to Scaramanga at the
Casino de Macau.

LEBANESE GANGSTERS

APPEARANCE
The Man With The Golden Gun (1974)
STATUS Living
CHARACTERISTICS Ill-tempered
PLAYED BY George Silver (owner),
Terry Plummer (Rahman), Rocky Taylor
(Hammud)

BUILT FOR TROUBLE *James Bond must face
off with this trio in order to retrieve the
golden bullet that killed agent 002.*

When Bond attempts to steal a
golden bullet held as a lucky charm
in the navel of a belly dancer called
Saida, the Lebanese nightclub
owner and his two bouncers,
Rahman and Hammud, attack.
Bond fights back, at one point using
a can of Fabergé Brut to sting the
eyes of one of his adversaries.

KRUG, MR.

APPEARANCE
Die Another Day (2002)
STATUS Living; whereabouts unknown
CHARACTERISTICS Burly, hostile
PLAYED BY Ian Pirie

Mr. Krug is a South African criminal
staying in Room 42 of the Gran
Blanco Hotel in Los Organos off
the Cuban coast. Here he waits with
other criminals to be taken to the
clinic of gene therapy specialist Dr.
Alvarez, where he will acquire a
new identity. Bond knocks Krug
unconscious and then uses his
admittance papers to gain
access to the clinic.

LA PORTE, MADEMOISELLE

APPEARANCE Thunderball (1965)
STATUS Unknown
CHARACTERISTICS Efficient, exotic
PLAYED BY Maryse Guy Mitsouko

When Bond attends the funeral of
SPECTRE No. 6, Colonel Jacques
Boitier, he brings the beautiful

Mademoiselle La Porte as his escort.
La Porte works for the British Secret
Service's French station. It transpires
that Boitier is actually alive and is
posing as his own widow at his
supposed funeral. La Porte helps
Bond escape from a trio of
SPECTRE gunmen after Bond
kills Boitier at his chateau.

LEE, CHUCK

APPEARANCE
A View To A Kill (1985)
STATUS Dead; strangled by May Day
CHARACTERISTICS Youthful, keen
PLAYED BY David Yip

Chuck Lee is a young Chinese-
American CIA agent who poses as a
Fisherman's Wharf seafood vendor
and gives Bond information regarding
tycoon Max Zorin's employee Bob
Conley and ex-Nazi Dr. Mortner. He
also introduces 007 to fisherman
O'Rourke, who tells Bond that
Zorin's oil pumping station ruined
an excellent crab patch.

May Day later strangles Chuck Lee in his truck outside geologist Stacey Sutton's home. San Francisco police recover his body in Chinatown.

Bond producers had planned to bring CIA agent Felix Leiter back as 007's contact in San Francisco. But with Chinatown such a key part of the city, they chose to make this character a Chinese-American CIA agent instead.

LEILA

APPEARANCE
From Russia With Love (1963)
STATUS Living; whereabouts unknown
CHARACTERISTICS Fit, superb dancer
PLAYED BY Lisa (Leila) Guiraut

At a gypsy camp in Istanbul, Turkey, Bond and head of Station T, Kerim Bey, are treated to a belly dance by a beautiful and talented woman who takes a great deal of interest in 007.

LEITER, DELLA

APPEARANCE
Licence To Kill (1989)
STATUS Dead; stabbed in the chest
CHARACTERISTICS Bubbly, beautiful
PLAYED BY Priscilla Barnes

Vivacious Della Churchill marries 007's close friend, DEA agent Felix Leiter, in a wedding ceremony in Key West, Florida. Her disapproving elderly uncle believes the marriage is a mistake. After the wedding, Bond travels to the airport to catch his Istanbul flight. On hearing that drug lord Sanchez has escaped custody, 007 returns to Leiter's house to find that Sanchez's henchmen have murdered Della and maimed Felix.

WELCOME TO THE GYPSY LIFE
Leila lets 007 in on her belly dancing secrets.

LEITER, FELIX

APPEARANCE Dr. No (1962),
Goldfinger (1964), Thunderball
(1965), Diamonds Are Forever (1971),
Live And Let Die (1973), The Living
Daylights (1987), Licence To Kill
(1989), Casino Royale (2006)
STATUS Living; whereabouts unknown
CHARACTERISTICS Reliable aide
and friend to Bond
PLAYED BY Jack Lord (Dr. No), Cec
Linder (Goldfinger), Rik Van Nutter
(Thunderball), Norman Burton
(Diamonds Are Forever), David Hedison
(Live And Let Die, Licence To Kill),
John Terry (The Living Daylights),
Jeffrey Wright (Casino Royale)

CIA CONTACT *Felix Leiter in* **Dr. No.**

Felix Leiter is Bond's Texas-born
CIA ally and close friend in six
Fleming novels and eight 007 films.
Fleming gives his age as 35 in *Casino
Royale*. The description of him in
that novel reads: "A mop of straw-
coloured hair lent his face a boyish
look which closer examination
contradicted."

An ex-member of the US Marine
Corps, jazz-lover Leiter joins the
CIA and comes to Bond's rescue at
the casino at Royale-les-Eaux in
northern France.

ON THE CASE *In*
Goldfinger, *Leiter tells
M 007 has landed.*

FAITHFUL FRIEND *In the
Bahamas, Leiter keeps his eye on
James Bond in* **Thunderball.**

BON VOYAGE *Leiter (on right) and Willard Whyte bid Bond and Tiffany farewell in* **Diamonds Are Forever.**

In the novel *Live And Let Die*, Leiter's friendship with Bond develops as the two barhop in Harlem and enjoy good meals together. Leiter loses his right arm and leg to a shark, courtesy of gangster Mr. Big's thugs. Bond finds his friend's body wrapped in a white sheet with a note attached to his chest, which reads: "He disagreed with something that ate him." This same scenario would be used by the filmmakers not for the film *Live and Let Die*, but as a key plot device for *Licence To Kill*, when drug baron Franz Sanchez feeds DEA agent Leiter to the sharks.

After being discharged by the CIA for his handicap, Leiter joins Pinkerton's Detective Agency and helps Bond in the novels *Diamonds Are Forever* and *Goldfinger*. CIA chief Allen Dulles calls Leiter back into CIA duty in the novel *Thunderball*, because he knows how well Bond and Leiter work together. Leiter arrives in Jamaica in the novel *The Man With The Golden Gun* and injures Scaramanga, paving the way for 007 to terminate the assassin.

In the films, Leiter first meets Bond at Kingston Harbour in *Dr. No*. He helps 007 discover more information about Dr. No's operation at Crab Key and arrives

with his marines at the end to rescue Bond and Honey Ryder. In *Goldfinger*, Leiter briefs Bond on Auric Goldfinger at the Fontainebleau Hotel in Miami, Florida. Later, with his colleague Johnny, Leiter keeps a sharp watch on Bond's activities in Kentucky. Once Bond prevents Operation Grand Slam, Leiter escorts 007 to a plane waiting to fly him to Washington, D.C., so that the US President can thank Bond personally. In *Thunderball*, Leiter flies around the islands of the Bahamas as 007 tries to locate two stolen nuclear weapons. In *Diamonds Are Forever*, Leiter provides ample assistance to Bond in Las Vegas and leads a helicopter raid on Blofeld's oil rig off the coast of Baja California, Mexico. *Live And Let Die* sees Leiter assisting 007 in New York City, New Orleans, and the island of San Monique as Bond investigates the activities of Dr. Kananga/Mr. Big. Leiter returns to the series in *The Living Daylights* keeping a sharp eye on American arms dealer Brad Whitaker's activities in Tangier, Morocco. Leiter instructs his two assistants, Ava and Liz, to bring 007 to the CIA's yacht after Bond fakes the assassination of KGB head General Pushkin. Leiter works for the DEA in Key West, Florida, at the time of the events of *Licence To Kill*.

In *Casino Royale*, Bond and Leiter meet for the first time at the casino in Montenegro. Leiter gives Bond $5 million to buy back into the Texas Hold 'Em poker game after Treasury officer Vesper Lynd refuses 007 further funds. In return, the CIA will get to apprehend Le Chiffre once 007 has cleaned him out.

> "What the hell are you trying to do, 007?
> # Start World War III?"
>
> **Felix Leiter to Bond**

DEA AGENT *Leiter hunts Sanchez on his wedding day.*

TEAM PLAYER *Leiter, partnered with his assistants Ava and Liz, reunites with Bond in Tangier, Morocco, to hunt arms dealer Brad Whitaker in* **The Living Daylights.**

LENKIN

APPEARANCE
Octopussy (1983)
STATUS Arrested
CHARACTERISTICS Nervous, extremely jittery art forger
PLAYED BY Peter Porteous

FABERGÉ FAKE *Lenkin worries that an inventory will reveal his and General Orlov's art forgery plot.*

Lenkin is a brilliant forger of Russian jewelry in league with Soviet General Orlov to replace the treasures in the Kremlin Art Repository with near perfect forgeries. Lenkin begs Orlov to retrieve an original Fabergé Egg stolen in transit by agent 009. An unscheduled inventory of the repository will take place in two days time, and Lenkin desperately needs the egg to guarantee that their forgery scheme will not be revealed.

Later, KGB head General Gogol becomes suspicious of General Orlov's activities within the Repository. Gogol brings in Hermitage Museum curator Borchoi to the Repository's vaults. Borchoi determines that the treasures are indeed fakes, leading KGB agents to arrest Lenkin.

LOPEZ, HECTOR

APPEARANCE
Licence To Kill (1989)
STATUS Living; whereabouts unknown
CHARACTERISTICS Adaptable, looks good in a uniform
PLAYED BY Pedro Armendáriz Jr.

Signs and banners around Isthmus City give the impression that Hector Lopez is a popular and effective president. However, he is merely a puppet ruler, completely under the control of drug lord Franz Sanchez, who reminds Hector that "you're only president for life."

After Sanchez is killed by James

Bond, Lopez's reign of power could be in doubt. Instead, Lopez manages to avoid both political upheaval at home and condemnation abroad and remains in power. What is more, he now boasts a trophy girlfriend: the beautiful Lupe Lamora, formerly Sanchez's mistress.

LOTI

APPEARANCE
Licence To Kill (1989)
STATUS Dead; shot by Heller
CHARACTERISTICS Purposeful, strong-willed, unflinching
PLAYED BY Diana Lee-Hsu

Loti is partnered with fellow Hong Kong narcotic agent Kwang who, posing as an Asian drug lord, conducts business with Franz Sanchez in Isthmus City. Loti, specially trained in ninja fighting techniques, attacks Bond when he attempts to assassinate Sanchez.

Loti and Kwang capture Bond and take him to their safe house outside of the city. They fear that Bond's attempt to kill Sanchez will ruin their infiltration of the drug lord's operation. After a force led by Heller, Sanchez's chief of security, destroys part of the house, Heller himself bursts in and shoots Loti dead.

M

APPEARANCE/PLAYED BY

Dr. No (1962), From Russia With Love (1963), Goldfinger (1964), Thunderball (1965), You Only Live Twice (1967), On Her Majesty's Secret Service (1969), Diamonds Are Forever (1971), Live And Let Die (1973), The Man With The Golden Gun (1974), The Spy Who Loved Me (1977), Moonraker (1979) (Bernard Lee); Octopussy (1983), A View To A Kill (1985), The Living Daylights (1987), Licence To Kill (1989) (Robert Brown); GoldenEye (1995), Tomorrow Never Dies (1997), The World Is Not Enough (1999), Die Another Day (2002), Casino Royale (2006) (Judi Dench)

STATUS Living; MI6 headquarters

CHARACTERISTICS Tough, decisive, disapproving, authoritative

M serves as the head of the British Secret Service, known alternately in the films as MI7 and MI6. M sends James Bond on missions from his wood-paneled London office. M stands as the bulwark of the British establishment, a Churchillian figurehead of England's glorious past and continued importance on the world stage.

> "If you carry a 00 number, it means you're **licensed to kill.** Not get killed."
>
> **M to Bond**

Ian Fleming created a stern, almost parental relationship between M and 007 that continues in the films. M recognizes Bond's unique skills and innate talent but barely tolerates his

NEW CHIEF *M (Robert Brown) hands 007 his assignment for Operation Trove in* Octopussy.

often-unorthodox methods and hedonistic lifestyle.

Fleming gave M's real name as Vice-Admiral (ret.) Sir Miles Messervy KCMG in his final novel *The Man With The Golden Gun*. M runs the secret service with naval efficiency, expecting his staff and agents to be available whenever duty calls. His gruff exterior and solid sense of judgment inspire unyielding loyalty from those who work for him, particularly his top agent, 007.

M's final naval appointment was to the battlecruiser HMS *Repulse*, sunk by Japanese torpedoes on December 10 1941. He keeps the ship's bell as the doorbell of his home. M resides in a small Regency manor-house on the edge of Windsor Forest called Quarterdeck.

M's hobby is painting watercolors of England's wild orchids (in the films his hobby is lepidoptery—the study of butterflies and moths). He smokes a pipe and keeps his tobacco in a jar made from an old navy shell. M is a member of two gentleman's clubs: the Seniors, a club for ex-Navy, and Blades. Fleming's M remains a lifelong bachelor.

The character of M was inspired by several figures from Fleming's past. At the top of the list is Rear Admiral John H. Godfrey, Fleming's commanding officer in Naval

Intelligence during World War II. Fleming acquired the idea for the letter M from Sir Mansfield Smith-Cumming, who, as head of the Secret Service, signed documents with the letter "C," a tradition continued by his replacements. Long before Fleming himself became involved in intelligence work, he addressed letters to his mother Eve with the letter "M."

For Bond's first 11 screen missions, M comes very close to Fleming's version of the character. In the film *Dr. No*, it appears that M may be relatively new to his position because he informs 007 that since he became "head of MI7, there's been a 40 per cent drop in 00 operative casualties, and I want it to stay that way."

M does not feature in the film *For Your Eyes Only*, and a new M gives 007 his assignment in *Octopussy*. This

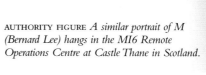

AUTHORITY FIGURE *A similar portrait of M (Bernard Lee) hangs in the MI6 Remote Operations Centre at Castle Thane in Scotland.*

M appears to be Admiral Hargreaves, who a few years earlier served as flag officer of submarines for the Royal Navy. He exhibits mild contempt for 007's reputation and personality and revokes Bond's "licence to kill" in the subsequent eponymous film.

By *GoldenEye*, a new, female M takes charge of MI6. She views Bond as a "sexist, misogynist dinosaur, a relic of the Cold War," but like her predecessors, she sees a use for Bond and his methods.

This M read law at Oxford and has children. She needles Bond about his womanizing reputation. Bond's

friend, senior analyst Bill Tanner, refers to her as "the evil Queen of numbers" for her reliance on statistical analysis.

In *Casino Royale*, M presides over Bond's initiation as an "00" agent, a narrative shift that relaunches both Bond and M in the 21st century. This M appears to be a veteran administrator of MI6 who dates back to the era of the Cold War and claims to miss the autonomy she formerly enjoyed. She lives in a modern secure flat accessed by a private elevator and has a husband or lover. M acts as a guiding force in Bond's painful

transformation from a skilled agent who sometimes fails to see the bigger picture to a hardened operative whose actions are guided by larger objectives.

When Bond sees M after convalescing in hospital in the novel *Dr. No*, he notes: "M was the symbol of normality he had longed for." M does represent a hoped-for normality. In a world filled with wars and upheavals, we all hope somewhere a sensible, reliable figure sits behind a desk addressing the outrages of the day with an even hand and watching over the great game of global espionage with clear gray eyes.

KIDNAPPED *M (Judi Dench) finds herself in deadly peril when Elektra King imprisons her in* The World Is Not Enough.

WISE WORDS *M briefs Bond, a new "00" agent, during his Casino Royale assignment.*

"**I have to know I can trust you and that you know who to trust.**"

M to Bond

MARY

APPEARANCE
Dr. No (1962)
STATUS Dead; brutally shot
CHARACTERISTICS Loyal, efficient
PLAYED BY Dolores Keator

Mary Prescott works as Commander Strangways's secretary in Kingston, Jamaica. After Dr. No's Three Blind Mice assassins eliminate Strangways, they target Mary, who prepares to contact London using an ultra-shortwave radio hidden in a bookcase. The Three Blind Mice fire bullets into Mary's chest, killing her instantly.

In Fleming's novel, her name is Mary Trueblood.

"Being dead doesn't mean one can't be helpful."

Mathis to 007

MATHIS

APPEARANCE
Casino Royale (2006)
STATUS Living
CHARACTERISTICS Charming and confident; a man of the world
PLAYED BY Giancarlo Giannini

René Mathis is 007's contact in Montenegro. Unable to outbid international criminal Le Chiffre for the Chief of Police's services, Mathis arranges for the Chief to be arrested.

Mathis helps Bond, giving him a bugging device that 007 slips into Le Chiffre's inhaler. Mathis also knows the rules of Texas Hold 'Em poker well enough to explain the game to Treasury official Vesper Lynd.

When Bond tries to rescue the kidnapped Vesper, Le Chiffre captures 007 and remarks, "your friend Mathis is really my friend Mathis." After 007 survives Le Chiffre's torture, Bond's suspicions intensify when Mathis tries to extract information from him as he recovers at a private clinic. Two MI6 agents appear behind Mathis, zap him with a taser, and drag him away for interrogation.

In the aftermath of Bond's betrayal by Vesper, M suggests to 007 that Vesper's actions have cleared Mathis of suspicion. Bond tells M to keep "sweating him," implying that he believes Mathis is a double agent, and his loyalties remain unclear.

Mathis appears in the two Fleming novels Casino Royale and From Russia With Love. An agent for the French Deuxième Bureau, he cheers Bond up in the hospital while 007 recovers from being tortured by Le Chiffre.

MAX

APPEARANCE
For Your Eyes Only (1981),
The Living Daylights (1987)
STATUS Living; whereabouts unknown
CHARACTERISTICS Talkative, good
listener, retentive memory
PLAYED BY Krone; voice: Jack Hedley

A Blue and Gold Macaw owned by marine archaeologist Sir Timothy Havelock and his wife, Iona, Max provides vital information to Bond during Operation Undertow. When Max hears 007 mention the "ATAC," he repeats the phrase he heard from Soviet agent Aris Kristatos, "ATAC to St. Cyril's," giving Bond a lead on where to find Kristatos.

MI6 later adopts Max and he appears in the Blayden safe house in The Living Daylights.

PRETTY POLLY *Max loves pistachio nuts, enjoys playing, and has excellent recall.*

MEI-LEI

APPEARANCE
Goldfinger (1964)
STATUS Living; whereabouts unknown
CHARACTERISTICS Highly attentive,
always on hand to help
PLAYED BY Mai Ling

Mei-Lei is the stewardess on Goldfinger's personal Lockheed JetStar. When pilot Pussy Galore flies Bond, who has been abducted, into Friendship Airport, Baltimore, Mei-Lei makes 007 a martini—shaken, not stirred. Pussy tells Mei-Lei to keep an eye on Bond while he changes his clothes, and she spies on him in the airplane lavatory. She reportedly moved to Japan after the collapse of Operation Grand Slam.

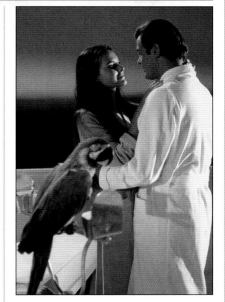

MENDEL

APPEARANCE
Casino Royale (2006)
STATUS Living; whereabouts unknown
CHARACTERISTICS Business-focused
PLAYED BY Ludger Pistor

A jovial Swiss banker representing the Basel Bank, Mendel oversees the transfer of all funds during the poker game at Casino Royale. He arrives with a briefcase computer at the clinic where Bond recovers so that Treasury officer Vesper Lynd can transfer Bond's winnings to the government. M later contacts 007 to ask why the Treasury hasn't received the money. Bond calls Mendel, only to learn that someone is withdrawing the funds. As Bond suspects, it is Vesper Lynd.

MIKLOS, ROSIKA

APPEARANCE
The Living Daylights (1987)
STATUS Living; whereabouts unknown
CHARACTERISTICS Resourceful
PLAYED BY Julie T. Wallace

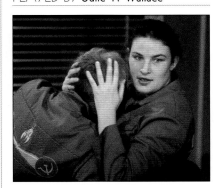

A Trans-Siberian pipeline worker based in Bratislava, Czechoslovakia, Rosika Miklos has assisted British Intelligence in the past. She helps Bond with KGB General Koskov's defection to the West. Rosika distracts the pipeline supervisor's attention with her ample cleavage while the control panel signals numerous alerts as a scouring plug, or "pig," shoots through the line with Koskov inside.

MINISTER OF DEFENCE

APPEARANCE
Tomorrow Never Dies (1997)
STATUS Living; based in London
CHARACTERISTICS Hears both
sides before reaching a decision
PLAYED BY Julian Fellowes

During the early hours of the South China Sea crisis, the Minister of Defence referees a tense debate between warmongering Admiral Roebuck and the more cautious M. He solves the dispute by giving M 48 hours to investigate the sinking of HMS *Devonshire* before Roebuck sends the British fleet into striking distance of the Chinese Air Force.

MISHKIN, DIMITRI

APPEARANCE GoldenEye (1995)
STATUS Dead; killed by Ourumov
CHARACTERISTICS Intelligent,
formidable, speaks his mind
PLAYED BY Tchéky Karyo

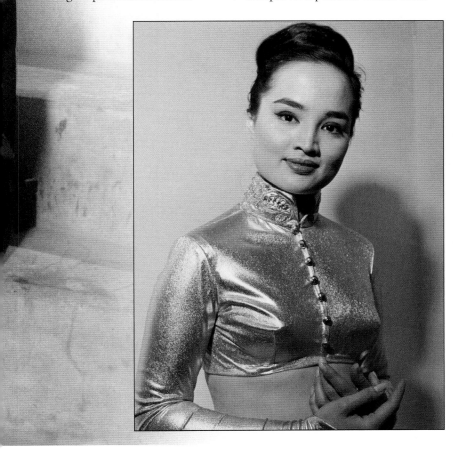

Defence Minister Dimitri Mishkin supervises the meeting where General Ourumov claims Siberian separatists detonated the GoldenEye and conducted the massacre at Severnaya. Mishkin considers this presumptuous.

He later interrogates Natalya Simonova and Bond and discovers Ourumov's connection to the GoldenEye detonation. Ourumov interrupts the interrogation and kills the defenseless minister.

MONEYPENNY, MISS

APPEARANCE/PLAYED BY
Dr. No (1962), From Russia With Love (1963), Goldfinger (1964), Thunderball (1965), You Only Live Twice (1967), On Her Majesty's Secret Service (1969), Diamonds Are Forever (1971), Live And Let Die (1973), The Man With The Golden Gun (1974), The Spy Who Loved Me (1977), Moonraker (1979), For Your Eyes Only (1981), Octopussy (1983), A View To A Kill (1985) (Lois Maxwell); The Living Daylights (1987), Licence To Kill (1989) (Caroline Bliss); GoldenEye (1995), Tomorrow Never Dies (1997), The World Is Not Enough (1999), Die Another Day (2002) (Samantha Bond)

STATUS Living

CHARACTERISTICS Highly efficient, tolerant, loyal, good sense of humor

Miss Moneypenny is the long-serving secretary to James Bond's boss, M. Ian Fleming sums up her character in the novel *Thunderball*, when he reveals that she "often dreamed hopelessly about Bond," but never acted on her feelings. Details Fleming reveals about her are that she has warm lips, doesn't smoke, owns a poodle, and started her career in the Cipher Department.

Moneypenny is not an especially memorable character in the novels— in fact, Fleming gives the secretaries Loelia Ponsonby and later Mary Goodnight more prominence. In the films, Moneypenny often has an important role to play. Her welcoming, easy-going flirtatiousness helps to establish Bond's irresistibility to women and contrasts well with the femme fatales and pliable heroines Bond encounters on his missions. In addition, Moneypenny often delivers important plot exposition.

When Ian Fleming first met Moneypenny actress Lois Maxwell, he said to her, "When I wrote Miss Moneypenny, I envisaged a tall, elegant woman with the most kissable lips in the world, and you, my dear, are the epitome of that dream of mine." Fleming based the character on two particular women— "Paddy" Bennett, who worked with him in Naval Intelligence, and Miss Pettigrew, private secretary to SIS chief

007: What gives?

Moneypenny:
Me, given an ounce of encouragement.

BOND BADINAGE *The verbal jousts between Moneypenny (Lois Maxwell) and 007 were a highlight of many movies, including* On Her Majesty's Secret Service *(left) and* The Man With The Golden Gun *(right).*

Stewart Menzies. In the first draft of *Casino Royale*, Fleming gave her the name of Miss Pettavel or "Petty," but he changed it during revisions, adopting the name Moneypenny from his brother Peter's incomplete novel, *The Sett*. Moneypenny's first name is never revealed in the novels or films, although sometimes Bond nicknames her "Penny."

Moneypenny's relationship with 007 has varied from film to film. In *Dr. No* and *From Russia With Love*, Moneypenny flirts with Bond, but there is nothing hopeless in her attitude. In *Goldfinger*, Moneypenny actively attempts to interest Bond in a relationship, making wistful comments about marriage, a theme repeated when *Goldfinger*'s director, Guy Hamilton, returns to the series with *Diamonds Are Forever*.

While in *You Only Live Twice*, Bond is nothing short of dismissive when Moneypenny urges him to say, "I love you" to her (a recognition code, as it turns out). In *On Her Majesty's Secret Service*, there is genuine emotion between the two. She rewrites Bond's letter of resignation and, at 007's wedding, Bond and Moneypenny share a look that conveys both tenderness and admiration.

In *Live And Let Die*, a sisterly Moneypenny helps to hide Bond's latest paramour to prevent M discovering her. This marks the

> ## "Moneypenny, what would I do without you?"
> ### 007

When Timothy Dalton took over as Bond, and Caroline Bliss became Moneypenny, the character found herself with a hair bun, a pencil behind the ear, librarian glasses, and a hopeless crush on 007. With Pierce Brosnan's introduction in *GoldenEye*, Samantha Bond's Moneypenny returned the character to that of Bond's sexual equal, willing to flirt as much on her terms as on his. In *Tomorrow Never Dies*, she teases 007 about him being asked to "pump" a former girlfriend "for information;" however, in *The World Is Not Enough*, she is dropping hints about marriage. In *Die Another Day*, Moneypenny finally manages to be alone with Bond, but only in virtual reality.

Moneypenny's entire character has been predicated on the premise of unrequited desire. Any relationship she may have with Bond can only be imagined by her as she sees Bond

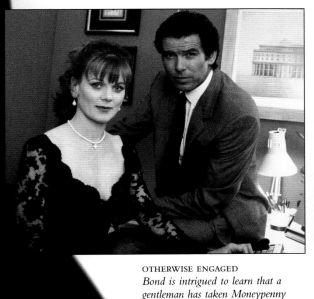

OTHERWISE ENGAGED
Bond is intrigued to learn that a gentleman has taken Moneypenny (Samantha Bond) to the theater in GoldenEye.

UP CLOSE BUT IMPERSONAL *Moneypenny finally gets a chance to live out her fantasy of a wild romantic fling with Bond, but only courtesy of Q's latest virtual reality gadget.*

point where Moneypenny's relationship with Bond changes, and the flirting temporarily stops. In *Octopussy*, Moneypenny has a younger assistant, Penelope Smallbone.

sweeping in and out on his adventures. She is, in many ways, a representative of the audience—an ordinary person, intrigued and seduced by the elegant secret agent whom she only occasionally encounters.

MUNGER, SIR DONALD

APPEARANCE
Diamonds Are Forever (1971)
STATUS Unknown
CHARACTERISTICS Business-minded
PLAYED BY Laurence Naismith

Sir Donald Munger serves as chairman of the Diamond Syndicate, which controls most of the legal diamond trading in the world. Sir Donald raises concerns with the Prime Minister regarding the increase in smuggling from South African mines, urging the British Secret Service to become involved.

NEVADA SHERIFF

APPEARANCE
Diamonds Are Forever (1971)
STATUS Unknown
CHARACTERISTICS Out of his depth
PLAYED BY Leroy Hollis

WW Techtronics security contacts the Clark County, Nevada Sheriff's office after Bond steals a moonbuggy. The Sheriff and numerous Las Vegas police cars pursue Bond as he drives them in circles in a Mustang Mach 1. After numerous crashes, the Sheriff finds he has the only remaining drivable car. He tries to follow Bond when the Mustang tilts onto two wheels to drive through a narrow ally, but the Sheriff merely flips his car over. He later transfers to the Louisiana State Police.

NIKOLI, CAPT.

APPEARANCE
The World Is Not Enough (1999)
STATUS Dead; poisoned
CHARACTERISTICS Too trusting
PLAYED BY Justus Von Dohnanyi

Nikoli, casino and caviar factory owner Valentin Zukovsky's nephew, is captain of a nuclear submarine in the Russian Navy. Billionaire heiress Elektra King pays Valentin $1 million to have Nikoli smuggle Russian machinery to Maiden's Tower in the Bosphoros. Ex-KGB assassin Renard poisons Nikoli and his crew, hides stolen plutonium in the submarine's reactor, and pilots it into Istanbul.

OLYMPE

APPEARANCE On Her Majesty's Secret Service (1969)
STATUS Living; whereabouts unknown
CHARACTERISTICS Skilled at chess
PLAYED BY Virginia North

Olympe is the secretary, lover, and chess opponent of Marc Ange Draco, head of the Union Corse. She is aware of most of his dealings, including trying to make Bond marry his daughter, Tracy. At Draco's birthday party, Olympe hints to Tracy that Draco is arranging something. Olympe's verbal slip causes Tracy to confront Draco and demand he give 007 information about Blofeld without obligation.

PEPPER, SHERIFF J. W.

APPEARANCE
Live And Let Die (1973), The Man With The Golden Gun (1974)
STATUS Living
CHARACTERISTICS Overbearing; uncouth
PLAYED BY Clifton James

Sheriff J. W. Pepper spends his afternoons ticketing speeders and taking care of local problems, like shooting Mrs. Pearson's rabid dog. When he catches Harlem gangster Mr. Big's henchman Adam in his car trying to cut off Bond's escape in a boat, Pepper relishes arresting a black man a little too much.

Pepper is unprepared for the arrival of Bond and the boats giving chase. Bond leaps his craft over Pepper's head and another boat crashes into Pepper's car. A third boat sails overhead, letting Adam escape. Pepper commandeers a State Trooper car, coordinates law enforcement efforts, and yells and screams at everyone to no avail. He enlists his brother-in-law Billy Bob but Adam steals Billy Bob's jet boat.

When Pepper catches up with Bond, he discovers that 007 is a British secret agent working with the cooperation of the CIA. Stunned at the destruction left by Bond, he asks, "A secret agent? On whose side?"

Bond meets Pepper again while chasing Francisco Scaramanga in Bangkok. Pepper first sees Bond when he tours with his wife, Maybel. Later, while improbably car shopping, Pepper finds himself in a stolen AMC Hornet with Bond. He makes for an enthusiastic passenger when Bond spiral-jumps across a canal. Unfortunately, Bond fails to catch Scaramanga, and the Thai police arrest a protesting Pepper.

A RELAXING HOLIDAY J.W. and Maybel Pepper (Jay Sidow) sail through the Bangkok klongs.

"What are you? **Some kinda doomsday machine, boy?**"

Sheriff Pepper to 007

SENSITIVE TO NOISE *Pepper covers his ears as Bond prepares to shoot off the lock on the doors of Scaramanga's garage in* The Man With The Golden Gun.

PINDER

APPEARANCE
Thunderball (1965)
STATUS Living; whereabouts unknown
CHARACTERISTICS Businesslike, calm
PLAYED BY Earl Cameron

TEAM PLAYER *Bond and Pinder discuss his mission to infiltrate Largo's house, Palmyra.*

Pinder, a native Bahamian, works for the British Secret Service in Nassau. He provides a location headquarters for Bond in the basement of his shop, which sells boating supplies. He coordinates with local officials, such as the governor, to provide Bond with the material and logistical support he needs.

PLEYDELL-SMITH

APPEARANCE
Dr. No (1962)
STATUS Living; whereabouts unknown
CHARACTERISTICS Likes bridge and pipe smoking
PLAYED BY Louis Blaazer

The Principal Secretary at Government House in Kingston, Pleydell-Smith offers assistance to 007. Unfortunately for him, his secretary, Miss Taro, works as a Dr. No minion who leaks vital information from his office.

At the end of the novel, Pleydell-Smith's wife, Betty, agrees to take Honey Rider, a beautiful Jamaican shell diver, under her wing and perhaps to help her acquire a job at The Jamaica Institute.

PRIME MINISTER

APPEARANCE
For Your Eyes Only (1981)
STATUS Living
CHARACTERISTICS World leader
PLAYED BY Janet Brown

Newly-elected Prime Minister Margaret Thatcher calls 007 to congratulate him on completing Operation Undertow. The call is placed to Bond's speaker Seiko watch on the *Triana*, where Bond and marine biologist Melina Havelock prepare for a moonlight swim. Bond leaves his watch next to Melina's talkative macaw, Max, who tells the Prime Minister to "give us a kiss." Thatcher blushes at "Bond's" flirtations.

PUSHKIN, GENERAL LEONID

APPEARANCE
The Living Daylights (1987)
STATUS Living; whereabouts unknown
CHARACTERISTICS Capable, tough
PLAYED BY John Rhys-Davies

When General Gogol departs as the head of the KGB to become head of the Foreign Service, Pushkin takes over his role. What Pushkin doesn't count on is KGB General Georgi Koskov, who defects to the West and informs the British that Pushkin has begun operation *smiert spionam* to eliminate western agents.

M orders 007 to kill Pushkin, but Bond, who knows that the KGB head is "tough and resourceful," confronts him at the Hotel Ile De France in Tangier, Morocco. Pushkin convinces Bond of his innocence, and they plan to turn the tables on Koskov and his ally Whitaker. Bond fakes Pushkin's death and foils

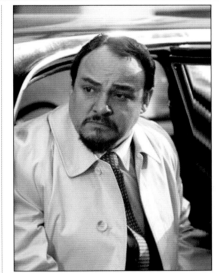

KGB CALLING *Pushkin arrives to take Kara Milovy in for questioning.*

Koskov's plan in Afghanistan. Pushkin later arrives at Whitaker's estate, arrests Koskov, and orders him sent back to Moscow.

PUSS-FELLER

APPEARANCE
Dr. No (1962)
STATUS Living; whereabouts unknown
CHARACTERISTICS Well-built, immaculate, affable
PLAYED BY Lester Prendergast

Puss-Feller owns a restaurant-nightclub on Kingston Harbour, Jamaica, where performers such as Byron Lee and The Dragoneers sing local hits like "Jump Up Jamaica." According to Bond's guide, Quarrel, Puss-Feller "wrestles alligators." In Fleming's novel, he acquires his name from wrestling an octopus and escaping with his life.

COLD LOOK *Puss-Feller is hostile to Bond, until put wise by the CIA's Felix Leiter.*

Q

STATUS Living; spends most of his
time at MI6 headquarters

CHARACTERISTICS An endlessly
inventive scientific genius

Q runs that rarified section of
British Intelligence that transforms
the ordinary into the lethal, the
pedestrian into the remarkable, and
the insignificant into the life-
saving. Q, also known as Major
Boothroyd, stands as proof of the
superiority of British ingenuity and
craftsmanship. His initial stands for
Quartermaster, but Q's duties reach
far beyond merely dispensing gear.
Q Branch runs a full research and
development operation of
monumental scale.

Q's origins can be traced to
World War II, where Ian Fleming
often had to liaise with the office
of Charles Frasier-Smith who
provided inventive ways to conceal
maps, compasses and guns to
those moving behind enemy
lines. Fleming mentions Q
briefly in the novel *Casino
Royale*, with M instructing
Bond, "Talk to Q about
rooms and trains, and any
equipment you want."

The cinematic character's
origins begin with the novel
Dr. No, where Fleming
introduces the Armourer, aka
Major Boothroyd. Fleming
based the Major on
Glasgow gun expert
Geoffrey
Boothroyd who
wrote the
author to

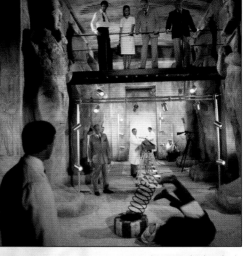

HIDDEN TREASURES Q *(Desmond Llewelyn)*
*gives Bond, Anya Amasova, General
Gogol, and M a tour of his
Egyptian facilities in* The Spy
Who Loved Me.

" I never
joke about my
work, 007. "
Q

complain about Bond's use of a Beretta .25, which he termed "a lady's gun." The filmmakers reproduce this scene in the first Bond film. With *From Russia With Love*, the filmmakers wished to echo the scene from *Dr. No* where 007 receives equipment in M's office before leaving on his mission. In that novel, Bond uses a trick

HANDY LUGGAGE
Q's suitcase is filled with gadgets to assist Bond in Isthmus City in Licence To Kill.

briefcase, and the filmmakers asked Richard Maibaum to script a scene where Major Boothroyd presents this to 007. When actor Peter Burton proved unavailable, Desmond Llewelyn stepped into the role, which was re-christened Q in the dialogue (but not the credits). Only KGB agent Anya Amasova refers to Q as Major Boothroyd in the films.

In *Goldfinger*, Q's irritation with 007 for destroying his equipment is clear. He displays his satisfaction with his ever-more lethal inventions. Bond treats him as a slightly dotty genius. The relationship between the pair

remains frosty when Q travels to the Bahamas (*Thunderball*) and Japan (*You Only Live Twice*) to equip 007 with customized gadgetry. Q attends Bond's wedding in Portugal, finally demonstrating affection for the man who has used his equipment to help save the world.

As the scope of Bond's adventures widened, so did the scope of Q's operation. Q Branch research labs servicing agents in Egypt, Brazil, and India hum with activity. Q's affection for 007 grows to the point that, in *Licence To Kill*, he travels to Isthmus City with a bag of gadgets to aid Bond on a private mission of vengeance.

Major Boothroyd retired in 1999, turning his department and title over to an assistant Bond dubbed R. The new Q proves to be just as effective in developing cutting-edge gadgetry and even more effective at topping Bond's quips with withering observations.

Q does not appear in *Casino Royale*, only the second film not to have any character called Q or Major Boothroyd.

GONE FISHING *Q manages to fit in a spot of relaxation while waiting for Bond in* Octopussy.

GADGET CENTRAL
Q *(John Cleese) shows 007 the room where he stores relics from past missions in* Die Another Day.

Whenever James Bond enters Q's MI6 laboratory, he always finds the ingenious inventor and his technicians hard at work experimenting with new and intriguing gadget prototypes . Below is just a small sample of the many technical wonders Q has devised over the years which have yet to be put to deadly purpose "in the field."

BLAST OFF! *Q's leg cast conceals a rocket launcher.*

DON'T LOSE YOUR HEAD
Q's technician demonstrates exploding bolos in MI6's monastery headquarters.

AN EAR FOR MUSIC
Q always has his finger on the pulse of contemporary culture, as demonstrated by this ghetto-blaster rocket launcher.

SLEEPING SOMBRERO
A gaucho taking a siesta splits in two, revealing a firing gun.

PIPE DOWN
In Castle Thane, Q's technician fires bagpipes that house a machine gun and a flamethrower.

SMASHING, Q!
Q's assistant Smithers demonstrates how his fake plaster cast can take out the enemy.

QUARREL

APPEARANCE
Dr. No (1962)
STATUS Dead; torched
CHARACTERISTICS Excellent
seaman, good navigator
PLAYED BY John Kitzmuller

Cayman Islander Quarrel, the most expensive charter fisherman in Kingston, Jamaica, provides vital help to 007 during his mission to investigate the murder of British secret service representative Strangways.

Quarrel works with Strangways to gather rock samples from nearby islands, including Crab Key, although Quarrel dislikes traveling there. Friends that visited never returned. Quarrel believes the local legend that a fire-breathing dragon roams Crab Key's swamps.

After the murder of Strangways, Quarrel meets CIA agent Felix Leiter, and the pair attempts to tail James Bond when he arrives in Jamaica. Soon, Quarrel, Leiter, and Quarrel's friend Puss-Feller learn 007's true identity, and they all join forces. Quarrel even offers to break the arm of a photographer who snaps a photo of 007. Discovering the rocks from Crab Key are radioactive, Bond requests that Quarrel take him to the island. Quarrel drinks heavily from a jug of rum during the journey and, after the pair link up with Honey Ryder, Quarrel is nervous about heading into the island's swamps. There he confronts the "dragon," a swamp vehicle equipped with a flame thrower, which burns him to death.

Quarrel appears in the Fleming novels Live And Let Die and Dr. No.

QUARREL JR.

APPEARANCE
Live And Let Die (1973)
STATUS Living
CHARACTERISTICS Even tempered, reliable, loyal
PLAYED BY Roy Stewart

Quarrel Jr., the son of Bond's Cayman Islander boatman in Dr. No, aids 007 in gaining access to remote parts of the island of San Monique during his investigation into the murders of three British agents.

Bond has known Quarrel Jr. for years, referring to him as "the man who shares my hairbrush."

007's CARIBBEAN CONTACT Quarrel Jr. aboard his fishing boat.

Quarrel adopts the façade of a lazy fisherman but works as a liaison agent for 007. He maintains communications gear and weapons behind a hidden door on his boat. Quarrel reveals the location of Solitaire's house to Bond and aids in 007's nighttime hang-glider incursions into Dr. Kananga's territory. He waits for Bond at a dock when 007 escapes with Solitaire, taking the pair to Santa Mina so they can catch a flight to New Orleans. When Bond and Leiter return to San Monique, Quarrel Jr. preps 007's shark gun and scuba gear, helps him get ashore to save Solitaire, and plants the incendiary bombs that destroy Kananga's poppies. He harbors no superstitions, urging Bond to shoot Baron Samedi, the voodoo god of cemeteries, "right between the eyes." Quarrel Jr.'s father performs a similar role in Bond's mission in the Ian Fleming novel.

RAOUL

APPEARANCE
Die Another Day (2002)
STATUS Living; residing in Havana
CHARACTERISTICS Loves his country and will never betray it
PLAYED BY Emilio Echevarria

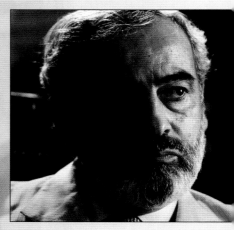

Raoul is a British sleeper agent in Havana, Cuba, whom Bond "rudely awakens" after thirty years when he arrives at his cigar factory. He tells Raoul's assistant that he's there "to pick up some delectados." The delectado cigar, thanks to the slow-burning Volado tobacco, never burns out, just like a sleeper.

Raoul provides Bond with vital information regarding North Korean terrorist Zao, who has traveled to Dr. Alvarez's gene therapy clinic on the island of Los Organos. Raoul loans Bond "a fast car"—a 1957 Ford Fairlane—to travel there as well as a book entitled Birds Of The West Indies and a pair of binoculars to help him with his cover as an ornithologist. Later, Raoul determines that a diamond from Zao's bullet pendant is chemically identical to African conflict diamonds. He helps Bond identify the diamond as belonging to Gustav Graves.

ROBINSON

APPEARANCE
Tomorrow Never Dies (1997),
The World Is Not Enough (1999),
Die Another Day (2002)
STATUS Living; whereabouts unknown
CHARACTERISTICS Statuesque, loyal
PLAYED BY Colin Salmon

Charles Robinson works as a Chief of Staff for M and is never far from her side.

In *Tomorrow Never Dies,* it is Robinson, from his post in the MI6 situation room, who communicates with 007 while Bond is on an anti-terrorism mission in the Khyber Pass. Robinson later informs Bond of media mogul Elliot Carver's background as M's limousine races through the London streets.

Robinson returns in *The World Is Not Enough,* where he briefs 007 and other MI6 agents at Castle Thane regarding the terrorist bombing at London's MI6 headquarters. Later in the same film, he escorts M to villain Elektra King's residence in Baku when King requests her protection.

In *Die Another Day,* Robinson plays a key role in Bond's virtual reality shooting gallery exercise through the corridors of MI6. As Robinson and Bond enter M's office, unidentified enemy agents shoot Robinson dead. Thankfully, it's only a simulation. He is later present at a US Command Bunker in South Korea where he briefs 007 and Jinx on the staged coup in North Korea.

RODNEY

APPEARANCE The Man With The Golden Gun (1974)
STATUS Dead; shot in the head with a golden bullet
CHARACTERISTICS A gruff old-style gangster out of his element
PLAYED BY Marc Lawrence

Rodney, a hood from Las Vegas, comes to a private island off the south-eastern coast of China at the

behest of Nick Nack. He hopes to kill the legendary assassin, Francisco Scaramanga for a fee. Rodney finds himself a live pawn in a training exercise for Scaramanga, the million-dollar-a-shot killer. When Rodney's first shot misses Scaramanga, Rodney becomes lost inside Scaramanga's fun house-like maze, designed to confuse and unnerve. As Rodney pursues Scaramanga, Nick Nack teases his boss, further confirming for Rodney the uneasy feeling that his grim fate is sealed. Scaramanga kills Rodney with a single shot to the head, using his custom component golden gun.

ROEBUCK, ADMIRAL

APPEARANCE
Tomorrow Never Dies (1997)
STATUS Living; whereabouts unknown
CHARACTERISTICS Not a fan of the spy business
PLAYED BY Geoffrey Palmer

Extreme patriot British Admiral Roebuck engages in a heated argument with M over firing a cruise missile from HMS *Chester* into the Khyber Pass, taking out half of the world's terrorists at an arms swap-meet. Although M wishes to give 007 more time to investigate, an overeager Roebuck orders the missile launched. His impatience nearly leads to disaster. Two nuclear torpedoes are among the arms on offer, and a tragedy is only averted when Bond removes them before the missile strikes. Later, Roebuck favors war against China after HMS *Devonshire* sinks at the supposed hands of the Chinese. M, however, again errs on the side of caution and asks the Minister of Defence for permission to investigate. Roebuck and M lock horns, with Roebuck barking at M, "Sometimes I don't think you have the balls for this job." M wittily retorts, "Perhaps. But the advantage is I don't have to think with them all the time."

> "Thank you, M. We've seen enough. This is now a military operation."
>
> **Admiral Roebuck**

RUBAVITCH

APPEARANCE
The Living Daylights (1987)
STATUS Living; whereabouts unknown
CHARACTERISTICS Elegant, discreet, dedicated
PLAYED BY Virginia Hey

Rubavitch is the beautiful mistress of KGB chief General Leonid Pushkin, whom she accompanies to the North African Trade Convention in Tangier, Morocco. She is present in the room as Bond confronts Pushkin about the KGB plot *smiert spionam* (Death to Spies). When Pushkin alerts his bodyguard that he is in trouble, Bond partially disrobes Rubavitch, distracting the guard long enough to knock him unconscious. When Leonid seemingly dies, Rubavitch displays enormous grief but is then relieved to find he's alive and well.

RUBLEVITCH

APPEARANCES
The Spy Who Loved Me (1977), For Your Eyes Only (1981), Octopussy (1983)
STATUS Living in a free world
CHARACTERISTICS Dedicated to her boss
PLAYED BY Eva Rueber-Staier

Rublevitch is the secretary to General Gogol in Moscow. In *The Spy Who Loved Me*, their relationship is strictly business. However, in *For Your Eyes Only*, she sits on the edge of his desk and he kisses her hand, showing their relationship has deepened. In *Octopussy*, Gogol admires Rublevitch's striking figure in the Moscow War Room as she walks past to deliver a message to General Orlov.

SADRUDDIN

APPEARANCE
Octopussy (1983)
STATUS Living; whereabouts unknown
CHARACTERISTICS Pleasant, friendly
PLAYED BY Albert Moses

This senior Indian gentleman runs the Station I, India office of MI6. Vijay, his main assistant, becomes 007's principal aide in Udaipur, India. Sadruddin books 007 into the Shiv Niwas Palace Hotel. He later provides Bond with the little information that is available on the mysterious woman Octopussy.

In early drafts, Sadruddin played a more central role in Bond's investigation, but the character of Vijay took over many of the field duties.

SAIDA

APPEARANCE The Man With The Golden Gun (1974)
STATUS Living
CHARACTERISTICS Skilled dancer
PLAYED BY Carmen Sautoy

The key to finding Scaramanga lies in Beirut belly dancer Saida's navel. In 1969, Saida was making love to agent 002 when he was shot. She later obtained the distinctive golden bullet and placed this "lucky charm" in her navel. Bond removes the bullet with his teeth just as gangsters hit him, causing him to swallow it.

SAUNDERS

APPEARANCE
The Living Daylights (1987)
STATUS Dead; killed by Necros
CHARACTERISTICS Diligent
PLAYED BY Thomas Wheatley

Head of Section V, Vienna, Saunders is furious when Bond refuses to kill Kara Milovy, KGB General Koskov's sniper. However, he comes to appreciate Bond's methods and supplies information about Koskov and arms dealer Brad Whitaker. Saunders is killed by a booby-trap set by Whitaker's henchman Necros. Bond finds a balloon inscribed with the Russian words smiert spionam ("death to spies") near his body.

SCOTT, COLONEL

APPEARANCE
Moonraker (1979)
STATUS Living; whereabouts unknown
CHARACTERISTICS Excellent soldier
PLAYED BY Michael Marshall

When Bond alerts NASA to the presence of a huge space station orbiting earth, the US launches a contingent of Space Marines to attack, led by Colonel Scott. A no-nonsense soldier, Scott leads his men into a battle in space, fighting aerospace magnate Hugo Drax's troops with laser weapons. Despite heavy losses, Scott manages to get his men on board the space station. Their assault causes so much damage that the station begins to disintegrate. Scott retreats with his men, and later rescues Jaws and his girlfriend, Dolly, as they float in space.

SFPD CAPTAIN

APPEARANCE
A View To A Kill (1985)
STATUS Living; whereabouts unknown
CHARACTERISTICS Blustering
PLAYED BY Joe Flood

San Francisco's Police Captain arrests Bond for the murders of corrupt bureaucrat W. G. Howe and CIA agent Chuck Lee, but Bond escapes in a fire truck with geologist Stacey Sutton. The captain and his men give chase, but Bond evades capture. Later, the captain is so shocked to see Bond hanging from an airship that he crashes his new police car.

SHAH, KAMRAN

APPEARANCE
The Living Daylights (1987)
STATUS Living; whereabouts unknown
CHARACTERISTICS Charming, well-spoken, dedicated to his cause
PLAYED BY Art Malik

Kamran Shah is an Oxford-educated mujaheddin rebel who is Deputy Commander of the Eastern District in Afghanistan during the Soviet-Afghan War.

Soviet troops capture Shah as he reconnoiters Colonel Feyador's airbase in preparation for a raid. The base's jailer informs Shah that he will be executed the following day. Thankfully, Bond rescues Shah, and he takes Bond and his companion, Kara Milovy, to his headquarters.

The next morning, Shah allows Bond and Kara to ride with him as he escorts Afghan drug dealers the Snow Leopard Brotherhood to an opium-for-diamonds trade with General Koskov. Shah doesn't realize until almost too late that Koskov plans to purchase American high-tech weapons and use them against the mujaheddin. Shah helps Bond obtain an explosive device and a timer and raids Colonel Feyador's airbase, killing Feyador in the process. As Shah and his men, on horseback, flee a convoy of Soviet armored vehicles, Bond drops a bomb from a cargo plane. The explosion destroys the convoy as they cross a bridge, to the great relief of Shah and his men. Bond then destroys the aircraft, which is loaded with Koskov's opium.

Unfortunately, Kamran Shah and his men arrive too late to witness Kara's triumphant cello concert in Vienna because, laden with weapons, they have had "trouble at the airport."

Kara: James is trapped. You must help him!
Shah: He'll have to take his chances.
Kara: You can't leave him. You owe him your life!

SHARKY

APPEARANCE
Licence To Kill (1989)
STATUS Dead
CHARACTERISTICS Kind-hearted, courageous, and loyal to his friends
PLAYED BY Frank McRae

Based in Key West, Florida, Sharky is a fisherman friend of DEA agent Felix Leiter. He presents Felix and his new bride, Della, with a box of hand-tied fishing lures as a wedding present. He later refuses to believe police detective Rasmussen's claim that a chainsaw removed his good

friend Leiter's left leg below the knee, informing Bond that the culprit was a shark.

Sharky helps Bond raid drug smuggler Milton Krest's marine warehouse in Key West and helps Bond to get the better of corrupt DEA agent Ed Killifer. He pilots his boat, the *Pa Ja Ma*, off the Cay Sol Bank, Bahamas, to enable Bond to get as close as possible to Krest's ship, the *Wavekrest*. However, while Bond sneaks aboard, two of Krest's henchmen, Clive and Oliver, kill Sharky and hang him over the stern of his boat suspended between two dead sharks.

LAUGHING OFF MURDER *The cruel death of Sharky underlines the viciousness of Milton Krest's smuggling racket.*

SIERRA

APPEARANCE
Goldfinger (1964)
STATUS Living; whereabouts unknown
CHARACTERISTICS Suspiciously still while everyone panics
PLAYED BY Raymond Young

Sierra is James Bond's contact in Mexico. He meets 007 at the El Scorpio bar and congratulates Bond on destroying drug baron Mr. Ramirez's heroin lab. Sierra recommends that Bond should not return to his hotel as Ramirez's men will be watching it. He suggests that 007 leave on a plane to Miami, Florida within the hour. Bond informs him that he will be on the flight, but only after he has taken care of some unfinished business.

SIMMONS, MR.

APPEARANCE Goldfinger (1964)
STATUS Living; whereabouts unknown
CHARACTERISTICS Gullible
PLAYED BY Austin Willis

Mr. Simmons plays gin rummy with Goldfinger for one week on the pool deck of the Fontainebleau Hotel for stakes as high as $5 per point. Unaware Goldfinger is cheating, Simmons continues to lose, racking up losses of $10,000. Bond quickly deduces Goldfinger's method of cheating and convinces Goldfinger to lose $15,000 back to Simmons.

In the Fleming novel, Goldfinger cheats Mr. Du Pont at canasta. Du Pont, who knew Bond from Casino Royale, asks 007 to figure out how.

SMALLBONE, PENELOPE

APPEARANCE Octopussy (1983)
STATUS Living; working somewhere in the MI6 secretarial pool
CHARACTERISTICS Former potential replacement for Miss Moneypenny
PLAYED BY Michaela Clavell

Penelope Smallbone is Miss Moneypenny's assistant and the second assistant to M. Moneypenny, who claims to have described Bond to Smallbone in "nauseating detail," assures Smallbone that a bouquet of flowers is all she will ever receive from Bond. Smallbone is never seen again; presumably she transferred to another MI6 department.

SMITHERS, COLONEL

APPEARANCE Goldfinger (1964)
STATUS Living; whereabouts unknown
CHARACTERISTICS Influential figure
PLAYED BY Richard Vernon

Colonel Smithers is head of the Bank of England. Smithers suspects Goldfinger is smuggling large quantities of gold out of Britain and wants the British Secret Service to investigate. To use as bait to catch Goldfinger, Smithers loans Bond a gold ingot worth £5,000 from a Nazi hoard at the bottom of Lake Toplitz Salzkammergut, Austria. Smithers also gives Bond the opportunity to display his knowledge of brandy, to M's irritation.

SNOW LEOPARD BROTHERHOOD

APPEARANCE
The Living Daylights (1987)
STATUS Living; whereabouts unknown
CHARACTERISTICS Tough traders
PLAYED BY Tony Cyrus (Chief)

The Snow Leopard Brotherhood is the biggest group of opium traders in the Golden Crescent, a mountainous area in Asia. The chief trades opium for diamonds with Soviet General Koskov and arms dealer Brad Whitaker. It is the chief's biggest deal since the Soviet invasion. According to Bond, his opium is "worth half a billion dollars on the streets of New York."

STRANGWAYS, JOHN

APPEARANCE Dr. No (1962)

STATUS Dead; murdered by the Three Blind Mice

CHARACTERISTICS Likes fishing and bridge; his routines are too easy to follow

PLAYED BY Timothy Moxon

Commander John Strangways is "the chief Secret Service agent for the Caribbean." Three men, disguised as blind beggars, gun down Strangways as he leaves The Queen's Club in Kingston. They then kill his secretary, Mary, and dispose of the bodies. Their disappearances lead Bond to Jamaica to investigate.

Strangways appears in the Ian Fleming novels *Live And Let Die* and *Dr. No*. He is described as a "tall lean man with a black patch over the right eye..." He drives a Sunbeam Alpine in the novels, which is the car Bond drives to Miss Taro's house in the film.

STREET URCHIN

APPEARANCE

The Man With The Golden Gun (1974)

STATUS Unknown

CHARACTERISTICS Industrious and persistent

PLAYED BY Unknown

A street urchin, or more exactly a klong urchin, pesters tourists by selling carved wooden elephants on the canals of Bangkok. Bond, pursued by Chula and other martial arts students, finds the longtail boat he has stolen slowing to a crawl.

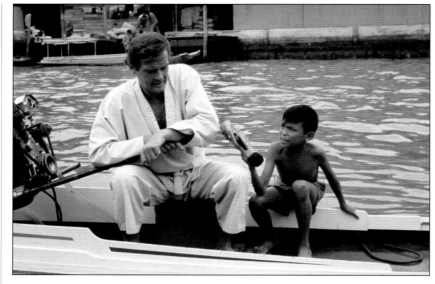

When the urchin pulls himself aboard, Bond offers him 20,000 baht to make his engine run faster. The urchin simply opens the fuel line and awaits his riches. Bond does not pay, but instead shoves the annoying child overboard into the klong as he speeds away.

STROMBERG'S ASSISTANT

APPEARANCE

The Spy Who Loved Me (1977)

STATUS Dead; eaten by a shark

CHARACTERISTICS Thankfully willing to betray her psychopathic boss

PLAYED BY Marilyn Galsworthy

The personal assistant of megalomaniac Karl Stromberg tries to sell the submarine tracking system developed by Dr. Bechmann and Professor Markovitz to a world power behind her boss's back. Stromberg announces his knowledge of the plot but pretends to be unaware of his assistant's involvement. While she stands in his elevator, he pushes a button that drops her into a tank, where a shark eats her.

QUICK SALE *A boy tries to sell Bond a carved elephant, but 007 has no time to lose.*

STRUTTER, HAROLD

APPEARANCE

Live And Let Die (1973)

STATUS Dead; laid to rest in New Orleans

CHARACTERISTICS Investigative mind

PLAYED BY Lon Satton

CIA agent Harold Strutter meets James Bond in New York. Strutter follows 007 to Harlem, then locates him in a back alley behind a Fillet of Soul restaurant. He explains that the gangster Mr. Big tracked Bond's movements, and only Big can pull together that kind of "black muscle in this town." Strutter travels to New Orleans to keep a close watch on the Fillet of Soul restaurant in the French Quarter, but suffers the same fate as British agent Hamilton when a faux jazz funeral passes by and becomes his own.

TALBOT, CMDR.

APPEARANCE

The Spy Who Loved Me (1977)

STATUS Dead

CHARACTERISTICS Ready for combat

PLAYED BY Bryan Marshall

Commander Talbot captains the HMS *Ranger*, one of Britain's four nuclear submarines. When the submarine encounters a strange phenomenon underwater, Talbot surfaces and cannot believe what he sees: a supertanker's bow open and ready to swallow his craft. Talbot remains a prisoner until James Bond frees him. He leads a raid on the ship's armory, providing weapons to the British, Soviet, and US sailors. A *Liparus* crew member kills him with a hand grenade during the resultant battle.

TANAKA, TIGER

APPEARANCE
You Only Live Twice (1967)
STATUS A closely-guarded secret
CHARACTERISTICS Professional,
friendly; a skilled ninja
PLAYED BY Tetsuro Tamba

Tiger Tanaka serves as head of the
Japanese SIS and provides vital
support to James Bond on his
mission to stop spacecraft from
disappearing in orbit and prevent
World War III.

Tiger has 007 delivered to his
office via a hidden chute beneath a
subway tunnel in Tokyo. Tanaka
works closely with Bond to uncover
Ernst Stavro Blofeld's plot to abduct
US and Soviet spacecraft, offering
Bond intelligence analysis of
materials obtained from Mr. Osato's
safe, the services of one of his top
female agents, Aki, as well as material
and logistical support on his mission.
He trains Bond as a modern ninja
and outfits him with weapons and
gear. When 007 goes undercover as a
Japanese fisherman, Tanaka arranges a
fake marriage with his local agent
Kissy Suzuki on an island of Ama
fishermen and pearl divers. He poses
as a local peasant farmer, bringing his
ninja fighters to the area to support
007. When Kissy returns to the Ama
village to report that Bond found a
secret rocket base inside a mainland
volcano, Tanaka leads the ninja
attack on Blofeld's headquarters
and skillfully fights the
SPECTRE guards and
technicians during the assault.
Tanaka reveals little of his
past in the film, but Ian
Fleming's novel fills many
gaps. Tanaka studied at
Trinity College, Oxford
before World War II,
gaining a first in
Philosophy, Politics and
Economics. He
worked as a spy for
Japan, serving as an
assistant naval
attaché for the
London embassy. During
World War II, he worked as
personal aide to Admiral
Ohnishi, the founder of the
official Kamikaze Corps, which
Tanaka joined before the
war ended.

TANNER

APPEARANCE The Man With The
Golden Gun (1974), For Your Eyes
Only (1981), GoldenEye (1995),
The World Is Not Enough (1999)
STATUS Living; MI6 headquarters
CHARACTERISTICS Learned, stuffy
PLAYED BY Michael Goodliffe (The
Man With The Golden Gun), James
Villiers (For Your Eyes Only), Michael
Kitchen (GoldenEye, The World Is
Not Enough)

M'S RIGHT HAND MAN *Tanner deputizes for
M during Operation Undertow.*

Bill Tanner first appears briefly in
The Man With The Golden Gun as the
Chief of Staff, listening to Bond
discuss Scaramanga's background.

He next surfaces in *For Your Eyes
Only*, when M is on leave, to give
007 his Operation Undertow
assignment. He becomes frustrated
with Bond when he learns that 007
was unable to question henchman
Gonzales because Melina Havelock
shot him with a crossbow. He
suggests 007 use Q's Identigraph to
identify who paid off Gonzales.

The Tanner in *GoldenEye* and *The
World Is Not Enough* is an MI6 senior
analyst. He calls M "the evil Queen
of numbers" and agrees with 007's
instinctual moves. In *The World Is Not
Enough*, Tanner advises M not to
travel to Azerbaijan at Elektra King's
request, but he fails to convince the
head of MI6.

BOND'S FRIEND *Tanner helps monitor
missions and unfolding global crises.*

TIBBETT, SIR GODFREY

APPEARANCE
A View To A Kill (1985)
STATUS Dead; strangled by May Day
CHARACTERISTICS Well-groomed, gentlemanly, long-suffering
PLAYED BY Patrick Macnee

Described as a "dapper trainer" in the script, Sir Godfrey Tibbett is a refined Englishman who works with MI6 to uncover the mystery of tycoon Max Zorin's winning racehorses. Bond poses as a wealthy English sportsman named St. John-Smythe at Zorin's annual thoroughbred racehorse sale, and Tibbett poses as his valet and chauffeur. Bond relishes ordering Tibbett about as part of their cover. They learn that Zorin's breeding consultant, Dr. Mortner, has injected steroids into the racehorses. When the pair's real identities are discovered, Tibbett is strangled by Zorin's lover, May Day.

Tibbett: Do we have to keep this up when we're alone?

007: A successful cover becomes almost second nature.

SUPER DRUG *Sir Godfrey Tibbett and Bond uncover Zorin's horse-doping plot.*

TRAIN CONDUCTOR

APPEARANCE
From Russia With Love (1963)
STATUS Unknown
CHARACTERISTICS Efficient, bribable
PLAYED BY George Pastell

The conductor on the Orient Express becomes an unwitting pawn in SPECTRE's game of murder and betrayal with the British and the Soviets. He has the grim duty of telling Bond of the death of his ally Kerim Bey, the head of Station T, Turkey. The conductor believes that Bey and Benz, the Soviet security man, killed each other. Bond requests that the conductor keep the deaths quiet until the train reaches Trieste, sealing the deal with a healthy bribe and the promise of more money from Bey's "influential friends."

MURDER ON THE ORIENT EXPRESS
The train conductor shows 007 the dead bodies of Kerim Bey and Benz—killed by SPECTRE assassin Donald Grant.

TYNAN, DR.

APPEARANCE
Diamonds Are Forever (1971)
STATUS Dead; killed by Wint and Kidd
CHARACTERISTICS Skilled at dental extractions
PLAYED BY Henry Rowland

An American dentist working at a Diamond Syndicate mine in South Africa, Dr. Tynan works as part of the mine's social services structure. Tynan makes contact with the miners, persuading them to bring him choice stones hidden in their mouths for cash payments. Tynan rides his motorcycle to a remote desert location for his regular appointments with Joe, a helicopter pilot who takes the diamonds to smuggler Mrs. Whistler. Tynan ultimately meets assassins Mr. Wint and Mr. Kidd who inform him Joe couldn't make the appointment. They then kill him with a scorpion, telling Joe that Tynan was "bitten by the bug."

STING IN THE TAIL *Dr. Tynan falls for Mr. Kidd's toothache ruse, leading to his death.*

UNNAMED FOREIGN AGENT

APPEARANCE Twelve Bond films to date
STATUS Living, whereabouts unknown
CHARACTERISTICS Chameleon-like; loves disguises
PLAYED BY Michael G. Wilson

This mysterious foreign agent fleetingly appears in several of Bond's assignments, always under a different identity. He first appears in *Goldfinger* as a tall Korean guard. In *Moonraker*, he walks past the Venini Glass Factory in Venice and later appears as a NASA control room technician. *For Your Eyes Only* sees the agent disguised as a Greek Orthodox priest, possibly shadowing a meeting between Bond and Q. *Octopussy* finds him on a boat in India acting as though he is an American tourist. This foreign agent heads to the opera in Vienna in *The Living Daylights*, shadowing British operative Saunders. In *GoldenEye*, the agent appears to be a member of the

ORTHODOX AGENT *The Unnamed Foreign Agent appears as a priest officiating at a wedding in* For Your Eyes Only.

Russian Defense Council, leading many to believe him to be a Russian agent. The agent then masquerades as an Elliot Carver media executive named Tom Wallace in *Tomorrow Never Dies*. In *The World Is Not Enough*, he appears as an employee in Zukovsky's Baku casino. He turns up twice in *Die Another Day*—first leaning against a car as Bond passes him on the streets of Havana, then as US General Chandler in a command bunker in South Korea. In *Casino Royale*, he is in disguise again—this time as the corrupt Chief of Police in Montenegro. As of this writing, this agent's agenda remains unclear, but his talent for rising quickly in any organization testifies to his creative instincts and tenacity.

BIG TOP THRILLS *The US General (left) and his aide (right) get a big bang out of Octopussy's Circus. Kamal Khan (center) prepares to leave the big top before an atomic bomb explodes.*

US GENERAL

APPEARANCE
Octopussy (1983)
STATUS Living; whereabouts unknown
CHARACTERISTICS Extremely focused on his job
PLAYED BY Bruce Boa

Octopussy invites the general in command of the US Air Force Base in Feldstadt, West Germany and his aide as her personal guests to a performance of her circus. When James Bond breaks into the heavily guarded tent disguised as a circus clown, he makes his way to Octopussy and informs the base commander that there is a bomb in the cannon. The general's aide tells his boss that Bond is either drunk or crazy. However, when Octopussy blasts the lock off the cannon, revealing the detonator, the general orders his men to release Bond so he can disarm the device.

VAVRA

APPEARANCE
From Russia With Love (1963)
STATUS Unknown
CHARACTERISTICS Friendly, earthy
PLAYED BY Francis de Wolff

Vavra and his rough-living gypsy tribe are used for dirty work by the head of Station T, Kerim Bey. The gypsies consider Bey to be a close family friend. They take in Kerim and Bond when they are trying to avoid Soviet agents. Bond and Kerim arrive at the camp and witness a fierce fight taking place between gypsy women Vida and Zora over the affections of one of Vavra's sons. When Bulgarian assassin Krilencu and his men attack the camp, Bond saves Vavra's life. In return, Vavra calls 007 an honorary son. The head of the gypsy tribe relents to Bond's request to call off the fight between Vida and Zora.

VENZ

APPEARANCE
A View To A Kill (1985)
STATUS Living; whereabouts unknown
CHARACTERISTICS Protective, loyal
PLAYED BY Dolph Lundgren

Venz and fellow KGB agent Klotkoff accompany General Gogol to meet errant agent Max Zorin at his racetrack. When May Day, Zorin's lover, lifts Klotkoff into the air and then throws him to the ground, Venz checks on his colleague's condition.

VERITY

APPEARANCE
Die Another Day (2002)
STATUS Living; whereabouts unknown
CHARACTERISTICS Defensive, possessive, ever watchful
PLAYED BY Madonna

Double agent Miranda Frost shares a close, protective relationship with Verity, her fencing instructor. It is mildly implied that Verity may be attracted to Miranda, and she certainly comes to Frost's defense when Bond reminds her that Miranda won the gold medal at the 2000 Olympic Games in Sydney, Australia by default. After giving 007 a fencing tip, she introduces him to Miranda's fencing partner, billionaire Gustav Graves. Verity declines to wager on a fencing match between these two men.

Gustav Graves: Care to place a bet Verity? **Verity:** No thanks, I don't like cock fights.

VIJAY

APPEARANCE Octopussy (1983)
STATUS Dead; killed by thugs
CHARACTERISTICS Resourceful, loyal
PLAYED BY Vijay Amritraj

Vijay works for Sadruddin, head of Section I, India and is Bond's main contact while 007 investigates Operation Trove. Vijay first meets Bond dressed as a snake charmer. He plays "The James Bond Theme" on a pungi to a cobra as 007 walks past. Vijay prefers his more usual cover, as part-time tennis pro at exiled Afghan prince Kamal Khan's club.

Vijay displays his tennis skills during a chase in a tuk-tuk taxi through the streets of Udaipur, making an overhand smash right onto a thug's head. Later, disguised as a fisherman, he keeps watch on jewel smuggler Octopussy's Floating Palace while 007 is in residence. During Vijay's watch, Khan's henchman Gobinda and Mufti's thugs attack and fatally wound him with a yo-yo buzz saw. Q finds Vijay before he dies. Vijay tells him, "It was Kamal's men."

VILLIERS

APPEARANCE Casino Royale (2006)
STATUS Living; whereabouts unknown
CHARACTERISTICS Young, keen
PLAYED BY Tobias Menzies

Villiers, M's aide, keeps his boss informed at all hours. He endures her temper, when she faces a Parliamentary inquiry after MI6's new 00 James Bond shoots a bomb maker in a foreign embassy. Villiers reports to M that 007 is using her password to conduct research in MI6's database. He provides key research into the target of a terrorist bombing in Miami.

WADE, JACK

APPEARANCE
GoldenEye (1995),
Tomorrow Never Dies (1997)
STATUS Living; retired
CHARACTERISTICS Jocular, feels like he's seen it all; amateur botanist
PLAYED BY Joe Don Baker

CIA agent Jack Wade provides indispensable help to Bond during two of his post-Cold War missions. Wade dislikes formality and has a cheerfully cynical view of his job. Married at least three times, he sports a rose tattooed on his hip with the name "Muffy," in honor of his third wife. A veteran of the Vietnam War, Wade developed a keen interest in gardening by accident while in Cambodia. He created explosives using plant fertilizer and diesel fuel and then realized that the mixture made excellent compost.

When Wade meets Bond in St. Petersburg, Russia during *GoldenEye*, he drives a decidedly unpretentious Moskvich automobile and initially finds Bond's manner irksome, calling him a "stiff-assed Brit." Wade soon takes a liking to 007 and comes to respect Bond's spycraft. Wade gives Bond important information concerning Russian Mafia boss Valentin Zukovsky that allows 007 to track down Alec Trevelyan, formerly Agent 006 of MI6.

Wade later meets Bond in the Caribbean, giving him and computer programmer Natalya Simonova a Cessna 172 and cover from the CIA to fly into Cuban airspace so that they can locate a satellite dish that will be used to detonate the second GoldenEye satellite. Wade tells Bond to get on the radio if he needs help, and he will send in the Marines. At the end of *GoldenEye*, Wade arrives

CIA ALLY *Jack Wade helps Bond investigate the sinking of HMS* Devonshire.

with his promised commando force to rescue 007.

In *Tomorrow Never Dies*, Bond meets Wade in Okinawa, Japan, while investigating the sinking of HMS *Devonshire*. They discover that the GPS encoder Bond took from media mogul Elliot Carver's office could have sent the frigate off course, launching a military confrontation between Britain and China.

WHISTLER, MRS.

APPEARANCE
Diamonds Are Forever (1971)
STATUS Dead; drowned
CHARACTERISTICS Kindhearted, but with a dishonest streak
PLAYED BY Margaret Lacey

BY THE BOOK *Mrs. Whistler leaves her young class to greet her colleagues in the diamond-smuggling racket, Mr. Wint and Mr. Kidd.*

Mrs. Whistler is a missionary teacher in South Africa, financing her school by smuggling diamonds. When she meets the killers Mr. Wint and Mr. Kidd, she says she is happy to see them again, implying they have had a role in her smuggling activities. Her desire to have photographs of the Amsterdam canals sent to the children at her school is sadistically fulfilled. Wint and Kidd drown Mrs. Whistler, and Kidd snaps pictures as police pull her body from the Amster.

WHYTE, WILLARD

APPEARANCE
Diamonds Are Forever (1971)
STATUS Living; whereabouts unknown
CHARACTERISTICS Eccentric, reclusive, but energetic when roused to action
PLAYED BY Jimmy Dean

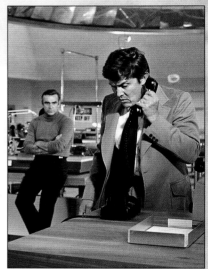

Billionaire Willard Whyte has a vast business empire that includes an aerospace complex, hotels, casinos, cruise ships, and oil wells. Whyte has become a notorious recluse, ensconced in the penthouse of his Las Vegas hotel, The Whyte House. He controls his empire through a few trusted subordinates, such as Tom at WW Techtronics and Bert Saxby. Bond's archenemy Ernst Stavro Blofeld convinces Saxby to betray Whyte, and together they kidnap him. They then seize Whyte's empire and use its resources to finance the building of a massive laser satellite powerful enough to blow up intercontinental ballistic missiles in their silos. Whyte becomes a prisoner in his own summer home, ten miles outside of Las Vegas. Gymnasts extraordinaire Bambi and Thumper guard the billionaire.

Bond rescues Whyte, but not before Blofeld, using a voice simulator to impersonate Whyte, successfully launches his deadly space weapon, destroying nuclear installations in the Soviet Union, the US, and China. Whyte reclaims control of his empire and helps 007 discover and destroy Blofeld's command center, situated in an oil rig off the coast of the Baja peninsula, Mexico.

ZUKOVSKY, VALENTIN

APPEARANCE GoldenEye (1995), The World Is Not Enough (1999)
STATUS Dead; shot by Elektra King
CHARACTERISTICS Roguish but dangerous head of the Russian Mafia
PLAYED BY Robbie Coltrane

Ex–KGB operative Valentin Dimitrovich Zukovsky runs the only major competition to the Janus crime syndicate in Russia, selling arms and engaging in numerous other extra-legal business ventures. During the Cold War, James Bond shot Zukovsky in the right knee and stole his car and his girlfriend. Years later, this not unnaturally proves a barrier to approaching Zukovsky for information on Janus, the alias of Alec Trevelyan.

Zukovsky operates out of building 23 in a warehouse district of St. Petersburg. According to Jack Wade and Zukovsky himself, Valentin has no compunction about killing uninvited guests. Zukovsky maintains a vast knowledge of firearms. He can tell Bond's Walther PPK merely from the sound of it cocking. He enjoys mocking Bond but demonstrates a flash of temper. Bond eventually negotiates a tenuous peace. Neither man likes the other, but they soon realize they occasionally share the same goals. In exchange for a rigged sale of C4 explosives where Zukovsky will be allowed to pocket a large profit, Zukovsky tells 007 all he knows about Janus and arranges an introduction.

A few years later, Valentin moves to Baku and claims to have become a legitimate businessman, opening his own casino and caviar factory. He still has a few shady dealings in the works, including one transaction with oil heiress Elektra King.

He smuggles Russian equipment and supplies for her, using his nephew Nikoli and a Russian navy submarine.

When Valentin realizes that Elektra and her lover Renard have killed Nikoli, he becomes furious. Elektra shoots him before he can take action. Zukovsky's final act before he dies is to fire his silver-handled walking stick, which conceals a rifle, at a wrist restraint, freeing 007 from Elektra's torture chair. In an ironic twist, the walking stick Valentin uses as a result of Bond's bullet to his knee saves 007's life.

A REUNION WITH 007 *"Walther PPK. 7.65mm,"* says Valentin Zukovsky. *"Only three men I know use such a gun. I believe I've killed two of them."*

ONE GIRL IS NOT ENOUGH *Zukovsky with his two girlfriends, Nina and Verushka.*

"I'm looking for a submarine. It's big and black and the driver's a very good friend of mine."

Zukovsky to Elektra King

VEHICLES

When Ian Fleming lovingly described James Bond's battleship-gray 4½-litre Bentley with the Amherst Villiers supercharger in *Casino Royale*, he tapped into the world's growing love of powerful machines. James Bond was the first hero of the Jet Age, and the novels and films offer a wonderful catalog of the most elegant, interesting, and deadly modes of transport ever conceived. The vehicles in the world of 007 speak to our love of the speed, power, and romance of travel. They transport us into a world where every ticket is first class, every journey is an adventure. They offer so much more than a gadget-laden Aston Martin or a submersible Lotus Esprit. They are a catalog of our aspirations, a reminder that life is a journey and the way we choose to move through it says more about us than the kind of car we drive. Anyone can look good behind the wheel of an Aston Martin DBS. When life hands you a Citroën 2CV or a Routemaster bus, can you still steer through the obstacles you face without breaking sweat? As you look through these pages at the amazing and the ordinary, remember, as Fleming noted in *You Only Live Twice*, "It is better to travel hopefully than to arrive."

ACROSTAR "BEDE" JET

APPEARANCE
Octopussy (1983)
FLOWN BY James Bond

EVASIVE ACTION *007 flies his Acrostar through the enemy's hangar to escape a missile.*

To escape troops in an unidentified Latin American country, Bond employs a jet small enough to fit inside a horse trailer. Jim Bede invented this remarkable aircraft, and a number were specially modified as Acrostars, one of which was obtained by Q Branch. The BD-5J "Acrostar" Microjet is just 12-ft (3.6-m) long, with a wingspan of only 13 ft (3.9 m). It is powered by a single TRS-18 microturbo jet engine, giving a top speed of 320 mph (514.9 kph).

Impersonating an officer named Colonel Toro, Bond is on a mission to sabotage a spy plane. Unmasked and captured, 007 manages to escape his guards. He leaps onto a Range Rover convertible pulling what looks like a horse trailer. In fact, the trailer contains the Acrostar. Bond jumps into the cockpit as trucks and motorcyclists roar toward him. The jet's folding wings descend, and Bond speeds toward the vehicles, taking off just over his pursuers' heads.

Troops fire a Rapier surface-to-air missile at the Acrostar and Bond tries to evade it through a series of ravines and mesas, to no avail. In an inspired maneuver, he then flies straight into the airplane hangar housing the spy plane. Colonel Toro's men race to close the doors at the far end, but Bond's plane zooms through the ever-diminishing gap. The pursuing missile smashes into the shut doors, obliterating the hangar in a massive explosion.

Bond flies off, but soon notices that the jet's fuel gauge is registering almost empty. Bond promptly lands on a country road, pulls into a petrol station, and nonchalantly asks the astonished attendant to "Fill her up."

GETAWAY PLANE *Enemy soldiers flee in panic as Bond's Acrostar roars over their heads.*

AEROSPATIALE/EUROCOPTER HELICOPTERS

APPEARANCES
You Only Live Twice (1967), Octopussy (1983), A View To A Kill (1985), Licence To Kill (1989), GoldenEye (1995), Tomorrow Never Dies (1997), The World Is Not Enough (1999), Die Another Day (2002)
USED BY James Bond, General Gogol, General Orlov, Stacey Sutton, Franz Sanchez, Dario, Heller, Xenia Onatopp, Natalya Simonova, Elliot Carver's men, Elektra King, M, Mr. Van Bierk

DIAMOND DELIVERY *Van Bierk's helicopter lands at Moon's base in* Die Another Day.

James Bond, his colleagues, and his enemies have often been transported to and from important locations in various French-built Aerospatiale helicopters.

In *You Only Live Twice*, an Aerospatiale Alouette 316B transports 007 to Japanese Secret Service agent Tiger Tanaka's ninja-training school in Japan.

In *Octopussy*, during Operation Trove, Bond takes an Aerospatiale SA-316 Alouette III to Udaipur, India. An Aerospatiale SA-365C Dauphin flies Soviet General Orlov to Kamal Khan's Monsoon Palace to finalize their plans to explode an atomic bomb on the US Air Force Base in Feldstadt, West Germany. KGB General Gogol also takes a 365 to the East/West German border to arrest Orlov for stealing jewelry from the Kremlin Art Repository.

A View To A Kill features state geologist Stacey Sutton arriving at businessman Max Zorin's French château in an Aerospatiale SA 341/342 Gazelle helicopter.

During the events of *Licence To Kill*, 007 arrives in Key West for the wedding of his good friend, DEA agent Felix Leiter. Bond, Leiter, and the DEA take control of a US Coast Guard HH–65A Dauphin when they learn that drug lord Franz Sanchez has arrived in US airspace. Leiter hoists Bond down on the rescue winch, and 007 lassoes the tail end of Sanchez's stolen Cessna 172 monoplane in mid-air, capturing the drug baron. Later in the film, Sanchez and his men Dario and Heller take an Aerospatiale 350B A-Star to the Olympiatec Meditation Institute that houses Sanchez's cocaine laboratories.

In 1992, Aerospatiale and Deutsche Aerospace merged to form the Eurocopter Group. All Aerospatiale helicopters were henceforth known as Eurocopters.

In *GoldenEye*, after Bond's plane crashes in the Cuban jungle, Janus member Xenia Onatopp slides down a rope from a Eurocopter 355 Twin Star and tries to squeeze 007 to death between her thighs. Bond fires the machine gun attached to her belt at the Twin Star, bringing it to a violent explosion. As the Twin Star crashes, the rope holding Onatopp quickly wedges her against a tree, squeezing her to death. Later in the film, computer programmer Natalya Simonova hijacks another 355 Twin Star to rescue 007. Bond leaps from the satellite antenna to the skids of the helicopter as it flies to safety.

In *Tomorrow Never Dies*, a Eurocopter Panther AS 565 Attack helicopter is observed by MI6 as one of the weapons for sale at a terrorist supermarket on the Khyber Pass. Another Eurocopter—an EC-135— remains in the background as Q gives Bond his new remote-controlled BMW 750iL at Hamburg Airport. In Saigon, media mogul Elliot Carver's men point the nose of a Eurocopter 350B A-Star to the ground and try to use the rotary blades to chop up Bond and Chinese agent Wai Lin as they speed through the streets on a stylish BMW R1200 motorbike.

The World Is Not Enough features a Eurocopter AS-365N Dauphin that pauses above the Caucasus Mountains to allow Bond and oil heiress Elektra King to jump from the helicopter onto the snow and ski to the pipeline. A Eurocopter EC-135 later flies M to Elektra's Azerbaijan oil pipeline station.

Die Another Day uses a very similar helicopter to an Aerospatiale SA 330 Puma, the Mil Mi-8 helicopter. Taking on the identity of diamond smuggler Mr. Van Bierk, Bond uses Van Bierk's helictoper to fly into Colonel Moon's base by the DMZ. When Moon learns Bond's true identity, he destroys the Mil Mi-8 with a tank-buster gun.
See also Eurocopter Tree-cutter; Tiger Helicopter

MARKET MAYHEM *(below) Carver's helicopter pursues Bond and Wai Lin through the streets of Saigon in* Tomorrow Never Dies.

JUMP OFF
Natalya Simonova arrives to rescue Bond in GoldenEye.

FIREBALL *(below)
Bond's adroit use of a washing line brings down Carver's chopper.*

AIRSHIP

APPEARANCE
A View To A Kill (1985)
USED BY Max Zorin, May Day,
Scarpine, Dr. Mortner

PUMPED UP *A Portakabin's roof folds back, and Zorin's airship rapidly inflates.*

Max Zorin owns two airships that play a role in his plan to destroy Silicon Valley. His larger airship, the Zorin Industries Skyship 6000, features a high-tech boardroom where he conducts a meeting with his cartel about seizing control of the microchip market. The airship also features collapsible stairs, which come in handy when a Taiwanese tycoon opts out of the plan. Zorin's lover, May Day, escorts the tycoon from the meeting to the stairs and, with the push of a button, sends him hurtling out of the ship.

Zorin also has a smaller airship, designated G-BIHN, hidden inside a Portakabin at his Main Strike mine. When Zorin, Nazi experimenter Dr. Carl Mortner, and henchman Scarpine depart the mine in the G-BIHN airship before setting off an explosion they believe will trigger a devastating earthquake, Zorin kidnaps geologist Stacey Sutton. Bond grabs onto a mooring rope, leading Zorin to attempt to knock

THE BALLOON BURSTS *Dr. Mortner's attempt to kill Bond and Stacey ends when he drops a lit bundle of dynamite and blows up himself and Zorin's airship.*

Bond loose in various ways. When Zorin tries to use the Golden Gate Bridge to force Bond free, 007 secures the mooring rope to one of the bridge's cables. Dr. Mortner destroys the airship when he inadvertently drops lit dynamite into the cabin.

"This'll hurt him more than me!"

Zorin to Scarpine, as Bond hangs from the airship's mooring rope

ALONG FOR THE RIDE *Bond seizes one of the airship's mooring ropes, determined to save Stacey Sutton from Max Zorin's clutches.*

AMC HORNET

APPEARANCE
The Man With The Golden Gun (1974)
USED BY James Bond, Sheriff Pepper

James Bond puts a 1974 AMC Hornet X Hatchback to the test in a chase with master assassin Francisco Scaramanga.

After the kidnapping of staff intelligence officer Mary Goodnight outside a kick-boxing arena, Bond spies Scaramanga's AMC Matador. Goodnight then informs him by walkie-talkie that she is trapped inside the trunk and has the prized Solex Agitator with her. Bond enters a car dealership and slips into a Hornet Hatchback only to discover he has a passenger along for the ride—Sheriff J. W. Pepper. Bond crashes the car through the showroom window and onto the Bangkok streets, weaving in and out of traffic at breakneck speed and even pulling a 180° reverse-to-forward maneuver.

Bond follows Pepper's advice on a turn by a klong and ends up on the opposite bank from Scaramanga, Goodnight, and the Solex. Spying a collapsed bridge, Bond accelerates to a speed between 39 and 41 mph (63–66 kph) and, using the remains of the bridge as a ramp, sends the Hornet rocketing into space. The weight of the Hornet, including passengers is between 3,214 and 3,228 lb (1,458–1,464 kg); the ramps sit between 51.9 and 52.09 ft (15.82–15.88 m) apart. Turning over once in mid air, the car lands precisely on the remains of the bridge on the opposite bank. Bond and Pepper then continue their pursuit of Scaramanga.

Unfortunately, despite this spectacular maneuver, Bond fails to catch Scaramanga who transforms his AMC Matador into a plane.

ANTONOV

APPEARANCE

Die Another Day (2002)

USED BY Gustav Graves, North Korean Generals, Jinx

The Russian Antonov An-124, one of the largest fleet aircraft in existence, serves as the flying headquarters of Gustav Graves/Colonel Moon as he directs the Icarus satellite's destruction of the South Korean defense lines along the De-Militarized Zone. Infiltrated by James Bond and Jinx, the plane depressurizes and flies into the blazing heat from the Icarus space mirror. As Icarus destroys the Antonov, James Bond and Jinx battle Graves and Miranda Frost to the death and escape via a Notar MD-600 helicopter from the cargo bay of the plane. They freefall in the helicopter as the plane explodes.

AMC MATADOR

APPEARANCE

The Man With The Golden Gun (1974)

USED BY Scaramanga, Nick Nack

As staff intelligence officer Mary Goodnight places a listening device in the trunk of Francisco Scaramanga's 1974 AMC Matador X Coupé, the master assassin shoves her inside and drives off. Bond steals an AMC Hornet and gives chase until

Scaramanga pulls into a hangar. Behind closed doors, Scaramanga converts the Matador into an airplane with a jet engine and wing attachment that locks onto the car. An airplane instrument panel flips down in the car's dashboard.

Delayed by the Bangkok police, Bond watches Scaramanga's car plane take to the skies. The AMC Matador is later found abandoned about 200 miles (322 km) west of Bangkok.

ASTON MARTIN DB5

TOP GEAR *The Bond DB5 in full bloom illustrates the wealth of gadgets installed by Q Branch.*

ORIGINAL DESIGNS *Ken Adam's sketches show a top-mounted search light, a flip-up bullet screen, and tire knives built into front and rear bumpers.*

APPEARANCES Goldfinger (1964), Thunderball (1965), GoldenEye (1995), Tomorrow Never Dies (1997), The World Is Not Enough (1999), Casino Royale (2006)

DRIVEN BY James Bond, Alex Dimitrios

The most well-known and sought-after Aston Martin ever made, the DB5 had a production run of only 1,023 cars and was produced between 1963 and 1965. No car is more closely identified with secret agent 007. The DB5's essential Britishness, bespoke craftsmanship, sleek, classic styling, and understated appearance made it a perfect fit for James Bond.

In the novel *Goldfinger*, Bond chooses an Aston Martin DB Mk III from the Service motor pool (Fleming refers to the car simply as a "DB III"—the Aston Martin DB3

its "up-to-date triptyque" (a form that kept British and European car owners from having to pay customs duties on cars driven from country to country), its "inconspicuous" battleship-grey color, "and certain extras."

"These included switches to alter the type and color of Bond's front and rear lights if he was following or being followed at night, reinforced steel bumpers fore and aft in case he needed to ram, a long-barreled Colt .45 in a trick compartment under the drivers seat, a radio pick-up tuned to receive an apparatus called the Homer, and plenty of concealed space that would fox most Customs men."

When Bond enters Q's laboratory in the film *Goldfinger*, Q tells 007 his Bentley has had its day and shows him a new Silver Birch Aston Martin DB5. The car's gadgetry not only offered Bond protection and weaponry, but it also subtly mocked a growing concern over automobile safety at the time.

Bond uses the car's tracking system to follow Goldfinger's Rolls Royce Phantom III to Switzerland. He later engages the tire scythe to disable Tilly Masterson's car in order to discover why she fired a shot at him. When Bond and Tilly attempt to escape from the Auric Enterprises compound, Bond uses the car's smoke screen and oil slick

> ## "Ejector seat? You're joking!"
>
> ### Bond to Q

functions. Trapped in a dead end, Bond protects himself with the rear bulletproof screen. Once captured, Bond fires the guard riding with him out of the roof with the ejector seat. The bulletproof windscreen comes in handy when the elderly gatekeeper sprays the car with machine-gun fire. Bond soon employs the front wing machine guns and the extending front bumpers while trying to escape the plant—without any success. He ends up playing chicken not with another car but his own reflection in a mirror and crashes into a brick wall.

Bond's DB5 has been recovered and repaired by *Thunderball*. Bond uses it to escape SPECTRE gunmen, washing them down with high-pressure water jets. Later, Bond drives the car on his return from his visit to the Shrublands health clinic, and

ARMREST OPTIONS *These switches control the DB5's formidable defense mechanisms, which include fixed front-firing machine guns.*

PRE-GPS *Q's onboard moving map system predated in-car analog systems by 19 years and commercial GPS systems by 30 years.*

DON'T TOUCH IT! *Pushing this red button causes part of the roof to blow away and activates the passenger ejector seat.*

was purely a racing model retired two years before *Goldfinger* was written. The Mark III was introduced in 1957, the year before Fleming wrote *Goldfinger*). The car serves as part of Bond's cover as "a well-to-do, rather adventurous young man with a taste for the good, the fast things of life." Bond chooses the car because of

WASHED AWAY *Bond and Mlle. La Porte blast gunmen with water cannons. This part of the scene was cut from* Thunderball *but can be seen in the documentary* The Incredible World of James Bond.

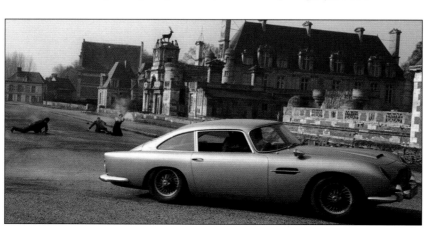

Count Lippe pursues him in a black Ford Skyliner. Before Bond can engage any gadgets, Fiona Volpe fires a rocket from her BSA Lightning motorbike which destroys the Skyliner.

The DB5 does not return for 30 years, when it serves as 007's personal car in *GoldenEye*. Bond engages in a playful but dangerous chase with Xenia Onatopp on the road to Monte Carlo, while being evaluated by Caroline of MI6. This car's special equipment includes a cooler for a bottle of 1988 Bollinger and a digital color fax printer/communicator built into the CD player.

Bond uses his DB5 to visit Professor Inga Bergstrom at Oxford in *Tomorrow Never Dies*. It saves 007 valuable time when he must return to London in a hurry. Few viewers ever notice the DB5 in *The World Is Not Enough*. It can be seen on the satellite image provided by R at the film's end. A deleted scene shows Bond arriving at the funeral for Sir Robert King in the DB5.

Casino Royale tells the story of how Bond acquired the DB5. At the One and Only Club, Bond discovers the identity of Alex Dimitrios thanks to his distinctive, left-hand drive 1964 Silver Birch Aston Martin. Bond later wins the car in a poker game with Dimitrios.

Goldfinger DB5 modifications (BMT 216A):
- Extending front and rear ramming bumpers
- Secret drawer (not seen) under driver's seat holding a 7.63 mm Mauser, silencer, Armalite rifle, telescopic sight, throwing knife, hand grenade
- Radio telephone (not seen) in compartment in driver's door
- Homer receiver: range 150 miles (241 km), works via radar scanner in racing mirror (not seen)
- Homer "moving map" display behind dashboard radio speaker grill
- Bulletproof windscreen and windows
- Revolving number plates, valid all countries (or at least UK, Switzerland, and France)
- Caltrop dispenser behind driver's rear light cluster (not seen)
- Tire knife mechanically extends from passenger-side rear wheel hub
- Smoke screen, fired from exhaust pipe
- Oil-slick dispenser behind passenger rear light cluster
- Retractable bulletproof screen in rear
- Front wing machine guns behind left and right indicator lights
- Passenger ejector seat, engaged and fired by pressing red button in gear lever knob

Thunderball modifications:
- High-pressure water cannons

GoldenEye modifications (BMT 214A):
- Champagne cooler in center armrest
- Digital color fax printer/communicator CD unit

THE FINER THINGS *Alex Dimitrios may have no morals, but he has exquisite taste in cars and women, as 007 soon discovers on Paradise Island in* Casino Royale.

CLASSICS *(below) James Bond looks out at the golf course beside the Aston Martin DB5 in* Goldfinger. *The relationship between Bond and the DB5 has lasted more than 40 years.*

THE NEXT GIRL *Bond plays cat and mouse with Xenia Onatopp in her Ferrari on the famous hairpin bends of the Corniche in* GoldenEye.

ASTON MARTIN DBS

APPEARANCE

On Her Majesty's Secret Service
(1969)

Diamonds Are Forever (1971)

Casino Royale (2006)

USED BY James Bond, Tracy di Vicenzo

The Aston Martin DBS, originally produced from 1967 to 1972, features in *On Her Majesty's Secret Service* and *Diamonds Are Forever.* A new version of the DBS, based on the DB9 model, awaits 007 when he arrives in Montenegro for the high-stakes poker game at the Hotel Splendide in *Casino Royale.*

In *On Her Majesty's Secret Service,* Bond, driving a silver DBS, pursues a suicidal Tracy Di Vicenzo in her red Mercury Cougar. Finding her car abandoned on a Portuguese coastal road, Bond opens the glove compartment to reveal a sniper rifle with a telescopic sight. Bond uses the sight to spy on Tracy as she enters the water, intent on drowning herself. 007 speeds the DBS across the dunes to rescue her. At the end of the film, Bond and Tracy leave on honeymoon in the DBS. When Bond stops on a mountain road to remove the wedding flowers from the car, Ernst Stavro Blofeld drives past in a Mercedes. Irma Bunt in the back seat fires a machine gun at the DBS, killing Tracy.

The DBS appears only briefly in *Diamonds Are Forever,* in the background of Q's workshop.

In *Casino Royale,* 007 discovers that the glove compartment of his new Aston Martin DBS contains a Walther PPK with silencer, a Medipac, and several combipens. When Valenka poisons Bond, he stumbles to the DBS and, with Vesper Lynd's timely intervention, uses the Medipac to counteract the digitalis in his system.

Bond later uses the DBS to pursue Le Chiffre and his men when they kidnap Vesper. When he sees Vesper tied up in the middle of the road, he swerves the speeding DBS, launching the car into seven barrel rolls before finally crashing.

THE RIGHT CAR *MI6 presents Bond with a top-of-the-range Aston Martin DBS to support his cover as a top professional poker player in* Casino Royale.

OVER AND OUT *Bond spins the wheel to avoid Vesper's body and sends his DBS somersaulting across the road.*

ASTON MARTIN V8

APPEARANCE
The Living Daylights (1987)
USED BY **James Bond, Kara Milovy**

Bond uses his gray Aston Martin V8 Volante to escape with cellist, Kara Milovy, through the Czech mountains. As the police try to stop them crossing the border to Austria, 007 uses various gadgets to evade them. These include a police band scanner radio, ice tires, retractable outriggers for use on snow and ice, and a jet engine booster rocket, which is concealed behind the rear licence plate. Bond also uses laser beams built into the front hubcaps to cut the chassis off a police car. A heads-up display on the windshield targets a pair of heat-seeking missiles hidden behind the fog lights that 007 uses to destroy roadblocks. The car also boasts a self-destruct system.

SMOOTH AS ICE *(left) The winterized V8 races across a frozen lake near the Czech— Austrian border.*

EXPLOSIVE ACCELERATION *(below) The V8 exits a boathouse just before a shell blasts it to matchwood.*

ASTON MARTIN VANQUISH

APPEARANCE
Die Another Day (2002)
USED BY **James Bond**

Bond drives the Aston Martin Vanquish V12 with Tungsten Silver coachwork and charcoal leather interior on his mission in Iceland. Q presents 007 with the brand new Vanquish at MI6's secret London Underground station headquarters and the car's most remarkable feature is its adaptive camouflage. Cameras on all sides of the car record images which are then displayed onto a light-emitting polymer skin on the opposite side, giving the illusion of transparency—but only if viewed from the appropriate angles and in the proper environment. The car also houses a remarkable array of weaponry, including a thermal imaging mechanism concealed within the car's CD player, heat-seeking missiles housed behind the grille, two machine-fired 12-gauge target-seeking shotguns hidden in the car hood, tire spikes for ice driving, and an ejector seat capable of blasting the passenger seat out with enough force to flip the Vanquish 180°—a feature Bond discovers during his mission. Additionally, the bodywork, windscreens, and windows are all bulletproof.

Bond uses the Vanquish to great advantage during his investigation of billionaire diamond tycoon Gustav Graves/Colonel Moon. Although the camouflage fails under a fusillade from a Jaguar XKR driven by henchman Zao. When driven on a frozen lagoon, the Vanquish manages to out-maneuver the XKR. The thermal imaging system locates Jinx inside the melting Ice Palace. The car also transports the pair to a hot spring, where 007 revives the nearly drowned NSA agent.

HOT ROD *A heat-seeking targeting system reveals the Vanquish; its adaptive camouflage makes it invisible to the naked eye.*

SNOW TIRES *Bond uses these ice spikes to literally climb a wall.*

FIRE AND ICE *Four heat-seeking missiles are concealed in the Vanquish's grille.*

READY FOR BATTLE
Two mighty vehicles face off on a frozen lake in Die Another Day: *Bond's Aston Martin Vanquish and Zao's Jaguar XKR.*

AUDI 200 QUATTRO

APPEARANCE
The Living Daylights (1987)
USED BY James Bond, Saunders

Bond uses an Audi 200 Quattro belonging to Saunders, head of Section V, Vienna, to help smuggle defecting Soviet General Georgi Koskov from communist Czechoslovakia into Austria. With the Czech police hunting for Koskov, Saunders stows the general in the car's trunk. "First place they'd look," says Bond. Installing Koskov in the front passenger seat, Bond drives to the Trans-Siberian Pipeline complex. With help from local contact Rosika Miklos, Bond sends Koskov through the pipeline to freedom. Bond later collects Saunders in the Audi, and they also safely cross the border.

BANGKOK LONGTAIL

APPEARANCE
The Man With The Golden Gun (1974)
USED BY James Bond, Chula and kickboxing school students

Bond escapes from Hai Fat's kickboxing school and star pupil Chula by leaping into a longtail boat. Powered by car engines and propellers, the boats are a common sight in Bangkok's floating market. In the resulting chase, Bond slices Chula's boat in half before cruising down the klong.

BATH-O-SUB

APPEARANCE
Diamonds Are Forever (1971)
USED BY Ernst Stavro Blofeld

Blofeld has a one-man submarine, known as a bath-o-sub, in case he needs to make a quick escape from his satellite control center on an oil rig off the coast of Mexico. When 007 releases a weather balloon on the oil rig, US government helicopters launch an attack. As the attack becomes more fierce, Blofeld orders his sub to be prepared. Bond takes over the crane lowering the sub into the ocean. He then uses the bath-o-sub, with Blofeld in it, as a wrecking ball to destroy the computers and thus prevent the satellite from blasting Washington DC.

BEDFORD, HMS

APPEARANCE
Tomorrow Never Dies (1997)
USED BY The Royal Navy

As tensions rise to a boiling point with China, the British fleet prepares for war in the South China Sea under its flagship HMS Bedford, commanded by Admiral Kelly. When James Bond triggers an explosion aboard press baron Elliot Carver's stealth ship, the Bedford sees the craft on its radar. HMS Bedford pursues the stealth ship and attempts to blow it out of the water. After Carver's stealth ship explodes, HMS Bedford searches for Bond and his ally Wai Lin of the Chinese People's External Security Force. Safe amid the wreckage, Bond and Wai Lin decide to remain "under cover" a little longer.

BEECH 18

APPEARANCE
Octopussy (1983)
USED BY Kamal Khan, Gobinda

AERIAL DUEL Gobinda battles Bond in mid air outside of Khan's Beech 18.

Kamal Khan uses his personal Beech 18, a twin-engine, low-wing, conventional-gear aircraft, to escape justice with counterfeit currency plates. Bond leaps from horseback onto the tail during take off to rescue Khan's hostage Octopussy. When Bond climbs out on a wing and pulls out engine wires, Khan sends his henchman Gobinda to kill him. Bond uses the plane's aerial to swat Gobinda off the plane. He then kicks at the ailerons, and Kamal struggles with the controls as the Beech 18 loses altitude. 007 crawls into the cabin, grabs Octopussy, and jumps out as the plane skids toward the edge of a cliff. Bond and Octopussy survive, but the Beech 18 crashes and explodes, killing Khan instantly.

BELL HELICOPTERS

APPEARANCES
Thunderball (1965), You Only Live Twice (1967), On Her Majesty's Secret Service (1969), Diamonds Are Forever (1971), Live And Let Die (1973), The Spy Who Loved Me (1977), Moonraker (1979), For Your Eyes Only (1981)
USED BY James Bond, Felix Leiter, CIA, Irma Bunt, Draco's men, Willard Whyte, Kananga's men, Dr. Bechmann, Prof. Markovitz, Naomi, Corinne Dufour, Blofeld, General Koskov, Necros

Bell helicopters have proved useful tools to 007 in foiling several madmen's plots. Equally, many megalomaniacs have used Bell helicopters to try to stop Bond.
During Operation Thunderball, CIA agent Felix Leiter flies Bond in a Bell 47J helicopter on a search for a

AIR TAXI A Bell carries Bond to Blofeld's clinic in On Her Majesty's Secret Service.

scuttled Vulcan bomber in Bahamian waters. The helicopter's pontoons allow Bond to scuba dive directly from the 47J when the pair locates the plane.
In You Only Live Twice, as 007 circles Japanese volcanoes in the Little Nellie gyrocopter, four black Kawasaki/Bell 47G-3 helicopters attack with high-powered machine guns. Bond destroys all of them with Little Nellie's arsenal of weapons.
In On Her Majesty's Secret Service, Blofeld's henchman Irma Bunt flies with Bond to Piz Gloria in a Bell 206 JetRanger. Later, Bond returns with Draco's men in three Bell 204 Hueys with fake Red Cross markings to attack Blofeld's hideout.
Diamonds Are Forever features millionaire Willard Whyte and Felix Leiter leading an attack on Blofeld's oil rig headquarters in a Bell 206B helicopter. Two UH-1H Hueys and three OH-6A Cayuses participate in the attack as well.
Live And Let Die features a Bell 206 JetRanger belonging to dictator Dr.

Kananga that tries to machine-gun Bond and clairvoyant Solitaire under the nets of Kananga's poppy fields.

The Spy Who Loved Me presents two enemy Bell 206 JetRangers, both owned by aquatic-obsessed Karl Stromberg. He destroys one carrying Dr. Bechmann and Prof. Markowitz after they have successfully developed the submarine tracking system for him. Later, Stromberg's pilot Naomi tries to eliminate Bond and Russian agent Anya Amasova with high-powered machine guns attached to her Bell helicopter. Bond destroys the JetRanger with a missile fired from his Lotus submersible.

Bell 206 JetRangers are also used by the villain of *Moonraker*, Hugo Drax. Drax's assistant, Corinne Dufour, flies 007 in one from LA airport to Drax's estate in the California desert.

In *For Your Eyes Only*, a man appearing to be Blofeld manages to tamper with an MI6 Augusta/Bell 206B helicopter (with Universal Exports painted on the side). He installs a remote control mechanism allowing him to fly the craft from a London rooftop location. Using a high-voltage line off the craft's generator, the man sends a deadly shock to the pilot, then takes the lone passenger—Bond—for a wild ride. Bond slips into the cockpit, disconnects the remote control, impales the man's wheelchair on the end of one of the skids, and drops the criminal mastermind down a 300-ft (91.4-m) chimney.

DIVING FOR COVER *Naomi's Bell 206 JetRanger drives Bond and Anya Amasova into the sea in* The Spy Who Loved Me.

BENTLEY MK IV

APPEARANCE
From Russia With Love (1963)
DRIVEN BY **James Bond**

James Bond's personal Mark IV drophead coupé (circa 1936) Derby Green Bentley can be seen briefly as Bond answers a call from Miss Moneypenny on the car's MTS radio telephone, which had recently been introduced in Britain. Bond also has a "cricket," an early form of a pager that informs him when he has a call.

In the Fleming novels, Bond owns a series of Bentleys. He first owns a 1930 4-cylinder 4 ½-liter Bentley convertible, which is destroyed during a car chase. Bond replaces that car with a 1953 Bentley Mark VI convertible with an open touring body. He later purchases a wrecked Bentley Continental that he has specially modified.

BIRD 1

APPEARANCE
You Only Live Twice (1967)
USED BY **Blofeld, SPECTRE astronauts**

Blofeld utilizes a two-stage rocket to capture US and Soviet spacecraft. A two-man craft with a large cargo bay, *Bird 1* is unique for its era, because it has a fully reusable main capsule. *Bird 1's* ability to land on four deployable legs as the craft nears touchdown also stands as a remarkable engineering achievement. The craft features a precision internal gyroscopic guidance system and retro-rockets which allow for vertical touchdown with safety and accuracy that has yet to be duplicated in manned spaceflight. *Bird 1* launches from Blofeld's rocket base headquarters in Japan, concealed inside a dormant volcano. 007 blows up *Bird 1* in orbit by unlocking and pressing the destructor button. Blofeld himself wipes out the ground-control technology when he sets off a series of explosions.

BMW Z3

APPEARANCE
GoldenEye (1995)
DRIVEN BY James Bond, Jack Wade

BMW Z8

APPEARANCE
The World Is Not Enough (1999)
DRIVEN BY James Bond

BMW 750IL

APPEARANCE
Tomorrow Never Dies (1997)
DRIVEN BY James Bond

James Bond's specially equipped BMW 750iL proves its worth when 007 visits Hamburg, Germany. Bond collects the car at the airport from Q, who poses as an Avis Rent-A-Car agent. Bond uses the traditional car as part of his cover as a banker. He makes a quick escape in the BMW from Elliot Carver's media complex. Later, Elliot Carver's men unsuccessfully attempt to break into the sedan on the fourth floor of the six-story car park to retrieve a GPS encoding device. The device remains hidden in the car's glove compartment, which doubles as a safe and carries a spare Walther PPK. Due to the car's top-level security system, attempts to break the its windshields with sledgehammers and tire irons prove fruitless. The electrified door handles further prevent entry to the would-be thieves.

The 750iL can be driven by remote, using the touch pad on 007's specially modified Ericsson mobile phone. Two taps cause the car's ignition to roar to life. A press of a button on the touch pad emits tear gas from the car. The touch pad allows Bond to drive the BMW from the backseat, where a German female voice warns him of potential driving

hazards. Bond remotely drives the 750iL to the first floor of the car park and then back to the fifth floor in attempts to escape from Carver's men.

The 750iL's top secret gadgetry includes twelve rockets hidden in the sunroof, caltrops spilling from the back bumper, re-inflatable tires, and a cable-cutting device that extends from the BMW's hood badge. On the fifth floor, Bond removes the GPS encoder from the glove compartment and leaps from the BMW as he sends the sedan flying off the roof of the garage straight into an Avis Rent-A-Car.

> "If you'd just sign here, Mr. Bond. It's the insurance damage waiver for your **beautiful new car.**"
>
> **Q to 007**

James Bond's blue BMW Z3 may be a small car, but Q assures Bond it's packed with all the usual refinements. With agile five forward gears, all points radar, a self-destruct system, and a parachute that fires out the back, it seems well-suited to any situation. Q is particularly proud of the Stinger missiles behind the headlights. It can also accelerate from 0 to 60 mph (96.6 kph) in 8.5 seconds with a top speed of 130 mph (209.2 kph).

While none of the more aggressive additions plays a role in Bond's mission, 007 does use the radar in the Caribbean. The screen pops up between the front seats to alert him of CIA contact Jack Wade's approaching Cessna 172. Wade temporarily trades Bond the Cessna for the Z3, with Bond admonishing him not to push any of the buttons. He looks mildly worried when Wade responds that he's just going to go "bombing around" in it.

Q provides Bond with a customized BMW Z8 for his mission to Baku to protect oil heiress Elektra King. The "fully loaded" car with the very latest in interceptive countermeasures, titanium armor, multitasking heads–up display, and the all-important six beverage cup holders, has enough firepower to blast a helicopter from the skies. Bond sacrifices the Z8 during his mission to Baku in order to save his own life.

At a caviar factory by the Caspian Sea, Bond and nuclear

physicist Dr. Christmas Jones question caviar factory owner Valentin Zukovsky about King when her Eurocopter AS-355F1 Ecureuil II "Twin Squirrel" helicopters, equipped with five-blade tree-cutting rigs, suddenly raid the factory. Bond uses his key fob to remotely drive his BMW toward him. Inside,

Bond activates a target-locking missile launcher concealed behind the car's exterior air vent by pressing buttons on the center of the steering column next to the BMW badge. Bond destroys one helicopter but has to evacuate the Z8 as another slices the car in half. Bond comments, "Q's not going to like this."

NIGHT RAID *(above left) King's tree-cutter copters hone in on Bond's Z8.*

SLICED *(above) Tree-cutting saws rip Bond's Z8 in half during the factory attack.*

BMW R1200

APPEARANCE
Tomorrow Never Dies (1997)
USED BY James Bond, Wai Lin

Carver's Eurocopter 350B A-Star helicopter pursues Bond and Wai Lin with its co-pilot firing a machine gun at them. Mounted on a BMW R1200 motorbike, they speed along streets, walkways, and rooftops, jumping from one building to another to escape a hail of bullets. When the chopper traps Bond and Wai Lin in a courtyard, they grab a washing line and lay the R1200 on its side, sliding just beneath the rotors. Bond slings the line into the helicopter's tail rotors, causing it to crash and explode.

THE HIGH WAY *(right) 007 and Wai Lin leap over rooftops to evade Carver's helicopter.*

EVASIVE ACTION *Seemingly trapped in a cul-de-sac by Carver's helicopter, Bond and Wai Lin skid beneath its whirling blades.*

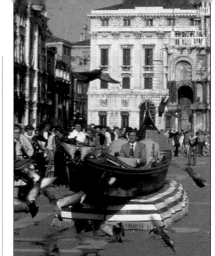

BOBSLED

APPEARANCE On Her Majesty's Secret Service (1969)

USED BY James Bond, Blofeld

Following the defeat of his guards by a force led by Bond and his ally Marc Ange Draco, Ernst Stavro Blofeld escapes from Piz Gloria, his mountaintop base, in a two-man racing bobsled. Bond, in another bobsled, pursues Blofeld down the mountain. Blofeld attempts to kill Bond with a grenade but only ends up blasting him across a hairpin turn, where 007 leaps on to Blofeld's sled. The two men battle on the sled until Blofeld pins Bond down. As Blofeld pummels Bond, a low-hanging branch sweeps the master criminal off the bobsled, breaking his neck.

BOMB SLED

APPEARANCE

Thunderball (1965)

USED BY SPECTRE frogmen, Emilio Largo

To transport two NATO atomic weapons, SPECTRE commissions a motorized underwater bomb sled. The sled is used to extract weapons from a hijacked Vulcan bomber. The bright orange sled is easily identifiable from the air, helping the US aquaparas to locate the craft. The sled is equipped with headlamps for night work and six forward-firing CO_2 spearguns for defense.

BONDOLA

APPEARANCE

Moonraker (1979)

DRIVEN BY James Bond

When a knife-thrower kills Bond's gondolier, Franco, Bond opens a hidden control panel on the left side of his gondola. He engages the throttle, and a propeller underneath the boat sends it speeding down the Venetian canals. Approaching St. Mark's Square, Bond unveils another control panel from the right side of the boat and pushes buttons that inflate a skirt underneath, turning the gondola into a hovercraft. He cruises through the square, using a steering wheel that emerges from the footrest. Tourists cannot believe what they see; even a pigeon does a double-take. Bond reenters the water and punts the boat like a normal gondola for a nighttime surveillance of billionaire Hugo Drax's secret nerve gas laboratory.

BSA A65L LIGHTNING

APPEARANCE

Thunderball (1965)

DRIVEN BY Fiona Volpe

The BSA A65L Lightning 650cc is one of the finest British motorcycles ever built. Manufactured by the Birmingham Small Arms Company, the twin cylinder 1965 Lightning hit the roads in late 1964, just in time for SPECTRE member Fiona Volpe to purchase one and outfit it with four front-firing rockets. Volpe uses the Lightning to eliminate fellow SPECTRE member Count Lippe, whom Blofeld feels has endangered the NATO project. While Lippe pursues 007's Aston Martin DB5 in a Ford Skyliner, Volpe drives the BSA close behind. She fires the rockets, which appear to skew wildly, but manage to hit their mark and blow up the rear portion of the car. As Lippe careens off the road, the gas tank ignites. Volpe takes the BSA to a nearby lake and disposes of it.

CABLE CAR

APPEARANCES

On Her Majesty's Secret Service (1969), Moonraker (1979)

USED BY James Bond, Grunther, Irma Bunt, Blofeld's Angels of Death, Holly Goodhead, Jaws

James Bond twice faces danger in connection with cable cars.

In On Her Majesty's Secret Service, he attempts to escape Blofeld's Piz Gloria base by going hand-over-hand down the guide cable from the cable car's wheelhouse. When a gondola ascends to Piz Gloria, Bond almost loses his hands as the guide-wheels roll over the cable.

In Moonraker, Bond and astronaut Dr. Holly Goodhead board an aerial tramway to descend Sugar Loaf Mountain. Jaws stops the cable car wheel and shears the tow-cable with his

JAW-DROPPING *Bond and Jaws grapple on top of a cable car in* Moonraker.

BLAME IT ON RIO *(below right) Bond and Holly climb atop the aerial tramway car at Sugar Loaf Mountain.*

teeth, causing the safety brake on the guide wheels to engage. Jaws then rides another car up to meet the pair. He leaps onto their car, but 007 and Goodhead escape by sliding down the guide cable on a chain. Jaws signals a helper to disengage the car's brake hoping to run Bond and Holly down; instead, he crashes into the station. Emerging from the wreckage, Jaws meets and falls in love with his soulmate Dolly.

WILD ONE *A leatherclad Fiona Volpe revs her lethal BSA Lightning.*

CAGIVA MOTORCYCLE

APPEARANCE
GoldenEye (1995)
DRIVEN BY James Bond, Soviet soldiers

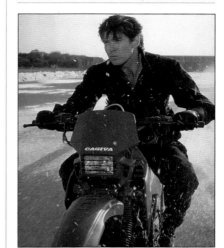

As Bond pursues a plane taxiing away from a Soviet chemical weapons facility, two soldiers on Mera Cagiva 600 W 16 bikes give chase. Bond climbs onto the plane, struggles with the pilot, and shoots one soldier off his bike. Bond and the pilot roll out of the plane and the second soldier's bike hits the pilot. Bond retrieves the bike and races after the plane, driving it over a cliff and diving off into a freefall.

CAPTURED TRAWLER

APPEARANCE
Tomorrow Never Dies (1997)
USED BY Wai Lin, Elliot Carver's men

Wai Lin hires a trawler to take her into Vietnamese waters, where HMS *Devonshire* sank. Upon reaching the surface with Bond—who parachuted into the sea on the same quest—Wai Lin indicates for the trawler to collect them. But Carver's enforcer, Stamper, fires a speargun harpoon into the helmsman's chest, and he and his men take control of the ship and capture Wai Lin and Bond.

CESSNA 140

APPEARANCE
Live And Let Die (1973)
USED BY James Bond, Mrs. Bell

The Cessna 140 N77029, used as a training plane by The Bleeker Flying School, makes a handy escape craft for Bond when Dr. Kananga/Mr. Big's minions try to capture him and take him for a "skydive" at Lakeside Airport in New Orleans. To the great relief of Mrs. Bell, the student pilot inside, Bond never actually takes the plane into the air. As Kananga's henchmen give chase, Bond drives the plane around the airfield and through the hangar, ripping the wings off in the process.

CESSNA 185 SEAPLANE

APPEARANCE
Licence To Kill (1989)
FLOWN BY Sanchez's pilot, James Bond

Off the coast of Key West, a Cessna 185 seaplane lands near the *Wavekrest*, Milton Krest's research ship and distribution base for Franz Sanchez's drug operation. The *Sentinel*, a remote-controlled submersible, delivers $5 million from the *Wavekrest* to the Cessna pilots in exchange for cocaine. Underwater, Bond destroys the drug shipment in the *Sentinel* and fires the harpoon of a CO_2 speargun into the pontoon of the seaplane. He barefoot skis behind the Cessna as it taxis, takes over the plane, disposes of the pilots, and flies away with Sanchez's drug money.

CHESTER, HMS

APPEARANCE
Tomorrow Never Dies (1997)
USED BY The Royal Navy

Admiral Roebuck orders the Royal Navy frigate HMS *Chester* to launch a missile strike into a terrorist arms bazaar. When Roebuck and MI6 learn that an L39 Albatross jet at the bazaar carries Soviet SB-5 nuclear torpedoes, Roebuck orders the Chester to abort the missile. The missile, however, is too far away to destroy.

CHEVROLET DELIVERY TRUCK

APPEARANCE
From Russia With Love (1963)
DRIVEN BY Rhoda, James Bond

This Chevrolet C30 1961 flatbed delivery truck plays an important role in SPECTRE's plot to steal the Lektor and humiliate James Bond. Driver Rhoda parks the truck across the Orient Express's track as though he has engine trouble in order to pick up assassin Donald "Red" Grant. Instead, Bond steals the truck and kidnaps Rhoda. In the truck, Bond dodges hand grenades from a SPECTRE helicopter and, after downing the chopper, forces Rhoda to guide him to SPECTRE's escape boat.

CITROËN 2CV

APPEARANCE
For Your Eyes Only (1981)
DRIVEN BY James Bond, Melina Havelock

Bond tests the limits of his driving skills when he is forced to escape in Melina Havelock's Citroën 2CV as a pair of Hector Gonzales's henchman pursue him in a couple of far more powerful Peugeot 504 sedans.

Created in 1939, the low-powered, low cost 2CV became Citroën's version of a "people's car." It is the antithesis of Bond's hand-built British sports cars.

After James Bond's white Lotus Esprit Turbo self-destructs when attacked outside a villa in Spain, 007 takes the passenger seat in marine archaeologist Melina Havelock's yellow 2CV. The two Peugeot 504 sedans, driven by Gonzales's henchmen, give chase through the Spanish countryside. In one small town, the 2CV overturns, allowing 007 to take over driving. Once Bond takes the wheel, he uses the 2CV's maneuverability and durability to his advantage in turning the tables on his pursuers.

"I love a drive in the country, don't you? Hold tight!"

007 to Melina

CROCODILE MINI-SUBMARINE

APPEARANCE
Octopussy (1983)
DRIVEN BY **James Bond**

James Bond uses a crocodile mini-submarine built by Q to inconspicuously approach the heavily guarded floating palace belonging to jewel smuggler Octopussy.

The jaws of the fake crocodile open and close to allow 007 entry and exit into the mini-submarine. Later, when Bond and one of Mufti's thugs crash into the quay, Bond pretends to be eaten by the crocodile, much to the distress of Octopussy. He actually escapes in the crocodile submarine and reports back to Q.

DEVONSHIRE, HMS

APPEARANCE
Tomorrow Never Dies (1997)
USED BY **The Royal Navy**

The British frigate HMS *Devonshire* becomes a pawn in Elliot Carver's plot to foment a war between China and Britain. Carver uses one of his satellites to beam a false GPS signal to the *Devonshire*. When the Chinese military accuses the *Devonshire* of being in their waters, the *Devonshire*'s captain, Commander Day, argues the ship is in international waters, In fact, it has been guided into Vietnamese waters. Secure in Carver's invisible-to-radar stealth ship, Stamper creates an international incident by sinking the *Devonshire* with the Sea Vac drill and shooting down a Chinese MiG fighter with a missile. Stamper then machine-guns the *Devonshire*'s 17 survivors while the stealth ship's crew

DOOMED *Sailors aboard the* Devonshire *fight for their lives as the sea pours through the gaping hole made by Carver's Sea Vac drill.*

salvage one of its cruise missiles. Bond and Wai Lin later locate the wreck and discover that a missile is missing. During their search, the *Devonshire* slips off the edge of a shelf and plunges into an abyss.

M - 265924

DISCO VOLANTE

APPEARANCE
Thunderball (1965)

USED BY Emilio Largo, SPECTRE

Emilio Largo purchased an early Rodriguez hydrofoil that he has customized with two Pratt & Whitney J12 jet engines to assist and supplant the onboard diesel. He has an outer shell, or cocoon, designed and built to give the appearance of a staid motor yacht. Behind the foils, Largo installs an underwater hatch. In the rear, he adds a smoke pot to create a smoke screen. On the cocoon, Largo mounts a front-facing WWII-era anti-aircraft gun. He also

BREAKING AWAY *Under fire by the US Navy and the US Coast Guard, the* Disco Volante *jettisons its cocoon, revealing itself to be a powerful hydrofoil.*

UP TO NO GOOD *A hatch in the hull enables Largo and his men to come and go unseen.*

installs placements for two smaller machine guns. Christening the motor vessel *Disco Volante* ("flying saucer" in English), Largo registers the craft in Panama. With the cocoon attached, the *Disco* can move at nearly 20 knots owing to the light catamaran design of the outer shell. Without the cocoon, the *Disco* can travel at 70 knots on her foil with her two rear jet engines at full thrust, a speed that enables the *Disco* outrun virtually any pursuing waterborne craft. The hydrofoil portion weighs 20 tons (18.1 tonnes)

and measures 65 ft (19.8 m) in length. The disguise allows Largo to secretly crew the vessel through the underwater hatch, collect and move the atomic weapons, and shed the cocoon for maneuverability and speed, if necessary.

The *Disco Volante* disintegrates in an explosion in Biscayne National Park while fleeing from the Royal Navy and US Coast Guard. All hands are lost except for Largo's mistress, Domino Derval, nuclear physicist Latislav Kutze, and uninvited passenger James Bond.

DRAGON TANK

APPEARANCE
Dr. No (1962)

USED BY Dr. No's men

Dr. No uses a swamp vehicle painted like a dragon and outfitted with a flame thrower to frighten away visitors to Crab Key. Both Honey Ryder and Quarrel know of the "dragon" and fear it. When Bond, Honey and Quarrel enter the island's

swamplands, the dragon tank hunts them down. The dragon's flame-thrower burns Quarrel to death, and Dr. No's men capture Bond and Honey.

In the novel, the dragon tank incinerates two wardens from the Audubon Society who live on Crab Key to monitor a population of roseate spoonbills. This initiates 007's battle with Dr. No.

ESCAPE POD

APPEARANCE
The Spy Who Loved Me (1977)

USED BY James Bond, Anya Amasova

When the USS *Wayne* torpedoes shipping magnate Karl Stromberg's *Atlantis* base, Bond and Soviet agent Anya Amasova flee in a handy escape pod. The pod, which rises to the ocean surface and emits a radio signal that allows it to be discovered, is equipped with a round bed and stocked with books, magazines, and spirits. Pressing a switch causes curtains to drape over the observation window.

PICKED UP *M, Q, Sir Frederick Gray, and KGB chief Gogol inspect Stromberg's pod.*

CURTAIN CALL *Bond and Anya demonstrate a new era of Western–Soviet cooperation inside Stromberg's escape pod.*

EUROCOPTER TREE-CUTTER

APPEARANCE
The World Is Not Enough (1999)
USED BY Elektra King's men

King Industries uses Eurocopter AS-355F1 Ecureuil II "Twin Squirrel" helicopters fitted with five giant vertically-suspended buzz saws to remove trees in the path of the future King oil pipeline. When Elektra King discovers Bond is alive at Valentin Zukovsky's caviar factory, she orders two tree-cutting choppers to eradicate Bond, Zukovsky, and Christmas Jones. As one of the helicopter's saws slices through buildings, Bond reaches his BMW Z8 and destroys the other one with a target-locking missile. The first chopper sneaks up behind, slices through the BMW, and chases Bond along a wooden walkway. Zukovsky and Christmas attempt to escape the deadly buzz saws by jumping into Zukovsky's Rolls-Royce and reversing along a walkway. The chopper slices the walkway to pieces, causing the Rolls to fall into the sea. Bond then opens a rusted gas jet, waits for the chopper to hover over it, and fires a flare gun at the gas. The resulting fireball sends the chopper's saws flying out of control and Zukovsky falling into a caviar pit.
See also Aerospatiale Helicopters

SLICED APART
The whirling blades of the tree-cutter zero in on 007's BMW.

FAIREY HUNTRESS SPEEDBOAT

APPEARANCE
From Russia With Love (1963)
DRIVEN BY James Bond, Morzeny, SPECTRE operatives

James Bond steals the Fairey Huntress speedboat on the Dalmatian Coast and uses it to escape with Soviet cipher clerk Tatiana Romanova and the Lektor decoder. The 23-ft (7-m) speedboat is confronted by SPECTRE's two Huntsmans and two Huntresses. While these boats have grenade launchers and machine-gunners, Bond's Huntress has a custom-made fuel drum rack. When bullets hit the drums, Bond releases them into the water and appears to surrender. Instead, he ignites the fuel slick with a flare which catches the SPECTRE boats on fire.

WATER RACE
Morzeny shouts orders to his fellow SPECTRE attackers in his Fairey Huntsman.

FERRARI F355 GTS

APPEARANCE
GoldenEye (1995)
DRIVEN BY Xenia Onatopp, Admiral Chuck Farrel

Xenia Onatopp, in a Ferrari Spider F355 GTS sports car with fake French registration plates, engages Bond, in his Aston Martin DB5, in a chase along the mountain roads of Monaco. Later, Bond sees the car—owned by Admiral Farrel—outside the Monte Carlo casino; Farrel and Onatopp drive it to the quayside as they travel to the yacht *Manticore*.

HOT PURSUIT
Xenia's Ferrari F355 speeds past cyclists on a training ride. Bond's Aston Martin DB5 follows.

FIRE TRUCK

APPEARANCE
A View To A Kill (1985)
USED BY James Bond,
Stacey Sutton

Bond and Stacey Sutton escape a
flaming San Francisco City Hall by
stealing a Tiller fire truck with an
unlocked mid-mount ladder. The San
Francisco police give chase, and
when Bond attempts to lock down
the rear ladder assembly, he finds
himself swinging dangerously over
busy city streets. After leaping a
drawbridge, the pair escapes and
uses the Tiller as cover to steal a
truck heading into Zorin's Main
Strike Mine.

FORD MUSTANG

APPEARANCES
Goldfinger (1964), Thunderball
(1965), Diamonds Are Forever (1971)
DRIVEN BY Tilly Masterson, Fiona
Volpe, Tiffany Case, James Bond

The Ford Mustang was a legendary
success in the 1960s, being unveiled
on all three major American
television networks on April 19,
1964. It proved to be the perfect
mass-production counterpart to
Bond's Aston Martin; over one
million 1964 1/2 Mustangs were sold
in comparison to 1023 hand-built
DB5s. Tilly Masterson drives a 1964

TOO CLOSE FOR COMFORT *Bond glimpses Tilly Masterson in his rear-view mirror in* Goldfinger.

1/2 cream Mustang convertible.
Unfortunately, her willingness to try
to shoot Goldfinger while Bond
stands in the way results in 007 using
the tire knife on his DB5 to blow
out both her tires and rip through
the body and door panels on the car.

In *Thunderball*, SPECTRE's Fiona
Volpe drives a 1965 powder-blue
Mustang convertible with a white
top in Nassau. After reconnoitering
Emilio Largo's yacht, Bond hitches a
ride with her to the Coral Harbour
hotel.

In *Diamonds Are Forever*, Tiffany

Case drives a red Mustang Mach 1
"Fastback." Tiffany and Bond use the
car to escape from guards at WW
Techtronics in the Nevada desert and
to elude the Las Vegas police and
Clark County Sheriff during a
spectacular chase in downtown Las
Vegas. Bond puts the strength of the
car's axels and its balance to the test
when he drives it through a narrow
alley on two wheels in order to shake
off his pursuer. The Sheriff attempts
to follow but, lacking Bonds'
expertise behind the wheel, turns
his police cruiser over.

FORD SKYLINER

APPEARANCE
Thunderball (1965)
DRIVEN BY Count Lippe

WHEELS ON FIRE *While pursuing Bond, Count Lippe's Ford Skyliner receives a direct hit from Fiona Volpe's motorbike.*

The 1957 Ford Fairlane 500 Skyliner, with its distinctive and celebrated retractable hardtop roof, provides a fiery end for SPECTRE operative Count Lippe when he decides to kill James Bond on a British motorway.

Lippe's Skyliner is in perfect working order when, in a fit of vengeance, he pursues Bond, firing a handgun at Bond's Aston Martin DB5. Bond prepares to defend himself by unleashing the furies of his car's arsenal, but he never gets the chance. Unknown to Lippe, his inefficiency has incurred the wrath of Ernst Stavro Blofeld, SPECTRE No. 1. He orders head executioner Fiona Volpe to extract the price of failure. Riding a BSA A65L Lightning 650cc motorcycle, Fiona Volpe fires rockets into the rear of Lippe's car. The explosion ignites the hydraulic system and eventually the gas tank, killing Lippe and destroying the car.

FORD THUNDERBIRD

APPEARANCES
Goldfinger (1964), Thunderball (1965), Diamonds Are Forever (1971), Die Another Day (2002)
USED BY Felix Leiter, Johnny, Emilio Largo, Mr. Wint, Mr. Kidd, Jinx

Four Ford Thunderbirds have been used by Bond's colleagues and enemies. In *Goldfinger*, Felix Leiter and CIA colleague Johnny drive a 1964 white Ford Thunderbird in Kentucky while investigating Goldfinger's activities. *Thunderball* features Emilio Largo driving a 1965 white Ford Thunderbird in Paris. In *Diamonds Are Forever*, assassins Wint and Kidd drive an unconscious Bond in a 1971 Ford Thunderbird through a tunnel from the Whyte House Hotel to the Nevada desert. *Die Another Day* showcases Jinx arriving in Iceland in a 2003 coral Ford Thunderbird. It is unknown whether this vehicle contains any special gadgetry.

TOP GEAR *Posing as Miss Swift from* Space Technology *magazine, Jinx arrrives in style at Gustav Graves's Ice Palace.*

GLASTRON SPEEDBOATS

APPEARANCES
Live And Let Die (1973), Moonraker (1979), A View To A Kill (1985)
USED BY James Bond, Adam, Kananga's thugs, Drax's minions, Jaws, May Day, Max Zorin

In *Live And Let Die*, James Bond escapes from Kananga's crocodile farm in a Glastron GT-150 and heads for the Irish Bayou in the Louisiana swamps. His pursuers drive the V-162 Futura, the V-145 Fireflite, the V-156 Sportster, and a V-184 Crestflite. The Sportster is the first casualty, crashing into a tree. When Bond finds his stretch of bayou leads to a causeway, he sends his GT-150 up an embankment, sailing over Sheriff J. W. Pepper's car and into the water on the other side. The pursuer in the Futura slams into the Sheriff's vehicle. Fuel spilling out of his engine due to a bullet hole from Pepper's gun, Bond ditches the GT-150 and steals a Glastron CV-19 from Deke Rodgers. The pursuers in the Firelite manage to get themselves stuck in the pool at Deke's home. Adam soon steals an even faster Glastron CV-21 jet boat from Louisiana wildlife ranger Billy Bob, Sheriff Pepper's brother-in-law.

Bond, the CV-21, and the Crestflight crash through a wedding ceremony, where the Crestflight ends up stuck in the catering tent. Bond leads Adam to Haley's Landing, douses him with gasoline, and then sends the CV-21 into a cargo ship where it spectacularly explodes.

While pursuing Sir Hugo Drax across the globe in *Moonraker*, 007 encounters Glastron boats driven by Drax's assassins in Venice. Bond himself takes a heavily customized silver flake Glastron/Carlson CV-23HT, specially outfitted with an array of gadgets from Q Branch, on a voyage up the River Tiparapé in Brazil. When Jaws and Drax's minions give pursuit in three SSV-189 boats armed with grenade launchers, Bond employs Q's defensive armaments, including a bulletproof shield, six mines ejected from the stern, a rear-launched torpedo hidden beneath the rear light fixture, and a roof-top hang glider. After Bond uses the hang glider to escape, the boat is destroyed when it tumbles down a massive waterfall.

In Paris, Max Zorin orchestrates the assassination of Achille Aubergine in *A View To A* Kill and collects May Day in a Glastron CVX-18 Intimidator.

LOW-FLYING BOAT *Sheriff Pepper is distracted from arresting Mr. Big's henchman Adam by 007's speedboat acrobatics.*

HERCULES C-130

APPEARANCE

The Living Daylights (1987)

USED BY M, 002, 004, James Bond

The Hercules C-130, one of the most common cargo planes in the world, serves as M's mobile headquarters as he briefs agents 002, 004, and 007 on war games with the SAS on the Rock of Gibraltar. The three double-0s skydive out of the open cargo bay and parachute onto the rock. M, who has allowed a desk to be loaded into the cargo bay, chases after his papers, which blow around in the wind.

ON MANEUVERS *Three MI6 agents, including 007, parachute from the Hercules to commence a training exercise.*

HILLER UH-12

APPEARANCES

From Russia With Love (1963), Goldfinger (1964)

USED BY SPECTRE, Pussy Galore, Goldfinger

SPECTRE uses the versatile Hiller UH-12C helicopter in *From Russia With Love*. The extremely stable, easy-to-fly craft is seen on SPECTRE Island bringing SPECTRE No. 3 Rosa Klebb to meet master assassin Donald "Red" Grant. Later, Bond encounters the helicopter when it begins chasing him and Tatiana as they make their escape from the Orient Express. Despite its safety record, the Hiller UH-12C cannot withstand the grenade explosion in the cockpit caused by the co-pilot.

In *Goldfinger*, Pussy Galore pilots a white Hiller UH-12E4 to Fort Knox. She transports Goldfinger, his associate Mr. Ling, and the atomic device Goldfinger plans to use to irradiate Fort Knox.

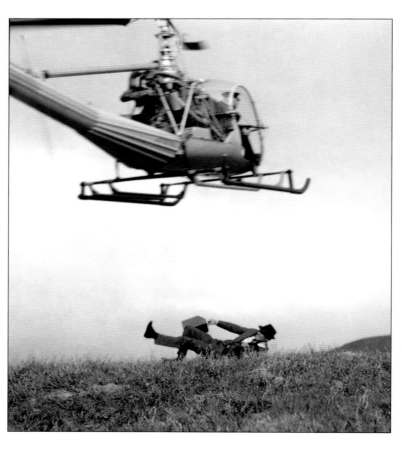

WANTED MAN *A SPECTRE Hiller helicopter hunts Bond in* From Russia With Love.

HONDA 3-WHEELER

APPEARANCE

Diamonds Are Forever (1971)

USED BY WW Techtronics Guards, James Bond

When 007 steals the WW Techtronics Moonbuggy, three guards give chase on Honda US 90 ATC 3-Wheelers. These vehicles can ride on most terrain and have greater stability than traditional motorcycles. Bond steals one from a Techtronics guard and uses it to reach smuggler Tiffany Case. The ATC uses a 90cc engine and drives on 22-in (55.8-cm) tires that are inflated with very low pressure. The machine can climb a gradient as steep as 35°.

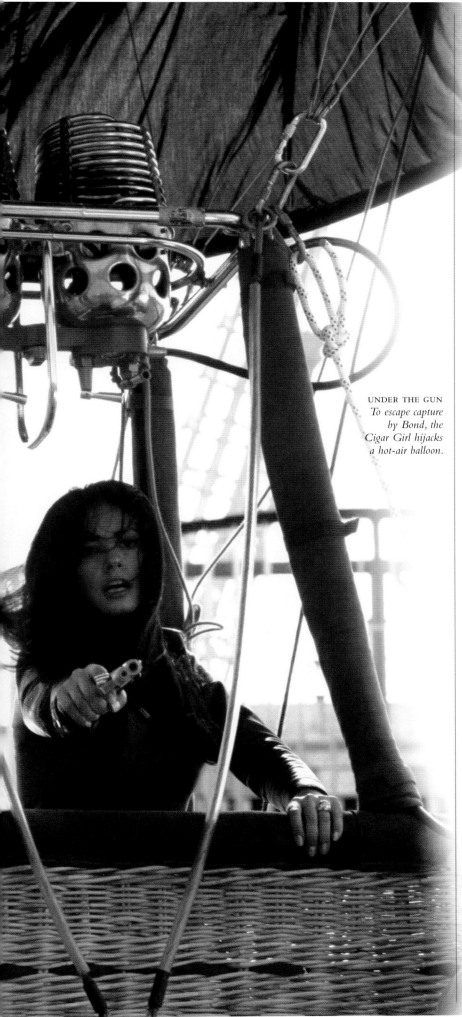

UNDER THE GUN
To escape capture by Bond, the Cigar Girl hijacks a hot-air balloon.

HOT AIR BALLOON

APPEARANCES
Octopussy (1983),
The World Is Not Enough (1999)
USED BY Q, James Bond, Cigar Girl

Bond rarely uses hot air balloons for transportation, but he does fly with Q in one that is decorated with a Union Jack in *Octopussy*. The pair use the balloon as they try to stop exiled Afghan prince Kamal Khan fleeing his Monsoon Palace. Television cameras attached to the balloon's structure allow for aerial surveillance of the palace.

In *The World Is Not Enough*, an assassin known as the Cigar Girl steals a hot air balloon to escape from 007. Bond leaps from a speeding boat onto one of the balloon's tethers. When the Cigar Girl commits suicide by blowing up the balloon's gas tanks, 007 has no choice but to let go of the tether and fall onto the Millennium Dome, painfully dislocating his collarbone.

ICEBERG SUBMARINE

APPEARANCE
A View To A Kill (1985)
USED BY James Bond

Following a dramatic ski chase, James Bond escapes Siberia in a submarine disguised as an iceberg. The iceberg has a Union Jack design on the inside of its hatch. Pilot and MI6 agent Kimberley Jones seems more than willing to enjoy vodka, caviar, and spending time with 007 during the five-day voyage to Alaska while the autopilot does the difficult work.

ICE DRAGSTER

APPEARANCE
Die Another Day (2002)
USED BY Gustav Graves, James Bond

Billionaire Gustav Graves enjoys racing his ice dragster to speeds of 324 mph (521.4 kph). To bring the ice jet to a stop, a parachute and grappling anchor emerge from the rear. Bond later steals the ice dragster to escape the heat beam of the Icarus satellite. Trapped on the face of a glacier, he uses the dragster's rear hatch and parachute to parasurf a tidal wave created as the heat beam destroys the glacier face.

LIVING THE DREAM *A braking parachute billows behind the dragster developed and raced in Iceland by diamond tycoon Gustav Graves.*

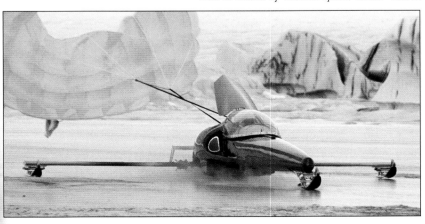

JAGUAR XKR

APPEARANCE
Die Another Day (2002)
DRIVEN BY Zao

In Iceland, Zao drives a gadget-laden 400-h.p. Jaguar XKR that rivals the most impressive vehicles from Q Branch. When Bond tries to use the adaptive camouflage on his Aston Martin Vanquish, Zao turns on a thermal imaging screen, giving him a perfect view. Zao hits a switch and a Gatling gun rises.and fires. The hail of bullets cause the Vanquish's adaptive camouflage to fail, rendering it visible. As Zao chases Bond over a frozen lake, Zao employs his battery of 18 heat-seeking missiles concealed behind the XKR's grille. Zao presses a button, revealing a rocket launcher. He fires at the Vanquish, overturning it. Another rocket barely misses as Bond uses his ejector-seat to right the car. Zao then launches a barrage of mortar bombs, which Bond

SHOOTING ON SIGHT *Zao targets Bond's Aston Martin with his XKR's Gatling gun.*

destroys with the Vanquish's target-seeking shotguns. Zao eventually corners Bond inside the melting Ice Palace and prepares to destroy the Vanquish with a battering ram protruding from his XKR's grille. The Vanquish's camouflage system corrects itself, the car seems to vanish, and Zao and his XKR fall into a lake of freezing water.

RACING DEMONS *Bond shunts Zao's XKR during their battle on the ice.*

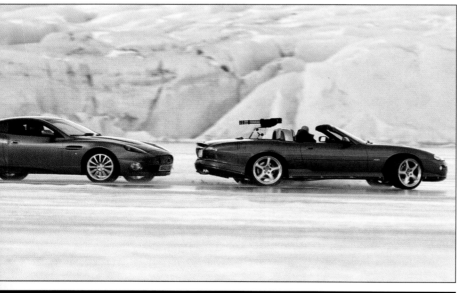

JUNK

APPEARANCES

The Man With The Golden Gun (1974), Tomorrow Never Dies (1997)
USED BY Scaramanga, James Bond, Nick Nack, Andrea Anders, Mary Goodnight, Wai Lin

In *The Man With The Golden Gun*, Scaramanga's diesel-powered junk survives the destruction of his island and allows Bond and staff intelligence officer Mary Goodnight to escape. When henchman Nick Nack interrupts the couple's lovemaking, Bond cages him in the crow's nest.

In *Tomorrow Never Dies*, Bond and Chinese agent Wai Lin hire a similar junk in Hao Long Bay to search for media mogul Elliot Carver's ship.

TOOLING UP *Aboard a rented junk, Bond and Wai Lin prepare to attack Carver's ship.*

JUPITER 16

APPEARANCE
You Only Live Twice (1967)
USED BY NASA

The US two-man spacecraft *Jupiter 16* becomes the first captured by Blofeld's *Bird 1* intruder rocket. While on an extended mission to practice EVAs (extravehicular activities) and conduct experiments, astronaut Chris exits the capsule using a maneuvering unit. Calls from Houston and Hawaii for Chris to re-enter the *Jupiter* capsule come far too late. *Bird 1*'s nose cone opens and swallows the capsule, snaps the astronaut's oxygen tether, and leaves Chris floating in orbit.

The *Jupiter* capsule mirrors the *Gemini* spacecraft used by NASA in 1965–66. The craft is called *Gemini* in the script, but filmmakers changed it to *Jupiter* because the *Gemini* program ended during the film's production.

KAWASAKI 900

APPEARANCE
The Spy Who Loved Me (1977)
DRIVEN BY Stromberg assassin

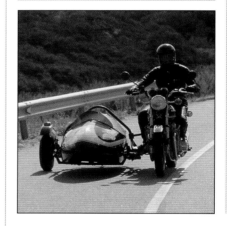

Leaving *Atlantis*, the marine research laboratory in Sardinia belonging to shipping tycoon Karl Stromberg, Bond and KGB agent Anya Amasova are pursued by an assassin riding a Kawasaki 900 motorcycle with sidecar. The sidecar is, in fact, a rocket that can be launched simply by pressing a button located on the motorcycle's handlebar. Driving his Lotus Esprit, Bond is able to maneuver between two lorries out of the path of the rocket, which ultimately destroys the trailer of a Sardadream mattress truck. The motorcyclist, blinded by the resulting cloud of feathers, goes careening off the road.

KAWASAKI-VERTOL KV107

APPEARANCE
You Only Live Twice (1967)
FLOWN BY Japanese SIS

The Japanese SIS uses a tandem-rotor Kawasaki-Vertol KV107-11, capable of lifting over 22, 000 lb (10,000 kg), to handle disruptive automobiles on the roads. When gunmen in a Toyota Crown S40 chase Bond and Aki in her Toyota 2000GT, the pair radios Tiger Tanaka. Aki asks Tiger for the "usual reception." The KV107-11 flies in, sets an industrial magnet on the roof of the Crown and flies off with the Toyota. The helicopter drops the pursuer's car in Tokyo Bay, despite the obvious disadvantage of not being able to question the occupants.

MAGNETIZED *Tanaka's Kawasaki uses a magnet to snatch up a car full of enemy agents on Bond and Aki's tail.*

KENWORTH TRUCKS

APPEARANCE
Licence To Kill (1989)

USED BY James Bond, Franz Sanchez, Sanchez's men, Pam Bouvier

Drug lord Franz Sanchez's team uses four Kenworth W900B tanker trucks to transport cocaine shipments. After setting Sanchez's lab on fire, Bond works with CIA contract pilot and agent Pam Bouvier to destroy the shipment. Bond jumps from a Piper crop-duster atop one tanker trailer. He takes control of the W900B, then shows his expert driving skills by tipping the truck and tanker up on its side wheels, allowing a Stinger missile to pass below. He also performs a wheelie on the tankerless truck to drive it through a wall of fire. Bond proceeds to destroy each of the tanker trailers. He forces one into a cliff face, where a Stinger missile strikes it. He takes out another two by releasing a tanker down a mountain where it crashes into another trailer being pulled below. Another wrecks when Sanchez cuts the hydraulic brake line as he tries to kill 007. Bond sets Sanchez on fire and he stumbles into the wreckage. As Sanchez immolates, the tanker and truck explode. Bond uses the one surviving W900B cab to ride to freedom with Pam.

FIREBALL Bond sends a tanker trailer down a slope and hits the lead truck in Sanchez's convoy.

L39 ALBATROSS

APPEARANCE
Tomorrow Never Dies (1997)

USED BY James Bond, unknown pilot

If a cruise missile hits the Soviet SB-5 nuclear torpedoes hanging from an L39 Albatross jet at a terrorist arms bazaar, mass destruction will result. Bond jumps into the cockpit of the Albatross, knocks out the co-pilot, and uses the jet's machine guns to wreak havoc. Bond takes off just before the missile hits. As he emerges from the fireball, so does a second Albatross with cannons blazing. The co-pilot in Bond's aircraft then revives and tries to garrote 007. With the second Albatross positioned overhead, Bond fires the rear-seat ejector. This sends the co-pilot smashing into the second Albatross, causing an explosion. "Backseat driver," Bond quips.

LAND ROVER

APPEARANCE
The Living Daylights (1987)
USED BY **Imposter agent, James Bond**

An imposter agent eliminates 004 in an exercise on the Rock of Gibraltar and escapes in a stolen Series III MOD Land Rover. Bond leaps onto the roof. The Land Rover smashes through a barrier and a soldier fires, hitting the gas tank; flames lick around explosives packed in the back. Bond grapples with the driver as the Land Rover crashes over a cliff. As the vehicle plummets toward the sea, Bond releases his reserve parachute, bailing out as the Land Rover explodes.

LINCOLN CONTINENTAL

APPEARANCES
Goldfinger (1964), Thunderball (1965)
USED BY **Oddjob, Mr. Solo, James Bond**

Goldfinger offers a luxurious 1964 Continental to gangster Mr. Solo after he refuses to take part in Operation Grand Slam. Oddjob drives Solo to a secluded spot, shoots him dead, then takes the car to a scrapyard where it is crushed and loaded into a waiting 1964 Ford Falcon Ranchero.

In *Thunderball*, Bond briefly drives a 1965 Continental convertible in the Bahamas when visiting the home of SPECTRE's Emilio Largo.

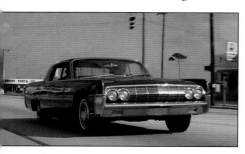

TAKEN FOR A RIDE *Oddjob pretends to drive Mr. Solo to the airport in* Goldfinger.

LIPARUS

APPEARANCE
The Spy Who Loved Me (1977)
USED BY **Karl Stromberg and his men**

Shipping tycoon Karl Stromberg's *Liparus* stands as a marvel of naval engineering. Designed to look like a supertanker—at over one million tons, it would be one of the largest ever built—the ship is, in fact, a floating submarine pen and command center. Stromberg builds the ship to take advantage of his submarine tracking technology and also to capture nuclear submarines.

Built in secret and manned by a loyal private navy, the *Liparus* has remained at sea for nine months. Stromberg uses the ship to kidnap both British and Soviet nuclear submarines (HMS *Ranger* and *Potemkin*, respectively). Armed with atomic weapons, Stromberg hopes to launch a nuclear war that will force civilization to rebuild beneath the sea. He later seizes the USS *Wayne*

"Now **where the hell is she?** By God, she's right behind us. **Impossible.**"

Commander Carter

with 007 aboard. The ship contains prisoner bays, a maglev monorail, and a substantial armory.

Bond ultimately initiates a battle to destroy the *Liparus*. Bond, Commander Carter, and the surviving crew members manage to climb back aboard the *Wayne*. They launch a torpedo to blast their way out of Stromberg's *Liparus* just before the ship meets its end at the bottom of the ocean.

PENNED IN *The* Liparus *houses the most sophisticated floating submarine command center ever built. The ship ends up where Stromberg hoped all humanity would—the ocean floor.*

LITTLE NELLIE

APPEARANCE
You Only Live Twice (1967)
FLOWN BY **James Bond**

James Bond uses the Wallis autogyro, no. G-ARZ B, for surveillance work in Japan while attempting to locate Blofeld's rocket base hidden on the southern islands. Operated under the code name Little Nellie, she proves to be a one-man air force, capable of defending herself and destroying a whole fleet of enemy aircraft.

Unlike a helicopter, only the Wallis autogyro's rear engine provides power during flight. Once airborne the top rotor freely spins by the force of air, creating an airfoil. Designed by Wing Commander Ken Wallis, the autogyro offers the advantages of precise handling, safe operation, high ground speed, and high altitude operation. The design also allows for safe descent should the engine fail in flight.

Tanaka: A toy **helicopter?** Q: No, it's certainly **not a toy.** You'll see.

Q Branch modifies the craft, outfitting it with an array of weapons and breaking it down so that it can fit into four alligator leather trunks. The weapons include two fixed machine-guns firing incendiary and high-explosive bullets harmonized for targets 100 yd (91.4 m) ahead, two forward-firing rocket launchers with seven rockets each, two heat-seeking air-to-air missiles, two rear-firing flame guns with a range of 80 yd (73 m) paired with smoke ejectors, and small high-explosive aerial mines. It also boasts radio communications and a helmet-mounted cine-camera triggered by using any of the forward-firing weapons. Bond uses these weapons as he battles four SPECTRE helicopters over the rocket base, destroying them one by one.

PORTABLE POWER *Q's technicians set to work assembling Little Nellie from parts supplied in four large alligator leather trunks.*

LOCKHEED JETSTAR PLANE

APPEARANCE
Goldfinger (1964)
FLOWN BY **Pussy Galore, Sydney**

Sold commercially starting in 1961, the Lockheed JetStar was the first and most luxurious private jet available for many years. Goldfinger's JetStar, piloted by Pussy Galore and copilot Sydney, comes with swivel seats, a wet bar, and a well-sized powder room. Goldfinger has installed two peepholes into the powder room and a two-way mirror on the medicine cabinet to keep his eye on passengers. He uses the plane to fly 007 from Switzerland to America, where it lands in Baltimore and travels on to Bluegrass Field in Lexington, Kentucky. The four-engine jet can achieve Mach 8, cruise at 41,000 ft (12,497 m), and travel over 2,000 miles (3,219 km) before refueling.

AIR FORCE 007 *Bond engages Little Nellie's rear-firing flame gun during his battle with SPECTRE helicopters in Japan.*

LOCKHEED US VC-140B

APPEARANCE

Goldfinger (1964)

USED BY Pussy Galore, Goldfinger, James Bond

The aircraft sent to collect James Bond after he has helped foil Goldfinger's mission to irradiate the US Treasury Bullion Depository is a Lockheed US VC-140B, the military VIP version of the JetStar, often used to fly the US President. This proves lucky for Goldfinger, as his pilot, Pussy Galore, flies Goldfinger's own JetStar. Goldfinger, dressed as a US Army General, kidnaps the crew and, with Galore, takes over the plane. When confronting Bond, Goldfinger discharges his gold-plated Colt .45, blowing out a window. As a result, Goldfinger finds himself sucked out of the cabin. The JetStar crashes but 007 and Galore parachute to safety.

LOTUS ESPRIT

APPEARANCE

The Spy Who Loved Me (1977)

USED BY James Bond, Anya Amasova

The modified Lotus Esprit S1 stands as one of the greatest cars ever built. Despite its size—165 in (419 cm) long, 73 in (185.4 cm) wide, and 44 in (111.7 cm) from ground to rooftop—Q modifies the Lotus to carry an arsenal of weapons and a full underwater conversion system, allowing the vehicle to operate as a submarine. All of this gadgetry exists on the car without sacrificing the Esprit's performance.

James Bond drives the Lotus in Sardinia during his joint mission with Major Anya Amasova of the KGB to investigate shipping tycoon Karl Stromberg. Although Q Branch designed and built the Lotus under strict security, Amasova stole the plans two years before her adventure with Bond. When Stromberg's assassins chase the pair, Bond employs a cement sprayer concealed under the rear license plate to blot out a pursuing car's windscreen.

Bond drives it into the sea to avoid a helicopter gunship and rapidly converts the Lotus into a submarine: the tires fold inside the car's body, rudders and fins emerge from the sides, rear screws and propellers deploy from the back bumper, louvers descend over the windows to cut surface glare, and a periscope rises from the car's roof. A video screen allows 007 a view behind the Lotus and digital readouts replace the analog dashboard. A targeting screen on the center console allows Bond to aim and fire a sea-to-air missile using the car's gearshift. Front-mounted torpedoes fire from controls on the steering wheel. The light switch initiates an ink cloud from the rear, and the hazard switch drops a mine from underneath. The Lotus is damaged during an underwater battle with Stromberg's men, but 007 reconverts it to a land car in the water and drives it up onto a beach.

BACK ON LAND *The Lotus converts back to normal car mode as it emerges from the waves.*

LOTUS ESPRIT TURBO

APPEARANCE

For Your Eyes Only (1981)

DRIVEN BY James Bond

Bond's white Lotus Esprit Turbo can achieve 0 to 150 mph (241.4 kph) in just 15 seconds. Bond doesn't get a chance to exploit the car's speed or use any of its gadgets. As Bond and Melina run to the car to escape a posse of gunmen, they see a thug smashing one of its windows. This triggers the self-destruct system, and the Lotus explodes.

Bond later drives a red Turbo in Cortina, Italy. He discovers the body of agent Ferrara in the car.

SELF-DESTRUCTIVE *A gunman inadvisedly attacks 007's Lotus.*

MAGLEV TRAIN

APPEARANCE

The Spy Who Loved Me (1977)

USED BY Karl Stromberg and his men, Anya Amasova, James Bond

A maglev (magnetic levitation) monorail train runs around the perimeter of the submarine pen inside Karl Stromberg's ship, the *Liparus*. Stromberg's maglev car shoots out of a hole in the side of the *Liparus*. The hull separates to reveal a motorboat, which Stromberg uses to take agent Anya Amasova to his *Atlantis* base. After escaping Stromberg's men, 007 forces the driver of a maglev car to take him to the prisoners's quarters, where 007 releases the captured sub crew.

M1 SUB

APPEARANCE

You Only Live Twice (1967)

USED BY M, Moneypenny, James Bond, Kissy Suzuki

M maintains a diesel-electric submarine for use by the British Secret Service. After the staging of Bond's death, 007's shrouded body is brought to the submarine. M briefs Bond on his upcoming mission in his office on the sub. When 007 finds himself adrift at sea with Japanese secret agent Kissy Suzuki at the end of the movie, HMS *M1* surfaces beneath the lifeboat and M orders Moneypenny to tell Bond to come below and report.

MANTIS

APPEARANCE

For Your Eyes Only (1981)

USED BY Mantis Man

The Osel "Mantis" One-Man Atmospheric Submersible, capable of working at depths of 1900 ft (579 m), attacks the *Neptune* submarine, with Bond and marine archaeologist Melina Havelock inside it, off the Albanian coast.

The Mantis arms have pincers and a destructive revolving drill with which it attacks the *Neptune*. Bond overpowers the Mantis, forcing it into a hole in the hull of the *St. Georges* wreck, where it remains.

MERCURY COUGAR

APPEARANCE On Her Majesty's
Secret Service (1969)
USED BY Tracy Di Vicenzo, James Bond

James Bond first meets Tracy Di
Vicenzo as she speeds along a
Portuguese coastal road past his
Aston Martin DBS in a red Mercury
Cougar convertible. Bond soon finds
the Cougar deserted on Guincho
Beach. After Bond rescues Tracy from
drowning and fends off Draco's men,
she abandons him and speeds off in
her Cougar. Later that day, he spots
the distinctive car parked outside the
Palacio Estoril Hotel and decides to
renew acquaintance with Tracy.

When 007 later finds himself
pursued by Irma Bunt and Blofeld's
men in the village of Grindenwald,
Switzerland, Tracy comes to the
rescue, and her Mercury Cougar
becomes the perfect escape vehicle.
As Bunt and her men give chase in a
black Mercedes, Tracy joins a stock
car race. The adventurous Tracy holds
her own with the professional stock
car drivers and puts the Cougar
through its paces, knocking several
cars out of the way, including the
black Mercedes, which flips over and
explodes. Tracy and Bond then brave
a blizzard and conceal the Cougar
inside a barn. That night, Bond
proposes marriage to Tracy. The car is
abandoned in the barn, and
apparently never recovered.

MEYERS 200A

APPEARANCE
You Only Live Twice (1967)
FLOWN BY Helga Brandt, James Bond

Helga Brandt tries to kill 007 in a
Meyers 200A, the 1966 speed
record-holder for single-engine
planes. Brandt, suspiciously wearing a
parachute, drops a lipstick flare and
triggers the rear arm rest side table to
slide over Bond's arms. After Brandt
bails out, Bond works a hand free,
karate chops the plank, and pilots the
aircraft to a no-gear crash landing
before it explodes.

MONORAIL

APPEARANCE
You Only Live Twice (1967),
Live And Let Die (1973)
USED BY Ernst Stavro Blofeld,
James Bond, Solitaire

Monorail systems have featured in
a number of Bond's adventures
because they are often ideal
transportation solutions for villains
with massive headquarters.

In You Only Live Twice, an elaborate
monorail network services Blofeld's
volcano rocket base in Japan. The
system features three types of electric
monorail carriages—a small, domed
carriage for moving people, a larger,
open-topped carriage for moving
equipment and supplies, and a similar
open-topped carriage for moving
groups of people. Bond secretes
himself in one of the cargo carriages
and finds himself in the astronaut
quarters near the cells where Blofeld
holds the US and Soviet astronauts
captured by Bird 1. When 007 dons a
spacesuit in the hope of flying in Bird
1, he travels to the launch pad on the
monorail. Later, Blofeld attempts to
shoot Bond from a small domed
carriage on the monorail, but Tiger
Tanaka, who is part of the invading
ninja force, foils the plan by hurling a
throwing star into Blofeld's wrist.
Blofeld engages the engine and
speeds away. After bandaging his
hand, Blofeld reappears in the
monorail carriage to set off a series
of explosions and utterly destroy his
already doomed rocket base.

In Live And Let Die, Dr. Kananga,
aka Mr. Big, maintains an
underground monorail as a potential
escape route from his underground
lair. Bond and Solitaire use it to
escape after killing Kananga.

MOONBUGGY

APPEARANCE
Diamonds Are Forever (1971)
DRIVEN BY WW Techtronics Guards, James Bond

The WW Techtronics moonbuggy receives quite a workout from 007 in the Nevada desert. When Professor Dr. Metz alerts security to an intruder, James Bond must figure out a way to escape the top secret facility.

Bond takes the moonbuggy, bursts through the wall, crashes through a security gate, and speeds into the desert. Able to attain speeds of up to 80 mph (129 kph) on tarmac, with a design based on a Corvair and steering from an Austin Healey Sprite, the craft easily outmaneuvers a pursuing security car. The moonbuggy has a harder time outrunning three Honda ATCs. Bond abandons the moonbuggy, kicks a WW Techtronics guard off an ATC, and rides to rendezvous with Tiffany Case.

In real life, the WW Techtronics moonbuggy never traveled to the moon, being rejected for the smaller and lighter, but less speedy and maneuverable LRV (Lunar Roving Vehicle), which was built by Boeing and Delco.

MOONRAKER SPACE SHUTTLE

APPEARANCE
Moonraker (1979)
FLOWN BY Hugo Drax, James Bond, Dr. Holly Goodhead

The Moonraker space shuttle can be launched into space by a rocket, orbit the earth, and reenter the atmosphere to land like a conventional aircraft. The shuttle is made at a facility owned by billionaire Hugo Drax in the California desert outside of Los Angeles. A number of Drax subsidiaries throughout the world produce components for the shuttle.

After one of his shuttles develops a fault during assembly, Drax's men steal a replacement as it is being flown to the British government piggybacked on a Boeing 747. Drax cannot afford to be one space shuttle down as he needs six shuttles to carry out his plan of global destruction and repopulation.

Investigating the missing space shuttle, Bond arrives at Drax's hidden South American launch facility in time to see the shuttle launch. Bond and CIA agent Dr. Holly Goodhead are taken into captivity, but the pair manages to escape and take over Moonraker 6. Holly pilots the shuttle on a pre-arranged flight program to Drax's secret space station.

Later, Bond and Holly use Drax's personal shuttle, Moonraker 5, to chase and destroy globes of lethal nerve gas that Drax has launched in order to wipe out Earth's population. With their mission accomplished, Bond and Holly make love in the shuttle's zero-gravity cargo bay.

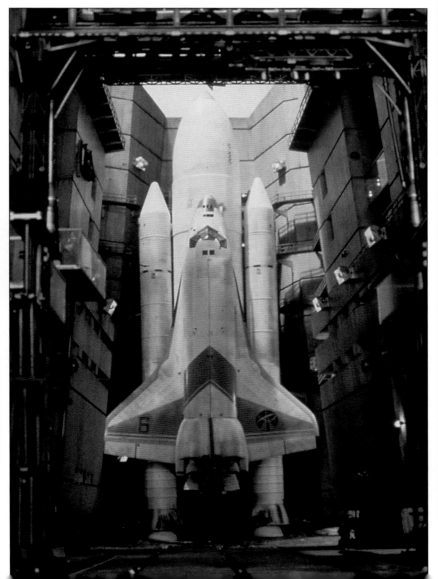

COUNTDOWN *A Moonraker space shuttle prepares to launch from Drax's base in the Brazilian jungle.*

MOSKVICH

APPEARANCE
GoldenEye (1995)
USED BY Jack Wade, James Bond

In St. Petersburg, Russia, James Bond's roguish CIA contact Jack Wade drives a little blue Moskvich car which, he proclaims, "hasn't let me down yet." When the car breaks down in St. Petersburg Square, Wade repairs it with the aid of a wrench, a screwdriver, and a whack from a sledgehammer. He then drives 007 in the Moskvich to the nightclub headquarters of arms dealer Valentin Zukovsky.

NEPTUNE

APPEARANCE
For Your Eyes Only (1981)
USED BY James Bond, Melina Havelock

The Neptune 2-Man Lock-out submersible, measuring 23 ft (7 m) by 8 ft (2.4 m), belongs to marine archaeologist Timothy Havelock. His daughter, Melina, and Bond use it to locate the sunken British spy ship the *St. Georges* off the Albanian coast. After retrieving the valuable ATAC transmitter from the ship, a Mantis one-man sub attacks the Neptune, but Bond and Melina use the Neptune's more powerful engines to win the clash.

NING-PO

APPEARANCE
You Only Live Twice (1967)
USED BY Ernst Stavro Blofeld, Helga Brandt

Bond discovers that Blofeld is using the *Ning-Po* to transport liquid oxygen—a key component of rocket fuel—to his secret base. When SPECTRE agents capture 007, they bring him aboard the *Ning-Po* to be interrogated by Helga Brandt.

Blofeld apparently named the ship after a notorious pirate ship of the Far East, which stood as a floating museum in Catalina Harbour for many years.

NOTAR MD-600N

APPEARANCES
Die Another Day (2002), Casino Royale (2006)
USED BY James Bond, Jinx, Villiers

As the Antonov flying command center disintegrates in *Die Another Day*, 007 and Jinx jump into a Notar MD-600N helicopter in the cargo hold. The chopper plunges backward off the ramp as the Antonov explodes. Bond frantically flicks switches trying to start the engine. 100 ft (30 m) from the ground, the engine kicks in, and Bond and Jinx fly the MD-600N to a Buddhist temple on the South Korean coast, where they make love amidst diamonds.

Bond also flies in a Notar MD-600N in *Casino Royale* as Villiers accompanies him from Miami to the estate of Alex Dimitrios.

OCTOPUSSY'S BARGE

APPEARANCE
Octopussy (1983)
USED BY Octopussy, Kamal Khan, James Bond, Magda

This lake barge, crewed by women, is the only legitimate means of accessing and leaving jewel smuggler Octopussy's heavily guarded palace in Udaipur, India. Afghan prince Kamal Khan visits Octopussy by traveling in this craft.

The crew rows to the command of an unidentified voice that instructs them with the words, "In, Out, In, Out." A flag depicting an octopus flies from the barge's mast. At the end of Operation Trove, Bond and Octopussy enjoy a romantic getaway on her barge.

OCTOPUSSY'S CIRCUS TRAIN

APPEARANCE
Octopussy (1983)
USED BY Octopussy, Octopussy's girls, Kamal Khan, General Orlov, Gobinda

Afghan prince Kamal Khan hide the bomb aboard the train in East Germany, knowing that the train will only receive a cursory look from

Jewelry smuggler Octopussy owns an S-class steam train, designated DR No 62 015. She uses it to transport her circus around Europe and to smuggle jewelry from East to West.

The train's smuggling activities are a perfect cover for Soviet General Orlov's plot to detonate an atomic weapon at Feldstadt Air Force Base in West Germany. Using the secret smuggling compartment in a prop circus cannon, Orlov and exiled

guards at the West German border. Bond, upon discovering the bomb is on the train, steals General Orlov's Mercedes and gives chase. Bond leaps onto the train in an attempt to warn Octopussy that she is being used for an act of nuclear sabotage. He does not get the chance. Attacked by Gobinda and later Grischka, Bond tumbles from the train, which arrives as scheduled at Feldstadt with its deadly cargo.

ORIENT EXPRESS

APPEARANCE

From Russia With Love (1963)

USED BY Bond, Tatiana Romanova, Kerim Bey, Donald Grant, Benz

The Orient Express remains the most famous train in the world. James Bond uses it as his escape route from Turkey to Italy with cipher clerk Tatiana Romanova and the Lektor cipher machine. Head of Station T Kerim Bey, Soviet security man Benz, and SPECTRE assassin Donald Grant all die inside its legendary carriages.

Bond uses the Orient Express because he can slip off it to smuggle the Lektor across the Yugoslavia/Italy border. SPECTRE No. 5 Kronsteen anticipates this plan, and thus Grant awaits Bond and Tatiana when they board, leading to a brutal confrontation in Bond's sleeper car.

The real train, founded in 1883, classically ran the Paris—Venice—Istanbul route. In February 1950, American Naval Attaché Captain Eugene Karpe died when pushed from the train after the exposure of his American spy ring. Karpe's murder inspired Ian Fleming to write *From Russia With Love*.

OSPREY HOVERCRAFT

APPEARANCE

Die Another Day (2002)

USED BY James Bond

Colonel Moon's hovercraft, equipped with RPGs, flame throwers, automatic weapons, gas masks, and enough ammunition for a small war, have been especially constructed to float over one million landmines in the Demilitarized Zone (DMZ) between North and South Korea. As Moon enters the DMZ on his hovercraft mothership, (actually a Griffin 2000TD model), a captured James Bond detonates a bomb in the diamond-filled briefcase using his Omega watch. Chaos ensues when 007 commandeers an Osprey hovercraft, fires rockets at Moon's headquarters building and his car collection from holes in the hovercraft's sides, and then pursues Moon in the DMZ. Moon uses his tank buster gun to detonate mines near Bond and then attempts to stop him by using automatic weapons and a flame thrower. Bond eventually boards the mothership and presses the accelerator, causing Moon to be thrown against a massive caged propeller. The mothership crashes through a temple, but 007 saves himself by grabbing onto a bell, leaving Moon and the hovercraft to tumble down a waterfall.

ONE-MAN ARMY Bond creates havoc in Moon's base aboard an Osprey hovercraft.

DANGER IN THE AIR Parahawks hunt Bond and Elektra in the Caucasus Mountains.

PARAHAWK

APPEARANCE

The World Is Not Enough (1999)

USED BY Renard's men

Parahawks are ultralight vehicles and hybrid snowmobiles that use parachutes instead of fixed wings.

While Elektra King shows Bond her family's future oil pipeline, four parahawks speed toward them. These are the property of the Russian Atomic Anti-Terrorist Unit and have been loaned to the terrorist Renard by Dr. Arkov. Bond orders Elektra to ski for a gully while he leads the parahawks into the trees. One parahawk's chute becomes entangled, destroying it. Two others land and turn into snowmobiles, their drivers firing machine guns. The remaining airborne parahawk drops a grenade at Bond but destroys a snowmobile instead. 007 then causes one to ski off a precipice; this parahawk deploys its reserve parachute and flies away. Bond destroys the two remaining parahawks by stabbing one parahawk's chute with his ski. Bond and Elektra look on as the parahawks crash into each other.

PILATUS TURBO-PORTER

APPEARANCE

GoldenEye (1995)

FLOWN BY James Bond

As Bond enters a Soviet Union mountain dam facility, a Pilatus PC-6/B2-H4 Turbo-Porter flies overhead. When Bond later escapes from the Arkangel Chemical Weapons Facility beneath the dam, the Pilatus rolls down the runway. Bond attempts to catch and hijack the plane. Although he pulls the pilot from the cockpit, the plane sails off the runway without Bond.

Knowing the slow dive-speed of the Pilatus, Bond seizes a Cagiva motorbike and drives off the cliff-face end of the runway as part of a desperate plan. Bond tucks himself into a speed-dive position, knowing that his terminal velocity is higher than that of the Porter. After precious seconds tick past, Bond catches the pilotless plane in mid-dive and pulls the exceptionally aerodynamically stable craft into level flight, moments before the plane would have crashed into the ground. Bond flies the plane to freedom as the chemical facility explodes below.

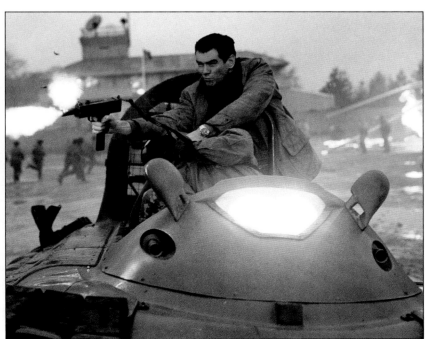

PIPER CHEROKEE

APPEARANCE
Goldfinger (1964)
USED BY Pussy Galore's Flying Circus

Pussy Galore's all-female flying circus uses Piper PA-28 Cherokees with varying engine sizes ranging from 140 hp to 235 hp. The pilots perform precision acrobatic maneuvers as part of Pussy Galore's Flying Circus, a traveling aerial show. The Cherokees play a key role in Goldfinger's plot to irradiate the gold in Fort Knox. They are intended to spray the area with the deadly Delta-9 nerve gas.

PIPER PA-18 SUPER CUB

APPEARANCE
Licence To Kill (1989)
FLOWN BY Pam Bouvier

Pam Bouvier steals a Piper PA-18 Super Cub crop-duster to aid Bond. She flies Bond over one of Sanchez's drug-laden tanker trucks, enabling Bond to leap onto it. She then dusts Sanchez's men with insecticide. Sanchez fires a Stinger missile at the Piper, destroying its tail, but Pam manages to crash-land the plane safely in the rocky terrain.

Q BOAT

APPEARANCE
The World Is Not Enough (1999)
DRIVEN BY James Bond

James Bond pilots a one-man aquatic jet craft custom-built by Bentz Boats with modifications by Q Branch. 007 commandeers the craft when an explosion damages MI6 HQ. He uses the Q Boat to chase the Cigar Girl, Renard's terrorist accomplice, in her Sunseeker Superhawk 34 speedboat, by leaping from a concealed torpedo ramp into the River Thames. Bond activates the boat's twin rear jet thrusters to catch up with and pass the Sunseeker.

The Q Boat's maneuverability allows it to turn 180° on a dime. Its stability and balance allow it to land on its hull after bounding over waves. When Bond slams the boat into the rear of the Sunseeker, sending it into a spiral, the Q Boat lands hull down. He employs the dive function, which briefly noses the bow underwater arcing the boat two to three ft (0.6–0.9 m) beneath the surface.

The boat's GPS auto-mapping system presents Bond an alternate route to catch his quarry when needed. The metal hull easily withstands bounding over a canal slipway, through the London Canoe Club boathouse, and the friction of grinding against pavement when Bond takes the Q Boat overland near Blackwall Basin on the Isle of Dogs. Bond fires the craft's two cannon-launched acoustic homing torpedoes. He damages the boat when he again ramps off the Sunseeker leaping onto a hot-air balloon tether.

The Q Boat makes an appearance in Q's lab at Castle Thane, MI6's remote operations center, where the damaged craft awaits repair. Q facetiously claims he will use the craft as a fishing boat during retirement.

RANGER, HMS

APPEARANCE
The Spy Who Loved Me (1977)
USED BY The Royal Navy, Karl
Stromberg and his crew

HMS *Ranger* is a Resolution-class Royal Navy submarine that carries sixteen Polaris nuclear missiles. While traveling at a depth of 500 ft (152.4 m), a loss of power forces the *Ranger* to surface. The submarine seems to vanish without a trace. Bond eventually discovers it, along with the *Potemkin*, a missing Soviet sub, in the bow of shipping tycoon Karl Stromberg's *Liparus*. Stromberg sends the *Ranger* and *Potemkin* out to fire their nuclear missiles and begin World War III, but Bond and Commander Carter send new target coordinates to the subs, causing them to destroy each other.

RED CROSS HELICOPTERS

APPEARANCE
On Her Majesty's Secret Service (1969),
The Living Daylights (1987)
USED BY Draco and his men, James
Bond, Necros, General Koskov

Although international humanitarian laws govern the use of Red Cross/ Red Crescent emblems, twice helicopters bearing false Red Cross markings have found their way into Bond's adventures. In *On Her Majesty's Secret Service*, Marc Ange Draco and Bond lead an attack on Piz Gloria in three faux Red Cross Bell 204 Hueys. In *The Living Daylights*, the tables turn when KGB General Koskov fakes his own kidnapping with a Bell UH-1H Huey painted with Red Cross markings.

BIG GAME FISHING *Bond blasts through the Thames in the Q Boat, looking for the assassin known as the Cigar Girl.*

RENAULT 11 TXE TAXI

APPEARANCE
A View To A Kill (1985)
DRIVEN BY James Bond

After May Day, henchman and lover of businessman Max Zorin, kills French detective Achille Aubergine and parachutes from the top of the Eiffel Tower, James Bond steals a 1984 front-wheel drive Renault 11 TXE taxi in order to intercept her. In his attempts to catch May Day, he proceeds to destroy the vehicle bit by bit.

Bond expertly spins the taxi down a flight of steps to the Seine quayside, dramatically leaps off a boat ramp, and drives over the top of a tour bus. The taxi then gets whittled down. Bond slices the top off with a metal gate arm, then, failing to avoid another car, the rear end gets sheared off in a collision.

Bond abandons the taxi on the Pont Alexandre III Bridge, failing to catch May Day and leaving the vehicle half the car it was.

RIO AMBULANCE

APPEARANCE
Moonraker (1979)
DRIVEN BY Hugo Drax's henchmen

After escaping from Jaws on Sugar Loaf Mountain, Bond and CIA agent Dr. Holly Goodhead are knocked out and subdued on gurneys inside a speeding ambulance. Holly attracts the attention of the attendant, whom Bond temporarily unnerves with a blast from a fire extinguisher. In the ensuing struggle, Bond and the attendant roll out the back of the vehicle on a gurney, leaving the ambulance to speed away with Holly held captive.

ALL FRONT *(left) Bond remains cool, calm, and collected behind the wheel of the sawn-off taxi.*

STAIR CRAZY *(below) A few moments earlier, Bond demonstrates the maneuverability of the Renault 11 TXE.*

ROLLS-ROYCE

Goldfinger (1964), On Her Majesty's Secret Service (1969), Octopussy (1983), A View To A Kill (1985), The World Is Not Enough (1999)
USED BY Auric Goldfinger, Marc Ange Draco, Kamal Khan, James Bond, Valentin Zukovsky, and others

SMOOTH RIDE *Kamal Khan arrives at his Monsoon Palace in his Rolls-Royce Phantom III in* Octopussy.

HIGH ROLLER *In* The World Is Not Enough, *Valentin Zukovsky owns a white Silver Shadow which his bodyguard, The Bull, drives.*

ROUTEMASTER BUS

Live And Let Die (1973)
DRIVEN BY James Bond

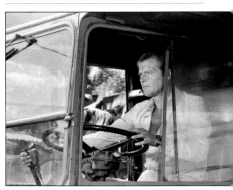

A double-decker Routemaster bus helps 007 escape the San Monique police. Bond spins the bus 180°, sending police motorcycles flying. He then swerves, forcing a police car off the road. Even when it appears 007 has made an error by turning down a road with a low bridge, he defeats his pursuers by driving under the bridge and shearing the top deck off, allowing him to get away.

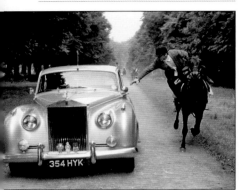

FOUL PLAY *007 finds May Day instead of Tibbett at the wheel in* A View To A Kill.

The Rolls-Royce is one of the most elegant and luxurious of all cars and a key vehicle in the world of James Bond, appearing briefly or prominently in numerous films.

In *Goldfinger*, Bond attaches a homing device to the trunk of Auric Goldfinger's 1937 Rolls-Royce Phantom III, allowing Bond to use his Aston Martin DB5's tracking system to follow Goldfinger from England to Switzerland. Bond soon discovers how Goldfinger transports his gold overseas: the bodywork of his Rolls is 24-karat gold.

In *On Her Majesty's Secret Service*, Che Che and Raphael escort Bond to crime boss Marc Ange Draco's Portuguese seaside headquarters in Draco's Rolls-Royce Mulliner Park Ward Drophead Coupé. The same Rolls later drops Bond off at Gebrüder Gumbold's office in Bern, Switzerland, and Tracy di Vicenzo then confides to her father that she is in love with Bond.

In *A View To A Kill,* Sir Godfrey Tibbett acts the role of Bond's chauffeur as he drives Bond, under the guise of James St. John Smythe, to Zorin's French chateau in a 1962 Rolls-Royce Silver Cloud II. May Day kills Tibbett in the car. Later, Zorin, May Day, and Scarpine try to drown Bond inside the car. He survives by breathing air from the tires.

Rolls-Royce makes the ultimate status statement, even for less-than-savory types. In *Octopussy*, Kamal Khan drives a Phantom III in India. In *The World Is Not Enough*, Valentin Zukovsky owns a white Silver Shadow to travel in style in Azerbaijan.

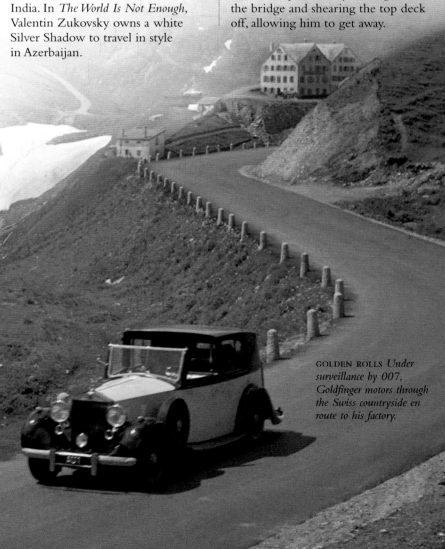

GOLDEN ROLLS *Under surveillance by 007, Goldfinger motors through the Swiss countryside en route to his factory.*

ST. GEORGES

APPEARANCE
For Your Eyes Only (1981)
USED BY British Intelligence

An innocent-looking fishing trawler, the *St. Georges* is really a British electronic surveillance ship which, upon capturing an old World War II contact mine in its nets, explodes and sinks off the Albanian coast. Inside the ship's false freezer is an array of surveillance equipment as well as the ATAC, which uses a low frequency coded transmitter to order British submarines to launch ballistic missiles. The person behind the sinking is smuggler Aris Kristatos. He arranges for the mine to be caught in the trawler's fishing nets, so that he can salvage the ATAC for the Soviets.

SANTA MAVRA

APPEARANCE
For Your Eyes Only (1981)
USED BY Aris Kristatos

Businessman Aris Kristatos uses his motor yacht, *Santa Mavra,* to hunt for the ATAC. After Bond and marine archeologist Melina Havelock recover the ATAC, Kristatos uses the *Santa Mavra* to drag the pair behind a paravane over coral reefs. While the ship turns, Bond wraps the rope around a coralhead. The tension against the *Santa Mavra* snaps the rope, sends the paravane sailing out of the water, and knocks a crew member into the sea. Believing his helmsman Kurt has run over Bond and Melina, Kristatos escapes with the ATAC.

SPY SHIP *A few fishermen on deck preserve the illusion that the* St. Georges *is a humble trawler, instead of a surveillance ship full of state-of-the-art equipment.*

SEABEE SEAPLANE

APPEARANCE
The Man With The Golden Gun (1974)
FLOWN BY James Bond

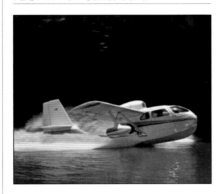

James Bond uses the Republic RC-3 Seabee seaplane to fly from Hong Kong to arch assassin Scaramanga's private island in Red Chinese waters. Staff intelligence officer Mary Goodnight has a tracking beacon, which Bond uses to guide his way. Bond flies so low that he scrapes the tops of trees in an attempt to avoid detection by radar. Chinese military spotters spot the plane despite his efforts and notify Scaramanga of Bond's arrival.

Soon after Bond, in the Seabee, touches down on the water and glides up onto the beach, Scaramanga destroys the plane using his powerful solar cannon.

PIRATE SHIP *The* Santa Mavra *cuts through the Ionian Sea with her illicit ATAC cargo.*

SEAPLANE, GONZALES'S

APPEARANCE
For Your Eyes Only (1981)
FLOWN BY Hector Gonzales

Cuban hitman Hector Gonzales masquerades as a Kerkyra Charter Service pilot and flies marine archaeologist Melina Havelock from Athens to Corfu in a Cessna U206G Stationair Amphibian seaplane. After he has dropped her off in Corfu Harbour at her parents's ship, the *Triana,* he circles around and fires 3,000 rounds per minute of high-velocity 222 bullets from a concealed gun that he has outfitted under the hull of the plane. Melina's parents,

Timothy and Iona, die instantly. Melina, having gone below deck, races to her parents's bodies. She stares at the seaplane speeding away and vows revenge.

SENTINEL SUBMERSIBLE

APPEARANCE
Licence To Kill (1989)
USED BY Milton Krest

The *Sentinel* is a remote-controlled exploratory submersible used by Milton Krest, the business partner of drug lord Franz Sanchez. The *Sentinel* transports cocaine and cash in its watertight storage container between the well area of Krest's ship, the *Wavekrest,* and a Cessna 185 seaplane operated by Sanchez's pilots. The *Sentinel,* 4 ft (1.2 m) long and 3 ft (0.9 m) wide, has a guidance system, a searchlight, and a built-in video camera, all of which are powered by an umbilical lifeline leading back to the *Wavekrest.* Atop the *Sentinel* are a periscope and the storage container.

Underwater, Bond opens the storage container, takes out a knife, and destroys the entire cocaine shipment. When Krest sees Bond on the surveillance screen ruining the shipment, he orders his men to bring the *Sentinel* to the surface. Bond then uses the knife to destroy the built-in video camera.

SHARK HUNTER

APPEARANCES
The Spy Who Loved Me (1977),
Licence To Kill (1989)
USED BY Karl Stromberg's men,
Milton Krest's men

The Shark Hunter two-man submersible is a "wet" submarine that fills with water as it submerges, requiring scuba-diving gear to be worn by the occupants.

In *The Spy Who Loved Me*, shipping magnate Karl Stromberg's men emerge in one from the underwater access tubes of his research laboratory *Atlantis*. They fire missiles at Bond and KGB agent Anya Amasova who are in the Lotus Esprit submersible. Bond ejects a cloud of black smoke from the Lotus, and Anya launches a mine on the seabed that destroys the craft.

In *Licence To Kill*, henchman Milton Krest owns a Shark Hunter. It helps drug lord Franz Sanchez escape from US custody. Krest also uses the sub to transport his men from a tunnel underneath his Ocean Exotica warehouse to his ship, the *Wavekrest*.

SHERPA VAN

APPEARANCE
The Spy Who Loved Me (1977)
USED BY Jaws, Anya Amasova,
James Bond

Jaws employs Egyptian Postal Telephone Service van no. 7124 in his attempt to recover microfilm blueprints of shipping tycoon Karl Stromberg's submarine tracking system. Bond follows Jaws and slips into the cargo hold of the Leyland Sherpa 240 van, where he is soon joined by Russian agent Anya Amasova. A microphone planted in the rear and a speaker in the cab allow Jaws to listen in on the conversation between Bond and Amasova as he drives them to an ancient Egyptian temple. When the pair recovers the microfilm, they attempt to escape in the van, which Jaws proceeds to rip and dent. The stress of the attack on the vehicle soon leads to the blowing of the cylinder head gasket, rendering the van useless.

SKYFLEET S570

APPEARANCE
Casino Royale (2006)
USED BY Unknown

Terrorist banker Le Chiffre targets the Skyfleet S570 prototype at Miami International Airport. Le

Chiffre believes he can destroy the Skyfleet S570, the world's largest passenger aircraft, at the introduction ceremony and cause Skyfleet stock to plummet. Le Chiffre, through buying "put options," will make tens of millions as a result. He hires Alex Dimitrios to find him a saboteur to blow up the plane. Dimitrios employs Carlos who attempts to drive a fuel tanker into the plane. Bond stops the truck and causes Carlos to obliterate himself.

SNOWMOBILES

APPEARANCES
A View To A Kill (1985),
Die Another Day (2002)
DRIVEN BY Siberian Research Centre
Officers, Gustav Graves's men

In *A View To A Kill*, Siberian Research Centre guards use Polaris Indy 600 snowmobiles to pursue Bond. Bond hijacks a Polaris, but a Soviet helicopter blasts it to bits. Bond recovers a broken runner to use as a snowboard. In *Die Another Day*, guards in Iceland ride Bombardier Ski-Doo MX ZREV

MOVING TARGET *Graves's guards try to get Bond in their sights.*

snowmobiles. Bond clotheslines one guard off a Ski-Doo. Another hits Bond's "invisible" Vanquish. Bond returns the favor by plowing through two Ski-Doos with the Vanquish.

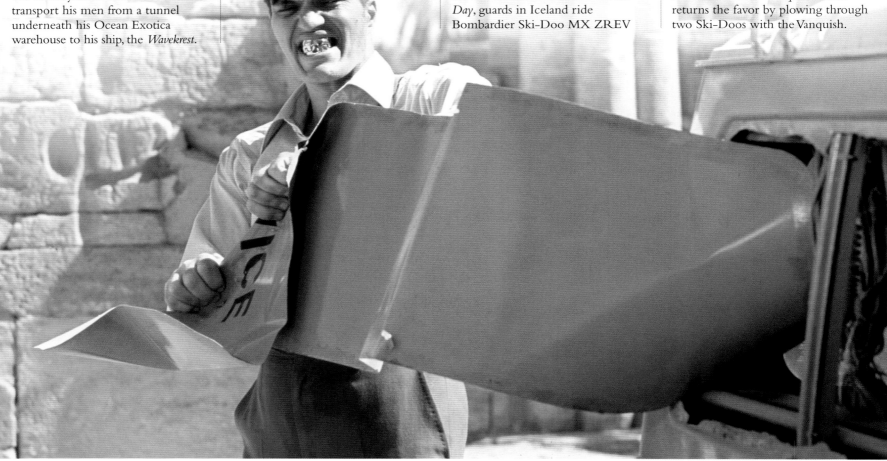

SOVIET ARMY UAZ-469

APPEARANCE
The Living Daylights (1987)
USED BY James Bond, Kara Milovy

Cellist Kara Milovy steals the basic Soviet army transport, a UAZ-469, during a mujaheddin raid on a Soviet airbase. Kara drives the UAZ up a cargo ramp into a Soviet transport plane piloted by 007, locking the vehicle in a specially built cargo sled. When the plane runs out of fuel, Bond and Kara jump in the UAZ and deploy the cargo sled parachute before the plane crashes. The UAZ survives the impact and Bond and Kara drive away toward dinner in Karachi.

SPIRIT 54 YACHT

APPEARANCE
Casino Royale (2006)
USED BY James Bond, Vesper Lynd

To celebrate their newfound love, and forget the brutal mission that flung them together, Bond and Vesper Lynd embark on an idyllic Mediterranean voyage in a Spirit 54 yacht. So assured is Bond of his new life with Vesper, he even sends a resignation email to M. However, Bond and Vesper's bliss is shortlived;

sailing down the Grand Canal, Vesper spots Gettler, and realizes she cannot escape her past.

After Vesper's tragic suicide, Bond remains on the yacht mourning the death of his dream to "float round the world" with her. A call from M informing him of Vesper's past and her deal to save his life jerks him back to reality, and he discovers that Vesper left him a vital clue on her cell phone.

STEALTH SHIP

APPEARANCE
Tomorrow Never Dies (1997)
USED BY Elliot Carver and henchmen

Media mogul Elliot Carver's stealth ship is vital to his plot to initiate a war between the UK and China. The craft, built with Chinese military materials on a catamaran design, produces very little wake disturbance. Its ultra-quiet all-electric engines powered by two 35-megawatt generators provide no acoustic (above water) or hydroacoustic (below surface) signature. The bow design minimizes pressure-wave propagation, another method of detecting a ship at sea. The angled radar-absorbing surface covers a carbon-fiber hull. The ship is virtually impossible to detect except with the naked eye. Carver bases the craft in Hao Long Bay off the Vietnamese coast. It lays in wait for the British frigate HMS *Devonshire* to

STEALTH SCIENCE *The bridge of Carver's stealth ship glitters with technology.*

sail off course, initiating a confrontation with the Chinese. The stealth ship launches a missile that shoots down a Chinese MiG jet and launches the Sea Vac drill that sinks the *Devonshire*. The ship serves as a platform to recover a missile from the *Devonshire*, which Carver later attempts to launch at Beijing. Bond blows a hole in the side of the stealth ship with a grenade, allowing the HMS *Bedford* to spot and shell the craft, blasting it to bits.

SUNBEAM ALPINE

APPEARANCE
Dr. No (1962)
DRIVEN BY James Bond

In Kingston, James Bond rents a marine blue Sunbeam Alpine Series 5 Sports Tourer convertible and drives it to secretary Miss Taro's house in Jamaica's Blue Mountains. A hearse carrying Dr. No's Three Blind Mice assassins accelerates behind Bond, attempting to run his Sunbeam off the cliffside road. Bond spots an angledozer ahead doing road repairs. He drives the Sunbeam under the angledozer's shovel-arm, which spans the road. Too high to follow, the hearse veers off the road and crashes in flames.

In the Fleming novel, Commander Strangways drives a Sunbeam Alpine.

SUNSEEKER YACHT

APPEARANCES
The World Is Not Enough (1999), Die Another Day (2002), Casino Royale (2006)
USED BY Cigar Girl, Renard, Jinx, Le Chiffre

In *The World Is Not Enough*, the Cigar Girl, positioned on a Sunseeker Superhawk 34 speedboat on the River Thames, uses a Heckler & Koch G36 rifle to fire at Bond as he stands amid the rubble following a bomb blast at MI6. Bond pursues her in a prototype Q boat. Cigar Girl beaches her Sunseeker and escapes in a hot-air balloon tethered near the Millennium Dome. Terrorist Renard later arrives at Maiden's Tower in Istanbul in a Sunseeker Manhattan 50 Flybridge motoryacht. This yacht also brings a captured Bond and nuclear physicist Christmas Jones to Maiden's Tower.

In *Die Another Day*, after backdiving off a cliff at Dr. Alvarez's clinic in Los Organos, NSA agent Jinx speeds away in a Sunseeker 48-50 speedboat.

In *Casino Royale*, terrorist banker Le Chiffre plays a game of poker aboard his yacht, a Sunseeker Predator 108. His Sunseeker also serves as the meeting place where Alex Dimitrios informs him he has hired a terrorist named Carlos to replace Mollaka in the plot to destroy the Skyfleet S570 at Miami International Airport.

SWITCHBLADE GLIDERS

APPEARANCE
Die Another Day (2002)
FLOWN BY James Bond, Jinx

To evade North Korean radar, Bond and Jinx bail out of the back of a US Air Force Chinook helicopter riding personal jet gliders, known as switchblades. The switchblade gliders are invisible to radar and are based on the PHASST glider (Programmable High Altitude Single Soldier Transport). Electrically powered retractable wings control the gliders's acceleration and trajectory. During the descent, Bond and Jinx jettison their switchblades and parachute down to land safely in North Korea.

T-80BV TANK

APPEARANCE
GoldenEye (1995)
DRIVEN BY James Bond

James Bond commandeers a Soviet T-80BV tank in an attempt to rescue computer programmer Natalya Simonova from General Ourmov, who has driven off in his car taking Natalya with him. The 46-ton vehicle chases after Ourmov, destroying a swath of historic St. Petersburg in the process. Powered by a 1250 hp gas-turbine engine, the T-80 crashes through a wall, plows through a narrow alley, squashes military jeeps and police cars, smashes through a truck, and knocks the plinth from beneath a statue of Tzar Nicholas sitting astride a winged horse.

When Ourmov takes Natalya aboard Alec Trevelyan's armored ICBM train, Bond rolls the tank down the railroad tracks in the train's path. He fires a shell and jumps out of the tank before the train smashes into it.

TANAKA'S TRAIN

APPEARANCE
You Only Live Twice (1967)
USED BY Tiger Tanaka

Tiger Tanaka, head of the Japanese Secret Intelligence Service, uses a private train to travel on the Tokyo subway system and possibly other rail lines. He tells Bond that it would be unwise, considering his position, to travel in the streets of Tokyo. The modern train includes servants, a well-stocked liquor cabinet, a high-

tech communications center, and precision optics for reading and projecting microdot information.

TEXRON TANKER

APPEARANCE
Casino Royale (2006)
DRIVEN BY Carlos, James Bond

Acting on the instructions of Dimitrios, a saboteur named Carlos uses a Texron fuel truck in an attempt to destroy the Skyfleet S570 prototype plane during its unveiling at Miami International Airport. Carlos attaches a key fob detonator to the fuel truck's undercarriage, intending to turn the truck's loaded fuel tank into a massive bomb. The truck's weight and ability to reach high speeds as well as the wide tarmac at MIA make the Texron vehicle nearly impossible to stop. When Bond leaps on top of the tanker, Carlos tries to dislodge him by swerving sharply and sideswiping a tow tug. Bond manages to climb back aboard and stay on the tanker as it smashes through a luggage flatbed and an articulated bus. The fuel truck continues on despite having numerous tires shot out, the brake line severed, and the tank itself punctured by machine gun fire. It also slams into police cars and smashes through a police SUV barricade. It is only when Bond manages to overcome Carlos and gain full control of the wheel that he can turn the truck into a controlled skid that brings it to a halt, just inches from the Skyfleet S570.

TIGER HELICOPTER

APPEARANCE
GoldenEye (1995)
USED BY Xenia Onatopp, Alec Trevelyan, General Ourumov

Bond first notices the Tiger helicopter aboard the French-built stealth ship *La Fayette*, when he spies on Admiral Chuck Farrel and Janus member Xenia Onatopp in Monaco.

The 170 knots helicopter, the first working prototype and Europe's answer to the electronic battlefield, not only uses stealth technology, but it is also the only helicopter to be hardened against all forms of electronic interference, radio jamming, and electromagnetic radiation.

Onatopp and ex-MI6 agent Trevelyan steal the helicopter from the deck of the *La Fayette*, having attacked and killed the pilots. Later, General Ourumov and Onatopp take the Tiger helicopter to the Space Weapons Control Centre in Severnaya, Russia. When they set off the GoldenEye satellite weapon Petya, the Russian MiG-29 jet fighters fail in the resulting electromagnetic pulse; the Tiger remains unaffected.

At MI6 headquarters, Bond, MI6's Senior Analyst Bill Tanner, and M view the heat radiation image of the Tiger at Severnaya, which spurs Bond to travel to Russia to investigate the missing helicopter. He soon sees the Tiger in the statue graveyard where Alec Trevelyan reveals that he turned traitor and has become the head of the Janus crime syndicate.

Shot with a knockout dart, Bond awakens bound and trapped inside the

TIGER ATTACK Ourmov and Onatopp arrive at the Severnya Space Weapons Control Centre. The Tiger's ability to withstand EMP makes it a vital component in their plot.

helicopter. Behind him sits computer programmer Natalya Simonova who screams for Bond to save them. The helicopter fires missiles that target the craft itself, but Bond headbutts the ejector seat button, sending the crew compartment—with Bond and Natalya in it—rocketing skyward moments before the Tiger explodes.

TOW SLED

APPEARANCE
Thunderball (1965)
DRIVEN BY SPECTRE frogmen, James Bond, Largo

SPECTRE uses underwater motorized tow sleds during its NATO project. The sleds allow the SPECTRE frogmen to cover more distance quickly. Additionally, they can help position cumbersome items underwater, such as the camouflage used to cover the hijacked Vulcan bomber. They also serve as an escort for the bomb sled, with two fixed underwater CO_2 spearguns that can be fired from the pilot's handles.

TOYOTA 2000 GT

APPEARANCE
You Only Live Twice (1967)
DRIVEN BY Aki

Japanese Agent 294 Aki drives a white Toyota 2000 GT with a closed-circuit telecommunications system built into the rear seat as her company car. The 2000 GT marked Toyota's entrance into the sports car market, but the company only produced 341 models, and no convertibles were ever sold to the public. Aki uses the car to take Bond to meet his contact Dikko Henderson, to twice rescue Bond outside of Osato Industries headquarters, to lead SPECTRE gunmen on a chase out of Tokyo, and to travel to Kobe to investigate the *Ning-Po*.

TRANSPORT ALLIANZ C-160

APPEARANCE
Tomorrow Never Dies (1997)
USED BY James Bond, Jack Wade

At a US Air Force Base in the South China Sea, Bond enlists the help of CIA agent Jack Wade to plan a High Altitude, Low Opening (HALO) jump to locate the HMS *Devonshire*.

Bond leaps from a Transport Allianz C-160 plane at 29,000 ft (8,839 m), freefalls for 5 miles (8 km) at 200 mph (321.8 kph), and then pops his chute 200 ft (60.9 m) below the Chinese and Vietnamese radars.

TREVELYAN'S TRAIN

APPEARANCE
GoldenEye (1995)
USED BY Alec Trevelyan, General Ourumov, Xenia Onatopp

After the fall of the Soviet Union, Russia dismantled much of its nuclear deterrent. This included retiring the trains designed to move the USSR's intercontinental ballistic missiles (ICBMs) from location to location.

After the retirement of one such train, ex-MI6 agent Alec Trevelyan takes it over. He knows its armor plating will provide good security and that the mobility of the train will make locating him difficult. Bond derails the train by positioning a T-80BV tank in its path. Trevelyan traps 007 and computer programmer Natalya Simonova inside and booby traps the train to explode. Bond and Natalya escape, using the onboard computer to discover that Trevelyan plans to travel to Cuba.

TRIANA

APPEARANCE
For Your Eyes Only (1981)
USED BY Melina Havelock, Timothy Havelock, Iona Havelock, James Bond

Marine archaeologist Sir Timothy Havelock owns the research vessel *Triana*. Its legitimate research is the perfect cover for British Intelligence to recover the ATAC, a submarine communications device. Cuban hitman Gonzales murders Sir Timothy and his wife, Iona, on the vessel. Melina Havelock, the couple's daughter, witnesses the killings and vows revenge. Melina and Bond recover the ATAC using the *Triana* as a base, and smuggler Aris Kristatos keelhauls them from its bow. After the death of Kristatos, Bond and Melina return to the *Triana*.

TUK-TUK TAXI

APPEARANCE
Octopussy (1983)
USED BY James Bond, Vijay, Gobinda

Vijay, Bond's contact in India, drives Bond in a tuk-tuk three wheeler taxi through the Udaipur streets. Kamal Khan's henchman Gobinda and his driver give chase in another tuk-tuk. A jeep bursts onto the scene, and a goon leaps onto Bond's tuk-tuk, plunging a knife into 007's heart. Bond is unaffected as the knife sticks in a wad of cash in his suit. Bond punches the man, and Vijay uses a tennis racket to battle Gobinda's other goons. Gobinda fires a blunderbuss at 007, but Bond manages to jump out of the taxi before the shot hits him. Bond later reunites with Vijay in the tuk-tuk. They escape Gobinda and his men by driving through a cinema poster that hides the entrance to the offices of Station I.

US ARMY AMBULANCE

APPEARANCE
Goldfinger (1964)
USED BY Kisch, Goldfinger

An ambulance plays a key role in Goldfinger's faux convoy of US Army vehicles that blast their way into the grounds of the US Treasury Bullion Depository at Fort Knox as part of Operation Grand Slam. The ambulance is, in reality, a mobile platform for Goldfinger's powerful industrial laser, housing a hinged roof, a hydraulic lift, and a remarkably resilient electric battery array to power the laser.

VULCAN BOMBER

APPEARANCE
Thunderball (1965)
HIJACKED BY SPECTRE

The Vulcan bomber served as the key nuclear deterrent aircraft of the UK from the early 1950s to the mid-1980s. Hard to track on radar, the Vulcan was very effective in the era of subsonic bombers. SPECTRE's hijacking of NATO flight 759 sparks Operation Thunderball, the British secret service's effort to retrieve the two atomic weapons on board. SPECTRE hires Angelo Palazzi to impersonate Major François Derval, take control of the craft, kill the crew, and fly the Vulcan to the Golden Grotto near Nassau, Bahamas. Palazzi ditches the Vulcan in the ocean but SPECTRE's Emilio Largo kills him. After removing the bombs, Largo's crew camouflages the plane. Bond locates it only hours before the first bomb is to be detonated.

WAVEKREST

APPEARANCE
Licence To Kill (1989)
USED BY Milton Krest

The *Wavekrest* is a marine research vessel owned by Milton Krest, who uses it to transport drugs for Franz Sanchez. Off the coast of Key West, Bond sneaks aboard the *Wavekrest*, destroys a cocaine shipment, and steals $5 million in drug money. Later, CIA contract pilot and agent Pam Bouvier disguises herself as the Isthmus City harbor pilot and crashes the *Wavekrest* through the dock to convince Sanchez that Krest wants him dead.

WAYNE, USS

APPEARANCE
The Spy Who Loved Me (1977)
USED BY James Bond, Anya Amasova, Commander Carter

Shortly after Bond and Russian agent Anya Amasova board the USS *Wayne*, the submarine has to surface because of an electrical failure. The *Liparus* swallows it, and shipping tycoon Karl Stromberg orders Commander Carter and his crew to evacuate or face death. When Bond and the crews of the American, British, and Soviet subs defeat Stromberg's army, they file back into the USS *Wayne*. Carter orders a torpedo to smash open the tanker's bow doors. The *Wayne* slides out of the sub pen as the ship explodes and sinks. The *Wayne* then proceeds to destroy Stromberg's base *Atlantis* under Pentagon orders.

WETBIKE

APPEARANCE
The Spy Who Loved Me (1977)
USED BY James Bond

Q sends an aquatic vehicle known as a wetbike to the USS *Wayne*, for Bond's use. Q obtained the first engineering prototype, which Bond uses to travel to the ocean laboratory *Atlantis* to rescue KGB agent Anya Amasova. With a 50 horsepower Suzuki engine, the wetbike's fixed nozzle outputs 500 lb (22.6 kg) of thrust, allowing it to safely transport Bond to *Atlantis*. When the USS *Wayne* attacks *Atlantis*, the torpedoes destroy the wetbike.

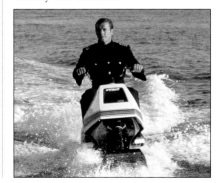

WEAPONS & EQUIPMENT

King Arthur had Merlin. James Bond has Q. With Major Boothroyd, 007 does not need magic spells to accomplish a mission. Bond is a hero created to embrace the power of technology. When the 007 films appeared in the 1960s, Bond spoke to the optimist in us who yearned to master technology, and who dreamed of GPS navigation systems and mobile phones. Bond understands that technology can destroy or liberate us. When the world was still wondering if a radium watch dial would slowly kill the wearer, Bond sported watches concealing Geiger counters, detonators, buzz-saws, and bullet-deflecting magnets. Bond relishes the danger of the modern age and harnesses it with confidence and style. He knows that in today's complex times, appearances can be deceiving. In Bond's world, a camera can be a tape recorder, and a tape recorder can be a book. A cigarette can kill your enemy in seconds. A mobile phone can drive your car. A hat may break your neck. On the following pages are the remarkable weapons and gadgets of James Bond's trade. Yet each one is simply a tool, to be applauded in the hands of the hero and feared when not. With 007, man is always the master; the gadget is the servant.

AEROSOL CAN

APPEARANCE
Live And Let Die (1973)
USED BY James Bond

When James Bond finds a snake in his bathroom at his hotel in San Monique, he uses a regular can of spray aftershave and his cigar to create a makeshift flame thrower. The highly-flammable propellant ignites and incinerates the serpent. In actual fact, Bond needn't have bothered—the snake was a desert kingsnake which is neither poisonous nor aggressive. CIA agent Rosie Carver receives quite a shock when she goes into the bathroom and sees the toasted reptile.

ASAT MISSILE

APPEARANCE
Die Another Day (2002)
USED BY US Navy

When the Soviet Union developed a "killer satellite" to topple other satellites in the 1970s, the US Air Force responded with the ASAT (Anti-Satellite Missile), designed to attack satellites in low Earth orbit.

Billionaire Gustav Graves plans to use his Icarus satellite to destroy the DMZ, allowing North Korean troops to overtake South Korea. A US warship launches an ASAT missile at Icarus, but the satellite's beam of sun-fueled heat easily destroys it.

ASSAULT RIFLE

APPEARANCE
The Living Daylights (1987)
USED BY Brad Whitaker

Brad Whitaker's assault rifle is actually a light machine gun with a ballistic face shield. When Bond exhausts the eight bullets of his Walther PPK against the bulletproof shield, Whitaker fires a round of 80 bullets from the light machine gun, obliterating his military museum in a vain attempt to eliminate Bond.

ATAC

APPEARANCE
For Your Eyes Only (1981)
USED BY British Navy

The ATAC is a secretive Automatic Targeting Attack Communicator utilized by the *St. Georges*, a British electronic surveillance spy ship. It uses an ultra-low frequency coded transmitter to order British submarines to launch ballistic missiles.

When a contact mine becomes trapped in the *St. Georges*'s nets, the ship explodes, and the ATAC is lost in the Ionian Sea off the Albanian coast. Both the Soviets and the British want this valuable device.

Bond and marine archaeologist Melina Havelock use the *Neptune* submersible to locate the *St. Georges* and retrieve the ATAC. When they surface, smuggler Aris Kristatos takes the ATAC, planning to deliver it to the KGB's General Gogol at St. Cyril's Monastery. Bond infiltrates the monastery and shatters the ATAC in front of Gogol. Bond's reason for destroying the device is détente-minded—if the British don't have it, the Soviets don't have it either.

ATOMIC DEVICES

APPEARANCES
Goldfinger (1964), Thunderball (1965),
The Spy Who Loved Me (1977),
Octopussy (1983),
The World Is Not Enough (1999)
USED BY Goldfinger, Mr. Ling, Kisch, Emilio Largo, Ladislav Kutze, Karl Stromberg, James Bond, Kamal Khan, General Orlov, Renard, Elektra King

Nothing says you have arrived among the most elite of the world's megalomaniacs like possessing your own atomic device.

Goldfinger receives a "dirty bomb" from the Chinese government in order to perpetrate economic chaos in the West. The device is designed to spread maximum lethal radiation with minimal explosive power. A CIA atomic specialist disarms the weapon with only seconds to spare.

In *Thunderball*, SPECTRE briefly becomes a nuclear power when a freelancer working for them—Angelo Palazzi—hijacks NATO flight 759, armed with two atomic weapons, MoS-type, as part of a plot hatched by Emilio Largo. When an attempt to place one of the bombs in Biscayne Bay, Miami, goes awry, US aquaparas seize one bomb. Nuclear specialist Ladislav Kutze throws the arming device for the second bomb into the sea when Largo attempts to escape with it aboard the *Disco Volante*. The bomb is destroyed when the *Disco Volante* crashes into a small coral island in Biscayne National Park.

The Spy Who Loved Me sees shipping magnate Karl Stromberg obtaining a host of sea-launched ballistic missiles (SLBMs) by building a submarine tracking system, a disabling beam, and a supertanker to swallow the craft. Bond uses one of the detonators to blow open the security shutters protecting the *Liparus*'s control room. Although 007 cannot stop Stromberg's crews from launching the SLBMs, he does order them to target each other, resulting in their mutual destruction.

Rogue Soviet General Orlov hijacks one of his country's weapons to stage an accident on a NATO airbase in Germany in *Octopussy*. Bond, dressed as a circus clown, extracts the detonator in time.

In *The World Is Not Enough*, Elektra King and her lover Renard hatch a plot to steal a nuclear weapon from a decommissioning site in the former Soviet Union. They plan to use part of the plutonium to make it appear that King's oil pipeline has been sabotaged and use the other part to force the nuclear reactor in a Russian submarine to explode, irradiating Istanbul. Bond stops the plot by shooting King and impaling Renard with a plutonium reactor rod.

ATTACHÉ CASE

APPEARANCES

From Russia With Love (1963), Goldfinger (1964)

USED BY James Bond, British Agent from Station Y

The black leather attaché case that Q presents to Bond in *From Russia With Love* is the first of Bond's lethal exotic gadgets.

The case contains forty rounds of .25-caliber ammunition in tubes hidden beneath two of the feet studs. Built into the lower section of the top is a flat throwing knife, released by a button concealed beneath the right latch. Inside the case is an ArmaLite AR-7 folding sniper's rifle, which has been modified from the standard .22

survival model and contains an infrared telescopic scope. In the base of the case are fifty gold sovereigns. A tear-gas cartridge disguised as a tin of talcum powder attaches magnetically to the top of the case. The latches must be turned horizontally before opening or the cartridge will explode.

Bond takes the case on his mission to Istanbul. Head of Station T, Kerim Bey uses the AR-7 when he kills assassin Krilencu. Later, 007 uses the gun to wound the copilot of a SPECTRE helicopter. Bond offers the gold sovereigns from his case to Grant as a bribe for a cigarette. He tricks Grant into opening an identical case he stole from a murdered contact from Station Y, and the explosion of the tear-gas cartridge briefly overcomes Grant. During the resulting fight, 007 extracts the throwing knife from one case and stabs Grant's shoulder, allowing him to gain the upper hand.

The case appears in *Goldfinger*, but Bond does not use it. When flying to the US, stewardess Mei Lei informs him that it was damaged when examined.

The attaché case in the novel *From*

COUNTDOWN *Bond desperately tries to disable Goldfinger's atomic device.*

Russia With Love includes a cyanide death-pill for Bond to take if captured. 007 washes this pill down the lavatory, a point referenced in the film *Die Another Day*.

AVALANCHE-RESCUE RECEIVER

APPEARANCE

A View To A Kill (1985)

USED BY James Bond

In Siberia, James Bond uses a handheld avalanche-rescue receiver in a weatherproof yellow plastic casing to locate the frozen body of

MI6 agent 003. On finding the body, Bond locates a chip hidden inside a locket around 003's neck. The chip, which proves to be impervious to an electromagnetic pulse, launches Bond's investigation into the activities of business tycoon Max Zorin.

BATTLESUIT

APPEARANCE

Die Another Day (2002)

USED BY Gustav Graves

Gustav Graves wears a high-tech battlesuit that controls his Icarus satellite during his attempt to destroy South Korean defenses from his flying command center. Designed by top scientist Vlad, the body armor-styled suit covers Graves's chest and arms. The wrist buttons of the suit control the Icarus satellite, a visor displays the coordinates of the Icarus, and a chest button emits 100,000 volts of electricity. Graves uses this feature to murder his father, General Moon, and in his ensuing battle with Bond he is electrocuted.

DEATH BRINGER *Encased in his battlesuit, Graves prepares to wreak havoc on South Korea with his Icarus superweapon.*

BELL-TEXTRON JET PACK

APPEARANCES
Thunderball (1965),
Die Another Day (2002)

USED BY James Bond

While Q Branch has often modified equipment and vehicles from other manufacturers, in the case of the Jet Pack, the British Secret Service merely purchased a pre-existing piece of technology. The US Army issued a contract to Bell Aerospace in 1959 to develop a Rocket Belt. Shortly after, Bell unveiled the 21-second flying machine, but the Army deemed it too dangerous for use in the field. Q did not agree, realizing it could be a perfect device for an agent to employ in certain circumstances.

In *Thunderball*, Bond uses the Jet Pack to escape from SPECTRE gunmen at the chateau of SPECTRE's Jacques Boitier in France.

Years later, Bond sees the Jet Pack in a storeroom for Q Branch in an abandoned London Underground facility used by MI6. The Jet Pack in *Die Another Day* appears to be modified because Bond flips on the thrust, something he was unlikely to do with the original as the exhaust consisted of exceedingly hot steam.

BERETTA AUTOMATIC

APPEARANCES
Dr. No (1962), Licence To Kill (1989),
Tomorrow Never Dies (1997),
Die Another Day (2002)

USED BY James Bond,
Pam Bouvier, Peaceful Fountains
of Desire, Jinx

James Bond uses a .25 Beretta Automatic in six of Ian Fleming's novels. The Beretta proves reliable in *Casino Royale*, *Live And Let Die*, *Moonraker*, *Diamonds Are Forever*, and *From Russia With Love*. In *Dr. No*, M insists the gun be replaced.

In the film *Dr. No*, Bond notes that the Beretta has been his sidearm for ten years, despite warnings from M that it was unsuitable. After it jams on a job, Bond spends six months in hospital, and M orders 007 to stop using the Beretta.

> **"**I've used a Beretta for ten years, and I've **never missed** with it yet.**"**
>
> **Bond to M**

GARTER GUN *Pam Bouvier shows Bond where she keeps her Beretta.*

Pam Bouvier in *Licence To Kill* and Peaceful Fountains of Desire in *Die Another Day* both use a Beretta 950, a .25 automatic known as the Jetfire.

In *Tomorrow Never Dies*, 007 uses a Beretta AR-70/90 assault rifle to infiltrate a terrorist supermarket.

NSA agent Jinx uses a Beretta Tomcat with silencer when she tracks down henchman Zao in *Die Another Day*. Jinx also uses a Beretta 84FS Cheetah, which she later surrenders to double agent Miranda Frost.

BINOCULAR/ MONOCULAR CAMERA

APPEARANCES
For Your Eyes Only (1981), GoldenEye (1995)
USED BY James Bond

In *For Your Eyes Only*, Bond spies on henchman Emile Locque paying off hitman Hector Gonzales in Spain using a Tasco binocular camera which combines 7 x 20 mm binoculars with a 110-format camera. Thugs destroy the film when they capture 007.

In *GoldenEye*, Bond uses a more advanced item in the form of a digital monocular to spy on Janus member Xenia Onatopp and Admiral Chuck Farrel in Monaco. With the push of a button, the monocular digitally transmits an image to MI6 for identification.

BOMBE SURPRISE

APPEARANCE
Diamonds Are Forever (1971)
USED BY Wint & Kidd, James Bond

Assassins Mr. Wint and Mr. Kidd attempt to kill Bond with a bomb inside a faux cake. Aboard an ocean liner, Wint and Kidd present Bond and smuggler Tiffany Case with a sumptuous meal, supposedly courtesy of billionaire Willard Whyte. When Bond confronts Wint, who poses as a sommelier, about his lack of knowledge of wines, a fight ensues. Case hurls the bombe dessert at Wint. She misses but reveals the bomb when the dessert hits the floor. 007 attaches the bomb to Wint's coattails and tosses him overboard. Wint explodes before hitting the water.

BOOK/TAPE RECORDER

APPEARANCE
Thunderball (1965)
USED BY James Bond

This sound-activated tape recorder is secreted inside a hollowed-out Nassau directory. Bond uses it to listen for intruders in his Coral Harbour hotel room in Nassau, Bahamas. When he plays the tape, he hears Quist, one of Emilio Largo's men, enter the room and hide in the bathroom. This allows Bond to scald Quist in the shower before the thug can shoot him. Bond knocks Quist senseless and sends him back to his "friends" with the words, "Tell them, the little fish I throw back in the sea."

BOUNDING MINES

APPEARANCE
Die Another Day (2002)
USED BY James Bond

Bounding mines are anti-personnel mines that are normally buried, and, when activated by pressure or a tripwire, burst 3–4 ft (0.9–1.2 m) in the air, causing severe injuries to a person's head and chest.

When James Bond and North Korean Colonel Moon engage in a chase on hovercrafts in the DMZ, Bond is pursued down a side road by one of Moon's men. Bond sees that this road is covered in bounding mines and detonates two of them with a machine gun. The flying shrapnel causes the North Korean hovercraft driver to crash into a tree.

BREITLING DIVER'S WATCH

APPEARANCE
Thunderball (1965)
USED BY James Bond

Following his arrival in the Bahamas on Operation Thunderball, Q gives Bond a modified Breitling Top Time chronograph with a built-in Geiger counter. The second hand measures radiation, allowing Bond to unobtrusively check if he is in the vicinity of the hijacked atomic weapons being ransomed by Emilio Largo and SPECTRE.

During the mission, Bond appears to find the watch uncomfortable, for he frequently wears his Rolex Submariner instead.

GETTING WARMER *Bond gets a radioactive reading on his Breitling watch.*

BRIEFCASE BOMB COMPARTMENT

APPEARANCE
Octopussy (1983)
USED BY James Bond

This briefcase contains a hidden compartment with a magnetic thermite explosive device. On a mission to destroy a spy plane, Bond infiltrates a Latin American airbase disguised as Colonel Luis Toro. He knocks out a technician, opens the briefcase, and places the explosive device against the inside of the spy plane's fuselage. The real Colonel Toro foils his efforts and takes possession of the explosive.

BROOM RADIO

APPEARANCE
Licence To Kill (1989)
USED BY Q

CLEAN SWEEP *Disguised as a humble gardener, Q utilizes his broom radio.*

This multi-band, low-frequency, high-level encryption walkie-talkie unit comes built into a standard broom. The unit scans channels for traffic and encrypts in sync with the capabilities of a designated receiver.

Disguised as a gardener, Q uses one outside drug lord Franz Sanchez's mansion to communicate with CIA contract pilot and agent Pam Bouvier. After making contact, he tosses the broom into the bushes.

BUG DETECTOR

APPEARANCES
From Russia With Love (1963),
Live And Let Die (1973)
USED BY James Bond

When James Bond checks into a hotel room on a mission, he finds it prudent to sweep the room for listening devices.

In *From Russia With Love*, Bond uses a device to check the voltage on the telephone line, which shows it is being monitored.

In *Live And Let Die*, Bond has a gadget inside his toiletries kit that reveals the location of listening devices.

CASSETTE TAPE

APPEARANCE
Diamonds Are Forever (1971)
USED BY Ernst Stavro Blofeld, Prof. Dr. Metz, James Bond, Tiffany Case

Prof. Dr. Metz uses a cassette control tape labeled "World's Greatest Marches" to guide Ernst Stavro Blofeld's satellite weapon. Bond first sees the cassette in Metz's lab and later spies the tape in Willard Whyte's penthouse when he meets Blofeld. Bond brings a hidden copy of the music cassette to Blofeld's oil rig command center in his suit lining. Guards find it, but Blofeld unwittingly allows 007 to switch the music tape for the control tape. Bond passes the control tape to Tiffany Case, who believes it is the music cassette, and she switches the tape in the machine. When she finds out this cassette is the control tape, she tries to swap the tapes again, but Blofeld catches her.

CELLO CASE

APPEARANCE
The Living Daylights (1987)
USED BY James Bond, Kara Milovy

This impact-resistant, felt-lined fiberglass cello case, equipped with watertight seals and stainless steel locking latches, seats two people comfortably.

Always ready to use available tools, Bond commandeers cellist Kara Milovy's cello case to use as a sled to traverse the Czechoslovakia—Austria border. Without a car, Milovy and 007 ride in the open cello case across the snow, evading bullets. Bond, holding the priceless Stradivarius cello, uses the tailpiece spike to steer. When they reach the border gate, Bond tosses the cello in the air and catches it on the other side. He and Kara tell the guards they have nothing to declare but a cello.

CENTRIFUGE TRAINER

APPEARANCE
Moonraker (1979)
USED BY James Bond

BUCKLE UP *Bond straps himself into the centrifuge and Dr. Holly Goodhead attaches a wire to his chest to monitor heart rate.*

The centrifuge trainer at Hugo Drax's Moonraker facility in California simulates the gravity force an astronaut feels when shot into space. An instructor in an observation booth controls the speed and monitors the subject's vital signs. The capsule seats one and spins on an extended gimbal arm. Restraints are not used to keep the subject seated; the force of the centrifuge accomplishes that. Instead, the restraints keep the subject from knocking themselves out with their hands and arms. The centrifuge can reach a speed of 20 g's (20 times the force of gravity), but pressure on the body and internal organs would be fatal. Take-off pressure of a vertical lift-off exerts three g's; according to Dr. Goodhead, most people pass out at seven. A "chicken switch" kills the power when the subject releases his finger from the button. Goodhead challenges 007 to take a spin. Chang tells Dr. Goodhead that Drax wishes her to call, then he hijacks Bond's session in the centrifuge, disabling the chicken switch. Chang slowly increases the rpms toward seven g's. Bond releases the chicken switch only to find that it does not work. Chang gleefully raises the speed even higher. When the centrifuge surpasses 7 g's, Bond realizes the chicken switch has been disabled. When the pressure reaches 13 g's, Bond, on the verge of passing out, fires his wrist dart gun to disable the centrifuge.

FEELING THE FORCE *Bond begins to suspect that something is wrong with the centrifuge— Hugo Drax's henchman, Chang, has taken over in the control room.*

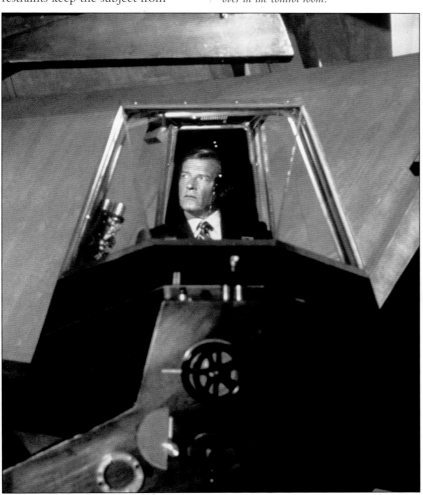

CHAKRA TORTURE KIT

APPEARANCE
Tomorrow Never Dies (1997)
USED BY Stamper, Dr. Kaufman

In Saigon, media baron Elliot Carver plans to have henchman Stamper torture Bond with his "toys," vicious-looking tools used in the ancient art of Chakra torture. According to Eastern philosophy, the body has seven Chakra points or energy centers. The Chakra tools probe a person's organs, inflicting the maximum amount of pain while keeping the victim alive for as long as possible.

Stamper was taught by the late Dr. Kaufman, whose record for keeping a victim alive was fifty-two hours. Stamper hopes to break the record, but before he can try, Bond and spy Wai Lin escape.

CHEQUE COPIER

APPEARANCE
A View To A Kill (1985)
USED BY James Bond

This Louis Vuitton cheque book is actually a device similar to a credit card flatbed imprinter, which allows the user to make an imprint of a previously written check. Bond employs this device to take a rapid copy of a check the mysterious industrialist Max Zorin has just written to Stacey Sutton in the study at his French chateau. The check is made out to Sutton for $5 million and dated May 3, 1985.

CIA STANDARD ISSUE EQUIPMENT

APPEARANCE
Moonraker (1979)
USED BY Dr. Holly Goodhead, James Bond

Suspicious of astronaut Dr. Holly Goodhead, James Bond breaks into her room at the Hotel Danieli in Venice. There Bond finds an array of CIA gadgetry, including a gold pen that contains a poison hypodermic needle (which he steals and later uses to kill Hugo Drax's python); a diary that fires a dart; a Christian Dior atomizer that shoots flames; and a handbag with a radio receiver and aerial. Bond realizes these items are all standard CIA equipment and deduces that the CIA has sent Goodhead to monitor Drax's activities.

IN THE BAG *The CIA fits Dr. Holly Goodhead's handbag with a radio receiver and a range of cunningly disguised gadgets.*

CIGARETTE CASE REMOTE CONTROL

APPEARANCE
Thunderball (1965)
USED BY Emilio Largo

SPECTRE's Emilio Largo possesses a remote control unit to enter the SPECTRE boardroom in Paris. The device, inside an ordinary-looking cigarette case, has one red button and one black. The black button slides back a large wooden cabinet. Pressing the red button opens a metal door behind the cabinet that leads to the boardroom.

CIGARETTE CASE SAFECRACKING UNIT

APPEARANCE
Moonraker (1979)
USED BY James Bond

When James Bond cracks into billionaire Hugo Drax's safe to find the blueprints for the Moonraker shuttle, he uses a safecracking unit disguised as a cigarette case. A panel in the case slides away to reveal an x-ray screen that shows the safe's tumblers and a digital readout that reveals the combination of the safe.

CIGARETTE LIGHTERS

APPEARANCES
The Spy Who Loved Me (1977),
Licence To Kill (1989)
USED BY James Bond

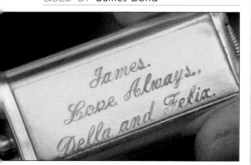

Non-gadget lighters play a key role in two 007 films.

In *The Spy Who Loved Me*, Major Anya Amasova learns 007 purchased his lighter in Berngarten, Austria and she realizes Bond killed her lover. She vows to kill Bond when the mission ends. Bond must convince Anya to put the past behind her.

In *Licence To Kill*, newlyweds Felix and Della Leiter present Bond with an inscribed lighter. When drug lord Franz Sanchez kills Della and maims Felix, Bond takes his revenge by igniting a gasoline-soaked Sanchez.

CIGARETTE PACKAGE DETONATOR

APPEARANCE
Licence To Kill (1989)
USED BY James Bond

Although cigarettes always come with a health warning, Q Branch guarantees this package to do harm when used as directed.

Bond squeezes "Dentonite toothpaste" plastic explosive along the ledge of Sanchez's office in order to blast through two inches of armored glass. He places a fake cigarette blasting cap from the detonator package in the explosive paste.

The rest of the package works as an encrypted radio receiver, accepting only Bond's detonation signal. From a roof across a street, Bond sets off

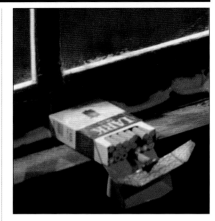

the blast, but before he can shoot, Hong Kong narcotics officers attack him. Later, in part because of the detonation, Bond convinces Sanchez that he needs protection.

CODE-CRACKING DEVICE

APPEARANCE
GoldenEye (1995)
USED BY James Bond, Alec Trevelyan

Breaking into the Arkangel Chemical Weapons Facility, MI6 agents James Bond and Alec Trevelyan use an electronic code-cracking device that slides into a card reader slot and activates by pushing a number sequence on a keypad. The number Trevelyan enters when he inserts the device to relock the door is incorrect, setting off an alarm that alerts Colonel Ourumov's guards.

CODE-CRACKER *Bond's mission to infiltrate the Arkangel Chemical Weapons Facility goes smoothly—until his partner Alec betrays him.*

COFFIN BODY COLLECTOR

APPEARANCE
Live And Let Die (1973)
USED BY New Orleans Mourners

Crime boss Mr. Big/Dr. Kananga has a macabre way of disposing of the bodies of those who try to spy on his New Orleans operation. The victim watches as a funeral procession passes. An assassin stabs the distracted victim. He falls to the street, whereupon the pallbearers set the empty coffin over him. A trio of claw mechanisms inside grabs and lifts the body. Two panels from the sides then slide over the open bottom.

COMMANDO KIT

APPEARANCE
Goldfinger (1964), Thunderball (1965), You Only Live Twice (1967), Live and Let Die (1973), A View To A Kill (1985), The Living Daylights (1987), GoldenEye (1995), Tomorrow Never Dies (1997), Die Another Day (2002)
USED BY James Bond

James Bond uses commando outfits to camouflage himself during dangerous insertion operations. Commando black clothing, similar to the type worn by cat burglars, holds the obvious disadvantage of immediate incrimination if one is caught. Bond first wears a special waterproof suit in *Goldfinger*, then standard black while entering Largo's compound in *Thunderball*, and gray for his ninja outfit in *You Only Live Twice*. Bond returns to black with a tan leather holster in *Live And Let Die*. In *A View To A Kill*, Bond quickly removes his commando outfit to bed May Day. In *The Living Daylights*, 007 parachutes onto Gibraltar in commando blacks. In *GoldenEye*, 007 joins 006 on a commando raid on a nerve gas plant. *Tomorrow Never Dies* features a commando attack on media baron Elliot Carver's stealth ship. In *Die Another Day*, 007 wears two commando outfits—during his raid of the Graves diamond mine facility and his insertion into North Korea with NSA agent Jinx.

COMMANDO KNIFE BEACON

APPEARANCE
Die Another Day (2002)
USED BY James Bond

On the Pukch'ong Coast in North Korea, one of Bond's South Korean colleagues cuts the power cable to a radar dish. Bond removes a combat knife from his surfboard saboteur kit and sticks it in the ground. The knife's handle splits open to form a radio beacon dish. It emits a signal that replaces the radar dish's signal and recalibrates the approaching Mil Mi-8 helicopter's flight plan. The occupants believe they are landing at Colonel Moon's North Korean compound; they are actually landing in a forest where 007 and his colleagues capture diamond trader Mr. Van Bierk. Bond assumes Van Bierk's identity and uses the Mil Mi-8 to fly to Moon's compound.

COMPACT COMMUNICATOR

APPEARANCE   On Her Majesty's Secret Service (1969)
USED BY Blofeld's Angels of Death

Upon opening this compact, a short-wave radio antennae emerges from the lid, allowing Blofeld to communicate with his Angels of Death around the world. Each night at midnight, the Angels must be alone so they can switch on the receiver and listen for Blofeld's voice. He will then tell them how to use their atomizers, which contain the deadly warfare agent Virus Omega. Fortunately, Bond and Marc Ange Draco destroy Piz Gloria, Blofeld's communications center.

COMPUTER MIRROR CAMERA

APPEARANCE
A View To A Kill (1985)
USED BY Max Zorin

This face-matching visual index computer system consists of a video camera, frame-grabbing software, and connection to a mainframe with contour-matching 3-D extrapolation software, which compares facial features to a large visual database.

Businessman Max Zorin uses this system when pretending to access The Progeny Index, the thoroughbred bloodline database, to find the perfect horse for his guest James St. John Smythe. In actuality, using a camera behind a wall mirror, Zorin accesses the mainframe to identify St. John Smythe as James Bond.

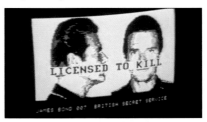

CROSSBOW

APPEARANCE
For Your Eyes Only (1981)
USED BY Melina Havelock

A crossbow is Melina Havelock's weapon of choice as she seeks revenge for her parents's murder. She "perforates" their killer Hector Gonzales at his Spanish villa and later hunts Aris Kristatos, who employed Gonzales. Before she can shoot Kristatos, Bond's ally Columbo hurls a knife into the villain's back.

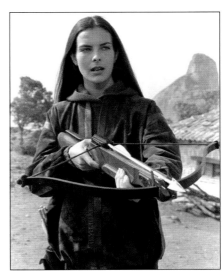

CYANIDE CIGARETTE

APPEARANCE
Dr. No (1962)
USED BY Mr. Jones

After arriving in Jamaica, Bond discovers that the supposed Government House chauffeur Mr. Jones works for the opposition. Bond demands that Jones reveal the identity of his employer. Instead, Jones bites into a cigarette that contains a vial of cyanide and dies quickly. Pleydell-Smith, the Government Secretary, later views the cigarette remains with good-natured bafflement.

DART-FIRING MIRROR

APPEARANCE
Live And Let Die (1973)
USED BY Whisper

Inside a white "pimpmobile," Dr. Kananga's henchman Whisper has a side-view mirror with a camera sight, a remote control aiming and firing device, and a metal dart that, when fired into the target's temple, causes the victim's right foot to involuntarily stomp the accelerator as he dies. Whisper uses this to send Charlie, 007's CIA driver, speeding out of control.

DA VINCI MACHINE

APPEARANCE
Die Another Day (2002)
USED BY MI6

The Da Vinci Machine is a $1.3 million surgical system that allows doctors to examine or perform surgery on a patient using the machine's robotic arms. MI6 uses this apparatus to examine Bond after his 14-month incarceration in a North Korean prison. The machine's four arms scour Bond's body, and an MI6 doctor monitors 007's condition. The machine discovers indications of neurotoxins, histamines, serotonin, enzyme inhibitors, and scorpion venom, as well as venom antiserum. The North Koreans stung 007 with scorpions and then administered the antidote. Bond's pulse is 72, and his blood pressure is 120 over 80. His internal organs remain unaffected, but his liver is not in great condition.

MASTERPIECE *The Da Vinci Machine allows physicians to perform delicate surgery via robotic arms that move with exact precision.*

DECOMPRESSION CHAMBER

APPEARANCE
Licence To Kill (1989)
USED BY Franz Sanchez, Milton Krest

A decompression chamber allows a diver to return to regular atmospheric pressure on the surface rather than underwater. Milton Krest's ship the *Wavekrest* has one in the vessel's launch area. After Bond and Pam Bouvier plant money in the decompression chamber to frame Krest, Franz Sanchez kicks Krest into the chamber and turns the pressure inlet valve to maximum. As the depth gauge drops to 500 ft (152 m) below sea level, Sanchez smashes the vent with a fire ax, causing the pressure to drop instantly and Krest's head to explode.

DENTONITE TOOTHPASTE

APPEARANCE
Licence To Kill (1989)
USED BY James Bond

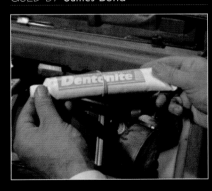

This looks like an ordinary tube of toothpaste, but is actually filled with plastique explosive. As part of his plan to assassinate drug lord Franz Sanchez, Bond squeezes the plastique from the tube along the ledge of Sanchez's study, which is protected by armored glass. Bond then places a remote-controlled cigarette-package detonator amidst the plastique. He later blows out the windows of Sanchez's office using a remote control switch and sets his signature gun's sights on Sanchez.

DETONATOR

APPEARANCES
The Spy Who Loved Me (1977),
A View To A Kill (1985),
Tomorrow Never Dies (1997)
USED BY James Bond, Max Zorin,
May Day, Wai Lin

STEADY HAND *Bond extracts a missile's detonator in* **The Spy Who Loved Me.**

Detonators often feature in Bond's adventures. In some cases, the detonator itself is used as a weapon.

In *The Spy Who Loved Me*, Bond works with the USS *Wayne* crew to remove a detonator from a sea-launched ballistic missile. He then blasts open the control room shutters on the *Liparus* in an attempt to stop shipping magnate Karl Stromberg from initiating nuclear Armageddon.

A View To A Kill sees microchip mogul Max Zorin place a detonator atop several tons of explosives within his Main Strike Mine, hoping to trigger a double earthquake. Unable to stop the timer on the detonator, Bond works with Zorin's lover, May Day, to remove the detonator from the explosives. The pair uses a rail car to push the detonator out of the mine. However, a faulty handbrake on the rail car leads May Day to ride the rail car out of the mine, blowing herself up to ensure the detonator does not set off the explosives.

While trying to stop media mogul Elliot Carver from launching a war between Britain and China in *Tomorrow Never Dies*, 007 uses a small detonator from his watch to set off a hand grenade remotely. Later, Wai Lin tosses Bond a set of magnetized detonators that, when ignited by a missile's tailfire, will cause the missile to blow apart before taking flight.

DIAMOND SATELLITE WEAPON

APPEARANCE
Diamonds Are Forever (1971)
USED BY Ernst Stavro Blofeld,
Professor Dr. Metz

Blofeld engages Professor Dr. Metz to build him a diamond satellite weapon. The weapon uses light refracted through diamonds to create a massive laser beam that can cook submarines, ignite ICBM missiles, and even destroy entire cities. Blofeld uses the weapon to demand nuclear disarmament, hold the world's superpowers hostage, and offer the satellite's unconquerable power to the highest bidder.

To create the satellite, Blofeld and Metz need a huge cache of diamonds. When he only needs one last packet of diamonds to complete the satellite's array, Blofeld orders the assassins Wint and Kidd to kill the smugglers as soon as they have completed their work. When Bond impersonates Peter Franks, a new member of the smuggling team, he temporarily prevents them from obtaining the last diamonds.

Soon, smuggler Tiffany Case delivers the diamonds to Metz. Blofeld then orders the launch of the satellite and takes control of it from his oil rig headquarters. When the US government fails to respond to Blofeld's demands, he threatens to incinerate Washington DC Bond uses Blofeld's bath-o-sub to destroy the computers controlling the satellite. Later, 007 ponders the difficult task of how to bring the diamonds safely back to Earth.

LASER SHOW *Blofeld demonstrates the power of his superweapon by destroying a US ICBM, a Soviet sub, and Chinese missiles.*

DICE, LOADED

APPEARANCE
Octopussy (1983)
USED BY Kamal Khan, James Bond

This pair of dice contains a small mercury load in the center cavity, which, when struck properly, shifts to force a roll of six.

Exiled Afghan prince Kamal Khan wins 220,000 rupees from retired Major Clive while playing backgammon at the Shiv Niwas Palace Hotel casino with loaded dice that always reveal a winning double six. When Clive refuses Khan's proposal to increase the stakes to 100,000 rupees, Bond takes his place, betting a real Fabergé egg, which Khan desperately wants. Bond then uses player's privilege and rolls Khan's loaded dice, winning 200,000 rupees and arousing Khan's interest and wrath.

DREAM MACHINE

APPEARANCE
Die Another Day (2002)
USED BY Gustav Graves/Colonel Moon, Zao

The Dream Machine consists of a face-enveloping mask that, with other components, produces a sleep-like state, allowing a body to repair and regenerate at a faster rate than normal. It is used as part of the DNA replacement therapy offered by Dr. Alvarez at his beauty parlor clinic in Cuba. Gustav Graves/Colonel Moon, who suffers from permanent insomnia as a result of his DNA replacement, uses the machine privately. Graves/Moon says an hour a day in the Dream Machine keeps him sane.

CURE FOR INSOMNIA *Zao arrives at Graves's base while Graves uses the Dream Machine.*

DUNHILL CIGARETTE LIGHTER GRENADE

APPEARANCE
Tomorrow Never Dies (1997)
USED BY James Bond

This gold Dunhill lighter has a hidden switch, which, when flicked, arms a grenade. In order to infiltrate a terrorist supermarket at the Khyber Pass, Bond flicks the hidden switch, and a red light flashes on the side of the lighter. Bond throws it behind a pile of oil drums, and it explodes. An automatic radar-guided Gatling gun spins and directs fire at Bond's grenade diversion, allowing Bond to race to an L39 Albatross jet and escape.

FIREBALL *Bond's Dunhill grenade lands near an oil depot at the terrorist arms bazaar.*

ELECTRIFIED CHAIR

APPEARANCE
Thunderball (1965)
USED BY Ernst Stavro Blofeld

When Blofeld discovers that SPECTRE's income from the distribution of Red China narcotics in the United States has been short-changed, he exacts an extremely

heavy price. Blofeld electrocutes SPECTRE No. 9 in his seat, has the chair with the smoking corpse lowered, and forces those working below to dispose of the body. Afterward, the smoking chair is raised back through the floor into its proper position.

ELEVATOR GAS CHAMBER

APPEARANCE
Diamonds Are Forever (1971)
USED BY Ernst Stavro Blofeld

When 007 enters the penthouse office of Willard Whyte, he finds himself in the presence of Blofeld. Surprisingly, Blofeld invites Bond to exit via his personal elevator. Bond does as suggested and soon finds himself trapped in a descending gas chamber. The gas does not kill Bond but knocks him out for many hours. When the elevator stops, Wint and Kidd collect 007's unconscious body and dump it in a pipeline that is soon buried under ground.

ELECTRIFIED HEADSET

APPEARANCE
For Your Eyes Only (1981)
USED BY Ernst Stavro Blofeld?

Sending a shock through a headset is an unusual way to kill a helicopter pilot. A man who resembles Ernst Stavro Blofeld takes advantage of the electricity generated by the Augusta/ Bell 206B's Allison 250 turboshaft engine. "Blofeld" uses a remote control unit to pump that charge into the temples of the pilot. This leaves the passenger, James Bond, at the mercy of "Blofeld's" remote-control flying skills.

ERICSSON MOBILE PHONE

APPEARANCE
Tomorrow Never Dies (1997)
USED BY James Bond, Dr. Kaufman

The Ericsson JB988 mobile phone, credited with saving James Bond's life numerous times in Hamburg, Germany, boasts several special features installed by Q Branch. These include a 20,000 volt stun gun, a fingerprint scanner, and an electronic

enter techno-terrorist Henry Gupta's secret lab on the top floor of Carver's Media Group Network headquarters. He also engages the stun gun terminals and fries the electronic access panel outside Gupta's private office. Bond uses the phone to scan Gupta's fingerprint and then uses that scan to gain entry into Gupta's safe.

007 later gains the upper hand against professional assassin Dr.

Q: Your new telephone. Talk here, listen here.
007: So that's what I've been doing wrong all these years.

lock pick hidden in the phone's antenna. The phone, when opened, reveals a touchpad and a color LCD screen. Together they can be used to remotely drive Bond's BMW 750iL.

When the British frigate HMS *Devonshire* sinks, M instructs Bond to investigate media mogul Elliot Carver's involvement. Bond uses the electronic lock pick in the mobile to

Kaufman by convincing him the only way to unlock Bond's 750iL is by hitting "recall-3-send." The sequence actually activates the stun gun in the mobile, shocking Kaufman.

Bond also uses the phone to drive and deploys the gadgets of the 750iL, using the phone, mostly from the backseat.

OPEN SESAME *Bond prepares to use the lock pick function of his Ericsson JB988 to gain access to Carver's Hamburg headquarters.*

STUN GUN *Bond disables the electronic lock with his phone's stun function to enter Gupta's office.*

WORK OF ART *This Imperial green-gold Easter Egg by Carl Fabergé contains a model of the state coach used by Tsar Nicholas II at his coronation in 1897.*

FABERGÉ EGG

APPEARANCE
Octopussy (1983)
USED BY James Bond

A forgery of an Imperial Fabergé Easter Egg places James Bond on the trail of a nuclear sabotage plot.

Rogue Soviet General Orlov pilfers the Fabergé egg and other valuable jewels from the Kremlin Art Repository in order to finance a plot to detonate a nuclear weapon on a US Airbase in West Germany. The Fabergé takes on great importance when agent 009 steals the forgery in East Germany. He reaches the residence of the British Ambassador but dies before he can explain its significance.

With the fake egg gone, General

Orlov tells his accomplices, exiled Afghan prince Kamal Khan and smuggler Magda, that he needs the real egg back. They must buy it at auction so it can be returned to the Kremlin in time for an inventory of the repository. During the auction, James Bond switches the real egg for the fake obtained from 009. Bond then uses the real egg as bait for Khan in India. Magda steals the real egg from Bond and gives it to Khan, unaware that it has a homing device and transmitter from Q Branch inside. This addition allows 007 to gain valuable information about Orlov and Khan's plan. General Orlov, believing the real egg to be the fake, smashes it with the butt of his gun.

FAKE ASSASSINATION KIT

APPEARANCE
The Living Daylights (1987)
USED BY General Leonid Pushkin

This fake assassination kit is perfect for spies who want to convince their

enemies they are dead. In order to convince General Koskov and Brad Whitaker that General Leonid Pushkin is out of the picture, 007 teams with Pushkin to "fake" his death using a bulletproof vest, a clear plastic bag containing "blood" or red dye, and a blood capsule for Pushkin to bite into at the time of the shooting. Bond fires at Pushkin at the North African Trade Convention in Tangier. The bullets burst the blood bag but are stopped by the vest. The fake assassination proves so convincing that everyone, including Pushkin's mistress, Rubavitch (shown grieving), is taken in.

FAKE FINGERPRINTS

APPEARANCE
Diamonds Are Forever (1971)
USED BY James Bond

Fake fingerprints allow an agent to undergo a rigorous background check without blowing his cover. To pose as smuggler Peter Franks, Bond covers his fingertips with false skin imprinted with the smuggler's own prints. When Bond meets smuggler Tiffany Case, she checks the prints and finds they match. Bond calls Q to congratulate him only to discover that the real Franks has escaped custody.

SHEDDING SKIN *Bond removes Q's ingenious fake fingerprints after passing muster with Tiffany Case.*

FAKE LEG CAST

APPEARANCE
Octopussy (1983)
USED BY James Bond

Bond apparently sustains several injuries while rescuing jewel smuggler Octopussy from exiled Afghan prince Kamal Khan's Beech 18 plane. Unable to travel from India to London, Bond retires to the bedroom on Octopussy's lake barge with a plastic cast on his right arm, a sling on his left, and one leg in traction. When Octopussy complains that she wishes he wasn't in such a weakened condition, the cast, the sling, and the traction suddenly fall apart, and Bond takes Octopussy in his arms. It has all been an elaborate ruse of Bond's to avoid returning to London.

FELIX LIGHTER

APPEARANCE
Live And Let Die (1973)
USED BY Harold Strutter, James Bond

A push-in car cigarette lighter doubles as a two-way radio for CIA agent Harold Strutter. Sitting in Strutter's car in Harlem, James Bond is surprised to hear CIA agent Felix Leiter joining in their conversation about a possible connection between dictator Dr. Kananga and businessman Mr. Big, because Felix is a few miles away in Midtown Manhattan. A built-in speaker allows Bond to hear Felix, and through a microphone, 007 informs his colleague that the gadget must be "a genuine Felix Lighter."

FINGER CLAMP

APPEARANCE
Diamonds Are Forever (1971)
USED BY James Bond

A finger clamp from Q's lab allows an agent being searched for a weapon to quickly gain the advantage. When Bond travels to Mexico to hunt down Ernst Stavro Blofeld, he infiltrates Blofeld's lab. Blofeld's double and two guards soon confront him. Bond raises his hands in surrender and that allows a guard to retrieve his Walther PPK from its shoulder holster. What the guard finds instead is a mousetrap-like device that clamps three of his fingers, slicing into them with razor-sharp teeth and giving Bond the upper hand.

FINGERPRINT SCANNER

APPEARANCE
Diamonds Are Forever (1971)
USED BY Tiffany Case

PETER FRANKS

To infiltrate Blofeld's diamond smuggling ring, Bond poses as smuggler Peter Franks and makes contact with Tiffany Case. A smuggler herself, Tiffany doesn't take unnecessary chances and uses a fingerprint viewer to verify the identity of her new contact. She dusts Bond's glass for fingerprints and takes a Polaroid photograph. She then slides the photo of Bond's thumbprint into the fingerprint scanner viewer hidden in her closet where it appears on a screen next to the real thumbprint of Peter Franks. When the prints match, Tiffany accepts Bond as the real Franks and gives him his mission. Little does she know that Q has supplied Bond with a set of fake fingerprints for the occasion.

FIVE-BLADED KNIFE

APPEARANCE
Octopussy (1983)
USED BY Gobinda's men

Among the many weapons used by Kamal Khan's henchman, Gobinda, and his goons is a five-bladed knife, that allows an assailant to swing,

thrust, or throw the weapon with potentially deadly results.

One of Gobinda's goons uses the five-bladed knife when chasing Bond through the streets in Udaipur, India. Bond, riding in a tuk-tuk taxi, has no room to escape when the thug leaps from a jeep and seemingly pushes one of the knife's blades deep into Bond's chest. Bond knocks his attacker off the speeding vehicle and reveals that a thick wad of rupees stashed in his jacket has just saved his life.

FLASH PAPER

APPEARANCE
You Only Live Twice (1967)
USED BY James Bond

Magicians commonly use flash paper because, once ignited, it burns so completely as to leave virtually no ash and no smoke. Because of this, it is perfect for passing written information that must be destroyed without a trace. Flash paper is treated with nitric acid and sulfuric acid to create a sheet of nitrocellulose, allowing it to self-oxidize when lit. When M sends Bond to Japan to hunt for clues to the loss of an American spacecraft, he gives 007 the name of his contact on a sheet of flash paper. Bond memorizes it, then sets the sheet aflame with his lighter.

GEIGER COUNTER

APPEARANCE
Dr. No (1962)
USED BY James Bond

GEIGER COUNTER
This piece of scientific hardware provides vital evidence toward uncovering Dr. No's network and plans.

A Geiger counter is a particle detector that measures ionizing radiation. One arrives for 007 in Kingston in the diplomatic pouch. Bond demonstrates the Geiger counter's effectiveness to local fisherman Quarrel by running it over his Rolex watch and explaining how the luminous dial activates it. Bond then runs the Geiger counter over the exact spot in Quarrel's boat where the assassinated British Secret Service representative Commander Strangways placed rock samples from Crab Key.

The Geiger counter indicates a strong radioactive count. Professor Dent's claim that the rocks were merely worthless chunks of iron ore confirms Bond's suspicions that Dent is working for the enemy. The presence of radioactivity in the rock samples also leads Bond to investigate Dr. No's base on Crab Key.

GEIGER COUNTER CAMERA

APPEARANCE
Thunderball (1965)
USED BY Domino Derval

Bond provides Domino Derval with a Q Branch Geiger counter camera to help her locate two atomic weapons stolen by her lover Emilio Largo. 007 gives Domino the fake camera believing Largo will bring the bombs aboard the *Disco Volante*. Bond tells Domino to go on deck if the signal indicates strong radiation. Largo confronts Domino when she leaves her cabin, discovers the camera, and tortures her for betraying him.

GLASSES DETONATOR

APPEARANCE
The World Is Not Enough (1999)
USED BY James Bond

These Calvin Klein 718F glasses (with clear lenses; 007 has 20/20 vision) boast a small protrusion, which, when pressed, triggers a blinding flash from 007's Walther P99 handgun. When Lachaise's men trap Bond in the Swiss banker's Bilbao office, 007 presses the protrusion, triggering the flash from the Walther P99 and temporarily blinding Lachaise's men. This flash allows Bond to gain the upper hand, take out Lachaise's men, and confront the Swiss banker.

GOLD INGOT

APPEARANCE
Goldfinger (1964)
USED BY James Bond, Goldfinger

007 uses a solid gold ingot, reputedly from the Nazi hoard at the bottom of Lake Toplitz (Toplitzsee) in Saltzkammergut, Austria, to entice Goldfinger into a £5000 wager on their golf match, which Bond wins. Goldfinger pays off gangster Mr. Solo with gold ingots in Kentucky, but then extracts them from the crushed remains of his Lincoln Continental. Bond later ineffectively uses a gold ingot as a weapon against Oddjob.

GOLDENEYE

APPEARANCE
GoldenEye (1995)
USED BY General Ourumov,
Alec Trevelyan

GoldenEye is a space-based nuclear weapons system designed to hit a large target on earth with a tremendous electromagnetic pulse. MI6 statistical analysis determined incorrectly during the Cold War that the Soviets had neither the finances nor technology to implement the system. The Soviets did, and the system consists of two satellites—Petya and Mischa—and two control stations in Russia and Cuba. Janus crime syndicate leader Alec Trevelyan takes control of GoldenEye. General Ourumov uses Petya to devastate Severnaya, and Trevelyan attempts to destroy London with Mischa. The Mischa weapon burns up in the atmosphere after programmer Natalya Simonova resets its orbit. James Bond destroys the Cuban control center through a series of sabotage efforts.

GOLDEN GUN

APPEARANCE **The Man With The Golden Gun (1974)**

USED BY **Scaramanga**

Master assassin Francisco Scaramanga uses a unique 4.2 mm golden gun that is likely to have been designed by Lazar, a specialist Portuguese weapons maker in Macau. The gun consists of components that can be disassembled and smuggled disguised as everyday objects. The pistol consists of a cigarette lighter, a cigarette case, cuff links, and a fountain pen. These items fit together to make a single-shot weapon. Lazar also makes the soft 23-karat golden bullets the gun fires. He uses nickel to strengthen the gold, which flattens on impact like a dum dum for maximum wounding effect. Lazar delivers these bullets in a cigarette box to an unknown contact at the Casino de Macau. The bullets and gun seal Scaramanga's reputation as the greatest living assassin.

Scaramanga uses the gun to kill 002 Bill Fairbanks in Beirut and dispatch hitman Rodney in his island fun house. He shoots Gibson outside the Bottoms Up Club in Hong Kong. Later, he turns the gun on his business partner Hai Fat in Fat's estate office. When 007 arrives at Scaramanga's island, the assassin engages him in a duel—Bond's Walther PPK against his golden gun. With a little subterfuge, Bond wins. Scaramanga also has a golden Colt .45, which he uses to shoot the top off a bottle of champagne offered to Bond by Nick Nack.

A SINISTER MESSAGE *The arrival of a golden bullet inscribed "007" prompts M to send Bond on a mission to kill the world's most feared assassin.*

GPS ENCODER

APPEARANCE **Tomorrow Never Dies (1997)**

USED BY **Elliot Carver, Henry Gupta, James Bond, Dr. Greenwalt**

This US military Global Positioning System (GPS) encoder sends a time signal to space-based navigation satellites equipped with atomic clocks. The GPS system calculates positions based on time-differences between signals received from multiple satellites.

Media mogul Elliot Carver instructs techno-terrorist Henry Gupta to alter the time signal on an encoder purchased at a terrorist swap meet. The HMS *Devonshire* receives a signal transmitted from a Carver Media Group satellite, which sends the ship off course. The Chinese believe the British are in Chinese waters and the British think they are in international waters. In reality, the British have strayed into Vietnamese waters. Bond steals the encoder from Gupta's safe and takes it to GPS expert Dr. Dave Greenwalt, who uses it to pinpoint where the *Devonshire* sank.

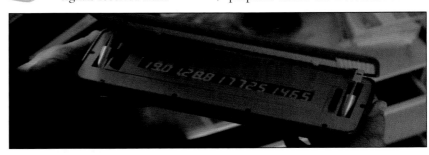

GRAPPLING HOOK GUN

APPEARANCE **Goldfinger (1964)**

USED BY **James Bond**

To allow quick entry into a walled compound, Q develops a grappling hook gun. The gun propels a grappling hook and the spooled high-test nylon ultra-thin climbing rope 40 ft (12 m) into the air. The use of the gun eliminates the problem of the climbing rope becoming tangled. Bond uses this device to enter the oil storage depots owned by heroin-manufacturer Mr. Ramirez in Mexico.

GRAVITY CONTROL UNIT

APPEARANCE **Moonraker (1979)**

USED BY **Hugo Drax**

Drax's space station has a radar-jamming system and an artificial gravity unit. The gravity control unit causes the station to rotate, creating a simulated gravitational pull. When Drax's men commence Operation Orchid, firing globes of nerve gas into the Earth's atmosphere, Bond and Dr. Holly Goodhead disable the radar-jamming system and make the space station visible from Earth. Drax orders the station's laser to destroy a fast-approaching US space shuttle, but Bond prevents this by engaging the gravity control unit's emergency stop and creating weightless chaos inside the station.

GRAVITY NORMAL *On arrival at the station, one of Drax's men engages the gravity control, enabling others to disembark with ease.*

QUICK THINKING *To save the attacking US shuttle, Bond flips open the cover on the emergency stop device and presses a button that shuts down the system.*

HAIRBRUSH TRANSMITTER

APPEARANCE
Live And Let Die (1973)
USED BY James Bond

In his hotel in San Monique, Bond unpacks a high-tech grooming kit. Removing the false back of a hairbrush, 007 reveals that it is also a radio transmitter. Before using it, Bond uses a bug-detector, disguised as a shaving kit, to sweep the room. Having located two hidden microphones, Bond employs the transmitter, using Morse code to send his message. To whom he communicates remains a mystery.

HANDBAG WALKIE-TALKIES

APPEARANCES
You Only Live Twice (1967),
Moonraker (1979)
USED BY Japanese SIS agents,
Dr. Holly Goodhead

When 007 enters the Ginza district of Tokyo looking for his initial contact in *You Only Live Twice*, two Japanese women watch him and radio his progress to an unknown person. It is likely they radio either Tiger Tanaka, the head of the Japanese Secret Service, or agent Aki, whom 007 is soon to meet at a Sumo wrestling arena.

In *Moonraker*, 007 discovers Dr. Holly Goodhead is really a CIA agent. In her hotel room in Venice, he finds a purse radio with a spring-loaded aerial among her standard CIA-issue equipment.

HANDCUFF CHAIR

APPEARANCE
Live And Let Die (1973)
USED BY Tee Hee, Mr. Big/
Dr. Kananga

With the pull of a switch on the back, this chair flips two arm shackles in place, pinning an unlucky occupant. Tee Hee locks 007 in the chair for questioning from Mr. Big/ Dr. Kananga about the state of Solitaire's virginity, which apparently effects her ability to tell the future. This proves to be a subject Bond remains eager to avoid. Despite a threat to have Tee Hee clip off Bond's little finger, Kananga releases 007 so he can be fed to crocodiles.

HECKLER & KOCH GUNS

APPEARANCES
Tomorrow Never Dies (1997),
Casino Royale (2006)
USED BY James Bond, Dr. Kaufman,
Elliot Carver's men, Gettler's men

James Bond and his enemies have used a variety of German-made Heckler & Koch guns.

In *Tomorrow Never Dies*, assassin Dr. Kaufman kills Paris Carver with a Heckler & Koch 9 mm P7 pistol and prepares to eliminate Bond with it before 007 turns the gun on him. Media mogul Elliot Carver's stealth ship is loaded with Heckler & Koch MP54 submachine guns that 007 and Carver's men fire at each other.

Casino Royale sees henchman Gettler's men fire UMP45 submachine guns at Bond as he tries to rescue treasury agent Vesper Lynd. 007 later fires a high-powered bullet from a Heckler & Koch UMP9 9 mm into terrorist middleman Mr. White's leg.

HELICOPTER REMOTE UNIT

APPEARANCE
For Your Eyes Only (1981)
USED BY A Blofeld-like villain

The helicopter remote unit consists of a console equipped with levers, buttons, switches, a joystick, and two TV screens. A man who could be Blofeld uses the unit to electrocute the pilot of his helicopter and eliminate 007. Bond climbs out of the helicopter, moves to the front seat, and pulls out a cable running into a black box near the instrument panel, disabling the remote unit. He then takes control of the chopper and goes after the villain.

HOLOGRAM MACHINE

APPEARANCE
The World Is Not Enough (1999)
USED BY MI6

This machine is based at MI6's Remote Operations Centre at Castle Thane, Scotland. It generates a huge 3-D image of the head of terrorist Renard. This hologram allows MI6 doctor Molly Warmflash to explain how a bullet fired by agent 009 is moving through the medulla oblongata in Renard's brain, gradually killing off his senses. This allows him to feel no pain and to push himself harder and longer than any normal man until the bullet finally kills him.

HOMER SYSTEM

APPEARANCE
Goldfinger (1964), The Man With The Golden Gun (1974)
USED BY James Bond, Felix Leiter, Mary Goodnight

The homer system consists of a small radio transmitter that works with a unique rotating receiver. This receiver fixes the direction of the homer signal. The homer emits signals enabling the receiving unit to calculate its distance, allowing for a continuous fix on the homer's location. The CIA and British Secret Service developed the homer, and both James Bond and Felix Leiter use the device during their pursuit of Goldfinger.

Bond plants a large, magnetized version of the transmitter in Goldfinger's Rolls-Royce in England, allowing him to follow the car to Switzerland. Leiter reports Bond's whereabouts to M when the CIA picks up the signal from Bond's own homer, secreted in the heel of his shoe. Bond plants the homer on gangster Mr. Solo at Goldfinger's stud farm with a note to the CIA alerting them to Goldfinger's plans.

In *The Man With The Golden Gun*, staff intelligence officer Mary Goodnight has a homer on her in Bangkok. When Scaramanga kidnaps Goodnight, the signal reveals his location.

HYDRAULIC DETONATOR

APPEARANCE
The Living Daylights (1987)
USED BY Necros

The hydraulic system that operates the sliding glass doors of the Prater Café in Vienna is rigged by former KGB assassin Necros so that it will work with unexpected speed when triggered by remote control.

As Saunders, head of Section V, exits the café, Necros presses one of the walkman's buttons, causing the doors to slam shut. The glass door slices Saunders in half. As Bond reaches Saunders, a balloon drifts past with the words *smiert spionam* on it.

ICARUS

APPEARANCE
Die Another Day (2002)
USED BY Gustav Graves/Colonel Moon

The Icarus satellite, launched by billionaire Gustav Graves, has a reflective surface that spans 437 yd (400 m). It is purportedly designed to reflect the sun's light to allow crops to be grown at any time of the year in areas facing potential famine. However, Icarus also has another level of power, where the sun's light can be focused on a particular target, creating a deadly beam of high-intensity heat.

Graves attempts to use the Icarus to kill Bond in Iceland. He also tries to melt his Ice Palace and drown NSA agent Jinx. Graves later uses Icarus to devastate the DMZ minefield between North and South Korea hoping to trigger a war with South Korea and ultimately Japan.

> "The bullet will kill him, but **he'll grow stronger every day** until the day he dies."
>
> **Dr. Molly Warmflash**

IDENTIGRAPH, VISUAL

APPEARANCE
For Your Eyes Only (1981)
USED BY James Bond, Q

The Visual Identigraph is an early digital imaging computer used by MI6 to identify suspects by matching facial features to photographs in the files of MI6, the Surete, Interpol, the Mossad, and the West German police.

Bond visits Q's workshop to use the Visual Identigraph and discovers the man who paid off Gonzales is Emile Leopold Locque.

INCENDIARY BOMBS

APPEARANCE
Live And Let Die (1973)
USED BY Quarrel Jr.

Quarrel Jr. is the son of 007's ally who helped him find Dr. No. Like his late father, Quarrel Jr. is a useful friend to Bond. First he leads Bond to the clairvoyant, Solitaire. Then, when Bond goes to rescue Solitaire, Quarrel plants incendiary bombs with thirty minute fuses. As Bond cuts Solitaire free from the sacrificial altar, the bombs blast Kananga's poppy fields, destroying his billion-dollar crop.

JIM DIVING SUIT

APPEARANCE
For Your Eyes Only (1981)
USED BY Kristatos

The JIM Atmospheric Diving Suit is larger than a normal diving suit. It has four windows in the headpiece as well as huge legs and arms fitted with deadly-looking pincers. The suit is named after Jim Jarratt who, wearing an "Iron Man" armored diving suit, located the sunken liner *Lusitania* 330 ft (100 m) down off the coast of Ireland in 1935. The modern JIM suit's purpose is for salvage work at depths exceeding 300 ft (91 m).

After Bond and Melina recover the ATAC transmitter from the command cabin of the sunken *St. Georges* spy ship, a Kristatos henchman in the JIM suit bursts into the cabin and uses the pincer arms to seize the ATAC from Melina. Bond removes the magnetic timer and thermite bomb from the ATAC console, attaches it to the back of the diving suit, and sets the timer for one minute. Kristatos's henchman pushes a console onto Bond's legs and traps him. Bond extricates himself, grabs the ATAC, and escapes with Melina from the wreck as the JIM diving suit explodes.

INHALER BUG

APPEARANCE
Casino Royale (2006)
USED BY James Bond

Bond notices that Le Chiffre uses an inhaler during their high-stakes poker game at Casino Royale. When Le Chiffre steps away from the table for a moment, 007 inserts a minuscule bugging and tracking device into the inhaler's base. With the aid of his Sony Ericsson phone, Bond tracks Le Chiffre back to his hotel room and overhears the part of the violent encounter between Le Chiffre and African terrorist Steven Obanno.

KEVLAR VEST

APPEARANCES

The Living Daylights (1987), Licence To Kill (1989), Die Another Day (2002)

USED BY General Pushkin, Pam Bouvier, James Bond

The high-strength polymer Kevlar was invented in 1965 to reinforce car tires, and became a key material used in bulletproof vests. In *The Living Daylights*, General Pushkin wears a Kevlar vest when he and 007 fake his death.

In *Licence To Kill*, Dario fires a bullet into Pam Bouvier's back. Bond thinks she's fatally wounded, but she's protected by Kevlar beneath her vest.

In *Die Another Day*, during a battle aboard a hovercraft, Bond blocks General Moon's bullets by holding a Kevlar vest in front of his body.

KEY FOB

APPEARANCES

The Living Daylights (1987), The World Is Not Enough (1999), Die Another Day (2002), Casino Royale (2006)

USED BY James Bond, Kara Milovy, Carlos

An innocent-looking key fob has saved James Bond's life on numerous occasions. In *The Living Daylights*, Q presents Bond with a Philips key fob with keys and a plastic rectangular box attached. Pressing a button on the box activates it. By whistling the first bars of "Rule Britannia," stun gas is released to a range of 5 ft (1.5 m), disorienting a person for about 20 seconds. The fob is also packed with a highly concentrated plastic explosive sufficient to remove the door of any safe. The activating signal is personalized, and Bond's code is a wolf whistle. The skeleton keys also open 90 percent of the world's locks.

Bond later whistles "Rule Britannia" to release the stun gas to disable the jailer and escape a Soviet air base jail in Afghanistan. Kara Milovy then uses one of the keys to unlock Bond's handcuffs.

In Tangier, while confronting Brad Whitaker in his military museum home, Bond attaches the

WRONG NUMBER *Carlos sends a signal from his cell phone that will detonate his exploding key fob.*

magnetic key fob to a bust of the Duke of Wellington. When 007 emits a wolf whistle, the bust explodes and crushes Whitaker to death.

In *The World Is Not Enough*, Bond uses his key fob to remotely drive his BMW Z8 along Valentin Zukovsky's caviar factory walkways in Baku. In *Die Another Day*, 007 presses a button on his key fob to engage the "adaptive camouflage" feature of his Aston Martin Vanquish. Bond also uses the fob to remotely drive the vehicle in his direction.

In *Casino Royale*, terrorist Carlos attaches a key fob detonator to the undercarriage of a Texron fuel truck, which he plans to crash into a Skyfleet S570 plane. Unbeknownst to Carlos, 007 attaches the key fob detonator to Carlos's belt buckle. Carlos triggers the detonator and obliterates himself.

KNOCKOUT CIGARETTE

APPEARANCE

The Spy Who Loved Me (1977)

USED BY Anya Amasova

As James Bond and Russian agent Anya Amasova travel on a traditional Nile felucca back to Cairo, Amasova interrupts a possible romantic interlude by putting Bond to sleep with a cigarette filled with narcotic dust. She then removes, from the inside pocket of Bond's tuxedo, a microfilm of blueprints detailing shipping tycoon Karl Stromberg's submarine tracking technology. When Bond meets Anya again in MI6's Egyptian headquarters, he says he wishes to know which brand of cigarettes she smokes.

LAPEL PIN

APPEARANCE

The World Is Not Enough (1999)

USED BY Sir Robert King, Elektra King

Sir Robert King wears a lapel pin, a Scottish heirloom called "The Eye of the Glens." His daughter, Elektra, replaces it with one that contains a transmitter. When King approaches his case of money, the urea-dipped cash and the metal anti-counterfeit strip serve as a detonator, blowing him up and devastating MI6 HQ.

LASER, INDUSTRIAL

APPEARANCES

Goldfinger (1964), Die Another Day (2002)

USED BY Goldfinger, Mr. Kil, James Bond

Goldfinger maintains an industrial laser for precision cutting sheets of gold at Auric Enterprises A. G. This laser, one of the first of its strength ever produced, is capable of projecting a beam of light to the surface of the moon or cutting through the metal security doors at the loading docks of Fort Knox. Goldfinger threatens to bisect 007 with the laser in Switzerland. He later hides it in the back of a disguised Army ambulance and uses it to enter the loading bay at the Bullion Depository vault.

Die Another Day sees 007 use another industrial laser. In the diamond cutting area of billionaire Gustav Graves's Icelandic mine, henchman Mr. Kil attempts to

DEATH RAYS *Bond battles Mr. Kil as deadly laser beams whirl around them in* Die Another Day.

eliminate spy Jinx, who is chained to a table, with a laser beam. Bond arrives and stops the laser with a remote device. Kil attacks and 007 knocks the remote against his face, switching on several lasers fired from a powerful robotic arm. Bond and Kil fight between the beams until Bond switches off the remote again. When Kil tries to stab Bond with a Maori bone hair comb, Jinx grabs the swinging remote and fires a laser beam into the back of Kil's head. The pair then cuts off Mr. Kil's hand with a laser to allow them to use his palm print to gain access to secure areas.

FINAL CUT *Goldfinger finds a novel use for his industrial laser— eliminating Bond.*

LASER CAMERA

APPEARANCE
Licence To Kill (1989)
USED BY Pam Bouvier

Pressing the shutter on this Polaroid camera shoots a brilliant red laser from the flash and takes an X-ray portrait of the subject.

In Bond's hotel room in Isthmus City, Pam takes a photo of Bond and Q with the camera and is amazed when the laser shoots from the flash, burning a hole through a framed photograph of President Lopez. The X-ray portrait shows Bond and Q leaping out of the way of the laser.

NEAR MISS *Carey's polaroid captures Bond and Q taking evasive action.*

LASER GUNS

APPEARANCE
Moonraker (1979)
USED BY Q Branch, James Bond, Hugo Drax's astronauts, space marines

One of Q's assistants demonstrates a laser rifle at Q's Brazilian laboratory.

The beams emitted by the laser rifle generate a heat great enough to melt the face of a mannequin in tests. Apparently, Q has shared the design with the US military, who go on to use similar weapons in their battle with Hugo Drax's men when they raid Drax's space station.

Drax himself has a laser cannon that can destroy approaching American space shuttles, but his plans are foiled before he can activate it.

The American space marines have lasers mounted over their shoulders on their life support packs and carry laser rifles. Drax's men are armed with chest-mounted laser weapons in the space battle, but on Drax's station, they have laser pistols. CIA agent Dr. Holly Goodhead commandeers one of these pistols as the battle ensues.

Drax's shuttle, Moonraker 5, is armed with a laser that Bond and Holly use to destroy Drax's nerve gas globes.

LEKTOR, THE

APPEARANCE
From Russia With Love (1963)
USED BY Soviet Intelligence, SPECTRE

The Soviet-built Lektor enables Eastern bloc intelligence agencies to communicate easily with each other. James Bond's mission is to bring the machine to the British Secret Service. The Lektor weighs approximately 22 lbs (10 kg) and is slightly larger than a typewriter. It can be easily carried in a brown case. It works using a series of rotating perforated disks, a light, and a mirror. Coded messages arrive via punch cards, which are then inserted into the machine, deciphered, and printed out. Fleming based the machine on the Enigma encoder used by the Nazis in World War II. In the novel, it is called the Spektor, but the name was changed for the film to avoid confusion with SPECTRE.

OPPORTUNIST THEFT *Tania steals the Lektor from the Soviet embassy.*

LIMPET MINES

APPEARANCES
From Russia With Love (1963), You Only Live Twice (1967), The Spy Who Loved Me (1977), A View To A Kill (1985), GoldenEye (1995) Tomorrow Never Dies (1997)
USED BY The Soviets, Japanese SIS ninjas, Karl Stromberg, Liparus crew, Klotkoff, Pola Ivanova, James Bond, Wai Lin

PRIMED TO KILL *Bond prepares to mine Carver's ship in* Tomorrow Never Dies.

A limpet mine is a magnetized explosive device that is attached to a ferrous object, then set off by remote control or via a timer. Soviet operatives set a limpet mine to kill Head of Station T, Kerim Bey, in *From Russia With Love.*

Japanese SIS ninjas use a limpet mine to blast a hole in the false lake in Blofeld's volcano to destroy SPECTRE's rocket base in *You Only Live Twice.*

The Spy Who Loved Me sees Karl Stromberg's men attaching a limpet speaker to the hull of the nuclear submarine USS *Wayne*, along with a cyanide bolt that they fire through the hull.

In *A View To A Kill*, KGB agents Klotkoff and Pola Ivanova attach a limpet to the jetty below Zorin's oil pumping station in San Francisco.

When 007 and 006 break into the Arkangel Chemical Weapons Facility in *GoldenEye*, Bond plants three magnetic explosives with digital timers. Though 007 sets them to detonate after six minutes, by pressing a button he reduces the count on one to three minutes. Nine years later, Bond plants a refined version of the mine on a nitrogen tank in Janus's Cuban GoldenEye satellite control facility. The timer on this version can be shut off by pressing a button on Bond's watch.

Bond uses limpets in his assault on an arms bazaar and, with help from spy Wai Lin, attaches limpets to the stealth ship belonging to Elliot Carver to prevent him from starting World War III in *Tomorrow Never Dies.*

LIPSTICK MAGNESIUM FLARE

APPEARANCE
You Only Live Twice (1967)
USED BY Helga Brandt

The lipstick magnesium flare belonging to SPECTRE No. 11, Helga Brandt, almost spells doom for James Bond. Brandt agrees to fly Bond from Kobe to Tokyo in her Meyers 200A airplane. Once at altitude, Brandt traps Bond in his seat and drops her lipstick compact, in reality a magnesium flare which starts to burn through the floor to the fuel lines. Helga bails out, and Bond soon breaks free. He struggles to crash land the burning plane before it explodes.

LOCATOR CARD

APPEARANCE
The World Is Not Enough (1999)
USED BY M

Every Russian nuclear warhead contains a locator card, a device similar in size and shape to a credit card, which emits a high-pitched signal on Russian emergency frequencies and allows the warhead to be tracked anywhere. Bond spots one of Renard's men removing the locator card from a warhead in a Kazakhstan underground nuclear test facility. 007 later retrieves it from the dead man's pocket and gives it to M when she arrives at Elektra King's oil pipeline station. Elektra later kidnaps M and holds her captive at Maiden's Tower on the Bosphorus near Istanbul, Turkey. When Elektra places an alarm clock on the ledge of M's cell to show M how much time is left before she and most of Istanbul are blown to kingdom come, M opens the back of the clock, removes the batteries and connects the wires to the locator card. Bond thus tracks M to Maiden's Tower.

FINAL CARD *M uses all her resourcefulness to escape incarceration.*

MANNEQUIN

APPEARANCE
Live And Let Die (1973)
USED BY Baron Samedi

During the sacrificial ceremonies on the Caribbean island of San Monique, the voodoo god of cemeteries, Baron Samedi, is called by worshippers. As the Baron rises from a grave, Bond pulls his Smith & Wesson 29 .44 Magnum and shoots Samedi in the head. The head breaks like plaster as the onlookers gasp. Bond fires two more shots, exploding the mannequin and revealing the trick, until the Baron in all-too-human form rises up from an adjacent grave.

MANTA RAY DISGUISE

APPEARANCE
Licence To Kill (1989)
USED BY James Bond

James Bond needs to gain entry into marine researcher and drug smuggler Milton Krest's research vessel, the *Wavekrest*, off the coast of Cay Sal Bank just north of Cuba. In order to avoid discovery, Bond covers himself underwater with a manta ray disguise. He fashions this disguise using a dark gray tarpaulin and two of his fisherman friend Sharky's fishing poles bent in a loop. When Krest's underwater probe, the *Sentinel*, passes over Bond's head, Bond drops the camouflage and swims after the craft, which is returning to the well area of the *Wavekrest*. Bond proceeds to climb aboard the *Wavekrest* undetected.

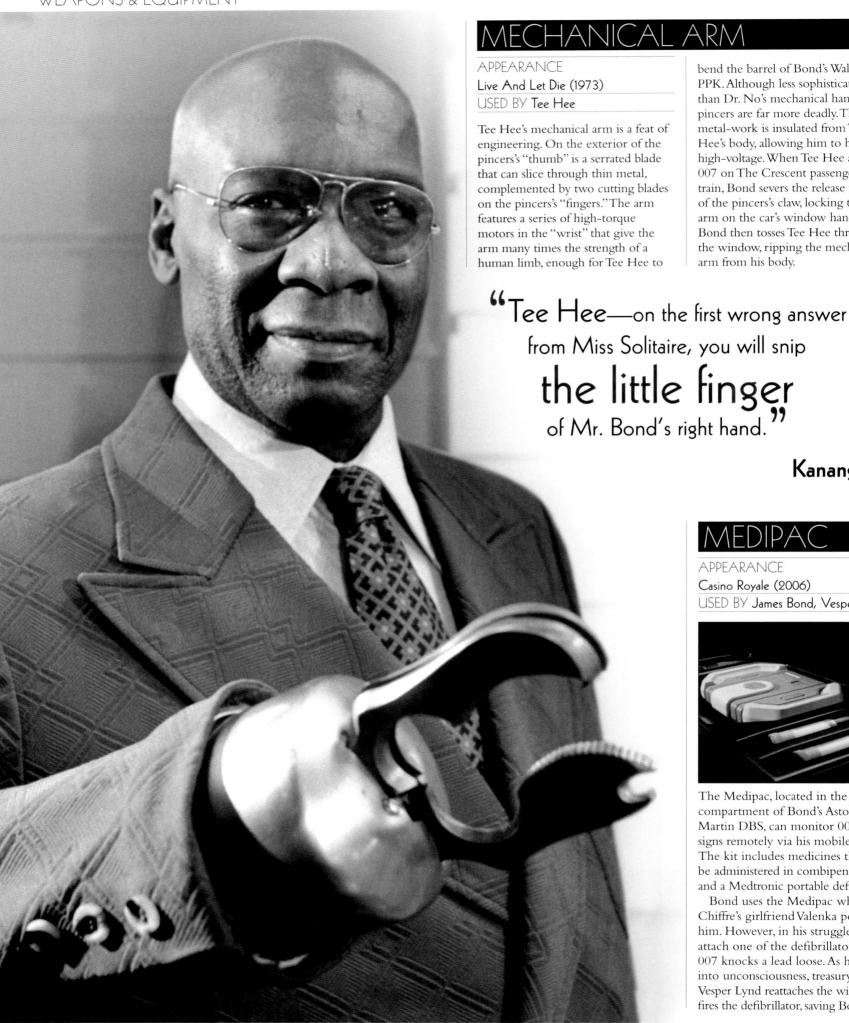

MECHANICAL ARM

APPEARANCE
Live And Let Die (1973)
USED BY Tee Hee

Tee Hee's mechanical arm is a feat of engineering. On the exterior of the pincers's "thumb" is a serrated blade that can slice through thin metal, complemented by two cutting blades on the pincers's "fingers." The arm features a series of high-torque motors in the "wrist" that give the arm many times the strength of a human limb, enough for Tee Hee to bend the barrel of Bond's Walther PPK. Although less sophisticated than Dr. No's mechanical hands, the pincers are far more deadly. The metal-work is insulated from Tee Hee's body, allowing him to handle high-voltage. When Tee Hee attacks 007 on The Crescent passenger train, Bond severs the release wires of the pincers's claw, locking the arm on the car's window handle. Bond then tosses Tee Hee through the window, ripping the mechanical arm from his body.

> "Tee Hee—on the first wrong answer from Miss Solitaire, you will snip **the little finger** of Mr. Bond's right hand."
>
> **Kananga**

MEDIPAC

APPEARANCE
Casino Royale (2006)
USED BY James Bond, Vesper Lynd

The Medipac, located in the glove compartment of Bond's Aston Martin DBS, can monitor 007's vital signs remotely via his mobile phone. The kit includes medicines that can be administered in combipen form and a Medtronic portable defibrillator.

Bond uses the Medipac when Le Chiffre's girlfriend Valenka poisons him. However, in his struggle to attach one of the defibrillator panels, 007 knocks a lead loose. As he slips into unconsciousness, treasury officer Vesper Lynd reattaches the wire and fires the defibrillator, saving Bond's life.

MICRO-COMPARATOR

APPEARANCE
A View To A Kill (1985)
USED BY James Bond

When James Bond returns from Siberia with a microchip recovered from 003's body, Q uses a micro-comparator to compare it to an electromagnetic pulse impervious chip developed by Zorin Industries for the British government. The chips are identical, proving that the KGB had access to the secret chip designed by Zorin Industries.

MICROFILM VIEWER

APPEARANCE
The Spy Who Loved Me (1977)
USED BY James Bond

On a Nile felucca, 007 uses a pocket microfilm viewer to inspect microfilm of shipping tycoon Karl Stromberg's submarine tracking system blueprint that he retrieved from Jaws.

The microfilm viewer is disguised as a cigarette case and lighter and has a top that slides back to reveal a tiny screen. The microfilm clips onto the projector unit, which is disguised as a cigarette lighter. This fits into the top of the microfilm viewer. Using this device, 007 sees that key information has been deleted from the blueprints photographed on the microfilm.

MILK BOTTLE GRENADES

APPEARANCE
The Living Daylights (1987)
USED BY Necros

These milk bottles are really high-powered concussion grenades based on the WWII German Model 24 or "Potato Masher" grenade.

Soviet assassin Necros disguises himself as a milkman and infiltrates MI6's Blayden safe house. Throwing the explosive milk bottles, Necros causes utter chaos. The grenades seriously damage the house,

resulting in "two dead, two in hospital," according to M. Necros and a group of conspirators then seemingly kidnap General Georgi Koskov.

MINI CAMERAS

APPEARANCE
On Her Majesty's Secret Service (1969), Moonraker (1979)
USED BY James Bond

In *On Her Majesty's Secret Service*, Bond uses a miniature Minox A/IIIs camera during the raid on Piz Gloria in Switzerland to photograph Blofeld's world map. The map features the locations of all of Blofeld's Angels of Death.

During the *Moonraker* mission, Bond takes blueprints of the Moonraker shuttle out of billionaire Hugo Drax's safe and photographs them with a miniature camera. The camera is engraved with 007, with the middle "0" being the camera lens.

MINI-REBREATHER

APPEARANCE   Thunderball (1965), On Her Majesty's Secret Service (1969), Die Another Day (2002)
USED BY James Bond

For use during short periods underwater when conventional Scuba gear is not available, Q developed the mini-rebreather, which can last for up to four minutes.

Bond first uses it in *Thunderball* during an underwater battle with a SPECTRE agent in a pool at Emilio Largo's Nassau home. Bond later uses the device during the fight with SPECTRE frogmen in Biscayne Bay.

In *On Her Majesty's Secret Service*, after 007 dictates a letter of resignation to Miss Moneypenny, he pulls the mini-rebreather out of his office drawer.

Bond utilizes an updated model when investigating activities at the Iceland diamond mine of Gustav Graves in *Die Another Day*.

MONT BLANC PEN

APPEARANCE
Octopussy (1983)
USED BY James Bond

This Solitaire Mont Blanc Pen writes poisoned pen letters as well as featuring state-of-the-art listening devices. A drop from the pen releases a mix of nitric and hydrochloric acid that can dissolve all metals. There is also a listening device in the pen's cap enabling one to listen in on a bug placed in the Fabergé Egg's coach model. 007 employs the acid to eat through the bars on the window of his room at Kamal Khan's Monsoon Palace and uses the listening device to eavesdrop on Khan and General Orlov, despite interference from Magda's hairdryer.

MURPHY BED

APPEARANCE
You Only Live Twice (1967)
USED BY Ling, James Bond

The British Secret Service stages Bond's death by using a spring-loaded Murphy bed that hurls Bond up against a wall at the touch of a button. Enemy machine gunners break in and spray the underside with bullets. The bed features a steel plate that protects 007, but fake blood convinces Hong Kong authorities that gunmen have killed Bond.

UP AGAINST THE WALL *Ling flips her Murphy bed back so that gunmen can "kill" Bond.*

NIGHT-VISION GOGGLES

APPEARANCE

The Living Daylights (1987) Die Another Day (2002)

USED BY Saunders, James Bond, South Korean agents

These goggles allow someone to view a person over 200 yd (183 m) away at night by amplifying tiny amounts of light so an image can be clearly seen. Saunders uses a pair in Bratislava as he and Bond watch for the sniper assigned to eliminate General Koskov. Bond and his South Korean colleagues later wear night-vision goggles as they surf into North Korea.

NINJA THROWING STARS

APPEARANCES

You Only Live Twice (1967), Tomorrow Never Dies (1997)

USED BY Tiger Tanaka, ninjas, Wai Lin

During *You Only Live Twice*, head of the Japanese Secret Service, Tiger Tanaka, gives 007 a tour of his training camp. Bond sees ninjas practicing with throwing stars. Later, Tanaka hurls a throwing star into Blofeld's wrist as he pulls the trigger to shoot Bond. Blofeld's shot goes wide, saving 007's life.

In *Tomorrow Never Dies*, Wai Lin throws a star into the neck of one of Elliot Carver's guards as she heads to the stealth ship's engine room.

ODDJOB'S HAT

APPEARANCE

Goldfinger (1964)

USED BY Oddjob, James Bond

DEADLY WARNING *For Bond's benefit, Oddjob's razor-sharp hat brim slices the head off a statue at Goldfinger's golf club.*

The deadly black hat with "a light but very strong alloy" ring for a brim is one of the most dangerous weapons in any henchman's arsenal. Oddjob's hat, which is a dressage top hat in the film, allows the manservant to accurately hit a target at a range of up to a hundred yards. He can hurl the hat with enough force to sever the head from a granite statue at 20 yd (18 m).

In Fleming's novel, Oddjob wears a flat-brimmed bowler. He uses the bowler to kill Tilly Masterton, the sister of Goldfinger's paid companion Jill Masterton, outside Fort Knox. In the film, Oddjob's dressage top hat snaps Tilly's neck while in Switzerland. Oddjob later throws the hat at Bond inside the US Treasury Bullion vault at Fort Knox but misses. A second throw sails high and

TIP OF THE HAT *In the gold vault at Fort Knox, James Bond considers turning the tables on Oddjob by hurling his metal-rimmed hat back at him.*

severs a high-voltage cable behind Bond. 007 takes hold of the hat, causing Oddjob some level of concern. Oddjob ducks Bond's throw, then goes to retrieve the hat stuck between metal bars in the gold vault. As Oddjob grabs the hat, 007 shoves the high-voltage cable against the bars, sending a deadly charge through Oddjob's body.

007: Remarkable. But what does the club secretary have to say? **Goldfinger:** Oh nothing, Mr. Bond. I own the club.

OMEGA SEAMASTER WATCH

APPEARANCES

GoldenEye (1995), Tomorrow Never Dies (1997), The World Is Not Enough (1999), Die Another Day (2002), Casino Royale (2006)

USED BY James Bond

Beginning with *GoldenEye*, Bond's watch of choice is an Omega Seamaster.

In *GoldenEye*, wearing the Omega Seamaster 300M Diver Quartz, 007 uses a laser emitted from the watch to cut an escape hatch in the floor of the train belonging to ex-agent 006 Alec Trevelyan. Trevelyan confiscates the watch in Cuba; by pressing the watch's helium release valve, he disarms the two limpet mines planted by Bond.

In *Tomorrow Never Dies*, Bond changes to an Omega Seamaster 300M Diver (self-winding, not a quartz movement). Bond slips on a version of the watch modified by the Chinese People's External Security Force in agent Wai Lin's bicycle shop. On media mogul Elliot Carver's stealth ship, Bond extracts the helium release valve from the watch, which is part of a remote detonator. He uses the detonator to make a booby trap with a grenade and a glass jar. Twisting the watch bezel triggers the detonator, which shatters the jar and allows the grenade's safety handle to release, blowing a hole in the ship.

In *The World Is Not Enough*, Bond activates LEDs on the Seamaster watch face by pressing the screw-down crown. These illuminate the inside of his inflating ski jacket when he and Elektra King are buried under an avalanche. Later, in an underground nuclear bunker, Bond fires a miniature piton with retractable high-tensile wire from the watch and raises himself to a gantry.

In *Die Another Day*, Bond again uses the helium release valve of his Seamaster as a detonator (this time a smaller version), sticking it into the C4 explosive he hides in smuggler Van

TIMED TO PERFECTION *Bond's Seamaster is an integral part of his style in* Casino Royale.

BRIGHT IDEA *Bond sheds some light by activating his Seamaster's LEDs in* The World Is Not Enough.

Bierk's briefcase underneath the diamonds. In Colonel Moon's compound, a twist of the bezel causes the detonator to explode the C4. After his released from captivity in North Korea, Bond receives a new watch from Q—his twentieth. At the ice palace of billionaire Gustav Graves, Bond uses the watch's laser function to cut a hole in the ice so he can rescue NSA agent Jinx.

Bond wears two different Omega watches in *Casino Royale*. He sports a black Seamaster Co-Axial Planet Ocean model before he earns his licence to kill. Afterwards, he wears the Omega Seamaster 300M Diver.

OPIUM BOMB

APPEARANCE

The Living Daylights (1987)

USED BY James Bond

In Afghanistan, Bond places a bomb inside a Red Cross relief sack in the hope of blowing up a cache of

opium. Bond ends up traveling with the opium and places the bomb inside a transport plane at a Soviet airbase. Bond sets the timer to explode in ten minutes and thirty seconds, shortly after Soviet General Koskov and his minions get airborne, but Koskov spots 007 before he can escape. Bond takes over the plane as the mujaheddin's Kamran Shah and his fighters attack the base. When 007 tries to defuse the bomb, Koskov's henchman, Necros, attacks. Bond throws Necros from the plane, resets the timer on the bomb to ten seconds, then uses it to blow up a bridge where Soviet troops pursue Shah and his men.

PARACHUTES

APPEARANCES
Goldfinger (1964), You Only Live Twice (1967), The Spy Who Loved Me (1977), Moonraker (1979), Octopussy (1983), A View To A Kill (1985), The Living Daylights (1987), Licence To Kill (1989), Tomorrow Never Dies (1997), Die Another Day (2002)

USED BY
James Bond, Pussy Galore, Helga Brandt, Jaws, Colonel Toro's paratroopers, May Day, 002, 004, Felix Leiter, Gustav Graves

James Bond's penchant for jumping or falling from planes, cliffs, and other high objects, and his enemies's desire to do the same, has made the parachute a vital piece of equipment in many of the Bond adventures.

In *Goldfinger*, Bond and Pussy Galore use round parachutes to evacuate from the Lockheed US VC-140B after it goes into a nosedive.

When Villain Helga Brandt flies Bond to Tokyo in *You Only Live Twice*, she drops a magnesium flare in her Meyers 200A plane and parachutes out in mid-flight.

The Spy Who Loved Me sees Bond base jump, or base ski, off a precipice near Berngarten, Austria, unfurling a Union Jack parachute to escape from pursuing KGB agents.

In *Moonraker*, Jaws pushes 007 out of a charter jet in mid-flight. Bond intercepts the free-falling pilot and steals his ram-air parachute in

ESCAPE CHUTE *May Day glides away from Bond after killing a detective in the Eiffel Tower's Le Jules Verne restaurant.*

RULE BRITANNIA *(from left to right) KGB assassins pursue Bond; 007 performs a back-twist somersault after shooting Sergei Barsov; Bond sails to safety with his patriotic parachute.*

mid-air. He then fends off an attack from Jaws, whose parachute fails to open.

During the action of *Octopussy*, Bond pulls the parachute cords of Colonel Toro's paratrooper guards in the back of a jeep in order to escape capture.

In *A View To A Kill*, henchman May Day performs a base jump from the Eiffel Tower, parachuting down to Max Zorin's boat on the Seine with a square ram-air parachute.

The Living Daylights begins with agents 002, 004, and 007 parachuting onto the Rock of Gibraltar to participate in war games with the SAS.

In *Licence To Kill*, 007 and Leiter parachute to the St. Mary's Star of the Sea Church in Key West after capturing drug lord Franz Sanchez's plane.

Bond pops his square ram-air parachute below the Chinese radar when he makes a HALO jump to investigate the sunken HMS *Devonshire* in *Tomorrow Never Dies*.

Die Another Day sees billionaire Gustav Graves parachuting in to a London press conference with a square ram-air Union Jack canopy.

PARKER PEN GRENADE

APPEARANCE
GoldenEye (1995)

USED BY
James Bond, Boris Grishenko

Bond's stainless steel Parker Jotter pen is actually a Class 4 grenade. Three clicks arm the four-second fuse; another three clicks disarm it.

At the GoldenEye control station in Cuba, computer programmer Boris Grishenko nervously clicks the pen. Mentally keeping track of the clicks, Bond slaps the pen from Grishenko's hand just before detonation; it explodes next to a fuel tank, setting off a chain reaction that devastates the control station.

PEN PAL *Boris Grishenko unknowingly plays with fire.*

PERISCOPE

APPEARANCE
From Russia With Love (1963)

USED BY
Kerim Bey, James Bond

Head of Station T, Kerim Bey, manages to have a submarine periscope installed beneath the Soviet Consulate in Istanbul. The lens allows him to see into the high-level security meetings at the consulate. The periscope is accessed through a great drainage tunnel that leads from the Yerebatan Saray Sarniçi, the sunken palace cistern.

PIPELINE PIGS

APPEARANCES

Diamonds Are Forever (1971),
The Living Daylights (1987),
The World Is Not Enough (1999)

USED BY Mr. Wint and Mr. Kidd, James Bond, Rosika Miklos, General Georgi Koskov, Dr. Christmas Jones

A "pig" is a device that travels through pipelines to seal them, check for cracks, or clean them.

In *Diamonds Are Forever*, 007 is buried alive in a section of pipeline in Nevada. He sees a pig approaching, manages to leap on top of it, then short-circuits the machine by touching the welding wires together.

In *The Living Daylights*, MI6 devises a pig for the Trans-Siberian pipeline that can carry a man. It is used by Bond and Czech technician Rosika Miklos to help Soviet General Koskov reach Austria from Czechoslovakia and defect to the West.

In *The World Is Not Enough*, terrorist Renard places a bomb on a pig in Elektra King's pipeline. 007 and nuclear scientist Dr. Christmas Jones use an observation rig to catch up to the speeding pig. When the pig and the rig lock together, Jones uses her HP Jornada 430SE computer to discover that half of the plutonium is missing from the bomb. Bond and Jones leap from the rig to the pipe and allow the pig bomb to explode in an attempt to convince Elektra that they are both dead.

CAPITALIST PIG *Bond and Rosika Miklos convince Koskov to ride the pig to Austria.*

RIDING THE PIPE *Dr. Jones prepares to speed through Elektra King's pipeline.*

PITON BELT

APPEARANCE

GoldenEye (1995)

USED BY James Bond

Though it appears to be a typical size 34 in (86.3 cm) leather belt, the buckle in this bit of wardrobe from Q Branch has a 75-ft (22.8-m) rappelling cord built in.

When fired, the piton shoots out at high-velocity, pulling a high-tensile wire designed to support Bond's weight. Bond uses it to escape from the Russian Military Intelligence Archives in St. Petersburg. He fires the piton into the cement ceiling, swings across an atrium, kicks a stunned soldier out of the way, and smashes through a window. Bond lands on a supply truck parked below the window in the compound's vehicle yard.

PITON GUN

APPEARANCE

Diamonds Are Forever (1971)

USED BY James Bond

Bond uses a piton-firing gun to gain entry into Willard Whyte's private suite at the Whyte House casino hotel in Las Vegas. Bond rides on top of the exterior express glass elevator to the Starlight Lounge. He uses the gun to shoot pitons with attached climbing ropes. Fastening the ropes to a climbing harness beneath his tuxedo, he pulls himself up to the otherwise inaccessible penthouse. Later, when confronted with two Blofelds in Whyte's office, Bond uses the piton gun to shoot one in the head.

PITON LASER GUN

APPEARANCE

GoldenEye (1995)

USED BY James Bond

The piton laser gun is a multi-purpose tool, able to fire its tempered ultra-high carbon steel mini-piton into granite. The 397 lb (180 kg) test cable attached to the piton retracts on an internal wrench as soon as the user gives the trigger a second squeeze. The laser can, at short-range, melt most ductile metals.

James Bond employs the gun when he infiltrates the Arkangel Chemical Weapons Facility in the USSR. Bond bungee jumps from a high dam above the plant and uses the cable from the gun to lower himself down to a ledge. From this point, he cuts through a metal plate on the roof and slips undetected into the interior.

POISON GAS

APPEARANCES

Goldfinger (1964), You Only Live Twice (1967), The Spy Who Loved Me (1977), Moonraker (1979)

USED BY Goldfinger, Kisch, Blofeld, Stromberg, Hugo Drax

Poison gas remains a potent weapon of the megalomaniac villain. While any criminal might use stun gas, tear gas, or knockout gas, only a select few employ deadly vapors.

Goldfinger reduces organized crime in the United States when he gasses the leaders of America's foremost crime families with Delta 9. James Bond convinces Pussy Galore to contact the CIA in order to switch the gas before her pilots spray Delta 9 over Fort Knox in Kentucky.

In *You Only Live Twice*, Blofeld protects his volcano rocket base by pumping phosgene gas into the venting caves that lead to the sea. However, when he launches *Bird 1*, the rocket's exhaust must travel out of the caves, and fans apparently disperse the gas, allowing Bond, Japanese agent Kissy Suzuki, and the ninjas to escape safely after a battle

DEADLY GLOBE *Drax's satellite is designed to distribute a poison lethal only to humans.*

with SPECTRE operatives.

In *The Spy Who Loved Me*, shipping magnate Karl Stromberg threatens to fill the *USS Wayne* with cyanide if Commander Carter refuses to surrender the submarine.

In *Moonraker*, billionaire Sir Hugo Drax rings the earth with satellite weapons filled with a deadly gas made from the plant Orchidea Negra. The gas made from this plant kills only humans. Bond must blast the weapons out of the sky before they enter the atmosphere.

DEATH AGONY
A scientist employed by Hugo Drax discovers the power of his poison gas concoction.

POISON STRING

APPEARANCE

You Only Live Twice (1967)

USED BY SPECTRE assassin

When SPECTRE attempts to kill James Bond, it sends an assassin armed with a deadly poison. As Bond sleeps with Japanese agent Aki, the assassin slithers into the attic, finds a gap in the ceiling, and lowers a black string. He then opens a bottle of a powerful poison that he pours down the string intending that drops will land in Bond's mouth. Before the drops can find their mark, Bond and Aki shift in their sleep. The drops spill into Aki's mouth and cause rapid death. Bond shoots the SPECTRE assassin, killing him instantly.

POLARIZING SUNGLASSES

APPEARANCE

A View To A Kill (1985)

USED BY James Bond

Standard sunglasses may have polarized lenses, but few offer adjustable settings that allow the wearer to cut glare and reflections from windows at almost any angle.

Q Branch provides these glasses to James Bond, allowing him to witness industrialist Max Zorin writing State geologist Stacey Sutton a check for $5 million at his French chateau. By moving the sliders at the bottom of the sunglasses frame, Bond can cut out the glare on the window of Zorin's room and see what is going on perfectly. On a sunny day at a garden party, nobody appears suspicious of the seemingly ordinary looking pair of sunglasses.

PUSHKIN'S WATCH

APPEARANCE
The Living Daylights (1987)
USED BY General Leonid Pushkin

By pushing the dial on the side of this watch, Pushkin can signal to the wearer of a receiver watch that he is in trouble with a low bleeping sound.

Bond confronts KGB head General Leonid Pushkin in his suite at the Hotel Isla De France in Tangier regarding Operation *Smiert Spionam*. Staring into the barrel of Bond's Walther PPK, Pushkin pushes the button on his watch to alert his bodyguard. Realizing what has happened, 007 knocks the bodyguard unconscious as he enters the suite.

RADAR-GUIDED GATLING GUN

APPEARANCE
Tomorrow Never Dies (1997)
USED BY Various terrorists

The Type 730 Chinese 30 mm Gatling gun is designed to be foolproof, firing at targets selected by radar.

When Bond encounters one at a terrorist supermarket on the Khyber Pass he easily distracts it by tossing a Dunhill cigarette lighter grenade behind a set of oil drums. When they explode, the 730 automatically turns and unleashes gunfire, allowing Bond to hijack an L39 Albatross fighter plane carrying Soviet SB-5 nuclear torpedoes. Once taxiing on the airfield, Bond fires a missile at the 730, destroying it instantly.

BITTER PILL
When Q presents Bond with "a recently developed harmess radioactive device," Bond is unsure what to do with it. "Swallow it," Q replies.

RADIOACTIVE PILL

APPEARANCE
Thunderball (1965)
USED BY James Bond

Q presents a radioactive pill to James Bond during Operation Thunderball. When swallowed, the pill sends out a signal to a special receiver, allowing the person's position to be tracked. When 007 finds himself trapped in the coral cavern that SPECTRE uses to store the stolen atomic weapons, he swallows the pill, allowing CIA agent Felix Leiter to guide a Coast Guard helicopter to Bond.

RAKE METAL DETECTOR

APPEARANCE
The Living Daylights (1987)
USED BY MI6 "Gardener" agent

This 60 in (152.4 cm) garden rake not only provides grounds maintenance, but its prongs also contain a metal detector to track armed intruders to the Blayden safe house.

When Bond arrives at the safe house to aid in the questioning of Soviet defector General Georgi Koskov, the prongs of the standing rake turn and beep. This alerts one of the MI6 agents posing as a gardener that Bond is carrying his Walther PPK. The agent disarms Bond, and allows him to enter the safe house.

RAPPELLING CUMMERBUND

APPEARANCE
Licence To Kill (1989)
USED BY James Bond

This broad sash, worn with a tuxedo, hides a nylon rappelling rope.

On top of the Isthmus casino, Bond removes his cummerbund, revealing a climber's rappelling rope. He ties the rope to the flagpole and rappels to the ledge outside of drug baron Franz Sanchez's office. Bond squeezes plastic explosive from a Dentonyte toothpaste tube and places a detonator from a cigarette package beneath Sanchez's office window, vital parts of a planned assassination attempt.

RAPIER MISSILE LAUNCHER

APPEARANCE
Octopussy (1983)
USED BY Colonel Toro's officers

The British Army and Royal Air Force began using this command-guided surface-to-air missile in 1967 to combat low-flying craft with high maneuverability.

After Bond escapes from Latin American officer Colonel Toro's paratroopers, he flies off in an Acrostar Bede jet. But a telephone call from one of Toro's officers has troops launching a rapier surface-to-air missile at 007. No matter what maneuver Bond makes, the missile remains locked on his tail. In a final attempt to rid himself of the missile, Bond flies the Bede jet through a spy plane hangar as Toro's men race to close the hangar doors. Bond makes it out safely through the other doors before they close, but the missile does not, resulting in a dramatic explosion that obliterates the hangar with the spy plane inside.

REMOTE-TRIGGERED IMPLANT

APPEARANCE
A View To A Kill (1985)
USED BY Max Zorin

This remote-control transmitter, which fits into a cane or jockey's whip, programs an injection of natural horse steroids, allowing a horse to overcome

fatigue while racing.

Amoral scientist Dr. Mortner implants a microchip into the racehorse Pegasus and installs a remote control transmitter into the silver-topped cane belonging to Pegasus's owner Max Zorin. At the press of a button, Zorin programs the horse steroids injection into Pegasus, allowing the horse to beat the others. Zorin later uses the cane transmitter to send Bond's horse Inferno into a frenzy when 007 begins to pull ahead in a steeplechase competing with Zorin.

REVERSIBLE JACKET

APPEARANCES
Live And Let Die (1973),
Octopussy (1983)
USED BY James Bond

One of the keys to confusing the enemy is good camouflage. But an outfit that may suit one circumstance can easily stand out when the situation changes. On a number of occasions, Bond has used a reversible jacket to blend seamlessly from one situation to another.

When visiting Tarot card reader Solitaire via hang glider, Bond wears black, but upon arrival he turns his jacket inside out and removes his trouser covers to reveal a more appropriate off-white, tropical suit.

On another mission, Bond arrives in a Latin American country to destroy a spy plane. He removes his hacking jacket and turns it inside out, revealing an officer's coat. It comes complete with medals, and with the addition of a holstered revolver, it allows him to pose as Colonel Luis Toro and enter the spy plane hangar.

RING CAMERA

APPEARANCE
A View To A Kill (1985)
USED BY James Bond

By simply bending one's ring finger, one can take black and white photos with this signet ring.

Bond wears this Q Branch ring camera at a party held by industrialist Max Zorin at his French chateau where he snaps shots of Zorin employees Bob Conley and Dr. Carl Mortner. CIA agent Chuck Lee later supplies 007 with biographical details on these men.

ROCKET-FIRING CIGARETTE

APPEARANCE
You Only Live Twice (1967)
USED BY Tiger Tanaka, James Bond

Head of the Japanese Secret Service, Tiger Tanaka, presents 007 with a rocket-firing cigarette. The rocket embedded in the cigarette is a real Finjet rocket, originally designed to be fired from a much larger weapon and saturate an area like a giant shotgun blast. Tanaka claims the rocket, adapted to fire from a cigarette, is accurate up to 30 yd (27.4 m). Bond uses the weapon to blast the SPECTRE crater-roof control operator, letting him briefly open the crater and enabling Tanaka's ninjas to enter Blofeld's volcano rocket base.

ROCKET GUN

APPEARANCE
You Only Live Twice (1967)
USED BY Tiger Tanaka

The Japanese SIS provides one of the few markets for the remarkable Gyrojet rocket guns, manufactured by the now defunct MB Associates out of San Ramon, California.

Head of the Japanese Secret Service, Tiger Tanaka, shows 007 an array of Gyrojet carbines and handguns and demonstrates a 12 mm model with an explosive incendiary charge in the rocket ammo.

The gun fires jet-propelled rockets that can carry explosive charges. Rocket guns are quiet and fire with almost no recoil, but accuracy depends on the precision achieved in the manufacturing of the ammo.

ROLEX WATCH

APPEARANCE
Live And Let Die (1973)
USED BY James Bond

James Bond wears a Rolex watch in a number of films, but one he wears in Live and Let Die is the most memorable. The Rolex Submariner watch comes with two very handy extra features. Firstly, by pulling out the cap or twisting the rotating 60 minute bezel, the watch can become a hyper-intensified magnetic field. According to Q, the magnet is powerful enough to deflect the path of a bullet. Secondly, the watch has a rotating saw blade built into its face.

Miss Moneypenny delivers the newly repaired watch to 007 at his home before Bond departs on a mission to investigate the deaths of three British agents. Bond demonstrates the watch's magnetism on a sceptical M.

When Dr. Kananga/Mr. Big wishes to know if Solitaire still has the power to predict the future, he asks her if he is correctly reading the registration number of Bond's watch.

When Kananga captures 007 and Solitaire, the Rolex comes in useful. Tied to a winch platform dangling over a shark pool. Bond engages the magnet, drawing a shark to him. He then sets the saw blade spinning. It cuts through the rope bindings, freeing Bond. 007 soon shoves the pellet in Kananga's mouth, causing him to explode.

ROLLEIFLEX CAMERA

APPEARANCE
From Russia With Love (1963)
USED BY **James Bond**

James Bond uses this simple ¼ in (0.64 cm) tape recording device built into the back of a Rolleiflex T Type 2 camera body to record his conversation with Soviet cipher clerk Tatiana Romanova. It allows Bond to act as a tourist while documenting valuable information about the Lektor decoder. After listening to this tape, the British Secret Service instructs Bond to move forward with obtaining the Lektor.

QUICK SPIN *The permutator checks every combination of Gumbold's safe.*

SAFE-CRACKER

APPEARANCES
**You Only Live Twice (1967),
On Her Majesty's Secret Service (1969)**
USED BY **James Bond**

In *You Only Live Twice*, James Bond employs a small pocket-sized safe-cracker unit to break into the office safe belonging to Blofeld's accomplice Mr. Osato. Although the unit detects the movement of the tumblers, it does not disengage the security alarm that sounds when 007 opens the safe. Bond grabs a few documents as Osato's guards approach, including a photo of the cargo ship *Ning-Po* and a paper with an explanatory microdot.

Bond also uses a safe-cracker/photocopy machine in Bern, Switzerland, in *On Her Majesty's Secret Service*. While lawyer Gumbold steps out to lunch, Bond infiltrates his office and collects a large tool chest sent over by a crane bucket. Bond opens the chest and removes a permutator programmed to electronically operate dials of a safe in all possible combinations. Bond attaches the permutator to a storage battery unit in the chest and places the permutator against the safe's dial. Once he cracks the safe, Bond removes papers concerning Blofeld and uses a photocopy machine located in the chest to make facsimiles of the documents. He packs up the chest, tosses it back in the crane bucket, and leaves the office as Gumbold returns.

CUTTING EDGE
Bond's Rolex proves not only stylish and durable, but in Dr. Kananga's grotto, it also saves him in the nick of time.

SCARECROW CAMERA/GUN

APPEARANCE
Live And Let Die (1973)

USED BY Tee Hee, Dr. Kananga

Dr. Kananga uses scarecrows outfitted with video cameras and remote-fired guns to protect his poppy fields on San Monique. Kananga kills CIA double agent Rosie Carver with a shot fired from one of his scarecrows when he fears she might confess her duplicity to 007. Bond later uses the scarecrows to find Kananga's poppy fields. In turn, the scarecrows help Kananga keep watch on Bond.

SCARECROW SENTRY *Kananga's security cameras transmit pictures back to his base.*

SUDDEN DEATH *A gun in one of Kananga's scarecrows cuts short Rosie Carver's life.*

SEAGULL SNORKEL

APPEARANCE
Goldfinger (1964)

USED BY James Bond

When 007 must infiltrate the oil storage depots where Mr. Ramirez has his heroin manufacturing plant, he approaches underwater. Rather than use scuba gear, Bond employs a snorkel disguised as a seagull atop his head. The seagull also makes it appear that Bond's natural wake as he moves beneath the surface is its own.

SEA VAC

APPEARANCE
Tomorrow Never Dies (1997)

USED BY James Bond, Elliot Carver

Media mogul Elliot Carver uses the deep sea rotary drill known as the Sea Vac as a tool to provoke an international incident between Britain and China.

In Carver's stealth ship, this device, with 6-ft (1.8 m) conical bits, can be lowered into the water beneath Carver's stealth ship. The Sea Vac is controlled through a cable that guides speed, direction, and the intensity of the drill itself. Carver and his henchman Stamper use the Sea Vac to cut into the generator room of the British frigate HMS *Devonshire*, leading the crew to believe they have been hit by a Chinese aerial torpedo. Stamper then instructs the control technician to drill the Sea Vac into the frigate's mess room. After the *Devonshire* sinks, Carver's divers enter the missile room and steal a Tomahawk-class missile. Later, Carver aims a gun at 007 in the stealth ship's control room. Bond engages the motor of the Sea Vac behind Carver, and it chews the media baron to bits.

SECURITY CAMERA

APPEARANCE
You Only Live Twice (1967)

USED BY SPECTRE No. 4

In the office of Blofeld's accomplice Mr. Osato, a secretary works at a tabulating machine. In reality, the man is SPECTRE No. 4, and the tabulating machine controls a security camera and gun and conceals a video screen showing the weapon's target. When 007 visits Osato, SPECTRE No. 4 trains the camera and gun on Bond for the entire visit.

CHEWED UP *Carver battles Bond shortly before his Sea Vac drill shreds him to pieces.*

SEIKO WATCH

APPEARANCES
The Spy Who Loved Me (1977),
Moonraker (1979), For Your Eyes
Only (1981), Octopussy (1983),
A View To A Kill (1985)
USED BY James Bond

ON TRACK *The directional finder on Bond's watch comes in useful in* **Octopussy.**

James Bond wears a Seiko watch on five different missions.

In *The Spy Who Loved Me*, he wears a Seiko 0674, which can receive a text messages that it prints on punch tape.

Moonraker sees Bond using a Seiko Digital LCD M354 Memory Bank Calendar watch. This watch includes detonating cord secreted in a rear compartment and a detonation cable attached to the start/stop timer button. It is detonated using the time/set button. 007 uses it to escape from the blast chute of the *Moonraker* shuttle.

In *For Your Eyes Only*, Bond wears a Seiko H357 Digital Analog Alarm watch with a display for scrolling

THE RIGHT TIME *The explosive device hidden in Bond's Seiko watch helps save his and Holly's lives in* **Moonraker.**

TEXT MESSAGE *Bond receives word from HQ in* **The Spy Who Loved Me.**

LED text messages and a radio transmitter for communication. At the end of the mission, Bond places the H357 near the macaw Max and lets him speak with the Prime Minister.

In *Octopussy*, Bond first wears a Seiko G757 Sports 100, containing a radio directional finder that allows him to track the fake Fabergé Egg, thanks to a homer in the egg. At the end of the mission, he wears a color model of the Seiko liquid crystal television watch, which allows him to see what Q's video cameras are filming from a hot air balloon.

Bond also wears a Seiko watch in *A View To A Kill*, but this watch has no known special features.

SHARK PELLET/GUN

APPEARANCE
Live And Let Die (1973)
USED BY James Bond, Dr. Kananga

The shark gun fires compressed CO_2 pellets, which kill by filling the prey's body with gas.

Island dictator Dr. Kananga acquires the gun after it is found on the beach with Bond's gear in San Monique. Bond uses a pellet to kill Kananga. He shoves it into Kananga's mouth, causing him to inflate and explode.

SHARK POOL SHOWDOWN *Bond shoves the shark gun's compressed-gas pellet into Kananga's mouth.*

SHARPER IMAGE CREDIT CARD

APPEARANCE
A View To A Kill (1985)
USED BY James Bond

In an attempt to ascertain a link between geologist Stacey Sutton and industrialist Max Zorin, Bond breaks into Stacey's house. Bond uses an electronic device disguised as a credit card from The Sharper Image, an electronics retailer. When placed between the jambs of a double-hung window, the card emits a signal that causes the window latch to rotate and unlock.

UNFORCED ENTRY *Bond breaks into Stacey Sutton's house with his special credit card.*

SHAVER BUG DETECTOR

APPEARANCE
A View To A Kill (1985)
USED BY Sir Godfrey Tibbett

This Norelco shaver conceals a sophisticated listening device locator.

When James Bond travels to Max Zorin's French chateau, he poses as James St. John-Smythe, a rich British eccentric wishing to dabble in horses. He brings with him Sir Godfrey Tibbett, a horse trainer working with the British Secret Service. Tibbett sweeps the room for bugs with the shaver. Once found, the pair plays a taped conversation to throw off those eavesdropping. When the pair searches the grounds at night, they leave a tape of snoring playing to fool Zorin's men.

SIGNATURE GUN

APPEARANCE
Licence To Kill (1989)
USED BY **James Bond**

An innocent-looking Hasselblad camera is actually a signature gun—a sniper's rifle that will fire only if the handprint signature of the shooter matches the one programmed into the gun's optical palm reader grip.

Q, on leave from HQ, brings the weapon to Isthmus City to assist James Bond, who has been removed from active duty by M. Components of the gun include an infrared Bushnell gun sight, an extension tube, a Bolex bi-pod, and the right-hand signature pistol.

Bond attempts to use the signature gun to assassinate drug lord Franz Sanchez, but Hong Kong narcotics agents attack him first. Unable to fire the weapon, the agents show it to British agent Fallon who confirms that the gun is government property.

Pam Bouvier: What kind of film does it take? 120? **Q:** No, .220 high-velocity.

SKI POLE ROCKET

APPEARANCE
The Spy Who Loved Me (1977)
USED BY **James Bond**

When Bond skis away from a cabin in Berngarten in the Austrian Alps, Sergei Barsov and three other KGB agents pursue him, armed with rifles and pistols. Though 007 appears to be unarmed, he is, in fact, well-prepared with an ingenious Q gadget. A twist of his ski pole causes a trigger to emerge. Skiing backwards, Bond aims the ski pole like a rifle and pulls the trigger, firing a four-bladed rocket dart into Barsov's chest, killing him instantly.

SKI SUIT ESCAPE POD

APPEARANCE
The World Is Not Enough (1999)
USED BY **James Bond, Elektra King**

By pulling a tab on this modified black ski suit jacket, an airbag inflates, enveloping the wearer in a protective cocoon. When an avalanche threatens Bond and Elektra King, 007 activates the airbag to protect them. He extracts a knife hidden in the jacket to cut through the airbag when the avalanche has finished, then punches through the snow to escape.

SNOWBALL *Bond and Elektra King find protection in his stylish yet functional ski jacket from Q Branch.*

SKYHOOK RESCUE SYSTEM

APPEARANCE
Thunderball (1965)
USED BY **James Bond, Domino Derval**

Developed by Robert E. Fulton, Jr., the Skyhook rescue system picks up 007 and Domino Derval after the *Disco Volante* explodes. The 90-lb (40.8-kg) kit consists of 500 ft (152.4 m) of nylon line, a harness, a helium tank, a balloon, and a jumpsuit.

Bond releases a balloon on a nylon line from a dinghy. A low-flying, unmarked CIA plane seizes the line and pulls Bond and Domino aloft. A crew member hooks the line into a winch, which allows Bond and Domino to be pulled into the plane.

HIGHFLIERS *The Skyhook rescue system allows James Bond and Domino to ascend to the skies.*

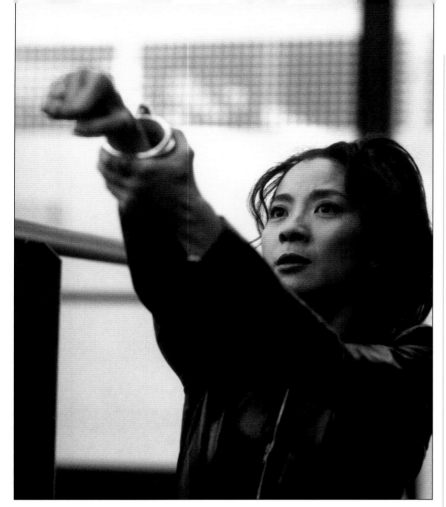

WRIST ROCKET *Wai Lin fires the piton into a metal column during her escape from Carver Media Group Network headquarters in Hamburg.*

SNAKE BRACELET/PITON

APPEARANCE
Tomorrow Never Dies (1997)
USED BY **Wai Lin**

This snake bracelet is not simply a beautifully-crafted piece of jewelry. The bracelet, which belongs to Chinese agent Wai Lin, also contains a piton and climbing wire that can be fired at a target.

Having broken into the Hamburg headquarters of Elliot Carver's Media Group Network, Wai Lin is on the run from Carver's men. She fires the piton from her snake bracelet at a metal column and attaches it to a hook on the belt of her leather catsuit. She then walks confidently down the column in order to make her final escape from Carver's men, waving goodbye to James Bond as he attempts to flee from the guards.

SNOOPER

APPEARANCE
A View To A Kill (1985)
USED BY **Q**

This dog-like, remote-controlled robot has video cameras for eyes and antennae for ears, allowing one to conduct undercover surveillance operations.

When Bond is presumed missing in action, Q uses this prototype of a highly sophisticated surveillance machine to search the countryside home of state geologist Stacey Sutton to discover if Bond is actually alive. Q monitors the snooper from a

van outside the house and determines that Bond is indeed alive and otherwise engaged, sharing a shower with Sutton. When asked to report on Bond's status, Q replies that he's "just cleaning up a few details."

SOLAR-POWERED LASER CANNON

APPEARANCE
The Man With The Golden Gun (1974)
USED BY **Scaramanga**

Scaramanga has an unorthodox "golden gun" in his arsenal—a powerful solar-powered laser cannon, which, as Scaramanga explains to Bond, "Goes with the Solex—no extra charge." Emitting a focused beam of sunlight with a heat of 3,500 °F (1,927 °C), the laser cannon has the power to explode Bond's seaplane at the push of a button. Scaramanga observes that the cannon makes him and the protection it affords him "undeniably, the man with the golden gun."

SOLEX AGITATOR

APPEARANCE
The Man With The Golden Gun (1974)
USED BY **Scaramanga**

The British government believes the Solex Agitator could be the solution to the world's energy needs. Developed by British scientist Gibson, the Solex converts sunlight into energy with 95 percent efficiency. Gibson defects from Britain to develop the Solex, and is assassinated by master assassin Francisco Scaramanga when he offers to return. Scaramanga takes possession of the Solex and plans to offer it up to the highest bidder. Bond saves the Solex before Scaramanga's island blows up, tucking it inside his shirt.

SONIC RING

APPEARANCE
Die Another Day (2002)
USED BY **James Bond, Q**

On a mission to Iceland, James Bond wears a ring, which by simply twisting it, turns into an ultra-high frequency, single-digit sonic agitator unit. Q demonstrates it on a sheet of bulletproof glass, placing his ringed hand on the glass and shattering it.

Bond first employs the ring at the fake diamond mine of Gustav Graves in Iceland. 007 uses it to shatter a glass floor of an office, allowing him to escape. Later, Bond uses the ring to rescue Jinx in the Ice Palace, shattering the windshield of his Aston Martin Vanquish to bring her inside the car.

SPEARGUNS

APPEARANCES
Thunderball (1965), For Your Eyes Only (1981), Licence To Kill (1989), Tomorrow Never Dies (1997)

USED BY James Bond, Domino Derval, SPECTRE frogmen, aquaparas, Columbo's men, Stamper

Spearguns become more than tools to hunt fish in the adventures of James Bond. They serve as dangerous weapons above and below water.

During Operation Thunderball, Bond uses a CO_2-fired gun on Love Beach to impale assassin Vargas. On board the *Disco Volante*, Emilio Largo's mistress, Domino Derval, fires a fatal spear into Largo's back. SPECTRE frogmen and aquaparas use dozens of spearguns during underwater battles.

In *For Your Eyes Only*, one of smuggler Columbo's men fires a spear into the back of Claus, a henchman for smuggler Aris Kristatos.

SHOOT TO KILL *Claudine Auger (Domino) poses with a speargun at Lyford Cay, Bahamas.*

In *Licence To Kill*, Bond steals a speargun from an attacker below the *Wavekrest*, fires the harpoon line into the pontoon of a seaplane, and skis barefoot with the gun as his handle.

Tomorrow Never Dies sees 007 witness Stamper shoot the pilot of Wai Lin's trawler with a speargun.

ADAPTABLE *Bond uses another diver's speargun as a ski-rope handle to barefoot ski behind a plane.*

STILETTO BOOT/SHOE

APPEARANCE
From Russia With Love (1963)

USED BY Morzeny, Rosa Klebb

This SPECTRE-developed weapon of a retractable stiletto blade built into the right toe of a shoe or boot was used by henchman Morzeny to kill SPECTRE's planner, Kronsteen, and used by SPECTRE's Rosa Klebb in an attempt to kill 007.

The blade, upon deployment, is coated from a concealed reservoir with the lethal poison tetrodotoxin— in this case extracted from the sex

organs of the pufferfish. There is no antidote.

Although tetrodotoxin is usually ingested, causing death in six to eight hours, direct application of a large amount into the cardiovascular system will result in death within seconds.

STILETTO FIGHTING STICK

APPEARANCE
You Only Live Twice (1967)
USED BY SPECTRE assassin

A traditional bamboo fighting stick becomes a deadly weapon when a disguised SPECTRE assassin has it outfitted with a poison-tipped stiletto blade inside the hollow chute.

Tiger Tanaka, the head of the Japanese Secret Service, educates Bond in Japanese culture. While training in bojutsu stick fighting, the SPECTRE assassin knocks Bond's staff away. Twisting a section of his weapon, the assassin locks his stiletto in position. Bond snatches the weapon from the assassin's grasp and kills him. Tanaka reveals to Bond that the assassin is an outsider.

STINGER MISSILES

APPEARANCE
Licence To Kill (1989)
USED BY Franz Sanchez, Perez

The shoulder-fired Stinger missiles allow ground troops to pose a serious threat to military aircraft as well as commercial aircraft. To that end, drug baron Franz Sanchez buys four infrared target lock Stinger missiles from the Contras and threatens to shoot down an American airliner if the DEA doesn't stop pursuing him. Heller, Sanchez's chief of security, makes a deal with CIA contract pilot and agent Pam Bouvier to return the Stingers if the US grants him immunity. When Bond tries to kill Sanchez, Heller tells Bouvier the deal is off. Sanchez and his henchman Perez fire two Stingers during their escape, one of which clips the tail of Bouvier's Piper PA-18 Super Cub.

SURFBOARD SABOTEUR KIT

APPEARANCE
Die Another Day (2002)
USED BY James Bond

The surfboard that Bond rides into the coast of Pukch'ong, North Korea contains a hidden saboteur kit. By twisting the surfboard fin, the surface of the board slides away to reveal a Walther P99 and ammunition, nylon rope, a tray of C-4 plastic explosive, a combat knife, and a GPS device. The combat knife conceals a small radio beacon transmitter in its handle that deploys when Bond sticks the knife into the ground. The knife emits a duplicate beacon to one used to guide in an approaching Mil Mi-8 helicopter. The kit allows Bond to send the helicopter off-course and plant a bomb in a case of conflict diamonds.

TANK BUSTER

APPEARANCE
Die Another Day (2002)
USED BY Colonel Moon

Korean Colonel Moon's Tank Buster is actually an OICW (Objective Individual Combat Weapon), which combines an assault rifle with semi-automatic, low velocity cannon-firing air-bursting munitions.

When Moon learns from henchman Zao that conflict diamond trader Mr. Van Bierk is, in fact, James Bond, he picks up his Tank Buster loaded with depleted uranium shells, which is located in his hovercraft mothership. He swings it around to aim at the Mil Mi-8 helicopter on which Bond flew into Moon's base. He fires the weapon, instantly blowing up the chopper. From his hovercraft mothership, he also detonates landmines in the DMZ with the Tank Buster in an effort to stop a pursuing Bond.

FIRE POWER Colonel Moon takes aim with his Objective Individual Combat Weapon, aka a tank buster.

TAROT CARDS

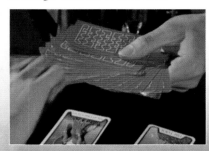

APPEARANCE
Live And Let Die (1973)
USED BY Solitaire, James Bond

Solitaire uses tarot cards to foretell the future and discern the unseen. She sees Bond's journey to New York and his purpose, as well as his journey with double agent Rosie Carver. With the turn of a card, she can tell Bond is armed.

The cards originally brand 007 "The Fool," but when Solitaire invites Bond to choose a card to see his future, it is "The Lovers"—a card she will turn again in San Monique when asked by her boss, Kananga, about the future. Solitaire sends Bond an upside-down Queen of Cups tarot card to warn him that Rosie Carver will betray him.

Bond uses the tarot, too. He invites Solitaire to choose a card, but she doesn't know that the deck is stacked with only Lovers cards. She considers this card an omen and loses her virginity to 007, and with it her supposed powers. Baron Samedi later taunts her and Kananga with the Death card.

MARKED CARDS The cards are fated in favor of 007—his number is visible on the card backs.

THERMOS BOMB

APPEARANCE
A View To A Kill (1985)
USED BY Scarpine

Max Zorin's henchman Scarpine places a radio-triggered bomb disguised as a coffee thermos into an explosives-filled mining car in the Main Strike Mine. The bomb blows through the bottom of the San Andreas Lake, flooding the fault. This sets the stage for a larger explosion to trigger a double earthquake and flood Silicon Valley. The explosion and flood kill dozens of miners, Pan Ho and Jenny Flex. May Day survives and resolves to foil Zorin's plot.

THIRD NIPPLE

APPEARANCE
The Man With The Golden Gun (1974)
USED BY James Bond

The superfluous papilla appliance or third nipple ranks as one of the most unusual Q Branch equipment requests. Bond calls it "a little kinky," but he hopes it will serve a valuable purpose. Bond places it on his chest to pose as master assassin Francisco Scaramanga for an unscheduled meeting with industrialist Hai Fat. Bond counts on Fat never having met Scaramanga face to face. Fat plays along during their meeting, even inviting Bond back to his estate that evening. Hai Fat, in fact, does know Scaramanga, and he quickly plots to have Bond taken captive.

THREE-FINGERED SNIPER RIFLE

APPEARANCE
The Man With The Golden Gun (1974)
USED BY James Bond

In Macau, Portuguese gunsmith Lazar asks 007 to fire a custom-built bolt-action rifle made for a client who has lost two fingers. Bond shoots, but the bullet hits low. Lazar brags that the gun is balanced for a person with three fingers, not five. Bond decides to test this and threatens Lazar with the rifle. This gesture forces Lazar to reveal to 007 details of a new shipment of arch assassin Scaramanga's trademark golden bullets.

THROWING KNIVES

APPEARANCES
From Russia With Love (1963), Thunderball (1965), On Her Majesty's Secret Service (1969), Moonraker (1979), For Your Eyes Only (1981), Octopussy (1983), The World Is Not Enough (1999), Die Another Day (2002)
USED BY Krilencu, Colonel Jacques Boitier, James Bond, Nick Nack, Venice assassin, Santos, Columbo, Mischka, Grischka, Cigar Girl, Jinx

Throwing knives have been used by Bond, his allies, and his enemies on numerous occasions.

Krilencu throws a knife into the stomach of a gypsy camp guard in *From Russia With Love* as he and his men prepare to raid it.

SPECTRE No. 6 Colonel Jacques Boitier attempts to eliminate 007 in *Thunderball* by throwing a knife; instead, he pins Bond's wrist to an antique cabinet.

In *On Her Majesty's Secret Service*, Bond throws a knife in Marc Ange Draco's office, hitting the date September 14th on a calendar. Draco notes the date is actually the 13th. Bond replies, "I'm superstitious."

In *Moonraker*, Drax's Venice assassin rises from the coffin atop a funeral boat and throws a knife, which hits Bond's gondolier. He throws another at Bond but misses. Bond throws the knife back, killing the assassin.

In *For Your Eyes Only*, Columbo's man Santos throws a knife into a guard's stomach during a raid on a warehouse owned by smuggler Kristatos. Columbo later kills Kristatos with a throwing knife at an abandoned monastery in Greece.

In *Octopussy*, expert knife throwers Mischka and Grischka throw a knife into 009's back when he steals a fake Fabergé Egg from Octopussy's circus. Grischka later pins Bond to a cabin door with throwing knives. Bond kills Grischka with one of his own blades.

In *The World Is Not Enough*, the assassin known as the Cigar Girl throws a knife into the neck of Swiss Banker Lachaise to stop him revealing information to 007.

In *Die Another Day*, NSA agent Jinx uses two throwing knives to great effect aboard the Antonov flying command center. She throws one into the neck of a North Korean guard and one at double agent Miranda Frost. It misses her and hits a book, *The Art Of War*. Jinx later grabs the knife-embedded book and stabs Miranda with it.

TORPEDO GUN

APPEARANCE
The Spy Who Loved Me (1977)
USED BY Karl Stromberg

Shipping tycoon Karl Stromberg has a gas-powered torpedo gun underneath his dining table onboard his *Atlantis* research laboratory. The gun fires an explosive missile through its long tube that runs almost the entire length of the table. When Stromberg fires at Bond, 007 dives out of the way as the missile destroys his chair. Bond then uses the tube to fire two Walther PPK bullets into Stromberg's abdomen, killing him.

TORTURE CHAIR

APPEARANCE
The World Is Not Enough (1999)
USED BY Elektra King, James Bond

The antique torture chair is a 19th century Ottoman Empire relic made of mahogany and inlaid with ivory. Elektra places Bond in this chair at her hideout at Maiden's Tower on the Bosphorus Sea. She secures 007's neck in a collar while he sits, shackled. A turn of the chair's wheel pushes a bolt into the back of 007's neck. Five turns will cause his neck to break.

Elektra is close to breaking Bond's neck when Russian casino owner Valentin Zukovsky enters the tower. Elektra shoots him, but Zukovsky lifts his walking stick (a single-action, single-shot rifle) and fires at a chair restraint, freeing one of 007's hands.

TRACKING DEVICE IMPLANT

APPEARANCE
Casino Royale (2006)
USED BY James Bond

INSIDE 007 *The portable sonic resonance unit allows an MI6 technician to see the placement of the tracking device in Bond's arm.*

At M's request, an MI6 technician fires a pea-sized tracking device from a syringe gun into the underside of James Bond's wrist. The device serves as both a longwave transmitter and 24 channel DGPS (Differential Global Positioning System) receiver. This allows it to transmit exceedingly accurate location data to MI6. After Le Chiffre and his accomplices force Bond into a car accident, they drag him from his wrecked Aston Martin DBS and dig the implant out of his arm with a knife. This prevents MI6 from locating 007 during the time Le Chiffre tortures him. Le Chiffre implies that he knew of the device's existence because Bond's contact René Mathis revealed this information.

HOLE IN ONE *Bond, fresh from receiving the tracking device implant, passes his hand through the Sonic Resonance Imaging unit.*

TRACTION TABLE

APPEARANCE
Thunderball (1965)
USED BY James Bond

At the Shrublands health clinic, osteopath Patricia Fearing suggests James Bond spend minutes on a motorized traction table—known by some patients as "the rack"—to help him recover from an injury to his lower back. While Bond is on the table, SPECTRE's Count Lippe enters. Lippe ratchets up the motor to full power. Bond passes out from the pain, but Patricia rescues him before he suffers possibly fatal injury.

TRANQUILIZER GUNS

APPEARANCES
Goldfinger (1964), Octopussy (1983)
USED BY Kisch, Pussy Galore, Octopussy and her army

Tranquilizer guns fire dart projectiles containing sedatives into wild animals, and in 007's adventures, into humans.

After James Bond talks his way out of being bisected by Auric Goldfinger with a laser beam in Switzerland, Goldfinger's henchman Kisch approaches with a tranquilizer gun and fires a projectile into Bond's side, knocking him unconscious. When 007 awakens on Goldfinger's Lockheed JetStar, he discovers Goldfinger is smuggling him into the United States. Pilot Pussy Galore shows him a similar gun and reveals it to be a tranquilizer.

During Operation Trove, jewel smuggler Octopussy's female army carries tranquilizer guns. Octopussy fires a tranquilizer dart into the neck of one of Mufti's thugs as they attack her and Bond in her floating palace. Later, when Octopussy and her army attack exiled Afghan prince Kamal Khan's Monsoon Palace, many of her gang fire tranquilizer darts into Kamal's remaining guards.

ANYTHING BUT TRANQUIL *One of Octopussy's gang takes aim with a tranquilizer gun.*

JUMP THE GUN *Pussy Galore discusses Bond's entry into the US with a Smith & Wesson .45. When Bond first wakes up, Miss Galore shows 007 a far less lethal tranquilizer gun.*

TRAPDOOR ELEVATOR

APPEARANCE
The Spy Who Loved Me (1977)
USED BY Karl Stromberg

When shipping tycoon Karl Stromberg surmises that his secretary has leaked his submarine tracking system plans, he casually asks her to excuse herself from his dining room. She steps into an elevator, and with the press of a button, Stromberg causes a trapdoor beneath her feet to open. The secretary falls through a chute into a pool where a shark eats her.

When Bond tries to rescue KGB agent Anya Amasova, Stromberg aims to dispose of 007 in the same way, but Bond saves himself by standing on the hinged edges of the trapdoor.

TRAPDOOR TABLES

APPEARANCE
Live And Let Die (1973)
USED BY Dr. Kananga/Mr. Big

At Mr. Big's Fillet of Soul clubs, a special table exists for unwelcome visitors—one that places them in Mr. Big's private offices. In New York, a booth spins Bond into Mr. Big's lair. In New Orleans, Bond's table and chair drop into a French Quarter basement. The trapdoor table first appeared in the novel, where Bond and Felix Leiter are lowered into the basement below The Boneyard, a Harlem club owned by Mr. Big.

TABLE FOR ONE Bond and Leiter at the Fillet of Soul shortly before the trapdoor opens.

TRAPDOOR SLIDE

APPEARANCE
You Only Live Twice (1967)
USED BY Tiger Tanaka, Aki

Head of the Japanese Secret Service, Tiger Tanaka, uses a unique method of bringing guests into his office: a trapdoor slide hidden in the flooring of a Tokyo subway station hallway.

Bond chases agent Aki to get information about the murder of his contact, Dikko Henderson, pursuing her into a closed subway station. Aki suddenly stops and turns around; puzzled, Bond halts. At that moment, a trapdoor opens at his feet and 007 falls down a slide, landing in a chair in Tanaka's office.

HIGH AND DRY Sean Connery wearing the underwater drysuit costume in Goldfinger.

UNDERWATER BREATHING UNIT/SHROUD

APPEARANCE
You Only Live Twice (1967)
USED BY James Bond

When assassins appear to shoot and kill James Bond, he receives a burial at sea with full military honors. What few know is that 007 remains very much alive, and his death has been staged to allow him to take on his next mission unnoticed. Wearing a rebreather to eliminate bubbles, packed inside a clear body bag, wrapped in a traditional sail-cloth shroud, and weighted with cannonballs, 007 endures his own funeral in Hong Kong Harbor before scuba divers carry him to the M1 submarine to receive his assignment.

BURIAL AT SEA James Bond disappears into the deep only to rise again in You Only Live Twice.

UNDERWATER DRYSUIT

APPEARANCE
Goldfinger (1964)
USED BY James Bond

Developed by Q Branch, the underwater drysuit offers a light, waterproof covering for an agent, allowing them to use an aquatic approach to insert themselves into an area, then discard the drysuit to reveal ordinary clothes or even a dinner jacket and bow tie beneath. A series of one-way vents allow for the wearer to expel air bubbles that would otherwise remain trapped inside when putting on the suit. Bond uses the underwater drysuit when infiltrating the drug manufacturer Ramirez's heroin lab.

UNDERWATER GRENADE

APPEARANCE
Thunderball (1965)
USED BY James Bond

A part of 007's underwater arsenal, an underwater grenade is used by Bond to blow up two SPECTRE frogmen during the subaquatic battle at the conclusion of Operation Thunderball. A TNT charge triggers the grenade, killing with its concussive force rather than through the spread of shrapnel.

UNDERWATER INFRARED CAMERA

APPEARANCE
Thunderball (1965)
USED BY **James Bond**

The auto-film advance motor on this camera allows the user to take eight photos in rapid succession. With the use of infrared film, the camera can take photos in very low light situations. Bond uses the camera to photograph the underwater hatch in the bottom of the *Disco Volante* during Operation Thunderball.

UNDERWATER PROPULSION UNIT

APPEARANCE
Thunderball (1965)
USED BY **James Bond**

James Bond's most unusual weapon used during Operation Thunderball is a large underwater propulsion unit with forward-firing exploding torpedoes, complete with oxygen tanks. The unit comes with a yellow-green "smoke screen," which 007 sets off when he hits the water. The speed of the device allows Bond to swerve through the existing underwater battleground, ripping off enemy masks and dislodging air hoses. Bond kills a SPECTRE frogman with an underwater grenade, destroying the propulsion unit in the process.

IN THE DARK *Bond takes photos at night beneath the* Disco Volante *with Q's camera.*

VEREY PISTOL

APPEARANCES
From Russia With Love (1963), Thunderball (1965), On Her Majesty's Secret Service (1969), A View To A Kill (1985), Tomorrow Never Dies (1997)
USED BY **James Bond**

When SPECTRE attacks James Bond's Fairey Huntress speedboat in *From Russia With Love*, Bond releases the leaking fuel drums into the water and fires a Verey pistol. The flare ignites the fuel, engulfing the pursuing boats in flame.

During Operation Thunderball, SPECTRE frogmen trap Bond in an underwater cave. Finding a vent from the cave to the sky, 007 fires his mini Verey pistol through the opening to alert Felix Leiter and the US Coast Guard to his position. The pen-sized tube gun fires a bright red flare approximately 70 ft in the air.

On Her Majesty's Secret Service sees Blofeld using a flare to illuminate the route of his night escape from Piz Gloria during Operation Bedlam.

During an escape from Siberia in *A View To A Kill*, 007 fires a bright flare into the cabin of a Soviet helicopter, causing it to fill with smoke and crash.

Bond uses an underwater magnesium flare in a more conventional fashion while he is searching the wreck of HMS *Devonshire* in Vietnamese waters in *Tomorrow Never Dies*.

AND THE KITCHEN SINK *Bond's underwater propulsion unit turns him into a one-man navy.*

VIRTUAL REALITY GLASSES

APPEARANCE
Die Another Day (2002)
USED BY **James Bond, Miss Moneypenny**

Virtual reality glasses allow one to interact with a computer-simulated environment. In the virtual shooting range chamber located in MI6's disused London underground station, Bond dons these glasses, stands on a motion-sensing floor plate, and interacts with the computer-simulated MI6 offices and corridors. In the simulation, Bond finds himself sitting in his office cleaning his

Walther P99. He hears gunshots and soon finds Moneypenny dead in her office with a bullet in her forehead. After taking out four gunmen, he joins Robinson, and they burst into M's office where a gunman holds M hostage. Two other gunmen stand in corners of the office. One shoots Robinson, and Bond takes out both of them. 007 then shoots M in the shoulder, and once she's out of the way with a flesh wound, fires his Walther into the chest of the gunman. Later, Moneypenny uses the glasses to enjoy her own romantic fantasy about Bond. When Q interrupts Moneypenny's simulation, she rises from the motion-sensing floor plate and quickly buttons her blouse.

VISA CARD SKELETON KEY

APPEARANCE
The World Is Not Enough (1999)
USED BY **James Bond**

Part of this ordinary-looking Visa credit card slides back, allowing a skeleton key to emerge. After spending a passionate evening with Elektra King, Bond approaches the office behind Elektra's mansion in Baku, uses the Visa credit card skeleton key to pick the lock, and searches for clues regarding an insider

in the King Industries organization. The arrival of security chief Sasha Davidov soon interrupts his infiltration.

VOICE SIMULATOR

APPEARANCE
Diamonds Are Forever (1971)
USED BY **Ernst Stavro Blofeld, James Bond**

As well as using doubles, Blofeld has a voice box—which records voice

patterns on tape—to complete his impersonation of Willard Whyte. A desktop unit allows Blofeld, or one of his doubles, to speak like Whyte on the phone. A miniature unit planted in the necks of the doubles also allows them to speak like Blofeld.

Q constructs a desktop unit in Las Vegas to help 007 sound like Bert Saxby on the phone. Using the unit, Bond calls Blofeld and discovers where the real Willard Whyte is being held.

WAI LIN'S BIKE SHOP

APPEARANCE
Tomorrow Never Dies (1997)
USED BY Wai Lin, James Bond

The bike shop spy Wai Lin enters in Saigon is actually a safe house for the Chinese People's External Security Force.

While at the safe house, Wai Lin and Bond battle goons sent by corrupt Chinese General Chang. Wai Lin also reveals the safe house's impressive armory of weapons and gadgets. At the push of a few buttons, old cabinets ascend to the ceiling and others swivel, revealing high-tech

PEDAL POWER *Wai Lin of the Chinese Secret Service blends in with the Saigon crowd.*

gadgets, guns, knives, and banks of computers. The gadgets include a dragon statue, which is really a flame thrower; a Chinese fan which, when unfolded, fires wire restraints across the room; a new Walther P99 (more powerful than Bond's Walther PPK 7.65), which Bond has been requesting from Q for some time; an Omega Seamaster watch, which 007 later uses as a detonator aboard Elliot Carver's stealth ship; and a stack of limpet mines.

The high-tech safe house also includes a computer (complete with Chinese keyboard) and several bike rickshaws, one of which can be fired as a projectile, as Wai Lin demonstrates by knocking out one of Chang's men.

HELL ON WHEELS *Wai Lin battles Chang's goons in the bike shop safe house.*

WALKIE-TALKIE FLUTE

APPEARANCE
Live And Let Die (1973)
USED BY Baron Samedi

When Bond and Solitaire search for Kananga's poppy fields, they discover an imposing man in peasant rags playing a flute in a graveyard. Unbeknownst to both of them, the man is Baron Samedi. He communicates to Kananga's hook-handed henchman, Tee Hee, via a walkie-talkie unit hidden in his reed flute, that Bond and Solitaire "are heading for the hill."

WALKING STICK GUN

APPEARANCE
The World Is Not Enough (1999)
USED BY Valentin Zukovsky

Russian casino owner Valentin Zukovsky's silver-handled walking stick conceals a .22 caliber single-shot rifle. Bursting into assassin Renard's hideout looking for his missing nephew, Zukovsky realizes he has been murdered and finds his enemy, Bond, shackled in Elektra King's torture chair. King shoots Zukovsky, but he finds the strength to aim his stick. He fires, not at 007, but at a chair restraint, freeing one of Bond's hands.

WALL-WALKING DEVICE

APPEARANCE
You Only Live Twice (1967)
USED BY James Bond

James Bond uses four large rubber suction cups to descend the sloping interior walls of Blofeld's volcano rocket base. When Bond discovers that the lake atop a volcano's crater is actually a metal roof, he sends agent Kissy Suzuki to alert head of the Japanese Secret Service Tiger Tanaka. Bond removes his fisherman's clothes to reveal a ninja suit. He places the large suction cups on his hands and knees and uses them to climb down from the roof to the floor of the rocket base.

WALTHER P99

APPEARANCES
Tomorrow Never Dies (1997),
The World Is Not Enough (1999),
Die Another Day (2002),
Casino Royale (2006)
USED BY James Bond

The Walther P99, introduced in 1996, is a semi-automatic pistol and an updated version of the Walther PPK 7.65 mm. With a magazine capacity of ten to sixteen rounds as opposed to the 7.65's seven rounds, this weapon offers more firepower.

Although Bond has repeatedly asked Q for a P99, it's not until he's in a safe house for the Chinese People's External Security Force in *Tomorrow Never Dies* that he acquires one for the first time. Attaching a silencer to the P99, he uses it to help him effectively attack media mogul Elliot Carver's stealth ship.

In *The World Is Not Enough*, the P99 includes a blinding flash mechanism, activated when Bond pushes a small protrusion on his Calvin Klein glasses. In *Die Another Day*, a P99 is hidden in Bond's surfboard saboteur kit.

Casino Royale sees Bond get into trouble with M when he shoots the terrorist Mollaka with his P99 in front of CCTV cameras at the Nambutu Embassy in Madagascar. When Bond arrives in Montenegro, he discovers a P99 fitted with a silencer in the glove compartment of his new Aston Martin DBS and places it in a brown envelope. During a break in the poker game with Le Chiffre, Bond returns to his hotel, collects the envelope from reception, and steps into the elevator with Vesper Lynd. Hearing angry voices coming from Le Chiffre's room (thanks to a bug), Bond pulls the P99 from the parcel (*opposite page, main picture*), though he never gets the chance to use it.

BOND'S NEW GUN *Major Boothroyd presents 007 with his new sidearm, a Walther PPK 7.65 mm.*

WALTHER PPK 7.65 MM

APPEARANCES
Dr. No (1962), From Russia With Love
(1963), Goldfinger (1964), Thunderball
(1965), You Only Live Twice (1967),
On Her Majesty's Secret Service
(1969), Diamonds Are Forever (1971),
Live and Let Die (1973), The Man
With The Golden Gun (1974), The
Spy Who Loved Me (1977),
Moonraker (1979), For Your Eyes
Only (1981), Octopussy (1983), A
View To A Kill (1985), GoldenEye
(1995), Tomorrow Never Dies (1997)
USED BY James Bond

The Walther PPK 7.65 mm was first introduced to German officers and police in 1931. It eventually became James Bond's most trusted weapon over the course of 18 missions.

In *Dr. No*, after Bond's Beretta jams on a job, M assigns 007 a new gun— the PPK 7.65 mm. SPECTRE soon becomes aware this is Bond's weapon of choice, as Ernst Stavro Blofeld points out to his henchman Mr. Osato in *You Only Live Twice*.

Bond uses a PPK on nearly all his missions up to and including *Tomorrow Never Dies* (though he never fires it *Moonraker*). The exception is *Octopussy* when Bond uses a Walther P5; he mentions to Q in India that he has mislaid his PPK.

Bond last uses his PPK in Hamburg, Germany while investigating media mogul Elliot Carver in *Tomorrow Never Dies*. He acquires a Walther P99 in spy Wai Lin's bike shop in Saigon.

WALTHER WA 2000 RIFLE

APPEARANCE
The Living Daylights (1987)
USED BY James Bond

Bond uses a Walther WA 2000 on a mission to protect a defecting Soviet General. Manufactured from the late 1970s to 1988, the WA 2000 uses .300 Winchester magnum cartridges, and is accurate to 1,000 m (3,281 ft). In Bratislava, Bond loads the rifle with steel-tipped bullets as he waits to shoot a KGB sniper posted to eliminate General Koskov as he defects to the West. Bond sees the sniper is the female cellist he noticed at a concert earlier in the evening. He senses she is not a professional assassin and, taking advantage of the WA 2000's accuracy, shoots her rifle out of her hands.

WATCH WITH GARROTE WIRE

APPEARANCE
From Russia With Love (1963)
USED BY Donald Grant

Concealed inside his ordinary-looking watch, SPECTRE assassin Donald "Red" Grant has 4 ft (1.2 m) of high-tensile strength garrote wire, accessed by pulling the crown out. Inside the watch, the wire feeds from a spring-loaded reel, which spools when tension is released. He uses the garrote to kill a James Bond double during a training exercise on SPECTRE Island. Grant later uses the garrote again in an attempt to kill 007 in their fight aboard the Orient Express but he becomes the victim, when 007 stabs him in the shoulder, then whips the garotte wire around Grant's neck.

KILLING TIME *Donald Grant awaits his moment to take the life of a James Bond double with his garrote wire watch.*

WAVE-WALKER

APPEARANCE
Diamonds Are Forever (1971)

USED BY James Bond

James Bond parachutes into the Pacific Ocean inside an icosahedron (20-sided) silver pod. The odd-looking device, made of water-proofed vinyl and supported by positive interior air pressure and inflated tubular ferrules, serves as a wave-walker. Ditching the chutes from an interior quick release, 007 walks within the pod, moving across the water's surface. He wave-walks to the base of an oil rig that houses Blofeld's control center. Blofeld's crew recovers the object, believing the occupant might have come to negotiate a peace deal.

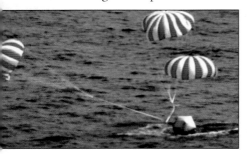

UNIDENTIFIED OBJECT (above) A strange-looking silver pod lands near Blofeld's oil-rig base.

"Good morning. The Acme Pollution Inspection. We're cleaning up the world. We thought this was a suitable starting point."

James Bond arriving at Blofeld's oil rig

WEIGHTED SKIRT

APPEARANCE
Octopussy (1983)

USED BY Magda

Magda wears a beautiful weighted Indian skirt, which she can remove from her body in an instant and use as a handy weapon. When Octopussy's army attacks Kamal Khan's Monsoon Palace, Magda uses her skirt to knock out one of Kamal's guards.

POWER DRESSING Magda adopts a traditionally peaceful pose, but her skirt is a dangerous weapon.

WRIST DART GUN

APPEARANCE
Moonraker (1979)
USED BY James Bond

The wrist dart gun is a unique weapon that can be used effectively and covertly against man and machine. Worn on a man's watch-style bracelet, the firing mechanism rests against the underside of the wrist. It is easily concealed, waterproof, and able to withstand the rigors of space travel. The gun senses nerve impulses when the hand rapidly flips upwards. For a short period, Q Branch offers it as standard issue with five red-tipped cyanide-coated darts that cause death in thirty seconds and five more blue-tipped darts with armor-piercing heads. Bond fires an armor-piercing dart to disable an out-of-control centrifuge at Hugo Drax's astronaut training facility. In Drax's secret space station, 007 fires a cyanide-coated dart into Drax's chest, before quickly ejecting the megalomaniac into orbit.

TRICK SHOT *(below) A dart from Bond's wrist dart gun finds its target.*

EYE OPENING *(above) Bond's X-ray glasses reveal a well-armed clientele at the bar.*

X-RAY SPECS

APPEARANCE
The World Is Not Enough (1999)
USED BY James Bond

Q Branch utilizes a transparent polymer video screen for interior coating of these light blue lenses. Filtered infra-red video reveals objects beneath a single layer of clothing, simulating X-ray vision capabilities. At Valentin Zukovsky's Casino Noir d'Or in Baku, Bond dons the glasses, which disclose that the patrons are concealing all manner of guns and weapons.

X-RAY DESK

APPEARANCE
You Only Live Twice (1967)
USED BY Mr. Osato

On a mission to investigate the disappearance of various space capsules, James Bond arranges to meet with Blofeld's accomplice, Mr. Osato. In the guise of Mr. Fisher, managing director of Empire Chemicals, Bond goes to Osato's office. Osato uses a fluoroscope built into his desk to X-ray 007's chest area. This provides Osato with a silhouette of Bond's Walther PPK. When Blofeld examines the X-ray film, he declares that only one man he knows uses this gun—James Bond.

YO-YO BUZZ SAW

APPEARANCE
Octopussy (1983)
USED BY Mufti's thugs

The weapon of choice for one of Mufti's thugs hired by Kamal Khan to kill Bond at Octopussy's Floating Palace is a large, steel-bladed yo-yo buzz saw attached to a steel wire. The thug first uses the weapon to kill Bond's contact Vijay. The gang then sneaks into Octopussy's palace, and attempts to murder Bond and Octopussy, who fight back and take refuge in a sitting room. The thug uses the saw to cut through the locked door. Bond and the thug, still clutching his saw, fall through a window and into the palace moat where a crocodile eats Bond's assailant.

"Take a giant step for **mankind!**"

007 to Drax, after shooting him with the wrist dart gun

THE MOVIES

With every 007 film, there are two great stories. The first is the one viewers see on the screen—the intrigue, adventure, and spectacle that begin with the signature gun-barrel opening of each Bond movie. The other tale is far more complex but filled with just as many twists and turns and just as much excitement and suspense. This second tale is the story of the making of the film. The James Bond series is the longest-running and most successful in cinema history, and the credit for that rests on the shoulders not only of Ian Fleming and the producers and directors, but also on the thousands of individuals who have worked on the movies since 1962. On the following pages, take a look at the Bond films from the other side of the camera. View the adventures in the order they were made, through the perspective of the challenges the filmmakers faced. Meet 23 of the key creative talents who have contributed to the legacy of 007, from the producers, directors, and writers who shaped the series, to other key individuals who helped create the character of James Bond through music, stunts, and special effects. The following pages celebrate the stories behind the 007 cinematic adventures, the men and women who made the films, and the entertainment they have provided to billions around the world.

DR. NO (1962)

CAST Sean Connery (James Bond),
Ursula Andress (Honey), Joseph Wiseman
(Dr. No), Jack Lord (Felix Leiter), Bernard Lee
(M), Anthony Dawson (Professor Dent), John
Kitzmuller (Quarrel), Zena Marshall (Miss Taro),
Eunice Gayson (Sylvia), Lois Maxwell (Miss
Moneypenny), Lester Prendergast (Puss-Feller),
Tim Moxon (Strangways), Marguerite LeWars
(Photographer), Reginald Carter (Jones),
Peter Burton (Major Boothroyd), William Foster-Davis
(Duff), Louis Blaazer (Pleydell-Smith), Michel Mok
(Sister Rose), Yvonne Shima (Sister Lily), Dolores
Keator (Mary), Colonel Burton (General Potter),
Eric Coverley, Charles Edghill, Henry Lopez
(The Three Blind Mice), Adrian Robinson
(Hearse driver)
PRODUCED BY
Harry Saltzman & Albert R. Broccoli
DIRECTED BY Terence Young
SCREENPLAY BY Richard Maibaum,
Johanna Harwood & Berkely Mather
BASED ON THE NOVEL BY Ian Fleming
MUSIC COMPOSED BY Monty Norman
ORCHESTRATED BY Burt Rhodes
"The James Bond Theme" played by the
John Barry Orchestra, conducted by
Eric Rodgers
DIRECTOR OF PHOTOGRAPHY
Ted Moore, BSC
PRODUCTION DESIGNER Ken Adam
PRODUCTION MANAGER L. C. Rudkin
EDITOR Peter Hunt
MAIN TITLES DESIGNED BY
Maurice Binder
ANIMATION
Trevor Bond & Robert Ellis
ART DIRECTOR Syd Cain
MAKEUP John O'Gorman
SPECIAL EFFECTS Frank George
CONTINUITY Helen Whitson
ASSISTANT DIRECTOR Clive Reed
CAMERA OPERATOR John Winbolt
HAIR STYLIST Eileen Warwick
SOUND RECORDISTS
Wally Milner & John Dennis
COSTUMES Tessa Welborn
SET DRESSING Freda Pearson
DUBBING EDITORS
Archie Ludski & Norman Wanstall
ASSISTANT EDITOR Ben Reyner

MONTY NORMAN *The composer of
"The James Bond Theme" on set.*

Throughout the 1950s, Ian Fleming flirted with the idea of
bringing James Bond to the silver screen, but none of these
ventures bore fruit. In 1961, Canadian producer Harry
Saltzman optioned the rights to the Bond novels, but could
not find financing. Saltzman had all but given up on Bond
when American producer Albert R. "Cubby" Broccoli, who
was also interested in making 007 films, entered the picture.
He secured financing with United Artists, and the pair set
off with a budget of just under $1 million to make the first
James Bond adventure.

Initially, Broccoli and Saltzman hoped *Thunderball* might
be the first film, but legal battles over the film rights to the
novel led to them selecting *Dr. No*, a story also set in a
tropical location with plenty of action and a topical plot.

With strong support from United Artists, especially
production executive David Picker, Broccoli, and Saltzman
assembled the cast and crew. For director, they selected
Terence Young, whom Broccoli knew would bring style and
elegance to the film. To adapt Fleming's sixth novel, they
hired Wolf Mankowitz, who had introduced Broccoli to
Saltzman, and Richard Maibaum, who had written
Broccoli's first hit film, the Alan Ladd war adventure *The*

Red Beret (1953). Maibaum and Wolf Mankowitz, however,
raised eyebrows when, in their first treatment, they made
the chief villain Buckfield, a shipping magnate with a spider
monkey named Li Ying perched on his shoulder. Disguised
as the deceased, esoteric Dr. No, he plans to destroy the
Panama Canal locks. Broccoli and Saltzman quickly
demanded a more faithful adaptation of Fleming's text.

The most important question remained: who would play
Bond? The producers considered everyone from Richard
Burton to Cary Grant (the best man at Broccoli's wedding)
but, in the end, they chose a young, dynamic Scottish actor
named Sean Connery.

While Young helped to provide Connery with a more
sophisticated image, the producers turned their attention to
casting the leading lady, Honey Ryder. They soon focused
their attention on the Swiss actress Ursula Andress and sent
her the script. Prompted by her husband John Derek and
the actor Kirk Douglas, Andress accepted the assignment.
For the role of chief villain, Dr. No, Ian Fleming
recommended friend and playwright Noel Coward. Coward
answered Fleming with a telegram that read, "Dear Ian, the
answer to Dr. No is No! No! No!" The producers soon

FILM !

ZENA
MARSHALL

ALSO STARRING
BERNARD

EUNICE
R·GAYSON LEE

...EON PRODUCTIONS LTD

selected the classically trained New York actor Joseph Wiseman for the role.

Filming began in Jamaica on January 16, 1962 and moved along relatively smoothly. When the cast and crew returned to England, where production designer Ken Adam had constructed the film's imaginative sets, they realized they had something special on their hands. The film's polished look, sharp script, exotic settings, thrilling set-piece action sequences, and modern attitude to sex and violence elevated it far above the standard thriller of the time.

One important element remained—the music. Composer Monty Norman wrote some songs while visiting the production in Jamaica, working with the legendary Byron Lee to bring a Caribbean feel to the score. Yet the piece that would define Bond came from a discarded song from a musical version of V. S. Naipaul's novel *The House of Mr. Biswas*. Norman turned the music into "The James Bond Theme." During post-production, John Barry came in to orchestrate, arrange, and record a version of the theme that stepped away from the "Colonel Bogey" march sound of Norman's original, using a driving, reverb-laden electric guitar to play the tune. Editor Peter Hunt used Barry's recording throughout the film, and Barry soon became closely associated with the Bond sound.

The filmmakers' faith in their movie was fully vindicated when United Artists released *Dr. No* in England in October 1962. The film also performed excellently in the US, where it premiered six months later in April 1963. Quite simply, *Dr. No* was an extremely fresh film for its time, ushering in a new cinematic screen hero who would still delight audiences 45 years later.

VIP VISITOR *(below) Bond's creator, Ian Fleming, chats with Sean Connery in Jamaica during production.*

SHOOTING DR. NO *(left, top to bottom) Sean Connery, Terence Young, and Jamaican actor Reginald Carter discuss a shot at the start of production; the crew shoots near Ocho Rios, Jamaica, in early 1962; Ursula Andress being dressed by Tessa Welborn, who designed the film's famed white bikini; Ursula Andress being attended to by makeup artist John O'Gorman.*

ALBERT R. BROCCOLI

Albert R. "Cubby" Broccoli is one of the most legendary of all Hollywood producers; the James Bond series is the most successful film franchise in the history of cinema.

Broccoli's uncle, Pasquale, emigrated to the US from Italy in the 1870s, bringing a strain of broccoli seeds with him and establishing a successful vegetable farm. His father Giovanni immigrated at the turn of the century, and Cubby was born in Astoria, Queens, New York, in 1909.

In his youth, his resemblance to comic-strip character Abie Kabibble caused his cousins to call him Little Kabibbee, later shortened to Cubby.

After a stint as a coffin salesman, a vacation to Los Angeles in 1934 introduced him to Howard Hughes and Cary Grant, who would become lifelong friends. Deciding to stay in LA, Cubby worked several jobs over the next 15 years, including a jewelry and Christmas tree salesman; a talent agent; a studio mailroom runner; and an assistant director on *The Black Swan* (1942) and *The Song Of Bernadette* (1943). When World War II erupted, he joined the Navy and arranged for stars to appear in shows for servicemen.

Cubby's wonderful way with people paid off when he entered into a producing partnership with Irving Allen, forming Warwick Pictures and making movies with American actors in England to take advantage of British production subsidies.

After the death of his second wife, Nedra, Broccoli married actress/writer Dana Wilson. His partnership with Allen dissolved just before the birth of his daughter Barbara. A year later, in 1962, 007 came into his life, and the rest is history.

Cubby always believed that a film's budget should be reflected in the production values on the screen, and he consistently strove to attain the highest technical standards.

Albert R. Broccoli passed on the mantle of the Bond series with *GoldenEye* (1995) and died in 1996.

FROM RUSSIA WITH LOVE
(1963)

CAST Sean Connery (James Bond),
Daniela Bianchi (Tatiana Romanova),
Pedro Armendariz (Kerim Bey) Lotte Lenya
(Rosa Klebb), Robert Shaw (Donald "Red" Grant),
Bernard Lee (M), Eunice Gayson (Sylvia),
Walter Gotell (Morzeny), Francis de Wolff (Vavra),
George Pastell (Train conductor), Nadja Regin
(Kerim Bey's Girlfriend), Lois Maxwell (Miss
Moneypenny), Aliza Gur (Vida), Martine Beswick
(Zora), Vladek Sheybal (Kronsteen), Leila (Gypsy
dancer), Hansan Ceylan (Foreign agent),
Fred Haggerty (Krilencu), Neville Jason (Kerim Bey's
chauffeur), Peter Bayliss (Benz), Mushet Auaer
(Mehmet), Peter Brayham (Rhoda),
Desmond Llewelyn (Boothroyd), Jan Williams
(Masseuse), Peter Madden (McAdams),
Arlette Dobson (Hotel receptionist)
PRODUCED BY
Harry Saltzman & Albert R. Broccoli
DIRECTED BY Terence Young
SCREENPLAY BY Richard Maibaum
ADAPTED BY Johanna Harwood
DIRECTOR OF PHOTOGRAPHY
Ted Moore, BSC
EDITOR Peter Hunt
PRODUCTION MANAGER Bill Hill
ART DIRECTOR Syd Cain
TITLE SONG WRITTEN BY Lionel Bart
"FROM RUSSIA WITH LOVE" SONG
PERFORMED BY Matt Munro
"THE JAMES BOND THEME" WRITTEN BY
Monty Norman
ORCHESTRAL MUSIC COMPOSED
AND CONDUCTED BY John Barry
ASSISTANT DIRECTOR David Anderson
SECOND UNIT CAMERAMAN
Robert Kindred
CAMERA OPERATOR Johnny Winbolt
CONTINUITY Kay Mander
MAKEUP Basil Newall & Paul Rabiger
HAIRDRESSER Eileen Warwick
LOCATION MANAGER Frank Ernst
ISTANBUL PRODUCTION ASSISTANT
Ilham Filmer
SPECIAL EFFECTS John Stears,
assisted by Frank George
STUNT WORK ARRANGED BY
Peter Perkins
SOUND RECORDISTS
John W. Mitchell & C. le Messurier
ASSEMBLY EDITOR Ben Rayner
DUBBING EDITORS
Norman Wanstall & Harry Miller
COSTUME DESIGNER Jocelyn Rickards
WARDROBE MISTRESS Eileen Sullivan
WARDROBE MASTER Ernie Farrer
ASSISTANT ART DIRECTOR Michael White
SET DRESSER Freda Pearson
TITLES DESIGNED BY Robert Brownjohn,
assisted by Trevor Bond

The phenomenal success of *From Russia With Love* transformed James Bond from a literary spy to a cinematic hero. The film's integration of modern filmmaking techniques, Cold War ethics, elegance, gadgetry, adventure, and sex both defined Bond in the popular consciousness, and ushered in a new cinematic style that influences films to this day.

Producers Albert R. "Cubby" Broccoli and Harry Saltzman and the director Terence Young needed to make an October 1963 UK release date. They felt that since many readers and critics, including US president John F. Kennedy, saw the novel as one of Fleming's best, a screenwriter would only have to make minor changes. They did decide to shift the acts of villainy from the Soviet Union's SMERSH to the independent criminal organization SPECTRE, a conscious decision to, as Broccoli recalled, "steer 007 and the scripts clear of politics." Novelist Len Deighton worked briefly on the project before Richard Maibaum and then Joanna Harwood wrote drafts.

With a cast that included Academy Award-nominee and famed chanteuse Lotte Lenya, actor/novelist Robert Shaw, and Mexican character actor, Pedro Armendariz (hired at the suggestion of John Ford), director Terence Young believed he could solve any remaining script issues during production. There was one remaining hurdle—finding the right actress for the role of Tatiana Romanova. Press releases went out around the world announcing that EON Productions was looking for a "young Greta Garbo." Italian actress Daniela Bianchi, a runner-up in the Miss Universe competition, won the role.

Shooting started on April 1, 1963 with Bond receiving his orders from M. On April 8-9, Terence Young shot Bond's meeting with Tatiana, a scene so perfectly realized filmmakers have used it to audition Bond actors and actresses for over 40 years. Harry Saltzman suggested shooting the SPECTRE training camp to parody the gladiator school scene in *Spartacus* (1960).

When the production moved to Istanbul in late April, Terence Young continued to alter the script on set. He brought Donald Grant into scenes that previously only included Bond and Soviet agents. The work to perfect the story proved difficult. Actor Peter Bayliss changed parts twice before Young cast him as Benz. Everywhere the crew set up to shoot, crowds gathered, causing delays. Young scrapped the climactic boat chase—scheduled for shooting off the coast of Turkey—because the boats moved too slowly. More seriously, Young noticed that Pedro Armendariz was masking a limp and at times appeared to be in great pain. Armendariz confessed he was dying of cancer.

Shaken by this news, the producers rearranged the schedule to immediately complete Armendariz's work at Pinewood Studios. Young worked hard to keep the film's energy high and demanded a chaotic and action-filled gun battle scene through which James Bond could move with seeming ease. Stunt coordinator Peter Perkins diligently rehearsed actresses Martine Beswick and Aliza Gur for the violent gypsy fight.

Armendariz completed filming in the early hours of Saturday, June 8. On Tuesday, June 18, he fatally shot himself at UCLA Medical Center. Armendariz's legacy to the Bond films did not end there. His son Pedro Armendariz Jr. appeared as a corrupt dictator in *Licence To Kill* (1989).

on just how well we have captured the split-second pace." Young and editor Peter Hunt worked closely to bring *From Russia With Love* together. They soon realized the film might be something quite remarkable. They rearranged the opening, and, at Hunt's suggestion, placed the scene of Grant apparently murdering 007 before the titles, creating the template of the pre-title sequence that has gone on to become a hallmark of the series. Hunt experimented with a faster, kinetic editing style that ignored traditional continuity in favor of movement and action. His influential innovations launched the modern style of action-film editing. Young's rapid shooting style worked perfectly with Hunt's cutting, drawing viewers into the action. Nowhere could this be better seen than the visceral fight between Bond and Donald "Red" Grant on the Orient Express. Using doubles in only two shots, shooting mostly handheld, Young captured what is still believed by many to be the most exciting fight scene in cinema history.

The completed cut proved remarkably entertaining. While filming had been every bit as challenging as an actual Bond adventure, the finished movie captured more excitement than most big-budget epics. The near-perfect pitch of Connery's performance as Bond, the staccato editing and the combination of suspense, wry humor, and action delivered a film experience like no other.

Composer John Barry delivered a lush, rich score that perfectly complemented the energy in film. The composer of the musical *Oliver!*, Lionel Bart, wrote the title song and hit singer and television personality Matt Munro provided silky vocals. John Barry combined Bart's melody with elements of "The James Bond Theme" and added a new composition, "007" that captured the soaring confidence of Bond's character. Barry's distinctive, modern score quickly became an audience favorite. The title song rose to #20 in the UK singles charts, and the soundtrack album charted on both sides of the Atlantic.

From Russia With Love premiered on October 10, 1963. Acclaimed by critics and public, it became the highest-grossing film ever released in the UK to that date, and broke records throughout Europe. Bond's place as the cultural phenomenon of the era had been secured.

For the next month, the production moved to Scotland, to film the speedboat chase as well as the helicopter assault on Bond. Disaster was narrowly averted when Terence Young and art director Michael White's helicopter ran into trouble. Thankfully the lightning reactions of the pilot saved all those on board from serious injury or worse. When shooting the giant petrol explosion, a miscommunication caused the special-effects charges to explode during a rehearsal, causing a significant delay.

"Because of the violent action scenes," Young stated in a press release at the end of principle photography, "This has been a difficult film to shoot...of course, everything depends

GOLDFINGER
(1964)

CAST Sean Connery (James Bond),
Honor Blackman (Pussy Galore), Gert Frobe
(Goldfinger), Shirley Eaton (Jill Masterson),
Tania Mallet (Tilly Masterson), Harold Sakata
[Tosh Togo] (Oddjob), Bernard Lee (M),
Martin Benson (Solo), Cec Linder (Felix Leiter),
Austin Willis (Simmons), Lois Maxwell (Miss
Moneypenny), Desmond Llewelyn (Q), Bill Nagy
(Midnight), Alf Joint (Capungo), Varley Thomas
(Swiss gatekeeper), Nadja Regin (Bonita),
Raymond Young (Sierra), Richard Vernon (Smithers),
Denis Cowles (Brunskill), Michael Mellinger (Kisch),
Burt Kwouk (Mr. Ling), Hal Galili (Strap), Lenny
Rabin (Henchman), Peter Cranwell (Johnny),
Mai Ling (Mei-Lei), Margaret Nolan (Dink),
Tricia Muller (Sydney), John McLaren (Brigadier),
Robert MacLeod (Atomic scientist),
Victor Brooks (Blacking), Gerry Duggan (Hawker)
PRODUCED BY
Harry Saltzman & Albert R. Broccoli
DIRECTED BY Guy Hamilton
SCREENPLAY BY
Richard Maibaum & Paul Dehn
PRODUCTION DESIGN BY Ken Adam
DIRECTOR OF PHOTOGRAPHY
Ted Moore, BSC
EDITOR Peter Hunt
PRODUCTION MANAGER L.C. Rudkin
ART DIRECTOR Peter Murton
"GOLDFINGER" TITLE SONG SUNG BY
Shirley Bassey
TITLE SONG LYRICS BY
Leslie Bricusse & Anthony Newley
MUSIC COMPOSED AND CONDUCTED BY
John Barry
ASSISTANT DIRECTOR Frank Ernst
CAMERA OPERATOR John Winbolt
CONTINUITY Constance Willis
MAKEUP Paul Rabiger & Basil Newall
ACTION SEQUENCES BY Bob Simmons
SPECIAL EFFECTS
John Stears, assisted by Frank George
ASSEMBLY EDITOR Ben Rayner
DUBBING EDITORS
Norman Wanstall & Harry Miller
SOUND RECORDISTS
Dudley Messenger & Gordon McCallum
HAIRDRESSER Eileen Warwick
WARDROBE SUPERVISOR Elsa Fennell
WARDROBE MISTRESS Eileen Sullivan
WARDROBE MASTER John Hilling
ASSISTANT ART DIRECTORS
Michael White & Maurice Pelling
SET DRESSER Freda Pearson
TITLES DESIGNED BY Robert Brownjohn

Goldfinger remains the most iconic of all Bond films,
certainly the film most referenced in popular culture.
Despite the tremendous financial success of both *Dr. No* and
From Russia With Love, *Goldfinger* did more to define the
cinematic James Bond than any other film. The story of its
creation shows the strength of the collaborative process that
has helped keep the Bond series going strong.

Screenwriter Richard Maibaum began adapting the novel
Goldfinger in April 1963, as *From Russia With Love* started
production. Maibaum immediately recognized plotting
problems for the film and set about strengthening Fleming's
original story. Maibaum let Bond discover Jill Masterson's
gilded body rather than hear about it from Jill's sister, Tilly.
He strengthened Goldfinger's motivation for keeping 007
alive. Most importantly, he changed Goldfinger's plot from
stealing the gold to destroying its value with an atomic blast.

Producers Broccoli and Saltzman approached Guy
Hamilton to direct the third Bond film. During pre-
production, Hamilton witnessed the tremendous success of
From Russia With Love in the UK, and was inspired to
develop an approach that would redefine the Bond series.
Working with British writer Paul Dehn and an uncredited
Berkeley Mather, Hamilton brought a greater emphasis on
humor to the film. Perhaps the clearest example of his
influence was the transformation of Bond's Aston Martin
DB Mk III from Fleming's novel into the film's gadget-filled
DB5, complete with machine guns and an ejector seat.
Viewers could both smile at the vehicle's outrageousness and
covet its deadly elegance.

Albert R. "Cubby" Broccoli brought in the accomplished
German actor Gert Frobe to play Goldfinger. To play Pussy
Galore, Hamilton suggested one of the most popular
actresses in England at the time, Honor Blackman, fresh
from playing judo expert Cathy Gale in the hit television
series *The Avengers*. Hamilton also spotted a wrestler by the
name of Tosh Togo, whom he realized would make a perfect
Oddjob. It turned out that Togo's real name was Harold
Sakata and he had won a Silver Medal in the 1948
Olympics. The filmmakers had to convince him that he
should use his real name in the credits. He insisted both
names appear on-screen.

While Hamilton and the producers were confident that
Goldfinger would be a huge success, other organizations were
still unaware of the Bond franchise's rapidly growing status.
Officials at the Bullion Depository at Fort Knox, were
reluctant to give the filmmakers access, despite the
production's well-connected technical advisor, US Air Force
Lt. Col. Charles Russhon. The aerial shots of Pussy Galore's
Flying Circus over the real Gold Depository attracted

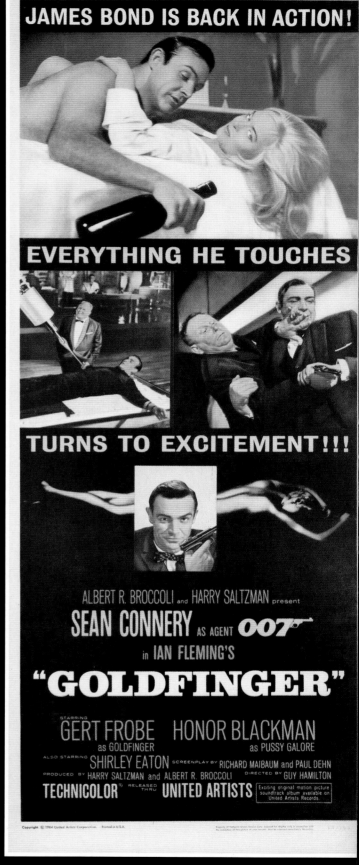

particular protest from officialdom.

Although shooting began in late January in Miami, Sean
Connery was unable to join the production until mid-
March, leaving less than five months to complete the film.
Connery was then forced to miss a week of shooting when
Harold Sakata failed to pull his punch sufficiently while
slamming Bond with a karate chop.

Throughout the production, cast and crew felt sure they

DYNAMIC DUO *(facing page) Harold Sakata (Oddjob) and Gert Frobe (Goldfinger) on location at Stoke Poges Golf Club.*
GOLD FOR GOLDFINGER *(near left) Shirley Bassey with her Gold Record for the **Goldfinger** soundtrack. The album charted at #1 in the US in early 1965.*

THE MIDAS TOUCH *(clockwise from top left) Sean Connery (James Bond) and Honor Blackman (Pussy Galore) on the backlot set of Auric Stud at Pinewood Studios; Guy Hamilton directs Gert Frobe (Goldfinger) to shoot US soldiers; Hamilton and Blackman on the Rumpus Room set; Harry Saltzman and Albert R. Broccoli meet with Honor Blackman for photos of her signing her contract with EON Productions; Sean Connery and Shirley Eaton (Jill Masterson) meet Ian Fleming a few months before the author's death; Basil Newall paints Shirley Eaton gold for her iconic moment.*

were working on something special. Production designer Ken Adam created a series of magnificent sets, including a drug lab hidden in an oil storage tank, a rumpus room that transforms into a strategy center, and the Auric Enterprises laser room. For the climax inside the Fort Knox gold vaults, Cubby Broccoli declared that he wanted "a cathedral of gold." Adam rose to the challenge, creating a set fitting for the epic battle between Bond and Oddjob.

With its ingenious blend of humor, action, gadgets, sex, sophistication, and exotic locations, *Goldfinger* defined what audiences would come to expect from a Bond film. However the film was almost banned in the US because of the name Pussy Galore. Cubby Broccoli had to plead his case to MPAA chief Geoffrey Shurlock before the film gained a certificate of approval. The film went on to be ranked by the *Guinness Book of World Records* as the fastest-grossing film ever released.

Goldfinger also defined the "Bond sound." Composer John Barry convinced the producers he should not only write the score but also the title song. "Goldfinger," featuring vocals by the incomparable Shirley Bassey, became a worldwide hit (#8 in the US; #21 in the UK singles charts). Its success propelled the soundtrack album to the top of the US charts, replacing The Beatles. The film's other sounds drew praise, too, with the film winning the Academy Award for Best Sound Effects, awarded to Norman Wanstall.

Sadly, *Goldfinger*'s worldwide success came too late to be enjoyed by Ian Fleming, who died on August 12, 1964, barely a month before the film premiered in London. The creator had passed away but, with *Goldfinger*, James Bond was destined to live forever.

RICHARD MAIBAUM

Born in New York City in 1909, Richard Maibaum attended New York University and the University of Iowa. After receiving his master's degree, he returned to New York and performed in plays with the Shakespearean Repertory Theatre. Besides acting, he also wrote plays. His first produced, *The Tree*, an anti-lynching drama, opened in New York in April 1932 but closed within a week. Undeterred, he wrote other plays, including *Birthright* (1933), which tackled Hitler's anti-Jewish fanaticism; *Sweet Mystery Of Life* (1935), a comedy about life insurance; *The Lonely Man* (1935), suggested by Calvin Coolidge; and the musical *Catch-As-Catch-Can* (1935).

In 1935, agent Sam Marx signed Maibaum to a Hollywood contract and brought him to Los Angeles, where he became a screenwriter at MGM. While working on the 1940 spy thriller, *Foreign Correspondent*, the director, Alfred Hitchcock, advised Maibaum that he knew he had a film when the story had at least 13 "bumps," or big moments.

During World War II, Maibaum became the head of the US Army's Industrial Film Unit and later director of the Combat Films Division. Leaving the service as a lieutenant colonel, Maibaum became a writer and producer at Paramount Pictures on such films as *O.S.S.* (1946), the suspense classic *The Big Clock* (1948), and *The Great Gatsby* (1949). In the 1950s, he began writing scripts for Warwick Pictures, a venture begun by Irving Allen and Albert R. Broccoli, providing the screenplay for their first film, *The Red Beret* (1953), as well as *Hell Below Zero* (1954), *Cockleshell Heroes* (1955), and *Zarak* (1956).

When Broccoli went on to produce the Bond films, he turned to Maibaum to bring Ian Fleming's novels to the screen. Maibaum contributed to 13 Bond films. He claimed that he always tried to work 39 "bumps" into a 007 script. His final screen credit came in 1996, five years after his death, when his 1956 thriller *Ransom!* was remade starring Mel Gibson.

THUNDERBALL
(1965)

CAST Sean Connery (James Bond), Claudine Auger
(Domino Derval), Adolfo Celi (Largo), Luciana Paluzzi
(Fiona Volpe), Rik Van Nutter (Felix Leiter),
Bernard Lee (M), Martine Beswick (Paula),
Guy Doleman (Count Lippe), Molly Peters (Patricia
Fearing), Desmond Llewelyn (Q), Lois Maxwell (Miss
Moneypenny), Ronald Culver (Foreign Secretary),
Earl Cameron (Pinder), Paul Stassino (Palazzi),
Rose Alba (Madame Boitier), Philip Locke (Vargas),
George Pravda (Kutze), Michael Brennan (Janni),
Leonard Sachs (Group Captain Pritchard),
Reginald Beckwith (Keniston), Anthony Dawson
(Ernst Stavro Blofeld), Bob Simmons (Jacques
Boitier),
Bill Cummings (Quist), Maryse Guy Mitsouko
(Mademoiselle La Porte), Edward Underdown
(Air Vice Marshall)
PRODUCED BY Kevin McClory
PRESENTED BY Harry Saltzman &
Albert R. Broccoli
DIRECTED BY Terence Young
SCREENPLAY BY Richard Maibaum &
John Hopkins
BASED ON AN ORIGINAL SCREENPLAY BY
Jack Whittingham
BASED ON THE ORIGINAL STORY BY
Kevin McClory, Jack Whittingham & Ian Fleming
PRODUCTION DESIGN BY Ken Adam
DIRECTOR OF PHOTOGRAPHY
Ted Moore, BSC
SUPERVISING EDITOR Peter Hunt
MUSIC COMPOSED AND CONDUCTED BY
John Barry
TITLE SONG "THUNDERBALL"
lyrics by Don Black, sung by Tom Jones
ART DIRECTOR Peter Murton
PRODUCTION SUPERVISOR
David Middlemas
ASSISTANT DIRECTOR Gus Agosti
CAMERA OPERATOR John Winbolt
CONTINUITY Joan Davis
MAKEUP Paul Rabiger & Basil Newall
ACTION SEQUENCES BY Bob Simmons
SPECIAL EFFECTS John Stears
2ND UNIT CAMERAMAN Egil Woxholt
EDITOR Ernest Hosler
ASSEMBLY EDITOR Ben Rayner
DUBBING EDITORS
Norman Wanstall & Harry Miller
SOUND RECORDISTS Bert Ross &
Maurice Askew
HAIRDRESSER Eileen Warwick
COSTUMES DESIGNED BY
Anthony Mendleson
WARDROBE MISTRESS Eileen Sullivan
WARDROBE MASTER John Brady
ASSISTANT ART DIRECTOR Michael White
SET DRESSER Freda Pearson
MAIN TITLE DESIGNED BY Maurice Binder
UNDERWATER SEQUENCES
Ivan Tors Underwater Studios Ltd.
UNDERWATER DIRECTOR Ricou Browning
UNDERWATER CAMERAMAN
Lamar Boren
UNDERWATER ENGINEER Jordan Klein

Thunderball has sold more tickets than any Bond film before or since. Its production history and legacy, however, remain controversial. When Harry Saltzman partnered with Albert R. Broccoli to produce James Bond films, they initially considered making *Thunderball*, which, having been published in 1961, was the most recent 007 novel. However, the novel was the subject of a lawsuit; a young director, Kevin McClory, claimed that work McClory and screenwriter Jack Whittingham had contributed to the story had been used by Fleming without credit or compensation.

Believing the lawsuit would soon be dismissed, Saltzman and Broccoli asked Richard Maibaum to write a script. When it became apparent that McClory's lawsuit against Ian Fleming and Fleming's friend Ivar Bryce would prove lengthy, Saltzman and Broccoli chose to adapt *Dr. No* as the first Bond adventure.

McClory settled his lawsuit in November 1963, as *From Russia With Love* broke box-office records in the UK. McClory gained screenrights to the novel and treatments and a credit in future editions of the novel. While McClory attempted to mount his own Bond film, Saltzman and Broccoli entered negotiations with Broccoli's old employer, agent-producer Charles K. Feldman, to make a film of the first Bond novel *Casino Royale*. When Feldman's terms proved too difficult, Saltzman and Broccoli struck a deal with McClory.

McClory had worked with the showman producer Michael Todd on *Around The World In 80 Days* (1956), and he pushed to make this Bond film an event movie with more of a "travelogue" feel. Thus, *Thunderball* became the first true widescreen Bond film.

In late 1964, Maibaum began rewriting *Thunderball*, this time with the knowledge of the success of the previous three Bond films. During production, respected British writer John Hopkins also contributed to the completed film's narrative polish and witty dialogue.

To direct, the producers returned to Terence Young, who quickly realized that *Thunderball*, as written, could not be shot without the addition of strong second-unit directors. He enlisted Ricou Browning, creator of *Flipper*, to direct the underwater scenes; underwater cameraman Lamar Boren shot the epic undersea battle. Broccoli's Hollywood friend, director André de Toth, filmed the aerial assault over Biscayne Bay.

Young wanted to keep 007's gadgetry from becoming a simple series of jokes. He and the filmmakers searched for real equipment for Bond's technological arsenal, including the Bell-Textron Jet Pack Bond uses to escape from SPECTRE agent Jacques Boitier's chateau in the film's opening sequence and the Skyhook rescue system that whisks Bond and Domino to safety at the film's close. Other gadgets proved so believable they even fooled military experts. After the film's opening, a Royal Navy representative called to inquire about Bond's mini-rebreather, only to be informed it wasn't real.

The film's cast was a testament to Bond's international appeal. Italian actors Adolfo Celi and Luciana Paluzzi led the villains. French actress Claudine Auger captured the role of Domino. Jamaican beauty Martine Beswick and British model/actress Mollie (Molly in the credits) Peters rounded out the cast.

The film required extensive work with sharks. Special effects supervisor John Stears found himself surrounded in a pool by frenzied sharks while working on one scene. On another occasion, Sean Connery found himself swimming through a plexiglass-walled tunnel in Largo's shark pool.

AQUATIC ADVENTURES *The crew prepares for a shot near Golden Cay, Bahamas.*

One missing piece of plexi allowed a lone shark to swim into the tunnel with Connery, resulting in a genuine expression of concern on Bond's face that one can see in the film. During scenes set in the open ocean, cameraman Lamar Boren used a unique way to fend off sharks he felt got too close—he rammed them with his 134-lb (61-kg) underwater camera. For the climactic underwater battle, 38 divers appeared on screen, requiring experienced scuba divers to be flown to Nassau from as far away as Richmond, Virginia.

The film's greatest challenge came during post-production. Young left the film as soon as shooting wrapped. At this point, the film was overlong. Editor Peter Hunt promised United Artists that he could bring the film together if they delayed the film's opening. Hunt helped to reshoot scenes, restructure the film's middle-third, and cut the movie down to 130 minutes from a first assembly that ran roughly 270 minutes.

Composer John Barry returned to score the film, creating a lush, mysterious soundtrack. He wrote the original opening credits song, "Mr. Kiss Kiss Bang Bang," the Italian nickname for 007, with Leslie Bricusse and recorded it twice: first with Shirley Bassey and then with Dionne Warwick. Concern that the song never mentioned the film's title resulted in Barry quickly writing "Thunderball" with Don Black, a hit in the US and UK for Tom Jones.

When the film opened in December 1965, audiences were awe-struck. *Thunderball* broke box-office records around the world and set a new standard for action-adventure films with its scale, scope, and amazing underwater battle sequences. John Stears won an Academy Award for the film's innovative special effects work.

For all its success, *Thunderball*'s legacy cast a small but troubling cloud over the Bond series from 1975 until 2000. During those years, McClory continually tried to parlay the rights he had into a James Bond series of his own. In 1983, Connery appeared in a non-EON produced Thunderball re-make, *Never Say Never Again*, based on McClory's rights. Then, in 1997, McClory struck a deal with Sony Pictures. After the settlement and disposition of the resulting lawsuits, McClory's Bond rights were severely limited. Sony severed their relationship with McClory and, most importantly, Sony ceded to the Bond producers the rights to *Casino Royale*. Every cloud has a silver lining.

k OUT!

HERE COMES THE BIGGEST BOND OF ALL!

TZMAN and R. BROCCOLI present

SEAN CONNERY in IAN FLEMING'S

"THUNDERBALL" A

CLAUDINE AUGER · ADOLFO CELI · LUCIANA PALUZZI · RIK VAN NUTTER

IN McCLORY Directed by **TERENCE YOUNG**   PANAVISION® TECHNICOLOR®

MAIBAUM & JOHN HOPKINS · Based on the original story by KEVIN McCLORY, JACK WHITTINGHAM and IAN FLEMING

TERENCE YOUNG

Born the son of an English police commissioner in the International Sector of Shanghai in 1915, Shaun Terence Young was educated in England. At Cambridge University, he excelled in rugby, tennis, and cricket. He also wrote film reviews for his college paper and had a summer job at BIP Studios. He gained a reputation as a talented screenwriter with the melodrama *Dangerous Moonlight* (1941).

During World War II, Young served with Britain's famed Guards Armoured Tank Division and was twice wounded in action. After the war, he returned to screenwriting and then became an assistant to directors Jacques Feyder, Alexander Korda, Josef von Sternberg, and King Vidor.

His directorial debut came in 1948 with *One Night With You*. His next film, *Corridor Of Mirrors* (1948), starring Lois Maxwell, won the "Best Film of the Year" award in France. *The Red Beret* (1953) marked his first teaming with 007 screenwriter Richard Maibaum and producer Albert R. Broccoli.

With an established reputation as an action director, Young was the ideal choice to helm *Dr. No* (1962). Many of those who worked with him thought he embodied the same qualities as 007—elegance, humor, and a knowledge of bespoke tailoring and fine wines. His staging of James Bond's introduction in *Dr. No* became a cinema classic, though he modestly claimed "it was really a steal of Paul Muni's introduction in *Juarez*." Young also directed the second film in the series, *From Russia With Love* (1963), and then, after a one film break, returned for his third and final Bond adventure, *Thunderball* (1965).

Young left *Thunderball* during post-production to direct a film for the United Nations, *The Poppy Is Also A Flower* (1966). His later films included *Wait Until Dark* (1967), *Mayerling* (1968), *Red Sun* (1971), *The Valachi Papers* (1972), *Bloodline* (1979), *Inchon* (1981), *The Jigsaw Man* (1983), and *Run For Your Life* (1988). In 1994, while preparing to direct a major European film, Young fell ill and died of a heart attack in hospital at Cannes, France.

ROCKET MAN *(left) One of the two stunt pilots flies the Bell Textron Rocket Belt in France.*

THE BIGGEST BOND OF ALL *(right) Crowds at the Paramount Theatre, Manhattan; like* **Goldfinger, Thunderball** *played 24 hours a day in New York throughout the Christmas holiday.*

WELCOME TO PARADISE *(above) Martine Beswick (Paula Caplan), Claudine Auger (Domino Derval), and Luciana Paluzzi (Fiona Volpe) during shooting on Paradise Beach.*

UNITED ARTISTS *(left) United Artists Exec. David Picker, Saltzman, and Broccoli at the Paramount Theatre.*

UNDERSEA SHOOT *(right) Lamar Boren shoots the beginning of the film's final battle.*

277

YOU ONLY LIVE TWICE (1967)

CAST Sean Connery (James Bond), Akiko Wakabayashi (Aki), Mie Hama (Kissy Suzuki), Tetsuro Tamba (Tiger Tanaka), Teru Shimada (Mr. Osato), Karin Dor (Helga Brandt), Donald Pleasence (Blofeld), Bernard Lee (M), Lois Maxwell (Miss Moneypenny), Desmond Llewelyn (Q), Charles Gray (Dikko Henderson), Tsai Chin (Ling), Ronald Rich (Hans), Burt Kwouk (SPECTRE No.3), Michael Chow (SPECTRE No.4), Jeanne Roland (Bond's masseuse), David Toguri (Assassin [bedroom]), John Stone (Submarine Captain), Paul Carson, Norman Jones, Laurence Herder, Richard Graydon, Bill Mitchell, George Roubicek (Astronauts)
PRODUCED BY
Harry Saltzman & Albert R. Broccoli
DIRECTED BY Lewis Gilbert
SCREENPLAY BY Roald Dahl
ADDITIONAL STORY MATERIAL
Harold Jack Bloom
DIRECTOR OF PHOTOGRAPHY
Freddie Young, BSC
SUPERVISING EDITOR & 2ND UNIT
DIRECTOR Peter Hunt
PRODUCTION DESIGNED BY Ken Adam
ART DIRECTOR Harry Pottle
PRODUCTION SUPERVISOR
David Middlemas
SPECIAL EFFECTS John Stears
ACTION SEQUENCES BY Bob Simmons
MAIN TITLE DESIGNED BY
Maurice Binder
MUSIC COMPOSED, CONDUCTED AND
ARRANGED BY John Barry
TITLE SONG LYRICS BY Leslie Bricusse
TITLE SONG SUNG BY Nancy Sinatra
TECHNICAL ADVISOR Kikumaru Okuda
2ND UNIT CAMERAMAN Bob Huke
AERIAL UNIT CAMERAMAN
John Jordan
UNDERWATER CAMERAMAN
Lamar Boren
ASSISTANT DIRECTOR
William P. Cartlidge
LOCATION MANAGER Robert Watts
CAMERA OPERATOR Ernie Day
CONTINUITY Angela Martelli
MAKEUP Basil Newall & Paul Rabiger
DUBBING EDITORS
Norman Wanstall & Harry Miller
SOUND RECORDISTS
John Mitchell & Gordon McCallum
ASSEMBLY EDITOR Robert Richardson
WARDROBE MISTRESS Eileen Sullivan
HAIRDRESSER Eileen Warwick
SET DECORATOR David Ffolkes

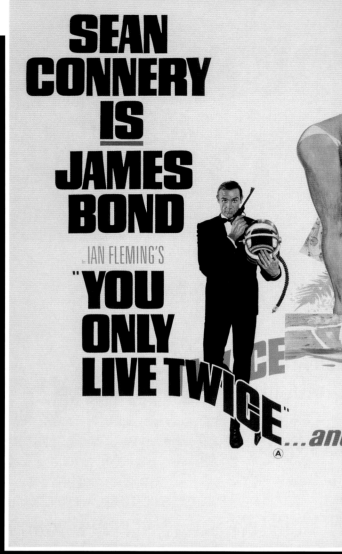

You Only Live Twice became the Bond movie where the filmmakers first turned away from Ian Fleming's original plot. In its place, they created the most fantasy-laden Bond adventure of the 1960s, an epic film that reflected the immense global success of 007.

Producers Albert R. "Cubby" Broccoli and Harry Saltzman wanted *You Only Live Twice* to surpass the expectations of an audience flush with a glut of Bond competitors in movie theaters and on television. Initially, Broccoli and Saltzman hired television writer Harold Jack Bloom to adapt Fleming's novel. They then invited famed short-story writer Roald Dahl, who had been friends with Fleming and shared story ideas with him over the years, to write the final script. By 1966, the development of the Bond films had become a group effort. Ideas for gadgets, scenes, and stunts in *You Only Live Twice* came from all quarters. Dahl's job was to link these ideas into a coherent storyline.

To direct the film, Broccoli called Lewis Gilbert, who had recently won many accolades for *Alfie* (1966). Gilbert's expertise with epic films such as *Damn The Defiant!* (1962) and *The 7th Dawn* (1964) proved he could handle a production the size of a Bond adventure.

The filmmakers hired English-speaking Japanese actor Tetsuro Tamba to play Tiger Tanaka. German actress Karin Dor took the role of the leading villainess, Helga Brandt. Two leading Japanese actresses, Akiko Wakabayashi and Mie Hama, signed to play Kissy and Suki, respectively. Yet language difficulties prompted the filmmakers to switch their roles, and Akiko suggested that her character be renamed Aki. For the important role of Blofeld, the filmmakers initially cast Czech actor Jan Werich, but shortly after filming began, Gilbert suggested replacing him with a more sinister-looking figure, and Donald Pleasence, famed from *The Great Escape* (1963), took over the part. Pleasence wore a disfiguring scar on his face, with grafted skin stretched partially over one eye to complete the eerie look.

Production designer Ken Adam played a key role in the film's development, traveling to Japan with Broccoli, Saltzman, and Gilbert for location scouting. In Tokyo, they ran into former Bond editor Peter Hunt. Seizing the moment, Broccoli talked Hunt into returning as a second unit director.

The filmmakers searched Japan for a coastal castle similar to the one in Fleming's novel. A guide informed them that there are no castles by the sea in Japan. The filmmakers then began a search for a suitable location to serve as Blofeld's lair. While Harry Saltzman thought they should film in a series of vaults in a Japanese salt mine, Broccoli came up with a different idea.

While location scouting in a helicopter, the filmmakers spotted a string of volcanoes. Broccoli suggested that the

villain could be hiding a rocket base inside one of them. Ken Adam soon drew up plans for the largest enclosed set ever built, Blofeld's volcano rocket base, which would tower 120 ft (37 m) over Pinewood Studios in England. The set cost a million dollars, required more structural steel than the London Hilton, housed a working monorail and had a retractable roof large enough to allow a helicopter to fly in and out.

While building the volcano set, the filmmakers shot in Japan during the sweltering heat of the summer of 1966, beset by Japanese paparazzi. The press hounded Sean Connery, even on location at a remote fishing village.

Peter Hunt faced more significant problems directing the dogfight between the autogyro Little Nellie and four SPECTRE helicopters. Despite expert flying by Commander Ken Wallis and a group of Japanese helicopter pilots, the crew experienced a tragic accident when cameraman John Jordan lost his leg as two helicopters collided in mid-air. Aerial shooting in Japan ceased, and Hunt completed the scene in the Torremolinos Mountains in Spain months later.

Location work for the film included more than Spain. Off

WICE" is the only way to live!

Y SALTZMAN and ALBERT R. BROCCOLI · Directed by LEWIS GILBERT · Screenplay by ROALD DAHL

SALTZMAN and ALBERT R. BROCCOLI · Music by JOHN BARRY · Production designed by KEN ADAM · **PANAVISION**

N:COLOR · Released through **UNITED ARTISTS**

of Gibraltar, a unit filmed Bond's funeral. An underwater unit shot Bond's recovery at sea by Royal Navy divers. A Unit travelled north of the Arctic Circle to shoot one shot of a radar dome doubling as an emergency summit location for Soviet, US and British diplomats. In Bermuda, yet another unit shot a navy plane dropping life rafts and Bond and Kissy being rescued by M's submarine. An entire effects unit worked at Pinewood Studios to create realistic space flight footage. The battle in Blofeld's volcano proved another major challenge. First, the Academy Award-winning cinematographer Freddie Young had to light an area spanning more than 450 ft (137 m) for the wide shots. He needed virtually every light at Pinewood Studios to do it. The script called for invading Japanese ninjas to abseil down ropes from the top of the set, a 12-story drop. Future Bond second unit director Vic Armstrong, using a piece of rubber tubing around the rope to slow his descent, became the first to make the drop.

After completing second unit work, Hunt was asked by Broccoli and Saltzman to take over primary editing duties from Thelma Connell. Hunt cut approximately 15 minutes, tightening the film to a running length of under two hours.

John Barry returned to score the film, penning a haunting title song performed by Nancy Sinatra with lyrics by Leslie Bricusse. The score incorporated Japanese elements along with beautiful guitar and brass orchestrations. The title song became a minor hit for Sinatra and became a theme for her comeback tour in the 1990s. The film opened only weeks after Charles K. Feldman's *Casino Royale* Bond spoof, but it was *You Only Live Twice* that triumphed at the box office. The film represented the culmination of a period of remarkable productivity for Broccoli and Saltzman. In just over four and a half years, the producers had premiered five 007 adventures, creating a phenomenon unequalled in film history. While the pace of making Bond films would shift to accommodate ever more complex movies, the dedication to exceeding audience expectations would continue.

ON LOCATION *(facing page, from top) Kobe, Japan: Lewis Gilbert, Sean Connery, William P. Cartlidge and crew await the next shot; Tetsuro Tamba (Tiger Tanaka) and Mie Hama (Kissy) share a joke; Mie Hama has her hair reset after a plunge in the water.*

ON SET *(this page, clockwise from above left) Production Designer Ken Adam thoughtfully surveys the scene as his spectacular hollowed-out volcano set is constructed; the sheer scale of the volcano set stunned visitors; Sean Connery jokes between takes with his co-star Karin Dor (femme fatale Helga Brandt).*

KEN ADAM

Born in Berlin in 1921, Ken Adam (real name Klaus Adam) left Germany with his family in 1934. After training as an architect at London University, he joined the RAF and took part in the Battle of Normandy. In 1946, Adam landed a job as a junior draftsman at Riverside Studios. Over the next decade, he became known as one of Europe's best film designers, earning his first Academy Award nomination for *Around The World In 80 Days* (1956).

In 1960, the producer Albert R. Broccoli hired Adam as production designer for *The Trials Of Oscar Wilde* (1960). Incidentally, Adam had already met Harry Saltzman, soon to be Broccoli's partner, while working in Italy. When Saltzman and Broccoli produced *Dr. No* (1962), they asked Adam to join the team. Adam set out to design imaginative sets using the very latest techniques and materials, setting the tone for the whole James Bond series.

Adam was unable to work on the second 007 film owing to a commitment to Stanley Kubrick's *Dr. Strangelove* (1964), but he returned for the next three, surpassing himself each time. Blofeld's hideout inside a volcano in 1967's *You Only Live Twice* resulted in a massive $1 million set on the Pinewood backlot. Greatly in demand, Adam only contributed to one of the next four Bond films, 1971's *Diamonds Are Forever*. After winning an Academy Award for his work on Kubrick's *Barry Lyndon* (1975), he returned for two more 007 assignments. His supertanker set for *The Spy Who Loved Me* (1977) required a space so huge that a special stage had to be constructed to house it. The resulting structure was christened the 007 Stage. Adam's designs for *The Spy Who Loved Me* earned him his third Academy Award nomination.

Adam continued to work on a variety of films in the 1980s and 1990s. He was nominated for an Oscar for 1993's *Addams Family Values*, and scored his second win with *The Madness Of King George* (1994). In 2003, he was knighted by Queen Elizabeth II.

ON HER MAJESTY'S SECRET SERVICE (1969)

CAST George Lazenby (James Bond), Diana Rigg (Tracy Di Vicenzo), Telly Savalas (Blofeld), Gabriele Ferzetti (Draco), Ilse Steppat (Irma Bunt), Lois Maxwell (Miss Moneypenny), George Baker (Sir Hilary Bray), Bernard Lee (M), Bernard Horsfall (Campbell), Desmond Llewelyn (Q), Yuri Borienko (Grunther), Virginia North (Olympe), Geoffrey Cheshire (Toussaint), Irvin Allen (Che Che), Terry Mountain (Raphael), James Bree (Gumbold), John Gay (Hammond), Angela Scoular (Ruby Bartlett), Catherina von Schell (Nancy), Brian Worth (Manuel), Julie Ege (Scandinavian Girl), Mona Chong (Chinese Girl), Sylvana Henriques (Jamaican Girl), Dani Sheridan (American Girl), Joanna Lumley (English Girl), Zara (Indian Girl), Anoushka Hempel (Australian Girl), Ingrit Back (German Girl), Helena Ronee (Israeli Girl), Jenny Hanley (Irish Girl)
PRODUCED BY
Harry Saltzman & Albert R. Broccoli
DIRECTED BY Peter Hunt
ASSOCIATE PRODUCER Stanley Sopel
SCREENPLAY BY Richard Maibaum
ADDITIONAL DIALOGUE Simon Raven
DIRECTOR OF PHOTOGRAPHY
Michael Reed, BSC
PRODUCTION DESIGNED BY Syd Cain
MUSIC COMPOSED, CONDUCTED & ARRANGED BY John Barry
SONG "WE HAVE ALL THE TIME IN THE WORLD" SUNG BY Louis Armstrong
SONG "DO YOU KNOW HOW CHRISTMAS TREES ARE GROWN?" SUNG BY Nina
LYRICS BY Hal David
EDITOR & 2ND UNIT DIRECTOR John Glen
SPECIAL EFFECTS John Stears
ASSISTANT DIRECTOR Frank Ernst
CONTINUITY Joan Davis
PRODUCTION SUPERVISOR
David Middlemas
CAMERA OPERATOR Alec Mills
STUNT ARRANGER George Leech
2ND UNIT CAMERAMEN
Egil Woxholt & Roy Ford
AERIAL CAMERAMAN John Jordan
SKI CAMERAMEN
Willy Bogner Jr & Alex Barbey
MAIN TITLE DESIGNED BY Maurice Binder
DUBBING EDITORS
Nicholas Stevenson & Harry Miller
SOUND RECORDISTS
John Mitchell & Gordon McCallum
ART DIRECTOR Bob Laing
WARDROBE DESIGNER Marjory Cornelius
SET DECORATOR Peter Lamont
HAIRDRESSER Eileen Warwick
MAKEUP Paul Rabiger & Basil Newall
WARDROBE SUPERVISOR Jackie Cummins
STOCK CAR SEQUENCE DIRECTOR
Anthony Squire

THE STARS *(above) Diana Rigg (Tracy Di Vicenzo) and George Lazenby (James Bond) pose atop the Schilthornbahn in Switzerland.*

On Her Majesty's Secret Service is one of Ian Fleming's most complex and action-packed James Bond novels; it would also become one of the knottiest Bond adventures to bring to the screen.

Originally, producers Albert R. "Cubby" Broccoli and Harry Saltzman hoped to make the film after *Goldfinger*, and in early 1964, screenwriter Richard Maibaum worked on a script treatment. An agreement with producer Kevin McClory to make *Thunderball* in 1965 changed Broccoli's and Saltzman's plans.

When filming on *Thunderball* wrapped, the producers turned their attention to *OHMSS*. The plot required a mountaintop lair in the Swiss Alps, but the producers could not find a suitably snowy location, so *OHMSS* was postponed once more.

Near the start of filming *You Only Live Twice* in 1966, Sean Connery announced his retirement from the role of Bond. After the film's release in June 1967, the producers again chose to tackle *OHMSS*.

THE PRODUCER *(below) Producer Harry Saltzman on the lot at Pinewood Studios.*

THE DESIGNER *(bottom) Production Designer Syd Cain examines a large-scale model of Piz Gloria. Cain designed the sets for* **From Russia With Love,** *and* **Live And Let Die.** *He also contributed designs to* **GoldenEye,** *particularly the GoldenEye key.*

Impressed by editor Peter Hunt's work on the previous five Bond films, the producers signed him to make his directorial debut with *OHMSS*. Broccoli and Saltzman believed that Hunt's quick cutting had helped set the style of the series. Hunt felt that, following the science fiction elements of *You Only Live Twice*, the Bond series needed to return 007 to his Ian Fleming roots. He asked Richard Maibaum to faithfully adapt Fleming's novel. His credo was, "We mustn't become imitators of our imitators." Hunt wanted to make a glossy film, but one that maintained the emotional rawness of Fleming's novel. He subsequently brought in British novelist and literary critic Simon Raven to sharpen and intellectualize the dialogue.

The filmmakers' first challenge was finding a new James Bond. One idea considered to account for the change of the lead actor was to have Bond undergo plastic surgery to fool his countless enemies, but this idea was dropped. Hunt and the producers narrowed the search to five actors, who were presented to the public in *Life* magazine: Hans De Vries, Anthony Rogers, Robert Campbell, John Richardson, and George Lazenby. After extensive screentesting, Lazenby won the role.

For the crucial role of Tracy, the woman who briefly becomes Mrs. Bond, the team selected Diana Rigg, an experienced actress who was as comfortable in action roles as playing Shakespeare. As the star of *The Avengers* television series, Rigg was also a worldwide name.

After Hunt declared he wanted a more powerfully built actor to play Ernst Stavro Blofeld, Broccoli's friend, American actor Telly Savalas, was cast. Saltzman had originally suggested the Italian actor Gabriele Ferzetti for the role of Blofeld, but Hunt and casting director Dyson Lovell convinced Saltzman that Ferzetti would be better suited to play Bond's ally, Marc Ange Draco. Completing

MAKING OHMSS *(below, left to right) Peter Hunt, on the set at Pinewood Studios, directs Lazenby and Rigg as they film Bond and Tracy's first night together; Telly Savalas (Blofeld) and producer Albert R. Broccoli socialize; Peter Hunt and Ilse Steppat (Irma Bunt) discuss the scene in Murren, Switzerland. Steppat never got to enjoy the success of the film. She passed away only four days after the release of OHMSS.*

the main casting, Hunt brought in German actress Ilse Steppat as Blofeld's evil accomplice, Irma Bunt.

Searching for the right location for Blofeld's hideout, Saltzman wondered if the tunnels at the Maginot Line could possibly be used. Then, above the tiny village of Murren, Switzerland, production designer Syd Cain and the Bond team learned that construction was nearly complete on a mountaintop restaurant that closely matched the location in Fleming's novel. The owners allowed the Bond crew to film in exchange for constructing a helipad and furnishing the restaurant.

Production began in October 1968, but the elaborate action sequences, bad weather, hard-to-access locations, and short daylight hours during winter contributed to *OHMSS* having the longest shooting schedule (nine months) and post-production schedule (over six months) of any Bond film to date. A foot chase over London rooftops and into the tunnels of the Royal Mail underground rail system was jettisoned altogether to save time.

Although the film itself contained remarkable action, the studio worried about the ending. Audiences expected to see 007 triumphant in the arms of a woman, not shattered, cradling a corpse. Hunt suggested ending the film with Bond's and Tracy's wedding and opening the next Bond film with Tracy's death. When Lazenby announced that he would not be returning as James Bond, the filmmakers decided the movie's finale would followed Fleming's novel.

John Barry's score was a triumph, perfectly reflecting the film's more serious tone. Barry used the newly invented Moog synthesizer to give a modern edge to the breathtaking action sequences. He composed an instrumental march for the title theme, since *On Her Majesty's Secret Service* didn't seem suited to a contemporary song. Barry suggested Louis Armstrong for the romantic ballad "We Have All The Time In The World," which serves as the theme for Bond and Tracy's relationship. Barry and lyricist Hal David also wrote a cheerful Christmas song, "Do You Know How Christmas Trees Are Grown?" performed by Danish singer Nina Van Pallandt (of the singing duo Nina & Frederik), which is part of the diegetic sound as Bond runs for his life in the village of Murren.

A month after the film's December 1969 opening, United Artists, Broccoli and Saltzman were all in agreement. While *OHMSS* had made money, the entire film had been a major risk which nobody wished to attempt again. The next film would need to adhere to the tried-and-true 007 formula. But the passing of time does something to movies, and time has been very good to *On Her Majesty's Secret Service*. Because of its memorable action and gripping emotional moments, many Bond aficionados and critics view the film as one of the best James Bond films ever made.

PETER HUNT

Born in 1928, Peter Hunt grew up in London's East End and spent school holidays at a documentary film company run by an uncle. He helped with the production of instructional films until 1942, when he joined the army and was sent to Italy. After the war, he worked in the cutting rooms of feature films, rising to the position of assembly editor of *The Man Who Watched The Trains Go By* (1952). He worked on *The Tall Headlines* (1952), directed by Terence Young, and became an editor with 1956's *A Hill In Korea*.

Hunt came to edit *Dr. No* (1962) through the recommendation of director Terence Young, giving the film a dynamic feel that suited 007. Hunt changed the way action films were edited by introducing a now widely imitated style called "crash cutting." Hallmarks of Hunt's editing style include jump cuts in a fight sequence; an abundance of insert shots to add suspense; the acceleration of certain shots for dramatic effect; a refusal to stop the film by fading in and fading out of a scene; and a dislike of close-ups, except when crucial to the story.

After editing and performing second unit director duties on *From Russia With Love* (1963), *Goldfinger* (1964), *Thunderball* (1965), and *You Only Live Twice* (1967), Hunt was announced as director of *On Her Majesty's Secret Service* in September 1967. Hunt gave the film a personal style and ensured the movie remained true to Fleming's novel.

In 1971, Hunt directed episodes of TV series *The Persuaders*, starring Roger Moore; and later directed Moore in *Gold* (1974) and *Shout at the Devil* (1976). His directing career in the 1980s included *Death Hunt* (1981), the miniseries *The Last Days Of Pompeii* (1984), and 1987's *Assassination*. In 1990, Michael Cimino hired Hunt to supervise editing of *Desperate Hours*. Afterward, Hunt retired to California, where he died in 2002.

DIAMONDS ARE FOREVER
(1971)

CAST Sean Connery (James Bond), Jill St. John (Tiffany Case), Charles Gray (Blofeld), Lana Wood (Plenty O'Toole), Jimmy Dean (Willard Whyte), Bruce Cabot (Bert Saxby), Putter Smith (Mr. Kidd), Bruce Glover (Mr. Wint), Norman Burton (Leiter), Joseph Furst (Dr. Metz), Bernard Lee (M), Desmond Llewelyn (Q), Leonard Barr (Shady Tree), Lois Maxwell (Moneypenny), Margaret Lacey
(Mrs. Whistler), Joe Robinson (Peter Franks), David de Keyser (Doctor), Laurence Naismith (Sir Donald Munger), David Bauer (Mr. Slumber), Donna Garrett (Bambi), Trina Parks (Thumper), Henry Rowland (Dr. Tynan), Edward Bishop (Klaus Hergersheimer), Leroy Hollis (Nevada sheriff), Denise Perrier (Marie)
PRODUCED BY
Harry Saltzman & Albert R. Broccoli
DIRECTED BY Guy Hamilton
SCREENPLAY
Richard Maibaum & Tom Mankiewicz
ASSOCIATE PRODUCER Stanley Sopel
MUSIC COMPOSED, CONDUCTED & ARRANGED BY John Barry
LYRICS BY Don Black
TITLE SONG SUNG BY Shirley Bassey
DIRECTOR OF PHOTOGRAPHY
Ted Moore, BSC
PRODUCTION DESIGNED BY Ken Adam
EDITORS Bert Bates & John W. Holmes, ACE
PRODUCTION MANAGERS
Claude Hudson & Milton Feldman
MAIN TITLE DESIGNED BY Maurice Binder
DUBBING EDITORS Teddy Mason, Jimmy Shields & Christopher Lancaster
DUBBING MIXER Gordon McCallum
SOUND RECORDISTS
John Mitchell & Alfred J. Overton
SPECIAL EFFECTS
Leslie Hillman & Whitney McMahon
WARDROBE SUPERVISORS
Elsa Fennell & Ted Tetrick
VISUAL EFFECTS
Albert Whitlock & Wally Veevers
STUNT ARRANGERS
Bob Simmons & Paul Baxley
LOCATION MANAGERS
Bernard Hanson & Eddie Saeta
MISS ST. JOHN'S COSTUMES BY
Don Feld
2ND UNIT CAMERAMAN
Harold Wellman
ART DIRECTORS Jack Maxsted & Bill Kenney
SET DECORATORS Peter Lamont & John Austin
PRODUCTION BUYER Ronnie Quelch
ASSISTANT DIRECTORS
Derek Cracknell & Jerome M. Siegel
CONTINUITY Elaine Schreyeck & Del Ross
CAMERA OPERATORS
Bob Kindred & Bill Johnson

SCENES FROM THE PRODUCTION
(clockwise from top) Sean Connery (James Bond) and Jill St. John (Tiffany Case) follow the direction of Guy Hamilton on stage at Pinewood Studios; Sean Connery jokes with Jill St. John as producer Harry Saltzman and his son Steven look on; on location in San Pedro, California, for the sailing of the Whyte Line's cruise ship; Connery and St. John relax for a moment while shooting Bond and Tiffany's tense first meeting in Amsterdam.

Diamonds Are Forever became the first "make or break" 007 film with the fate of the series resting on its ability to reach an audience. The film's worldwide success lay not just with the decision to bring back director Guy Hamilton and star Sean Connery, but also with the skill of the filmmakers to adapt Bond to a changing audience and changing times.

In January 1970, producer Albert R. "Cubby" Broccoli met with United Artists to discuss the future of Bond. The studio and the producers felt that while *On Her Majesty's Secret Service* had been a good film, they needed to deliver the kind of entertainment *Goldfinger* provided, and they needed to do it for a reasonable budget.

First, United Artists wanted assurance that it was the old James Bond that the public wanted to see. They re-released *Thunderball* and *You Only Live Twice* as a major double-bill barely six months after *OHMSS*'s opening. Audiences packed theaters and cheered. The message was clear—cinemagoers wanted the return of the classic Bond.

Working with screenwriter Richard Maibaum, the filmmakers fashioned a first-draft script that involved Auric Goldfinger's twin brother and a boat chase set on Lake Mead. After searching for a new Bond, they selected John Gavin, an American actor who would become US Ambassador to Mexico during the 1980s. With no fanfare, they signed him to a contract, although the producers knew that United Artists President of Production David Picker hoped to cast a different actor as 007: Sean Connery.

Connery returned with the reluctant blessing of Broccoli and Saltzman for a world record salary, ten percent of the gross, and the right to green light two United Artists films of modest budgets.

Picker suggested hiring American writer Tom Mankiewicz, a writer he felt could bring wit and pace to the script while still capturing the essentially British tone of

Bond. After the first draft, all agreed to bring back Bond's nemesis, Ernst Stavro Blofeld, whose story it was felt had been left unresolved. To direct, the producers chose Guy Hamilton, who vowed to bring back the "*Goldfinger* touch" to the series. Mankiewicz's final script, developed with input from the producers and Hamilton, featured a return to intriguingly sinister henchmen—Wint and Kidd—a grand plot, and most of all, humor.

The filmmakers originally thought of shooting *Diamonds*, which was largely set in the US, in Hollywood. Pre-production work began at Universal Studios, but later the production moved back to Pinewood.

Shooting began on April 5, 1971 with the desert outside of Las Vegas doubling for South Africa. Cooperation from the billionaire Howard Hughes (whose reclusive behavior and use of doubles inspired the storyline) helped pave the way for an amazing car chase through downtown Las Vegas. The scene in which 007 turns a Ford Mustang on two wheels had to be shot three times: once at Universal Studios and then twice more with different stunt drivers in Las Vegas in order to properly capture the shot of the car emerging from the alley. The drivers performed the stunt on different sides of the car, resulting in much consternation on the part of the filmmakers. Most audience members never noticed.

The filmmakers staged the movie's climax at an oil rig off the coast of Oceanside, California. An assistant director miscued the explosions but, thankfully, one lone aerial cameraman captured nearly all the fireworks, saving the scene from a total re-shoot.

The biggest challenge occurred as the filmmakers moved back to Pinewood Studios, as every shot with Connery had to be completed in 18 weeks. On August 13, 1971, director Hamilton called cut on Connery's last shot. Everyone shook hands, and Connery left the role of 007 until his non-EON

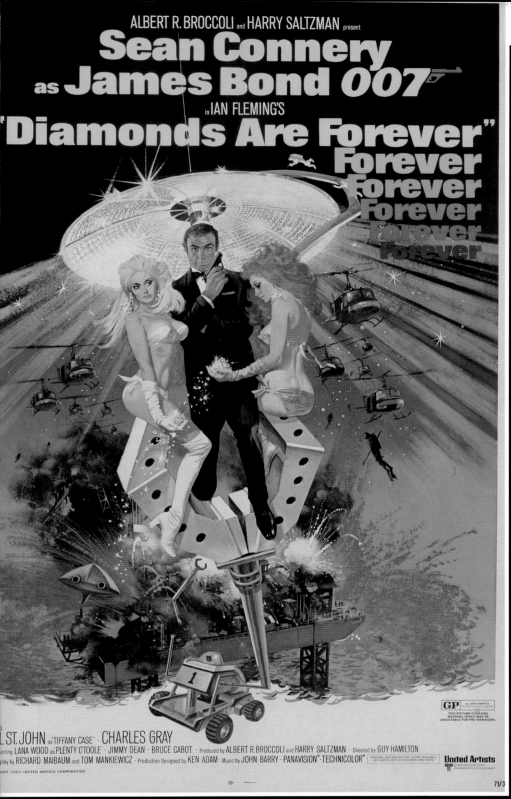

ALBERT R. BROCCOLI and HARRY SALTZMAN present

Sean Connery as James Bond 007

in IAN FLEMING'S

"Diamonds Are Forever"
Forever
Forever
Forever

L ST.JOHN as TIFFANY CASE · CHARLES GRAY
arring LANA WOOD as PLENTY O'TOOLE' · JIMMY DEAN · BRUCE CABOT · Produced by ALBERT R.BROCCOLI and HARRY SALTZMAN · Directed by GUY HAMILTON
play by RICHARD MAIBAUM and TOM MANKIEWICZ · Production Designed by KEN ADAM · Music by JOHN BARRY · PANAVISION® TECHNICOLOR · ORIGINAL MOTION PICTURE SCORE AVAILABLE ON UNITED ARTISTS RECORDS AND TAPES

GP

THIS PICTURE CONTAINS
MATERIAL WHICH MAY BE
UNSUITABLE FOR PRE-TEENAGERS

United Artists
International Inc.
Transamerica Corporation

GHT ©1971 UNITED ARTISTS CORPORATION

71/3

PERSIANS AND PRODUCERS (below, top to bottom) The cat trainer shows the many doubles for Blofeld's white Persian cat on set. The name of his company? "Pussies Galore"; on the Moon set, producers Harry Saltzman and Albert R. Broccoli and director Guy Hamilton discuss the gravity of the situation.

appearance in *Never Say Never Again* 12 years later.

John Barry returned to score the music, bringing back Shirley Bassey to lend her seductive vocals to the title song. The score managed to capture in sound the glitter of diamonds sparkling in the light, adding a glamorous allure to Guy Hamilton's often humorous visuals.

The blend proved a perfect recipe for Bond's first film of the 1970s. Audiences flocked to cinemas, and the film sold 11 million more tickets in the US than its predecessor. The Oscars recognized *Diamonds Are Forever*'s brilliant use of sound, earning the film a nomination for Best Sound for Bond veterans Gordon K. McCallum, John Mitchell, and Alfred J. Overton.

James Bond had returned, but, with the role of 007 again up for grabs, further challenges lay ahead.

GUY HAMILTON

The son of a British diplomat, Guy Hamilton was born in Paris in 1922 and spent his early childhood in France. At 16, he got his first film job as clapper boy for director Julien Duvivier. At the beginning of World War II, he was evacuated aboard a coal ship and found himself sleeping on coal piles near another refugee, Somerset Maugham. Arriving in London, he worked in the film library at Paramount News before joining the Royal Navy. After the war, he became an assistant director, working with such distinguished filmmakers as Carol Reed and John Huston. Reed helped Hamilton get his first directing job with 1952's *The Ringer*. While *The Intruder* (1953) and *The Colditz Story* (1955) showed that Hamilton was very adept with mostly male casts, he also branched out with a musical comedy, *Charley Moon* (1956), and the melodrama *Manuela* (1957).

By the end of the decade, he had proven himself a skilled director of big-budget films with spectacular action set-pieces, like *The Devil's Disciple* (1959) and *The Best of Enemies* (1962). He turned down an offer to direct *Dr. No* to make *The Party's Over*, a film about swinging London that wasn't released until 1965 due to censor issues. When Hamilton finally directed a Bond film, 1964's *Goldfinger*, he played up the humor and gadgetry, made Bond the most knowledgeable man alive, and set the template for the Bond films that followed. Hamilton directed two more films for Harry Saltzman, *Funeral In Berlin* (1966) and *The Battle Of Britain* (1969) before returning to the Bond series with *Diamonds Are Forever* (1971), *Live And Let Die* (1973), and *The Man With The Golden Gun* (1974), overseeing the transition from Sean Connery to Roger Moore.

After Bond, Hamilton directed the World War II action film *Force 10 From Navarone* (1978), the Agatha Christie mysteries *The Mirror Crack'd* (1980) and *Evil Under The Sun* (1981), and two 007-style adventures, *Remo Williams: The Adventure Begins* (1985) and *Try This One For Size* (1989), before retiring to the island of Mallorca.

LIVE AND LET DIE (1973)

CAST Roger Moore (James Bond), Yaphet Kotto
(Dr. Kananga/Mr. Big), Jane Seymour (Solitaire),
Clifton James (Sheriff J. W. Pepper),
Julius W. Harris (Tee Hee), Geoffrey Holder
(Baron Samedi), David Hedison (Felix Leiter),
Gloria Hendry (Rosie Carver), Bernard Lee (M),
Lois Maxwell (Moneypenny), Tommy Lane
(Adam), Earl Jolly Brown (Whisper), Roy Stewart
(Quarrel Jr.), Lon Satton (Strutter), Arnold Williams
(Kananga's cab driver), Ruth Kempf (Mrs. Bell),
Joie Chitwood (Charlie), Madeline Smith (Miss
Caruso), Michael Ebbin (Dambala), Kubi Chaza
(Sales girl), Dennis Edwards (Baines), James Drake
(Dawes), Robert Dix (Hamilton), Dan Jackson (Fillet
of Soul waiter), B. J. Arnau (Fillet of Soul singer)
PRODUCED BY
Harry Saltzman & Albert R. Broccoli
DIRECTED BY Guy Hamilton
SCREENPLAY BY Tom Mankiewicz
MUSIC BY George Martin
TITLE SONG COMPOSED BY
Paul & Linda McCartney
TITLE SONG PERFORMED BY
Paul McCartney and Wings
DIRECTOR OF PHOTOGRAPHY
Ted Moore, BSC
PRODUCTION SUPERVISOR Claude Hudson
SPECIAL EFFECTS Derek Meddings
EDITORS Bert Bates, Raymond Poulton, GBFE &
John Shirley
SOUND RECORDISTS
John Mitchell & Ken Barker
ASSISTANT DIRECTOR Derek Cracknell
LOCATION MANAGER Bernard Hanson
CHOREOGRAPHER Geoffrey Holder
COSTUME DESIGNER Julie Harris
MAIN TITLE DESIGNER Maurice Binder
CASTING DIRECTOR Weston Drury Jr.
STUNTS Bob Simmons, Joie Chitwood,
Ross Kananga, Jerry Comeaux, Eddie Smith,
Bill Bennet
DUBBING EDITORS Teddy Mason,
Jimmy Shields, Chris Lancaster
SUPERVISING ART DIRECTOR Syd Cain
CO-ART DIRECTORS
Bob Laing, Peter Lamont
OPTICAL EFFECTS Charles Staffell
CONTINUITY Elaine Schreyeck
CAMERA OPERATOR Bob Kindred
SECOND UNIT CAMERAMAN John Harris
WARDROBE SUPERVISOR Laurel Staffell
MAKEUP SUPERVISOR Paul Rabiger
HAIRDRESSER Colin Jamison
CONSTRUCTION MANAGER Leon Davis
PROPS Patrick Weymouth
USA Crew
PRODUCTION MANAGERS
Stephen F. Kesten, Steven P. Skloot
ASSISTANT DIRECTOR Alan Hopkins
UNIT MANAGER Michael Rauch
LOCATION CO-ORDINATOR Jack Weis
ART DIRECTOR Stephen Hendrickson
CAMERA OPERATORS
George Bouillet & Warren Rothenberger
SHARK SCENES BY William Grefe

The success of *Live And Let Die* proved that the character of James Bond was a bigger star than the actor playing the role. With Sean Connery gone, producers Albert R. "Cubby" Broccoli and Harry Saltzman, working closely with United Artists President David Picker, began searching for a new 007. Although Broccoli and Saltzman considered many actors over the years, they always returned to the idea of bringing Roger Moore in to play 007. As Simon Templar in *The Saint* television series, Moore played a James Bond type: debonair, adventurous, unflappable. His success had made him a household name, and his reputation for professionalism was second to none. The studio approved the casting and also the producers' decision to bring back Guy Hamilton as director and Tom Mankiewicz as screenwriter.

Faced with the challenge of introducing a new actor as 007, Guy Hamilton suggested that Moore be careful not to in any way imitate Connery's Bond. "The fatal thing would be for Roger to step into Sean's shoes," Hamilton told TIME magazine. "He must have his own way." By stripping away the vestiges of the past, the filmmakers offered a Bond who felt fresh and new.

The early 1970s saw a vogue for blaxploitation films, and the filmmakers decided to place Bond in the modern world of African-American cinematic culture. The production team toured the Caribbean and plot elements soon fell into place—voodoo ceremonies in Haiti, talk of drug smuggling riches, a large crocodile farm in Jamaica whose gate bore a sign, "Trespassers will be eaten." Impressed with the crocodile farm's owner, Ross Kananga, the filmmakers set a major sequence on his property, hired him to perform a major stunt, and named the lead villain after him. Hamilton's fondness for jazz led to the suggestion of sending Bond to New Orleans, which dovetailed nicely with the film's voodoo subplot.

The filmmakers cast up-and-coming actor Yaphet Kotto in the dual role of Dr. Kananga/Mr. Big. Harry Saltzman cast

Jane Seymour as Solitaire. Seymour's career in movies and television after *Live And Let Die* would distinguish her as one of the most successful Bond actresses of her generation. Legendary choreographer Geoffrey Holder agreed to play Baron Samedi, a role he originated in Truman Capote's 1954 musical *House of Flowers*. He also staged the distinctive San Monique dance sequences in the film. Holder suggested the idea of closing the film on his character, the man who cannot die, riding on the front of Bond and Solitaire's train.

Filming began on Friday, October 13, 1972 in the Irish Bayou in Louisiana, shooting the boat chase between Bond and Mr. Big's men, the most complex and original ever conceived. The scene required 26 speedboats to leap over roadways and skid across lawns. Stuntman Jerry Comeaux set a world record leaping a Glastron GT-150 110 ft (33.5 m) over a road. Stunts destroyed 17 speedboats before the completion of filming.

The production filmed in Jamaica in late 1972, using some of the same locations seen in *Dr. No* a decade earlier. They also filmed at a set of banana boat docks adjacent to the late Ian Fleming's estate, Goldeneye, where the author wrote the novel *Live And Let Die*.

The emerald tree boa, used in the voodoo ceremonies, proved dangerous. While not poisonous, the snake sports very real fangs. After it bit Dambala actor Michael Ebbin, Dennis Edwards, playing Baines, was briefly overcome with nerves as Ebbin waved the snake in his face. The most serious case of jangled nerves, however, belonged to Ross Kananga, who dashed across the backs of three of his crocodiles five times while doubling 007. After the first take, the crocodiles began to anticipate Kananga's movements, snapping at him and nearly taking off his foot.

Bond composer John Barry could not schedule sufficient time to score *Live And Let Die*, so the producers sought out

ALBERT R. BROCCOLI and HARRY SALTZMAN present

ROGER JAMES
MOORE as BOND

7

in IAN FLEMING'S
"LIVE AND LET DIE"

...OTTO · JANE SEYMOUR · Produced by ALBERT R. BROCCOLI and HARRY SALTZMAN · Directed by GUY HAMILTON
...M MANKIEWICZ · Title Song Composed by PAUL and LINDA McCARTNEY and Performed by PAUL McCARTNEY and WINGS
...EORGE MARTIN   Original Motion Picture Soundtrack Available on United Artists Records and Tapes   **PG** PARENTAL GUIDANCE SUGGESTED   **United Artists** Entertainment from Transamerica Corporation

WEST HEMI.   73/35

"LIVE AND LET DIE"

ARMED AND DANGEROUS *(facing page, top to bottom) Roger Moore (James Bond), Tommy Lane (Adam), Jane Seymour (Solitaire), Arnold Williams (Cab Driver), and Yaphet Kotto (Dr. Kananga / Mr. Big) on location at Lakeside Airport in New Orleans; Roger Moore, the new 007, greets a bus full of young fans.*

Barry's friend, the producer for The Beatles, George Martin. Martin worked with Paul and Linda McCartney and their band Wings to construct a brilliant title song that became the biggest Bond hit yet (#2 in the US; #7 in the UK). The song earned Paul and Linda McCartney an Academy Award nomination, and the score's richly produced sound helped create a new generation of Bond music fans.

Live And Let Die swept into theaters in the summer of 1973, becoming a solid success in the US and performing far better than the two previous Bond films overseas. It launched Roger Moore as a natural successor to Sean Connery and provided Bond fans with a new 007 for the next 12 years.

LOCATION, LOCATION, LOCATION *(right, top to bottom): Robert Dix (Hamilton) awaits his fate in the French Quarter; the filmmakers shoot a key stunt on Jamaica's North Shore; producer Harry Saltzman and actress Jane Seymour on location in Louisiana.*

TED MOORE

Ted Moore is remembered as one of the great widescreen cinematographers, equally adept at location and studio cinematography. His lavish color photography and clear compositions made him the perfect choice to realize James Bond's cinematic adventures. Moore's style set the photographic look of the Bond films, eschewing gritty realism for an elegance that mirrored the élan of Ian Fleming's writing.

Born in Cape Province, South Africa on August 7, 1914, Moore emigrated to England in 1930 with his family. Before the outbreak of World War II, Moore worked as a cameraman on films like *Sons Of The Sea* (1939) before joining the RAF. He flew combat missions during the war, earning a DFC from Britain and the Croix de Guerre from France. He worked with the RAF's Film Unit before deciding on a career in the movie industry after the war.

Moore's controlled work as a camera operator on difficult-location films such as *The African Queen* (1951) won him widespread praise within the industry. Working on early films produced by Albert R. Broccoli and his then partner Irving Allen, such as *Hell Below Zero* (1954) and *The Black Knight* (1954), Moore graduated to cinematographer the following year, lensing *A Prize Of Gold* (1955) and *Cockleshell Heroes* (1955). Moore's speed and ability to capture complex shots particularly impressed Terence Young, who would go on to direct three Bond films shot by Moore.

Moore photographed using wide-angle lenses, frequently employing deep-focus techniques and emphasizing bold colors. His clear images allowed Bond editor Peter Hunt to cut action scenes with great speed. With Moore's images, the viewer could always clearly see what was happening, even in the briefest of shots.

Ted Moore shot seven James Bond films, and won an Academy Award for 1966's *A Man For All Seasons*.

He died in 1987, at the age of 72.

THE MAN WITH THE GOLDEN GUN (1974)

MAKING GOLDEN GUN (clockwise from right) Director Guy Hamilton lines up a shot with Christopher Lee (Scaramanga) on the set of Hai Fat's office; Roger Moore (Bond), W. J. Milligan (the car stunt arranger), Albert R. Broccoli and Michael Redding (construction manager [location]) celebrate after the successful Astro Spiral jump; Maud Adams (Andrea Anders) listens to Christopher Lee (Scaramanga) discuss his golden gun; Guy Hamilton offers direction to Britt Ekland (Mary Goodnight) on location in Bangkok.

CAST Roger Moore (James Bond), Christopher Lee (Scaramanga), Britt Ekland (Mary Goodnight), Maud Adams (Andrea Anders),
Hervé Villechaize (Nick Nack), Clifton James (Sheriff J. W. Pepper), Richard Loo (Hai Fat), Soon-Taik Oh (Lt. Hip), Marc Lawrence (Rodney), Bernard Lee (M), Lois Maxwell (Moneypenny), Marne Maitland (Lazar), Desmond Llewelyn (Q), James Cossins (Colthorpe), Chan Yiu Lam (Chula), Carmen Sautoy (Saida), Gerald James (Frazier), Michael Osborne (Naval lieutenant), Michael Fleming (Communications officer), Michael Goodliffe (Tanner), Gordon Everett (Gibson), George Silver (Nightclub owner), Terry Plummer (Rahman), Rocky Taylor (Hammud), Sonny Caldinez (Kra), Françoise Therry (Chew Mee), Joie Pacharintraporn (Cha), Cheung Chuen Nam, aka Yuen Qiu (Nara)
PRODUCED BY Harry Saltzman & Albert R. Broccoli
DIRECTED BY Guy Hamilton
SCREENPLAY BY Richard Maibaum & Tom Mankiewicz
MUSIC COMPOSED, CONDUCTED & ARRANGED BY John Barry
LYRICS BY Don Black
TITLE SONG PERFORMED BY Lulu
ASSOCIATE PRODUCER Charles Orme
DIRECTORS OF PHOTOGRAPHY Ted Moore & Oswald Morris
PRODUCTION DESIGNER Peter Murton
PRODUCTION SUPERVISOR Claude Hudson
LOCATION MANAGER (THAILAND) Frank Ernst
LOCATION MANAGER (HONG KONG) Eric Rattray
MAIN TITLE DESIGNED BY Maurice Binder
EDITORS John Shirley, Raymond Poulton, GBFE
DUBBING EDITORS Jimmy Shields, Christopher Lancaster, Charles Crafford
DUBBING MIXER Ken Barker
SOUND RECORDIST Gordon Everett
ASSISTANT TO THE PRODUCERS Reginald Barkshire
PRODUCTION ACCOUNTANT Brian Bailey
PRODUCTION CO-ORDINATOR (BANGKOK) Santa Pestonji
CASTING DIRECTORS Maude Spector & Weston Drury Jnr.
WARDROBE SUPERVISOR Elsa Fennell
MAKEUP SUPERVISOR Paul Engelen
HAIRDRESSER Mike Jones
PROPS Patrick Weymouth
CO-ART DIRECTORS Peter Lamont, John Graysmark
SPECIAL EFFECTS John Stears
MINIATURES Derek Meddings
CONSTRUCTION MANAGER Leon Davis
ASSISTANT DIRECTOR Derek Cracknell
CAMERA OPERATOR Bob Kindred
CONTINUITY Elaine Schreyeck
2ND UNIT CAMERAMAN John Harris

Best remembered for its flamboyant villains and spectacular locations, *The Man With The Golden Gun* was the last Bond film made under the partnership of producers Albert R. Broccoli and Harry Saltzman. After the great success of *Live And Let Die*, Saltzman and Broccoli dove into pre-production on *The Man With The Golden Gun*, which had originally been conceived as the follow-up to *You Only Live Twice* in 1968, with production slated for Cambodia. When civil war broke out in 1967, *Golden Gun* was shelved for six years.

Broccoli and Saltzman brought back director Guy Hamilton, writer Tom Mankiewicz, and much of the production crew of *Live And Let Die*. Peter Murton, who had worked with Ken Adam during much of the 1960s, signed on as production designer. The team originally visited Iran to scout locations, but the outbreak of the Yom Kippur-Ramadan War in October 1973 convinced the filmmakers not to shoot in the Middle East. Yet that very war did create the OPEC oil embargo, which launched the mid-1970s energy crisis, two events that inspired the film's plot. Broccoli's stepson, future Bond producer Michael G. Wilson, an engineer by training, was engaged to clarify the solar energy elements in the story for Richard Maibaum, who was rewriting Tom Mankiewicz's first draft script.

Guy Hamilton hoped to set the film's climax in Ha Long Bay in Vietnam. Although a peace accord had ended US involvement in the Vietnam War in January 1973, shooting in North Vietnamese territory proved impossible. Production designer Peter Murton saw a poster on the London Underground of similar spires near Phuket, Thailand, and the filmmakers soon departed to scout the location. They were impressed and decided to return the story to Southeast Asia, setting it largely in Hong Kong, Macau, and Thailand. On the Hong Kong location recce, Broccoli came up with the idea of using the hulk of the *Queen Elizabeth* in the harbor as M's Far East base.

The filmmakers did not have to look far to cast Mary Goodnight. Even before the script was written, Britt Ekland discussed the role with Broccoli. Swedish model Maud Adams

was chosen for the role of Andrea Anders. Guy Hamilton declared he wanted a miniature Oddjob for the henchman, leading to the casting of Hervé Villechaize as Nick Nack. Mankiewicz, who returned to rewrite Maibaum's draft before shooting began, originally suggested Jack Palance for Scaramanga, but Guy Hamilton soon turned to Christopher Lee. He proved ideal for the role, having also been a cousin by marriage to Ian Fleming. To round out the cast, flush from the success of *Live And Let Die*, the producers decided to bring back Clifton James as Sheriff J. W. Pepper.

The cast assembled in Bangkok in mid-April, proceeding to the village of Phang Nga. The remote village offered only the most rugged accommodation for cast and crew. Shooting began on Khow-Ping-Kan island, the setting for the exteriors of Scaramanga's lair. In Bangkok, the filmmakers shot a complex chase with longtail boats speeding through the city's famed floating market. This scene proved easy compared to the car chase involving Bond and Scaramanga, which involved the most harrowing car stunt ever conceived. The producers licensed a stunt designed by Raymond McHenry on a computer, inspired by his work on simulations of single-vehicle accidents. Perfected through trial and error by W. J. Milligan, Jr. and his stunt show crew, the Astro Spiral Jump had awed audiences in shows across America. Milligan worked with Peter Murton to create precisely built ramps that could look like a collapsed wooden bridge. Stunt driver Loren "Bumps" Willard performed the leap perfectly in one take; he had never attempted the stunt before.

Riots in Bangkok forced the second unit to leave earlier than scheduled, but other large challenges faced the first unit when it returned to England to complete the studio work. Broccoli, while in Thailand, found veteran Bond cinematographer Ted Moore was unable to complete the film. Upon arriving in London, Broccoli convinced Academy-Award-winning cinematographer Oswald Morris to replace him, a difficult task as Moore had shot seven of the previous Bond films. Despite the use of large pyrotechnic explosions on

Khow-Ping Kan island, the filmmakers needed to create images of a solar array rising from a rock spire and the island itself disintegrating. Miniature effects supervisor Derek Meddings built amazingly accurate copies of the island at Pinewood Studios. His most challenging effect proved to be creating shots of the sun passing behind clouds.

John Barry had only three weeks to score the film.

To reflect Guy Hamilton's style, his score had some humorous touches, including a penny whistle heard during the Astro Spiral jump. To create the flavor of Southeast Asian music, Barry worked with a Southern European instrument, the cymbalom, which he had used extensively for his score of *The Ipcress File* (1965). Barry lined up Scottish singer Lulu to perform Don Black's lyrics for the title song.

Soon after completion of *The Man With The Golden Gun*, Harry Saltzman sold his share of the Bond franchise to United Artists, leaving Broccoli as sole producer. The film opened on December 19, 1974 but, for a combination of reasons, sold fewer tickets in the US than any previous Bond film. Although the film made a profit, some thought it portended the end of the Bond franchise. Broccoli had different ideas.

ON LOCATION (top to bottom) Guy Hamilton waits patiently as the crew lines up a shot on the klongs; Hamilton and Britt Ekland look over the script in Bangkok, Thailand during production.

JOHN STEARS

John Stears made the most outlandish concepts in the early Bond films a reality. He was the real Q, the man who devised the inner workings of gadgets, built 007's deadly toys and, when the time came, he was the man who blew them all up. His clever, convincing, and spectacular effects gave the Bond movies a grand sense of scale.

Born in Middlesex in 1934, John Stears developed an interest in pyrotechnics and ballistics while serving in the British Army. When he returned to civilian life, he landed a job making a model of a Bristol Bulldog biplane for the film *Reach For The Sky* (1956), the true story of airman Douglas Bader. He then went to work for the Rank Organization as a matte artist.

Stears began his association with James Bond when he built and destroyed a miniature of the bauxite wharf for *Dr. No* (1962). Impressed with his work, the producers asked him to become the special effects supervisor on the next 007 film. Stears blew up a miniature model of a SPECTRE helicopter and set the sea afire for *From Russia With Love* (1963), as well as packing an arsenal of weapons inside an Aston Martin for *Goldfinger* (1964). While working on *Thunderball* (1965), he managed to obtain a quantity of rocket fuel to boost the explosion of the *Disco Volante*. This film saw Stears take home an Academy Award for special effects. He provided more miniatures and explosions and attached missiles to the Little Nellie one-seater autogyro for *You Only Live Twice* (1967) and destroyed a model Piz Gloria for *On Her Majesty's Secret Service* (1969). Work on other films kept him absent from subsequent 007 films until *The Man With The Golden Gun* (1974), for which he provided a radio-controlled model of Scaramanga's flying car.

Stears won a second Academy Award in 1977 for his work on *Star Wars*. He remained busy throughout the 1980s, working on films such as *Outland* (1981), *The Bounty* (1984), and *F/X* (1986). Stears died of a stroke a year after the release of his last film *The Mask Of Zorro* (1998), directed by Martin Campbell.

THE WORLD'S GREATEST VILLAINS TRIED TO KILL JAMES BOND

DR. NO.
He couldn't kill Bond with a cyanide cigarette and the world's largest tarantula.

ROSA KLEB.
She couldn't kill Bond with an assassin trained from birth.

GOLDFINGER AND ODD JOB.
They couldn't split Bond in half with a laser beam or with the world's deadliest hat.

BLOFELD.
He tried to kill Bond with a deadly virus and ten of the most beautiful women in the world.

NOW IT'S SCARAMANGA'S TURN TO TRY

ALBERT R. BROCCOLI and HARRY SALTZMAN present

ROGER MOORE
AS
JAMES BOND
007

IN IAN FLEMING'S
"THE MAN WITH THE GOLDEN GUN"

with CHRISTOPHER LEE · BRITT EKLAND · Produced by ALBERT R. BROCCOLI and HARRY SALTZMAN
Directed by GUY HAMILTON · Screenplay by RICHARD MAIBAUM and TOM MANKIEWICZ · Music by JOHN BARRY

PG PARENTAL GUIDANCE SUGGESTED   ORIGINAL MOTION PICTURE SOUNDTRACK AVAILABLE ON UNITED ARTISTS RECORDS AND TAPES · COLOR· United Artists

THE SPY WHO LOVED ME
(1977)

CAST Roger Moore (James Bond), Barbara Bach (Major Anya Amasova), Curt Jurgens (Karl Stromberg), Richard Kiel (Jaws), Caroline Munro (Naomi), Walter Gotell (General Gogol), Geoffrey Keen (Minister of Defence), Bernard Lee (M), George Baker (Captain Benson), Michael Billington (Sergei Barsov), Olga Bisera (Felicca), Desmond Llewelyn (Q), Edward de Souza (Sheik Hosein), Vernon Dobtcheff (Max Kalba), Valerie Leon (Hotel receptionist), Lois Maxwell (Miss Moneypenny), Sydney Tafler (Liparus Captain), Nadim Sawalha (Fekkesh), Sue Vanner (Log cabin girl), Eva Rueber-Staier (Rublevich), Robert Brown (Admiral Hargreaves), Marilyn Galsworthy (Stromberg's assistant), Milton Reid (Sandor), Cyril Shaps (Bechmann), Milo Sperber (Markovitz), Albert Moses (Barman), Rafiq Anwar (Cairo Club waiter), Felicity York, Dawn Rodrigues, Anika Pavel, Jill Goodall (Arab beauties), Shane Rimmer (Commander Carter), Bryan Marshall (Commander Talbot)
PRODUCED BY Albert R. Broccoli
DIRECTED BY Lewis Gilbert
SCREENPLAY BY
Christopher Wood & Richard Maibaum
ASSOCIATE PRODUCER William P. Cartlidge
SPECIAL ASSISTANT TO PRODUCER
Michael Wilson
PRODUCTION DESIGNED BY Ken Adam
MAIN TITLE DESIGNED BY Maurice Binder
MUSIC BY Marvin Hamlisch
TITLE SONG "NOBODY DOES IT BETTER"
performed by Carly Simon; lyrics by Carole Bayer Sager; composed by Marvin Hamlisch; produced by Richard Perry
DIRECTOR OF PHOTOGRAPHY Claude Renoir
EDITOR John Glen
PRODUCTION CONTROLLER
Reginald A. Barkshire
PRODUCTION MANAGER David Middlemas
ART DIRECTOR Peter Lamont
ASSISTANT ART DIRECTORS
Ernie Archer, John Fenner & Michael Lamont
ASSISTANT ART DIRECTOR (SET) Charles Bishop
CHIEF DRAUGHTSMAN Brian Savegar
SPECIAL EFFECTS SUPERVISOR Derek Meddings
SPECIAL OPTICAL EFFECTS Alan Maley
SPECIAL EFFECTS (STUDIO) John Evans
2ND UNIT DIRECTORS Ernest Day, John Glen
ACTION ARRANGER Bob Simmons
SKI JUMP PERFORMED BY Rick Sylvester
SET DRESSER Hugh Scaife
MAKEUP Paul Engelen
HAIRDRESSING Barbara Ritchie
FASHION CONSULTANT Ronald Paterson
WARDROBE SUPERVISOR Rosemary Burrows
SCRIPT EDITOR Vernon Harris
CAMERA OPERATOR Alec Mills
CONTINUITY June Randall
ASSEMBLY EDITOR Alan Strachan
ASSISTANT EDITOR John Grover
SOUND RECORDIST Gordon Everett
PRODUCTION ACCOUNTANT Brian Bailey
PRODUCTION ASSISTANT Marguerite Green
CASTING DIRECTORS
Maude Spector & Weston Drury Jr.
UNDERWATER PHOTOGRAPHY Lamar Boren
CONSTRUCTION MANAGER Michael Redding
ASSISTANT DIRECTOR Ariel Levy
ASSISTANT DIRECTOR (2ND UNIT) Chris Kenny

The Spy Who Loved Me became Albert R. "Cubby" Broccoli's first Bond film as sole producer. Its success helped define the legacy of one of the film industry's most beloved figures.

In Spring 1975, Broccoli, Harry Saltzman, and director Guy Hamilton began preparing the tenth Bond film. For the first time, the filmmakers only had a title as Ian Fleming did not wish this novel, written from the perspective of a woman who meets James Bond for one harrowing night, to be used for a film plot. Many talented writers took a shot at developing the story, including veteran Richard Maibaum, *A Clockwork Orange* author Anthony Burgess, and writer/director John Landis.

Harry Saltzman's outside investments had created large debts, and the banks saw Saltzman's share of EON Productions as his largest asset. Saltzman sold his share to United Artists, leaving Albert R. "Cubby" Broccoli as sole producer of *The Spy Who Loved Me*.

Resolving these matters resulted in delays to pre-production. Guy Hamilton left the project, requiring Broccoli to find a new director and, despite the number of writers involved, the numerous scripts and treatments had yet to coalesce.

Broccoli sought out *You Only Live Twice* director Lewis Gilbert to bring the project back on track. Gilbert brought in Christopher Wood to complete the screenplay. Gilbert also brought John Glen onboard as an editor and additional unit director. Gilbert introduced the key script element of Bond killing Anya Amasova's lover late in the pre-production stage, helping to create a solid story underpinning the action. The production draft of the script reflected the additional humor Gilbert wanted and the craftmanship sought by special assistant to the producer Michael G. Wilson.

FLYING THE FLAG *Stuntman Rick Sylvester performs Bond's amazing ski and parachute jump in the opening scene.*

Curt Jurgens, co-star of Gilbert's *Ferry To Hong Kong* (1958), landed the role of Karl Stromberg. An assistant saw Richard Kiel on the American television series *The Barbary Coast* and suggested him for the part of Jaws. The filmmakers searched for an appropriate actress to play Anya Amasova. When United Artists Executive Danton Rissner asked if there was a small role for his friend Barbara Bach, he was surprised to discover that Broccoli wanted her for the lead.

While brainstorming for an idea for the opening sequence, all eyes fell on a TV advert for Canadian Club featuring a skier sailing off El Capitan in California and then unfurling a parachute to land safely. Research showed the ad was faked, but the parachutist, Rick Sylvester, said the stunt could be done on Baffin Island. Weather threatened to scotch the stunt, but finally the winds died down and the clouds parted. Out of three cameras rolling, fortunately one captured the shot.

Location work in Egypt proved an ordeal. Despite location

ALBERT R. B...
ROG... MOO...
IAN Fl...
JAM... BO... OO...
"T...
starring BARBA...
and CURT JURGENS as...

MAKING SPY *(clockwise from above far left) Barbara Bach and Roger Moore sit with Albert R. Broccoli on the set of the interior of the* **Liparus** *supertanker; Lamar Boren and his underwater crew prepare to film the* **Atlantis** *miniature off Coral Harbour, Bahamas; Ken Adam's design sketch of Stromberg's* **Atlantis** *lair; production designer Ken Adam stands on his magnificent* **Liparus** *set.*

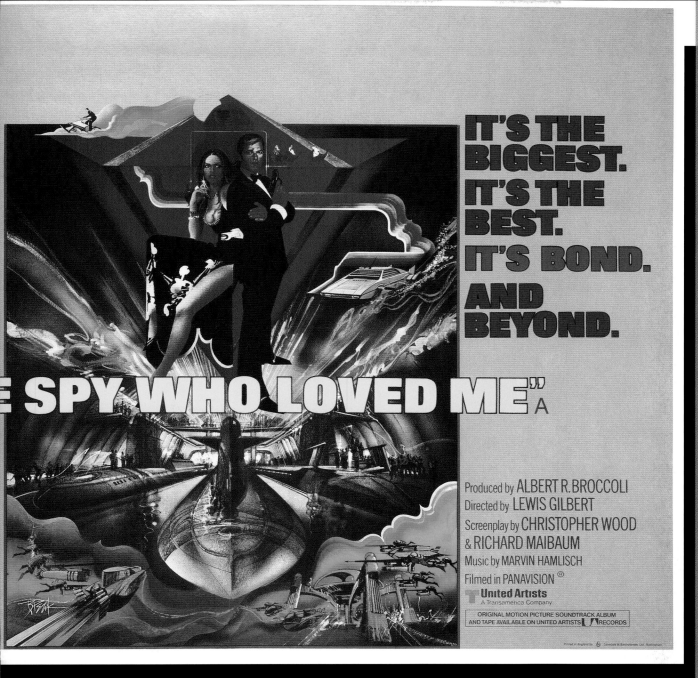

IT'S THE BIGGEST.
IT'S THE BEST.
IT'S BOND.
AND BEYOND.

E SPY WHO LOVED ME" A

Produced by ALBERT R. BROCCOLI
Directed by LEWIS GILBERT
Screenplay by CHRISTOPHER WOOD
& RICHARD MAIBAUM
Music by MARVIN HAMLISCH
Filmed in PANAVISION ®

United Artists
A Transamerica Company

ORIGINAL MOTION PICTURE SOUNDTRACK ALBUM
AND TAPE AVAILABLE ON UNITED ARTISTS RECORDS

LEWIS GILBERT

Lewis Gilbert brought scope and an incredibly wry sense of humor to the James Bond films, injecting his 007 adventures with a layer of elegant and exotic fantasy.

Born into a family of music-hall performers, Lewis Gilbert began his career as a child actor, appearing in such films as *Dick Turpin* (1933).

Legendary British producer Alexander Korda offered to send him to the Royal Academy of Dramatic Arts, but Gilbert had his sights set on directing. In 1939, he worked as an assistant on Alfred Hitchcock's *Jamaica Inn*.

When World War II broke out, he joined the Royal Air Force. Attached to the US Air Corps Film Unit, he directed several documentaries such as *Sailors Do Care* (1944) and *Arctic Harvest* (1946). He continued to write and direct documentary shorts after the war, before directing low-budget features starting with *The Little Ballerina* (1948). By the end of the 1950s, he had graduated to directing more expensive productions, like *Reach For The Sky* (1956) and *Carve Her Name With Pride* (1958). He was particularly adept at war and action films like *Sink The Bismarck!* (1960) and *H.M.S. Defiant* (1962), and he had a knack for translating plays to the big screen, scoring a hit with *Alfie* (1966), which made an international star of Michael Caine.

When Albert R. Broccoli approached Gilbert to direct *You Only Live Twice* (1967), Gilbert was reluctant to take the job but Broccoli eventually persuaded him. Gilbert brought a fresh eye to the series and returned a decade later to direct *The Spy Who Loved Me*, capitalizing on Roger Moore's 007 persona in the process. The immensely profitable *Moonraker* (1979) followed, after which Gilbert returned to making contained dramatic comedies.

In the 1980s, he had two major successes, *Educating Rita* (1983) and *Shirley Valentine* (1989). More recently, he directed the drama *Before You Go* (2002).

filming at some of the greatest temples along the Nile, including Karnak, Edfu and Abu Simbel, the day to day needs of the production were often difficult to meet. Communications with London were unreliable. The crew found the catering abysmal. Broccoli earned great goodwill by finding the supplies to cook a homemade pasta dinner for the cast and crew. At the *Son et Lumière* show at the pyramids, the crew discovered that they could not direct enough light onto the giant structures at night to get an exposure; as a result, all the pyramid shots were later created with mattes and miniatures back in England, at Pinewood Studios.

Sardinia provided the perfect backdrop for second unit director Ernie Day to film much of the car chase with the Lotus Esprit. Special visual effects supervisor Derek Meddings made a shell car to be fired into the sea from an air cannon. In the clear waters of the Bahamas, three additional cars showed the Lotus transforming into a submarine. Perry Oceanographics built a fifth effects Lotus, a true submarine in the shape of an Esprit, for the Nassau shoot. Meddings supervised a cable pulling a final Lotus body onto a Sardinian beach to end the scene. Meddings also built models of the *Liparus* supertanker and Stromberg's *Atlantis* laboratory, both shot in the Bahamas.

At Pinewood, production designer Ken Adam broke new ground with sets that deftly combined sweeping curves,

burnished metal finishes, and beautiful antiques. Yet no stage or location could be found for the interior of the *Liparus*, so Adam designed a permanent stage at Pinewood. Built in only 13 weeks, including the tanker interior, the 007 Stage became the largest film stage in the world. Adam secretly contacted the director Stanley Kubrick to help him devise a lighting design for the set. The 007 Stage opened with great fanfare, including a visit by former Prime Minister Harold Wilson.

John Barry was unavailable to score the film and suggested Marvin Hamlisch, then famed for his score for the 1976 Pulitzer-prize-winning musical *A Chorus Line*. Hamlisch wanted to create a big sound in keeping with the 007 style created by Barry. For the title song, Hamlisch thought, "Everything is bigger than life on a Bond film. So, I went right to Mozart, thinking, 'Go just the opposite.'" Hamlisch started the title song with a lone piano, waiting a full 30 seconds before introducing the sweeping orchestra. Lyricist Carole Bayer Sager came up with the title "Nobody Does It Better," a phrase that still defines Bond. Perfomed by Carly Simon, the song reached # 2 in the US and #7 in the UK. Both song and score earned Academy Award nominations, as did the art direction.

With a budget higher than any Bond film before it, *The Spy Who Loved Me* became a tremendous box office success and a touchstone film in the Bond series.

MOONRAKER
(1979)

CAST Roger Moore (James Bond), Lois Chiles (Holly Goodhead), Michael Lonsdale (Drax), Richard Kiel (Jaws), Corinne Clery (Corinne Dufour), Toshiro Suga (Chang), Bernard Lee (M), Geoffrey Keen (Frederick Gray), Desmond Llewelyn (Q), Lois Maxwell (Miss Moneypenny), Emily Bolton (Manuela), Blanche Ravalec (Dolly), Irka Bochenko (Blonde beauty), Michael Marshall (Colonel Scott), Leila Shenna (Hostess private jet), Anne Lonnberg (Museum guide), Jean-Pierre Castaldi (Pilot private jet), Walter Gotell (General Gogol), Douglas Lambert (Mission Control Director), Arthur Howard (Cavendish), Alfie Bass (Consumptive Italian), Brian Keith (US Shuttle Captain), George Birt (Captain Boeing 747) Guy Delorme (Tree assassin)
PRODUCED BY Albert R. Broccoli
DIRECTED BY Lewis Gilbert
SCREENPLAY BY Christopher Wood
EXECUTIVE PRODUCER Michael G. Wilson
ASSOCIATE PRODUCER William P. Cartlidge
MUSIC BY John Barry
TITLE SONG "MOONRAKER"
performed by Shirley Bassey
composed by John Barry
lyrics by Hal David
PRODUCTION DESIGNED BY Ken Adam
MAIN TITLE DESIGNER Maurice Binder
EDITOR John Glen
DIRECTORS OF PHOTOGRAPHY
Claude Renoir, Jean Tournier
VISUAL EFFECTS SUPERVISOR Derek Meddings
VISUAL EFFECTS ART DIRECTOR Peter Lamont
LOCATION MANAGERS Frank Ernst (Brazil), Phillippe Modave (Italy), John Comfort (USA)
UNIT MANAGERS Robert Saussier (France), Chris Kenny (UK)
ASSISTANT DIRECTOR Michel Cheyko
ACTION SEQUENCES Bob Simmons
PRODUCTION CONTROLLER
Reginald A. Barkshire
PRODUCTION ACCOUNTANT Brian Bailey
ART DIRECTORS
Peter Lamont, Max Douy & Charles Bishop
CASTING DIRECTORS
Margot Capelier & Budge Drury
SET DECORATOR Peter Howitt
2ND UNIT CAMERAMAN Jacques Renoir
VISUAL EFFECTS CAMERAMAN Paul Wilson
OPTICAL EFFECTS CAMERAMAN
Robin Browne
ASSEMBLY EDITOR John Grover
2ND UNIT DIRECTORS Ernest Day & John Glen
SPECIAL EFFECTS John Evans, John Richardson, René Albouze, Serge Ponvianne
PRODUCTION MANAGERS Jean-Pierre Spiri-Mercanton (France), Terence Churcher (UK)
CAMERA OPERATORS Alex Mills, Michel Deloire, John Morgan
STUNT ARRANGER Bob Simmons
CONTINUITY Elaine Shreyeck
DUBBING EDITOR Allan Sones
DUBBING MIXER Gordon K. McCallum
SOUND MIXER Daniel Brisseau
SCRIPT EDITOR Vernon Harris
SPACE CONSULTANT Eric Burgess
COSTUME DESIGNER Jacques Fonteray
WARDROBE MASTER Jean Zay
MAKEUP ARTISTS
Monique Archambault & Paul Engelen
HAIRDRESSERS Mike Jones, Pierre Vade
STILLS CAMERAMAN Patrick Morin

The eleventh EON James Bond film, made at the height of the worldwide science-fiction craze brought on by the success of *Star Wars* (1977), remains the most fantasy-laden Bond adventure ever. Its scope, scale, and sense of spectacle provided unique challenges to the Bond team.

At the end of *The Spy Who Loved Me* (1977), the title card announced James Bond would return in *For Your Eyes Only*. Within weeks of the release, producer Albert R. "Cubby" Broccoli and United Artists felt Bond's next adventure should be an adaptation of Ian Fleming's third novel, *Moonraker*. The concept was simple: take James Bond into space. Realizing that *Moonraker* could be made to coincide with the launch of the first NASA space shuttle, Broccoli declared he wanted *Moonraker* to be "science fact," not science fiction.

As with all the Bond films since *Live And Let Die* (1973), the script flowed from extensive location scouting. When Broccoli visited Brazil during the opening of *The Spy Who Loved Me*, his hosts took him to Iguazu Falls. Broccoli decided that the next Bond film would shoot in Brazil taking advantage of the unique opportunities provided by the location. The creative team returned, dreaming up a scene to take place during the Rio Carnival.

For financial reasons, Broccoli decided to move the production of *Moonraker* from Pinewood to Paris. With an early draft of the script in hand, production designer Ken Adam agreed this was feasible, but suggested that Broccoli book every studio in Paris to house the film. For months, the French film industry came to a standstill as *Moonraker* monopolized the stages and studio crafts departments.

Broccoli's desire to make, as executive producer Michael G. Wilson termed it, "an extravagant film" brought on a flurry of expensive scenes and ideas, not all of which could be included. A scene with microlight jets ended up being reworked for *Octopussy* (1983). Another scene at the Eiffel Tower was dropped, only to be transformed into the spectacular base jump in *A View To A Kill* (1985).

One element that could not be dropped was the climax in space. Broccoli turned to visual effects supervisor Derek Meddings to solve the problem. With limited time available, Meddings proposed a risky plan to create all the effects in the camera by shooting one element, winding back the film, and then shooting the next.

When the numbers came in, Broccoli discovered this film would cost more than twice the amount of any previous Bond film. Looking at the profits of *The Spy Who Loved Me*, both Broccoli and United Artists signed off. Never had more been riding on one of 007's cinematic adventures.

For the opening sequence, Michael G. Wilson wanted Bond to be pushed from a plane without a parachute. Locating some of the best parachutists in the world, the filmmakers overcame two problems: how to hide the parachutes and how to mount a 35mm camera on a helmet that would not injure the cameraman when his chute opened. Wilson and second unit director and editor John Glen traveled to California to film the sequence using an ultra-light titanium camera body and an experimental plastic Panavision lens, capturing amazing footage.

The filmmakers cast French actor Michael Lonsdale as Hugo Drax, American actress Lois Chiles as Dr. Holly Goodhead, and French actress Corinne Clery as Corinne Dufour. To play Drax's henchman Chang, the filmmakers cast Michael G. Wilson's aikido teacher, Toshiro Suga. Following his popularity in *The Spy Who Loved Me*, Richard Kiel returned as Jaws. Sadly, *Moonraker* would prove to be the last Bond film to feature Bernard Lee as M.

Filming was an endurance test, with complex shooting across the globe. In Brazil, stuntman Richard Graydon hurled himself over the edge of a cable car for a shot that took everyone's breath away. At Iguazu Falls, neither Bond's speedboat nor the hang glider could be filmed properly for the sequence, requiring miniatures to be built in England. In Venice, careful negotiations took place to allow the high-speed boat chase through the centuries-old canals. In France, weightless sequences required days of rigging wires for over a dozen performers.

DEREK MEDDINGS

Both of parents of Derek Meddings worked for producer Alexander Korda; his father was a master carpenter, and his mother was a stand-in for actress Merle Oberon. Born in 1931, Meddings attended art school and, after a stint in the RAF, tried to break into the film industry. He eventually landed a job at Denham Labs creating movie titles and met matte painter Les Bowie. Bowie took him under his wing, and Meddings worked as a matte painter until he discovered that he was slightly color-blind. However, by then, he had discovered a talent for building miniatures.

While working with Bowie at Bray Studios, Meddings began moonlighting for TV producer Gerry Anderson in the evenings, painting backdrops and doing special effects work. Anderson soon had a hit with the *Thunderbirds* television series, and Meddings was busier than ever.

Meddings later did special effects for Anderson's feature film *Doppelgänger* (aka Journey To The Far Side Of The Sun, 1969). Next came *UFO* (1970), a live-action TV series. When that ended, Meddings returned to film work.

Production designer Syd Cain recommended Meddings to the Bond producers and he soon began what would become a six-film affiliation with James Bond. He was responsible for the exploding poppy fields in *Live And Let Die* (1973); the destruction of Scaramanga's island for *The Man With The Golden Gun* (1974); the extensive models built for *The Spy Who Loved Me* (1977); the outer space models and effects for *Moonraker* (1979); and he created the illusion of Roger Moore and Carole Bouquet's underwater scenes in *For Your Eyes Only* (1981). He won an Oscar for his work on 1978's *Superman* and was nominated for *Moonraker*. He returned to Bond with *GoldenEye* (1995), where he did extensive miniature work.

Sadly, Meddings died from cancer before the film's premiere. *GoldenEye* is dedicated to his memory.

The pressure on Derek Meddings and his crew at Pinewood was great. Hundreds of effects shots needed to be completed. Meddings and his team created dozens of models of space shuttles, the space station, and space debris customized for each individual shot. Any mistakes meant starting again. For one shot of the space battle, a single piece of film endured 48 exposures. The slightest lens flare or speck of dirt would have ruined the work. To create the effect of the space station disintegrating, the team obtained two shotguns, closed the stage at Pinewood, and blew the model part. The effects work earned Meddings an Oscar nomination.

John Barry returned to the series to score the film. Shirley Bassey once again sang the title song, which featured lyrics by Hal David. *Moonraker* marked the last time the "007 Theme" would be heard in a John Barry Bond score, and Barry's use of it in the boat chase sequence is magisterial.

Moonraker's technical achievements and sense of grandeur make it a memorable addition to the Bond canon. The film broke numerous box-office records upon its release in the summer of 1979. *Moonraker* literally took 007 to new heights, but it also signaled a close to an era of introducing elements of science-fiction fantasy into the world of James Bond.

FOR YOUR EYES ONLY
(1981)

CAST Roger Moore (James Bond), Carole Bouquet (Melina Havelock), Topol (Columbo), Lynn-Holly Johnson (Bibi Dahl), Julian Glover (Kristatos), Cassandra Harris (Countess Lisl Von Schlaf), Jill Bennett (Jacoba Brink), Michael Gothard (Emile Locque), John Wyman (Kriegler), Jack Hedley (Havelock), Lois Maxwell (Moneypenny), Desmond Llewelyn (Q), Walter Gotell (General Gogol), Geoffrey Keen (Minister of Defence), James Villiers (Tanner), John Moreno (Ferrara), Charles Dance (Claus), Paul Angelis (Karageorge), Toby Robins (Iona Havelock), Jack Klaff (Apostis), Alkis Kristikos (Santos), Stag Theodore (Nikos), Stefan Kalipha (Hector Gonzales), Graham Crowden (First Sea Lord), Noel Johnson (Vice Admiral), William Hoyland (McGregor), Eva Rueber-Staier (Rublevich), Janet Brown (Prime Minister), John Wells (Denis)
PRODUCED BY Albert R. Broccoli
DIRECTED BY John Glen
SCREENPLAY BY Richard Maibaum & Michael G. Wilson
EXECUTIVE PRODUCER Michael G. Wilson
ASSOCIATE PRODUCER Tom Pevsner
MUSIC BY Bill Conti
TITLE SONG performed by Sheena Easton; music by Bill Conti; lyrics by Michael Leeson; produced by Christopher Neil
PRODUCTION DESIGNED BY Peter Lamont
MAIN TITLE DESIGNED BY Maurice Binder
DIRECTOR OF PHOTOGRAPHY Alan Hume
EDITOR John Grover
SPECIAL EFFECTS SUPERVISOR Derek Meddings
PRODUCTION SUPERVISOR Bob Simmonds
PRODUCTION MANAGERS Mara Blaseti, Phil Kohler, Aspa Lambrou
PRODUCTION CONTROLLER Reginald A. Barkshire
PRODUCTION ACCOUNTANT Douglas Noakes
DIRECTOR OF PUBLICITY Charles Juroe
ASSISTANT DIRECTOR Anthony Waye
CAMERA OPERATOR Alec Mills
VISUAL EFFECTS PHOTOGRAPHY Paul Wilson
CONTINUITY Elaine Schreyeck
SOUND MIXER Derek Ball
ART DIRECTOR John Fenner
SET DECORATOR Vernon Dixon
ACTION SEQUENCES Bob Simmons
DRIVING STUNTS Rémy Julienne
2ND UNIT DIRECTION & PHOTOGRAPHY Arthur Wooster, BSC
UNDERWATER PHOTOGRAPHY Al Giddings
AERIAL PHOTOGRAPHY James Devis
SKI PHOTOGRAPHY Willy Bogner
UNIT AND LOCATION MANAGERS Vincent Winter, Peter Bennett, Michaelis Lamrinos, Redmond Morris, Umberto Sambuco
2ND UNIT ASSISTANT DIRECTOR Gerry Gavigan
2ND UNIT CONTINUITY Phyllis Townshend
2ND ASSISTANT DIRECTORS Terry Madden, Michael Zimbrich, Gareth Tandy, Tony Broccoli
CASTING BY Maude Spector & Deborah McWilliams
COSTUME DESIGNER Elizabeth Waller
WARDROBE MASTER Tiny Nicholls
MAKEUP George Frost & Eric Allwright
HAIRDRESSERS Stephanie Kaye & Marsha Lewis
SPECIAL EFFECTS John Evans

Following Moonraker's enormous success, producers Albert R. "Cubby" Broccoli and Michael G. Wilson decided it was time to bring 007 back to earth and closer to Ian Fleming's conception of the character.

Although Broccoli had considered producing non-007 features from time to time, including *The Detective* in 1979, he decided to stick with James Bond. To help shape the 12th 007 adventure, Broccoli brought back Bond screenwriting veteran Richard Maibaum, who began collaborating with Michael G. Wilson. For inspiration they turned to Fleming's short stories, *For Your Eyes Only* and *Risico*, as well as an unused keelhauling scene from the novel *Live And Let Die*, which was originally scripted to follow the cable car sequence in *Moonraker*.

To direct the new film, Broccoli turned to Bond editor and second unit director alumnus John Glen. With Roger Moore on board, attention turned to casting. Publicity director Charles "Jerry" Juroe recommended French actress Carole Bouquet for the revenge-seeking Melina Havelock. Broccoli's wife, Dana, suggested Israeli-born actor Topol of *Fiddler On The Roof* fame for pistachio-chewing rogue Columbo. American ice-skating champion and actress Lynn-Holly Johnson took the role of Olympic hopeful Bibi Dahl. British actor Julian Glover, once considered for the role of Bond, starred as the villainous Kristatos. British actress Jill Bennett, who starred in the early Broccoli production *Hell Below Zero* (1954), portrayed Bibi's coach Brink.

Budgeted at $28 million, *For Your Eyes Only* began filming on September 15, 1980 at the Villa Sylva at Kanoni above Corfu Town, which doubled as the villa of hitman Gonzales. Nearby, driving-stunts arranger Rémy Julienne and second unit director Arthur Wooster filmed a thrilling, gadget-free car chase involving Melina's Citroen 2CV.

When it came time to film Locque's Mercedes sliding off a cliff, Moore debated with Michael G. Wilson and John Glen how best to complete the scene. Should Bond just drop an incriminating pin to tip the balance? Or should Bond kick the car over the edge? The filmmakers chose to have Bond deliver the kick, signaling a harder-edged interpretation of the role.

Filming moved to the Meteora region of Greece, where Bond scales the mountain to the monastery hideout used by Kristatos. The local monks tried to disrupt filming by hanging their laundry from the windows. This didn't stop the filmmakers from shooting the sequence, in which Kristatos henchman Apostis kicks Bond over a cliff. Climber Rick Sylvester, doubling Moore, performed a 300 ft (91.4 m) fall from the mountain, and special effects wizard Derek Meddings built a 30-ft (9-m) trough partially filled with sandbags to ease the jarring impact on his body as the climbing rope pulled taut. To capture the death of Apostis, Glen filmed an empty patch of ground and then cut to a shot of actor Jack Klaff lying on the ground. With a harsh sound effect, it created the effect of Apostis violently hitting the ground.

Back in England, Glen filmed the remote-controlled helicopter pre-credits sequence at Becton Gas Works in East London. The idea for the scene originated one day when he saw a technician's son playing with a remote-controlled car at Pinewood Studios.

New Year arrived with mixed emotions. Beloved actor Bernard Lee proved too ill to shoot his scenes as M, so the filmmakers, hopeful that Lee would eventually recover, brought in James Villiers to play Tanner for the film. Sadly, Lee passed away shortly afterwards.

When the crew arrived in the Italian Alpine resort of Cortina d'Ampezzo, they discovered the town and mountains in the midst of a snow drought. Twenty-five truckloads of virgin snow had to be brought in for the street scenes. Ski champion and filmmaker Willy Bogner returned for his third Bond film. Using a pair of skis that allowed him to ski both forward and backward, Bogner filmed breathtaking action. Actor John Wyman, playing ski champion Erich Kriegler, spent many hours learning the sport to convincingly play the role.

Another challenge occurred when the production team learned Carole Bouquet wasn't comfortable filming underwater. Again, Derek Meddings came to the rescue. Bouquet and Moore filmed on a dry sound stage with wind machines. Meddings then wound the film back in the camera, and superimposed bubbles onto the film negative.

No one comes close to JAMES BOND 007

ALBERT R. BROCCOLI
presents
ROGER MOORE
as
IAN FLEMING'S
JAMES BOND 007
in
FOR YOUR EYES ONLY

Starring CAROLE BOUQUET · TOPOL · LYNN-HOLLY JOHNSON · JULIAN GLOVER
Produced by ALBERT R. BROCCOLI · Directed by JOHN GLEN
Screenplay by RICHARD MAIBAUM and MICHAEL G. WILSON · Executive Producer MICHAEL G. WILSON
Music by BILL CONTI · Production Designer PETER LAMONT
Associate Producer TOM PEVSNER · PANAVISION® · TECHNICOLOR®   United Artists

DOLBY STEREO

Title Song Performed by SHEENA EASTON

THE EYES HAVE IT
*(clockwise, starting below)
Roger Moore (James Bond)
and his son Christian during
production; Moore gives Lynn-
Holly Johnson (Bibi Dahl) a
hug during rehearsals at the
indoor ice rink at Cortina
d'Ampezzo; Maurice Binder
directs the title sequence with
singer Sheena Easton;
Al Giddings and his crew
work on the Greek temple set
off the coast of the Bahamas;
Albert R. Broccoli, Sheena
Easton, John Glen, and
Michael G. Wilson pose for a
publicity photo following the
announcement that Easton
would sing the film's title
song; Roger Moore and Carole
Bouquet (Melina Havelock)
share a joke during a break on
location in Cortina.*

BOB SIMMONS

Born in Fulham, London, in
1933, Bob Simmons first
teamed with Bond producer
Albert R. Broccoli on the film
The Red Beret (1953). He
became a legend in the world
of film action stunts; his work
on many Bond films, from *Dr.
No* (1962) to *A View To A
Kill* (1985), raised the bar for
fight and action scenes.

Simmons holds the
distinction of being the first actor to
portray 007 on the big screen, as it
is he who appears in the famed gun
barrel opening at the beginning of
Dr. No. Simmons did not work on
From Russia With Love (1963), but
his work on *Goldfinger* (1964)
through *You Only Live Twice*
(1967) contained innovative and
exciting stunts seamlessly designed to
make audiences believe that Sean
Connery himself was taking incredible
risks. A double high-fall at the
Japanese Kobe docks in *You Only
Live Twice* illustrates the stunt
arranger's skill. When Simmons
disappears behind a container for a
fraction of a second, Connery steps
into view to replace him.

Bob Simmons' preparation and skill
helped save him when an explosion
blew through the back of Count
Lippe's Ford Skyliner in *Thunderball*
(1965). Simmons kept his cool as
flames poured into the driver's
compartment, hurling himself out at
the last moment to ensure not only
his safety but also that director
Terence Young got the shot.

Simmons passed away in 1988, but
his legacy of hard-hitting action and
stunts done for real lives on in the
Bond films to this day.

DRY RUN *Bob Simmons rehearses
with Roger Moore and stuntman Tom
Haggerty in Greece while shooting
For Your Eyes Only.*

Bill Conti composed and recorded
the title song with Scottish singer
Sheena Easton, who became the only
singer to date to appear in the main
titles. Easton scored a major hit on
both sides of the Atlantic (#4 in the
US; #8 in the UK), and the song
earned an Academy Award
nomination. Conti's score employed a
bazouki, a Greek-Turkish stringed
instrument, to add an ethnic flavor to
several tracks.

For Your Eyes Only set a new
direction for James Bond in the 1980s:
less fantasy-laden and based upon
more realistic premises. The film
proved a major success during the
summer of 1981.

OCTOPUSSY
(1983)

CAST Roger Moore (James Bond), Maud Adams (Octopussy), Louis Jourdan (Kamal Khan), Kristina Wayborn (Magda), Kabir Bedi (Gobinda), Steven Berkoff (General Orlov), David Meyer (Mischka), Tony Meyer (Grischka), Vijay Amritraj (Vijay) Desmond Llewelyn ("Q"), Robert Brown ("M"), Walter Gotell (Gogol), Geoffrey Keen (Minister of Defence), Suzanne Jerome (Gwendoline), Cherry Gillespie (Midge), Albert Moses (Sadruddin), Douglas Wilmer (Fanning), Andy Bradford (009), Lois Maxwell (Miss Moneypenny), Michaela Clavell (Penelope Smallbone), Philip Voss (Auctioneer), Bruce Boa (US General), Richard Parmentier (US aide), Paul Hardwick (Soviet Chairman), (Dermot Crowley (Kamp), Peter Porteous (Lenkin), Eva Rueber-Staier (Rublevich), Jeremy Bullock (Smithers), Tina Hudson (Bianca), William Derrick (Thug with yo-yo), Stuart Saunders (Major Clive), Ken Norris (Colonel Toro), Gabor Vernon (Borchoi), Tony Arjuna (Mufti)
PRODUCED BY Albert R. Broccoli
DIRECTED BY John Glen
SCREEN STORY AND SCREENPLAY BY George MacDonald Fraser and Richard Maibaum & Michael G. Wilson
EXECUTIVE PRODUCER Michael G. Wilson
ASSOCIATE PRODUCER Thomas Pevsner
MUSIC COMPOSED AND CONDUCTED BY John Barry
THE SONG "All Time High," performed by Rita Coolidge; music by John Barry; lyrics by Tim Rice
PRODUCTION DESIGNED BY Peter Lamont
MAIN TITLE DESIGNER Maurice Binder
DIRECTOR OF PHOTOGRAPHY Alan Hume
SUPERVISING EDITOR John Grover
SPECIAL EFFECTS SUPERVISOR John Richardson
2ND UNIT DIRECTOR AND PHOTOGRAPHER Arthur Wooster
COSTUME DESIGNER Emma Porteous
CASTING Debbie McWilliams
PRODUCTION SUPERVISOR Hugh Harlow
PRODUCTION MANAGERS Philip Kohler, Barrie Osborne, Leonhard Gmür, Gerry Levy
PRODUCTION ACCOUNTANT Douglas Noakes
ASSISTANT DIRECTOR Anthony Waye
CAMERA OPERATOR Alec Mills
CAMERA GRIPS W.C. "Chunky" Huse, Colin Manning
SOUND RECORDIST Derek Ball
CONTINUITY Elaine Schreyeck
ACTION SEQUENCES ARRANGED BY Bob Simmons
DRIVING STUNTS ARRANGED BY Rémy Julienne
AERIAL TEAM DIRECTOR Phil Wrestler
ART DIRECTOR John Fenner
SET DECORATOR Jack Stephens
MAKEUP SUPERVISOR George Frost
HAIRDRESSING SUPERVISOR Christopher Taylor
PRODUCTION CONTROLLER Reginald A. Barkshire
DIRECTOR OF PUBLICITY Charles Juroe
EDITORS Peter Davies, Henry Richardson
SOUND EDITOR Colin Miller
LOCATION MANAGERS Peter Bennett, Rashid Abassi
2ND UNIT ASSISTANT DIRECTOR Gerry Gavigan
ADDITIONAL ASSISTANT DIRECTORS Baba Shaikh, Don French
EXECUTIVE ASSISTANT Barbara Broccoli

In 1967, *You Only Live Twice* beat the spoof version of *Casino Royale* at the box office by advertising "Sean Connery IS James Bond." In 1983, producers Albert R. "Cubby" Broccoli and Michael G. Wilson faced another rival Bond film, *Never Say Never Again*, but this time the rivals had Connery. *Octopussy* rose to the challenge, exciting audiences worldwide with a winning mixture of audacity, romantic adventure, humor, and suspense.

Scripting for *Octopussy* began with a new Bond writer, George MacDonald Fraser, author of the Flashman novels. His first draft included a pre-titles sequence set at the Isle of Man Tourist Trophy car races as well as a story based in India. Richard Maibaum and Wilson rewrote Fraser's script, retaining some of his ideas, including a deadly yo-yo buzz saw and Bond evading capture by hiding in a gorilla suit.

John Glen returned to direct his second Bond film, and with Roger Moore agreeing to terms for a sixth Bond film, focus shifted to casting other roles. Broccoli cast Maud Adams as Octopussy, bringing her back for her second starring role in a Bond film. French actor Louis Jourdan, a friend of Broccoli's, secured the role of villain Kamal Khan. Swedish actress Kristina Wayborn, who had played Greta Garbo in a television mini-series, took the part of Magda. George MacDonald Fraser suggested Indian actor Kabir Bedi for Khan's henchman Gobinda. For the part of the crazed Soviet General Orlov, Barbara Broccoli spotted British actor/director Steven Berkoff in the play Greek in Los Angeles. Moore recommended Robert Brown, his co-star from the television series Ivanhoe and godfather to his daughter Deborah, for the crucial role of M. Broccoli, a

HOLD THAT TIGER *(opposite page, top) Assistant director Anthony Waye inspects a stuffed tiger on loan from the Maharana of Udaipur.*

ACCESS ALL AREAS *(opposite page, left to right) Louis Jourdan, who plays Afghan Prince Kamal Khan, meets HRH Prince Charles at the Octopussy premiere. Maud Adams (Octopussy) can be seen foreground left and Kristina Wayborn (Magda) is in the background; Peter Robb King applies clown makeup to Roger Moore (James Bond) during shooting; on set with (left to right) camera operator Michael Frift, focus Simon Hume, camera operator Alec Mills, camera grip W. C. "Chunky" Huse, and producer Cubby Broccoli.*

THE DIRECTOR *(opposite page, right) John Glen sits behind the camera contemplating a shot.*

great tennis fan, cast Davis Cup champion Vijay Amritraj in his screen debut as Bond's Indian contact, Vijay.

Second unit and aerial unit work on Octopussy began weeks before principal photography, with Moonraker skydiving experts B. J. Worth, Jake Lombard and cameraman Randy DeLuca filming a mid-air fight on top of Kamal Khan's Beech 18 airplane. In addition, J. W. "Corkey" Fornof piloted his Acrostar Bede jet over Southern Utah for much of the pre-credit sequence. In fact, the Bede jets had originally appeared in an early Moonraker script draft. While in Utah, aerial team director Phil Wrestler attempted to film the destruction of Khan's plane for the movie's climax. He projected a full-sized plane along a railroad track and shot it off a cliff, hoping the plane would fall 1,000 ft (304 m) to its destruction. The plane, filled with explosives, leveled out and began flying on its own. Wrestler was horrified that it might fly into Utah State Route 9 but, thankfully, the plane banked and crashed into a nearby gully out of camera range. Special effects supervisor John Richardson subsequently blew up a

model plane at Pinewood Studios.

First unit filming then began in West Berlin on August 10, 1982, with production designer Peter Lamont's crew painting a section of the graffiti-covered Berlin Wall to make it look like the East Berlin side. At RAF Northolt in England, the producers shot the Acrostar's trip through a military hangar. John Richardson stripped an old Jaguar down to its chassis and attached a pole from the car to a mock-up of the jet. As the Jaguar sped through the hangar, Glen had soldiers running in front of the car to conceal it. Moore even sat in the cockpit. Richardson then blew up a miniature of the hangar. For the closer shots of the plane and the missile pursuing it, Richardson built a model plane and attached a flaming firework behind it.

To film the Germany train scenes, the team traveled to the Nene Valley Steam Railway near Peterborough, England. For close shots of Moore hanging from the undercarriage of the train, Peter Lamont used an old silent film trick. He had two of the Nene Valley carriages delivered to stages at Pinewood. He suspended the carriages from cranes and placed a looped painting of railway track beneath the rail cars. With Moore hanging on beneath the train, and the painting moving, it appeared the star was really beneath a speeding train.

At the end of September, filming moved to one of the most exotic Bond locations yet, Udaipur, India, where the Maharana rolled out the red carpet for the crew. One of Lamont's most difficult tasks was the creation of Octopussy's barge. He found two derelict ceremonial barges in Bombay, and the Maharana gave permission to destroy both of them to make one working barge. The Maharana also gave the filmmakers permission to film the tiger hunt sequence in his overgrown garden. To create the effect of a tiger leaping out at Bond, Glen borrowed the Maharana's stuffed tiger, had it placed it in a wheelbarrow and then pushed through the bushes at Moore.

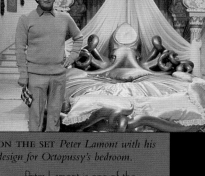

ON THE SET *Peter Lamont with his design for Octopussy's bedroom.*

PETER LAMONT

Peter Lamont is one of the world's most renowned production designers. A veteran of 18 James Bond films, including nine as production designer, Lamont is a constant sustaining member of the Bond creative team and has helped keep the Bond films innovative and visually spectacular.

Having left art school in 1946, Lamont acquired a job at Pinewood Studios where he spent two years as a print boy runner. After spending two years in the RAF, he returned to Pinewood Studios as a junior draughtsman. In early 1964, Lamont was asked by Ken Adam's art director, Peter Murton, if he wanted to join *Goldfinger* as a draughtsman. Lamont had just seen *From Russia With Love* (1963) and was completely "knocked out" by the film. He immediately joined the Bond team, and Ken Adam gave him the exterior of Fort Knox to draw as his first task.

Over the years, Lamont stayed with the Bond films, receiving promotions from chief draughtsman to set decorator, then to art director, and finally becoming Ken Adam's right-hand man on both *The Spy Who Loved Me* (1977) and *Moonraker* (1979). When Adam left to design the film *Pennies From Heaven* (1981) in the US, Lamont was asked who he would like to work with next as production designer. He answered, "Why not me?" Within hours he was the production designer of *For Your Eyes Only* (1981), and he has remained in that position. He sat out for only one film, *Tomorrow Never Dies* (1997), so that he could design the sets for James Cameron's blockbuster *Titanic* (1997), for which he won an Academy Award. Lamont has also been nominated three other times for an Academy Award for his work on the films *Fiddler On The Roof* (1971), *The Spy Who Loved Me* (1977), and *Aliens* (1986). He won the Art Directors Guild's Excellence in Production Design Award for *Casino Royale* (2006).

For the Tuk-Tuk taxi chase, local crowds descended upon the set, much to the distress of the stunt drivers. One man on a bicycle got past the security and rode through a shot that remained in the film.

John Barry returned to compose his ninth Bond film score. He collaborated with Tim Rice on six different songs, and "All Time High" was the one selected by the production team, despite not mentioning the title of the film in its lyrics. Rita Coolidge performed the song, which reached #36 on the US charts.

In the end, production delays caused the rival Connery Bond film, *Never Say Never Again* to be pushed back to an October 1983 release date. *Octopussy* premiered in June 1983 and became the biggest Bond film of the 1980s in the US, out-grossing Connery's by a large margin.

DRESSED TO KILL
(clockwise from top)
The crew filming on location in Iceland; Christopher Walken (Max Zorin), Grace Jones (May Day) and producer Michael G. Wilson listen to director John Glen set the scene on the Seine; Broccoli and Moore relax during shooting of the Renault taxi chase in Paris.

A VIEW TO A KILL (1985)

CAST Roger Moore (James Bond), Christopher Walken (Max Zorin), Tanya Roberts (Stacey Sutton), Grace Jones (May Day), Patrick Macnee (Tibbett), Patrick Bauchau (Scarpine), David Yip (Chuck Lee), Fiona Fullerton (Pola Ivanova), Manning Redwood (Bob Conley), Alison Doody (Jenny Flex), Willoughby Gray (Dr. Carl Mortner), Desmond Llewelyn (Q), Robert Brown (M), Lois Maxwell (Miss Moneypenny), Walter Gotell (General Gogol), Geoffrey Keen (Minister of Defence), Jean Rougerie (Achille Aubergine), Daniel Benzali (Howe), Papillon Soo Soo (Pan Ho), Mary Stavin (Kimberley Jones), Dominique Risbourg (Butterfly Act compere), Carole Ashby (Butterfly girl), Lucien Jerome (Paris taxi driver), Joe Flood (SFPD Captain), Bogdan Kominowski (Klotkoff), Dolph Lundgren (Venz)
PRODUCED BY
Albert R. Broccoli & Michael G. Wilson
DIRECTOR John Glen
SCREENPLAY BY
Richard Maibaum & Michael G. Wilson
ASSOCIATE PRODUCER Thomas Pevsner
MUSIC COMPOSED AND CONDUCTED BY
John Barry
TITLE SONG
performed by Duran Duran
composed by Duran Duran and John Barry
produced by Bernard Edwards
PRODUCTION DESIGNED BY Peter Lamont
MAIN TITLE DESIGNED BY Maurice Binder
DIRECTOR OF PHOTOGRAPHY Alan Hume
2ND UNIT DIRECTOR & PHOTOGRAPHER
Arthur Wooster, BSC
SKI SEQUENCES DIRECTED & PHOTOGRAPHED BY Willy Bogner
COSTUMES Emma Porteous
CASTING Debbie McWilliams
EDITOR Peter Davies
SOUND EDITOR Colin Miller
SPECIAL EFFECTS SUPERVISOR John Richardson
PRODUCTION SUPERVISOR Anthony Waye
PRODUCTION MANAGERS Philip Kohler, Serge Touboul, Leonhard Gmür, Ned Kopp & Company, Jón Thor Hannesson
UNIT MANAGER Iris Rose
PRODUCTION ACCOUNTANT Douglas Noakes
ASSISTANT DIRECTOR Gerry Gavigan
CAMERA OPERATOR Michael Frift
SOUND RECORDIST Derek Ball
CONTINUITY June Randall
ELECTRICAL SUPERVISOR John Tythe
ACTION SEQUENCE ARRANGER
Martin Grace
DRIVING STUNTS ARRANGER Rémy Julienne
ART DIRECTOR John Fenner
SET DECORATOR Crispian Sallis
CONSTRUCTION MANAGER Michael Redding
MAKEUP SUPERVISOR George Frost
HAIRDRESSING SUPERVISOR Ramon Gow
PRODUCTION CONTROLLER
Reginald A. Barkshire
DIRECTOR OF MARKETING Charles Juroe
LOCATION MANAGERS Nick Daubeny, Agust Baldursson, Stefan Zürcher, Jean-Marc Deschamps, Steph Benseman, Rory Enke
2ND UNIT ASSISTANT DIRECTOR Peter Bennett
2ND UNIT CONTINUITY
Penny Daniels, Daphne Carr
ADDITIONAL ASSISTANT DIRECTORS
Edi Hubschmid, Laurent Bregeat, Serge Menard, Terry Madden, Andrew Warren, Simon Haveland, Nick Heckstall-Smith, Barbara Broccoli

A View To A Kill marked the end of Roger Moore's 12-year tenure as Bond. The film's blend of humor and action exemplifies the qualities Moore brought to the role. Richard Maibaum and Michael G. Wilson returned to co-write their third Bond film. It was Wilson's idea to set the film's story around Silicon Valley, and the pair decided to have the villain attempt to destroy this high-tech center by flooding the San Andreas Fault and creating a double earthquake.

To flesh out the script, the writers looked to unused ideas from previous Bond films. One such idea came from *Moonraker* (1979) and involved a poisonous bee brooch killing Bond's contact at the Eiffel Tower's Le Jules Verne Restaurant. For this film, director John Glen suggested the deadly insect should be a butterfly marionette.

The producers cast Oscar-winner Christopher Walken as Max Zorin, chose Tanya Roberts to play geologist Stacey Sutton, signed disco diva Grace Jones as the villainous May

Day, and awarded the role of Bond's ally Sir Godfrey Tibbett to Patrick Macnee, star of *The Avengers* television series.

Ski unit director Willy Bogner's plans to film the Siberian pre-titles sequence in Scotland ended when, after five weeks of planning, the snow melted. Bogner turned to alternative locations in Iceland and Switzerland. In Iceland, it took the production team three tries before they successfully crashed the model helicopter into a glacier.

In June 1984, disaster struck: the 007 soundstage at Pinewood Studios burned down during production of *Legend* (1985). EON Productions set about rebuilding the stage, but this meant that production designer Peter Lamont's mine set could not be completed until the end of the shooting schedule. Any delay would mean postponing the film's release.

In August, filming began in Paris. To perform May Day's jump off the Eiffel Tower, parachute/skydiving expert B. J. Worth made 22 test jumps from a hot-air balloon. When, after lengthy negotiations, the French authorities finally approved the stunt, a man and woman suddenly parachuted off the Eiffel Tower. The production team worried that the authorities might revoke their permission, but the thrillseekers actually showed that the jump could be performed safely. B. J. Worth successfully executed the stunt in a single take with numerous cameras rolling, creating one of the iconic images from the film. Filming continued at Chantilly Chateau outside Paris. The Silver Cloud Rolls-Royce driven by Patrick Macnee in the film actually belonged to Broccoli. When it came time to sink the Rolls back in England, the crew used a duplicate car.

After filming at the Amberley Chalk Pits Museum in West Sussex, which served as the exterior to Zorin's mine, the production moved to San Francisco. Mayor Dianne Feinstein gave the crew unprecedented permission to film in the city, including simulating a real fire at City Hall and capturing a fire truck chase over three weeks of night shooting.

For the film's climactic battle atop the Golden Gate Bridge, action sequence arranger Martin Grace supervised shots of stuntmen fighting on one of the main suspension cables. With two VistaVision cameras, the crew filmed plate shots to be used in the studio. At Pinewood, Lamont built full-scale replicas of the bridge. Front projectionist Charles Staffel projected the VistaVision footage below the actors on the studio floor. Editor Peter Davies then assembled location, model, and studio shots into a seamless whole.

The production celebrated the rebuilding of the 007 Stage on January 7, 1985. At a special ceremony, Pinewood renamed it the Albert R. Broccoli 007 Stage in honor of the producer's contribution to the British film industry.

John Barry returned to compose his tenth Bond film score. John Taylor of the rock group Duran Duran asked Broccoli if the group could create the title song. Broccoli agreed, and Duran Duran, working with Barry, created the most successful Bond movie theme to date, hitting #1 on the US charts and reaching #2 in the UK

A View To A Kill marked the end of an era for the Bond series. Afte this, his seventh film as James Bond, Roger Moore stepped aside from the role. His tremendously successful tenure brought legions of fans to the series, making 007 just as much a popular culture icon of the 1970s and 1980s as he had been in the 1960s.

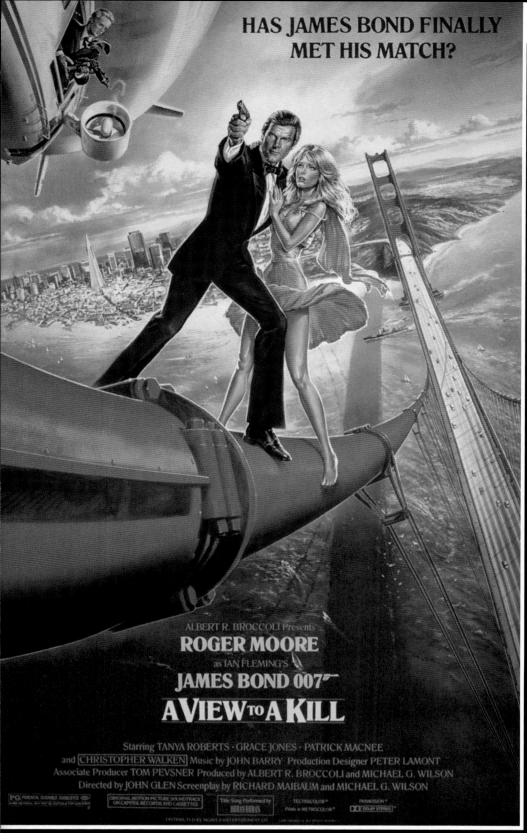

HAS JAMES BOND FINALLY
MET HIS MATCH?

ALBERT R. BROCCOLI Presents
ROGER MOORE
as IAN FLEMING'S
JAMES BOND 007
A VIEW TO A KILL

Starring TANYA ROBERTS · GRACE JONES · PATRICK MACNEE
and CHRISTOPHER WALKEN Music by JOHN BARRY Production Designer PETER LAMONT
Associate Producer TOM PEVSNER Produced by ALBERT R. BROCCOLI and MICHAEL G. WILSON
Directed by JOHN GLEN Screenplay by RICHARD MAIBAUM and MICHAEL G. WILSON

THREE POINTS OF VIEW
(below, left to right)
Director John Glen on the
set; director of marketing
Charles "Jerry" Juroe.
Princess Diana attends the
London premiere of **A**
View To A Kill, *meeting*
members of Duran Duran
who performed the film's
title song.

JOHN BARRY

John Barry created the musical sound of James Bond. His arrangement and orchestration of "The James Bond Theme" combined his own twangy-guitar signature (from his earlier career as leader of the British rock-instrumental group The John Barry Seven) with a jazzy big-band kick. Recurring throughout *Dr. No* (1962), it guaranteed Barry's subsequent involvement with 007.

Barry's innovative approach, combined pop, jazz, and classical styles to create a new genre of movie music that was exciting, romantic, and suspenseful. After he scored the next Bond film, *From Russia With Love* (1963), *Goldfinger* (1964) became the first of many Bond films for which Barry wrote title song and score.

He was born John Barry Prendergast in York, England, in 1933. His father ran a chain of theaters, and Barry gravitated toward a career that combined movies and music. While on national service in the early 1950s, Barry studied playing the trumpet, via a correspondence course, with famed Stan Kenton arranger Bill Russo. By the late 1950s, he was a prominent figure on the British rock 'n' roll scene. His group backed the popular singer Adam Faith, and Barry duly supplied the music for Faith's film debut, *Beat Girl* (1960). Barry's future as a film composer was assured.

Barry composed the scores for 11 Bond films (and, with *Dr. No*, contributed to a 12th). He continually updated his style, incorporating a Moog synthesizer in *On Her Majesty's Secret Service* (1969) and the rock sounds of The Pretenders on 1987's *The Living Daylights*. He collaborated with top pop vocalists and bands, from Shirley Bassey (*Goldfinger*, 1971's *Diamonds Are Forever*, 1979's *Moonraker*) to Duran Duran (*A View To A Kill*, 1985), and a-ha (*The Living Daylights*, 1987); and established a musical framework for Bond to which the current 007 composer David Arnold adheres to this day.

Beyond Bond, Barry's film career encompasses some of the most significant films of the past five decades. He has won five Academy Awards, for *Born Free* (1966, song and score), *The Lion In Winter* (1968), *Out Of Africa* (1985) and *Dances With Wolves* (1990).

THE LIVING DAYLIGHTS
(1987)

CAST Timothy Dalton (James Bond), Maryam d'Abo (Kara Milovy), Jeroen Krabbe (General Georgi Koskov), Joe Don Baker (Brad Whitaker), John Rhys-Davies (General Leonid Pushkin), Art Malik (Kamran Shah), Andreas Wisniewski (Necros), Thomas Wheatley (Saunders), Desmond Llewelyn (Q), Robert Brown (M), Geoffrey Keen (Minister of Defense), Walter Gotell (General Gogol), John Terry (Felix Leiter), Caroline Bliss (Miss Moneypenny), Nadim Sawalha (Chief of Security, Tangier), Virginia Hey (Rubavitch), John Bowe (Col. Feyador), Julie T. Wallace (Rosika Miklos), Kell Tyler (Linda), Catherine Rabett (Liz), Dulice Liecier (Ava), Carl Rigg (Imposter 00 Agent), Tony Cyrus (Chief of Snow Leopard Brotherhood), Ken Sharrock (Jailer) Frederick Warder (004), Glyn Baker (002)
PRODUCED BY Albert R. Broccoli & Michael G. Wilson
DIRECTOR John Glen
SCREENPLAY BY
Richard Maibaum & Michael G. Wilson
ASSOCIATE PRODUCERS
Tom Pevsner & Barbara Broccoli
TITLE SONG performed by a-ha; composed by Pal Waaktaar and John Barry; produced by Jason Corsaro, a-ha, and John Barry
SONGS "Where Has Everybody Gone?" & "If There Was A Man" performed by The Pretenders; music by John Barry; lyrics by Chrissie Hynde; produced by John Barry and Paul O'Duffy
MUSIC COMPOSED AND CONDUCTED BY John Barry
PRODUCTION DESIGNER Peter Lamont
MAIN TITLE DESIGNED BY Maurice Binder
DIRECTOR OF PHOTOGRAPHY Alec Mills
2ND UNIT DIRECTOR & PHOTOGRAPHER
Arthur Wooster, BSC
COSTUME DESIGNER Emma Porteous
CASTING Debbie McWilliams
EDITORS John Grover & Peter Davies
SOUND EDITOR Colin Miller
SPECIAL EFFECTS SUPERVISOR John Richardson
PRODUCTION SUPERVISOR Anthony Waye
PRODUCTION ACCOUNTANT Douglas Noakes
DIRECTOR OF MARKETING Charles Juroe
PRODUCTION MANAGERS Philip Kohler, Sparky Greene, Arno Ortmair, Leonhard Gmür, Denise O'Dell
UNIT MANAGER Iris Rose
ASSISTANT DIRECTOR Gerry Gavigan
CAMERA OPERATOR Michael Frift
SOUND RECORDIST Derek Ball
CONTINUITY June Randall
ELECTRICAL SUPERVISOR John Tythe
STUNT SUPERVISOR Paul Weston
DRIVING STUNTS ARRANGER Rémy Julienne
AERIAL STUNTS ARRANGER B. J. Worth
ART DIRECTOR Terry Ackland-Snow
SET DECORATOR Michael Ford
CONSTRUCTION MNGR. Anthony Graysmark
MAKEUP SUPERVISOR George Frost
HAIRDRESSING SUPERVISOR Ramon Gow
PRODUCTION CONTROLLER
Reginald A. Barkshire
LOCATION MANAGERS Nick Daubeny, John Bernard, Arie Bohrer, Stefan Zuercher, Driss Gaidi
ACTION UNIT ASSISTANT DIR. Terry Madden
ACTION UNIT CONTINUITY Jean Bourne
ADDITONAL ASSISTANT DIRS. Callum McDougall, Crispin Reece, Nick Heckstall-Smith, Terry Blyther, Urs Egger, Ahmed Hatimi, Mohamed Hassini

MAKING DAYLIGHTS
*(below, left to right)
Associate producer
Barbara Broccoli studies
the next shot on location
in Weissensee, Austria;
Maryam d'Abo (Kara
Milovy) discusses a scene
with director John Glen
at Pinewood Studios;
Producer Albert R.
Broccoli and Timothy
Dalton (James Bond)
give a tour of Q's lab set
to HRHs Princess Diana
and Prince Charles.
Desmond Llewelyn (Q),
Maryam d'Abo, and John
Glen stand in the
background.*

The Living Daylights, the 15th Bond film, proved to be a watershed for the series. The film offered insightful moments exploring the character of 007, a sign of the increasing awareness on the part of the filmmakers of the dramatic potential in the James Bond stories.

Once the decision came from producer Albert R. "Cubby" Broccoli to recast the role of James Bond, Michael G. Wilson and Richard Maibaum began hammering out story ideas. The pair initially looked at exploring 007's roots and developed a story involving Bond as a rebellious young naval officer, who lives his life according to the family motto "The World Is Not Enough." Broccoli rejected the concept, feeling audiences wanted to see Bond as a professional, not an amateur. He also felt it was too soon to re-launch the Bond storyline. Wilson and Maibaum turned to the Fleming short story *The Living Daylights* as a launching point for the script. As inspiration for

the character of Koskov, the writers looked to the real-life story of KGB officer Vitaly Yurchenko, who defected to the CIA for a short time in 1985, then re-defected to the Soviet Union. Leadership changes in the Soviet Union helped define the story, and the increasingly grim war in Afghanistan provided a unique setting.

As the script took shape, Bond screen tests continued. With top choice Timothy Dalton unavailable, the producers settled on Pierce Brosnan, but NBC renewed Brosnan's contract to appear in the television series *Remington Steele* at the last moment. With some shifts to the shooting schedule, Dalton was able to take the role.

To fill out the cast, the filmmakers drew together an assortment of international actors. European actress Maryam d'Abo took the role as Czech cellist Kara Milovy. For Russian defector villain Georgi Koskov, the producers cast Dutch

DESIGNS FOR LIVING (above and left) Art department concept drawing of Bond's new Aston Martin; a sketch by costume designer Emma Porteous of an elegant evening gown for Kara Milovy.

actor Jeroen Krabbe, who had previously impressed them in the film *Soldier Of Orange* (1979). American actor Joe Don Baker of *Walking Tall* (1973) fame landed the role of arms dealer Brad Whitaker. The filmmakers originally hoped series regular Walter Gotell could play a larger role as KGB chief General Gogol, but health insurance restrictions led to the creation of a new KGB chief, General Pushkin. Welsh character actor John Rhys-Davies took the part. Caroline Bliss also landed the role of Miss Moneypenny.

Second unit filming began on Gibraltar on September 17, 1986. When Dalton later joined the Gibraltar second unit, he impressed everyone by performing many of his own stunts atop a speeding Land Rover.

Production quickly moved to Vienna, where a major press conference introduced the new James Bond to the world. Glen and his crew filmed in the Viennese opera houses, the Volksopera and the Schönbrunn Palace concert hall. Glen also shot at the Prater Amusement Park, the scene of the memorable confrontation between Orson Welles and Joseph Cotton in the classic thriller, *The Third Man* (1949), on which Glen had been a junior editor.

In the US, above California's Mojave Desert, parachute experts B. J. Worth and Jake Lombard filmed the fight sequence in which a cargo net falls out of the back of a plane in flight with Bond and henchman Necros hanging on for dear life.

The first unit moved to Morocco, shooting in the Forbes Museum in Tangier, where publisher Malcolm Forbes housed his lavishly detailed dioramas of important battles. They also shot exteriors in the city, including the rooftop chase when Bond eludes the Moroccan police. Filming continued in Ouarzazate, the location doubling for the Soviet airbase in Afghanistan. The film's climactic battle remains the largest ever in a Bond movie.

The crew returned to Pinewood Studios, where Prince Charles and Princess Diana paid a visit to the set in December. Jeroen Krabbe suggested to Diana that she smash a prop bottle over the head of the Prince as a joke. The next day, the picture landed on the front pages of newspapers around the globe.

In Weissensee, Austria, 007's new Aston Martin led a chase on an ice lake. Glen suggested that, at the end of the sequence, Bond and Kara should abandon the crashed car and use Kara's cello case as a sled to escape across the border. Steering the modified case as it sped across the snow became quite a challenge for actress Maryam d'Abo.

Filming wrapped at Pinewood Studios on February 13, 1987. One week later, Broccoli was awarded an honorary Order of the British Empire.

Ray Still, director of Warner Brothers Records, suggested the Norwegian pop trio a-ha, and their title song, written with John Barry, reached #5 in the UK. Barry returned to score his 11th and final film score, writing 57 minutes of music in just four weeks and using a synthesizer to give the score a fresh sound. He also co-wrote two additional songs which The Pretenders performed. Barry fittingly made a cameo as a conductor at the end of the film, an appearance that served as a coda to his career with 007.

The Living Daylights was a worldwide smash when released in the summer of 1987. It proved once again to Cubby Broccoli that the star of the picture is James Bond, not the actor who portrays him.

JOHN GLEN

John Glen holds the record for helming five James Bond films, the most of any director. He is responsible for bringing a more realistic, espionage-driven feel to the films.

Born on May 15, 1932, in Sunbury-on-Thames, England, Glen began work in the film industry as a messenger at Shepperton Studios under director Alexander Korda. In 1947, he worked as a runner in the cutting room and then as an assembly editor on such films as *The Third Man* (1949) and *The Wooden Horse* (1950). After two years in the Royal Air Force, he entered the business once again as a sound editor. Glen then worked his way up to second unit director and editor on such British television series as *Danger Man* and *Man In A Suitcase*.

Peter Hunt, director of *On Her Majesty's Secret Service* (1969), gave Glen the opportunity of a lifetime to direct second unit and edit the film. They had been assistants in the editing room at Shepperton Studios. His work on the bob-run sequence for *OHMSS* greatly impressed Bond producer Albert R. "Cubby" Broccoli.

Throughout the 1970s, Glen's services as a second unit director and editor were in constant demand on such films as *Murphy's War* (1971), *Catlow* (1971), *Gold* (1974), *Shout At The Devil* (1976), *The Wild Geese* (1978), the Bond film *Moonraker* (1979) and *The Sea Wolves* (1980). He also edited the films *Pulp* (1972), *Dead Cert* (1974), and Bond director Lewis Gilbert's *Seven Nights in Japan* (1976). Glen's work on the classic ski parachute jump in *The Spy Who Loved Me* (1977) established him as a master of filming action material.

In 1980, Cubby Broccoli gave Glen the opportunity to make his feature film directing debut with the 12th James Bond film, *For Your Eyes Only*. After that film's enormous success, Glen directed four more Bond films.

Since leaving the series, he has directed the films *Aces: Iron Eagle III* (1992), *Christopher Columbus: The Discovery* (1992), and *The Point Men* (2001).

LICENCE TO KILL (1989)

CAST Timothy Dalton (James Bond), Carey Lowell (Pam Bouvier), Robert Davi (Franz Sanchez), Talisa Soto (Lupe Lamora), Anthony Zerbe (Milton Krest), Frank McRae (Sharkey), Everett McGill (Killifer), Wayne Newton (Professor Joe Butcher), Benicio del Toro (Dario), Anthony Starke (Truman-Lodge), Pedro Armendariz, Jr. (Hector Lopez), Desmond Llewelyn (Q), David Hedison (Felix Leiter), Priscilla Barnes (Della Churchill), Robert Brown (M), Caroline Bliss (Miss Moneypenny), Don Stroud (Heller), Grand L. Bush (Hawkins), Cary-Hiroyuki Tagawa (Kwang), Alejandro Bracho (Perez), Guy de Saint Cyr (Braun), Rafer Johnson (Mullens), Diana Lee-Hsu (Loti), Christopher Neame (Fallon)
PRODUCED BY
Albert R. Broccoli & Michael G. Wilson
DIRECTED BY John Glen
WRITTEN BY
Michael G. Wilson & Richard Maibaum
ASSOCIATE PRODUCERS
Tom Pevsner & Barbara Broccoli
PRODUCTION DESIGNED BY Peter Lamont
DIRECTOR OF PHOTOGRAPHY Alec Mills
VISUAL EFFECTS John Richardson
ORIGINAL SCORE COMPOSED AND CONDUCTED BY Michael Kamen; title song lyrics by Narada Michael Walden, Jeffrey Cohen, Walter Afanasieff, performed by Gladys Knight
CASTING BY Jane Jenkins & Janet Hirshenson
MAIN TITLE DESIGNED BY Maurice Binder
COSTUME DESIGNER Jodie Tillen
2ND UNIT DIRECTED & PHOTOGRAPHED BY Arthur Wooster, BSC
EDITOR John Grover
SOUND EDITOR Vernon Messenger
ART DIRECTOR Michael Lamont
SET DECORATOR Michael Ford
CONSTRUCTION MANAGER Tony Graysmark
MAKEUP SUPERVISORS
George Frost & Naomi Donne
HAIRDRESSING SUPERVISOR Tricia Cameron
ELECTRICAL SUPERVISOR John Tythe
CONTINUITY Jean Randall
ASSISTANT DIRS. Miguel Gil, Miguel Lima
CAMERA OPERATOR Michael Frift
SOUND RECORDIST Edward Tise
CONTINUITY June Randall
DIRECTOR OF MARKETING Charles Juroe
PRODUCTION SUPERVISOR MEXICO
Hector Lopez
PRODUCTION MANAGER Philip Kohler
UNIT MANAGER Iris Rose
STUNT CO-ORDINATOR Paul Weston
DRIVING STUNTS ARRANGER Rémy Julienne
AERIAL STUNT SUPERVISOR "Corkey" Fornof
PRODUCTION SUPERVISOR Anthony Waye
UNDERWATER SCENES DIRECTED & PHOTOGRAPHED BY Ramon Bravo
PRODUCTION ACCOUNTANT
Douglas Noakes
PRODUCTION COORDINATOR
Loolee Deleon
2ND ASSISTANT DIRECTOR Callum McDougall
PRODUCTION ASSISTANTS Ignacio Cervantes, Marcia Perskie, Gerardo Barrera, Monica Greene
PRODUCTION SECRETARY Ileana Franco
ACCOUNTANTS
Jane Meagher, Rosa Maria Gomez
ASSISTANT ACCOUNTANT Andrew Noakes
ASSEMBLY EDITOR Matthew Glen
SOUND EDITORS Peter Musgrave, Mark Auguste

James Bond is out on his own and out for revenge

ALBERT R. BROCCOLI
presents
TIMOTHY DALTON
as IAN FLEMING'S
JAMES BOND 007
LICENCE TO KILL
15
STARRING CAREY LOWELL ROBERT DAVI TALISA SOTO ANTHONY ZERBE
DIRECTOR OF PHOTOGRAPHY ALEC MILLS PRODUCTION DESIGNER PETER LAMONT MUSIC BY MICHAEL KAMEN ASSOCIATE PRODUCERS TOM PEVSNER AND BARBARA BROCCO
WRITTEN BY MICHAEL G. WILSON AND RICHARD MAIBAUM PRODUCED BY ALBERT R. BROCCOLI AND MICHAEL G. WILSON DIRECTED BY JOHN
DISTRIBUTED BY UNITED INTERNATIONAL PICTURES DOLBY STEREO SR FILMED IN PANAVISION® COLOUR BY DELUXE® PRINTS BY TECHNICOLOR® Original Motion Picture Soundtrack Album on MCA Records, Cassettes and Co
Gun Logo Symbol © 1962 Danjaq, S.A. and United Artists Company © 1989 Danjaq, S.A. and United A
All R

The success of Timothy Dalton's first Bond film, *The Living Daylights*, led producer Albert R. "Cubby" Broccoli to tailor his 16th 007 film to Dalton's harder-edged persona.

During Fall 1987, the filmmakers went on a recce to China, where they imagined a chase sequence on the Great Wall and a fight scene involving the uncovered terracotta soldiers at Xian. Screenwriter Richard Maibaum and writer/producer Michael G. Wilson wrote two treatments concerning a drug warlord in the Golden Triangle, but plans to film in the country fell through.

The filmmakers soon decided that Mexico provided an array of locations and production services with which they could mount a new incarnation of the film. Wilson and Maibaum recast their story with a Central American drug lord. They chose to shoot the film's interiors at the famed Churubusco Studios in Mexico City. The writers used Milton Krest, a character from Fleming's short story *The Hildebrand Rarity*, as one of the villain's main henchmen. They also took unused scenes from Fleming's novel *Live And Let Die* and incorporated those into the plot.

After Cubby Broccoli and Maibaum saw Robert Davi in the 1988 TV movie *Terrorist on Trial—The U.S. Vs. Salim Ajami*, they decided he would make the perfect Franz Sanchez. Davi researched drug lords and had the script translated into Spanish to learn his lines with the proper cadence. Davi also performed the role of 007 to help audition actresses for the role of Sanchez's mistress, Lupe. Brooklyn-born actress Talisa Soto won the part. Carey Lowell landed

the role of CIA pilot Pam Bouvier, while David Hedison reprised the role of Felix Leiter, which he played in *Live And Let Die*. Future Academy Award-winner Benicio del Toro secured one of his first roles as the knife-wielding henchman Dario. Desmond Llewelyn returned for his largest role ever as Q, providing a welcome sense of familiarity to this darker-than-usual film. Las Vegas entertainer Wayne Newton always wanted to be in a Bond film, and Broccoli cast him as the oily televangelist Professor Joe Butcher. Pedro Armendariz Jr., whose father Pedro Armendariz played Kerim Bey in *From Russia With Love* (1963), portrayed Isthmus City's puppet President Hector Lopez.

Upon arriving in Mexico, production designer Peter Lamont found he needed to totally refurbish the studio to make it operational for a Bond film. Filming began on July 18, 1988, at Churubusco. On August 1st, the production moved to Key West, Florida, where second unit director Arthur Wooster supervised the filming of Bond lassoing Sanchez's plane in mid-air with Jake Lombard doubling Dalton. Special consultants Sparky Greene and Jillian Palenthorpe suggested the sequence involving Bond's escape from the Wavekrest underwater and then via plane to Wilson. Waterskiing champion David Reinhardt doubled for Bond barefoot skiing behind a plane. Skydiving experts Lombard and B. J. Worth, along with aerial supervisor J.W. "Corkey" Fornof, took over for the Cessna plane hijacking. Famed underwater photographer Ramon Bravo filmed the underwater scenes at Isla Mujeres near Cancun, Mexico.

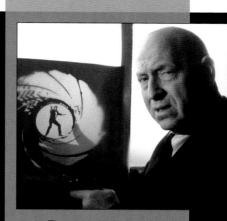

challenge of performing the grueling stuntwork on the dangerous location. The curving road had seen so many fatal accidents that locals claimed the area was cursed. Each accident on the location set off new rounds of speculation as to possible supernatural causes.

During post-production, MGM changed the film's title from *Licence Revoked* to *Licence To Kill*. It became the first Bond film to receive a PG-13 rating in the US and, in many countries, several cuts for violence were made to achieve a more family-friendly rating. In the UK, the film received a 15 certificate, the only James Bond film to receive that rating.

Composer Michael Kamen, hot off the action films *Lethal Weapon* (1987) and *Die Hard* (1988), scored *Licence To Kill*, working closely with Glen to give the film a Bond feel. Soul singer Gladys Knight performed the title song (which reached #6 in the UK), and Patti Labelle sang the end title song "If You Asked Me To," which became a hit for Celine Dion almost three years later.

Despite receiving high test screening ratings, *Licence To Kill* failed to achieve a breakout American audience when it was released during the summer of 1989. Sadly, *Licence To Kill* would prove to be the last Bond film for many veterans of the series: Maurice Binder, Richard Maibaum, John Glen, and Alec Mills.

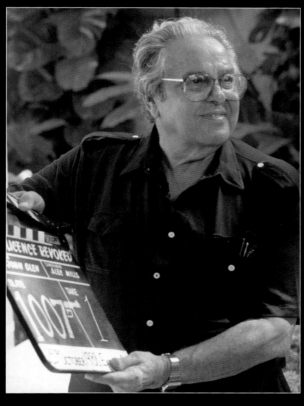

ADVENTURE IN MEXICO
(top to bottom) Robert Davi (Franz Sanchez) receives gun instruction from stunt coordinator Paul Weston; director John Glen on location in the Florida Keys with (from left to right) camera grip W. C. "Chunky" Huse, camera trainee Tom Kopp, camera operator Michael Frift, script supervisor June Randall, camera focus Frank Elliot, director of photography Alec Mills, and clapper boy Simon Mills; producer Albert R. Broccoli holds the slate for a scene shot on 25th October, 1988. Peter Lamont stands in front of his spectacular set for the second floor of the Casino d'Isthmus, Sanchez's headquarters.

Other key Mexico locations were utilized to ensure this film would be as exotic as its predecessors. For Sanchez's mansion, Broccoli's close relationship with Baron Ricky di Portanova allowed for filming at his palatial home in Acapulco known as Arabesque. The Centro Ceremonial Otomi near Toluca, built for the Otomi Indians but now deserted, was chosen as the site of Professor Joe Butcher's Meditation Institute.

A Coast Guard law enforcement friend of Wilson's told him that one way drug dealers smuggled cocaine was to dissolve it in airplane fuel and then recover it once in the US. Wilson took this idea and had the villain Sanchez dissolve his cocaine in four tanker trucks. During the film's climax, Bond must destroy the tankers. In order to perform the incredible tanker side and back wheelies of the chase, vehicle stunt supervisor Rémy Julienne contacted Larry Orr, chief engineer of Kenworth Trucks, who modified and sent the stunt trucks, known as Pamela 1, 2, and 3 (after the film's heroine), to Rumorosa Pass, an hour from Mexicali. There, the first and second unit faced the seven-week shooting

MAURICE BINDER

The main title designs of Maurice Binder are true works of art and contain many of the signature images of the James Bond films. His feeling for color, shape, and mood helped define the world of 007. His sense of humor, seen in the trailers he cut for the Bond films, helped build anticipation for Bond adventures all over the globe.

Born in 1925, Binder studied engineering and attended the Art Students' League. He started as a teaboy at Macy's department store in New York City but soon became their art director. During World War II, Binder served on an army salvage ship. On a stop near Hollywood, Binder made some contacts in the film studios leading to work as a stills photographer. After the war, he moved into movie advertising and designed opening film credits, especially for director Stanley Donen. His titles on the 1961 film *The Grass Is Greener* received a tremendous reaction from the audience at the premiere. The next day, Binder received a phone call asking him to design the titles and trailer for a film called *Dr. No*. Binder showed the producers his idea for the opening gunbarrel logo, which became a signature image on all the Bond films to follow. Although absent from *From Russia With Love* (1963) and *Goldfinger* (1964), he designed the titles for *Thunderball* (1965) through to *Licence To Kill* (1989), using a combination of the most sophisticated and basic filmic techniques to create stunning, dreamlike visuals.

Binder became one of the most sought-after title designers, working on films as diverse as *Billion Dollar Brain* (1967), *Barbarella* (1968), *The Private Life of Sherlock Holmes* (1970), *The Wild Geese* (1978), and *The Last Emperor* (1987). In 1980, Binder used his optical printing experience to create the special visual effects for the time travel movie, *The Final Countdown*.

In addition to his work on titles, Binder owned a remarkable modern art collection. He died in 1991.

GOLDENEYE
(1995)

CAST Pierce Brosnan (James Bond), Sean Bean (Alec Trevelyan), Izabella Scorupco (Natalya Simonova), Famke Janssen (Xenia Onatopp), Joe Don Baker (Jack Wade), Judi Dench (M), Robbie Coltrane (Valentin Zukovsky), Tchéky Karyo (Dimitri Mishkin), Gottfried John (General Ourumov), Alan Cumming (Boris Grishenko), Desmond Llewelyn (Q), Samantha Bond (Moneypenny), Michael Kitchen (Bill Tanner), Serena Gordon (Caroline), Billy J. Mitchell (Admiral Farrel), Michelle Arthur (Anna), Minnie Driver (Irina)
PRESENTED BY Albert R. Broccoli
PRODUCED BY
Michael G. Wilson & Barbara Broccoli
DIRECTED BY Martin Campbell
SCREENPLAY BY Jeffrey Caine & Bruce Feirstein
STORY BY Michael France
EXECUTIVE PRODUCER Tom Pevsner
"GOLDENEYE" performed by Tina Turner; written by Bono & The Edge; produced by Nellee Hooper
MUSIC BY Eric Serra
PRODUCTION DESIGNER Peter Lamont
DIRECTOR OF PHOTOGRAPHY
Phil Méheux, BSC
EDITOR Terry Rawlings
COSTUME DESIGNER Lindy Hemming
2ND UNIT DIRECTOR Ian Sharp
2ND UNIT CAMERAMAN Harvey Harrison, BSC
ADDITIONAL UNIT DIRECTED &
PHOTOGRAPHED BY Arthur Wooster, BSC
SPECIAL EFFECTS SUPERVISOR Chris Corbould
MINIATURE EFFECTS SUPERVISOR
Derek Meddings
STUNT COORDINATOR Simon Crane
CASTING Debbie McWilliams
MAIN TITLE DESIGNED BY Daniel Kleinman
VISUAL EFFECTS PHOTOGRAPHY
Paul Wilson, BSC
SUPERVISING SOUND EDITOR Jim Shields
SUPERVISING ART DIRECTOR Neil Lamont
SET DECORATOR Michael Ford
CONSTRUCTION COORDINATOR
Tony Graysmark
PROPERTY MASTER Barry Wilkinson
MODEL UNIT ART DIRECTOR Michael Lamont
MODELLER HEAD OF DEPARTMENT
Brian Smithies
MAKEUP SUPERVISOR Linda Devetta
HAIRDRESSING SUPERVISOR Colin Jamison
WARDROBE SUPERVISOR John Scott
STILLS PHOTOGRAPHER Keith Hamshere
PUBLICITY & MARKETING Gordon Arnell
PARACHUTE COORDINATOR B. J. Worth
CAR CHASE STUNTS Rémy Julienne
PRODUCTION MANAGER Philip Kohler
UNIT MANAGER Iris Rose
LOCATION PRODUCTION MANAGERS
Serge Toubol, Valery Yermolaev, Ellen Gordon, Leonard Gmür, Stefan Zürcher
ASSISTANT DIRECTOR Gerry Gavigan
CAMERA OPERATOR Roger Pearce
SOUND RECORDIST David John
SCRIPT SUPERVISOR June Randall
ELECTRICAL SUPERVISOR Terry Potter
2ND UNIT ASSISTANT DIR. Terry Madden
ASSOCIATE PRODUCER Anthony Waye
FINANCIAL CONTROLLER Douglas Noakes
PRODUCTION ACCOUNTANT Andrew Noakes
COSTINGS ACCOUNTANT John Roebuck
ADDITIONAL PRODUCTION MANAGER
Callum McDougall
DANJAQ VP OF MARKETING John Parkinson
LEGAL SERVICES David Pope

No limits. No fears. No substitutes.

After the release of *Licence To Kill* in 1989, Albert R. "Cubby" Broccoli and Michael G. Wilson decided that a new team should write and direct the next 007 adventure. Within months, the Berlin Wall fell, Communism in Europe collapsed, and the Cold War that spawned Bond ceased to exist. Was James Bond still relevant? The producers developed a new script, but MGM/UA began a painful financial journey that resulted in lawsuits and a lengthy delay for 007.

When the dust settled in 1992, Broccoli and Wilson declared they wanted to make a new Bond film. The pair brought in a new producer who had known Bond all her life. Barbara Broccoli took on the job of producing her first Bond film with a determination to make the characters in the film

as rich and varied as in the Ian Fleming novels.

Working with screenwriter Michael France, the producers developed the premise of Bond facing his MI6 mentor, Alec Trevelyan, 006, who has now turned into a master criminal in control of a devastating space weapon. Screenwriter Jeffrey Caine introduced the motivation for the former 006: the purported betrayal of the Leinz Cossacks by the British army at the end of World War II.

Although, Cubby was still very much part of the key decisons made during this vital period, he had passed on the day-to-day film production to Michael G. Wilson and Barbara Broccoli. As the script developed, Timothy Dalton announced he would not return as Bond. Pinewood Studios booked other films, forcing the filmmakers to look for another studio.

Michael G. Wilson and Barbara Broccoli confronted these challenges head-on. They discovered an abandoned Rolls Royce aircraft factory that production designer Peter Lamont transformed into a new film studio dubbed Leavesden. They brought in the experienced New Zealand director Martin Campbell and cast Pierce Brosnan as the new James Bond. By late summer 1994 the filmmakers were ready to start; however the producers and the studio decided to do more work on the script. Writer Bruce Feirstein joined the team, honing dialogue and tightening the story. During this time, the idea of a female M came to pass.

To play the vengeful Alec Trevelyan, the filmmakers turned to an actor they felt could have been a contender for the role of Bond, Sean Bean. Casting director Debbie McWilliams searched all over the world before finding Izabella Scorupco in Sweden to play Russian programmer Natalya Simonova. Dutch actress Famke Janssen landed the part of Xenia Onatopp, Joe Don Baker returned to play CIA agent Jack Wade, and Judi Dench became the new M.

With a budget more than twice that of any previous 007 film, production began on January 16, 1995, the exact month and day *Dr. No* began lensing in Jamaica 33 years before. The filmmakers sent Ian Sharp and his second unit to St. Petersburg, Russia, to film the location shots for the tank chase. The city authorities worried about damage to streets and the foundations of historic buildings, so the filmmakers undertook an engineering study to see if the chase could be completed safely. Working with the utmost care, the crew staged stunts and explosions in the heart of the city. To complete the sequence, production designer Peter Lamont built a two-block stretch of a St. Petersburg street at Leavesden. There, the filmmakers used a real T-55 tank to smash through a wall, roll over cars, grind through narrow alleys, and ram into a statue.

The film's opening sequence featured two incredible stunts.

Firstly, stuntman Wayne Michaels performed the world's highest bungee jump off a fixed point, the Verzasca dam in Switzerland. Secondly, parachutist Jacques "Zoo" Malnuit drove a motorcycle off a cliff-face in Switzerland, launching into a free-fall after a plane. In another Swiss valley, B. J. Worth and his team tried to actually have a freefalling jumper catch a diving plane. Unable to complete the stunt, the filmmakers created the effect using a digital composite image.

Location work in Puerto Rico and Monaco included not only Bond's classic Aston Martin DB5, but the BMW Z3, a sleek sports car that was only in the prototype stage.

In Puerto Rico, the filmmakers shot at the giant Arecibo Observatory, the world's largest single-dish radio telescope. To shoot the scripted scene of the observatory appearing from beneath a draining lake, the filmmakers turned to miniature effects supervisor Derek Meddings. The stunning array of miniatures created by Meddings included a vast stretch of Siberian wilderness, Alec Trevelyan's armored train, several fighter jets, both giant satellite dishes, and the entire Soviet chemical weapons facility, seen in the opening sequence as it explodes.

For the music, the filmmakers chose Eric Serra, composer of the music for *La Femme Nikita* (1990) and asked John Altman to record a version of "The James Bond Theme" to accompany the tank chase through the streets of St. Petersburg. The filmmakers asked Bono and The Edge of U2 to compose the title number. Sung by Tina Turner, "GoldenEye," reached #10 in the UK.

Audiences embraced Pierce Brosnan as Bond in overwhelming numbers. In the US, the film sold just shy of three times the number of tickets as *Licence to Kill*, the best box-office of any Bond film since *Moonraker*. The success of *GoldenEye* emphasized Bond's relevance in the post-Cold War world and marked the passing of the torch from Albert R. Broccoli to a new generation of producers: Michael G. Wilson and Barbara Broccoli.

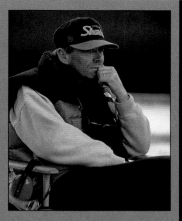

MARTIN CAMPBELL

Few directors bring such energy and passion to a film set as Martin Campbell. His desire to glean the most from every shot has helped launch both Pierce Brosnan and Daniel Craig in the role as James Bond.

Born in New Zealand in 1940, Martin Campbell moved to England in 1966 to become a cinematographer. He graduated to assistant director with the 1972 exploitation film *The Love Box.* The following year, he made his directing debut with an adult comedy, *The Sex Thief,* followed in 1975 by *Eskimo Nell,* a satire of the adult comedy genre. He produced the film *Black Joy* (1977) and was associate producer of *Scum* (1979), a tough and controversial exposé of the British borstal system for young offenders.

Moving into television in the late 1970s, Campbell made his name as a superior director of action dramas, helming episodes of *Minder, Shoestring,* and *The Professionals.* In the early 1980s, he directed two critically acclaimed miniseries, *Reilly: Ace of Spies* (1983) and *Edge Of Darkness* (1985), the latter winning a BAFTA TV Award for Best Drama Series.

Campbell returned to feature directing with the American thriller *Criminal Law* (1988), starring Gary Oldman and Kevin Bacon, followed by *Defenseless* (1991) and *No Escape* (1994). His work in the spy genre with *Reilly* and *Edge Of Darkness* impressed producers Michael G. Wilson and Barbara Broccoli, who chose him to introduce Pierce Brosnan as 007 in *GoldenEye* (1995). The result was an exciting and hugely profitable film that relaunched the franchise after a six-year hiatus.

After *GoldenEye,* Campbell directed *The Mask Of Zorro* (1998), *Vertical Limit* (2000), *Beyond Borders* (2003), and *The Legend Of Zorro* (2005). He returned to the world of Bond for 2006's *Casino Royale.*

MAKING GOLDENEYE
(clockwise from above left)
Pierce Brosnan (James Bond) performs a slide on a set re-creation of the Arecibo radio telescope; Derek Meddings poses on his miniature of the area surrounding the Severnaya Space Weapons Centre; Sean Bean (Alec Treveylan) and Pierce Brosnan shoot the film's climax (turned 90°) on a green screen stage at Leavesden Studios; Brosnan poses with Desmond Llewelyn on the set of Q's lab; script writer Bruce Feirstein.

TOMORROW NEVER DIES
(1997)

CAST Pierce Brosnan (James Bond), Jonathan Pryce (Carver), Michelle Yeoh (Wai Lin), Teri Hatcher (Paris Carver), Ricky Jay (Gupta), Götz Otto (Stamper), Joe Don Baker (Wade), Vincent Schiavelli (Dr. Kaufman), Judi Dench (M), Desmond Llewelyn (Q), Samantha Bond (Moneypenny), Colin Salmon (Robinson), Geoffrey Palmer (Admiral Roebuck), Julian Fellowes (Minister of Defense), Terence Rigby (General Bukharin), Cecilie Thomsen (Professor Inga Bergstrom), Nina Young (Tamara), Daphne Deckers (Carver's PR), Mark Spalding (Stealth Boat Captain), Bruce Alexander (Captain, HMS *Chester*), Anthony Green (Firing Officer, HMS *Chester*), Christopher Bowen (Commander Richard Day), Michael Byrne (Admiral Kelly), Pip Torrens (Captain, HMS *Bedford*)
PRODUCED BY
Michael G. Wilson & Barbara Broccoli
DIRECTOR Roger Spottiswoode
SCREENPLAY BY Bruce Feirstein
LINE PRODUCER Anthony Waye
"TOMORROW NEVER DIES" written by Sheryl Crow & Mitchell Froom; produced by Mitchell Froom; performed by Sheryl Crow
MUSIC BY David Arnold
PRODUCTION DESIGNER Allan Cameron
DIRECTOR OF PHOTOGRAPHY Robert Elswitt
EDITORS Dominique Fortin, Michael Arcand
COSTUME DESIGNER Lindy Hemming
2ND UNIT DIRECTOR & STUNT COORDINATOR Vic Armstrong
SPECIAL EFFECTS SUPERVISOR Chris Corbould
STUNT SUPERVISOR Dickey Beer
CASTING Debbie McWilliams
MAIN TITLE DESIGNED BY Daniel Kleinman
MINIATURE EFFECTS John Richardson
AERIAL COORDINATOR Marc Wolff
HALO JUMP COORDINATOR B. J. Worth
2ND UNIT CAMERAMAN Jonathan Taylor
MINIATURE PHOTOGRAPHY Paul Wilson
UNDERWATER PHOTOGRAPHY Pete Romano
ADDITIONAL PHOTOGRAPHY Eddie Collins
AERIAL PHOTOGRAPHY Adam Dale
SET DECORATOR Peter Young
CONSTRUCTION COORDINATOR Ray Barrett
PROPERTY MASTER Ty Tieger
ART DIRECTORS Stephen Scott, Giles Masters, Tony Reading, Jonathan Lee, Ken Court
MAKEUP SUPERVISOR Norma Webb
HAIRDRESSING SUPERVISOR Eithne Fennell
WARDROBE SUPERVISOR John Scott
ELECTRICAL SUPERVISOR John Higgins
STILLS PHOTOGRAPHER Keith Hamshere
PUBLICITY & MARKETING Gordon Arnell
FAR EAST PROD. SUPERVISOR Philip Kohler
UNIT MANAGER Iris Rose
PRODUCTION MANAGER Janine Modder
LOCATION PRODUCTION MANAGERS Terry Bamber, John Bernard, Leonhard Gmür, Neil Ravan
ASSISTANT DIRECTOR Gerry Gavigan
CAMERA OPERATOR Ian Foster
SCRIPT SUPERVISOR Angela Wharton
SOUND MIXER Chris Munro
SUPERVISING SOUND EDITOR Martin Evans
2ND UNIT ASSISTANT DIR. Terry Madden
PRODUCTION SUPERVISOR Callum McDougall
SUPERVISING PRODUCTION ACCOUNTANT Andrew Noakes
LEGAL & BUSINESS AFFAIRS David Pope

"How do we make the 18th Bond an event?" United Artists production executive Jeff Kleeman asked producers Michael G. Wilson and Barbara Broccoli in May 1995, while *GoldenEye* was still shooting.

Bruce Feirstein, the final contributing writer to the *GoldenEye* script, had a nine-word pitch about a media baron villain, "Words are the new weapons; satellites, the new artillery." Wilson and Broccoli were intrigued and commissioned Feirstein to write a first draft.

Numerous rewrites followed as the producers brought in director Roger Spottiswoode, who began as an editor for directors Sam Peckinpah and Walter Hill in the 1970s. Spottiswoode brought a strong sense of pace to the film, which became the first 007 adventure to run less than two hours since 1971's *Diamonds Are Forever.*

Hong Kong action star Michelle Yeoh accepted the role of Wai Lin, a Chinese secret agent and very much Bond's equal. For the role of power-hungry Elliot Carver, the filmmakers recruited British actor and Miss Saigon star Jonathan Pryce. American Teri Hatcher, from the hit television series *Lois and Clark*, signed to play Paris Carver, Bond's former lover-turned-villain's wife. The filmmakers shot the emotional love scene between Bond and Paris in a suite at Stoke Poges Golf Club, the setting of the golf game in *Goldfinger* (1964).

With both Pinewood and Leavesden Studios completely booked, the filmmakers once again needed to create a new studio. They turned a former grocery warehouse in Frogmore, England into a production facility.

Long-time production designer Peter Lamont could not work on the film due to his commitment to James Cameron's *Titanic* (1997); production designer Allan Cameron was hired and gave the film very high-tech yet realistic sets.

Second unit director Vic Armstrong filmed many remarkable action scenes, including the pre-titles sequence, set at a Khyber Pass terrorist arms bazaar. The cameras rolled in January 1997 in the French Pyrenees to take advantage of the snow. Armstrong and his crew later filmed a spectacularly contained car chase with the Brent Cross Shopping Centre car park doubling for a multi-story car park in Hamburg. To create the effect of Bond driving his car via a touchpad on his cell phone, special effects supervisor Chris Corbould's crew rebuilt four BMW 750iLs to be driven by hidden stunt driver Steve Griffin crouched on the back floorboard watching video monitors. In the end, 17 BMW 17 750iL were used by the production to put the four minute car chase on film. The filmmakers also staged a hair-raising motorcycle-helicopter chase seamlessly melding Bangkok locations and English sets. At Frogmore, French motorcycle expert Jean-Pierre Goy, astride a BMW R1200 motorbike, insisted on performing an incredible leap between two buildings over a prop helicopter.

Simultaneously, miniature effects supervisor John Richardson commandeered the Baja Studios tank in Mexico after Titanic finished production to film models of the stealth ship and HMS *Devonshire*. To perform the film's spectacular HALO jump, parachute specialist B. J. Worth conducted 80 parachute jumps, falling 12,000 ft (3,658 m) over Arizona and 14,000 ft (4,267 m) over Florida.

MAKING TOMORROW *(below top left) Roger Spottiswoode directs Pierce Brosnan (Bond) and Michelle Yeoh (Wai Lin) on a rooftop in Bangkok.*

OUR MAN IN FROGMORE *(below top right) Production designer Allan Cameron on his recreated Saigon street at Frogmore Studios.*

EVERY PICTURE TELLS A STORY *(below bottom left): Original storyboards of the helicopter attack on Bond and Wai Lin.*

CITYSCAPE *(below, middle right) A scenic artist touches up a photographic transparency of Saigon used for the sequence in Carver's media headquarters in Vietnam.*

Spottiswoode's editing skills were invaluable in designing these sequences so they would cut smoothly. When Bond and Wai Lin leap from a Saigon skyscraper and rip a banner of Carver's face, Spottiswoode combined shots of the lead actors, stunt performers, miniatures of the actors, the real location at Sinn Sathorn Tower in Bangkok, a 60 ft (18.3 m) replica of the building and banner on the Frogmore backlot, and digital compositing to create the finished sequence.

During the final weeks of production, the crew filmed the interior of the stealth ship climax inside the Albert R. Broccoli 007 Stage at Pinewood Studios during the day. At night, the crew switched to filming the underwater sequences beneath the ship interior in the 007 stage tank. The sequences had to be filmed with different electrical power setups and at different times of the day to avoid injuring anybody.

To make the December 9, 1997 premiere date, David Arnold composed and recorded the score in sections during production. When the filmmakers first heard the opening bars from Arnold's outstanding "White Knight" cue, they knew they had found the heir apparent to John Barry. With one foot in the 1960s and the other set firmly in the 1990s, Arnold created a fresh-sounding score with several references to Bond music of the past. Sheryl Crow wrote and performed the brooding title song, which received Golden Globe and Grammy nominations, and Arnold, David McAlmont, and Bond lyricist alumnus Don Black wrote the haunting end-title song "Surrender," a sexy, brassy number belted out by k.d. lang in the style of Shirley Bassey.

Tomorrow Never Dies opened to a whirlwind of publicity during the 1997 Christmas season. It topped *GoldenEye*'s grosses in the US and played to packed cinemas around the world, solidifying Pierce Brosnan's place as the perfect James Bond for the 1990s.

DAVID ARNOLD

David Arnold made James Bond music exciting for a new generation of fans. He is the first composer since John Barry to score more than one Bond film. Like Barry, he has an inherent sense of the James Bond sound. Born in Luton in 1962, Arnold saw his first Bond movie, *You Only Live Twice* (1967), as a child and was mesmerized by the film and its music. Years later, he taught himself to write, orchestrate, and compose scores for filmmaker Danny Cannon and scored with the hit Bjork-performed song "Play Dead" for the film *The Young Americans* (1993). After winning a Grammy for his rousing score for the sci-fi blockbuster *Independence Day* (1996), he set to work on an album entitled *Shaken And Stirred*, for which modern artists performed new interpretations of classic Bond songs. As he finished these recordings, he sent them to MGM Music and the Bond producers. They were extremely impressed with what they heard, and, when John Barry proved unable to score *Tomorrow Never Dies* (1997), the film was offered to Arnold with Barry's blessing. Arnold has gone on to compose soundtracks for *The World Is Not Enough* (1999), *Die Another Day* (2002), and *Casino Royale* (2006).)

STREET PERFORMERS
An extra prepares for his moment on the Frogmore backlot (below left); Pierce Brosnan and Michelle Yeoh shoot close ups for the motorcycle chase in a Saigon market (below right).

COOL CUSTOMER *(right) Vic Armstrong directs Bond and Elektra's ski tour.*

ELECTRIFYING
(far right) Original design sketch by Lindy Hemming of Elektra King's red gown.

THE WORLD IS NOT ENOUGH
(1999)

THE MEN BEHIND
THE MAYHEM
*(clockwise from right)
Michael Apted
discusses motivation
with Robert Carlyle
(Renard) at Pinewood
Studios; Special
Effects Supervisor
Chris Corbould poses
by Bond's BMW Z8;
Desmond Llewelyn
(Q) talks with Apted.*

CAST Pierce Brosnan (James Bond), Sophie
Marceau (Elektra King), Robert Carlyle (Renard),
Denise Richards (Christmas Jones), Robbie Coltrane
(Valentin Zukovsky), Judi Dench ("M"), Desmond
Llewelyn ("Q"), John Cleese (Q's Assistant),
Samantha Bond (Miss Moneypenny), David Calder
(Sir Robert King), Michael Kitchen (Tanner), Colin
Salmon (Robinson), Serena Scott Thomas (Dr. Molly
Warmflash), John Seru (Gabor), Claude-Oliver
Rudolph (Colonel Akakievich), Ulrich Thomsen
(Sacha Davidov), Goldie (The Bull), Maria Grazia
Cucinotta (Cigar Girl), Patrick Malahide (Lachaise),
Jeff Nuttall (Dr. Arkov), Diran Meghreblian (Priest)
PRODUCERS Michael G. Wilson & Barbara
Broccoli
DIRECTOR Michael Apted
WRITTEN BY Neal Purvis & Robert Wade
LINE PRODUCER Anthony Waye
'THE WORLD IS NOT ENOUGH'
PERFORMED BY Garbage
MUSIC BY David Arnold
PRODUCTION DESIGNER Peter Lamont
DIRECTOR OF PHOTOGRAPHY
Adrian Biddle, BSC
EDITOR Jim Clark
COSTUME DESIGNER Lindy Hemming
2ND UNIT DIRECTED BY Vic Armstrong
SPECIAL EFFECTS SUPERVISOR Chris Corbould
STUNT CO-ORDINATOR Simon Crane
CASTING Debbie McWilliams
MINIATURES John Richardson
VISUAL EFFECTS SUPERVISOR Mara Bryan
MAIN TITLE DESIGNED BY Daniel Kleinman
2ND UNIT PHOTOGRAPHY Jonathan Taylor
MINIATURE PHOTOGRAPHY Paul Wilson,
BSC
UNDERWATER PHOTOGRAPHY Tim Wooster
AERIAL COORDINATOR Marc Wolff
ADDITIONAL UNIT DIRECTED &
PHOTOGRAPHED BY Arthur Wooster, BSC
SUPERVISING ART DIRECTOR Neil Lamont
SET DECORATOR Simon Wakefield
CONSTRUCTION CO-ORDINATOR
Peter G. Williams
PROPERTY MASTER Barry Wilkinson
ART DIRECTORS Andrew Ackland-Snow,
Steve Lawrence, Fred Hole, Simon Lamont,
Mark Harris, Jim Morahan
MAKEUP SUPERVISOR Linda De Vetta
HAIRDRESSING SUPERVISOR Colin Jamison
WARDROBE SUPERVISOR John Scott
ELECTRICAL SUPERVISOR Kevin Day
STILLS PHOTOGRAPHER Keith Hamshere
PUBLICITY & MARKETING Anne Bennett
UNIT MANAGER Iris Rose
PRODUCTION SUPERVISORS Philip Kohler,
Janine Modder, Hugh Harlow
LOCATION PRODUCTION MANAGERS
Terry Bamber, John Bernard, Tim Lewis, Ali
Akdeniz, Yousaf Bokhari, Carlos Taillefer
ASSISTANT DIRECTOR Gerry Gavigan
2ND UNIT ASSISTANT DIRECTOR Terry
Madden
SCRIPT SUPERVISOR Nikki Clapp
SOUND MIXER Chris Munro
SUPERVISING SOUND EDITOR Martin Evans
CAMERA OPERATOR David Worley
ASSOCIATE PRODUCER Nigel Goldsack
FINANCIAL CONTROLLER Andrew Noakes
PRODUCTION EXECUTIVE David Pope

The World Is Not Enough brought James Bond's adventures in the 20th century to a close, and the producers were determined to create a dramatic plot with emotionally complex characters that would twist the audience's preconceptions of 007 at every turn.

In November 1997, Bond producer Barbara Broccoli watched an episode of *Nightline* that detailed how the untapped oil in the Caspian Sea was ripe for the taking after decades of Soviet control. Every major oil company now had a stake there. Broccoli wondered what might happen if the next Bond villain tried to eliminate all the competition to provide the only pipeline from the Caspian to the West.

Broccoli and her producing partner Michael G. Wilson approached British screenwriters Neal Purvis and Robert Wade. The duo pitched two villains: one who was close to death and the other a woman; the characters of Renard and Elektra King grew from these early conversations. During the scripting process, Broccoli reminded the writers, "With Elektra, Bond thinks he has found Tracy [his short-lived wife from OHMSS] but he's really found Blofeld."

Since Elektra was the key to making the film work, the producers wanted a filmmaker skilled at eliciting strong performances from women. They appointed Michael Apted to helm *The World Is Not Enough*, a title taken from the family motto of a branch of the Bond family in the novel *On Her Majesty's Secret Service*. Apted had directed Sissy Spacek in an Academy Award-winning performance and Sigourney Weaver and Jodie Foster to Academy Award nominations. He immediately saw great potential in involving M more in the plot. To strengthen the women's roles, Apted brought in his screenwriter wife Dana Stevens. To strengthen Bond's role, Apted brought screenwriter Bruce Feirstein back to the fold.

With the script complete, the producers focused on casting. French actress Sophie Marceau was chosen for the central role of Elektra and, after a mesmeric performance as a psychopath in the British television crime series *Cracker*, Scottish actor Robert Carlyle was chosen to play terrorist

Renard. American actress Denise Richards landed the role of nuclear physicist Dr. Christmas Jones. Robbie Coltrane reprised his popular character from *GoldenEye*, Russian arms dealer Valentin Zukovsky. In this film, Zukovsky owns a casino and caviar factory in Baku.

Filming began at Pinewood Studios on January 11, 1999, the first 007 film to be based at the studio since 1987's *The Living Daylights*. Filming continued in Bilbao, Spain, which Apted chose for the backdrop of the Guggenheim Museum. When the crew arrived, 100,000 excited Spaniards came to view the production. Apted and his crew returned to Spain later in the shoot after the cancellation of extensive filming in Turkey. Second unit director Vic Armstrong and stunt coordinator Simon Crane had their hands full with two major stunt sequences: the boat chase on the River Thames and the parahawk—ski chase (filmed in Chamonix, France). Production designer Peter Lamont's team built the set of Zukovsky's caviar factory—a complicated set of walkways and night walls complete with fiber-optic stars—in the Paddock Tank at Pinewood. The set was now ready to film the difficult sequence where Bond is pursued by Elektra's helicopters equipped with murderous buzzsaws. Since the local community would not allow real helicopters to be flown above the studio, a unit shot footage of helicopters at Long Valley, later enhanced with CGI effects. Miniature helicopters also appeared in shots. For realism, special-effects supervisor Chris Corbould and his team suspended an Aerospatiale Squirrel helicopter sans rotors on a computer programmed gimble arm to swoop over the set. In the Bahamas, miniature effects supervisor John Richardson shot the 45-foot (13.7 m) submarine model for the film's climax.

During the film's test screening, the Thames boat chase followed the main titles. But audience feedback indicated that the pre-titles sequence needed to be bigger. Apted and the producers decided to do some tight editing and move the boat chase so that it came before the main titles, resulting in the longest pre-titles sequence to date.

David Arnold returned to compose the film's electronic-driven score, using an Arabic string instrument, the qanun, to give a Middle Eastern feel. Since the lyrics of the title song, written with Don Black, were from Elektra's point-of-view, Arnold chose Shirley Manson of the rock band Garbage, since he felt her voice had a "steel fist in a velvet glove" quality. The song reached #11 on the UK charts.

The World Is Not Enough premiered in November 1999 and proved a huge worldwide success. The producers had gambled on a more complex storyline and won.

ALBERT R. BROCCOLI'S EON PRODUCTIONS PRESENTS
PIERCE BROSNAN AS IAN FLEMING'S JAMES BOND 007

The World Is Not Enough 007

DANIEL KLEINMAN

After Maurice Binder died in 1991, director Daniel Kleinman faced the unenviable task of stepping into his shoes as the designer and creator of one of the most important sequences in every Bond film: the main titles. His first assignment was *GoldenEye* in 1995, and he has remained with the Bond team ever since.

After graduating from art school in 1977, Kleinman worked as an illustrator of album covers. His work caught the attention of music video directors, and he became one himself in 1983 when he directed the video "Crushed By The Wheels Of Industry" for Heaven 17. Over 100 music video directing assignments followed, including one-hour HBO specials for Madonna, Prince, and Van Halen. He came to the notice of the Bond producers when he directed Gladys Knight's video for *Licence To Kill* (1989).

Kleinman has used digital technology to update the look of the titles, choosing images that reflect the themes of each film. For *GoldenEye*, he used falling Soviet statues to symbolize the end of Communism. For *Tomorrow Never Dies* (1997), he took viewers behind video screens into a seemingly transparent world where everything is visible. In the titles for *The World Is Not Enough* (1999), Kleinman showcased Elektra King's obsession with oil. For *Die Another Day* (2002), Kleinman broke new ground by intercutting the film's motifs of ice and fire with Bond's grueling 14 months of torture in a North Korean prison.

For *Casino Royale* (2006), Kleinman found inspiration in a first edition cover of Ian Fleming's novel *Casino Royale* that featured red hearts on a playing card dripping blood. The title sequence's bold colors and complex line patterns served as a backdrop for showcasing the masculine appeal of Daniel Craig's James Bond.

One of the world's top commercial directors, Kleinman has stayed true to his dictum that he only creates titles for 007.

DIE ANOTHER DAY (2002)

CAST Pierce Brosnan (James Bond), Halle Berry (Jinx), Toby Stephens (Gustav Graves), Rosamund Pike (Miranda Frost), Rick Yune (Zao), Judi Dench (M), John Cleese (Q), Michael Madsen (Falco), Will Yun Lee (Colonel Moon), Kenneth Tsang (General Moon), Emilio Echevarría (Raoul), Mikhail Gorevoy (Vlad), Lawrence Makoare (Mr. Kil), Colin Salmon (Robinson), Samantha Bond (Moneypenny), Ben Wee (Snooty desk clerk), Ho Yi (Hotel Manager), Rachel Grant (Peaceful), Ian Pirie (Creep), Simón Andreu (Dr. Alvarez), Mark Dymond (Van Bierk), Deborah Moore (Air hostess), Tymarah (Scorpion Guard)
PRODUCED BY
Michael G. Wilson & Barbara Broccoli
DIRECTED BY Lee Tamahori
WRITTEN BY Neal Purvis & Robert Wade
EXECUTIVE PRODUCER Anthony Waye
CO-PRODUCER Callum McDougall
"DIE ANOTHER DAY" PERFORMED BY
Madonna
MUSIC David Arnold
PRODUCTION DESIGNER Peter Lamont
DIRECTOR OF PHOTOGRAPHY
David Tattersall, BSC
EDITOR Christian Wagner
COSTUME DESIGNER Lindy Hemming
2ND UNIT DIRECTOR Vic Armstrong
SPECIAL EFFECTS SUPERVISOR Chris Corbould
STUNT COORDINATOR George Aguilar
CASTING Debbie McWilliams
MAIN TITLE DESIGNED BY Danny Kleinman
MODEL EFFECTS SUPERVISOR John Richardson
VISUAL EFFECTS SUPERVISOR Mara Bryan
2ND UNIT PHOTOGRAPHY Jonathan Taylor
MODEL PHOTOGRAPHY Paul Wilson
ADDITIONAL UNITS PHOTOGRAPHY BY
Shaun O'Dell, Arthur Wooster BSC, Don King
SUPERVISING ART DIRECTOR Simon Lamont
SET DIRECTOR Simon Wakefield
CONSTRUCTION MANAGER Paul Hayes
PROPERTY MASTER Ty Tieger
ELECTRICAL SUPERVISOR Eddie Knight
ART DIRECTORS James Hambidge, Mark Harris, Fred Hole, Stephen Scott, Alan Tomkins
PUBLICITY & MARKETING Anne Bennett
MAKEUP SUPERVISOR Paul Engelen
HAIRDRESSING SUPERVISOR Colin Jamison
WARDROBE SUPERVISOR Graham Churchyard
STILLS PHOTOGRAPHER Keith Hamshere
PRODUCTION MANAGERS
Terry Bamber, Tim Lewis
UNIT MANAGER Iris Rose
PRODUCTION SUPERVISOR Janine Modder
LOCATION PRODUCTION SUPERVISORS
Philip Kohler, Mark Albela, Chris Brock, Glenn Beadles
ASSISTANT DIRECTOR Gerry Gavigan
2ND UNIT ASSISTANT DIRECTOR
Terry Madden
SCRIPT SUPERVISOR Anna Worley
SOUND MIXER Chris Munro
SUPERVISING SOUND EDITOR Martin Evans
CAMERA OPERATOR Peter Robertson
POST PRODUCTION SUPERVISOR
Michael Solinger
FINANCIAL CONTROLLER Andrew Noakes
PRODUCTION EXECUTIVE David Pope

Die Another Day in 2002 marked the release of the 20th James Bond film, the 40th anniversary of the 007 film series. Screenwriters Neal Purvis and Robert Wade began work on "Bond 20" in the summer of 2000, brainstorming ideas with producers Michael G. Wilson and Barbara Broccoli. Agreeing they wanted the new film to be on a grand scale, similar to 1967's *You Only Live Twice.* Purvis and Wade suggested structuring the film around Ian Fleming's third novel, *Moonraker,* with a villain who transforms his identity, becomes a knighted industrialist, and plans to use a space weapon in a mad act of vengeance. Choosing the long-running political tensions between North and South Korea as the film's main theme, they plotted a grand, globe-hopping adventure on a scale never before seen in a Bond movie.

To direct, the producers chose New Zealand-born Lee Tamahori, who had helmed *Once Were Warriors* (1994), a movie Broccoli called "one of the best films made in the last 50 years." Tamahori brought a sense of spectacle and history to *Die Another Day,* peppering it with clever nods to James Bond's past. Eagle-eyed viewers will note, for example, the name of the Hong Kong hotel, The Rubyeon Royale, which pays homage to the Ruby Anniversary of EON Productions as well as the first Bond novel *Casino Royale.*

The producers cast Halle Berry as NSA agent Jinx; British stage actor Toby Stephens joined the cast to play the villain Graves; and newcomer Rosamund Pike took the role of duplicitous MI6 agent Miranda Frost. Rick Yune pursued the smaller role of Colonel Moon, but Tamahori cast him in the larger role of terrorist Zao.

On Christmas Day, 2001, a small unit began work off the coast of Maui, Hawaii, where Laird Hamilton and his surfing team rode some of the world's largest waves for the film's opening scene—a sign of the scale to come. The precredits sequence alone required a small fleet of hovercraft, bounding mines, the destruction of several sports cars, and a miniature of a vast waterfall. Everyone involved wanted this film to be the biggest Bond ever: the filmmakers changed the climax from an indoor Japanese beach to an out-of-control Antonov plane, the largest aircraft in the world, and Tamahori continued a car chase that began on a frozen lake into Peter Lamont's magnificent, melting Ice Palace set. Filming also took place in the largest greenhouse in the world, The Eden Project, in Cornwall, England.

Five weeks into filming, Pierce Brosnan injured his knee while sprinting on the set of Colonel Moon's compound on the Pinewood backlot. Brosnan flew to Los Angeles for emergency surgery, which ignited worries about the schedule. However, according to Broccoli, Pierce "was almost bionic in his recovery."

The production received some morale-boosting news in

March when Halle won the Best Actress Academy Award for *Monster's Ball* and sound mixer Chris Munro won the Oscar for Best Sound for *Black Hawk Down*. The Academy Awards also featured nominations for Dame Judi Dench and Dame Maggie Smith, mother of Toby Stephens, for *Iris* and *Gosford Park* respectively.

Halle Berry soon returned to the production to shoot Jinx's dramatic emergence from the sea in an orange bikini, deliberately recalling Ursula Andress's iconic first appearance as Honey Ryder in *Dr. No.* (1962). The scene was shot in Cadiz, Spain (doubling for Havana, Cuba) during a cold but thankfully clear day after five days of steady rain.

By June 2002, seven units were filming simultaneously to deliver the movie by November 2002. Aerial, underwater, and miniature units, as well as first, second,

performed the title song and also had a cameo role as fencing instructor Verity; she thus became the first title-song performer to play a role in a Bond film.

On November 18, 2002 when *Die Another Day* premiered at London's Royal Albert Hall. Her Majesty Queen Elizabeth II made this the only film premiere of her Jubilee year celebrations, viewing the movie with former James Bond actors George Lazenby, Sir Roger Moore, Timothy Dalton, and 3,000 guests.

Die Another Day thrilled audiences around the globe. However, while the film successfully brought James Bond into the new century, it also marked the end of an era. It would prove to be Pierce Brosnan's last performance as James Bond.

PAUSE FOR THOUGHT *(facing page, top left) Senior vice president of marketing and publicity Anne Bennett confers with producer Michael G. Wilson.*

ON AND OFF SET *(clockwise from left) Pierce Brosnan shoots in front of a blue screen for close ups during the hovercraft sequence; costume designer Lindy Hemming warms Halle Berry (Jinx) on a chilly location shoot in Spain; assistant director Gerry Gavigan lines up the background action for a major shot; supervising art director Simon Lamont with his uncle, production designer Peter Lamont.*

THE DIE IS CAST *(far left and left) Casting director Debbie McWilliams; Lee Tamahori directs Brosnan during the virtual reality sequence.*

KEEPING COOL *Pierce Brosnan and producer Michael G. Wilson await the next shot.*

and third units pulled together to create remarkable images of action.

Special effects supervisor Chris Corbould provided numerous practical special effects, including one shot for the film's climax that involved a staggering 70 explosions.

David Arnold returned to compose his third Bond film score, this time experimenting by recording an orchestra playing sections of his score in reverse. He also used a Korean stringed instrument, the yanggeum, to give the Korean scenes a distinctive feel. Madonna wrote and

NEAL PURVIS & ROBERT WADE

Screenwriters Neal Purvis and Robert Wade have contributed highly inventive plots, characters, and action scenes to the James Bond film series and have succeeded in giving the stories of the recent 007 adventures a highly modern feel while simultaneously tipping their hats to Bond's creator Ian Fleming. They are noted for creating rich villains and exploring the complex character of 007.

Purvis, born outside London, and Wade, born in Cardiff, Wales, met at the University of Kent at Canterbury, where Purvis studied philosophy and Wade studied English. They subsequently began collaborating on film scripts, enjoying their first success in 1991 when their script *Let Him Have It*, the story of the Craig-Bentley murder case, was made into a feature film by director Peter Medak. The film was screened for Parliament and played a role in Derek Bentley's posthumous pardon. Purvis and Wade continued to work in a variety of genres, and one of their scripts for the highwayman adventure *Plunkett And MacLeane* (1999) came to the attention of Bond producers Michael G. Wilson and Barbara Broccoli.

The pair wrote the storyline and co-wrote the screenplay of *The World Is Not Enough* (1999) and were the only writers on *Die Another Day* (2002). They took time off from the Bond series to co-write the spy spoof *Johnny English* (2003) starring Rowan Atkinson, and then wrote the story outlines and formative drafts of *Casino Royale* (2006) and the 22nd Bond adventure (2008). They also wrote and co-produced both *Return to Sender* (2004) and *Stoned* (2005).

WRITTEN IN ICE *(above) Neal Purvis and Robert Wade discuss the script with Lee Tamahori on the ice palace set.*

CASINO ROYALE (2006)

CAST Daniel Craig (James Bond), Eva Green (Vesper Lynd), Mads Mikkelsen (Le Chiffre), Judi Dench (M), Jeffrey Wright (Felix Leiter), Giancarlo Giannini (Mathis), Caterina Murino (Solange), Simon Abkarian (Dimitrios), Isaach De Bankolé (Obanno), Jesper Christiansen (Mr. White), Ivana Milicevic (Valenka), Tobias Menzies (Villiers), Claudio Santamaria (Carlos), Sébastien Foucan (Mollaka), Malcolm Sinclair (Dryden), Richard Sammel (Gettler), Ludger Pistor (Mendel), Joseph Millson (Carter), Daud Shah (Fisher), Clemens Shick (Kratt), Obanno's lieutenant (Michael Offei), Ade (Infante), Urbano Barberini (Tomelli), Tsai Chin (Madame Wu), Charlie Levi Leroy (Gallardo), Lazar Ristovski, (Kaminofsky), Tom So (Fukutu), Veruschka (Gräfin Von Wallenstein)
PRODUCERS
Michael G. Wilson & Barbara Broccoli
DIRECTOR Martin Campbell
SCREENPLAY WRITERS
Neal Purvis & Robert Wade & Paul Haggis
BASED ON THE NOVEL BY Ian Fleming
EXECUTIVE PRODUCERS
Anthony Waye & Callum McDougall
"YOU KNOW MY NAME" PERFORMED BY
Chris Cornell
"YOU KNOW MY NAME" WRITTEN & PRODUCED BY Chris Cornell & David Arnold
MUSIC BY David Arnold
PRODUCTION DESIGNER Peter Lamont
DIRECTOR OF PHOTOGRAPHY
Phil Méheux, BSC
EDITOR Stuart Baird, ACE
COSTUME DESIGNER Lindy Hemming
2ND UNIT DIRECTOR Alexander Witt
SPECIAL EFFECTS & MINIATURE EFFECT SUPERVISOR Chris Corbould
MAIN TITLE DESIGNER Daniel Kleinman
CASTING Debbie McWilliams
STUNT COORDINATOR Gary Powell
UNIT PRODUCTION MANAGER
Jeremy Johns
2ND UNIT PRODUCTION MANAGER
Terry Bamber
FIRST ASSISTANT MANAGER Bruce Moriarty
VISUAL EFFECTS & MINIATURE SUPERVISOR
Steve Begg
SUPERVISING ART DIRECTOR Simon Lamont
PROPERTY MASTER Ty Teiger
CONSTRUCTION MANAGER Stephen Bohan
POST PRODUCTION SUPERVISOR
Michael Solinger
SOUND RECORDIST Chris Munro
ELECTRICAL SUPERVISOR Eddie Knight
STILLS PHOTOGRAPHER Jay Maidment
MAKEUP SUPERVISOR Paul Engelen
HAIRDRESSING SUPERVISOR Christine Blundell
WARDROBE SUPERVISOR Dan Grace
CAMERA OPERATOR Roger Pearce
2ND UNIT ASSISTANT DIRECTOR
Terry Madden
SCRIPT SUPERVISOR Jean Bourne
PUBLICITY & MARKETING Anne Bennett
PROMOTIONS Keith Snelgrove
ASSISTANT PRODUCER David G. Wilson
ASSOCIATE PRODUCER Andrew Noakes
PRODUCTION EXECUTIVE David Pope

ALBERT R. BROCCOLI'S EON PRODUCTIONS PRESENTS DANIEL CRAIG AS IAN FLEMING'S JAMES BOND 007 IN

CASINO ROYALE 007

NOVEMBER 16

casinoroyale-movie.co.uk

After the completion of *Die Another Day* (2002) producers Michael G. Wilson and Barbara Broccoli discussed the future of James Bond. They decided to make a film of *Casino Royale*, the first, darkest, and most literary of the Bond novels, which had been previously unavailable to EON Productions. Wilson and Broccoli felt the storyline of Bond going after a Soviet operative who has squandered money and now desperately needs to win it back at the gaming tables could be adapted to the world of modern terror networks and those that finance terrorist attacks.

To film Ian Fleming's first novel and the story of how Bond became a "00", presented the producers with many new

FUN IN THE SUN *(clockwise from above right) Daniel Craig (James Bond) prepares for his entrance from the sea in the Bahamas; Sébastien Foucan receives weapons training on location; director Martin Campbell in his element.*

challenges. Not only did they need to find a new actor to play James Bond, but MGM was soon sold to a consortium that included Sony Pictures. Sony would now finance and distribute the new Bond film. The careful development of the script, the change of studios, and the long process of casting contributed to a four-year gap between Bond films.

Screenwriters Neal Purvis and Robert Wade returned to adapt Fleming's novel. The filmmakers worked to capture the spirit of Fleming's novel while focusing on the story of "how James became Bond." In early 2005, Martin Campbell signed to direct the film. His success with *GoldenEye* (1995) had launched Pierce Brosnan as 007; he now faced the task of launching another actor to take on the character of James Bond. Paul Haggis, soon to win two Oscars for writing and

directing *Crash* (2004), joined to work on the script. With a script finally in place, Campbell and the producers conducted two days of screen testing and formally approached their first choice to play 007—Daniel Craig.

The filmmakers assembled an international cast to fill the key remaining roles. French actress Eva Green signed on for the critical role of Vesper Lynd, and Danish actor Mads Mikkelsen took the part of Le Chiffre. To play Bond's liaison in Montenegro, the filmmakers chose Italian acting legend Giancarlo Giannini. African-American actor Jeffrey Wright became the seventh actor to portray Felix Leiter.

Production began on the 27th January 2006 at Modrany Studio, outside Prague. The rigorous fitness regime Daniel Craig had embarked on in preparation for the shoot immediately paid off: Craig's first scene was the pulse-pounding chase sequence in which Bond pursues would-be bomber Mollaka through the Nambutu Embassy.

On the 17th February the production moved to the Bahamas. A derelict hotel in Coral Harbour provided the perfect location for the filmmakers to stage an amazing foot chase through a construction site. The scene was inspired by footage Purvis and Wade had seen of Sébastien Foucan demonstrating his sport of free running, also known as parkour, in the 2003 documentary *Jump London*. The filmmakers cast Foucan as the bomb-maker Mollaka and employed his amazing skills to make the stunts as real as possible. The jaw-dropping leap from one construction crane to another and then to a roof below was done in one shot. While the jumpers wore safety harnesses connected to an even higher crane, and a 15 in by 28 in (38 cm by 7 cm) landing platform was digitally removed from the shot, the leap was done for real.

Back at the Barrandov Studio in Prague, the filmmakers shot the poker game between Bond and Le Chiffre on one of Peter Lamont's most beautifully designed sets. Producer Michael G. Wilson, along with poker expert Thomas

Sambrook taught the actors the intricacies of Texas Hold'em poker, a game requiring a great deal more strategy than baccarat, the game Fleming chose for the novel.

In England, the stunt team tested ways to somersault one of the few Aston Martin DBS models then in existence. Stunt co-ordinator Gary Powell and driver Adam Kirley used an 18-in (46-cm) ramp to launch the $200,000-plus car into a roll, but the vehicle quickly slammed back down, shattering a mannequin of Vesper used in the shot. Special-effects supervisor Chris Corbould's team then mounted an air cannon in the car, hoping it would launch the vehicle into the air. The car flipped over seven times, a new world record.

At Dunsfold Aerodrome in Surrey, England, second unit director Alexander Witt staged other major stunts, including launching a car into the air as if it had been blasted by the slipstream of a 747 airliner. On the Albert R. Broccoli 007 Stage at Pinewood, special and visual effects supervisors Chris Corbould and Steve Begg helped create the most complex set ever built for a Bond film, the interior of a Venetian villa that crumbles into the Grand Canal. They also created the villa in miniature at 1/3 scale—26 ft (7.9 m) tall—in Pinewood's 800,000-gallon (3,636,872-liter) Paddock Tank.

MICHAEL G. WILSON & BARBARA BROCCOLI

Michael G. Wilson and Barbara Broccoli have been the producers of the James Bond films since 1995. Their vision has kept the 007 series and the character of James Bond both exciting and relevant.

Born in New York to actress-writer Dana Wilson, Michael G. Wilson studied engineering and then law. His mother married Bond producer Albert R. "Cubby" Broccoli in 1960, allowing Michael to witness firsthand Bond's success and development. In 1972, Wilson began working for his stepfather and Harry Saltzman in a legal-administrative capacity. He worked on many aspects of *The Spy Who Loved Me* (1977), earning the title, Special Assistant to the Producer. Wilson became executive producer on *Moonraker* (1979). For the next five Bond films, Wilson collaborated on the screenplays. With *A View To A Kill* (1985), Wilson became a full producing partner with Albert R. "Cubby" Broccoli. Michael G. Wilson is the Chairman of the National Media Museum of Photography, Film and Television.

Barbara Broccoli grew up with the Bond films. After earning a film degree from Loyola University in Los Angeles, she became an assistant director on *A View To A Kill*, although also she worked on the crew of both *For Your Eyes Only* (1981) and *Octopussy* (1983). With the next two films in the series, Broccoli graduated to associate producer, and first became a producer with Michael G. Wilson on *GoldenEye* in 1995.

Outside of Bond, Broccoli executive produced the acclaimed *Crime Of The Century* for HBO in 1996. Broccoli is also Chair of First Light, the UK Film Council's filmmaking initiative for young people.

Throughout the physically gruelling shoot, Daniel Craig continued to surpass the crew's expectations. The three months of training he undertook before filming had given his body a lean, dangerous look. His performance did not echo his predecessors as much as it brought Fleming's words to life. But would audiences accept a harder, colder Bond? Would they endure the stomach-wrenching torture scene from Fleming's novel? Would they feel betrayed by a Bond film where 007 does not get the girl, but only ends up with the bitter taste of her death and betrayal? As with the film's poker game, the stakes for the filmmakers were enormous.

Composer David Arnold faced a unique challenge with his fourth 007 score. The script specifically stated that the Bond theme would not be played until the end credits. Arnold and title song performer Chris Cornell, formerly of the rock band Soundgarden and later Audioslave, co-wrote a theme, "You Know My Name," which they felt contained the musical DNA of James Bond without relying on Monty Norman's "The James Bond Theme." The result was a hard-driving theme song that celebrated the essence of Bond's character in the film.

Casino Royale premiered on Tuesday, 14th November 2006, at the Odeon Leicester Square, London. The premiere had been chosen as the 60th Royal Film Performance, and was attended by Her Majesty, Queen Elizabeth II. The response around the globe was phenomenal: *Casino Royale* became the highest-grossing Bond film ever. In the UK, it became the first Bond film to earn more than $100 million at the box office. Daniel Craig's performance won universal praise and a BAFTA nomination for Best Actor. For producers Wilson and Broccoli, the gamble of making *Casino Royale* had paid off: a new standard had been set and a path for 007's future had been laid.

HOW JAMES BECAME BOND
(top to bottom, left to right)
Second unit director Alexander Witt; Martin Campbell discusses an important cinematic moment with Eva Green (Vesper Lynd) and Daniel Craig; executive producer Callum McDougall; Eva Green, Daniel Craig and Caterina Murino (Solange) pose for a publicity photo in the Bahamas; associate producer Andrew Noakes and executive producer Tony Waye on location; screenwriter Paul Haggis.

SENIOR EDITOR Alastair Dougall
SENIOR ART EDITOR Jill Clark
SENIOR DESIGNER Lisa Crowe
PROJECT EDITOR Laura Gilbert
DESIGNERS Ron Stobbart, Hanna Ländin,
Lynne Moulding
EDITORS Julia March, Amy Junor
DESIGN ASSISTANT Mika Kean-Hammerson
BRAND MANAGERS Lisa Lanzarini, Mark Richards
PUBLISHING MANAGER Simon Beecroft
CATEGORY PUBLISHERS Alex Allan, Siobhan Williamson
DTP DESIGNER Almudena Diaz
PRODUCTION CONTROLLER Amy Bennett
COLOR RETOUCHING Peter Pawsey
INDEXER Marian Anderson

First published in Great Britain in 2007; reprinted 2008

by Dorling Kindersley Limited,
80 Strand, London, WC2R 0RL

2 4 6 8 10 9 7 5 3

JD070 – 14/09

007 (Gun Logo) and related James Bond Trademarks

A CIP catalogue record for this book is available from the British Library

ISBN: 978-1-40533-427-3

Colour reproduction by Media Development and Printing Ltd., UK

Printed and bound by Hung Hing Ptg Co., China

Discover more at
www.dk.com

The authors would like to thank those who helped fact-check and research various bits of info, including John and Laurie Barry, Anne Bennett at EON Productions, Raymond Benson, James Burkart Jr., Martin Campbell, John Cox, Corinne Erard at Omega SA, Bruce Feirstein, Gary Firuta, Julie Graham, Charles Helfenstein, Andrew Lycett, Duncan Mac, Scott McIsaac, Tom Mankiewicz, Doug Redenius, Hillary Saltzman, David Sulzberger, Michael Van Blaricum, and Dean Williams. Doug Oliver at the Cessna Aircraft Company was extremely helpful in identifying some of the more obscure aircraft seen in the Bond films. Brian and Ray McHenry verified the parameters for the Astro-Spiral car jump as detailed in the AMC Hornet entry. There are certainly more who need to be thanked, but whose names are, for the moment, lost in a sea of emails related to this project.

This book, of course, would not exist without the novels of Ian Fleming, the creator of James Bond. We have tried to note the characters, vehicles, and gadgets that originally appeared in the literary universe. Just as importantly, the creators of this book are in debt to all those who contributed ideas, performances, and labor to the making of the Bond films. In particular, the great unit still photographers and the cinematographers deserve special mention. The images presented inside are memorable because of their skill and artistry. In the movie section, space has only been afforded to highlight 21 of the artists and technicians who have greatly contributed to the 007 series. Many more could be included. Their contributions are just as vital to the success of 007. In the end, this book is nothing more than a celebration of the creative work of others. Ultimately, these films exist because of the guidance of four individuals: Albert R. Broccoli, Harry Saltzman, Michael G. Wilson, and Barbara Broccoli. Every character, every gadget, every vehicle was deemed Bond-worthy by at least one of these individuals before it was ever committed to celluloid. We may have typed the text, but they wrote the book on Bond.

DK would like to thank Dan Bunyan for design work; Catherine Saunders and Heather Scott for editorial assistance; Guy Harvey and Robert Perry for color correction and retouching; Santosh Kumar G, Viv Ridgeway, and Siu Yin Chan for additional DTP work; Sarah Ashun for additional photography; Martin Copeland for picture research. DK would also like to thank Jenni McMurrie and Tara Barnes at EON Productions for their invaluable help. Thanks also to Nathan Clark.